The Ethnic Quilt

udies

thridge
49
aphical Studies
7
merica

ard Number: 97–66216

er

eets the minimum requirements of the
ormation Sciences—Permanence of Paper
984.

The Ethnic Q

Population Diversity in Southern

James P. Allen and Eugene T

The Center for Geographical Studies   California Stat

Contents

List of Illustrations   vi

List of Tables   viii

Preface and Acknowledgments   ix

1. The Concept and the Data   1

2. Urban Patterns and Ethnic Transformation   10

3. Distributions: Whites and Blacks   43

4. Distributions: American Indians and Hispanics   90

5. Distributions: Asians and Pacific Islanders   119

6. Narrowing the Gap?   167

7. Probing the Income Gap   182

8. Ethnic Niches at Work   201

9. A Multiethnic Society?   230

10. Conclusion   254

References   261

Index   275

Illustrations

Graphs

1.1   Ethnicity, Socioeconomic Status, and Place   2

6.1   Men's Income Distribution by Ethnicity, 1959 and 1989   174

6.2   Difference in Minority-White Income Ratios, 1959 and 1989   175

6.3   Difference in Minority-White Status Ratios, 1960 and 1990   177

7.1   Difference in Minority-White Income Ratios, Los Angeles and Orange Counties and the United States, 1959 and 1989   184

7.2   Income by Class of Employment by Ethnicity for Males, 1989   188

7.3   Difference in Adjusted Minority-White Income Ratios, 1989   191

7.4   Women's Income Distribution by Ethnicity in Selected Occupations, 1989   195

7.5   Men's Income Distribution by Ethnicity in Selected Occupations, 1989   196

9.6   Socioeconomic Status, 1990   238

9.7   Cultural Assimilation, 1990   238

9.17   Rates of Ethnic Intermarriage, 1990   251

Maps

2.1   Population Distribution, 1990   19

2.2   Cities and Other Places In and Around Los Angeles   20

2.3   Land Use, 1990   21

2.4   Major Communities and Streets, Central Los Angeles   22

2.5   Median Year of Housing Construction, 1990   23

2.6   Single-Unit Detached Houses, 1990   24

2.7   Owner-Occupied Housing, 1990   25

2.8   Persons per Room, 1990   26

2.9   College Graduates, 1990   27

2.10   Managers and Professionals, 1990   28

2.11   Physicians, 1990   29

2.12   Lawyers, 1990   29

2.13   Police and Detectives, 1990   29

2.14   Computing Equipment Manufacturing Workers, 1990   29

2.15   Aircraft and Missile Manufacturing Workers, 1990   30

2.16   Theater and Motion Picture Workers, 1990   30

2.17   Private Household Service Workers, 1990   30

2.18   Apparel Manufacturing Workers, 1990   30

2.19   Persons in Poverty, 1990   31

2.20   Persons Over Age 64, 1990   32

2.21   Persons Under Age 15, 1990   33

Maps

3.1   Major Shifts in Ethnic Populations After 1940 ... 51
3.2   Ethnic Populations, 1960 ... 52
3.3   Non-Hispanic White, 1990 ... 53
3.4   English Ancestry, 1990 ... 54
3.5   Russian Ancestry, 1990 ... 55
3.6   Israeli Ancestry, 1990 ... 56
3.7   Arab Ancestries, 1990 ... 57
3.8   Armenian Ancestry, 1990 ... 58
3.9   Iranian Ancestry, 1990 ... 59
3.10 Turkish Ancestry, 1990 ... 60
3.11 Non-Hispanic White Household Income, 1989 ... 61
3.12 Black, 1990 ... 62
3.13 Belizean Ancestry, 1990 ... 63
3.14 Jamaican Ancestry, 1990 ... 64
3.15 Nigerian Ancestry, 1990 ... 65
3.16 Black Household Income, 1989 ... 66

4.1   American Indian, 1990 ... 99
4.2   Mexican Origin, 1990 ... 100
4.3   Guatemalan Origin, 1990 ... 101
4.4   Salvadoran Origin, 1990 ... 102
4.5   Cuban Origin, 1990 ... 103
4.6   Puerto Rican Origin, 1990 ... 104
4.7   Other Central American Origins, 1990 ... 105
4.8   Hispanic South American Origins, 1990 ... 106
4.9   Hispanic Origin Household Income, 1989 ... 107

5.1   Chinese, 1990 ... 131
5.2   Japanese, 1990 ... 132
5.3   Filipino, 1990 ... 133
5.4   Korean, 1990 ... 134
5.5   Asian Indian, 1990 ... 135
5.6   Pakistani, 1990 ... 136

5.7   Vietnamese, 1990 ... 137
5.8   Cambodian, 1990 ... 138
5.9   Laotian, 1990 ... 139
5.10 Thai, 1990 ... 140
5.11 Indonesian, 1990 ... 141
5.12 Samoan, 1990 ... 142
5.13 Hawaiian, 1990 ... 143
5.14 Guamanian, 1990 ... 144
5.15 Asian and Pacific Islander Household Income, 1989 ... 145

9.1   Leading Ethnic Population, 1990 ... 233
9.2   Second Leading Ethnic Population, 1990 ... 234
9.3   Ethnic Diversity, 1990 ... 235
9.4   Asian and Black Populations in Central Los Angeles, 1990 ... 236
9.5   Hispanic and White Populations in Central Los Angeles, 1990 ... 237
9.8   Foreign-Born Non-Hispanic White, 1990 ... 239
9.9   Foreign-Born Black, 1990 ... 239
9.10 Foreign-Born Mexican Origin, 1990 ... 239
9.11 Foreign-Born Japanese, 1990 ... 239
9.12 Persons Immigrating 1980-1990 ... 240
9.13 Foreign-Born Mexican Origin: Proficiency in Speaking English, 1990 ... 241
9.14 Foreign-Born Guatemalan and Salvadoran: Proficiency in Speaking English, 1990 ... 241
9.15 Foreign-Born Chinese: Proficiency in Speaking English, 1990 ... 241
9.16 Foreign-Born Korean: Proficiency in Speaking English, 1990 ... 241
9.18 Non-Hispanic White Intermarriage, 1990 ... 242
9.19 Black Intermarriage, 1990 ... 242
9.20 Mexican Origin Intermarriage, 1990 ... 242
9.21 Japanese Intermarriage, 1990 ... 242

Tables

A   Small Ethnic Groups in Southern California, 1990   xiv

2.1   Populations in Group Quarters, 1990   16
2.2   Ethnic Population Change, 1960 to 1990   35
2.3   Ethnic-Group Fertility Rates, 1986   41

3.1   Largest Black Populations in Places, 1920   82
3.2   Racial and Hispanic Identification among Selected African and Middle American Ancestries, 1990   85

4.1   American Indian Populations, 1990   91

5.1   Leading Countries of Birth of Chinese Immigrants, 1990   120
5.2   Characteristics of Chinatown Residents and All Chinese Immigrants, 1990   121
5.3   Chinese-Vietnamese in Selected Areas, 1990.   123

6.1   Educational-Attainment Ratios, 1960 and 1990   170
6.2   Occupational-Status Ratios, 1960 and 1990   172
6.3   Median-Income Ratios, 1959 and 1989   173
6.4   Homeownership Ratios, 1960 and 1990   178

7.1   Adjusted Median-Income Ratios of U.S.-Born Men, 1989   190
7.2   Adjusted Median-Income Ratios of U.S.-Born Women, 1989   190
7.3   Median-Income Ratios of Men in Selected Occupations, 1989   193
7.4   Median-Income Ratios of Women in Selected Occupations, 1989   193
7.5   Ethnic Percentages in Selected Occupations, 1990   194

8.1   Selected Occupational Niches, 1960 and 1990   202
8.2   Ethnic Representation in Detailed Occupations, 1960 and 1990   204
8.3   Class of Employment, 1990   208
8.4   Disproportionate Representation of Ethnic Groups in Selected Occupations, 1990   211–212
8.5   Mexican Immigrants and Mexican Americans in Overrepresented Occupations, 1990   214
8.6   Leading Industries of Employment, 1990   216–221

9.1   Residential Segregation Between Ethnic Groups, 1990   232
9.2   Most and Least Ethnically Diverse Urban Places, 1990   243
9.3   Ethnic Intermarriage Rates, 1990   249
9.4   Structural Assimilation and Related Characteristics, 1990   250

Preface and Acknowledgments

In this book we try to help the reader better understand the varied racial and ethnic populations of Southern California. Our perspective differs from that of some authors who deal with these important and sometimes sensitive matters. This is because our book is not written to support a particular viewpoint or policy regarding multiculturalism, assimilation, or the treatment of certain ethnic groups. Nor is the book a polemic about racism or the need to either eliminate or preserve race- and ethnic-based preferences. On the contrary, our descriptions of thirty-four racial and ethnic populations in Southern California are designed to provide a broad foundation of knowledge about the people and places of this region.

Our most important primary source for this book is the 1990 U.S. census. Although the census is not perfect, as we explain in chapter 1, it is the standard by which other statistics on the American people are judged. No other source equals the detail and quality of its data.

We hope that the availability of the factual base represented by this book will help local residents see how their own lives and those of their neighbors and friends fit into the larger society, economy, and places of this region. Some of our results may also be useful in providing a common ground for policy discussion and future research.

Some people stress a distinction between race and ethnicity, racial groups being those with memberships mostly defined by aspects of physical appearance, such as skin color, as interpreted by the dominant group. In contrast, ethnic groups are those not visibly different from the general white population. Both racial and ethnic groups stress their distinctive cultures and identities. With the intermixing of populations, it is not surprising that a distinction between racial and ethnic groups must be blurred and unsatisfactory. Although we recognize that an individual's physical appearance is a significant factor in how he or she is assessed and treated by others, we do not attempt to make a racial-ethnic distinction. We consider all people as belonging in varying degrees to ethnic groups—whether defined by physical appearance, language, religion, national origin, or some other criterion.

The Importance of Ethnic Identities

There would be no point in writing this book unless we acknowledged what most Southern Californians already know from their daily experiences—that Southern California is substantially fragmented by ethnicity, by social class, and by locality. In this book we study especially the ethnic dimension of that fragmentation, and we also examine how ethnic groups intersect with class and place. At the end of the book we look at intermarriage rates between groups to determine how much the walls between ethnic groups have broken down and the extent to which various groups have come together socially.

Some people believe that ethnic groups are no longer important in our nation, that we are all simply Americans. We share the belief that America is richer to the extent that friends, employees, and political and business leaders are chosen and people judged as individuals without regard to physical appearance, religion, language heritage, or national origin. However, in both Southern California and the United States ethnic cultural differences and various prejudices make many people most comfortable with members of their own ethnic group and sometimes unfavorably disposed to certain other groups.

Even if no one were evaluated for employment or housing opportunities or in other public situations lower or higher than other people because of his or her perceived ethnic identity, ethnicity would continue to affect our private lives. Racial and ethnic identity would still make a difference in our choice of close friends, marriage partners, and where we lived.

In recent decades ethnic identities in the United States have been particularly emphasized. This is partly because government policy at various levels has accentuated certain racial and ethnic identities in the collection of statistics and in contracting, hiring, and promotion. Statistics on minority populations provide a basis for measuring progress toward overcoming discrimination.

Another major reason has been the resurgence of immigration. Most immigrants are more strongly tied to the culture and society from which they emigrated and their corresponding ethnic group in the United States than to the broader American culture and society. Although most of these immigrants and their descendants become much more integrated into American society as the years pass, their relatively recent arrival as of the 1990s accentuates ethnic pluralism.

Understanding Southern California and Its People

Many people have never heard of some of the ethnic groups who are living in their midst, and most people have glimpsed the various cities of Southern California only from freeways. Most of us are acquainted only with our small worlds, connected by freeway travel. The populated part of Southern California appears undifferentiated and uninteresting because we know little of it and because single-family houses and apartments in one area look so much like those in another. However, this book demonstrates that ethnic and other differences between areas which appear superficially similar are often real and important.

Swelling especially during the 1980s, immigration has grown so large that by 1990 a fifth of all foreign-born people in the United States lived in Southern California. Many of the international transplants are highly educated, cosmopolitan,

and wealthy. At the other extreme are many who attended only a few grades of school in their home country. The flood of new arrivals has transformed Southern California in ways that are often observable but not well understood, and these recent changes have partially masked underlying tensions among established white, black, Mexican American, and some Asian communities.

Americans often know nothing of the backgrounds from which immigrants have come. Older residents may be friendly toward their new neighbors, but beneath a veneer of welcoming acceptance lie anxieties about these strangers and their potential impact here. Immigrants themselves are often so overwhelmed by the difficulties of daily survival that they make little attempt to understand the larger multiethnic society of Southern California. Societal tensions may also result from suspicions about other groups with respect to appearances of great wealth or poverty as well as the somewhat distinctive occupations and business activities of some groups. People's concerns about all these matters are seldom stated in public because Americans are uncomfortable with such differences in a society that is ostensibly democratic and is symbolized, some believe, by a "melting pot."

We try to confront the reality of Southern California's new ethnic pluralism head-on by measuring, analyzing, and interpreting the region's varied ethnic groups and their characteristics. This is a step toward understanding the reality of life in Southern California—a reality which is sometimes distorted by images and rhetoric but which nonetheless undergirds interethnic relations and the functioning of society as a whole. Lack of knowledge about the similarities and differences among groups opens the way to unfounded rumors and feelings of deep resentment. If people can better grasp what has been happening around them, they will be better able to cope with the changes. Enhanced mutual understanding may help to alleviate mistrust.

Although this book describes and analyzes several basic characteristics of the various racial and ethnic populations, it does not attempt to cover everything. We do not treat the interrelations of ethnicity with politics and power, with religion, or with values, lifestyles, health, or crime.

An Urban Geography

The themes of our book link it strongly to urban geography, urban sociology, and urban history. The discipline of geography is usually defined by its special viewpoint or perspective on the world, rather than by any specific subject matter or content area. The perspective of geography emphasizes the characteristics and relative locations of places. Geographers investigate and explain the spatial or areal patterns of things and people, as well as the interrelationships of these. Urban geography simply applies this perspective to cities and suburbs. Sociology's focus on social groups and history's emphasis on change over time and on interconnections between phenomena in time mean that those disciplines are complementary to and intimately related to any geographical study of ethnic groups. We have tried to interweave research from all three disciplines because they all investigate the same real world.

With our emphasis on both the socioeconomic status and location of ethnic populations, we continue a tradition of research on intraurban differentiation that began in the early twentieth century. In recent decades, however, much urban research has neglected localities or treated them perfunctorily. This book may better balance the status and geographical aspects of urban differentiation. Also, most research in sociology and much in geography has stressed theory and generalizations, but some of the most fascinating and provocative aspects of a region lie in its specifics. Because we think that details are at least as interesting as broad generalizations, our book is distinctive in its wealth of detail about places and ethnic groups.

About the Chapters

Chapter 1 explains the basic concepts underlying our analyses of ethnic groups. We view Southern California as having a social structure with three primary dimensions—ethnic identity, socioeconomic status, and geographical distribution. The book explores these dimensions and how they intersect and interrelate with each other.

In chapter 2 we explain how and why the region's basic urban spatial patterns developed. This provides a background for interpreting the distributions of ethnic populations in subsequent chapters. The chapter also explains the several factors that have resulted in the increased ethnic diversity in Southern California since about 1960.

Chapters 3, 4, and 5 describe and explain the distributions of thirty-four ethnic groups. Our treatment is thoroughly historical as well as geographical, providing rich details on specific groups and places that we hope will make their presence here more real and understandable.

Chapter 6 examines the relative socioeconomic status of minorities compared with whites and compares minority positions in 1960 with those of 1990. Our finding that the income gap between whites and both blacks and Hispanics is no narrower in 1990 than it was in 1960 prompted chapter 7, which explores the reasons for this lack of income convergence.

Chapter 8 focuses on ethnic differences in particular occupations and industries, and it measures the extent of ethnic-group specializations at work. We also look at how such specializations have changed over the past few decades. The chapter is very specific in its coverage of ethnic groups and types of work and in its explanations for the likely reasons behind many of the specializations.

In chapter 9 we bring the ethnic groups together for several additional analyses. These concern the degree of residential differences among groups, the ethnic diversity of places, and the comparative socioeconomic status and acculturation of different groups. Then, rates of intermarriage between ethnic groups are used as indicators of the degree to which ethnic groups are integrating socially. This last analysis shows clearly the extent to which Southern California has become a multiethnic society and the relative importance of social linkages among the various groups.

Chapter 10 presents our major conclusions.

Group and Area Coverage

We especially want to portray those populations that have partially transformed Southern California's ethnic composition over the last several decades. Thus, we concentrate on people of color and ethnic groups with high proportions of immigrants. We attempt to be comprehensive with respect to ethnic groups of African, Middle Eastern, Asian, Pacific Island, West Indian, and Latin American origins. The book includes all such ethnic groups numbering more than 5,000 persons in Southern California, according to the 1990 U.S. census. For practical reasons the maps and text do not treat smaller groups, although their total populations are listed in the notes.[1] However, whites are considered a major ethnic group, and they are often the standard for socioeconomic comparisons among groups. Also included are the English- and Russian-ancestry populations because of their size and special importance.

This book deals only with residents of the five counties—Los Angeles, Orange, Riverside, San Bernardino, and Ventura—that constitute the heart of Southern California. This is the area that the Bureau of the Census calls the Los Angeles Consolidated Metropolitan Statistical Area (CMSA). In 1990 the 14.5 million residents of the Los Angeles CMSA represented 49 percent of California's population. Moreover, this massive Southern California megalopolis contains one-fifth of all the foreign-born population of the United States and more than the comparable New York CMSA. The somewhat separate and peripheral portions of Southern California—Santa Barbara, San Diego, and the large areas of desert to the east—are not treated.

About the Maps

Within this large area, our maps focus on that portion which contains the greatest ethnic diversity. That diversity is concentrated in the more densely populated sections of Los Angeles and Orange Counties. Because more distant suburbs are still closely connected socially and by daily commuting to these counties, our map coverage extends to nearby parts of Ventura, Riverside, and San Bernardino Counties. However, the area represented on maps does not extend into the heart of the three outlying counties because the required decrease in map scale would result in too great a loss of detail in the more intricately patterned areas. Only whites, blacks, American Indians, Filipinos, and people of Mexican origin have ethnic concentrations outside the area mapped in this book.

Most of our maps show spatial patterns in terms of small, neighborhood-sized areal units called census tracts. Census tracts average only 4,000 inhabitants and have long been the most common areal units for examining neighborhood characteristics and mapping within a metropolitan area. In contrast, the sets of quarter-page maps show much larger areal units called PUMAs or Public Use Microdata Areas. PUMAs have a minimum population of 100,000 and are typically composed of entire cities. Although the PUMA-based maps lack the locational detail of the tract-based maps, they make possible the mapping of highly specific data that are not even available for census tracts. To orient the reader geographically, maps label many places referred to in accompanying sections of text as well as other distinctive locations visible on map patterns. Also, details on maps can be located and identified quite precisely because most maps show freeways in red, municipal boundaries in bluish green, and census tract boundaries in white.

Nearly all of our maps are of the choropleth type, in which areal units are colored according to percentages or median values. There has been considerable discussion concerning how data distributions should be aggregated into a limited number of classes: no approach seems to satisfy both statistical and perceptual needs. Unfortunately, most systematic procedures result in a large range in the highest category, where values are few and differences large. Our strategy was to break data distributions into percentiles: the 95th, 90th, 80th, and the bottom 10th or 20th. In some cases the top 5 percent category was further subdivided to isolate the locations of extremely high percentages. In this way we have attempted to reveal where a particular group is absent and where concentrations are particularly strong. In maps of household income those census tracts with fewer than 100 households in each ethnic group are masked. This was done to counter sampling error and to help the reader focus on those areas which are especially important in each group's distribution.

The legend of each choropleth map indicates the number of tracts or PUMAs within each category by numbered bars whose length is proportional to that number. The bar length and number are based on the number of PUMAs or tracts in the entire five-county area (not just the portion shown on the map), and on income maps they include the tracts that are masked as having fewer than 100 households.

In interpreting maps based on PUMAs as areal units, it is important to note that PUMAs are usually composed of contiguous areas. However, a few were defined by the Census Bureau to include noncontiguous places. Three such PUMAs involve well-known places. In the San Fernando Valley, the cities of San Fernando and Burbank are combined in this way. Maps showing PUMAs must also treat Beverly Hills, Culver City, Ladera Heights, Marina Del Rey, View Park, and West Hollywood as one unit. Lastly, the independent cities of the Palos Verdes Peninsula are included with El Segundo and the three "Beach" cities of the South Bay in a single PUMA.

On dot distribution maps the dots are located randomly within census tracts. However, in very large rural tracts, we moved dots out of unpopulated areas.

Maps were created on a Macintosh 8500 computer using AtlasPro and ArcView 2.1 software. Map finishing was accomplished with Deneba Canvas 3.5 and Adobe Illustrator 6.0. Boundary files for tracts came from GDT Inc., Wessex Inc., and Strategic Mapping Inc. Additional geographical features were produced from TIGER files using TIGER Massage software. PUMA boundary files were created by merging place and tract boundaries in Adobe Illustrator. A resulting postscript file then was converted to a boundary file for AtlasPro.

Most of the population totals which lead off the statistics on the maps of ethnic groups are from complete-count (nonsample) data; however, totals for ancestry groups are based on a 12.7 percent sample. These are the best census measures of the sizes of the groups. All other statistics on those maps represent a 5 percent sample from the special Public Use Microdata Sample (PUMS) file, which we explain in chapter 1.

Acknowledgments

Many knowledgeable and busy people took time to help us with the preparation of *The Ethnic Quilt*.

Investigations by geography majors in the course on ethnic Los Angeles taught at California State University (CSU), Northridge, uncovered historical origins and the evolution of certain ethnic enclaves reported in this book. We are grateful for the help provided by Dennis Andal, David Deis, Mike Ferguson, George Glaab, Steve Gonzalez, Tom Jones, Steve Kennedy, David MacDonald, Chris Mayda, Marsha Otchis, Joanne Quinn, Anthony Reyes, Jeffrey Roth, Howard Shain, and Robert Vinas.

Scholars and other knowledgeable people freely answered our questions, and they are named in specific notes. In addition, Shiva Bajpai, James Curtis, Lawrence de Graaf, Yen Espiritu, Darrin Gitisetan, Gilbert Gonzalez, Stephen Koletty, Kian Kwan, Bruce Phillips, Hammam Shafie, Ronald Tsukashima, and Eui-Young Yu read drafts of parts of chapters and offered valuable suggestions for improvement, for which we are deeply appreciative.

Some scholars read and commented on one or more entire chapters. The detailed suggestions and insights of Kenyon Chan, William A.V. Clark, Gloria Lothrop, Paul Ong, Curtis Roseman, and Roger Waldinger enabled us to make important additions and corrections.

Census data for our book came from two sources, the Bureau of the Census and the CSU Social Sciences Database Archive (SSDBA) located at CSU, Los Angeles. Dona Bailey and Stuart Wugalter of Academic Technology Support at CSULA were most helpful in acquiring and processing various census tapes. Our work could not have been completed without the detailed California digital census data that this important CSU specialty center provided. In the Van Nuys regional office of the Bureau of the Census, Larry Hugg was always particularly helpful in answering questions and in being certain that we were able to obtain the data we needed. The digital file for the 1990 land-use map was provided to the Department of Geography by Terry Bills, director of research at the Southern California Association of Governments.

Photographs on the front cover are of Southern Californians at the time they became new U.S. citizens in 1996. The pictures, taken just after an official naturalization ceremony, were graciously provided by Elliott Barkan.

We deeply appreciate the support and assistance of Ralph Vicero, former dean of the College of Social and Behavioral Sciences at CSU, Northridge. Dean Vicero shared our vision of the importance of the book. Years ago his office provided us with a grant to support publication. The use of color in this volume would not have been possible without his assistance.

Blenda Wilson, president of CSU, Northridge, and Louanne Kennedy, provost and vice president for Academic Affairs, encouraged us in our efforts. In addition, William Flores, dean of the College of Social and Behavioral Sciences, has been strongly supportive in the months since he took over that office.

Arrangements to publish the book at the Center for Geographical Studies at CSU, Northridge were made by I-Shou Wang, chair of the Department of Geography, and by William Bowen, Antonia Hussey, and Elliot McIntire, the board of directors of the Center. Their willingness to take on this unusually large project is much appreciated.

We thank all of the above for their kindness in graciously donating their time, thought, and support to this project.

Lastly, we are indebted to our wives for their patience over the past three years—the period of planning, data extraction and analysis, writing, and mapmaking. Thank you, Nancy and Carol.

Notes

1. The table lists ethnic groups numbering between 1,000 and 5,000 persons in the five-county Southern California area.

Table A   Small Ethnic Groups in Southern California, 1990

Ethnic Group	Population
Aleuts	1,447
Afghans	4,171
Assyrians	3,521
Bangladeshi	1,083
Brazilians	4,112
Burmese	1,465
Eskimos	1,036
Ethiopians	3,613
Guyanese	1,609
Haitians	2,253
Hmong	1,557
South Africans	2,330
Sri Lankans	2,673
Tongans	3,220
Trinidadians[a]	2,315
West Indians	4,500

Source: U.S. Bureau of the Census (1991, 1993d). We used race (complete-count) data whenever they were available; when they were not, we used sample ancestry figures.

[a] Includes Tobagonians.

1. The Concept and the Data

In some ways the people of the United States constitute a society of free individuals and their families. However, a great deal of our lives involves formal and informal connections with other people. Consciously or subconsciously, our opinions and feelings about other individuals are often based on their probable group affiliation.

Many of us derive part of our personal identity from a larger and often loose affiliation based on race, religion, language, national origin, or other heritage—what most people call ethnicity. A person may also feel an affiliation based on occupation, political philosophy, avocation, residence, or class. For some people this shared sense of belonging is weak or nonexistent, but for others it is extremely important. There is abundant evidence that people generally form their closest ties with others who are like themselves.[1] Thus, to understand society we must see it not only as an irregular collection of individuals and families but also as a set of larger groups, some of which are based on shared ethnic identities.

Many Southern Californians attempt to cope with the diversity of ethnic groups by trying to appreciate the cultures they represent. This perspective emphasizes learning about the traditional cultures of others—their distinctive foods, dances, religions, special holidays, and so forth. This is the view stressed by the schools and the media. It is also the underlying foundation for nearly all efforts to improve relations among groups. Its utility was illustrated after the 1992 riots by efforts to help Korean merchants and black residents of South Central Los Angeles recognize how their two groups view each other differently.

A focus on cultural awareness is insufficient, however, for it merely scratches the surface of relationships among ethnic groups. In stressing the equal value of all cultures, the cultural perspective ignores group differences in political power, educational attainment, and economic position. It also seems blind to the importance of where different people live and the type of work they do as factors in ethnic group perceptions and relationships.

Perhaps the most basic flaw of the cultural perspective is its implicit denial of the underlying competitive relationship among groups. An important but often unacknowledged motivation behind the creation and maintenance of ethnic group categories is competition for economic resources and status.[2]

The Central Concept: Structure

We base this book on a structural perspective rather than a cultural one. Structure can be thought of as the fundamental form or pattern by which people differentiate themselves and others.[3] It is the basic composition of society—the underlying arrangement of individuals and groups. Individuals interact and conduct their work and play from their position within the structure. Groups are aggregations of individuals who share a position in the structure, although some individuals may be but dimly aware of their places.

In emphasizing structure, we assume that people are conditioned in important ways by their ethnic identities and their geographical and economic positions in the larger society. Group similarities and differences in those positions are important in understanding intergroup relations. Admittedly, aspects of culture such as a predisposition to enter some lines of work much more than others or a special emphasis on education or homeownership do help shape the structural position of a group. People—with their values, lifestyles, and prejudices—are a part of the life of their group, and their group is embedded in the structural matrix of society as a whole.

A structural perspective, like a cultural perspective, tempers but does not deny the importance of individual decisions. Although one's place in the structure will affect one's opportunities, people are not forced by the structure into achieving certain levels of education, lines of work, income levels, or residential locations. Structure is an influence on or predisposition rather than a determinant. The many individuals who make occupational, political, and lifestyle choices that are atypical of their friends and relatives are demonstrating a very real freedom to choose.

Thus, our book describes and explains how ethnic groups fit together into the larger society, economy, and geography—the structure—of Southern California. Although our main goal is to investigate the structure in order to better understand people and places in this region, we also believe that knowledge of different groups' structural positions is a prerequisite to any realistic reduction of tensions between them.

The Three Dimensions of Structure

The structure of population in any region can best be conceived of as having three basic dimensions: ethnic identity, social class or socioeconomic status, and geographical distribution. These dimensions are often called the ethnic structure, the class or socioeconomic structure, and the spatial structure.

Although structure is an abstraction, it can be conveniently diagrammed in such a way that it is more easily grasped (Fig. 1.1). The first two dimensions are represented by a rectangle. The horizontal dimension represents identities, each of which is represented by a vertical column. The vertical dimension represents socioeconomic status. On the graph each column is divided into smaller segments to differentiate people by status. Geographical distribution can be thought of as the location of rectangles on a horizontal plane.

In this way it is possible to differentiate a poor Thai immigrant from a middle-class Salvadoran along both the status and the ethnic dimensions. Ethnic composition and status

vary substantially from place to place, and residential and work locations affect potential contact among people of different ethnic identities and classes. For these reasons the spatial patterns or distributions of ethnic groups and socioeconomic status must be added.

Ethnic structure. Ethnic structure is the ethnic composition of an area—the proportions of people in various ethnic groups. Ethnic identity and its corollary, ethnic group, are difficult to define but nonetheless indispensable. It is best to explain these terms simply and then characterize them briefly. Ethnic identity can be thought of as a sense of peoplehood, having its roots in one's ancestry or family heritage and likely to continue into the future.[4] An ethnic population is the collection of people within the larger society who share a specific identity.

In the United States identities and groups have usually been defined in terms of the country of origin of a person or a person's ancestors. However, racial or religious affiliation may also be a basis for ethnic identity. Thus, blacks and whites are

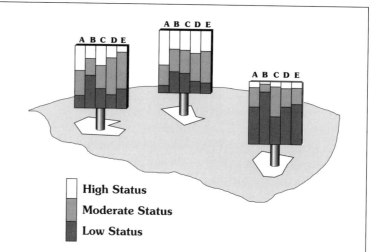

Figure 1.1 Ethnicity, Socioeconomic Status, and Place

Columns identified by letters represent ethnic groups in different places. The vertical dimension shows variations in socioeconomic status within ethnic groups. Both socioeconomic status and ethnic composition can vary from one place to another.

really large ethnic groups, within each of which can be nested other identities such as Jamaican or Irish. Identities based on race or physical appearance are different from those based on religion or country of origin, however, in that they are not necessarily voluntary. People of color in the United States have long known that white society has given them a separate racial identity, whether they wish it or not.

Class structure. The stratification of society according to economic and closely related characteristics is recognized in the concept of social class or socioeconomic status. A higher position on the status scale is generally preferred over a lower position, and position is usually indicated by general type of occupation or level of income. Status can also be described by characteristics like educational attainment or specific occupation because these can be significantly related to income. Thus, individuals who belong to an ethnic group can range from very high to very low in status, and the average status of entire ethnic groups can be compared.[5]

Spatial structure. In the context of this book, spatial structure is the areal pattern or distribution of socioeconomic status and ethnic groups. However, understanding the spatial structure usually involves more than just mapping spatial patterns. It requires knowing both the processes by which patterns were created and the characteristics of various places that may relate to the patterns. Such place descriptions include type of land use, terrain, general appearance and age of houses and apartments, proportion of single-family houses, and statements about the most typical people who live there. Other basic characteristics of places are their ethnic and class composition. In this way, all three dimensions of structure are closely interconnected.

Relative ease of access to other places is also an important characteristic of any place and may be an appropriate part of the characterization of an area. The presence of nearby shopping centers and business districts, prestigious residential areas, beaches, and mountain amenities are part of a place's geographical situation. Conversely, proximity to unattractive land uses such as railroad yards, industrial corridors, or slum areas is also significant.

Ethnic compartmentalization. The concept of structure is a useful way to understand probable patterns of social differentiation and association. People can be imagined as living much of their lives in a social compartment defined by ethnic identity, social class, and residential location (Fig. 1.1). To say that society is compartmentalized is to acknowledge that most people's regular and more personal associations are with others in the same compartment as their own.

Measuring Structure with U.S. Census Data

Each of the three dimensions of structure has variables that describe and measure it. Within the ethnic dimension, each ethnic group is a variable. The dimension of status is most commonly measured by educational attainment, occupation, and income. These allow individuals and groups to be located or ranked vertically in the structure. The spatial dimension of structure locates people geographically. In contrast to the ethnic and class dimensions, the location of people changes frequently during an average day or week. Despite this, the location of residence normally defines the spatial pattern of groups.

The best source of information on ethnic identity, socioeconomic status, and residential location is the U.S. census of 1990. The bulk of the data summarized in our tables, graphs, and maps originated in Summary Tape Files (STFs) 1, 3, and 4 and in the PUMS file for California. We generally used the STF data to describe the population living in census tracts, whereas PUMS data were tabulated by PUMA, a region of at least 100,000 persons.

Wherever possible, we used the complete count (STF 1) or nonsample data rather than STF 3 and STF 4, which are based on a 12.7 percent sample of the Southern California population.[6] The PUMS file is a 5 percent sample of all households and individuals.[7] PUMS data made it possible for us to obtain information on an ethnic population in much more detail than we could have from any published volumes or from other computer files. They also enabled us to determine, for instance, the characteristics of a specific age or educational group within an ethnic population. For 1960 data, we used various published volumes as sources of data.

Data on Ethnic Populations

Census questions as data sources. The 1990 census questionnaire included four questions related to ethnic identity. We make use of all four in this book. The first two items—race and Hispanic origin—were asked of all respondents; the third and fourth—ancestry and country of birth—were part of the more detailed form of the questionnaire completed only by the 12.7 percent sample.

In answering the race question, respondents had to select the race they considered themselves to be from a list of fifteen categories. The categories included white, black, American Indian, and several Asian countries and Pacific Island groups, as well as "other race." If no appropriate racial group was listed, people could write in smaller Asian and Pacific Islander groups in a blank space. Many people reported their identity in this way, and we make use of these data. The second question, on Hispanic origin, was completely separate. It was designed to identify the specific countries of origin of people who considered themselves of Spanish or Hispanic origin, either by filling in the circle opposite a label such as Mexican or Cuban or by writing in the name of another country.

Together, these two items on the census questionnaire are particularly important in categorizing people ethnically. This is because neither was based on a sample and because a great number of national origins were tabulated from the write-in spaces. Also, only a cross-tabulation from the two questions can provide the most appropriate category for the dominant ethnic group in Southern California—non-Hispanic whites.

The third question regarding ethnic identity asked people to write in their ancestry or ethnic origin. The responses were particularly useful in characterizing specific European and Middle Eastern national identities within the larger white race population, as well as specific African and West Indian origins within the black race population. The best measure of ancestry as an indicator of identity and population size is the first ancestry reported by any individual, which is the basis for the ancestry data used in this book.

Lastly, the question about place of birth is a source of specific information on the foreign-born within specific ethnic groups. The responses also allowed us to investigate subgroups within the larger ethnic populations of Armenians, Chinese, and Indonesians.

Selection of white ethnic identities. To a large extent, people of European origin have assimilated into a single English-speaking, Americanized white society. Although some individuals retain a strong sense of ethnic identity for an ancestral homeland in Europe, intermarriage and distance from the immigrant experience have resulted in weakened, blurred, and multiple senses of ethnic identity. For this reason, we do not generally distinguish among European ethnic groups. Instead, we characterize people of European heritage as racially white but not Hispanic. The non-Hispanic restriction is important to distinguish the European-origin whites from the more recently arrived and culturally distinct groups from Latin America. Various ethnic groups from the Middle East are also white, but each should be identified separately.

Within the broad non-Hispanic white population, we also distinguish two groups of European origin because of their exceptional significance. First, the English-ancestry group contains few immigrants but large numbers whose ancestors arrived from England a century or more ago. This group is important because it includes the descendants of the people who once defined the mainstream or core culture in America and controlled it economically as a power elite: white Anglo-Saxon Protestants. Although most people of English ancestry have never been connected with any social or economic elite, others are wealthy and remain highly influential. Because the group is large, it effectively represents traditional, English-speaking American culture and appropriately includes some "old," high-status families.

The second European-origin group is people of Russian ancestry. We selected Russian ancestry because it is a useful surrogate for the Jewish population, an important ethnic group which is at the same time a religious group. Because of concern over religious privacy and potential religious discrimination, the U.S. Congress decades ago prohibited the Bureau of the Census from asking any question concerning religion in decennial censuses. Nevertheless, the status and locations of Jews in Southern California can be approximated by using ancestry data for people of Russian ancestry. This association is substantiated by a mid-1970s national survey which showed that 70 percent of Americans of Russian ancestry were Jewish.[8]

The Jewish component of the Russian-ancestry population in Southern California in 1990 should be even greater. Since World War I many thousands of Jews have moved to Los Angeles from New York and other eastern cities where their parents and grandparents had settled after emigrating from Russia. Jews have also constituted a high proportion of Russian émigrés to Los Angeles since the mid-1970s. As a result, we estimate that people of Jewish heritage or faith constitute about 85 to 90 percent of the people of Russian ancestry in Southern California.[9]

Russian ancestry is not a good indicator of the total numbers of Jews because many Jews have family origins in countries other than Russia. However, the tendency of Jews to cluster residentially near other Jews without much regard to national origin and to share socioeconomic characteristics means that Russian ancestry is an appropriate substitute for describing the Jewish population.

Quality of the data. Not all residents were enumerated by the census, and the resulting undercount was greater for blacks and Hispanics than for whites and Asians.[10] Analyses of the coverage of past censuses suggest that the undercount was also greater among poorer people and those who are not legal residents of this country.[11] For this reason the estimated national undercount of 4 to 6 percent among blacks and Hispanics probably means that poorer blacks and Hispanics are less well represented, so that the socioeconomic status of these groups appears slightly higher in census data than it should be.

The undercount of illegal residents may have been smaller in 1990 than in 1980 because many such people had already applied to legalize their status under the amnesty provisions of the Immigration Reform and Control Act of 1986. In 1990 they were presumably less fearful of divulging their presence. Nevertheless, a significant undercount in Southern California must have occurred. Because Mexico has been by far the largest source of illegal immigration, the actual status of Mexican immigrants is probably lower than what is indicated by census data. Similarly, their numbers in various low-status work specializations (see chapter 8) are probably greater than the census data show.

Because inconsistency in people's responses to the race, Hispanic-origin, and ancestry questions may have weakened the data, the Bureau of the Census reinterviewed a national sample of individuals. Results showed a high consistency of responses for race and Hispanic origin, but only moderate consistency for an American Indian identity. With respect to ancestry, immigrants are understandably consistent in their responses. However, ethnic intermarriage and some loss of a sense of origins on the part of the U.S.-born resulted in Russian and English ancestries being reported with only moderate consistency. Moderate consistency means that group characteristics may not appear as distinctive as they would be if the groups were more clearly and tightly defined.[12]

Inconsistencies typically occurred when people with multiethnic family backgrounds were forced to choose a single identity for the race and Hispanic-origin questions. The resulting census data give the impression of sharply defined ethnic populations where, in fact, an unknown proportion of people have mixed backgrounds and identities.

The prohibition against identifying people's religion also limits data on people from the Middle East, where religious groups within most countries are separate socially but cannot be distinguished in census data. Religious data would help identify Muslims, Christians, and Jews—especially significant subgroups among Egyptians, Lebanese, Syrians, and Iranians.

Data on Socioeconomic Status

The foundation of status rests theoretically on educational attainment, because occupation and income are largely dependent on education. Although decades ago a high-school education typically led to a good job, by 1990 a decline in such jobs, together with a generally rising level of education, meant that the basic standard of educational attainment is now a college education. Thus, our key measure of educational status is the percentage of those individuals aged 25 and older who are graduates of a four-year college or university.

Occupations are not easily ranked on the basis of status or prestige, but people in the managerial and professional occupations generally have more education and earn more money than do those in other occupations.[13] This means that the best occupational measure of status is the percentage of workers who are employed as managers (also referred to as executives and administrators) and professionals. We sometimes call these "upper-level, white-collar" workers.

In chapter 8 we use highly detailed occupation and industry categories to describe work specializations or niches—but without regard to status. Ethnic groups, especially newer immigrant groups searching for opportunities in the United States, can be differentiated by their concentrations in certain types of businesses and occupations, which are a form of ethnic compartmentalization.

A third aspect of work is the type of ownership of the employing organization. We group all workers into three categories: private wage and salary workers, government workers, and self-employed workers. Unpaid workers in a family business are included in the self-employed category. These distinctions can be important in comparisons of ethnic groups because groups often differ in the degree to which members are in business for themselves, and some groups have exceptionally high or low proportions of government workers.

The major purpose of work is the earning of money. This suggests that income is probably the most important indicator of status. Both median household income and median personal income are useful variables. Because families share incomes and because many key decisions are made by households rather than individuals, household income is the most widely used income variable. It is the total income reported by all people living together in a housing unit, such as a single-family dwelling or an apartment.[14] Differences among ethnic groups

in the average number of workers in a household can distort household-income comparisons. For this reason the median personal income of individual men and women is also valuable.

Whereas income measures money received during a single year, homeownership is an indicator of longer-term wealth. We use the percentage of households that own their homes as a basic measure of economic status.

The timing of the taking of the census is significant in measuring socioeconomic status. Monthly economic indicators show that the April 1 census date was just prior to a major recession. This means that the census measures the results of economic growth during the 1980s, but it does not reveal any features of the recession of the 1990s.

The Permeable Walls of Ethnic Compartments

We have suggested that the residents of Southern California can be viewed as occupying various specific compartments in the larger structure—compartments defined by ethnic identity, socioeconomic status, and place. The concept of structure seems to emphasize the walls or boundaries between ethnic groups. However, in many cases people cross these boundaries. Close contact between people of different ethnic identities may lead to weaker or more permeable social boundaries between groups and, ultimately, to the merging of some groups and the disappearance of some identities.

In the remainder of this chapter we explain the processes that lead to closer contact among ethnic groups. There are no data to measure the permeability of boundaries between classes within an ethnic population. However, we can measure the potential for interaction among groups by language ability and other variables, which we discuss as acculturation. Rates of intermarriage between groups can show the social integration of groups (the permeability of compartments).

Acculturation

Acculturation, or cultural assimilation, is normally a first step in the process of immigrant or minority adjustment to the culture of the dominant group.[15] It means the adoption, at least partially, of the leading group's ways of thinking and behaving. The most important aspect of acculturation is language, because improved skills in the common language open up other avenues of assimilation, such as education and a greater range of employment possibilities.

With a few exceptions concerning Spanish speakers, most communication among different ethnic groups in Southern California takes place in the English language. This means that an ethnic group's average English ability compared with that of other groups is an excellent indicator of the possibilities of interaction. More important, the group that wields most economic influence and sets the cultural tone is U.S.-born, English-speaking whites. As people spend more time in this country and or have more contact with those whites, they come to understand more of the culture represented by whites and typically adopt aspects of it. The economic payoff expected from acculturation, in terms of a better job or higher income, is usually a powerful motivating force.[16]

We recognize that in contemporary Southern California there are aspects of acculturation that are detrimental to individuals and families and that many people resist it.[17] However, we stress the language aspect of this pervasive and powerful process because fluency in standard English speech is so widely acknowledged as important for most economic success.

People who use a language other than English at home at least some of the time were asked on the census questionnaire to rate their ability to speak English as not at all, not well, well, or very well. The extent of an ethnic group's acculturation is best measured by the most demanding of these criteria: the percentage of adults who speak only English in their home or who speak English very well even if other languages are also spoken.

Individuals and ethnic groups that arrived in this country earlier than other groups tend to be more acculturated.[18] Two variables that indirectly measure the relative recency of immigration suggest the probability of acculturation. The first is the percentage of adults (aged 25 and older) who are immigrants (born outside the United States), and second is the percentage of the foreign-born who arrived during the 1980s.

In addition, we calculated the median personal income for the foreign-born compared with the U.S.-born in an ethnic group. Although ostensibly a measure of status, we use it to suggest the extent of an assimilation lag between immigrants and the U.S.-born within any one ethnic group.

Social Integration and Structural Assimilation

Social integration—the breakdown of compartmentalization—occurs much more slowly than does acculturation. This is because social integration is characterized by close personal ties, friendships that continue beyond the workplace, frequent social gatherings, and possibly marriage between people in different groups.[19] It means entering into the cliques and institutions of another ethnic group.

The most common form of social integration is structural assimilation. This is the name given to the integration of a minority group with the dominant ethnic group in an area. In the case of Southern California and the United States, structural assimilation occurs when members of other ethnic groups enter into the social group of non-Hispanic whites. Both cultural and structural assimilation become less necessary if economic power and influence become less concentrated within the white group. This has already been demonstrated by the success of some Asian immigrants relying on Asian capital.

It is usually the children of immigrants, rather than the immigrants themselves, who achieve substantial structural assimilation. They often speak English with little or no accent and feel comfortable doing so, and they often form close friendships at school and elsewhere because of shared interests rather than shared ethnic identities.

The degree to which ethnic groups are structurally assimilated into white society or closely connected socially with other groups can be measured by rates of intermarriage. Because it is so deeply personal and reflects at least strong personal connections between individuals in different groups, intermarriage is a very stringent measure of social integration.

Census data from the PUMS file permit us to examine the ethnic identities of married couples. This is the basis for our measurement of the extent of social integration between ethnic groups and our assessment of the relative unity or separateness of Southern California's multiethnic society.

Ethnic-Identity Labels

In this book the non-Hispanic white group, sometimes called "Anglos," is generally called "whites" where it is clear that the reference excludes Hispanics. Although "emerging majority" might be the more appropriate term in this region for the aggregate of all other groups, we use the traditional terms "minorities" and "minority groups" for everyone other than non-Hispanic whites. "Japanese," "Chinese," and "Filipino," for example, include people regardless of country of birth. To distinguish those born in the United States from others, the former are called "U.S.-born," or the word "American" is added to the ethnic label. Others are referred to as "foreign-born" or "immigrants." The term "immigrant" does not imply either legal or illegal status with respect to U.S. immigration law.

People of any Spanish heritage or origin, regardless of nationality, are described as "Latino," "Hispanic," or "of Hispanic origin." In this book the terms are interchangeable. Following Bureau of the Census practice, however, we generally use "Hispanic" when referring to the size or other characteristics of these populations as described in U.S. census data. "Latino" is often used in other contexts. Consistent with Census Bureau terminology on the questionnaire, specific Hispanic groups are described by their national origin, such as "people of Mexican origin." These labels include all people in the ethnic group, regardless of country of birth.

Because the Mexican-origin population includes large numbers of both immigrants and U.S.-born, we often call the former "Mexicans," "Mexican immigrants," or "Mexican-born people." Those born in the United States are either "U.S.-born people of Mexican origin" or "Mexican Americans." Changes in census terminology and ethnic-group preferences mean that labels for ethnic groups can be confusing. We have tried to use labels that are short, widely accepted, and not laden with political connotations. African Americans are referred to as "blacks," although in earlier census data they were "Negroes." Similarly, although the 1960 census identified Latinos by means of distinctive Spanish surnames rather than a "Hispanic origin," we ignore this minor change and refer to the group in both 1960 and 1990 as "Latino" or "Hispanic."

Where maps or measures of ethnic groups based on the sample ancestry data are used, we always identify the group as an ancestry group.

Fitting It All Together

Subsequent chapters are designed to show how ethnic groups are positioned within the larger socioeconomic and spatial structures of Southern California. In the next chapter we describe and explain the basic spatial structure of the region into which the ethnic groups are placed, and in chapters 3, 4, and 5 we focus on the differing spatial structures or distributions of the groups. Other chapters deal with the placement of ethnic groups along the socioeconomic dimension of the regional structure. Thus, the three dimensions of structure and the varying permeability of its compartment walls are valuable concepts for organizing our thinking about the patterned relationships among ethnic groups, class, and place.

Notes

1. Blau (1994), 17, 21.
2. Competition for jobs, housing, and higher income is not necessarily expressed in terms of ethnic groups. However, to the extent that people provide more help to those in their own group than to others outside the group as all attempt to maintain and improve their status, the indirect cumulative effect is to produce competition among ethnic groups. Some ethnic groups are roughly equal to each other in status; others may be higher or lower. Competitive tensions among ethnic groups fluctuate in pattern and strength due to shifts in group numbers, labor-market niches, and economic expansion or contraction in a local area (Olzak and Nagel 1986; Nagel 1995). Competition may appear to be absent during periods of economic growth. The best recent study of varied ethnic networks and niches in the inherently competitive job market is Waldinger (1996). At the same time, a basic, persistent conflict which is indirectly one of ethnic competition is that between the economically dominant (and mostly white) class and other classes and minority groups that are less powerful (Feagin and Feagin 1994). Elaborations of these ideas and additional perspectives on relations between ethnic groups can be found in Rex and

Mason (1986); Omi and Winant (1986); and Stanfield (1995).

3. Our emphasis on people as members of groups and comparative group structures is derived theoretically from Gordon (1964) and Blau (1994).

4. Gordon (1964), 23–24, 29. Ethnic identities may change over time because they reflect ongoing social-psychological processes that are responsive to cultural shifts in the wider society. Identities and labels that are salient at any one time are not immutable, even though they may appear so.

5. Technically, the socioeconomic structure of any ethnic group or place should be defined by the distribution of people in several categories of educational status or income. However, because our purpose is primarily to compare the relative status of different groups, we simplify and describe the group's socioeconomic structure by a single measure, usually some median or percentage value.

6. U.S. Bureau of the Census (1991, 1993d).

7. U.S. Bureau of the Census (1992).

8. These were the findings of a general social survey conducted in the 1970s and reported in Archdeacon (1983), 238.

9. The Russian-ancestry population in Southern California includes people who are neither practicing Jews nor Jewish by heritage. Nearly all of these have a Christian family heritage, but the paucity of Russian Orthodox churches and other Russian-oriented congregations in Southern California argues that they constitute a very small proportion of the area's Russian-ancestry population. Because there were an estimated 639,000 Jews in the five-county Southern California area in 1990 (Kosmin and Scheckner 1991), Jews among the 197,000 persons of Russian ancestry must constitute at least a quarter of the total Jewish population of Southern California.

10. A special section in an issue of the *Journal of the American Statistical Association* is the most authoritative source concerning the estimated undercount in 1990 (Schenker 1993).

11. Passel and Woodrow (1984); Fein (1990).

12. McKenny et al. (1993).

13. Stevens and Cho (1985); Farley and Allen (1987). Other occupations, such as sales, clerical, technical, administrative support, machine operator, and precision production, have roughly similar educational standards and pay; and occupations that may be lowest in status are handlers, helpers, laborers, and private-household workers. However, these occupations vary so much in job requirements and pay that they are almost impossible to differentiate in status.

14. Although some households consist of just one person, about 70 percent of households in Southern California contain a family (two or more related people), and 52 percent of all households contain married couples (U.S. Bureau of the Census 1991).

15. The clearest conceptual discussion of acculturation and structural assimilation is found in Gordon (1964), chapters 3 and 4.

16. Acculturation is not necessarily required for economic success or high income in those businesses in which markets and employees are restricted to a single ethnic group—what is sometimes called an ethnic economy.

17. Many people resist acculturation emotionally because it seems to imply at least a corresponding loss of group's culture and identity. However, this is not necessarily the case. People who are fully acculturated can conform to the culture of English-speaking whites when they wish, such as in work and public situations. At the same time, they usually retain their ethnic identity and aspects of the ethnic culture with which they are more comfortable, typically expressing these with close friends and families in private or ethnic settings.

18. Borjas (1990); Portes and Rumbaut (1990), 201–9; LaLonde and Topel (1992); Myers (1995).

19. Gordon (1964), 70–71, 80–81. Gordon refers to intermarriage as marital assimilation and sees it as following inevitably from structural assimilation.

2. Urban Patterns and Ethnic Transformation

This chapter has two main parts, each distinct from the other. The first sets the geographical context of Southern California for the rest of the book. It does this by introducing some of the most basic processes and spatial patterns that define the region's urban geography. The focus is on the major patterns of land use, population, housing, social class, and age.[1] The general principles and features often interrelate with the other dimension of race and ethnicity and, for this reason, should make the maps and text in chapters 3 through 5 more understandable.

The second part of the chapter explains the basic factors behind the rapid change in Southern California's ethnic composition since about 1960. It summarizes the reasons for the greatly increased immigration, especially from Asia and Latin America, and it points out how the ethnic transformation is also the result of ethnic differences in both fertility (birth rate) and net migration to Southern California. In this section we bring the people to Southern California, so to speak, so that in later chapters we can discuss what has happened to them here.

The Creation of Population and Land-Use Patterns

Initially a home only to Indians, Southern California became part of New Spain and, after 1821, Mexico. During their 79 years of rule, those powers accomplished the region's first ethnic transformation—from Indian to Mexican.

The second ethnic transformation was initiated in 1848, when California was taken over by the United States after Mexico was defeated in war. By 1880 the Spanish-speaking inhabitants of Southern California were outnumbered by English-speakers from the eastern United States. After the

Santa Fe Railroad connected Los Angeles with the Midwest in 1886, the pace of the influx skyrocketed. Americans arrived from all parts of this country to make their new homes here.

From that time on, landowners, developers, and realtors actively promoted Southern California to other Americans. Most of the people who responded by settling here were whites, who were happy to forsake life on Midwestern farms and towns for the warmth and dryness of Southern California. In the first half of the twentieth century these migrants set the dominant cultural tone in Southern California. They also stimulated the growth of various industries designed to capture the market the newcomers represented. For more than a hundred years the character and growth of the region have been controlled by whites, though they have thought of themselves as just ordinary Americans rather than as whites.

Immigrants from China, Japan, Mexico, and Europe also came in the late nineteenth and early twentieth centuries, but it was in the 1960s that immigration—migration from other countries—increased substantially. Immigrants of varied backgrounds, together with whites, blacks, American Indians, Mexicans, and Asians already here, have begun a third ethnic transformation. Although only partial in scope compared with the previous two, this most recent transformation has introduced an ethnic diversity unparalleled in the region's history.

Mountains and flatlands. Within Southern California, almost all settlement has taken place in the flatlands, which stretch from the coast to the mountains, and between the various mountain ranges (Fig. 2.1). The high and rugged San Gabriel Mountains, which separate Los Angeles and most of Southern California from the Mojave Desert to the north, have always been a barrier to transportation and development. The Santa Ana Mountains of eastern Orange County are also steep sloped and composed of hard rock. They lie mostly within a national forest, thus precluding subdivision into lots for homes. However, the Santa Monica Mountains, the foothills of the San Gabriels, and the Palos Verdes Peninsula are much lower and have been much prized as settings for homes, with correspondingly higher prices than homes on the adjacent flatlands. More distant from the major centers of population, the gently sloping San Jose Hills, Puente Hills, and Chino Hills have been developed only more recently. All these areas continue to be associated with higher status and greater wealth.

With those minor exceptions, homes, stores, offices, and industries have been located on the flatlands of Southern California. The largest contiguous flat area stretches south from the Santa Monica and San Gabriel Mountains through Orange County and far east through the San Gabriel Valley to the cities of San Bernardino and Riverside. To the north of the Santa Monica Mountains is the San Fernando Valley, which is connected with the larger basin by a gap in the mountains through which flows the Los Angeles River. The original pueblo of Los Angeles, founded in 1781, was sited by the Spanish in order to easily tap the waters of this once-perennial river for irrigation farming. The downtown part of Los Angeles (hereafter referred to as "Downtown") developed near this original center, and it is from this area that Los Angeles has been expanding outward since the 1880s.

Dispersal of population. Interurban railways were laid out to newly founded towns and villages like Santa Monica, Pasadena, Redondo, Norwalk, Downey, Santa Ana, Monrovia, and Riverside by companies involved in land sales in those areas and along those routes (Fig. 2.2). By the 1920s, as the automobile was replacing the railways, new highways—financed by government—were opening up new areas in all directions for land subdivision. In the 1950s and 1960s a basic grid of freeways was constructed, vastly extending the residential fringe of the metropolitan area. Since that time the metropolitan periphery has continued to expand as new freeways have increased accessibility over a much larger area.

In the first half of the twentieth century much of the flatland between the scattered towns and subdivisions was farmed. Vineyards; fields of grain and hay; rows of irrigated beans, celery, strawberries, melons; and groves of orange and walnut trees seemed to stretch for miles. Fields and orchards, punctuated by occasional poultry houses and dairy barns, occupied most of the better agricultural land, especially in the San Gabriel and Pomona Valleys, southern Los Angeles County, and northern Orange County. Between World War II and 1949 Los Angeles County was the leading county in the United States in the value of agricultural products sold.[2] After about 1950, however, the pace of urbanization increased, leading to the virtual demise of farming in most parts of Los Angeles and Orange Counties by 1990.

The development of affordable housing in an expanding metropolitan periphery, the widespread availability of automobiles, and improved transportation connections between these new suburbs and the older city center made it possible for many whites to move into what they saw as superior housing in the suburbs. A cultural preference for single-family houses surrounded by lawns and gardens gave further impetus to suburbanization.

In parts of southern Los Angeles and northern Orange Counties the location of oil fields and refineries stimulated nearby suburban developments before 1930.[3] The demand for homes for oil workers in El Segundo, Torrance, Signal Hill, San Pedro, Huntington Beach, Brea, and Santa Fe Springs led to home construction nearby. The rapid expansion of automobile and other manufacturing also prompted homebuilding for workers' families. In the early 1940s new planned communities for defense workers were built near aircraft factories, and after World War II other residential developments were designed and located for workers at other large industrial facilities.[4] The net result was a dispersal of industry which gave an economic base and a working-class character to many suburbs.

By the 1960s residential suburbs and industry had already filled much of the flatland near Los Angeles, and new homebuilding became more active in surrounding areas—Orange County, the eastern San Gabriel Valley and western San Fernando Valley, and the Santa Clarita and Simi Valleys.

The trend of increasing dispersal has continued, so that residents of Southern California are scattered over most of the region—wherever the terrain is not too steep or where nonresidential land uses prohibit housing (Fig. 2.1). Densities of people per square mile tend to be higher in the older settled areas. Because minorities usually had lower incomes than whites and faced discriminatory restrictions on where they could live, they tended to live in those older areas. Minority groups often established enclaves in such neighborhoods, many of which were still significant as of 1990. Streets in the older, more central part of Los Angeles are mapped in some detail, so that the ethnic-group settlements referred to in chapters 3 though 5 can more easily be located (Fig. 2.4).

Housing development and mobility. The detailed distribution of people of varied status and identity within any metropolitan region like Los Angeles is limited by the distribution of housing of different types and cost.

The basic process of residential development has been the subdivision of large tracts of land into small parcels and the construction of single-family detached houses on those parcels. Realtors and developers judged future demand and made all the key decisions regarding the location and timing of land purchase and subdivision, the income level of the desired home buyers, and the style and characteristics of the homes they built.[5] After World War II the government helped to simulate further subdivision by subsidizing the cost of new freeways and guaranteeing mortgage loans with good terms for new home buyers, including working-class families and others with low incomes.

Once new housing becomes available, it normally entices residents from other parts of Southern California who can afford that housing. A chain of housing openings appears, as those who move into the new house or apartment leave behind a vacancy, which is then usually filled by others, which then results in another housing vacancy, and so forth. Households insert themselves into these vacancy chains, including the initial one based on new construction. They choose their new residence based on the number and ages of people in their household, their financial resources, and their

general areas of preference and avoidance. Ethnic identity and networks play a role in these locational decisions, which in large part determine ethnic distributions.

Industrial location before 1960. As hundreds of thousands of migrants poured into Los Angeles in the first two decades of the twentieth century, the oil, movie, apparel, automobile, rubber, and aircraft industries all built facilities and expanded. The oil industry preceded the others, and the location of its larger operations determined much of the dispersed pattern of manufacturing in the region. Other types of manufacturers responded to the opportunities provided by the region's climate and ample buildable land, its supply of potential workers and consumers, and the weakness of most unions in Southern California.

Railroad lines had already linked Los Angeles with points east by means of three routes through the San Gabriel Valley, with the harbor at Wilmington by way of Alameda Street, and with San Francisco through the San Fernando Valley (Fig. 2.3). These arteries became corridors for the location of those industries that required rail transportation. Certain municipalities like Torrance, Vernon, and Industry were planned to emphasize large industrial operations. Aircraft factories were dispersed in Santa Monica, Inglewood, Downey, Burbank, and Hawthorne; and in 1941 Douglas Aircraft built a large new assembly plant in Long Beach.

Apart from dispersed aircraft factories and narrow industrial corridors along railroad lines, large industrial plants were typically located around Vernon and in the harbor area. In general, the more southern areas of Los Angeles County were preferred for industrial development. This was because they provided easy access to ocean transportation and contained large parcels of former farmland for potential development. This greater concentration of industry in the southern part of Los Angeles County has meant that blue-collar workers have been more strongly represented in that area than in areas to the north.[6] In contrast, professional, managerial, and clerical (white-collar) workers tended to live in the other directions away from Downtown: to the west as far as Santa Monica and in and near Pasadena.

Deconcentration of stores, offices, and industries after 1960. The suburbanization that began with nineteenth-century residential development has gathered steam more recently. Building projects have included single-family houses, as before, but have no longer been restricted to that type of development. Because the more distant areas of Orange County, eastern Ventura County, and the eastern San Gabriel Valley were still mostly small towns and agricultural land until the 1960s and 1970s, this more varied form of deconcentration has especially characterized those areas.

Beginning in the 1960s, modern industrial plants, shopping centers, and residential subdivisions began to replace the fields and orchards. All urban functions have tended to move away from the old downtowns. Massive enclosed shopping centers, industrial parks, corporate and government office buildings, restaurants, and hotels have appeared in various clusters, their locations often close to higher-status neighborhoods and suburbs (Fig. 2.3). New apartment and townhouse complexes have been built, as have many new subdivisions of modern single-family houses. All have been designed not for pedestrians but for people with automobiles.

Because homogeneity of land use in any one area remains important to the people who will use and buy homes and other buildings, distinct functions are each given their own area. A mosaic of land uses describes the urban and suburban patterns of Southern California: agricultural, industrial, office, shopping, and transportation land uses cluster in different places. Even the locations of apartment housing are evident on a detailed land-use map. Altogether, the highly intricate distributions of various land uses are a change from the loose collection of suburbs and vacant land beyond the urban fringe that characterized the early 1960s.

A multinucleated urban pattern. The new malls, the industrial zones, and the clusters of office buildings can all be considered nuclei that attract local residents and outsiders for work, shopping, or other services. Various tracts of new housing are priced to preserve the homogeneity of income level, as in earlier decades. The outer cities are "large conglomerates of technologically advanced industry, services, and information processing. They are sharply differentiated by class, income, and life-styles."[7] The post-1960 spatial pattern reflects a high degree of urbanization—but with no clear center. Because new construction is no longer restricted to tracts of single-family houses, this has been called "postsuburban" development.

The business centers that have been built far from the old central business district of Los Angeles have siphoned away much of the business activity that in earlier times was focused on Downtown. These new office complexes have been appropriately described as "edge cities."[8] In Southern California such "suburban downtown" centers include Warner Center in the San Fernando Valley, Century City in the Westside of Los Angeles, the area adjacent to Los Angeles International Airport (LAX), and the redeveloped downtowns of Glendale and Pasadena, Irvine Spectrum, and Newport Center–Fashion Island. The largest of these developments are found on extensive tracts of vacant or former agricultural land that escaped earlier development. In size and scope the city of Irvine in Orange County epitomizes these trends. "By design Irvine has no downtown but is a deconcentrated mosaic of residential villages, small shopping centers, and industrial parks. Irvine's city hall is not a routine walk from any of the city's villages."[9]

When viewed as an entire metropolitan area, including the area of older development, Southern California can be characterized as essentially polycentered or multinucleated (Fig. 2.3).[10] Centers or nuclei can be shopping malls, complexes of business and government offices, industrial areas and warehousing areas, airports, or universities. Between these centers lies a residential mosaic—a set of housing areas each somewhat homogeneous in terms of price and type of dwelling. Some more traditional urban patterns, such as the location of small stores along major highways and industries near railroad tracks, still characterize older sections of the metropolitan area. However, areas developed since about 1970 and the entire built-up area of Southern California are polycentered. This spatial pattern is different from that of the pre-1960 period when Orange County was essentially a bedroom appendage of Los Angeles County. Southern California suburbs were nearly all residential, whereas shopping and office work were much more concentrated in central business districts or downtowns.

This multinucleated mosaic of varying land uses is hidden from most of the maps in this book because the maps are based on only the residential population. Some census tracts have relatively few people because they contain large industrial complexes, commercial districts, or open areas. For instance, the city of Irwindale in the San Gabriel Valley appears on maps as a large tract, but it is mostly empty land with gravel pits and contains only 1,050 people. Only in consultation with the land-use map (Fig. 2.3) can some significant aspects of tracts be identified.

Patterns of Housing

Age of housing. Of all the housing units (single-family houses, apartments, mobile homes, and so forth) in Southern California in 1990, only 19 percent were constructed prior to 1950. Another 19 percent were built during each of the three decades subsequent to 1950. In the 1980s the pace of construction increased: 22 percent of all Southern California's housing units were constructed during that decade. Although many buildings dating from before 1950 were later demolished to make room for newer housing or other land uses, in the poorest areas less money has been available for reconstruction and in-filling. As a result, a few tracts, primarily in South Central Los Angeles, contain a majority of houses built before 1940.

Because housing development has not followed an overall plan, the varied timing and location of new subdivisions and the in-filling of buildable spaces have resulted in a somewhat helter-skelter pattern (Fig. 2.5). If the variability in percentage of single-family houses is also considered, the spatial pattern of development is indeed complex (Fig. 2.6).

Nevertheless, a general pattern of age of housing can be discerned. Older houses are found near the centers of cities, because these areas were developed earlier. This is especially evident in Los Angeles, which had 1.2 million residents in 1930. Other leading cities of the day—those with populations of about 30,000 or more in 1930—had proportionately smaller areas of old housing, which have been more easily modified by urban renewal. For this reason Long Beach, Pasadena, Glendale, Santa Monica, Riverside, San Bernardino, and Santa Ana have fewer tracts in which the majority of housing was constructed prior to 1951. Old neighborhoods in smaller outlying places, like San Pedro, Torrance, Santa Ana, Burbank, South Gate, and Long Beach can also be seen on the map. In Irvine and scattered other areas of new development, those tracts which show a pre-1951 median year of housing construction have few residents and are essentially office buildings and industry.

The extensive area subdivided in the 1950s is easily visible. Because the single-family houses that typify these areas are not obsolete or decaying, they have experienced only in-filling and little demolition of older housing.

The most recent housing construction tends to be near the outer edges of suburbs—in the urban fringe. Easy access by means of interstate highways and the vast extent of buildable land to the east and west meant that during the 1980s some new subdivisions were located far beyond the bounds of maps in this book. By 1990 many people were commuting from new homes in very distant places, like Lancaster and Palmdale in the Antelope Valley far to the north and Hemet, Lake Elsinore, and Moreno Valley in Riverside County. Houses in such subdivisions were priced lower than were those closer to the core, and the lower prices enabled many families to become first-time home buyers. The drawback of locations on the urban fringe is the long drive required in the commute to work.

There are numerous exceptions to this general pattern of more recent housing near the urban fringe. This is partly because many older houses remain in what were once outlying farm areas, such as in and near Piru, at the top of Figure 2.5. Also, unused parcels within many older subdivisions were built up much later, and older housing has sometimes been destroyed and replaced with modern apartment complexes. Most pockets of new housing on once-vacant land surrounded by older neighborhoods are too small to be evident on maps at the scale of census tracts. In many cases the in-filling is as small as one or two houses or apartment buildings on tiny parcels. Nevertheless, some larger examples of this redevelopment in older areas can be seen on Bunker Hill in Downtown, near Marina del Rey, and in parts of Burbank, Industry, Inglewood, and Torrance (Fig. 2.5).

Single-unit detached housing. Single-unit detached houses (including mobile homes) are often referred to as single-family homes. Most people distinguish these from other types of housing such as townhouses and apartment buildings. Single-unit houses constitute 59.5 percent of all housing units in Southern California.[11] Despite the importance of this type of residence in this region, it is less frequently found here than in U.S. metropolitan areas in general (62.0 percent). In the older, more densely settled Los Angeles City, single-family housing represents only 45.4 percent of residential units.

Few areas contain very low percentages of single-unit detached houses (Fig. 2.6). These are either the poorer and more central sections of the older cities or newer residential sections of apartment and condominium complexes. Since 1960 many apartment buildings and larger complexes have been constructed, especially for rental housing. Because the number of apartments may represent far less than half the housing units in the entire tract, small pockets of apartment development often do not show up on tract-level maps. Where the developments are larger, however, often with large complexes of several buildings, they are evident and widespread. Such larger apartment and condominium developments characterize parts of Santa Monica, Marina del Rey, Culver City, Redondo Beach, Glendale, Woodland Hills, and Irvine.

Single-unit detached houses constitute more than 97 percent of all housing in some areas. A very large and homogeneous single-family-housing area can be seen most clearly in Lakewood (Fig. 2.6). In the early 1950s old hay and grain fields were covered with tract after tract of houses in what was one of the largest subdivision developments ever. Other census tracts that are homogeneous in their single-family housing are home to wealthier families. Those pockets are widespread, but the largest areas with almost entirely single-family housing are in the Santa Monica Mountains and the northern and western parts of the San Fernando Valley.

Homeownership. Of the total of 4.9 million households in Southern California, 54.0 percent own the home they are living in—or are considered to, even if most of them still have a mortgage to pay off. Homeownership is less likely in Southern California than in U.S. metropolitan areas as a whole (61.8 percent).[12] Homeownership is partly an indicator of wealth, and areas with high percentages of owners are typically areas of moderate to high income (Fig. 2.7). Conversely, people with low incomes are apt to be renters, and housing is more apt to be rented when the structure itself is older. These reasons combine to explain the fact that only 39.4 percent of households in Los Angeles City are homeowners. Older single-family houses and apartment buildings are likely to need remodeling or roofing, plumbing, and electrical repairs. Such older structures are less attractive to buyers.

Some contrasts of wealth within short distances are evident, and this juxtaposition can be a source of neighborhood tension. The Los Feliz section in the hills of Hollywood, with its high percentage of owners, is a different world from that of the renters who live south of Hollywood Boulevard. The same comparison holds for the Cheviot Hills and the adjacent flatlands east of Robertson Boulevard. The wealthiest section of Santa Monica is also easily distinguishable from areas in that city with a high percentage of renters.

However, high rates of homeownership are occasionally found in areas of moderate income: much of the city of Carson, the Avalon section of South Central Los Angeles, and parts of Huntington Beach and Westminster.

Overcrowded households. The ratio between the number of people in a household and the number of rooms in their home is called the housing ratio. It can be a useful indicator of relative crowding. A housing unit is usually considered overcrowded if the number of persons living in it is greater than the number of rooms. Most households in Southern California are not overcrowded. However, 6 percent of the households have between 1.01 and 1.50 persons per room, and another 10 percent are severely overcrowded, with more than 1.5 persons per room. Households are overcrowded because of poverty, but the large size of Hispanic immigrant families is part of the reason for the fact that Hispanics constitute 73 percent of all Southern California households that are severely overcrowded.

Thus, overcrowding of between 1 and 3 persons per room shows many areas with high proportions of recent Hispanic immigrants (Fig. 2.8). It is not surprising that some of the greatest household crowding occurs in the poorest part of Los Angeles—the area immediately south of Downtown and Little Tokyo, characterized by poorly maintained and sometimes abandoned apartment buildings, wholesale markets, trucking operations, and garment factories. The other area of intense overcrowding is in the Westlake barrio, west of Downtown.

Also overcrowded, but less so, are surrounding areas that received many Latino immigrants during the 1980s, including East Hollywood, Koreatown, Boyle Heights, Pacoima, and Huntington Park. In these and other areas, immigrant families and groups of men have often shared housing units meant for many fewer people. To illustrate, during the 1980s the southeastern part of Los Angeles (adjacent to Vernon and Huntington Park) recorded a gain of more than 47,000 residents but a net increase of only 198 housing units.[13] In the case of Long Beach and one part of Santa Ana, some of the overcrowding is due to the presence of Cambodian refugees with many children. Overcrowding in poor areas that are mostly black is not as severe a problem because the birth rate among blacks has been much lower than the birth rate among Hispanics or Cambodians.

College dormitories, prisons, and residential hospitals. Housing ratios that are even higher than those that indicate household overcrowding can identify a completely separate phenomenon: large institutions that provide housing for people in group quarters rather than households. All mapped census tracts in which the ratio of persons to rooms is greater than 6 are such places (Fig. 2.8). Because their special character may affect details of some map patterns, institutions that house two-thirds or more of the total tract population are identified in Table 2.1 and in Figure 2.8.

Patterns of Social Class

Differentiation of neighborhoods in terms of social class has been an important feature in American cities and suburbs in the twentieth century. Street railways, interurban trolleys, and automobiles led to the opening up of many new housing

areas, but any one subdivision was designed and priced for buyers of a specific income level. This was the first step in creating a residential geography defined by income.

Another factor in class differentiation was political. As cities grew and new housing was extended outward, most new subdivisions did not join up with the central city. Many incorporated as separate suburban entities. The government of the suburb could set lower property tax rates, apportion revenues,

Table 2.1 Populations in Group Quarters

Institution	Number	Percent of Tract Population
California Institution for Men (prison, Chino, San Bernardino County)	8,271	100
California Narcotics Rehabilitation Center (Norco, Riverside County)	4,966	100
Metropolitan Detention Center (federal prison, Downtown)	2,567	100
Lanterman Developmental Center (state rehabilitation center, Pomona)	1,088	100
California State University Long Beach (student dormitories)	855	99
Federal Correctional Institution (prison, Terminal Island)	1,122	98
Rancho Los Amigos Medical Center (county rehabilitation center, Downey)	357	97
CSU Polytechnic, Pomona (student dormitories)	1,190	97
West Los Angeles V. A. Medical Center	907	96
Long Beach V. A. Medical Center	322	91
University of California, Los Angeles (student dormitories)	4,629	90
Claremont Colleges (student dormitories)	3,524	87
University of Southern California (student dormitories)	2,313	84
Los Angeles County Central Jail (Downtown)	6,739	73
Metropolitan State Hospital (mental hospital, Norwalk)	838	67

Note: All institutions are in Los Angeles County unless otherwise indicated. These institutional populations are included in Figure 2.8 and other 1990 maps.

and create regulations that would have the effect of excluding poor people and minorities.[14] Suburban governments could refuse to provide public housing for low-income families, and they could limit apartment construction, mobile homes, or any other type of housing. For poor people and minorities, such restrictions certainly reduced housing opportunities in those suburbs that had such policies.

Although many people have moved from older housing to newer developments in the suburbs, the location of rich and poor neighborhoods has changed very little over the last thirty years.[15] Despite the aging of all housing, neighborhoods that began as high status have remained higher than neighborhoods that were originally of lesser status. Neighborhoods tend to decline slightly as housing ages and as new housing appears near the urban fringe. This is because some residents leave and buy homes in the new subdivisions. In the older areas the relative status of neighborhoods is usually stable and slower to change than is ethnic composition.

Since 1940 neighborhoods have become more differentiated in terms of status. Between 1940 and 1970 rich and poor families in Los Angeles came to live increasingly in separate areas.[16] Improved transportation, the land-development process, and the separatist politics of suburban governments have increased income and ethnic differences among places. In the 1980s this divergence was accentuated by a growing income polarization (see chapter 7). Differences in values, lifestyles, and social networks among occupational-status groups may be an especially important factor in differentiating neighborhoods.[17] Wider gaps in status between neighborhoods means that the geography of class becomes still more important.

Together, the maps of educational attainment, occupational status, people in specific occupations and industries, and poverty are sufficient to describe the general geography of status in Southern California. Income is another important facet of status, but it is saved for use in maps of income levels for each group—whites, blacks, Hispanics, and Asians (see Figs. 3.11, 3.16, 4.9, and 5.15).

Educational attainment and occupational status.
Whereas poverty focuses on the lower end of the continuum of social class, our maps of education and occupational status are a good means of describing areal patterns at the upper end of that continuum.

In Southern California 22 percent of the people aged 25 and older have graduated from a four-year college or university. Where that percentage is doubled and even tripled, the residents have exceptionally high status in terms of educational attainment (Fig. 2.9). The sharpness of many of the boundaries is striking and shows powerful contrasts between places. More than half of all adults are college graduates in many special places. The higher status of Hancock Park, Belmont Shore, Porter Ranch, and parts of Fullerton, compared with surrounding areas, is clear. Exceptionally low percentages of college graduates are associated with either poverty (Fig. 2.21) or a high percentage of Hispanic residents (Figs. 7.2–7.4).

Twenty-eight percent of all employed Southern Californians are professionals or managers, executives, and administrators. Areal variations in this percentage are pronounced, with many roots in the patterns of development in the early twentieth century. In 1940 people in professional, clerical, domestic, and service occupations tended to live between Downtown and Beverly Hills and south as far as Slauson Boulevard.[18] Within this area the proportion of blacks was particularly high east of Main Street. In contrast, craftsmen, operatives, and laborers were common east of the Los Angeles River, in Santa Monica, and in the entire area between Slauson Boulevard and the harbor. Although the residential location and occupations of blacks have changed radically since 1940, the 1990 occupational pattern confirms the greater percentage of blue-collar or working-class people in the southern and southeastern part of Los Angeles County, compared with the white-collar central and western area.

Some of the same pattern is evident today, although, with the expansion of the metropolitan area, there are more separate areas with high percentages of managers and professionals (Fig. 2.10). Pockets of high percentages of managers and professionals are often clearly differentiated from surrounding areas. In Long Beach this can be seen in Belmont Shore and in Bixby Knolls just east of Interstate 710. Also, over 60 percent of all employed people living in the gated community of Rancho Los Alamitos are in high-status occupations.

As expected, the pattern is similar to that of educational attainment. The few areas in which men and women are more likely to be professionals or managers than they are to be college graduates are probably not significant. The residential preferences of physicians and lawyers confirm these patterns for general regions within Southern California. However, police officers with lower incomes tend to live in very different areas (Figs. 2.11–2.13).[19] Employment in these three occupations is found widely in Southern California.

On the other hand, the distribution of people who work in certain specific industries is related to both income and employment location. An example is the high-tech industries in southern Los Angeles and northern Orange Counties (Figs. 2.14 and 2.15). Moreover, sometimes ethnic groups are highly represented in certain industries (see chapter 8), so that the location of ethnic concentrations is an additional factor. We demonstrate a Russian-ancestry niche in the theater and motion-picture industry, as well as Guatemalan and Salvadoran overrepresentation in the manufacturing of apparel and in private household services. The distribution of workers in these industries shows special concentrations, with the pattern based on a combination of income level, work location, and ethnicity (Figs. 2.16–2.18). Such distinctive distributions may also characterize other occupations and industries.

Poverty. The Census Bureau's definition of the level of income below which people are considered to be in poverty is based on both the total income of the household and the number of people living in it. The actual dollar value is adjusted by means of the national Consumer Price Index, which means that in Los Angeles, where housing prices were extremely high as of 1990, the percentage of people in poverty is understated.

A map of varying percentages of people in poverty portrays a fundamental aspect of the geography of social class, and the details of the pattern show real neighborhood differences (Fig. 2.19). The largest area of poverty extends from Downtown south past Watts, but the percentage in poverty typically decreases fairly abruptly beyond this area.

The pockets of greatest poverty are in the large public-housing projects built in the 1940s and 1950s (Fig. 2.19). Most of the tracts in which more than half the people are in poverty are such places, and some of these are identified on the map. These poverty tracts include Long Beach's Carmelitos Housing Project, built in 1939, and most of the seventeen projects in Los Angeles. Jordan Downs, Imperial Courts, and Nickerson Gardens in Watts are visible, as are Ramona Gardens in Boyle Heights and Pueblo del Rio in South Central.[20]

Other census tracts contain public-housing projects but are not so completely characterized by them. These include San Fernando Gardens in Pacoima, Rose Hill Courts in Lincoln Heights, Mar Vista Gardens in West Los Angeles, Dana Strand Village in Wilmington, and Rancho San Pedro in San Pedro. Occasionally the newer type of low-income, federally subsidized housing is large enough to be visible on the map. A good example of this is the privately owned Park Parthenia complex in Northridge.

Some focused concentrations of poverty also appear without these types of housing, but the proportions of people in poverty are usually less: the Skid Row southeast of Downtown and the poorest sections in many cities. In the San Fernando Valley the Blythe Street neighborhood just west of the General Motors plant in Van Nuys has long been notorious for poverty, drugs, and crime.

Two tracts easily noticed on Figure 2.19 have so few people that they are not significant. The first, a poverty tract in Santa Fe Springs, is almost all industrial but does contain 27 people. A similar situation occurs in Anaheim, where a modern industrial and warehousing area has completely engulfed the few old, run-down houses that date from the days when Mexicans worked nearby fields along the Santa Ana River floodplain. In 1990 the tract contained only 81 residents, mostly poor Mexican immigrants and their families.

Because this measure of poverty is so dependent on income, some tracts with college students also appear as pockets of poverty: for example, the University of Southern California and a section of Westwood next to the campus of the University of California, Los Angeles.

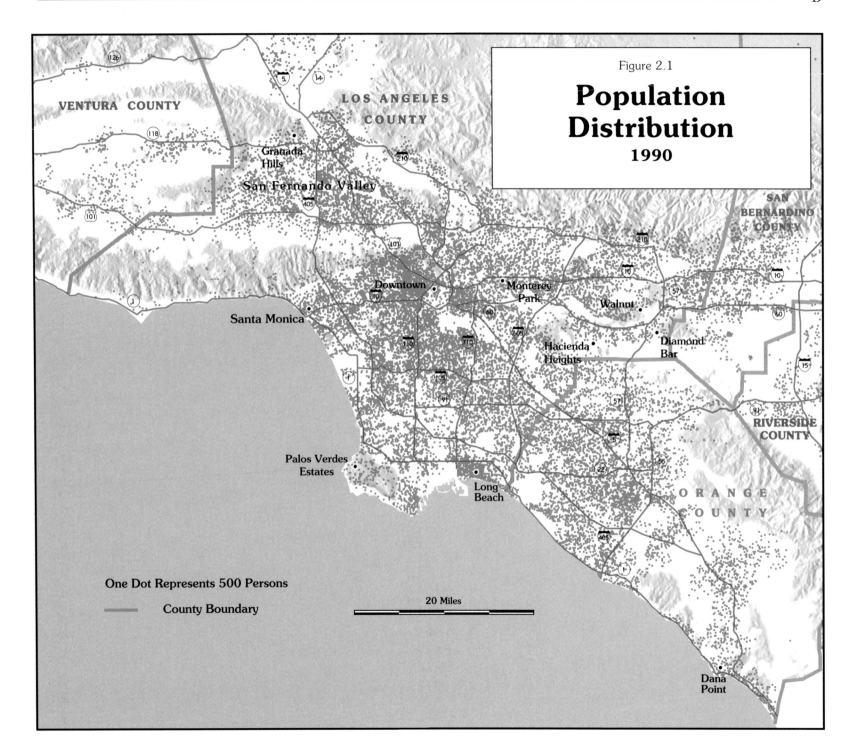

Figure 2.1

Population Distribution
1990

VENTURA COUNTY

LOS ANGELES COUNTY

SAN BERNARDINO COUNTY

Granada Hills

San Fernando Valley

Downtown

Monterey Park

Walnut

Diamond Bar

Santa Monica

Hacienda Heights

RIVERSIDE COUNTY

Palos Verdes Estates

Long Beach

ORANGE COUNTY

Dana Point

One Dot Represents 500 Persons

County Boundary

20 Miles

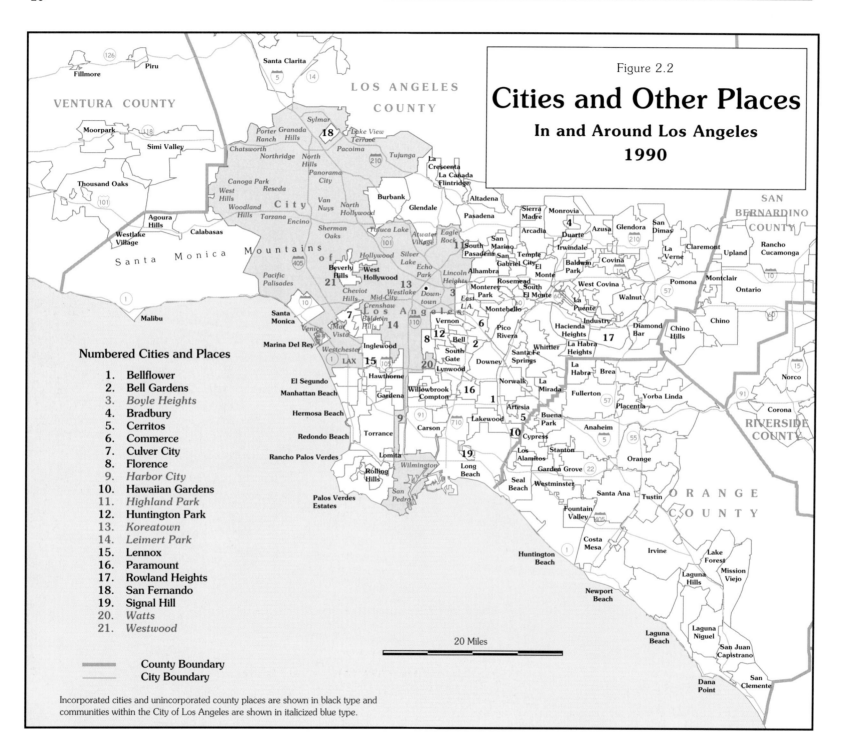

Figure 2.2

Cities and Other Places

In and Around Los Angeles
1990

Numbered Cities and Places

1. Bellflower
2. Bell Gardens
3. *Boyle Heights*
4. Bradbury
5. Cerritos
6. Commerce
7. Culver City
8. Florence
9. *Harbor City*
10. Hawaiian Gardens
11. *Highland Park*
12. Huntington Park
13. *Koreatown*
14. *Leimert Park*
15. Lennox
16. Paramount
17. Rowland Heights
18. San Fernando
19. Signal Hill
20. *Watts*
21. *Westwood*

━━━ County Boundary
─── City Boundary

20 Miles

Incorporated cities and unincorporated county places are shown in black type and communities within the City of Los Angeles are shown in italicized blue type.

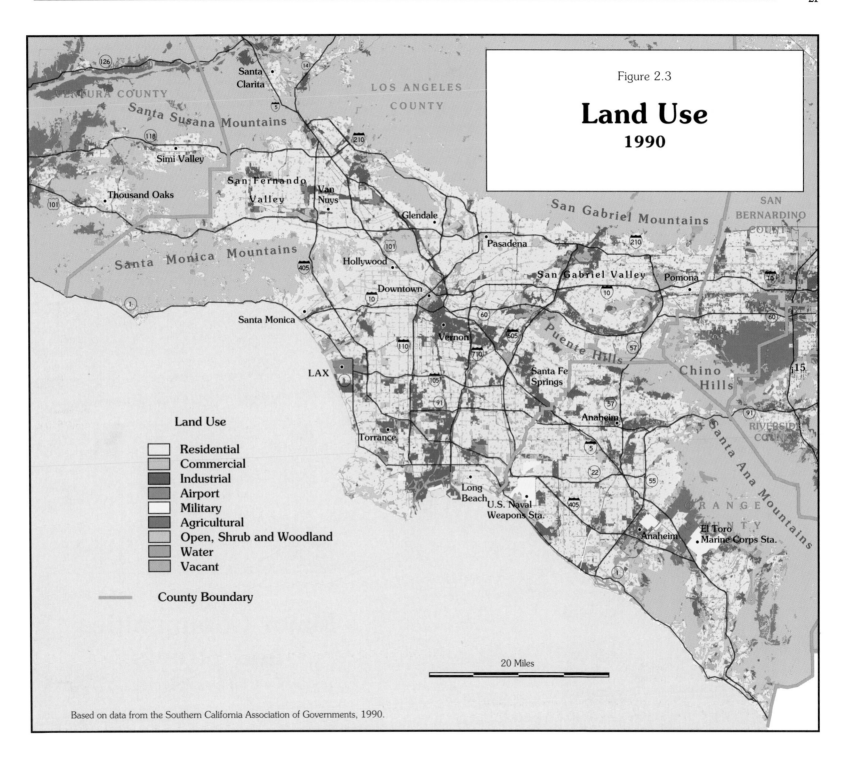

Figure 2.3

Land Use
1990

Land Use

- Residential
- Commercial
- Industrial
- Airport
- Military
- Agricultural
- Open, Shrub and Woodland
- Water
- Vacant

— County Boundary

20 Miles

Based on data from the Southern California Association of Governments, 1990.

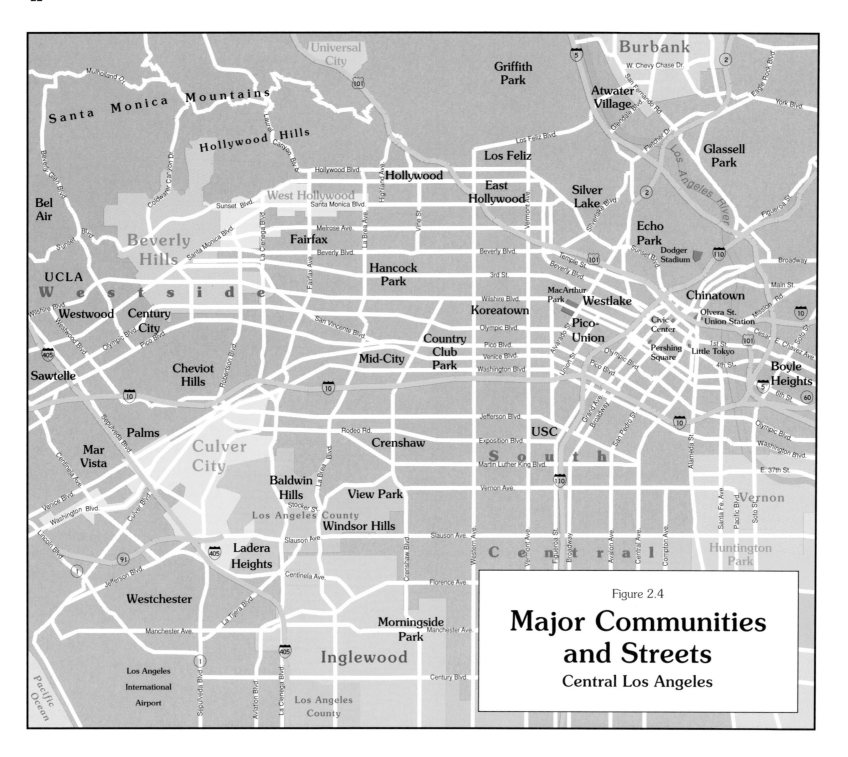

Figure 2.4

Major Communities and Streets

Central Los Angeles

Figure 2.5

Median Year of Housing Construction
1990

Number of Tracts	Median Year of Construction
369	Before 1951
857	1951 - 1960
718	1961 - 1970
460	1971 - 1980
160	1981 - 1990

County Boundary
City Boundary

20 Miles

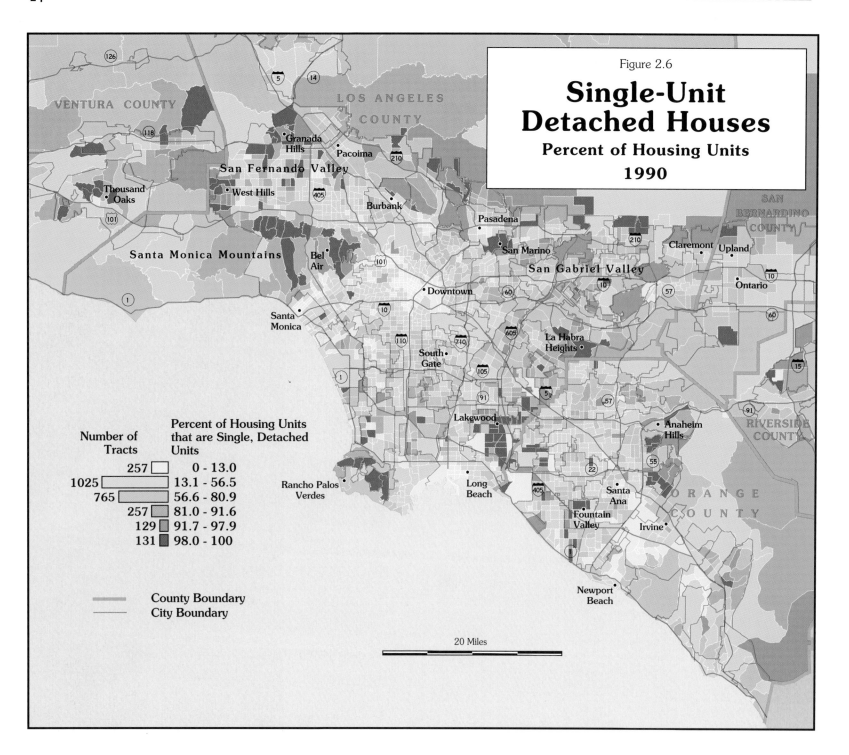

Figure 2.6

Single-Unit Detached Houses

Percent of Housing Units
1990

Number of Tracts	Percent of Housing Units that are Single, Detached Units
257	0 - 13.0
1025	13.1 - 56.5
765	56.6 - 80.9
257	81.0 - 91.6
129	91.7 - 97.9
131	98.0 - 100

County Boundary
City Boundary

20 Miles

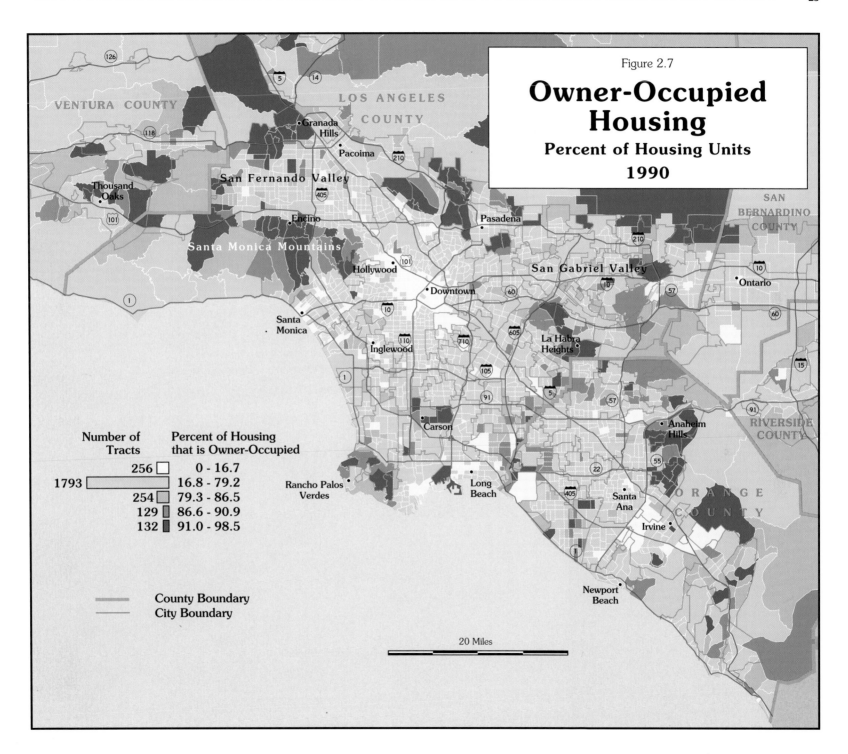

Figure 2.7

Owner-Occupied Housing

Percent of Housing Units

1990

Number of Tracts	Percent of Housing that is Owner-Occupied
256	0 - 16.7
1793	16.8 - 79.2
254	79.3 - 86.5
129	86.6 - 90.9
132	91.0 - 98.5

County Boundary
City Boundary

20 Miles

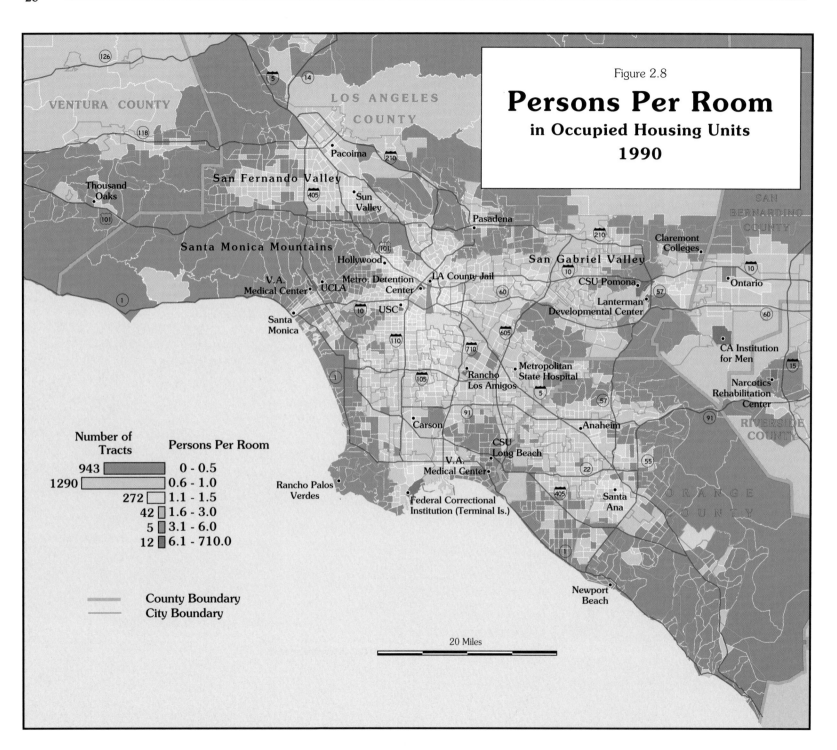

Figure 2.8

Persons Per Room
in Occupied Housing Units
1990

VENTURA COUNTY

LOS ANGELES COUNTY

Thousand Oaks

SAN BERNARDINO COUNTY

Pacoima

San Fernando Valley

Sun Valley

Pasadena

Claremont Colleges

Santa Monica Mountains

Hollywood

San Gabriel Valley

Ontario

V.A. Medical Center

UCLA

Metro. Detention Center

LA County Jail

CSU Pomona

Lanterman Developmental Center

USC

Santa Monica

CA Institution for Men

Metropolitan State Hospital

Narcotics Rehabilitation Center

Rancho Los Amigos

RIVERSIDE COUNTY

Carson

Anaheim

CSU Long Beach

V.A. Medical Center

Santa Ana

ORANGE COUNTY

Rancho Palos Verdes

Federal Correctional Institution (Terminal Is.)

Newport Beach

Number of Tracts	Persons Per Room
943	0 - 0.5
1290	0.6 - 1.0
272	1.1 - 1.5
42	1.6 - 3.0
5	3.1 - 6.0
12	6.1 - 710.0

County Boundary

City Boundary

20 Miles

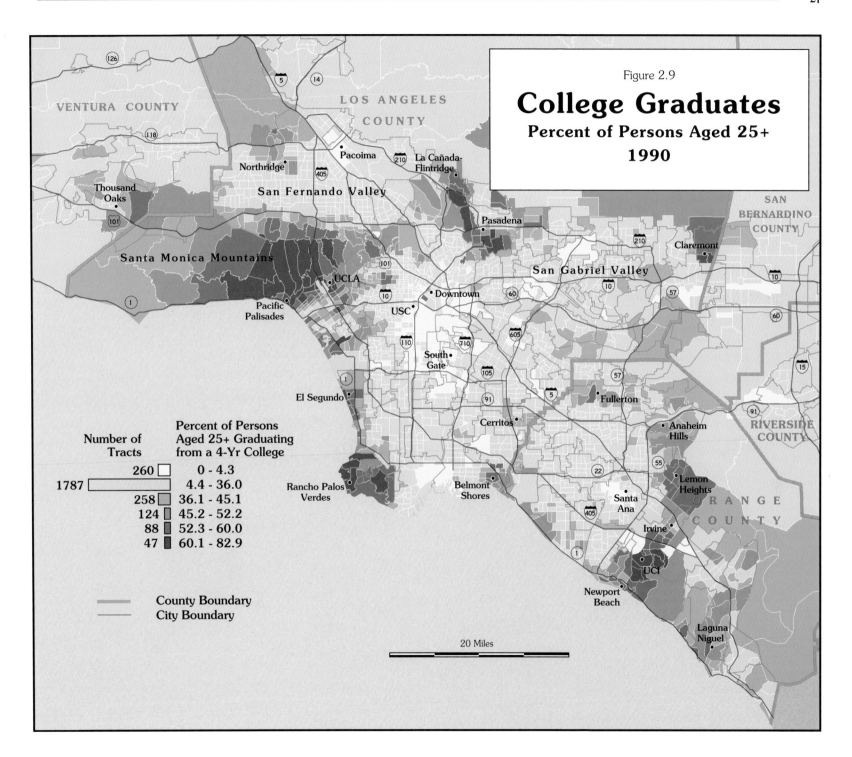

Figure 2.9

College Graduates
Percent of Persons Aged 25+
1990

Number of Tracts		Percent of Persons Aged 25+ Graduating from a 4-Yr College
260		0 - 4.3
1787		4.4 - 36.0
258		36.1 - 45.1
124		45.2 - 52.2
88		52.3 - 60.0
47		60.1 - 82.9

County Boundary
City Boundary

20 Miles

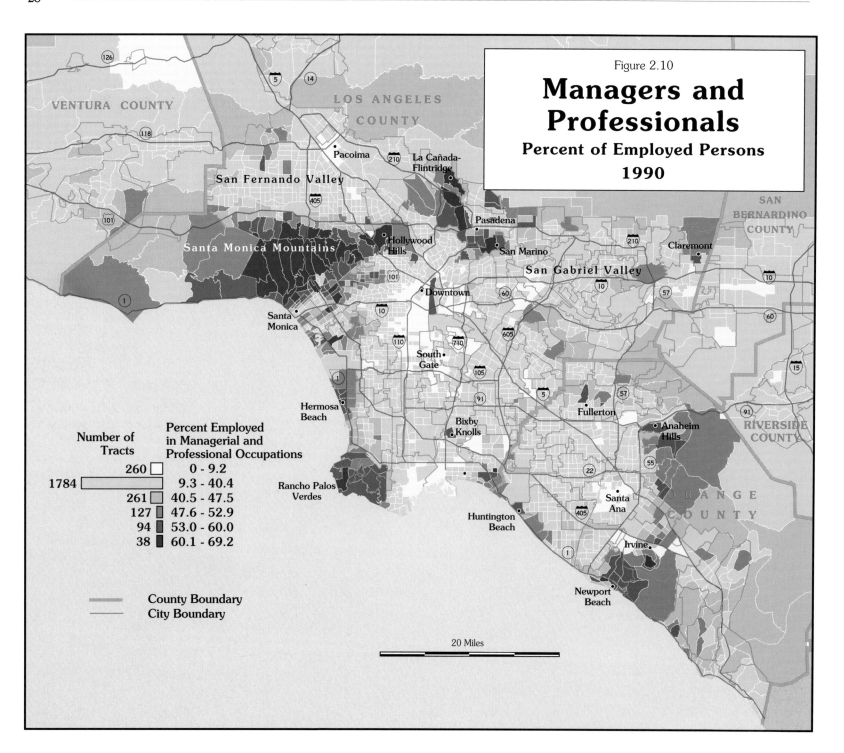

Figure 2.10

Managers and Professionals

Percent of Employed Persons

1990

Number of Tracts		Percent Employed in Managerial and Professional Occupations
260		0 - 9.2
1784		9.3 - 40.4
261		40.5 - 47.5
127		47.6 - 52.9
94		53.0 - 60.0
38		60.1 - 69.2

County Boundary

City Boundary

20 Miles

29

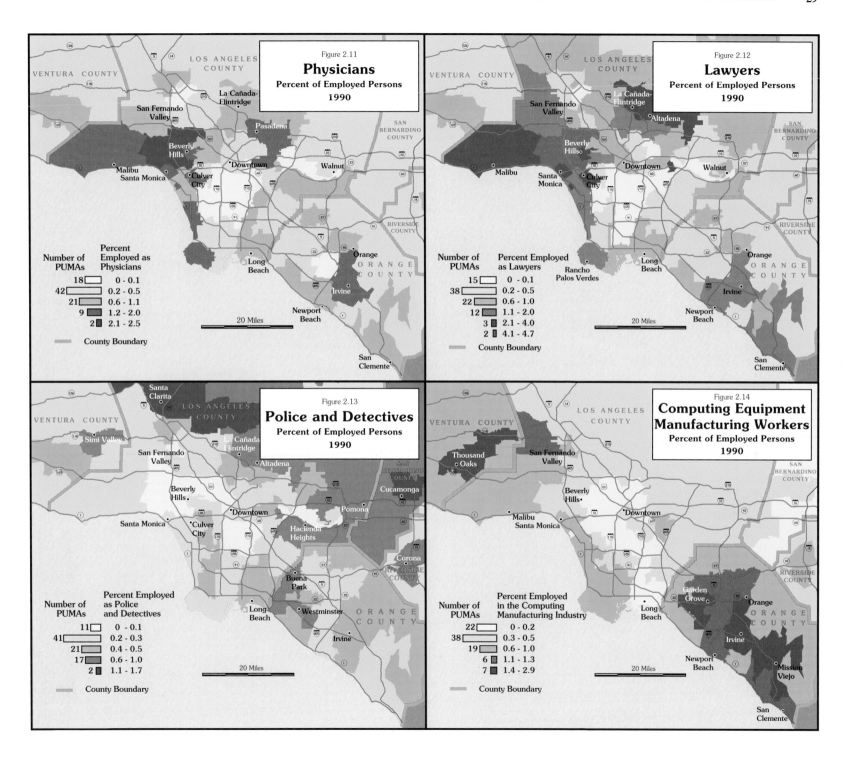

Figure 2.11
Physicians
Percent of Employed Persons
1990

Number of PUMAs | Percent Employed as Physicians
18 | 0 - 0.1
42 | 0.2 - 0.5
21 | 0.6 - 1.1
9 | 1.2 - 2.0
2 | 2.1 - 2.5

County Boundary

20 Miles

Figure 2.12
Lawyers
Percent of Employed Persons
1990

Number of PUMAs | Percent Employed as Lawyers
15 | 0 - 0.1
38 | 0.2 - 0.5
22 | 0.6 - 1.0
12 | 1.1 - 2.0
3 | 2.1 - 4.0
2 | 4.1 - 4.7

County Boundary

20 Miles

Figure 2.13
Police and Detectives
Percent of Employed Persons
1990

Number of PUMAs | Percent Employed as Police and Detectives
11 | 0 - 0.1
41 | 0.2 - 0.3
21 | 0.4 - 0.5
17 | 0.6 - 1.0
2 | 1.1 - 1.7

County Boundary

20 Miles

Figure 2.14
Computing Equipment Manufacturing Workers
Percent of Employed Persons
1990

Number of PUMAs | Percent Employed in the Computing Manufacturing Industry
22 | 0 - 0.2
38 | 0.3 - 0.5
19 | 0.6 - 1.0
6 | 1.1 - 1.3
7 | 1.4 - 2.9

County Boundary

20 Miles

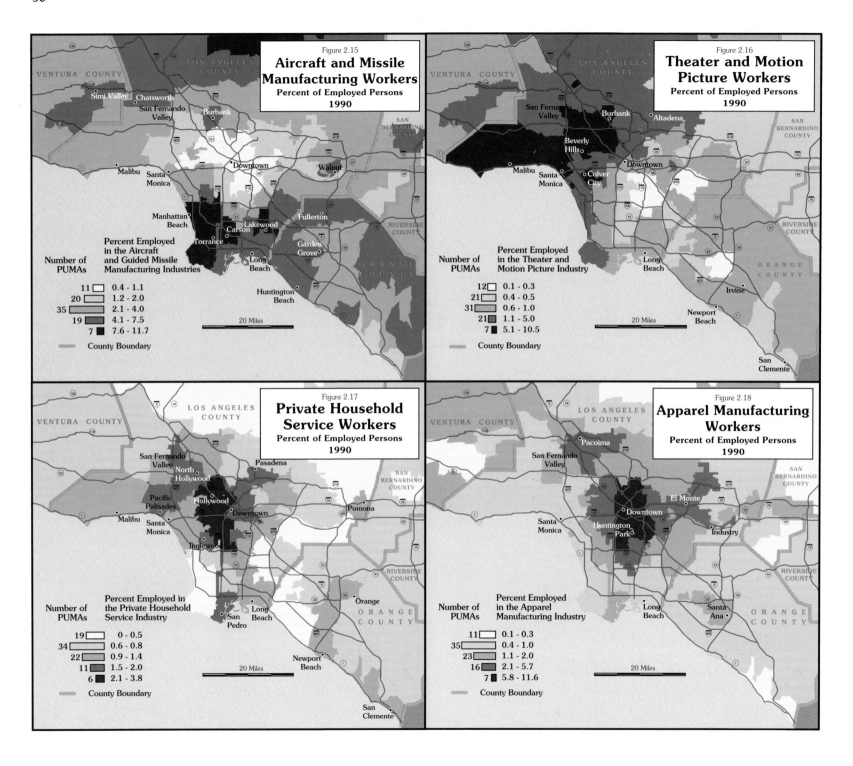

Figure 2.15

Aircraft and Missile Manufacturing Workers

Percent of Employed Persons
1990

Percent Employed
in the Aircraft
and Guided Missile
Manufacturing Industries

Number of
PUMAs

11 — 0.4 - 1.1
20 — 1.2 - 2.0
35 — 2.1 - 4.0
19 — 4.1 - 7.5
7 — 7.6 - 11.7

County Boundary

20 Miles

Figure 2.16

Theater and Motion Picture Workers

Percent of Employed Persons
1990

Percent Employed
in the Theater and
Motion Picture Industry

Number of
PUMAs

12 — 0.1 - 0.3
21 — 0.4 - 0.5
31 — 0.6 - 1.0
21 — 1.1 - 5.0
7 — 5.1 - 10.5

County Boundary

20 Miles

Figure 2.17

Private Household Service Workers

Percent of Employed Persons
1990

Percent Employed in
the Private Household
Service Industry

Number of
PUMAs

19 — 0 - 0.5
34 — 0.6 - 0.8
22 — 0.9 - 1.4
11 — 1.5 - 2.0
6 — 2.1 - 3.8

County Boundary

20 Miles

Figure 2.18

Apparel Manufacturing Workers

Percent of Employed Persons
1990

Percent Employed
in the Apparel
Manufacturing Industry

Number of
PUMAs

11 — 0.1 - 0.3
35 — 0.4 - 1.0
23 — 1.1 - 2.0
16 — 2.1 - 5.7
7 — 5.8 - 11.6

County Boundary

20 Miles

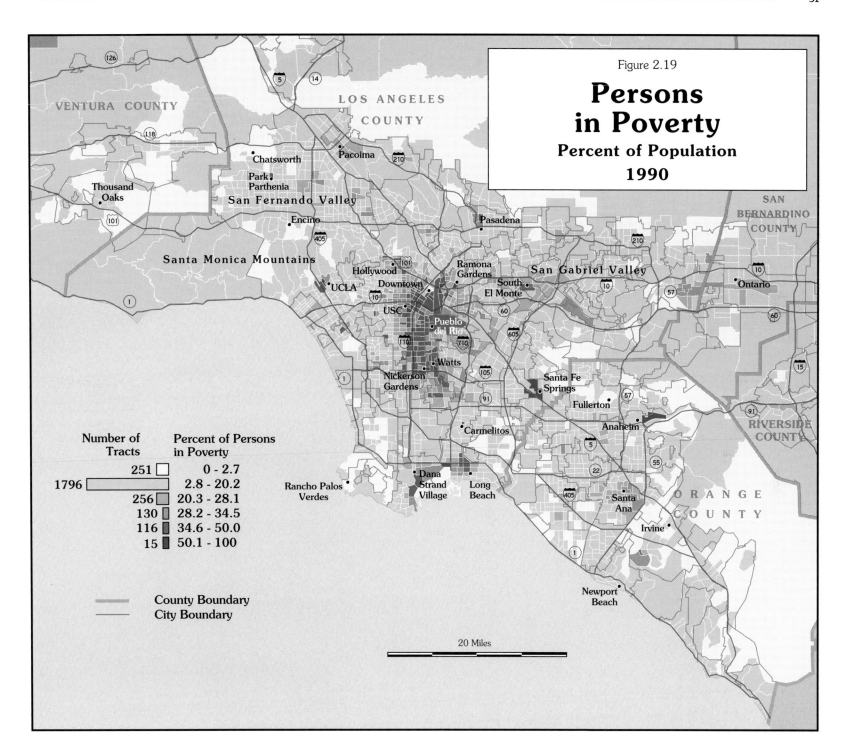

Figure 2.19

Persons in Poverty
Percent of Population
1990

Number of Tracts	Percent of Persons in Poverty
251	0 - 2.7
1796	2.8 - 20.2
256	20.3 - 28.1
130	28.2 - 34.5
116	34.6 - 50.0
15	50.1 - 100

County Boundary
City Boundary

20 Miles

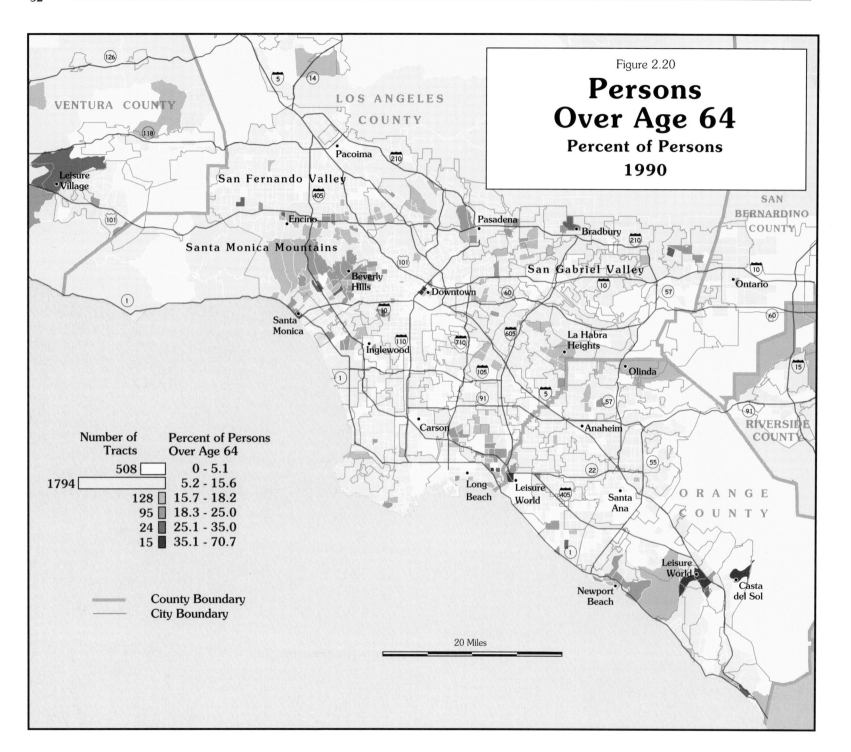

Figure 2.20

Persons Over Age 64

Percent of Persons

1990

VENTURA COUNTY

LOS ANGELES COUNTY

SAN BERNARDINO COUNTY

Leisure Village

Pacoima

San Fernando Valley

Encino

Pasadena

Bradbury

Santa Monica Mountains

San Gabriel Valley

Beverly Hills

Ontario

Downtown

Santa Monica

La Habra Heights

Inglewood

Olinda

RIVERSIDE COUNTY

Carson

Anaheim

Long Beach

Leisure World

Santa Ana

ORANGE COUNTY

Newport Beach

Leisure World

Casta del Sol

Number of Tracts	Percent of Persons Over Age 64
508	0 - 5.1
1794	5.2 - 15.6
128	15.7 - 18.2
95	18.3 - 25.0
24	25.1 - 35.0
15	35.1 - 70.7

County Boundary
City Boundary

20 Miles

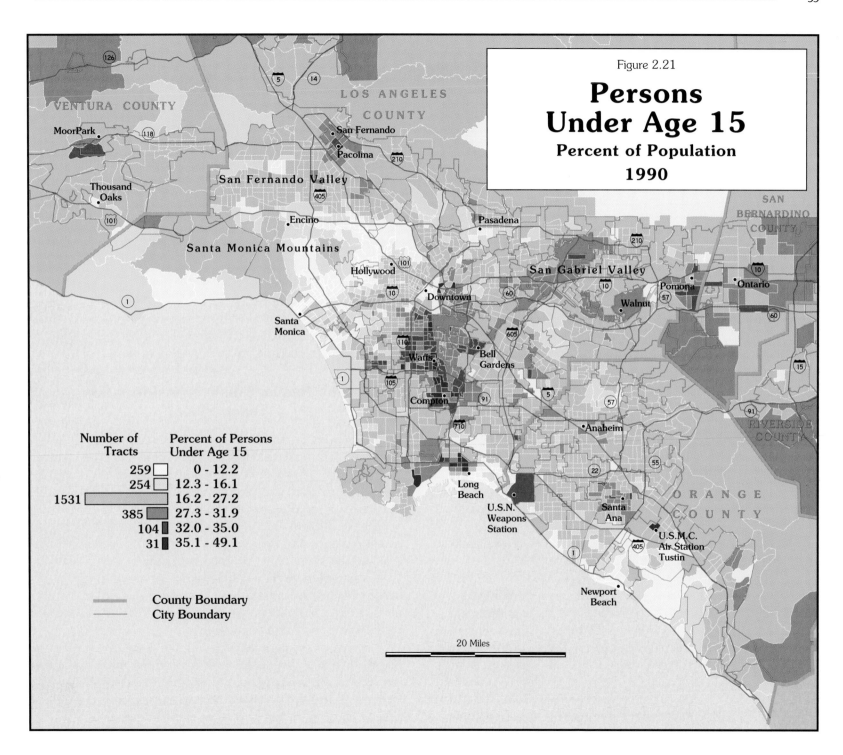

Figure 2.21

Persons Under Age 15

Percent of Population

1990

Number of Tracts		Percent of Persons Under Age 15
259		0 - 12.2
254		12.3 - 16.1
1531		16.2 - 27.2
385		27.3 - 31.9
104		32.0 - 35.0
31		35.1 - 49.1

County Boundary
City Boundary

20 Miles

Patterns of Age

We look first at the patterns of older people—the elderly—and then at areas with very youthful populations. Following traditional practice, we have defined elderly people as those over the age of 64, whereas those under 15 are children or youth.

Until the 1970s most older people in American cities were poor. Because they usually had not accompanied their sons and daughters to the suburbs, they remained in familiar housing in the city or moved to nearby small apartments that were sometimes cheaper and certainly easier to maintain. Both factors tended to result in higher proportions of elderly people in the older parts of cities and much lower proportions in the newer suburbs.

In the past two decades, the young couples who moved to the suburbs forty or fifty years ago have aged but have chosen to remain in their old homes or find apartments not far away. As a result, by 1990 the older suburbs were home to many elderly people as well as to younger families.

New suburbs near the urban fringe have relatively few elderly people, as is illustrated in Santa Clarita and the southern half of Orange County (Fig. 2.20). Older suburbs, like the San Fernando Valley, the South Bay cities, and northern Orange County, have higher percentages of elderly people. Even the Crenshaw area is an older suburb. Although blacks predominate, that area's aging Japanese American population is sufficient for the tract to qualify as being at least one-quarter elderly.

Elderly constitute the highest percentages of tract populations in certain special situations. In Orange County are two planned retirement communities for people aged 55 and older: the Leisure Worlds in Seal Beach and in Laguna Hills. Also, within the city of Mission Viejo is the Casta del Sol retirement community. In Ventura County is Leisure Village, a seniors-only community originally connected with the Leisure Worlds. The two Veterans Administration hospitals in Long Beach and West Los Angeles care for many elderly patients. Large apartment buildings and complexes have often attracted a disproportionate number of elderly residents. The map shows

older areas—Park La Brea, dating from the 1940s, and the Fairfax district, home to many elderly Russian Jews. There are newer developments, too—Oakwood Garden Apartments in Woodland Hills, the Rancho Park and Century City area, and the new apartments on Bunker Hill in Downtown.

High percentages of children are most commonly associated with both poverty and highly Latino areas, particularly those in which immigrants are overrepresented (Fig. 2.21). A single large area stands out: the area in South Central that extends south from the Interstate 10 to Carson. That is the area that received the largest numbers of immigrants from Mexico during the 1980s. The population in this area is more youthful than are the populations of Boyle Heights or East Los Angeles, the old traditional barrios. The high percentage of children in an old part of Long Beach is due to the presence of both Latino and Cambodian immigrants. Other tracts with high proportions of children contain public-housing projects, such as Ramona Gardens in Boyle Heights, Dana Strand Village in Wilmington, and Carmelitos in Long Beach.

Why Has an Ethnic Transformation Taken Place?

Immigration to Southern California since 1960 is the most important factor behind the region's ethnic change. However, the departure of many whites and an ethnic differential in birth rate also play significant roles. Essentially, the non-Hispanic white population has been growing slowly in Southern California as a whole, and in Los Angeles County its absolute number has decreased by 25 percent since 1960 (Table 2.2). At the same time, the black population in Southern California has more than doubled, and the much smaller numbers of American Indians have increased sixfold. By far the most important trend, however, has been the sheer growth of the Hispanic and Asian populations.

So many immigrants arrived from Asia and the Pacific Islands that these populations were ten times more numerous in 1990 than in 1960. Increased immigration from Mexico and Central America, as well as the natural increase of families already here, led to the growth of a Latino population which, by 1990, was rivaling non-Hispanic whites numerically. By 1990 non-Hispanic whites constituted only 50 percent of all Southern Californians. Los Angeles and Orange Counties contained 78 percent of the five-county region's population but were only 46 percent white.

In our explanation of the trend, we provide only general answers. Three of the sections concern the immigration of minorities. These are followed by sections on white out-migration and high Latino fertility. We make no attempt to delve into the details concerning any one country or region of origin. Where particularly significant, such factors are discussed in the treatment of specific groups in chapters 3 through 5.

Growing Linkages with Other Countries

Since 1960 Southern California and the United States as a whole have become more strongly linked with other countries in the world than ever before. This greater globalization of the American economy has resulted in a myriad of new contacts and information. As a result, people in other countries seriously consider migration and, in some cases, actually immigrate. American companies search for materials, cheap labor, workers, and markets in countries we had barely heard of three decades ago, and other countries ship goods for sale here. In other cases the economic and personal connections that have grown so rapidly in recent decades were begun more than a century ago. The total amount of foreign investment in the world (money invested in all countries except the country where it originated) increased 1,400 percent between 1960 and 1987.[21] The net effect of these growing economic interconnections has been to stimulate migration in many countries.

The source region for early Chinese immigration to California illustrates the importance of prior contacts in creating migrations. The first Chinese to immigrate to the United States came from the Guangdong region of China. That region's proximity to Hong Kong, the British colony that had just been taken from China in 1842, meant that they were some of the first Chinese to hear about the 1848 gold strike in California. Because people in that region were being particularly ravaged by a combination of loss of land from inability to pay high taxes, sporadic warfare, and starvation, many men borrowed money for the passage and seized the opportunity that a few years of work in California offered.[22] Connections established in and near Hong Kong were then followed by the brokers who supplied labor for Hawaiian sugar plantations. Later, in order to achieve a linguistically divided labor force, recruiters for Hawaiian and California growers went to Japan, other Asian countries, Puerto Rico, and Mexico. Thus, word of opportunities in the growing U.S. and California economies

Table 2.2 Ethnic Population Change by County

County	Total Population 1960	Total Population 1990	Percent of Total Population 1960	Percent of Total Population 1990
Non-Hispanic Whites				
Los Angeles	4,877,150	3,618,850	80.8	40.8
Orange	641,778	1,554,501	91.2	64.5
Riverside	253,148	754,140	82.7	64.4
San Bernardino	422,018	862,113	83.8	60.8
Ventura	158,584	440,555	79.6	65.9
Blacks				
Los Angeles	461,546	992,974	7.6	11.2
Orange	3,171	42,681	0.5	1.8
Riverside	12,485	63,591	4.1	5.4
San Bernardino	17,234	114,934	3.4	8.1
Ventura	3,598	15,629	1.8	2.3
Asians and Pacific Islanders				
Los Angeles	115,250	954,485	1.9	10.8
Orange	5,670	249,192	0.8	10.3
Riverside	2,631	41,591	0.9	3.6
San Bernardino	2,298	59,201	0.5	4.2
Ventura	2,773	34,579	1.4	5.2
Hispanics				
Los Angeles	576,716	3,351,242	9.6	37.8
Orange	52,576	564,828	7.5	23.4
Riverside	36,224	307,514	11.8	26.3
San Bernardino	60,177	378,582	11.9	26.7
Ventura	33,980	176,952	17.1	26.4

was spread to many parts of the world. After initial contacts had been made and the flow of immigrants had begun, the new migration systems were maintained through networks of friends and relatives by means of letters and money sent home, return visits, and new immigrants traveling along these migration "chains."

Sometimes initial contact with people who became immigrants was made by Christian mission activities, as was the case in Korea. In other situations, the U.S. government has played a role. Since World War II the U.S. military has been an important stimulus to migration from Japan, South Korea, Taiwan, the Philippines, and Thailand. Friendships and knowledge of the United States resulted from training under American specialists, from contacts established in the daily operations of U.S. military bases overseas, and from ties developing out of the love interests of American troops.

When corporations penetrate the economies of Europe, Latin America, the West Indies, and a great range of Asian countries, traditional economic systems are disrupted. Wholesalers and retailers, craft and clerical workers, and managers and owners can find themselves out of work. Some find employment in the new branch plants and offices. Those who do not get jobs are more likely to consider migration, either within the country or internationally.[23]

In the tourist industry, for instance, satisfying the demand for safe and comfortable visits to more exotic places opens up opportunities for some citizens of faraway lands and leads to migration toward jobs connected with tourism. At the same time it may put out of business owners of small stores, restaurants, or hotels. Peasants often lose their livelihood when the land they worked is made part of a large farm for the production of fresh vegetables or fruit for American supermarkets; others may migrate toward the farm in hopes of work. Young women from rural Mexico, the Philippines, and Haiti are enticed to work long hours assembling telephones or computers or stitching shirts or shoes for cash wages. Life in the workers' dormitories may be stressful and restricting, but work is so difficult to find that most of them feel they have little choice.

Directly or indirectly, economic penetration has increased awareness of opportunities in distant places. Although most people probably prefer not to leave their home area, many others think for the first time about migrating to the United States. In some cases the assistance of an American employer can even help people qualify for an immigration visa.

Superior Earnings in the United States

People in other countries will not actually wish to migrate unless the sum of good and bad points at the destination positively outweighs that of the area in which they currently live.[24] Thus, the old notion of migration as resulting from either "push" or "pull" factors is too simplistic in its dichotomy.

People generally migrate for economic reasons. Although they may express this in terms of "a better life for the children" or other glowing phrases, they usually seek employment, higher pay, better working conditions, greater business or professional opportunities, and the like. This means that most people will not move to another country unless economic prospects are substantially better there. The volume and timing of migration to a richer country is correlated with the size of both wage-rate and unemployment-rate differences between countries.[25] For example, for most of this century Mexican workers have earned about four or five times as much per hour in the United States as they could earn in Mexico. Given the proximity and size of the two countries, it is not surprising that the flow from Mexico to the United States is the largest sustained migration of workers in the world. Similarly, the earnings and professional opportunities for engineers, physicians, optometrists, and others are much lower in most Asian and Middle Eastern countries than in the United States, prompting many of them to try to immigrate.

Earnings differentials for migrants can sometimes vary by the migrant's educational level.[26] For example, educated Mexicans have generally migrated toward better positions within their own country because they sensed that middle-class Mexicans would not be rewarded in the United States for their skills. (With the stumbling of the Mexican economy in the mid-1980s, however, some educated Mexicans ventured north of the border.) On the other hand, poorly educated migrants from Mexico have had good opportunities in the United States because they fill the menial, physically difficult, and low-paying jobs that most U.S.-born Californians refuse to fill.[27]

The importance of this earnings differential as a factor behind migration is shown by the fact that most immigrants to Southern California come from countries with incomes that are lower than those in the United States. Between about 1890 and 1924 immigration from Japan and Europe was much greater than it is now because those areas were relatively much poorer than the United States was. Now, prosperity and pay are not very different, so that fewer Japanese and Europeans feel a strong desire to migrate to the United States.

The economic improvement sought through migration is usually for the larger extended family, not just the migrant and his or her spouse and children. Other family members help pay for travel costs, and most migrants send money home to help support their families. These remittances help the families buy things they otherwise could not afford or invest in housing improvements, equipment for family businesses, and so forth. The economic advantages of migration thus become quite visible for everyone in the local area, which tends to encourage further migration. The same basic motivation applies to migrants who plan to work only a few years in another country and to others who intend a permanent change. Both groups have been important, and many who imagined they would not stay long in Southern California later changed their minds.

One underlying reason for the growing earnings differential between countries since about 1950 is the more rapid population growth in developing countries compared with that in the United States and other developed countries. Death rates in those poorer areas have been substantially lowered with the advent of improved medical treatment and public-health measures. Although traditionally high birth rates have dropped somewhat, in many countries in Latin America, Africa, and Asia they still remain high enough to produce rapid population growth. Because expansion of the economy in those countries has usually not been as rapid as population growth, jobs and housing are increasingly in short supply. Thus, overcrowding in many developing countries tends to exacerbate the earnings differential over time. It clearly adds to people's motivation to migrate to the United States or another developed country.

Economic reasons for migrating are sometimes mixed with political reasons, such as a desire for freedom, stability, or the avoidance of war or persecution. Even though it is difficult to separate the various motivations, the earnings differential is very significant for nearly all migrants who come from countries that are much poorer than the United States.

The Immigration Act of 1965 and Other Changes in Immigrant Selectivity

As more people have become aware of migration possibilities and the superior earnings they expect to receive after migration, it is not surprising that increasing millions of people have wished to migrate to the United States. In recent decades the large supply of potential immigrants in other countries has meant that U.S. policies and laws have had to be selective regarding potential immigrants.

Pre-1965 policies. In the first half-century of our country's existence, when new land and growing cities needed farmers, workers, and shopkeepers, the president and Congress encouraged immigration from the familiar source—Europe. Unskilled laborers from China and other Asian countries were recruited for some of the most hazardous and demanding jobs. However, the much lower wages they would accept compared with white workers in similar jobs prompted Congress to protect the wages and jobs of white workers by limiting the entry of Asian groups. Such limitations were not applied to Mexico, however, because California farmers believed that cheap, tractable labor was vitally important to their survival and because Mexicans were not far away and eager to oblige.

Immigration from Europe continued strong until World War I. The large numbers of European immigrants crowding into industrial cities and their lack of English skills made many Americans feel that the society was being overwhelmed by foreigners. Although the immigrants were white, they spoke a range of languages and clustered together in enclaves. It seemed at the time that an English-speaking America was being balkanized by the separate communities of Germans, Italians, Greeks, Hungarians, Poles, Russians, and Jews.

southern and eastern Europe and Asia. For more than twenty years (the mid-1920s to the mid-1940s) the United States received few immigrants from other countries, although Mexican immigration continued until the Great Depression. During this period, when immigrant communities were not replenished by new arrivals from old countries, much of the cultural and structural assimilation of previous European, Asian, and Mexican immigrants occurred. After the surge of European immigration before World War I, the interlude allowed time for the United States to incorporate the newcomers. World War II continued this process, as European immigrants and their children participated in the common effort.

After the mid-1940s Congress opened up the gates slightly for a few special groups of immigrants, refugees, and students. However, no fine tuning of earlier immigration law was as momentous as that of 1965.

For over a century abrupt shifts in acceptance or denial of different categories of immigrants have affected Asian countries most intensely. Thus, the precise wording of U.S. immigration laws and their judicial interpretation have been major subjects of concern for Asian ethnic communities in Southern California.[28]

The Immigration Act of 1965. The Amendments to the Immigration and Nationality Act ushered in radical changes in immigration policy. Congress eliminated race as a consideration in immigration and scrapped the old system of quotas favoring Western European countries and instituted a single limit of 20,000 immigrants a year for each country in the Eastern Hemisphere. The law favored close relatives or immigrants or citizens already in the United States, but some room was left for people with specific occupational skills who had no close relative here.[29]

Although the Immigration Act of 1965 was designed to eliminate the low quotas for Italy and other southern and eastern European countries, its greatest effect over the past thirty years has been to open up immigration from Asian countries. Close relatives of Asians already here could apply for entry, and numerous other Asians entered the United States first as students or refugees and then later became permanent immigrants. That status has enabled them to sponsor their family members.

The great increases in Southern California's Asian populations are a net cumulative effect of the old and new family-based migration chains made possible by the Immigration Act of 1965. At the same time, most Asians would not have immigrated if there had been no economic differentials between their countries and the United States.

Some changes in immigration law have been made since 1965, but none of them has been as momentous as those of 1965. Until 1976 the annual 20,000 quota was not applicable to countries in the Western Hemisphere. Thus, immigration from Mexico and other Latin American countries was not affected by the new law of 1965. Since 1976 the limit has resulted in a backlog of qualified potential Mexican immigrants, as has been the case in some Asian countries. Other changes involve shifts in the number in various occupations allowed to immigrate because of the changing U.S. demand for certain skills.

Refugee policies. People who are designated by the U.S. government as refugees have been accepted for special entry above and beyond the regular immigration laws. When such people apply to the U.S. embassy for refugee status, they have left their normal country of residence and have not returned because they are justifiably fearful of persecution. (If they enter the United States and then apply to remain in this country, they are called "asylees.")

After World War II Europeans entered as displaced persons or refugees. Since then the United States has quite willingly accepted people from Communist countries as refugees, and after 1980 the U.S. government gave much greater credence to those fleeing rightist or fascist totalitarian regimes. After the Communists took over China in 1949, refugees from that country found their way to Hong Kong or Taiwan, and some later entered the United States. In the early 1960s the first of several waves of anti-Castro Cuban refugees arrived in Miami. As these refugees later dispersed to places like Los Angeles, the Cuban-born population in Southern California came to mirror the socioeconomic status and timing of these various waves.

With the defeat of American forces in Vietnam and the

loss of Saigon in April of 1975, Vietnamese who were closely connected with the U.S. war effort and their families became the first wave of Vietnamese refugees to be accepted into the United States. Many in this first wave were processed and connected with sponsors at Camp Pendleton, the Marine Corps Reservation just south of Orange County.

Two years later a second large exodus occurred, as the Vietnamese government forced thousands of Vietnamese and Chinese-Vietnamese to flee in boats. Most of those who made it to the shores of Thailand and Malaysia were accepted as refugees in some other country, many in the United States. Another year later massacres in Cambodia by the Khmer Rouge forced Cambodians to search for safety across the Mekong River in Thailand. These people were some of the first Cambodians to settle in the Long Beach area.

Because all of Indochina saw the devastation of war, the United States was obligated to help other people, like the Hmong, who had assisted the U.S. war effort. Thus, most Indochinese who came to the United States in the late 1970s and early 1980s were refugees. Later arrivals often entered with immigrant visas because by that time their close relatives were either immigrants themselves or U.S. citizens.

When diplomatic relationships with the Soviet Union became less tense, that country often permitted more of its citizens to emigrate. In the late 1970s many Jews and some Armenians were able to leave the Soviet Union; a large proportion settled in Los Angeles. Another similar wave appeared in the late 1980s, to augment the Soviet Armenian and Russian-speaking Jewish populations of Los Angeles.

With the downfall of the U.S.-supported regime of the shah of Iran and the rise to power of an anti-American and antimodernization leader, the United States had little difficulty in according refugee status to those who escaped from Iran during the 1980s. Just the opposite situation characterized Guatemala and El Salvador. Although persecution and massacres have been widespread in those countries over the past twenty years or more, the fact that the United States supported those governments made it seem inconsistent to acknowledge those arriving illegally in the United States as asylees. By 1990, however, the United States was modifying laws to accept

more Salvadorans, at least temporarily.

Numerous changes in the laws dealing with refugees have been made since 1965, the details of which are not of concern at this point. Some changes have recognized that there are legitimate refugees from non-Communist countries, and some accommodate political events or war in specific countries and subsequent refugee flows.

The significance of changes in selectivity. The main point is that the United States chooses whom it permits to immigrate legally. With the large numbers of potential migrants, the government must devise ways of selecting which and how many immigrants should be approved. Yet because selectivity changes, the number of immigrants in specific occupations and of certain age groups from specific countries has fluctuated. This means that ethnic groups in Southern California with a large proportion of immigrants may differ from each other in characteristics that relate to the timing of their arrival and modifications of U.S. law.

Once the gates to immigration from Asia were opened wide in 1965, old and new networks of personal contact were elaborated, producing a multiplier effect. This has built up the potential number of legal immigrants and, to a lesser extent, the actual flows.[30] This, then, becomes another mechanism by which linkages with immigration source countries have grown.

Illegal immigration. Many thousands of residents of Southern California are not living in the United States legally. Considering the limitations imposed by U.S. law on migration flows previously set up by the globalization of the American economy and by the earnings differential, this is not surprising. Many enter the United States temporarily as students or tourists and simply remain here after their visas expire. Others, mostly Mexicans and Central Americans, cross the U.S.–Mexican border and enter illegally.

No one knows exactly how many people are living illegally in Southern California, but the numbers are substantial. From 1988 through 1991 more than 765,000 formerly illegal (undocumented) residents of this region and another 318,000 special agricultural workers have received legal-immigrant status agricultural workers have received legal-immigrant status under the Immigration Reform and Control Act of 1986.[31] Although the latter group includes some migrant workers, their base was Southern California. The 765,000 figure includes only people who were living in Southern California continually since 1982. If those who arrived after 1982 are included, the total number of illegal residents of Southern California during much of the 1980s must have been at least 1.3 million. Mexico was by far the largest source of these formerly illegal residents, but El Salvador, Guatemala, Iran, China, and the Philippines were also important.

White Movement out of Los Angeles County

Although the largest and most dramatic aspects of the change in ethnic composition involved the immigration of Asians and Latinos, patterns of net migration of whites have also furthered ethnic change in Los Angeles County. The earlier in-migrations of whites and blacks that had built up Los Angeles' white and black populations after World War II were much reduced during the 1970s and, especially, the 1980s. In fact, since at least 1970 the net outflow of whites from Los Angeles County has been massive.

Most people, regardless of ethnic affiliation, would rather live in newer, suburban housing than in older units near the city centers. Those who can afford to move into or toward the suburbs are likely to do so. For this reason, residential deconcentration characterizes all ethnic groups to some degree—although the timing and importance of suburbanization have differed among groups.[32]

Compared with other groups, whites moved first and in greatest numbers to suburban areas. Movement from Los Angeles County into newer homes in the outlying counties became great in the 1960s and has continued unabated since that time. The percentage of whites in Los Angeles County fell from more than 80 to near 40 between 1960 and 1990, and in absolute numbers the white population of that county declined by 25 percent (Table 2.2). The motivations for this massive deconcentration are varied. They include the desire to purchase a newer house for reasons of investment, a preference

for single-family housing, and the desire to escape the higher crime rates of most older, poorer areas. Many people, especially whites, also move to avoid neighborhoods with moderate or increasing proportions of low-income minorities, particularly blacks or Latinos.

In addition to shifts into adjacent counties, many Los Angeles County whites moved out of Southern California altogether. This trend has grown since the early 1970s and became particularly strong in the last half of the 1980s.[33] Washington, Oregon, Nevada, Colorado, and Arizona have been the leading destinations of this large net outflow.

Ethnic Differentials in Fertility

The birth rate, or fertility, of ethnic groups in Southern California differs substantially. Like net migration, fertility has affected the changing ethnic composition.[34] By far the most significant differential, however, is the comparatively high birth rate among Latinos compared with non-Hispanic whites (Table 2.3). Latina mothers in Los Angeles County have more than twice the number of children that whites have. Over time Latino immigrants living in the United States and later generations have shown reduced fertility, but that trend will be delayed in Southern California because 64 percent of Mexican-origin adults as of 1990 were immigrants and 37 percent of these had arrived in the United States during the 1980s.[35] Fertility among some groups of Indochinese is also high, but on average Asian groups have sufficiently low fertility that the rate of new births contributes much less than immigration to their ethnic population growth.

The effect of the fertility differential on population growth can be estimated by projecting the 1980 population of Hispanics in Los Angeles County forward to 1990 under an assumption of zero net migration.[36] The percentage of the total 1980–1990 increase that is accounted for by the projected population increase is the proportion of the growth that can be attributed to natural increase.

The projected total for Hispanics was 48 percent of the actual 1990 Hispanic total for the county. In other words, if none of the Hispanics who had been living in Los Angeles

Table 2.3   Ethnic Group Fertility Rates, Los Angeles County 1986

Group	Total Fertility Rate
Non-Hispanic Whites	1.49
Blacks	2.45
Asians and American Indians	2.10
Hispanics	3.19

Source: Los Angeles County, Department of Health Services.

Note: These total fertility rates can be thought of as the number of babies an average woman would have during her lifetime if the age-specific birth rates of 1986 were in effect throughout her reproductive years.

County in 1980 moved out and no others moved in during the next ten years, Hispanic growth would have been 48 percent of the actual increase reported.

The fertility differential reinforced the effect of the net migration differential. Because the relative fertility of groups does not vary a great deal among the five counties, both factors are important in explaining the relative decline of whites compared with Latinos in Southern California.

Establishing the Foundations

In this chapter we have described and explained some of the basic spatial patterns of Southern California. Although this sketch of the urban geography was brief, it should help make the maps of the various ethnic populations more understandable. Also, we have summarized the general processes that have resulted in the region's increasing ethnic diversity and its partial ethnic transformation. The latter part of the chapter has, in a sense, brought the new immigrants to Southern California.

These two parts of the chapter constitute the foundations for the rest of the book. We are now ready to look at what has happened to both the newcomers and the old residents. In the next three chapters we examine in detail the thirty-four largest ethnic groups in Southern California and where the people in those groups have lived.

Notes

1. More detailed descriptions and explanations of earlier spatial patterns and other aspects of the geography of Los Angeles can be found in Steiner (1981) and Nelson (1983). Soja (1989), chapters 8 and 9, interprets the economic geography of Southern California, emphasizing spatial changes associated with economic restructuring since the 1960s.

2. Nelson (1959).

3. Viehe (1981).

4. Hise (1993).

5. Fogelson (1967), 103.

6. Shevky and Williams (1949), 36–41 (maps).

7. Kling, Olin, and Poster (1991), 10.

8. Garreau (1991).

9. Kling, Olin, and Poster (1991), 10.

10. Gottdiener and Kephart (1991).

11. U.S. Bureau of the Census (1993a), Table 1.

12. U.S. Bureau of the Census (1993a), Table 1.

13. Los Angeles Department of City Planning (1991).

14. Danielson (1976), 5–8. For examples of such suburban incorporation in the Los Angeles area, see Davis (1990), 165–69.

15. Marchand (1986), 98–102, 192, 120; Myers (1990), 282. This persistence in the status position of neighborhoods is the major reason why maps of socioeconomic characteristics at the census-tract level, such as those in this book, remain valuable for many years and decades.

16. Marchand (1986), 174.

17. Scott (1988), 223–25.

18. Shevky and Williams (1949), 36–41 (maps).

19. Data are not available by census tract on the number of people employed in specific occupations and industries. It is necessary to use the 1990 PUMS data explained in chapter 1. Areal units for those data are PUMAs, which have a minimum of 100,000 residents and are generally composed of one or more municipalities. The City of Los Angeles, however, is divided into 22 PUMAs.

20. The location of public-housing projects in clearly minority areas of Los Angeles City followed partly from the outcome of a struggle in the early 1950s over segregation versus integration in public housing. The city's Housing Authority had designed a large, racially and ethnically integrated housing project for the Chavez Ravine area. It was to have been occupied by residents of Bunker Hill, whose deteriorated housing was due to be cleared, and other

low-income people. Those plans were killed, Chavez Ravine became the Dodgers' new home, and future public housing was located in intensely minority areas rather than in mixed areas. This decision heightened subsequent racial segregation and has, in combination with other factors, concentrated poverty more completely in minority areas. See Gottlieb and Wolt (1977), 262–68; Wilkinson (1991).

21. Sassen (1991), 36. There have been many studies of the effects of these expanded connections on various countries, much of them based on world systems theory. That theory assumes that capitalism and capitalist enterprises based in powerful core countries like the United States have a built-in tendency to try to make increasing use of the raw materials, cheap labor, and potential markets in other countries—the periphery.

22. Takaki (1989), 32–37.

23. Massey et al. (1994), 724–25. A detailed case study shows how capitalist penetration of the agricultural economy in several Central American countries led to migration (Hamilton and Chinchilla 1991).

24. Lee (1966).

25. Massey et al. (1994), 701–11.

26. Massey et al. (1994), 701–11.

27. One aspect of the economic motivation is whether migration is influenced primarily by working conditions in the place of origin or by the desire of employers in the country of destination for more, cheaper, or better workers. In other words, is migration driven more by supply or by demand? This is the economic component—the most important one—of the old "push–pull" terminology. Actual recruitment of workers in other countries would clearly demonstrate demand-driven migration, for example, whereas annual fluctuations in migration which follow changing economic conditions in the country of origin indicate that supply-driven forces are paramount. We find it not especially helpful to try to distinguish the supply or demand side or the push or pull side as more important. People considering migration have to try to assess their prospects both at home and at their possible destination.

28. These details are thoroughly covered in Hing (1993).

29. Some categories of immigrants are exempt from annual quota limitations. Spouses, parents, and children of U.S. citizens can immigrate without regard to the annual quota. This is the major reason why annual immigration from the Philippines, Mexico, Korea, and India is greater than 20,000. Also not included in that limit are immigrants originally classified as refugees, which explains why there have been far more than 20,000 immigrants from Vietnam, the Soviet Union, and El Salvador in certain years. The most concise source for data and changes in the law is the annual *Statistical Yearbook of the Immigration and Naturalization Service*.

30. Jasso and Rosenzweig (1986).

31. U.S. Immigration and Naturalization Service (1992), Tables 22, 23.

32. Ethnic-group gains and losses during the 1980s in Los Angeles and Orange Counties are mapped by census tracts in Turner and Allen (1991).

33. Allen (1990).

34. Ethnic differences in mortality play a minor role in the shift of ethnic composition, tending to reinforce the migration and fertility differentials. Asians and Hispanics in California have lower age-adjusted death rates than do whites; the rate for blacks is higher (California Department of Health Services 1994, Tables 5, 1A–1D).

35. Stephen and Bean (1992); Allen and Turner (1996b), 146.

36. Our cohort-component projection made use of age-specific fertility rates provided by the Department of Health Services for 1986. Interactive Population Statistical System was the projection software.

3. Distributions: Whites and Blacks

The spatial structure of Southern California's ethnic diversity can be described by maps that show the residential locations of the various ethnic groups. This chapter and the two that follow contain the maps and basic descriptive data on the thirty-four different groups, as well as explanations of their distributions.

The maps for each of the thirty-four ethnic groups are designed to show the relative importance of each ethnic group in the total residential population of each census tract. Chapters 3 through 5 also include maps of the median income of white, black, Hispanic, and Asian households. These four maps appear in the chapters directly after the text treatment of the specific groups within each of the categories.

"Concentration," "cluster," "enclave," and "neighborhood"—can be used to indicate the clustering of an ethnic group. Although other writers occasionally define certain of these words with special precision, we use them in a general sense and synonymously.

Explaining Ethnic Distributions in General

In general, ethnic residential patterns can be explained by: (1) areal variations in the cost and availability of housing; (2) group differences in population size, economic resources, employment locations, timing of settlement, and familiarity with American culture; (3) group differences in attitudes toward various places, environments, and other groups; and (4) past restrictions on minority residential locations. Most of these can be thought of as either economic, cultural, or exclusionary factors behind the distributions.

No simple explanation of ethnic distributions is possible. After all, an individual household's decision about where to live is usually not simple. The patterns visible on the maps in this chapter represent the cumulative effect of numerous locational decisions.

Explanations for contemporary ethnic concentrations involve details of history. Thus, it is necessary to understand the above factors in the context of earlier decades, sometimes a half-century or more ago. Because we set the 1990 distributions in a historical context, the reader can see the growth and decline of various ethnic concentrations, the partial or almost complete displacement of one group by another in a neighborhood, and the appearance of areas that are ethnically mixed.

However, the process of changing distributions is normally slow. Even though individuals and families may change their addresses frequently, in-movement and out-movement from neighborhoods usually balance each other to some degree. Thus, the distributions for some groups show the presence of ethnic neighborhoods that originated more than half a century ago. Although such enclaves have typically become diffused or blurred, the fact that they are recognizable demonstrates the stability of many of these patterns. Just as most people do not change their ethnic identity quickly, it is likely that the important features of the 1990 group distributions will still be recognizable for decades to come.

Economic factors. Lowest-cost housing tends to be older and located closer to the traditional downtowns, the oldest of which are Los Angeles, Long Beach, Santa Ana, Pasadena, and Pomona. Those groups with lower average incomes and wealth will tend to be concentrated in areas closer to those downtowns. The exception to this occurs when the homes of poor people have been destroyed through urban renewal while the more expensive homes and apartments built in their place have attracted residents with higher incomes. In other types of urban renewal, low-income housing is replaced by nonresidential land uses, such as convention centers, shopping centers, offices, parking lots, freeways, or recreation centers. This renewal typically forces the former residents to scatter to other housing, reducing the concentration of poorer people.

Ethnic groups with the highest average incomes or wealth will have higher proportions living in areas of expensive housing. However, in nearly all groups there is a wide range of household income, and many households, regardless of ethnic affiliation, have similar levels of income. This means they qualify economically for housing in the same areas. If income were the sole determinant of residential location, many members of ethnic groups would be thoroughly intermingled in such areas.

Easy accessibility to employment is sometimes a factor, but the presence of freeways and the wide availability of automobiles means that this locational factor is less important now than it used to be. Eighty years ago, immigrants from a particular village or region or members of an ethnic group would often find jobs in the same type of industry located in the same general area of a city. Thus, proximity to past or contemporary employment can be a factor behind the present-day location of ethnic settlements.

Cultural factors. People who are less comfortable in American society usually have a greater tendency to live closer together for mutual support. Among immigrant groups, those that have arrived more recently or are less acculturated typically show more clustered residential distributions.[1] It makes sense that newcomers, especially those who speak little English, look to friends and relatives for assistance in the search for housing and jobs and to help make them feel at home. As individuals become more acculturated and economically successful, they typically leave the ethnic concentration and disperse into areas in which U.S.-born whites are the largest group.

However, residential clustering also occurs among ethnic groups that are highly acculturated if the sense of group cohesion is strong or if the group is concerned about its acceptance

in the larger society. For American blacks, the attractions of living in a geographically based black community and a wariness about their reception in predominantly white areas retard the dispersal of some blacks who could financially afford to leave the concentration. In a more subtle way a shared Jewish identity remains a powerful force, binding most Jews to the general sections of a metropolitan area where the Jewish community is strong.

Locational decisions based on the images of certain places or feelings about certain types of environments or other ethnic groups have been little studied but presumably play some role in explaining the varying ethnic distributions. It is difficult to imagine, for instance, that Chinese and other Asian immigrants with strong cultural preferences for urban life are attracted to rural environments on the metropolitan fringe as much as are many U.S.-born whites.

Exclusionary factors. Nowadays, the choice of residential location is mostly the result of household decisions constrained by financial resources and influenced by cultural factors such as those previously mentioned. However, ethnic groups differ in their attitudes toward other groups, and the cumulative effect of widespread ethnic avoidances can affect the geographical separation of specific groups.[2]

In the past, whites often achieved residential exclusion by refusing to rent or sell housing to minorities. This was widespread and legally permissible from about 1920 until after World War II. Discrimination against blacks by white landlords and lending institutions continued well after the 1968 Fair Housing Act.[3] Such discrimination resulted in extremely high levels of residential segregation of blacks and whites between 1920 and about 1980. In 1960 Los Angeles County was second only to Chicago (Cook County) as the most highly segregated large metropolitan county in the United States.[4]

Thus, 1990 settlement patterns of long-settled minorities, especially blacks, show clear effects of past exclusion. Discrimination in housing still exists, although the aggregate spatial pattern of black and other minority population shifts in the 1980s was probably little affected.[5]

Maps of Changing Ethnic Patterns

Two of our maps depict some historical ethnic distributions and directions of residential movement. The first displays the most important and distinctive shifts of group locations during the past half century (Fig. 3.1). It shows the largest concentrations of blacks, Mexicans, Japanese, and Chinese near Downtown in 1940 and the leading directions of movement out of these areas.[6] Whites are not shown as having any area of concentration because they were found nearly everywhere.

The second map is designed to capture evolving ethnic distributions at a single point in time—1960 (Fig. 3.2).[7] In 1960 blacks were moving into what had been all-white neighborhoods to the west and south of the former black ghetto (South Central). Also, Japanese were buying new homes in Gardena, and many sons and daughters of Mexican immigrants were leaving the barrio and moving eastward into the San Gabriel Valley. By that year the proportion of whites in Los Angeles County had dropped to 81 percent but remained much higher in Orange County. The processes which created these distributions are discussed in detail in this and the two subsequent chapters. However, the pervasiveness of whites in the new, low-density suburbs is striking, especially when compared to 1990 distributions.

Non-Hispanic Whites

The United States, representing a white population based far to the east, defeated Mexico in war in the 1840s and officially took over Southern California in 1848. Over the next thirty years that shift of political control, together with the arrival of many more Americans, led to English-speaking white dominance over the Spanish-speaking Mexican residents. Thus, non-Hispanic whites have been the most powerful ethnic group in Southern California for more than a century.

Not all white migrants from eastern states settled in Los Angeles and the larger towns. Some newcomers were particularly attracted to the new little towns that were being planned amid thousands of acres of orange groves in the foothills of the San Gabriel Mountains.

Citrus Belt towns. The zone just downhill from the rugged face of the San Gabriel and San Bernardino Mountains to the east was a major destination for white settlers as early as the 1870s. A special attractiveness of this foothill climate zone was its potential for growing navel oranges. Navel oranges were already known to grow better on those slopes than on the floors of the valleys or near the coast, where the less valuable Valencias could grow. Groves were lovely and fragrant, and growing oranges was considered a clean, beautiful, and prestigious type of agriculture. However, the cost of setting up these handsome groves meant that their owners had to be wealthy.

Land developers attracted potential owners by building a luxury hotel, museum, or small college as the nucleus of their projected town and then advertising for investors in eastern and Midwestern newspapers. Railroads brought thousands of visitors, and many retired business and professional people bought land and moved to Southern California. A series of exclusive towns was founded in this Citrus Belt, the most prominent of which were Pasadena, Monrovia, Glendora, and Claremont (Fig. 2.2) and Riverside and Redlands farther east.

Many new settlers were members of elite families from New England or the Midwest. They and their children played major roles shaping the character of these foothill towns. Because the towns have retained much of their heritage and their charm, they remain especially attractive to whites, who can often afford to purchase homes. For these reasons the percentage of whites is larger in the higher elevations of Citrus Belt towns like Sierra Madre, Monrovia, and Glendora in 1990 than on the floor of the San Gabriel Valley (Fig. 3.3).

White absence from central sections of cities. Whites formerly lived in the central parts of cities and were the predominant group there in the early twentieth century. However, they began to leave the older areas as newer and less crowded housing was built farther from the city center. They were often able to purchase a new house, which became an important investment. The cumulative effect of such purchases resulted in the transfer of money out of central-city areas. After a time only people with lower incomes remained. As older housing filtered down to poorer people, its price declined.

Whites left the older areas of Los Angeles, Long Beach, and Santa Ana to take advantage of the availability of newly built homes, to buy a house in a location where it was likely to increase in value, and to distance themselves from poor people. The fact that the poorer people who were replacing the whites in their old neighborhoods were often black, Asian, or Mexican American meant that discomfort with these groups added to the desire of white residents to leave.

The actual mix of reasons behind white departure from older areas will probably always remain hidden. In the neighborhoods near growing black and Latino settlements, "white flight" may have been the paramount reason for leaving. However, in other, less threatened, areas the more typically economic and housing-related motivations probably outweighed white flight as a motivation. The fact that in more recent decades Asians, blacks, and Latinos have also participated in the same suburban moves indicates clearly that the motivations behind such deconcentration are much deeper and more pervasive than merely white avoidance of other groups.

The net geographical effect of white suburbanization and replacement by minorities over more than half a century is dramatic (Fig. 3.3). A very large area extending south from Downtown has very few whites. Whites used to be the dominant group in almost all of this area before it was filled in by the merging and areal expansion of black settlement concentrations. A second area of lowest white percentages is east of Downtown and the Los Angeles River. In the very early twentieth century whites were enjoying new homes in Boyle Heights, but by World War I the area was declining in value and attracting Eastern European Jews, Mexicans, and other immigrants.

In the 1960s whites were also leaving older suburbs like Inglewood, Compton, South Gate, Lynwood, Pacoima, and Hollywood. By 1990 the exodus from such areas and in-movement by blacks and Latinos had produced a ring of fairly low white percentages surrounding the extremely low percentages of the very oldest, more central areas.

Environmental amenities. In Southern California, many of the more affluent whites would rather live up in the hills than in the more crowded flatlands. The association between income and elevation has existed for at least a century in this area, and some towns had a series of status belts, grading downslope from the wealthy through the middle-class families to the poorest people and minorities on the valley bottoms and often across the railroad tracks.[8]

The largest attractive developed area of hill or canyon terrain is the Santa Monica Mountains, stretching from the Hollywood Hills west past Malibu and Calabasas to Thousand Oaks in Ventura County (Fig. 2.1). Other important areas are the Palos Verdes Peninsula, the foothills of the San Gabriel Mountains. The San Jose Hills in the San Gabriel Valley, the Puente Hills between eastern Los Angeles and Orange Counties, and the Chino Hills separating northern Orange County from San Bernardino and Riverside Counties are only partially developed as of 1990. Most of the rugged Santa Ana Mountains in eastern Orange County are part of Cleveland National Forest and have not been subdivided. Much smaller sections like the Cheviot Hills and Mount Washington near central Los Angeles and Bixby Knolls in Long Beach are also more expensive than the surrounding flatlands because they have both varied terrain and a location near centers of employment and recreation for people of higher status.

Proximity to the beaches of the Pacific Ocean is also desired by many people, resulting in high housing prices in most coastal areas. Such places are most attainable by whites. Most whites who live near the beaches at Malibu, Pacific Palisades, and Newport Beach are wealthy; the South Bay cities of Manhattan, Redondo, and Hermosa are not as expensive (Fig. 3.11). The latter locations are ideal for many workers in the computer and aerospace industries that are so concentrated in the southern part of the county (Figs. 2.13 and 2.14). But even near the coast a few lower-cost areas exist—Venice, San Pedro, and Huntington Beach—in which white proportions are lower.

Newer suburban developments. The newest residential subdivisions are often located near the outer edges of metropolitan areas, where land is cheaper but freeways provide access to jobs in previously developed areas. The major attraction of moving to such areas is the fact that homes cost much less there than they do in areas that are more accessible to jobs, shopping, and entertainment. Thus, homeownership is often traded for a long commute. Most such places are too distant to show on the maps in this book, but many of their names are familiar: Lancaster and Palmdale to the north and Rialto, Victorville, and Moreno Valley to the east. Although most home buyers and renters in such areas are whites, the lower prices make these distant areas also accessible to blacks, Latinos, and others.

In contrast, developers can command higher prices for their homes in areas that are not as distant and have attractive environmental settings. Because fewer minorities qualify as buyers, these areas will usually have higher percentages of whites. Eastern Ventura County and southern Orange County are the leading examples (Fig. 3.3). However, cities like Walnut, Hacienda Heights, and Diamond Bar on the floor of the eastern San Gabriel Valley are exceptions. White proportions tend to be lower in such places because large numbers of Asians and Latinos are ready to move into these suburbs from older settlements like East Los Angeles and Monterey Park.

People of English Ancestry

An estimated 985,000 Southern Californians listed English as their first or only ancestry in 1990. This group outnumbered all other European ancestries except German. Over the years people of British heritage have intermarried, and their ancestral identities have become blurred. For the sake of simplicity, however, we focus on people of strictly English ancestry. If the 167,000 who reported a Scottish ancestry and the 99,000 who wrote in either a British or a Welsh ancestry were included, people in Southern California whose primary ancestry was British would number 1.25 million.

Despite this large total, this ethnic group is widely scattered (Fig. 6.4.). This is shown by the fact that only 13 census tracts had populations that were more than 20 percent English. In fact, the group's distribution is similar in many ways to that of the total white population. The blurred spatial patterns parallel the cultural characteristics of people of English ancestry— their pervasive influence, their intermingling with people of other European ancestries, and their almost ubiquitous cultural presence. For these reasons, this interpretation of Figure 6.4 is shorter than the group's numbers might seem to warrant. Nevertheless, the distribution does have features that illuminate the character of certain parts of Southern California.

People of English ancestry include both English immigrants and others whose ancestors arrived in the United States generations ago. British immigrants were the largest foreign nationality in Los Angeles County in 1937. Many well-known film and music stars have been immigrants from Britain, and numerous British societies and festivals serve that immigrant population.[9] Nevertheless, most Southern Californians of English ancestry are not immigrants. Most have American-born parents and often grandparents, and many families trace their roots to colonial days.

The traditional elite. In the United States and in Southern California, this ancestry group has long been the most important one among non-Hispanic whites. Because people of English family heritage were easily the largest ancestry group at the time of the founding of the United States, they were able to dominate subsequent business, political, technical, and cultural development in the United States. The expression "WASP," for white Anglo-Saxon Protestant, became a widely used acronym acknowledging this group's traditional influence and power in the United States. It was not until after World War II that WASP control of most of the powerful and prestigious institutions in this country was substantially reduced.

Thus, in Southern California, as of 1990, men and women of English ancestry are probably represented among members of the social, political, scientific, and business elite more than the one-seventh proportion they constitute in the total white population. This is strongly suggested by their distribution (Fig. 3.4). English-ancestry residential concentrations, though never at all exclusive and rarely very strong, most frequently are found in areas of moderate and high incomes.

Despite the association of WASPs with power and their concentrations in certain higher-status areas, the large English-ancestry group contains many millions of people of rural origins and with little formal education.

Anti-urban preferences. Also significant is fact that most English-ancestry clusters are located in suburban areas often far from Downtown. This reflects a widespread antipathy toward high-density cities on the part of this ethnic group and most other migrants from small towns and rural areas in the East and the Midwest. Their conception of the good community was one of "single-family houses, located on large lots, surrounded by landscaped lawns, and isolated from business activities."[10] This idealized image helped set the direction of suburban development in America.

Pasadena. Although not far from Downtown, Pasadena contains a concentration of English ancestry (Fig. 3.4). The exceptional presence of this group in Pasadena relates to the city's special origins, identity, and character, which have made it distinctive from Los Angeles. Founded in the early 1870s as the Indiana Colony, Pasadena later attracted many Bostonians and other New Englanders, who bought land and homes. The first Tournament of Roses in 1889 was organized by a transplant from New England.[11]

Wintertime visits by train brought thousands of prospective migrants, and Pasadena was able to entice many business owners and wealthy families from the East and the Midwest.[12] The concentration of old wealth (mostly WASP) in Pasadena was later tapped for the founding of the California Institute of Technology, the Jet Propulsion Laboratory, and other research-related organizations, as well as the Huntington Library in adjacent San Marino. These activities presumably enhanced an identity for Pasadena and a commitment among its influential families. When Carey McWilliams wrote in 1946 about an "early Bostonian atmosphere, traces of which can still be detected in such communities as Pasadena," he may actually have underestimated the cultural persistence of this heritage.[13] Despite all the changes that have occurred during the past half century, Pasadena south of Colorado Boulevard has remained an oasis for the old-guard Protestant and Episcopalian elite.

The most intensely English sections of Pasadena are the tract west of the Rose Bowl and Arroyo Seco, where elegant homes are nestled against a backdrop of spectacular hills, and the tract to the southeast, where Ambassador College is located (Fig. 3.4). Other tracts with higher-than-usual proportions of English ancestry stretch eastward past the California Institute of Technology to the Huntington Library.

Rustic hill environments and selected coastal areas. The English-ancestry association with suburban or lower-density settings can be found in Lakeview Terrace at the east end of the San Fernando Valley, La Cañada–Flintridge on the slopes of the San Gabriel Mountains, the city of La Habra Heights, and in the hilly portions of northern Whittier, Brea, and the Tustin area (Fig. 3.4). The Bixby Knolls section of Long Beach, with its Virginia Country Club, also stands out in English-ancestry percentage.

Many places near the Pacific Coast have relatively high proportions of people with English ancestry. Some tracts, as in Costa Mesa and Huntington Beach, are middle-income areas. However, most are expensive: parts of Pacific Palisades, Manhattan Beach, Hermosa Beach, the Naples section of Long Beach, and the Palos Verdes Peninsula. In Orange County, English ancestry is overrepresented in the Leisure World communities, in South Laguna Beach, and in parts of East Tustin and Newport Beach. The Lido Isle section of Newport Beach is easily the most strongly English area in Southern California: 29 percent of its people listed English as their first ancestry.

Special situations. Higher English-ancestry percentages in a section of tract homes in Lakewood and Long Beach represent nonelite people. Many of them worked for decades in aircraft assembly and other manufacturing jobs and are now retired.

English-ancestry clusters are not located in places where English immigrants congregate, partly because immigrants generally do not have the incomes or wealth to live in such areas. However, one well-known gathering place for English tourists may have remained in the same locality over many decades. In the late nineteenth century, tourists flocked to the coast, especially at Santa Monica,[14] and a short stretch of Santa Monica Boulevard between Ocean Avenue and 4th Street continues to be popular among English émigrés and other Anglophiles. With its pubs, English specialty foods, and British-oriented newsstands and gift shops, the area has long provided a flavor of England.

Two tracts shown as more than 20 percent English ancestry contain small populations, which make high percentage values of little consequence (Fig. 3.4). The tract in Long Beach Harbor, mostly docks and container-storage areas, contains only 27 residents. Similarly, the large tract in Simi Valley has a total population of only 268.

Contrast with Russian ancestry (Jews). The distributions of the two groups of European origin that we cover in this book—English ancestry and Russian ancestry—differ strikingly (Figs. 6.4 and 6.5). Whereas the former group tends to have its clusters dispersed in outlying suburbs, the latter is highly concentrated in a single large area. Because both distributions include numerous areas of high-priced homes, the contrasting patterns are not a function of group differences in financial resources. Rather, they are a geographical indication of real differences in culture, relative cohesiveness, and environmental and locational preferences. For people who might think of non-Hispanic whites as an essentially homogeneous single group, this contrast between the English and Russian-ancestry groups, as well as the unique distributions of Armenians and Iranians, demonstrates that such a simplistic conception of whites is fallacious.

People of Russian Ancestry (Jews)

The 639,000 Jews estimated to live in the five-county Southern California region constitute 4.4 percent of the region's population and 8.8 percent of its non-Hispanic white population.[15] Although Figure 3.5 maps people of Russian ancestry, we argue in chapter 1 that Russian ancestry in Southern California is a useful surrogate for the Jewish population. Moreover, the 1990 distribution of people of Russian ancestry bears a close resemblance to the most recent map of Jewish population based on a privately collected 1979 survey.[16] For these reasons, our interpretation is written in a way that portrays a Jewish distribution.[17]

Early social integration. At least eight Jews were present in Los Angeles as early as 1850, when Southern California was just beginning its transition from a rural, Spanish-speaking portion of Mexico's northern frontier to a western outpost of the United States. Many Jews who settled in Los Angeles during the next three decades opened small shops to sell clothing and dry goods; and many of the merchants in the city were Jews. Other Jews became wholesalers, bankers, clerks, or salesmen.[18]

Before the 1890s Jews were highly integrated into the social and cultural life of Los Angeles. Many were also active in civic affairs and members of the leading clubs. At the same time, most of them retained their Jewish identity, and marriage had intertwined many of their leading families. During this period most Jews lived near Downtown, and a few had summer homes at the shore in Santa Monica or Wilmington, but no section of town was considered distinctively Jewish.

However, the massive influx of rural and small-town folks brought by railroad from the East and the Midwest, the increased anti-Semitism across the United States, and local resentment at what appeared to be the growing political influence of Los Angeles Jews produced a change of mood in Los Angeles.[19] By the turn of the century some Jews in Los Angeles were finding themselves excluded from influence and membership in the leading organizations and were, consequently, becoming more involved in the affairs of the Jewish community.

Growth and social separation. In 1904 the first wave of Eastern European Jews arrived in the city of Los Angeles. The typical Jewish migrants to Los Angeles between 1900 and 1920 were immigrants who had been born in Russia, Poland, or other parts of Eastern Europe but who had been living in New York, Philadelphia, or Chicago. Most were noticeably Jewish, poor, and conservative in religious ritual. Their Yiddish speech, occasionally exotic dress, and tendency to enter the second-hand junk business aggravated the anti-Semitic predispositions of some Christians. In addition, the established Jewish community found the newcomers embarrassing and worried that they would become overly dependent on charity.

Between 1900 and 1929 the number of Jews in Los Angeles grew from 2,500 to about 70,000.[20] Because Jews flooded into Los Angeles at a much greater rate than did other groups of newcomers, the percentage of Jews in the city's population increased from less than 3 percent in 1900 to more than 17 percent in 1930.

Extension of the city's street railway during the first two decades of this century and subdivisions built near those routes opened up homes for Jews and others. Many newcomers, plus those leaving the old and increasingly congested Downtown, moved just west of Downtown near Temple Street, or two miles to the south near Central Avenue. Some could afford the more expensive homes in the Wilshire Boulevard, Hollywood, or West Adams areas. Many others settled in Boyle Heights, which became the most important Jewish enclave in the 1920s.

The 1920s was the decade in which the Jewish community became much more socially separated from the non-Jewish whites (Gentiles), who were Christian in heritage. Jews who had been members of the leading clubs found their sons and daughters not accepted for membership. The tendency for Jewish adults who moved to Los Angeles after 1920 to be the sons and daughters of Eastern European immigrants, and thus more acculturated, did not lead to greater acceptance of Jews in politics or citywide cultural affairs. For several decades the Downtown-based law firms of the Los Angeles elite included no Jewish lawyers. Even in the late 1940s it was almost impossible for Jews to be accepted in medical schools or obtain an internship or residency in Los Angeles hospitals except at the two hospitals sponsored by Jews, Cedars of Lebanon and Mount Sinai.[21] The old-guard elite of Los Angeles excluded Jews from their country clubs and private schools.[22]

Jews socialized more and more with each other, created new fraternal organizations, and founded their own Hillcrest Country Club, just south of Beverly Hills. Through membership in Hillcrest, tensions between the old elite Jewish families of mostly German heritage and the rising Hollywood moguls, who were Eastern European immigrants, were mostly reconciled.[23] Their alliance became the foundation on which Westside Jewish economic and political strength developed during the 1950s and 1960s.

Communication between the Jewish and Gentile elite was at its nadir from the late 1920s until the early 1960s. Much of this was due to resentment by the Downtown-based Gentile business leadership at the development by A. W. Ross and other Jews of the "Miracle Mile" commercial axis along Wilshire Boulevard. That shopping and office area, so clearly oriented to the automobile rather than the street railway, drained much business from Downtown. In retaliation, the Downtown-oriented *Los Angeles Times* reported almost nothing concerning the Jewish community for the next three decades.[24] This policy changed only when Dorothy (Buff) Chandler, the wife of *Times* publisher Norman Chandler, approached wealthy Jewish businessmen for support in building the Music Center and did obtain large contributions.[25] Successful completion of the center in 1964 symbolized a partial rapprochement between the elites of the Jewish and Gentile communities.

Geographical concentration. Social separation of Jews and Gentiles was reflected in and reinforced by locational differences: Jews settled in some areas much more than in others. In general, Jews remained closer to Downtown than did other whites, who were often particularly attracted to new subdivisions in outlying areas. This was partly because Jews did not share most Christian whites' bias against high-density living and partly because Jews were more apt to be employed Downtown. The proportion of white-collar workers, managers, and professionals among Jews began a very rapid increase during the 1920s. Until about 1950 most managerial and professional work was in Downtown.[26] Also, the clothing business prior to about 1950 was predominantly Jewish. Tailors, factory workers, and owners desired easy access to Downtown, where most factories were located.[27]

Discrimination in housing was a minor and short-lived factor in the evolution of the Jewish distribution.[28] However, Gentiles did sometimes attempt to exclude Jews from certain residential areas. During the 1920s and 1930s, when anti-Semitism was widespread, the Ku Klux Klan in places such as Glendale and Inglewood worked to keep Jews as well as blacks out of certain areas. Restrictive covenants that prevented the

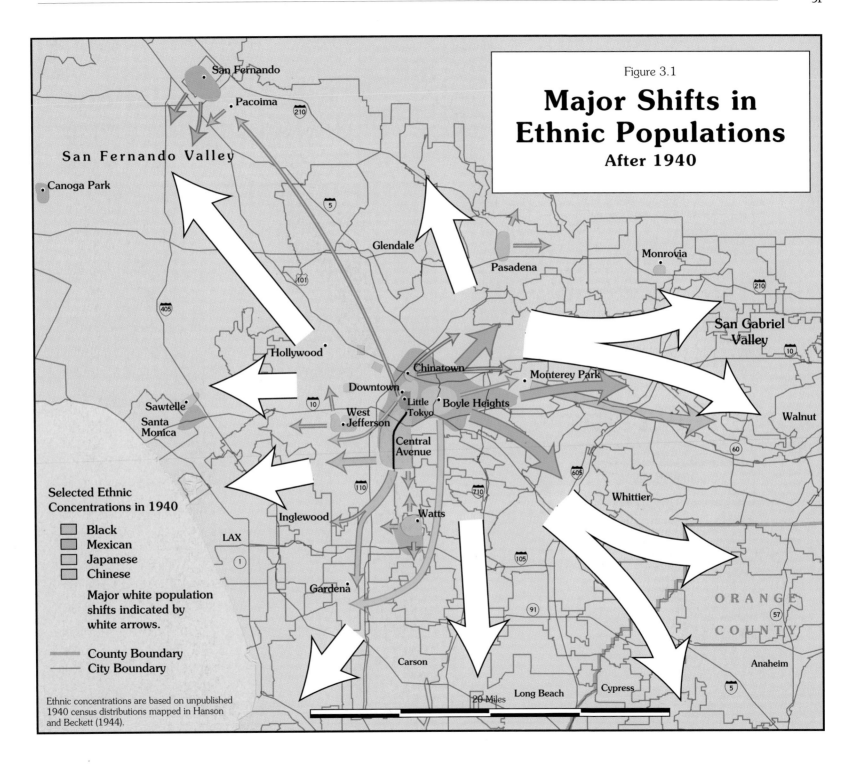

Figure 3.1

**Major Shifts in
Ethnic Populations**
After 1940

Selected Ethnic
Concentrations in 1940

- Black
- Mexican
- Japanese
- Chinese

Major white population
shifts indicated by
white arrows.

County Boundary
City Boundary

Ethnic concentrations are based on unpublished
1940 census distributions mapped in Hanson
and Beckett (1944).

52

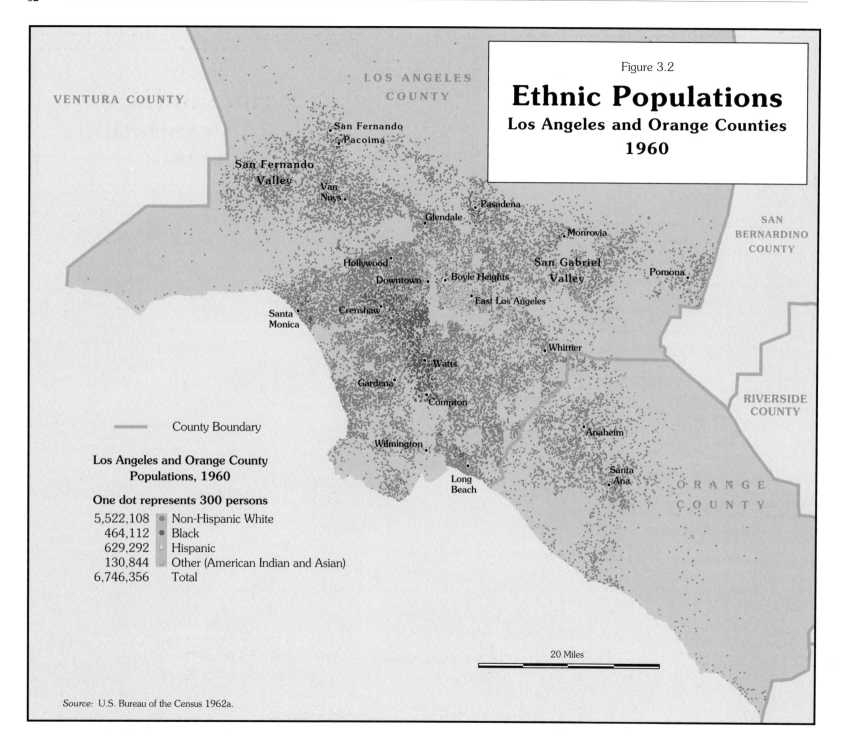

Figure 3.2

Ethnic Populations
Los Angeles and Orange Counties
1960

County Boundary

Los Angeles and Orange County Populations, 1960

One dot represents 300 persons

5,522,108		Non-Hispanic White
464,112		Black
629,292		Hispanic
130,844		Other (American Indian and Asian)
6,746,356		Total

20 Miles

Source: U.S. Bureau of the Census 1962a.

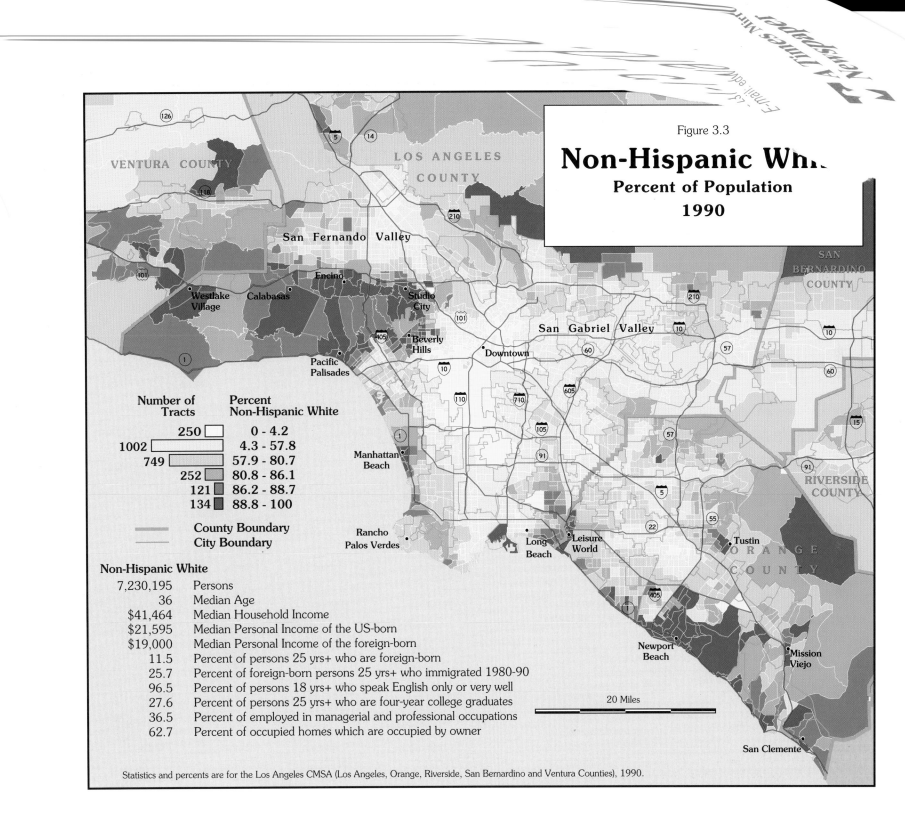

Figure 3.3

Non-Hispanic Whit[...]
Percent of Population
1990

Number of Tracts	Percent Non-Hispanic White
250	0 - 4.2
1002	4.3 - 57.8
749	57.9 - 80.7
252	80.8 - 86.1
121	86.2 - 88.7
134	88.8 - 100

County Boundary
City Boundary

Non-Hispanic White

7,230,195	Persons
36	Median Age
$41,464	Median Household Income
$21,595	Median Personal Income of the US-born
$19,000	Median Personal Income of the foreign-born
11.5	Percent of persons 25 yrs+ who are foreign-born
25.7	Percent of foreign-born persons 25 yrs+ who immigrated 1980-90
96.5	Percent of persons 18 yrs+ who speak English only or very well
27.6	Percent of persons 25 yrs+ who are four-year college graduates
36.5	Percent of employed in managerial and professional occupations
62.7	Percent of occupied homes which are occupied by owner

20 Miles

Statistics and percents are for the Los Angeles CMSA (Los Angeles, Orange, Riverside, San Bernardino and Ventura Counties), 1990.

54

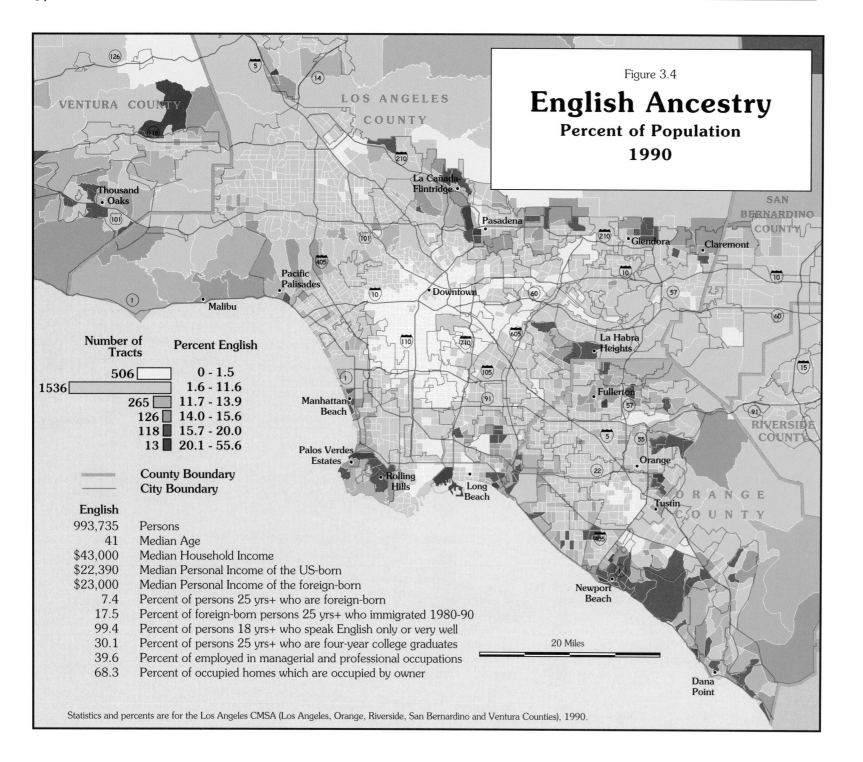

Figure 3.4

English Ancestry
Percent of Population
1990

Number of Tracts	Percent English
506	0 - 1.5
1536	1.6 - 11.6
265	11.7 - 13.9
126	14.0 - 15.6
118	15.7 - 20.0
13	20.1 - 55.6

County Boundary
City Boundary

English

993,735	Persons
41	Median Age
$43,000	Median Household Income
$22,390	Median Personal Income of the US-born
$23,000	Median Personal Income of the foreign-born
7.4	Percent of persons 25 yrs+ who are foreign-born
17.5	Percent of foreign-born persons 25 yrs+ who immigrated 1980-90
99.4	Percent of persons 18 yrs+ who speak English only or very well
30.1	Percent of persons 25 yrs+ who are four-year college graduates
39.6	Percent of employed in managerial and professional occupations
68.3	Percent of occupied homes which are occupied by owner

20 Miles

Statistics and percents are for the Los Angeles CMSA (Los Angeles, Orange, Riverside, San Bernardino and Ventura Counties), 1990.

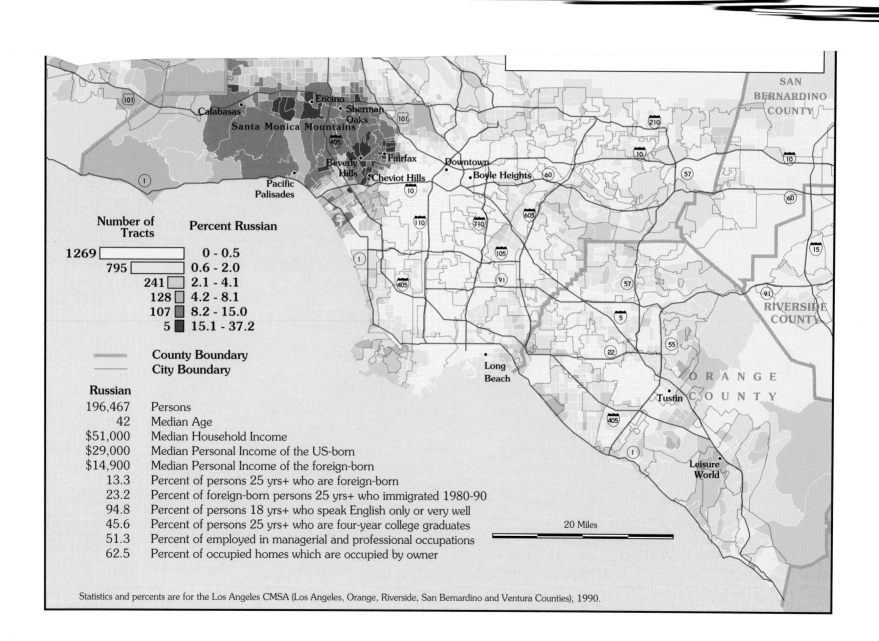

SAN BERNARDINO COUNTY

ORANGE COUNTY

RIVERSIDE COUNTY

Calabasas
Encino
Sherman Oaks
Santa Monica Mountains
Fairfax
Beverly Hills
Cheviot Hills
Downtown
Boyle Heights
Pacific Palisades
Long Beach
Tustin
Leisure World

Number of Tracts   **Percent Russian**

1269	0 - 0.5
795	0.6 - 2.0
241	2.1 - 4.1
128	4.2 - 8.1
107	8.2 - 15.0
5	15.1 - 37.2

County Boundary
City Boundary

Russian

196,467	Persons
42	Median Age
$51,000	Median Household Income
$29,000	Median Personal Income of the US-born
$14,900	Median Personal Income of the foreign-born
13.3	Percent of persons 25 yrs+ who are foreign-born
23.2	Percent of foreign-born persons 25 yrs+ who immigrated 1980-90
94.8	Percent of persons 18 yrs+ who speak English only or very well
45.6	Percent of persons 25 yrs+ who are four-year college graduates
51.3	Percent of employed in managerial and professional occupations
62.5	Percent of occupied homes which are occupied by owner

20 Miles

Statistics and percents are for the Los Angeles CMSA (Los Angeles, Orange, Riverside, San Bernardino and Ventura Counties), 1990.

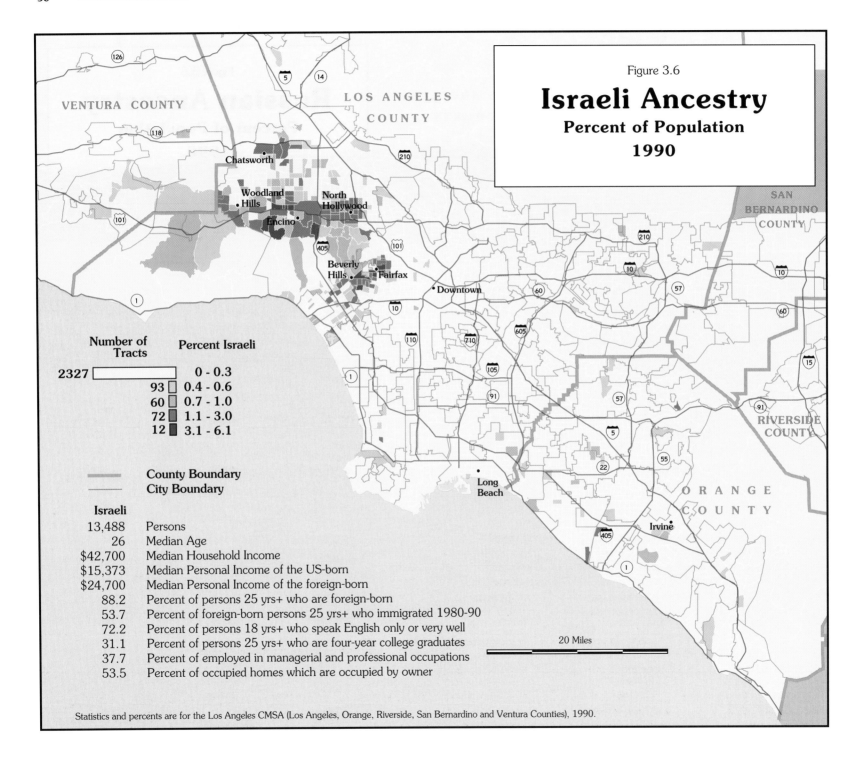

Figure 3.6

Israeli Ancestry
Percent of Population
1990

VENTURA COUNTY

LOS ANGELES COUNTY

SAN BERNARDINO COUNTY

Chatsworth

Woodland Hills

North Hollywood

Encino

Beverly Hills

Fairfax

Downtown

RIVERSIDE COUNTY

Long Beach

ORANGE COUNTY

Irvine

Number of Tracts

	Percent Israeli
2327	0 - 0.3
93	0.4 - 0.6
60	0.7 - 1.0
72	1.1 - 3.0
12	3.1 - 6.1

County Boundary
City Boundary

Israeli

13,488	Persons
26	Median Age
$42,700	Median Household Income
$15,373	Median Personal Income of the US-born
$24,700	Median Personal Income of the foreign-born
88.2	Percent of persons 25 yrs+ who are foreign-born
53.7	Percent of foreign-born persons 25 yrs+ who immigrated 1980-90
72.2	Percent of persons 18 yrs+ who speak English only or very well
31.1	Percent of persons 25 yrs+ who are four-year college graduates
37.7	Percent of employed in managerial and professional occupations
53.5	Percent of occupied homes which are occupied by owner

20 Miles

Statistics and percents are for the Los Angeles CMSA (Los Angeles, Orange, Riverside, San Bernardino and Ventura Counties), 1990.

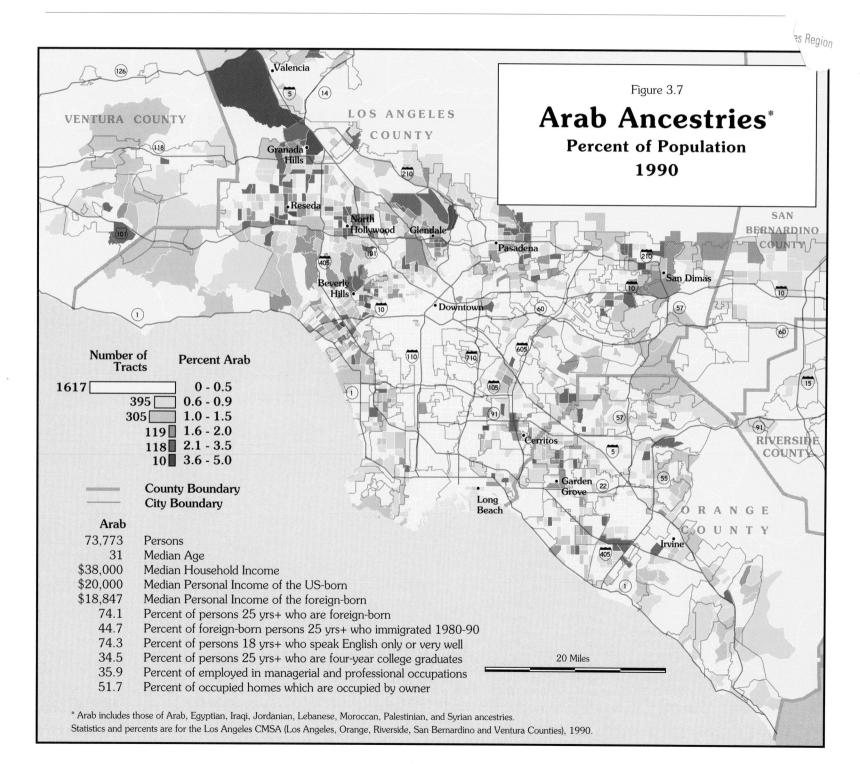

Figure 3.7

Arab Ancestries*
Percent of Population
1990

Number of Tracts — **Percent Arab**

1617	0 - 0.5
395	0.6 - 0.9
305	1.0 - 1.5
119	1.6 - 2.0
118	2.1 - 3.5
10	3.6 - 5.0

— County Boundary
— City Boundary

Arab

73,773	Persons
31	Median Age
$38,000	Median Household Income
$20,000	Median Personal Income of the US-born
$18,847	Median Personal Income of the foreign-born
74.1	Percent of persons 25 yrs+ who are foreign-born
44.7	Percent of foreign-born persons 25 yrs+ who immigrated 1980-90
74.3	Percent of persons 18 yrs+ who speak English only or very well
34.5	Percent of persons 25 yrs+ who are four-year college graduates
35.9	Percent of employed in managerial and professional occupations
51.7	Percent of occupied homes which are occupied by owner

20 Miles

* Arab includes those of Arab, Egyptian, Iraqi, Jordanian, Lebanese, Moroccan, Palestinian, and Syrian ancestries.

Statistics and percents are for the Los Angeles CMSA (Los Angeles, Orange, Riverside, San Bernardino and Ventura Counties), 1990.

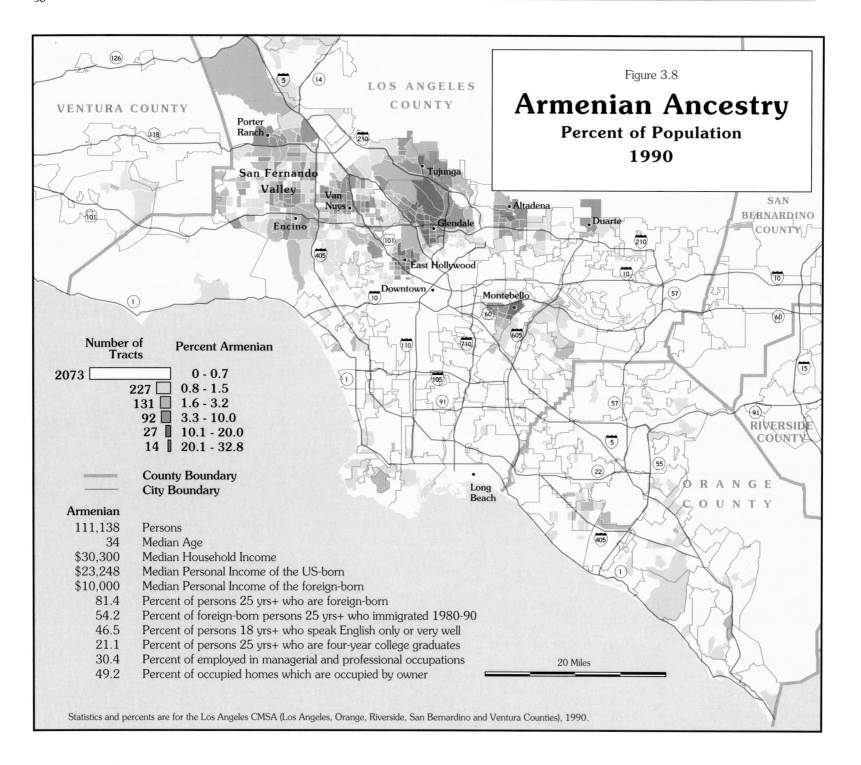

Figure 3.8

Armenian Ancestry
Percent of Population
1990

VENTURA COUNTY

LOS ANGELES COUNTY

SAN BERNARDINO COUNTY

RIVERSIDE COUNTY

ORANGE COUNTY

Porter Ranch

San Fernando Valley

Van Nuys

Encino

Tujunga

Glendale

Altadena

Duarte

East Hollywood

Downtown

Montebello

Long Beach

Number of Tracts	Percent Armenian
2073	0 - 0.7
227	0.8 - 1.5
131	1.6 - 3.2
92	3.3 - 10.0
27	10.1 - 20.0
14	20.1 - 32.8

County Boundary
City Boundary

Armenian

111,138	Persons
34	Median Age
$30,300	Median Household Income
$23,248	Median Personal Income of the US-born
$10,000	Median Personal Income of the foreign-born
81.4	Percent of persons 25 yrs+ who are foreign-born
54.2	Percent of foreign-born persons 25 yrs+ who immigrated 1980-90
46.5	Percent of persons 18 yrs+ who speak English only or very well
21.1	Percent of persons 25 yrs+ who are four-year college graduates
30.4	Percent of employed in managerial and professional occupations
49.2	Percent of occupied homes which are occupied by owner

20 Miles

Statistics and percents are for the Los Angeles CMSA (Los Angeles, Orange, Riverside, San Bernardino and Ventura Counties), 1990.

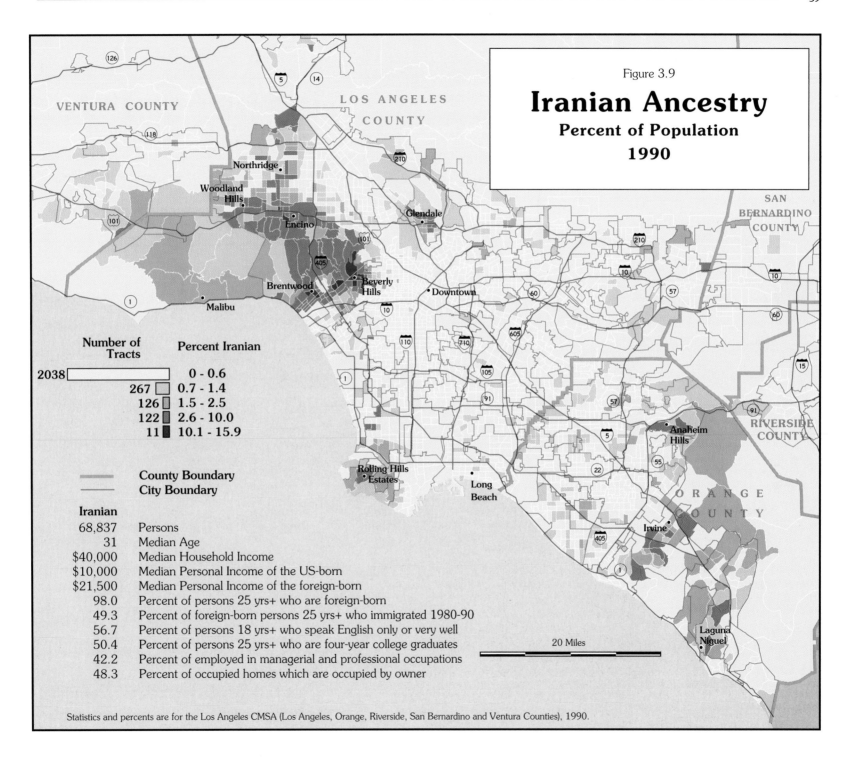

Figure 3.9

Iranian Ancestry
Percent of Population
1990

VENTURA COUNTY

LOS ANGELES
COUNTY

SAN
BERNARDINO
COUNTY

Northridge

Woodland
Hills

Encino

Glendale

Brentwood

Beverly
Hills

Downtown

Malibu

RIVERSIDE
COUNTY

Anaheim
Hills

ORANGE
COUNTY

Rolling Hills
Estates

Long
Beach

Irvine

Laguna
Niguel

Number of Tracts		Percent Iranian
2038		0 - 0.6
267		0.7 - 1.4
126		1.5 - 2.5
122		2.6 - 10.0
11		10.1 - 15.9

County Boundary
City Boundary

Iranian

68,837	Persons
31	Median Age
$40,000	Median Household Income
$10,000	Median Personal Income of the US-born
$21,500	Median Personal Income of the foreign-born
98.0	Percent of persons 25 yrs+ who are foreign-born
49.3	Percent of foreign-born persons 25 yrs+ who immigrated 1980-90
56.7	Percent of persons 18 yrs+ who speak English only or very well
50.4	Percent of persons 25 yrs+ who are four-year college graduates
42.2	Percent of employed in managerial and professional occupations
48.3	Percent of occupied homes which are occupied by owner

20 Miles

Statistics and percents are for the Los Angeles CMSA (Los Angeles, Orange, Riverside, San Bernardino and Ventura Counties), 1990.

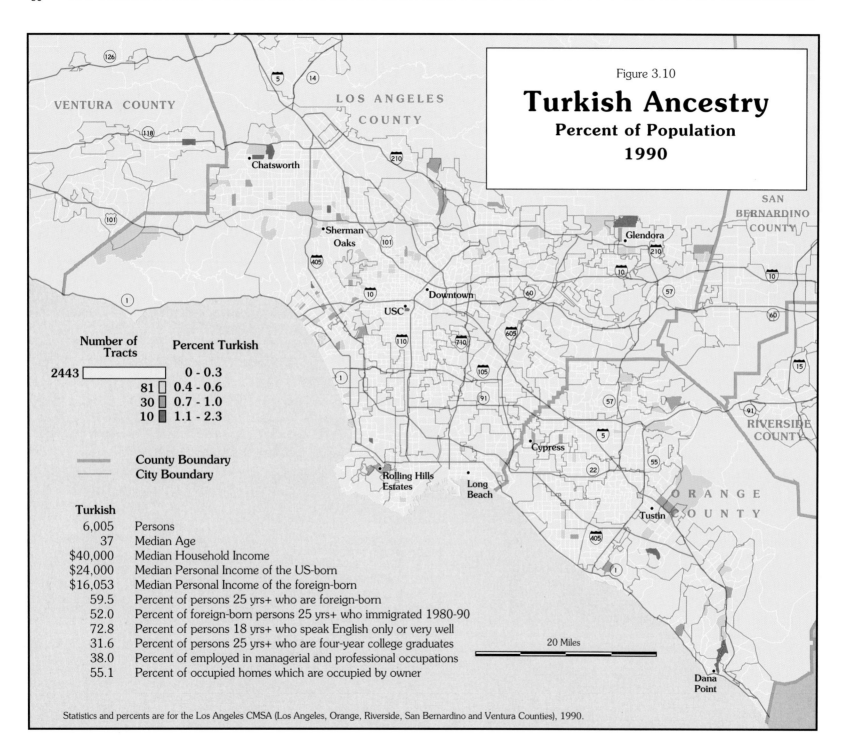

Figure 3.10

Turkish Ancestry
Percent of Population
1990

Number of Tracts | **Percent Turkish**

2443 | 0 - 0.3
81 | 0.4 - 0.6
30 | 0.7 - 1.0
10 | 1.1 - 2.3

County Boundary
City Boundary

Turkish

6,005	Persons
37	Median Age
$40,000	Median Household Income
$24,000	Median Personal Income of the US-born
$16,053	Median Personal Income of the foreign-born
59.5	Percent of persons 25 yrs+ who are foreign-born
52.0	Percent of foreign-born persons 25 yrs+ who immigrated 1980-90
72.8	Percent of persons 18 yrs+ who speak English only or very well
31.6	Percent of persons 25 yrs+ who are four-year college graduates
38.0	Percent of employed in managerial and professional occupations
55.1	Percent of occupied homes which are occupied by owner

20 Miles

Statistics and percents are for the Los Angeles CMSA (Los Angeles, Orange, Riverside, San Bernardino and Ventura Counties), 1990.

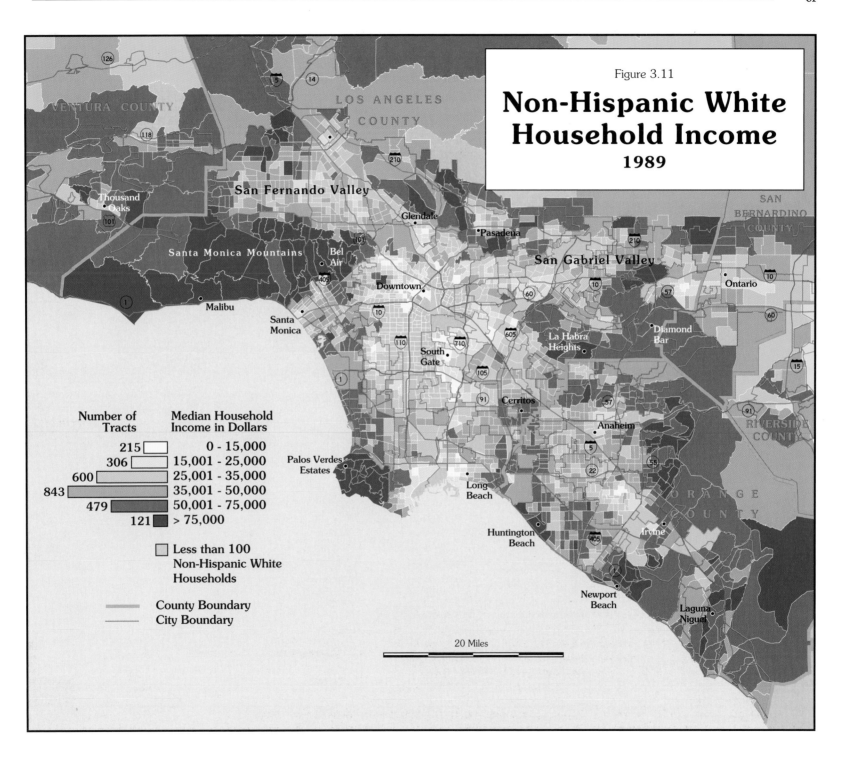

Figure 3.11

Non-Hispanic White Household Income
1989

Number of Tracts	Median Household Income in Dollars
215	0 - 15,000
306	15,001 - 25,000
600	25,001 - 35,000
843	35,001 - 50,000
479	50,001 - 75,000
121	> 75,000

Less than 100 Non-Hispanic White Households

County Boundary
City Boundary

20 Miles

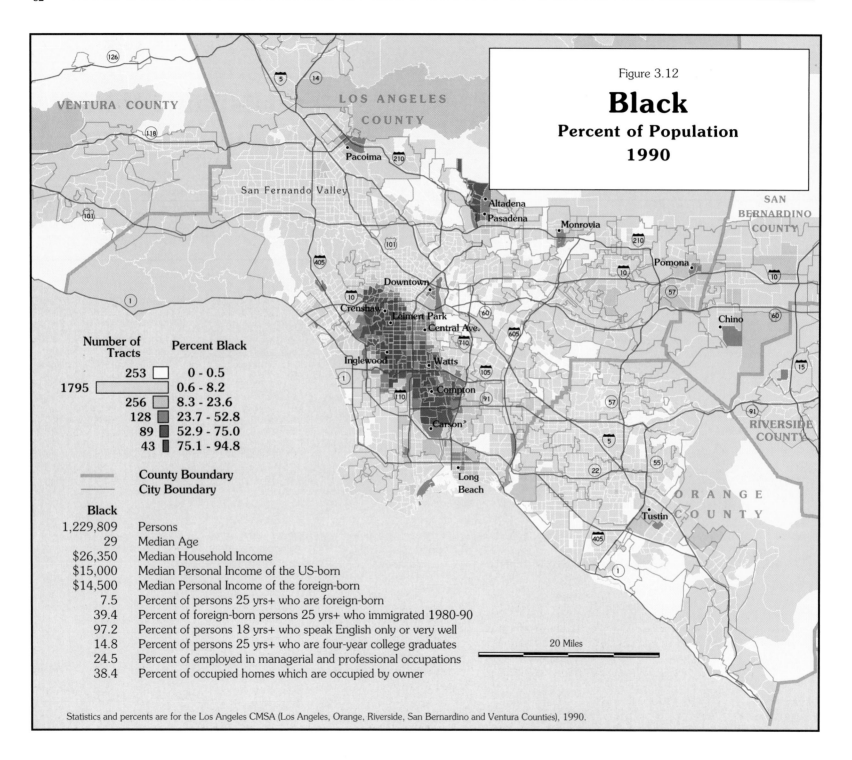

Figure 3.12

Black
Percent of Population
1990

VENTURA COUNTY

LOS ANGELES COUNTY

SAN BERNARDINO COUNTY

San Fernando Valley

Pacoima

Altadena
Pasadena

Monrovia

Pomona

Downtown

Crenshaw

Leimert Park

Central Ave.

Chino

Inglewood

Watts

Compton

Carson

RIVERSIDE COUNTY

Long Beach

ORANGE COUNTY

Tustin

Number of Tracts	Percent Black
253	0 - 0.5
1795	0.6 - 8.2
256	8.3 - 23.6
128	23.7 - 52.8
89	52.9 - 75.0
43	75.1 - 94.8

——— County Boundary
——— City Boundary

Black

1,229,809	Persons
29	Median Age
$26,350	Median Household Income
$15,000	Median Personal Income of the US-born
$14,500	Median Personal Income of the foreign-born
7.5	Percent of persons 25 yrs+ who are foreign-born
39.4	Percent of foreign-born persons 25 yrs+ who immigrated 1980-90
97.2	Percent of persons 18 yrs+ who speak English only or very well
14.8	Percent of persons 25 yrs+ who are four-year college graduates
24.5	Percent of employed in managerial and professional occupations
38.4	Percent of occupied homes which are occupied by owner

20 Miles

Statistics and percents are for the Los Angeles CMSA (Los Angeles, Orange, Riverside, San Bernardino and Ventura Counties), 1990.

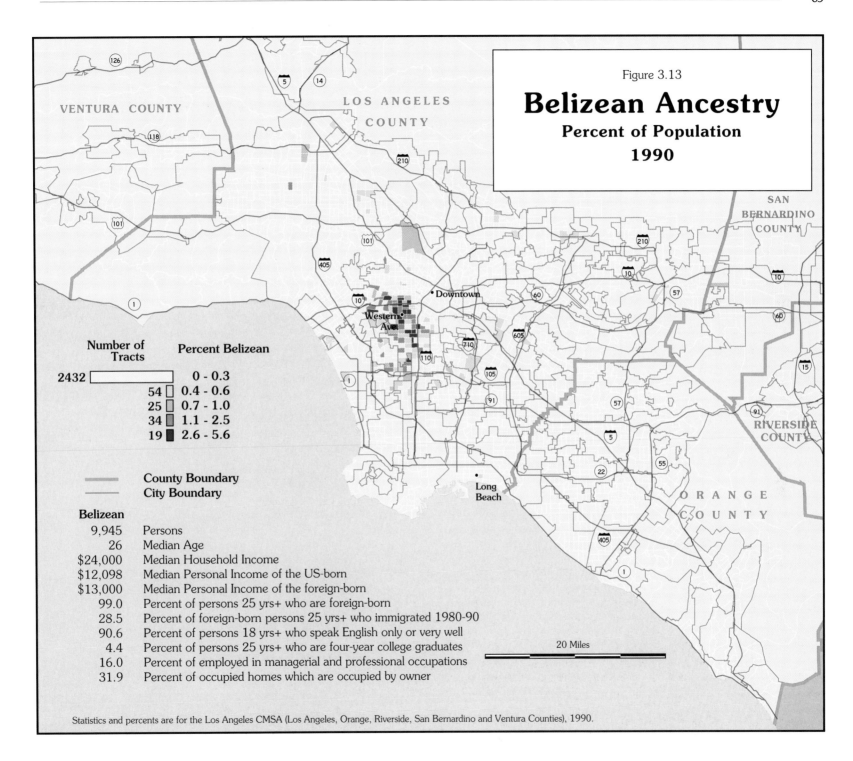

Figure 3.13
Belizean Ancestry
Percent of Population
1990

Number of Tracts — **Percent Belizean**

2432 — 0 - 0.3
54 — 0.4 - 0.6
25 — 0.7 - 1.0
34 — 1.1 - 2.5
19 — 2.6 - 5.6

County Boundary
City Boundary

Belizean

9,945	Persons
26	Median Age
$24,000	Median Household Income
$12,098	Median Personal Income of the US-born
$13,000	Median Personal Income of the foreign-born
99.0	Percent of persons 25 yrs+ who are foreign-born
28.5	Percent of foreign-born persons 25 yrs+ who immigrated 1980-90
90.6	Percent of persons 18 yrs+ who speak English only or very well
4.4	Percent of persons 25 yrs+ who are four-year college graduates
16.0	Percent of employed in managerial and professional occupations
31.9	Percent of occupied homes which are occupied by owner

20 Miles

Statistics and percents are for the Los Angeles CMSA (Los Angeles, Orange, Riverside, San Bernardino and Ventura Counties), 1990.

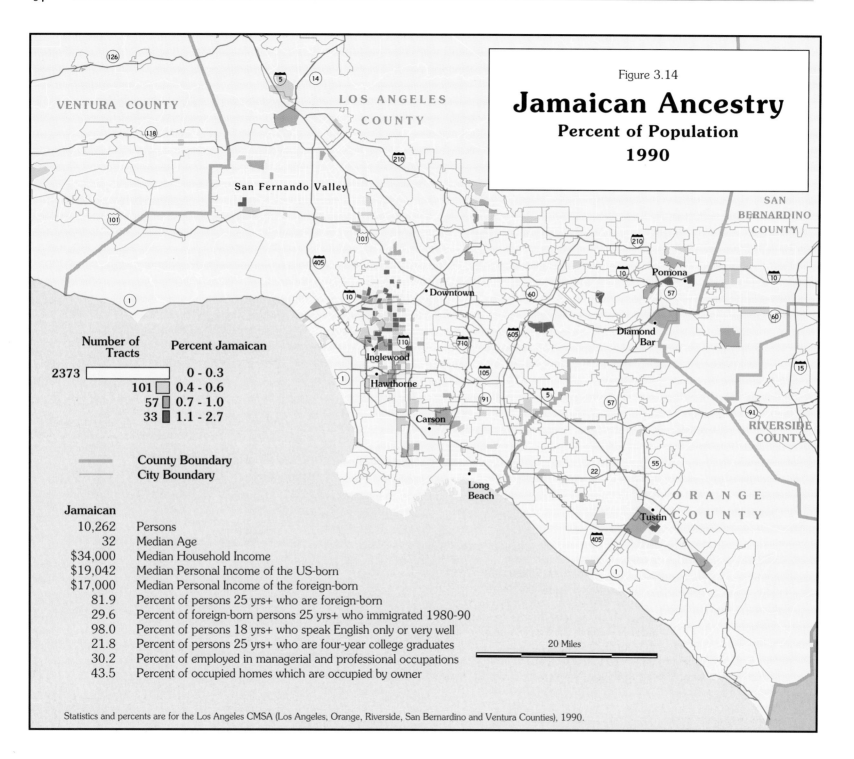

Figure 3.14

Jamaican Ancestry
Percent of Population
1990

VENTURA COUNTY

LOS ANGELES COUNTY

SAN BERNARDINO COUNTY

San Fernando Valley

Pomona

Downtown

Diamond Bar

Number of Tracts   **Percent Jamaican**

Inglewood

2373   0 - 0.3
101   0.4 - 0.6
57   0.7 - 1.0
33   1.1 - 2.7

Hawthorne

Carson

RIVERSIDE COUNTY

— County Boundary
— City Boundary

Long Beach

ORANGE COUNTY

Jamaican

10,262	Persons
32	Median Age
$34,000	Median Household Income
$19,042	Median Personal Income of the US-born
$17,000	Median Personal Income of the foreign-born
81.9	Percent of persons 25 yrs+ who are foreign-born
29.6	Percent of foreign-born persons 25 yrs+ who immigrated 1980-90
98.0	Percent of persons 18 yrs+ who speak English only or very well
21.8	Percent of persons 25 yrs+ who are four-year college graduates
30.2	Percent of employed in managerial and professional occupations
43.5	Percent of occupied homes which are occupied by owner

Tustin

20 Miles

Statistics and percents are for the Los Angeles CMSA (Los Angeles, Orange, Riverside, San Bernardino and Ventura Counties), 1990.

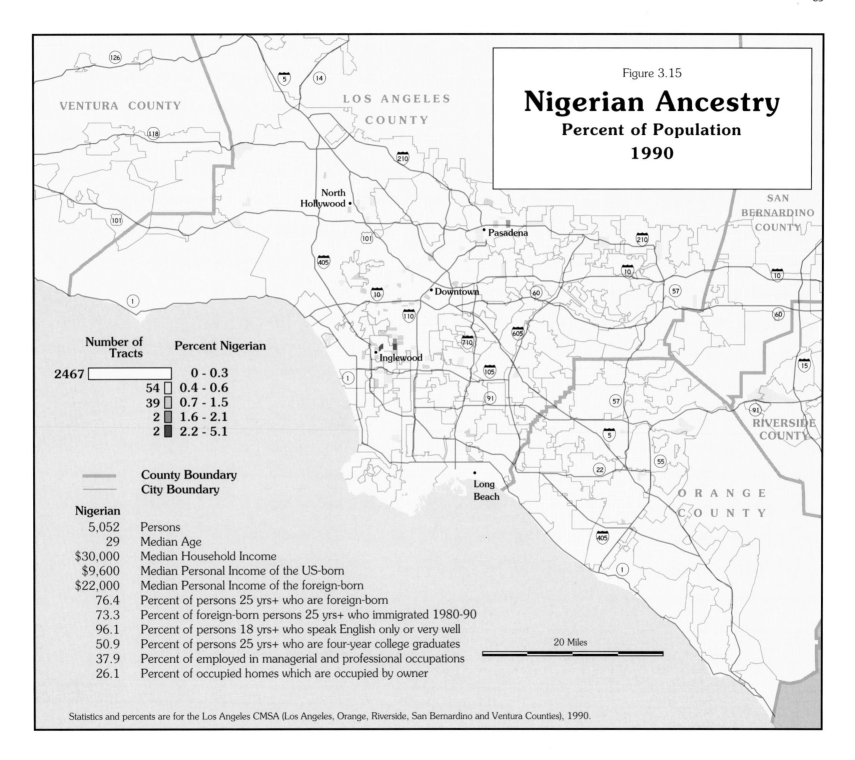

Figure 3.15

Nigerian Ancestry
Percent of Population
1990

VENTURA COUNTY

LOS ANGELES COUNTY

SAN BERNARDINO COUNTY

North Hollywood

Pasadena

Downtown

Inglewood

Long Beach

ORANGE COUNTY

RIVERSIDE COUNTY

Number of Tracts	Percent Nigerian
2467	0 - 0.3
54	0.4 - 0.6
39	0.7 - 1.5
2	1.6 - 2.1
2	2.2 - 5.1

County Boundary
City Boundary

Nigerian

5,052	Persons
29	Median Age
$30,000	Median Household Income
$9,600	Median Personal Income of the US-born
$22,000	Median Personal Income of the foreign-born
76.4	Percent of persons 25 yrs+ who are foreign-born
73.3	Percent of foreign-born persons 25 yrs+ who immigrated 1980-90
96.1	Percent of persons 18 yrs+ who speak English only or very well
50.9	Percent of persons 25 yrs+ who are four-year college graduates
37.9	Percent of employed in managerial and professional occupations
26.1	Percent of occupied homes which are occupied by owner

20 Miles

Statistics and percents are for the Los Angeles CMSA (Los Angeles, Orange, Riverside, San Bernardino and Ventura Counties), 1990.

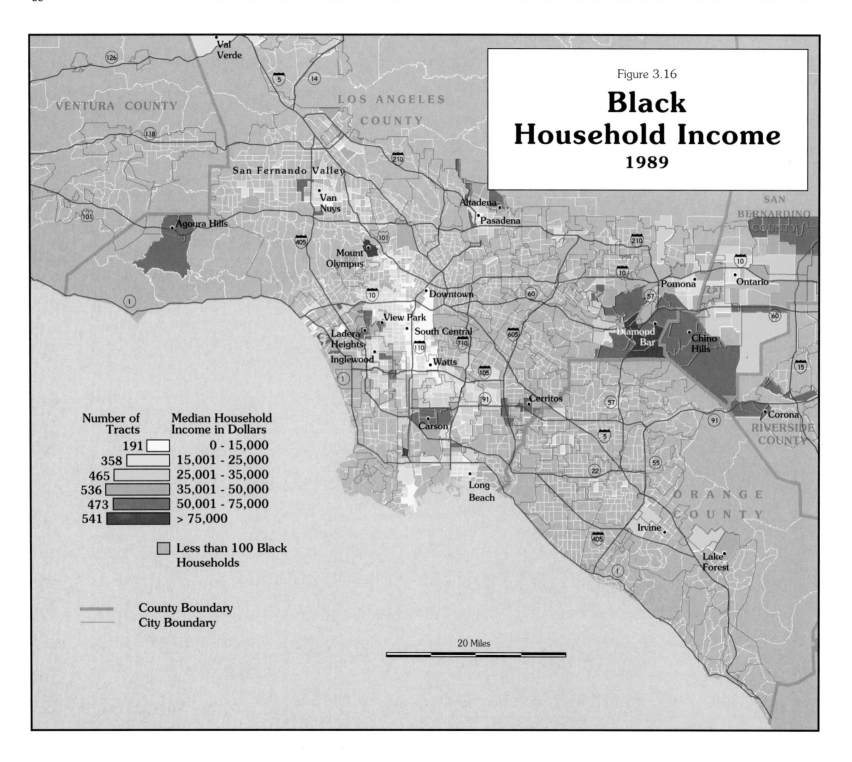

Figure 3.16

Black Household Income
1989

Number of Tracts		Median Household Income in Dollars
191		0 - 15,000
358		15,001 - 25,000
465		25,001 - 35,000
536		35,001 - 50,000
473		50,001 - 75,000
541		> 75,000

Less than 100 Black Households

County Boundary
City Boundary

20 Miles

sale of a house to Jews and non-whites were fairly common.[29] Palos Verdes Estates, incorporated in 1939, for a time limited ownership to "Caucasians and Gentiles."[30]

Boyle Heights. By 1890 the Boyle Heights section of Los Angeles, east of the Los Angeles River, was connected to Downtown by two street railways. The next decade saw the growth of this streetcar suburb, with numerous large, attractive homes built above the bluffs overlooking Downtown. With much additional homebuilding after 1910 and the departure of many of the original homeowners to newer suburbs, Boyle Heights soon became the leading destination for new immigrants. During the 1920s the sheer numbers of Eastern European Jews arriving in Los Angeles meant that Jews became the dominant ethnic group in Boyle Heights.

By the mid-1930s, about 35,000 Jews (almost a third of Los Angeles' Jewry) lived in Boyle Heights.[31] Mostly Orthodox in their Judaism and Yiddish speaking, they established a neighborhood Jewish presence and an active cultural and religious life. The area boasted ten synagogues, Jewish food and candy shops and bookstores, two theaters showing Yiddish films, an old folks' home, a Kosher slaughterhouse and restaurants, a Yiddish school, and Jewish social clubs. On Breed Street the Orthodox synagogue *(shul)* became the symbol of the Boyle Heights Jewish community. The hilly area called City Terrace, just outside the Los Angeles City boundary to the northeast of Boyle Heights, had homes that were newer and more expensive than those in Boyle Heights. It too became Jewish, but the fact that many of its residents were secular and politically active resulted in periodic conflicts with the more religious and traditional Jews of Boyle Heights.

Beginning in the 1920s it became possible for the more affluent Jews to move out of Boyle Heights and City Terrace. They found better homes to the west of Downtown, especially in Hollywood and in the increasingly Jewish Fairfax Avenue neighborhood north of Beverly Boulevard. By 1940 the settlements west of Downtown had more Jews than did Boyle Heights.[32] The contrast between the two general areas was clear. Boyle Heights remained the home of the more Yiddish, Orthodox, and working-class Jews; the more acculturated Jews

(particularly the Reform Jews) and the new professionals and managers lived in a completely separate area, to the west of Downtown.

In later decades the Jewish exodus from Boyle Heights continued. As the area became more and more Mexican, most evidence of its Jewish past was obliterated or lost. By the 1990s only the Breed Street synagogue—abandoned and vandalized— remained to suggest the vitality of Jewish neighborhood life in the past. However, many Jews still alive remember "the Heights" with fondness.[33] That area, more than any other in Los Angeles, was a transplantation of the intensely rewarding community life they had experienced earlier in New York, Chicago, and other large Jewish centers.

Shifts from older neighborhoods. Between 1920 and 1940 Jews and other whites moved out of the old Central Avenue area south of Downtown, and their places were taken by blacks.[34] The Sephardic Jewish immigrants who had settled two miles to the west in South Central during the 1920s and early 1930s did not leave so soon, but in the 1940s and 1950s most of them also moved farther west or north into the Westside.[35] The many black in-migrants to Los Angeles were being residentially segregated into a ghetto whose focus was Central Avenue, and nearly all whites moved out as the southward-advancing black settlement penetrated their neighborhoods. White flight was delayed from more expensive areas to the west, particularly the West Adams neighborhood west of the University of Southern California, where many large, architecturally distinctive homes dated from the early 1890s. However, in the late 1940s and 1950s most Jews left the West Adams area and moved farther north or west, toward what was coalescing as the Jewish Westside community.

Some Jews who lived in these parts of South Central had important ties to blacks in their area. They employed blacks as servants in their homes and in various menial jobs in Jewish-owned neighborhood stores, at which blacks shopped frequently.[36] Jews and blacks also recognized a common bond in their struggle against discrimination and worked together to eliminate it. In addition, Jews earned a reputation during the years of legalized segregation of being more willing than other whites to ignore restrictive covenants and sell their homes to blacks.[37] Later, in the 1950s and 1960s, the connections between Jews and blacks were forged into an influential political coalition that ultimately achieved the election of a black mayor, Tom Bradley, in 1973.

Departure from the Temple Street area occurred as early as 1920, but in this case white flight in advance of encroaching blacks was not one of the motives. The Temple Street area was two miles north of major black areas and was not viewed as being in the likely path of black-ghetto expansion. Out-movement from the Temple Street neighborhood was simply a response to neighborhood aging, a growing affluence among Jewish residents, and the availability and affordability of better neighborhoods elsewhere. Thus, the increasingly low-income Temple Street neighborhood became ethnically diverse rather than black.

Jews who left these disparate sections tended to move into a single large area which would become the large Jewish enclave stretching between Hollywood and the coast. Although Jews continue to live in small numbers in most parts of Southern California, this single concentration within a relatively small part of Los Angeles County is dramatically evident in 1990 (Fig. 3.5). In the next sections we will explore various areas within that Jewish enclave.

The Fairfax District and Pico-Robertson. During the 1940s and 1950s many Jews settled near Fairfax Avenue, between Wilshire Boulevard and Melrose Avenue.[38] This area contained numerous apartment buildings that attracted many Jews who were elderly or not affluent. Fairfax Avenue between Melrose Avenue and Beverly Boulevard emerged as the most important Jewish residential and shopping enclave— an updated and smaller-scale version of Boyle Heights. Fairfax was the symbolic focus of the Jewish community during the postwar years.

Since the 1940s this Fairfax District has been the best-known distinctively Jewish section of Los Angeles. Its Jewish identity is visible in its many Orthodox synagogues, kosher butcher shops, stores selling religious books and music from Israel, newspaper stands with Russian and Hebrew papers, and

service centers to help elderly Jews.[39] Canter's Restaurant and Delicatessen includes a Kibbutz Room, Bob's Fish Market sells only kosher fish, and the Diamond Bakery is famous for corn rye, raisin pumpernickel, and Sabbath *challah* bread. Strolling along Fairfax Avenue was once a favorite pastime in Los Angeles. However, as the neighborhood has declined, affluent and assimilated Jews visited Fairfax less often if ever. As the old generation died, as thrift stores and pizzerias and Chinese restaurants intruded, the district became a relic of the past rather than a vibrant enclave of contemporary Jewish life.

Two miles to the southwest, around the intersection of Pico and Robertson Boulevards, is another Jewish neighborhood. This one, however, has many younger families and is easily accessible to more affluent Jews in the Cheviot Hills. With kosher meat markets, Jewish day schools and bookstores, and several Orthodox and Conservative congregations, Pico-Robertson is an important Jewish enclave.[40]

Russian Jewish refugees in West Hollywood. During the 1940s and 1950s, Hollywood attracted many Jews who left Boyle Heights and others newly arrived in Los Angeles. As in Fairfax, housing in Hollywood has been mostly apartments in large buildings, though some old homes were remodeled into smaller rental units. In subsequent decades most of these Jews departed, their places to be taken by a very different group.

In the late 1970s West Hollywood and adjacent parts of Hollywood became a major destination for Jewish refugees from the Soviet Union. A similar flood of refugees occurred during the Soviet-American détente of the late 1980s, so that in 1990 a great many refugees had just arrived in Los Angeles. All spoke Russian, many were elderly, and most have found it difficult to learn English and adapt to the American economic system.

During the Soviet period religion was strongly discouraged, and Jews were not permitted to conduct religious services. As a result, Russian Jews in Los Angeles have typically arrived with little knowledge of Judaism. However, the close proximity of this area to the Fairfax district and its many synagogues has helped reconnect these Jews to their heritage. In Fairfax some elderly Russian Jews have become acquainted with elderly Jews who migrated many decades ago, although this poses some language difficulties because Russian Jews at that time spoke Yiddish rather than Russian.

The West Hollywood area has also been particularly attractive to Soviet Jews because it represents a Russian-speaking enclave. Plummer Park provides a convenient and pleasant place for the elderly to congregate, converse in Russian, and play dominoes.[41] Neighborhood businesses advertise in Russian, and there are Russian-speaking doctors, dentists, and salespeople in the various food, clothing, and appliance stores. In addition, a rabbi from the Soviet Union opened a center for refugee assistance and religious outreach across the street from Plummer Park.[42]

The West Hollywood enclave is located in the eastern-most set of tracts with 15 percent or more Russian ancestry (Fig. 3.5). It is precisely these Russian Jewish refugees, rather than a U.S.-born Russian-ancestry population, that distinguishes this area. With the assistance of relatives and local Jewish congregations, many refugees settled elsewhere in the Westside or in the Jewish sections of the San Fernando Valley. However, in the mid-1990s West Hollywood remained an enclave that was ostensibly part of the larger Westside Jewish population but was, in fact, culturally and socially distinct.

The Westside of Los Angeles. Since the 1940s younger Jewish families have been moving into newer neighborhoods, either farther west in what is usually called the Westside of Los Angeles or north into the San Fernando Valley. These two areas encompass the most important Jewish concentration in Southern California (Fig. 3.5).

The Westside is a regional label which is defined as much by the affluence of its predominantly white (and often Jewish) population as by its location (Fig. 2.4). Geographically it extends westward from approximately La Brea or Fairfax Avenue to the Pacific Ocean. Thus, within the Westside are the large, single-family houses of Beverly Hills, Bel Air, Cheviot Hills, Brentwood, and Pacific Palisades, as well as the more modest homes and apartments of Palms and Santa Monica.

The Westside and the San Fernando Valley were attractive to Jews because they were not far from earlier settlements like Boyle Heights and West Adams and were areas where new housing and the higher-status jobs were opening up. The Jewish concentrations in these areas are also partly due to Jewish internal cohesiveness—the desire of many Jews to be part of a geographically based Jewish community. However, the continual and substantial westward shift of the Jewish distribution over the last half century has isolated what was once the most prestigious and important Jewish temple in Los Angeles. At the time of its founding in 1929, the Wilshire Boulevard Temple was reasonably close to its members' homes. By 1990, however, this historic landmark seemed far out of place in its setting amid modern office buildings in Koreatown. It is certainly poorly located to serve its contemporary Westside congregation.

Jewish proportions, as indicated by Russian-ancestry percentages, are particularly high in Beverly Hills and the area to its south (Fig. 3.5).[43] The latter includes the Cheviot Hills, Beverlywood, and the less expensive Pico-Robertson area. The tract that contains the Fairfax enclave also appears on the map in the highest percentage-Russian category.

Much of the financial strength of Westside Jews has been based on their success in the film industry and, since World War II, in television, suburban real-estate development, and savings-and-loan operations.[44] Jewish residential concentration on the Westside has been reinforced by the area's commercial growth. This growth has been focused especially in Century City and on the "Miracle Mile" on Wilshire Boulevard between Fairfax and La Brea. These centers of exclusive stores, hotels and restaurants, and office buildings represent mostly Jewish competition with the monopoly of Los Angeles business functions formerly held by Downtown and the old "Anglo" elite. The offices of the largest Jewish community organization, the Federation Council, lie on Wilshire Boulevard at the eastern edge of Beverly Hills, an area with an unusually high percentage of Russian ancestry (Fig. 3.5). The Simon Wiesenthal Center and its associated Museum of Tolerance are also located in the heart of the Jewish Westside—on Pico Boulevard close to the 20th Century Fox Studio in Century City. It is likely that the majority of highly influential Jewish families in Los Angeles reside within two miles of these institutions.

The San Fernando Valley. For three decades following World War II this valley was a major focus of new homebuilding in the Los Angeles area. Population growth was rapid, and the number of Jews in the valley in 1979 was seven times what it had been in 1951.[45] Most Jews settled near the southern edge of the valley, at first in North Hollywood but later in a corridor that extended west on either side of Ventura Boulevard into Encino, Sherman Oaks, Tarzana, and Woodland Hills.[46] Ventura Boulevard, which stretches the length of the valley's southern margin, became a shopping center for the affluent, many of whom were Jewish.

To the north of the Ventura Boulevard axis of Jewish settlement lies an ethnic and economic transition zone, carefully defined by the price and appearance of housing and by the degree of industrialization, with cheaper apartment rentals commonly occupied by Latinos. To the east, Jewish settlement diminishes sharply beyond the 170 Freeway (Fig. 3.5). Burbank, Toluca Lake, and a few parts of North Hollywood remain to some extent a stronghold of "Anglo" whites. Similarly, the Russian-ancestry percentage is low in the more rugged areas west of the San Fernando Valley because few Jews have been attracted to those rustic but isolated pockets of settlement.

In the 1970s and 1980s the valley became less suburban and more urban. Employment, shopping, and entertainment opportunities became widespread, making trips over the mountains to the Westside less necessary and locations near Ventura Boulevard less advantageous. Jews avoided the low-income areas in the older central part of the valley and selected homes in the better sections of Northridge and near the valley's western and northern fringes (West Hills and Porter Ranch). During the 1980s many refugees from the Soviet Union settled in the southern corridor of the valley, accentuating the Jewish presence in that zone.

Santa Monica Mountains. These rugged mountains may be a barrier to transportation, but they do not divide Los Angeles Jewry geographically or socially (Fig. 3.5). Russian-ancestry percentages continue relatively high through this picturesque and expensive area. In the mid-1990s a highly visible new focus of Los Angeles Jewry was built at a key crossroads in the mountains—where Mulholland Drive crosses Interstate 405. Recent developments there include the Skirball Cultural Center, which stresses the American Jewish experience, and the University of Judaism. Nearby is the Stephen S. Wise Temple—the largest in the Los Angeles area—and its school, which provides education from prekindergarten through high school. All these institutions together constitute what is probably the largest Jewish learning center in the United States. It is located appropriately near the geographical center of Los Angeles Jewry, and it links symbolically the two most important settlement areas in Los Angeles—the Westside and the San Fernando Valley.

People of Israeli Ancestry

Nearly all people who identify their ancestry as Israeli are Jewish. Christian and Muslim migrants from Israel are much more likely to identify themselves as Palestinian or to use some label other than Israeli, because the latter term is inseparable from the Jewish dominance of Israel. The Jewish nature of Israelis means that Israelis share some characteristics with American Jews.

Jews in Southern California have provided social and economic support for newly arrived Israelis. Residential locations are also similar. Most Israelis live in neighborhoods where there are many other Jews (Figs. 3.5 and 3.6). Their percentages are relatively high in the Fairfax District, the section of Hollywood next to West Hollywood and Fairfax, the Pico-Robertson area, and the adjacent section of Beverly Hills. In the San Fernando Valley Israelis have concentrated somewhat in Sherman Oaks and Tarzana—both on expensive Santa Monica Mountain sites and on the valley floor. Israelis and the Russian-ancestry population share some industry niches although these are also common among other groups (Table 8.6).

Nevertheless, in a great many ways Israelis in Southern California are distinct from other Jews.[47] In Southern California (and the United States as a whole) the Reform and Conservative branches of Judaism are numerically much larger and more influential than is the Orthodox branch, but in Israel the Reform and Conservative groups hardly exist. Among

Israelis, much of life is directly or indirectly tied to Orthodoxy and its synagogues. Language is another reason why Israelis typically form independent social networks. They speak Hebrew, but Southern California Jews are rarely able to speak Israeli Hebrew. Israelis in Southern California miss the solidarity of the social community they knew in Israel, and Israeli women work hard to establish informal networks of mutual support and child rearing with other Israelis in order to overcome this deficiency in American life. Israelis and other local Jews have mixed feelings about each other. Israelis frequently consider American Jews to be soft and lacking in self-confidence and pride as Jews, whereas many U.S.-born Jews think of Israelis in Los Angeles as boorish and arrogant.[48]

American Jews often look critically at Israelis living in the United States, believing that they have too easily forsaken their obligations to Israel for the greater material prosperity of America. And the ambivalence of Israelis themselves concerning their emigration from Israel is indicated by the fact that most Israelis in Southern California agree with American Jews that they (the Israeli émigrés) should return someday to Israel.[49]

People of Arab Ancestries

People with origins in one of the predominantly Arabic-speaking countries identify with that country. In most cases they also consider themselves Arabs. The pervasive Arab identity throughout North Africa and much of the Middle East may well become stronger in Southern California relative to national identities, partly because there are too few people from any single Arab country to form a cohesive community.[50]

We combined several national ancestries into a single larger Arab ancestry total (Fig. 3.7). This Arab aggregation includes the following, listed here with their 1990 estimated populations in Southern California: Egyptian (13,584), Moroccan (1,482), Lebanese (24,925), Syrian (7,769), Jordanian (2,504), Palestinian (4,787), and Iraqi (2,373), as well as those who reported their ancestry as Arab (11,791). Other ancestries not included in this Arab aggregation because of their much smaller numbers are Algerian (299), Tunisian (130), Libyan (72), Bahraini (101), Kuwaiti (80), Saudi Arabian (100), and Yemeni (202).

Within our aggregation, Muslims and Christians constitute the leading religious groups, but in Southern California there are also Jews, especially from Morocco, and an active Druze community. No good data on the size of the various religious communities exist, because the U.S. census is not permitted to ask questions regarding religious adherence and no one has surveyed religious identity among Southern Californians of Arab origin.[51] Although most immigrants from many Arab countries are Muslim, it may well be that Southern Californians of Egyptian, Palestinian, Syrian, and Lebanese ancestries are predominantly Christian, represented by numerous Protestant, Catholic, and Orthodox denominations. The large immigration from Egypt, for instance, has produced a rapid increase in numbers of Coptic Christians.[52] Additionally, most Armenians (almost all of whom are Christian) who immigrated from Lebanon or Syria are fluent in Arabic and at home in Arab culture. Although most of them probably identified their primary ancestry as Armenian on the census, their ties to Arabs from those countries are often strong, both socially and politically.

Distribution. It seems likely that people of Arab ancestry have long been widely distributed across Southern California. A survey of Christian Lebanese about 1960 found something of a concentration in the Silver Lake–Los Feliz–East Hollywood area, but the majority were living elsewhere.[53] During the past thirty years many immigrants arrived first as college or graduate students sent by well-to-do parents, and their subsequent high-status employment has enabled many of them to live in more expensive but widely scattered areas near their work.

Widespread prejudice against Muslims, particularly Arabs, has also prompted many people to be discreet in expressing their identities in public.[54] Also, the absence of any distinctive Arab or Muslim enclave diminishes the public's awareness of local Arabs and Muslims. Although the Islamic Center of Southern California (Vermont Avenue near 4th Street) has become the most influential local media source for Islamic perspectives on a wide range of topics, it is not located near any residential cluster of Arabs or other Muslim populations.

Moreover, the other forty or so other mosques in the Los Angeles and Orange County area are unobtrusive.[55] The Arab-ancestry group's wide scattering is reflected in the varied locations at which formal group functions are held. These range from the Arab American Community Center near Silver Lake, the Beverly Hilton, and the Disneyland Hotel in Anaheim to a Middle Eastern restaurant and night club in Glendora, a banquet center in Monrovia, and a public park in Lakewood.

The location of specific tracts with relatively high Arab proportions may not be very significant because all of the percentages are so low. Nevertheless, the fact that Arab-oriented churches are located in or near clusters suggests possible connections (Fig. 3.7). For instance, there are Arab Protestant churches in Glendora, Pasadena, and Glendale; a Syrian Melkite Catholic Church in North Hollywood; and Coptic Orthodox churches in Arleta, Glendale, and Bellflower, and on Robertson Boulevard in Los Angeles within the tract that shows as at least 3.5 percent Arab ancestry.[56] One tract stands out visually at the top of Figure 3.7, less because of its importance in the Arab distribution than because its area is so large. This tract, west of Interstate 5 and Valencia, has 1,700 residents, but nearly all of them live in the new Stevenson Ranch subdivision. The remainder of the tract is rugged, wild country.

Other tracts with slightly high Arab percentages are widespread. It is possible that in 1990 some residential clustering would be more apparent in distributions of specific Arab nationalities because chain migrations and social networks normally tied to one specific country would not be masked by those of other countries. However, we found no evidence that this was the case. For example, the 1960 Christian Lebanese concentration is apparent in 1990 only in a single Los Feliz tract that was no more than about 3 percent Arab ancestry, and the thirteen organized Coptic Christian congregations are widely scattered through Southern California.[57]

People of Armenian Ancestry

A handful of students, health seekers, and rug merchants were probably the first Armenians to settle in Southern California, beginning in the 1890s. Most of these had lived for several years in the Boston or New York City areas.[58] More arrived during the first decade of the twentieth century, from the eastern United States, from the large Armenian colony to the north in Fresno, and directly from the Turkish (Ottoman) and Russian Empires. Most of these early Armenians did not cluster residentially but scattered—some as far as Santa Barbara, San Diego, and Riverside.

Los Angeles. The area just south of Downtown was the first focus of Armenian religious institutions. Many of the early Armenian immigrants to Los Angeles were Congregationalists or other Protestant Christians—a result of missionary work in parts of the Ottoman Empire during the mid-nineteenth century. They worshiped initially with the Congregationalists, whose church was at 9th and Hope Streets, before they formed their own church nearby. Later, an Armenian Gregorian (Apostolic) Church, which followed the traditional Armenian religion, was also founded near Downtown.

As Los Angeles expanded, both people and churches slowly left the older neighborhoods. By 1923 Armenians were living in many sections of the city, including some wealthy neighborhoods like West Adams and the Wilshire district. Considering the many decades of urban change in older neighborhoods, it is not surprising that in 1990 hardly any Armenians were living near Downtown or in West Adams.

Pasadena and Altadena. Armenian settlement in Pasadena dates from about 1901. Northeastern Pasadena, along Washington Boulevard between Allen and Hill Avenues, became the initial center of a thriving Armenian community. After World War I more immigrants arrived, especially from Turkey, and since World War II many Armenians from Lebanon and Syria have settled in Pasadena. Immigrants typically became shopkeepers, tailors, or barbers. Their more educated sons and daughters often remained in the area but became professionals. Over the past eighty years the Armenian settlement has expanded, especially northward into East Altadena, with its newer homes on large lots (Fig. 3.8). However, during the many decades since the community was first established in Pasadena, the geographical focus of its churches, shops, and other businesses has changed little.

Boyle Heights and Montebello. Before World War I a few Armenians migrated from the section of Armenia within the Russian Empire to Canada but later moved to Southern California. Their letters back to the homeland enticed others, so that by the early 1920s several hundred Russian Armenians were living in Boyle Heights—at that time the major immigrant district of Los Angeles. At first most Russian Armenians settled in a small area near the bluffs not far from the future route of the Interstate 5 Freeway, and many found work in brickyards, foundries, and local railroad shops. Others established themselves in the trucking business. In 1908 a few Armenians began to specialize in rubbish collection, which had previously been done by blacks, and some were highly successful. By the 1940s Armenians were said to control three-quarters of Los Angeles County's rubbish removal; and the BKK Company, founded by Ben K. Kazarian in 1918, has been prominent in the waste-disposal business.

By the early 1920s the more successful and assimilated Russian Armenians were moving eastward to newer homes and more space. This suburbanization led to the Armenian settlements in and around Montebello and ultimately to the departure from Boyle Heights of virtually all Armenians. Letters back to friends in Russian Armenia (known as Soviet Armenia from 1921 to 1991) directed many people from the same sections of Armenia to settle in Montebello, making for a cohesive community centered on the local Apostolic Church. The Montebello community grew again in the late 1940s and 1950s with the arrival of more than a thousand Armenian refugees from World War II. Most of these were men who had been soldiers in the Soviet army but were captured by German or Italian troops during the war. Under the Displaced Persons Act of 1948 they were permitted to leave the temporary camps in Germany and settle in the United States.

East Hollywood. In the 1960s and 1970s the section of Hollywood east of the 101 Freeway was the leading point of arrival for Armenian immigrants and refugees from Iraq, Lebanon, Syria, Turkey, and Soviet Armenia. East Hollywood's Armenian markets, clubs, churches, schools, and social-service centers, located between Santa Monica and Hollywood Boulevards, created a community called "Little Armenia."[59]

In August 1987 conditions in East Hollywood became still more crowded when thousands of Armenians from the Soviet Union suddenly began to arrive as a result of more liberal emigration under Mikail Gorbachev's *glasnost*. Because these people were poorer than most Armenian immigrants and had not been permitted to bring money out of the Soviet Union, they settled in the more modest apartments of East Hollywood, where they could at least obtain some help in finding jobs, learning English, becoming reacquainted with religious practices that had been forgotten under Communism, and coping with the numerous challenges of survival in America. Since the breakup of the Soviet Union, Armenia has again emerged as an independent country—the source of great symbolic pride and affection for Armenians everywhere but a nation racked by severe unemployment, shortages of supplies, and warfare with neighboring peoples.

Glendale. Throughout the 1980s, earlier Armenian immigrants who had established themselves financially found that they could escape East Hollywood and its crowded and somewhat run-down housing. Some moved a little to the north, into the better apartments of the Los Feliz area, but most moved to Glendale.

Although Glendale was home to only a dozen Armenian families in the 1950s, by the late 1970s many business and professional families from Iran and Lebanon had settled there. During the 1980s it emerged as the main destination for newly arriving middle- and upper-class Armenians, particularly those who fled Iran after that country's takeover in 1979 by a conservative Islamic faction. By 1990 Armenians formed an important part of the residents in most parts of Glendale and in the adjacent valley that stretches from La Cañada–Flintridge to the Tujunga section of Los Angeles (Fig. 3.8).

During the 1980s, as the Armenian population of Glendale grew rapidly, it became more mixed in origin and socioeconomic status. The city was becoming a popular symbol of

Armenian immigrant upward socioeconomic mobility. Those who were stepping up from East Hollywood generally settled in South Glendale (south of the 134 Freeway), where fine, old family homes of a bygone era were frequently remodeled into smaller apartments for Armenians. A larger Armenian church was also needed, and in 1985 this was bought from Christian Scientists. The imposing, domed edifice on Central Avenue became the new St. Mary's Armenian Apostolic Church. The sheer numbers of Armenian immigrants and their lack of familiarity with American culture have made for major ethnic tensions within Glendale, especially in South Glendale, which has become an intensely Armenian part of the city (Fig. 3.8).

The San Fernando Valley and more distant places. As the children and grandchildren of Armenian immigrants looked for homes for their families, most moved to suburbs in the San Fernando Valley. In the 1940s some Armenians had moved to the eastern San Fernando Valley near Van Nuys, where new homes were offered. During the following decades younger people settled in the newer homes to the west. Some of the more affluent were living in Porter Ranch in the northern fringe of the valley and on the valley's south side, in and near Encino. The homes of Armenians were scattered, with no residential enclave. For the many who have wished to preserve the cohesive community and strong sense of ethnic identity they knew as children, Armenian private schools have been built, and two large schools (in Encino and Canoga Park) provide instruction for all grades through high school.

Although the San Fernando Valley contains many foreign-born Armenians, its dispersed Armenian residences reflect the greater educational attainment and acculturation of the U.S.-born generations. Those Armenians who in 1990 were living in Orange County, Palos Verdes, Ventura County, and other places quite distant from the major centers of Armenian life are less likely to need frequent contact with the larger Armenian community.

Nevertheless, Armenian identity remains strong and is continually energized by memories of the early-twentieth-century genocide in Turkey, commemorated by the Armenian Martyrs Memorial Monument in Bicknell Park in Montebello.

People of Iranian Ancestry

In the mid-1970s immigration from Iran began to increase rapidly, as many parents who could afford to send their male children to colleges or universities in the United States did so.[60] Iran lacked opportunities for advanced education, which was in demand because of the nation's rapid development. Also, many families who had benefited from economic modernization recognized that as the power of the shah diminished, their security and affluence were threatened. Anticipating major changes, many Iranians put money into Swiss banks and left Iran, entering the United States under student or visitor visas.

When the shah's government collapsed in 1979 and members of an Islamic fundamentalist clergy grasped the reins of power, the revolution was both political and cultural. During the next few years the new Islamic Republic instituted severe restrictions in such matters as popular music, singing, women's clothing, and the use of alcohol. The government persecuted non-Islamic religious groups and individuals who did not support its narrow Islamic, anti-American, and antimodernist views. Entire families, including most of Iran's upper class and others in the oil industry, fled the country, usually first to Istanbul. The exodus included a large proportion of Iran's religious minorities—Armenians, Assyrians, Jews, Bahais, and Zoroastrians—as well as rich and more secular Muslims.

The majority of Iranians arriving in Southern California were from the Westernized middle and upper classes of Teheran.[61] Because they had known the good life in Iran, they did not share the motivation of economic betterment that has characterized most immigrants to the United States. Without the reversal of their political fortunes in 1979, most would have been happy to remain at home in Iran. The tendency of many Iranian women in Los Angeles to display expensive and stylish clothes, automobiles, and jewelry may represent their attempt to retain, at least on the surface, the prosperity and elegance they had known in Iran.

Religious and ethnic distinctions. People of Iranian ancestry have traditionally divided themselves into separate communities based primarily on religion. This derives from the pattern found over much of the Middle East, where religions and ethnic groups are socially separate, live in separate sections of cities, and often pursue different, specialized occupations.

To illustrate, a private survey in 1987–1988 found that, if at all possible, most Iranian entrepreneurs in Los Angeles selected business partners and hired workers from among their relatives or from their own religious or ethnic group.[62] The different religious communities also vary somewhat in industry niches, impossible to differentiate with census data but evident in the private survey. Among those who were self-employed, Jews were much more apt to be involved in wholesaling and retailing, particularly of clothing and jewelry. In contrast, Armenians from Iran tended to specialize more in financial and business services, Muslims in construction and durable-goods manufacturing, and Bahais in manufacturing and in health and legal services.

The majority of Iranian Muslims in Southern California do not form a distinct community, in contrast to other groups from Iran. They are also more secular than are Muslims from other countries and do not frequently socialize with even fellow Shi'i Muslims of other national origins. Many still expect to return to Iran and reunite with family members who remained in that country.

Iranian Jews have acculturated more rapidly in Southern California than have Muslims.[63] This is because of substantial contact with American Jews, the emigration of entire families from Iran, and their relative satisfaction with Southern California. Ironically, in Los Angeles there is more social contact between Iranian Muslim and Iranian Jewish women and families than there was in Iran, because both now enjoy each other's company in the context of their shared Iranian culture.

In general, Muslims and Bahais have more social ties with people outside their own group and with Americans than do Jews and Armenians from Iran.[64] It is not surprising, then, that English is replacing the Persian language most rapidly among Muslims and Bahais.

Iranian concentrations. The leading center of Iranian business and cultural activity is Little Teheran on Westwood Boulevard south of Wilshire Boulevard. Signs in Persian and English advertise the varied restaurants, clothing stores, news and cultural centers, and other businesses. Iranian investment and shopping have also invigorated and made more cosmopolitan the fashion scene along Rodeo Drive in Beverly Hills.

The strongest residential concentrations are in Beverly Hills, Westwood, and Brentwood. Iranians are also apt to live in the southern San Fernando Valley, particularly Encino and Tarzana, and in the Santa Monica Mountains (Fig. 3.9). Lesser Iranian concentrations also occur in more affluent outlying areas from eastern Ventura County to the Palos Verdes Peninsula, Laguna Niguel, and Newport Beach in Orange County. The tendency of Iranians to live in more expensive urban and suburban areas reflects both wealth brought from Iran and relatively high incomes earned here. This pattern is not the entire story, however. Some Iranians live in more modest neighborhoods in the San Fernando and San Gabriel Valleys and in northern Orange County.

Religious subgroup distinctions in residential location are blurred but are sometimes still evident. Armenians from Iran headed primarily to Glendale, where many Armenians from other countries also settled during the 1980s. Glendale became so well known among Armenians in Iran that they talked not of the United States but of Glendale as the hoped-for destination. Glendale is not distinctive on the map of Iranian ancestry because most Armenians reported their primary ancestry as "Armenian" rather than "Iranian." Similarly, many Assyrians and Kurds from Iran probably reported those specific ancestries rather than Iranian.

A large proportion of Iranian refugees were Jews, many of whom had been very wealthy in Iran.[65] They settled on the Westside of Los Angeles, particularly in Beverly Hills. The wealthier families bought large estates, but many could afford only apartments. Others moved to the Jewish corridor along Ventura Boulevard in the San Fernando Valley, especially Encino and Tarzana, and established businesses Downtown.

Iranian Jews joined temples near their residences, and by the early 1980s three Westside temples and one in Encino came to have largely Iranian congregations.[66] This settlement pattern is very similar to that of the Russian-ancestry population that represents the American Jewish population. Although many non-Jewish Iranians live on the Westside and in the southern San Fernando Valley, the strong Iranian concentrations in these areas suggest the importance of Jews among Southern Californians of Iranian ancestry.

Many Muslims chose to live in Westside communities, such as in Santa Monica and Palms or, for those who could afford it, Beverly Hills. They were more likely than Iranian Jews to have opened restaurants, grocery or clothing stores, professional offices, or other businesses along Westwood Boulevard south of the campus of the University of California, Los Angeles. Other Muslims settled in Irvine or on the Palos Verdes Peninsula. Bahais often live in West Los Angeles and Santa Monica. The religious focus of the few Zoroastrians has been their large center in Westminster in Orange County.

Because immigrant residential enclaves in American cities have usually been associated with relatively poor and less acculturated groups, the presence of a strong Iranian concentration in the Westside–Santa Monica Mountains area is unusual. Two factors help explain this. First, Iranian immigrants came from an intensely urban environment, and the Westside is one of the few areas in Southern California with both high density and affluence. Second, in 1979 and 1980, when the first refugees were arriving, Iranian Jewish settlement near American Jews may have encouraged other Iranians, regardless of religion, to settle in the same area because so many of them shared language, political ideology, class background, and the experience of persecution in Iran.

People of Turkish Ancestry

Almost all the people who reported this ancestry are ethnically Turkish. This is because Armenians, Kurds, Greeks, or others whose family lived in the country of Turkey were encouraged in the census to write in their ethnic affiliation, not the country of their birth. In Turkey and other multiethnic countries, especially in the Middle East, this ethnic precision makes the data more valuable than they would have been had a question concerning country of origin been asked.

People of Turkish ancestry are scattered over much of Southern California (Fig. 3.10). Such a dispersed distribution

reflects their high degree of cultural and economic assimilation. Paralleling this almost complete residential deconcentration is the absence of any enclaves of Turkish restaurants, other businesses, and institutions. There is nothing even approaching a Turkish neighborhood which could provide a central place for shopping and socializing. With Armenian feelings concerning the Turkish treatment of Armenians in 1915 still strong, the lack of an identifiable focus for the Turkish community may diffuse potential antagonism.

The actual tracts that represent minor Turkish residential clusters are probably not significant, because the numbers of people in each tract are so small. However, the types of places represented are important. They show a clear association of Turkish ancestry with middle- to upper-income suburban areas, reflective of the advanced education and high status of most Turkish immigrants.

In Orange County the two tracts with the highest percentages of Turkish ancestry are areas of expensive homes: one tract includes portions of Dana Point and San Juan Capistrano; the other is the Turtle Rock section of Irvine. In Los Angeles County the most strongly Turkish-ancestry tracts in the San Gabriel Valley are in the foothills of the San Gabriel Mountains, in the more affluent sections of Glendora and Azusa. Other tracts are an upper-middle-class part of Westchester near Loyola Marymount University and the campus of the University of Southern California. Although in the eastern San Fernando Valley two small Turkish-ancestry clusters are in poorer areas, farther west the most evident concentrations are in moderately priced parts of the San Fernando Valley and eastern Ventura County.

Non-Hispanic-White Median Household Income

Figure 3.11 provides the socioeconomic dimension of the total of the previously discussed ethnic groups plus other whites. Three features are striking.

First, there are few whites in the more central areas of older housing. Whites formerly lived there, but most moved away when they could afford to do so or when the presence of minorities in their neighborhood made them uncomfortable.

Second, although no areas of poor whites are extensive in Southern California in 1990, the largest such area shows up in the southeastern part of Los Angeles County. Most of the white industrial workers and their families who once dominated this area have moved away or died, and Latino immigrants eagerly took their places. However, some whites—mostly the elderly—remain. An additional area of poorer whites, also elderly and often living alone, is in the older, central part of Long Beach. They, too, represent the remnants of families who migrated a half-century or more ago from the Midwest.

Third, numerous geographically separated regions of wealth are evident, most of which are located in or near environmental amenities: within hilly or mountainous terrain or near the coast. In Los Angeles County the largest residential area for wealthy whites is the wedge of the Santa Monica Mountains, including the Malibu coast east to the Pacific Palisades. Other affluent areas include parts of Northridge and Granada Hills in the northern San Fernando Valley; portions of Glendale and Pasadena; and much of the Palos Verdes Peninsula. Wealthy households also characterize San Marino, Bradbury, and La Habra Heights in the San Gabriel Valley.

Smaller, distinctively affluent areas appear on the Westside of Los Angeles—the Cheviot Hills and Hancock Park. Near Marina del Rey, whites living in newer housing near Villa Marina have much higher incomes than Latinos and Asians in the older part of the same tract. In Orange County the highest household incomes are found in the Seacliff section of Huntington Beach just south of the Bolsa Chica Ecological Reserve, in Newport Beach, and in the recently built-up southern part of the county.

Blacks

When the pueblo of Los Angeles was first established in 1781, men and women of part-African ancestry constituted about half of the original settlers. The city has always been the center of the black population in Southern California. A brief statement concerning the general processes of black settlement and change will be useful before we treat the evolution of particular areas.

Segregation, expansion, and dispersal. Historic black residential areas and later changes can be understood as the result of the processes of residential segregation, contiguous expansion, and non-contiguous dispersal to more distant places.

In the early twentieth century the arrival of large numbers of blacks in cities like Los Angeles, combined with white dislike of blacks, led many whites to limit severely the areas available for black settlement. Sharp restrictions on black choices in the housing market produced a change from the more dispersed and mixed black settlement before about 1915. Such exclusion was backed by the law and the courts until various mechanisms for maintaining segregation were weakened by U.S. and California Supreme Court decisions between 1948 and 1967.

During the years of legal residential segregation, Los Angeles had one main black concentration. It was located directly south of Downtown, on either side of Central Avenue. There were also two smaller concentrations—in the West Jefferson area and in Watts (Fig. 3.1). Other cities had smaller but also segregated black populations.

Restricting the areas in which blacks could live was part of a much wider set of discriminatory and separationist practices. In the period from 1915 until the 1960s some whites made intense efforts to prevent blacks from using public facilities, working at better jobs, and joining white unions.[67] Blacks were also denied regular admittance at most movie theaters, restaurants, hotels, playgrounds, and swimming pools.

The areas with high proportions of blacks have changed over time, and the level of racial segregation has diminished. Nevertheless, the effect of exclusion by whites is evident in the high level of geographical concentration of blacks compared with that of other ethnic groups.

The second process—contiguous expansion of black residential areas—has occurred since World War II. Demand for housing on the part of blacks had built up intensely during the 1930s and 1940s because of the large black migration to Los Angeles, prompted by wartime employment opportunities and the relative affluence of California. By 1948 the legal basis for racial restrictions was being demolished, but some whites became violent in their objections to change. In the Allied

Gardens subdivision in Compton, for example, whites responded to black home buyers by throwing rotten fruit at the houses and smearing them with paint, tearing out rose bushes, cutting off the electricity, warping floor boards by flooding them with water via a garden hose, and burning crosses.[68]

In South Central the conditions that prompted blacks to move were most intense. The earlier departure of jobs and larger grocery and department stores to the suburbs, the crime and violence, and the harassment by the police led to poverty and frustration, which was expressed in the Watts uprising (or riot) of 1965. Most blacks believed that racial integration—in schools, housing, and work—was the key to a better life. Such a goal implied escape from the black ghetto, and many blacks made great efforts to leave. A 1967 California Supreme Court ruling requiring enforcement of the state's fair housing law (the Rumford Act) and the 1968 federal Fair Housing Act may have aided movement into other areas.

Prior to the 1970s blacks who relocated generally moved into nearby areas. White homeowners usually sold to blacks and fled to more distant suburbs. As a result, few areas remained racially mixed for more than a dozen years, and the areas into which blacks moved became resegregated as black. This is why the level of black-white residential segregation dropped only slightly until after 1970.

Dispersal of the black population to distant destinations has occurred primarily since 1970. Southern California has seen a significant scattering of blacks into predominantly white areas, but accompanying "white flight" appears to have been minimal. Cultural and legal changes in American society, a growing black middle class, and a much slower rate of black population growth have made this possible. In the past two decades whites have come to accept black neighbors more readily—though their acceptance may depend on whether the number of new black residents is small and on whether they are concentrated in certain blocks or neighborhoods.

The settlement since 1970 of Mexican immigrants in areas which had been mostly black also led to black dispersal. The immigrants found that the cheapest housing in Los Angeles was in the historic Central Avenue corridor, and by 1990 Latinos came to outnumber blacks in that area. As of 1990 this former black concentration directly south of Downtown appears as only 10–35 percent black (Fig. 3.12).

General dispersal and the Latino settlement have weakened all the black concentrations, including those in outlying areas. Thirty years ago black settlements in Pacoima, Pasadena, Monrovia, Pomona, Long Beach, and Santa Ana—as well as in South Central—had higher percentages of blacks within more sharply defined boundaries. Blacks left these areas when Latinos successfully rented or purchased housing, often by sharing incomes of two or more families. For black homeowners, selling to Latinos offered the chance to leave a concentration of poverty, drug use, and crime.

Los Angeles before 1915. After 1886, when the Santa Fe Railroad established more direct railroad connections with the Midwest, the opportunities Los Angeles offered for health and wealth beckoned both whites and blacks. Most early blacks were craftsmen and laborers. They lived in various neighborhoods but most commonly in rooming houses on 1st and 2nd Streets east of Los Angeles Street.[69] That area was where the hiring of construction gangs took place and where black businesses were becoming established. However, during the next twenty years of city growth, the black population shifted southward because of rapidly growing Japanese settlement in that lowest-rent area.

In 1910 a scattering of live-in servants in white homes meant that some blacks were found in nearly all parts of the city. However, most blacks lived on either side of Alameda Street north of Washington Boulevard—an area close to rail yards, warehouses, and industry—or near Central Avenue between 10th Street and Washington Boulevard.

At about this time some whites began to forcefully oppose the movement of blacks (as well as Japanese and Mexicans) into the better neighborhoods to the south. Despite occasional intimidation by whites, the black population continued to expand southward into white residential areas. For example, by 1910 a cluster of a few hundred blacks had formed near 33rd Street and Hooper Avenue, where in 1902 the first black resident had to defend his right to the house against a white mob by waving them off with his gun.[71] A mile to the south, another black residential focus was developing between 51st and 55th Streets, just west of Alameda, because the developer had welcomed black residents to his tract. In outlying areas black settlement in 1910 was focused in a few neighborhoods: a section of Boyle Heights, West Temple Street between Rampart and Reno Streets, and an area west of the University of Southern California.

Despite obstacles to black settlement, the years before about 1915 were full of hope for black Angelenos, who represented, to some extent, a selective migration which included many blacks who were well-to-do and many from other parts of California.[72] Newcomers riding waves of economic expansion were sometimes able to buy homes a few years after arriving and, like whites, frequently made a great deal of money during real-estate booms. Churches and black businesses were growing; Jews moving out of Boyle Heights willingly sold their homes to blacks; and the shops, men's clubs, and nightlife on Central Avenue thrived. As the largest settlement of blacks in the western United States, Los Angeles was sizable enough to attract business people and professionals intent on serving the local black community. In 1913 W. E. B. DuBois echoed the optimism of thousands of blacks when he wrote, "Los Angeles is wonderful. Nowhere in the United States is the Negro so well and beautifully housed, nor the average efficiency and intelligence in the colored population so high."[73]

Segregation and crowding in South Central. However, after about 1915 the black population of Los Angeles grew rapidly, and whites imposed more restrictions on blacks, including restrictions on where they could live. To eliminate black movement into their neighborhoods, many whites added "restrictive covenants" to their property titles or made written agreements among neighborhood homeowners stating that they would sell or rent only to other whites. In 1919 a California Supreme Court decision validated racial restrictions on the occupancy or use of a house and provided a legal basis for residential exclusion until 1948.

Restrictive covenants and intimidation kept most blacks trapped. By 1925 blacks and whites were mixed as far south as Slauson Avenue. Local whites decided to make Slauson a sharp

racial boundary so that in 1940 it still represented the southern boundary of the largest black concentration (Fig. 3.1). Restrictive covenants on property all the way south to 92d Street were strongly enforced by threats and violence against the homes of blacks who attempted to move into this area.

The black population of Los Angeles increased from fewer than 8,000 in 1910 to 335,000 in 1960. During the 1940s, as black migrants sought jobs in defense industries, the black population of the city grew by more than 100,000. Crowding became very intense within a sector extending from Downtown southward on either side of Central Avenue. This ghetto came to be called "South Central Los Angeles."

Between 1920 and the late 1940s the efforts by many whites to keep blacks out of their neighborhoods were never completely effective. Whites occasionally chose to sell despite the restrictions, especially if they were out of work during the Great Depression. Some houses were bought from whites just after old restrictive covenants had been known to expire, and other techniques were devised to weaken white resistance. For example, block busting was used by realtors to drive the opening wedge into white neighborhoods. A realtor might arrange for a white intermediary or a black who could pass as white to buy property for a black in a white neighborhood, and the imminent move-in was well publicized. Many white neighbors panicked, fearing a drop in home prices, and were easily persuaded to sell their own homes to black families at lower-than-market prices. Some Japanese and Mexicans followed blacks into a neighborhood after its all-white status had been broken.

Contiguous expansion and resegregation. Only after World War II did the legal base for racial exclusion begin to crumble. Most significant was the U.S. Supreme Court decision in 1948 to overturn the judicial enforcement of restrictive covenants, which led to later decisions that further weakened racial restrictions.[74]

As of 1950, however, black expansion south of Slauson Avenue had not yet reached west to Broadway or east past Alameda Street. White resistance was especially strong in the small, independent cities such as Huntington Park, Bell Gardens, and South Gate to the southeast. These cities were populated particularly by working-class whites from rural parts of Texas and Oklahoma, and their residents prevented nearly all blacks from renting or buying until the 1950s.

As the boundaries around the ghetto began to weaken, black settlement advanced neighborhood by neighborhood. Sections that were all white changed over to almost all black, sometimes in three or four years and sometimes over two decades.[75] Over the course of the last half-century the process whereby once-white neighborhoods became resegregated as mostly black has characterized a large portion of Los Angeles as well as some adjacent cities like Compton, Gardena, and Inglewood. Those blacks who first moved into new neighborhoods had typically formed stable families and were employed in steady jobs. They worried about the quality of those who would follow them into the neighborhood.

During the period of legalized racial segregation, blacks of all classes and backgrounds were forced into South Central. Once other housing became available, most of the middle class left. Their departure meant that the remaining residents were more uniformly poor. However, some successful black families have chosen to remain in the geographical heart of the black community, where they have felt more comfortable. Although true to a lesser extent in 1990 than in the 1930s, "poverty and prosperity exist side by side" in South Central.[76]

Poor Watts. At the turn of the century the area called Watts was mostly dusty, vacant fields with some nearby land in farms. Its growth began in 1902, when the Pacific Electric decided to locate its Los Angeles–Long Beach route through the area.[77] Soon afterward, Watts became the junction point of lines to Santa Ana and, later, Redondo, prompting land subdivision into home lots for people who could now commute easily to Los Angeles and many other places. The little town of Watts was incorporated in 1907 and in 1926 was annexed to the city of Los Angeles.

Most settlers in Watts as of 1920 were whites, but the town also included several hundred blacks (14 percent of the total population) and even more Mexicans (Fig. 3.1). Mexican workers had originally come to lay the Pacific Electric tracks and were living in a special section called *La Colonia* or, among

English speakers, the "Latin Camp." The increasing settlement of blacks in Watts began after 1910, when a developer advertised a tract specifically for black homeowners. That area attracted numerous black migrants directly from the rural South, who found Watts a good stopping place in Southern California. Although Watts was seven miles from Los Angeles, the interurban railway made it fairly convenient for women domestics working in different places and for men who needed to reach the main Southern Pacific and Santa Fe railroad stations in Los Angeles, the base for their work as Pullman car porters and waiters.

Watts was not ideal, however. Its drinking clubs flourished before the beginning of nationwide prohibition in 1919, when neighboring Los Angeles was legally "dry." In the wintertime, runoff from the rains collected in Watts from the higher lands to the north. The Ku Klux Klan chapter based in nearby all-white Compton occasionally flexed its muscle, and the unpaved streets in the black part of Watts led locals to dub that section "Mudtown." When jobs opened in the defense industries in the early 1940s, some residents of Watts found jobs in the Long Beach shipyards and the Northrop, Douglas, North American, and Lockheed aircraft factories. Nevertheless, in the minds of Los Angeles blacks, the name Watts continued to connote country hicks and chicken farmers.

Not surprisingly, many people left this semirural town to be closer to work and entertainment in Los Angeles. But with massive black in-migration during the 1930s and 1940s, Watts became more crowded, and by 1950 was it was 71 percent black. A few years later black settlement in both South Central and Watts had expanded sufficiently to coalesce (Figs. 3.1 and 3.2). Watts became part of South Central, though it would retain a symbolic distinctiveness because of later events.

As early as 1946 a few developers built tracts of single-family houses specifically for purchase by blacks, many of whom had saved money from military service or defense jobs. Such tracts were exceptional, but they played a role in the dispersal of middle-class blacks out of crowded housing. For instance, Carver Manor was a tract of 250 houses built for black home buyers in the Willowbrook area just south of Watts, and Parkside Manor was a similar development in Watts east of

Central at 103d Street. A few families have remained in those tracts for decades, providing a stable base for a long-lived community.[78]

In the mid-1950s the city supplemented the public housing (Hacienda Village) that had been built in Watts in 1942 with three large projects (Jordan Downs, Nickerson Gardens, and Imperial Courts), for a total of more than 7,000 residents. This provided needed housing, but it also accentuated Watts as a focus of poverty. Low home prices and high black unemployment led to an avoidance of the entire area by businesses whose loans and investments might have brought jobs and services. The area's increasing black concentration made white business leaders even more wary of investment in Watts and the rest of South Central.

High prices charged by local white merchants provoked resentment. The poverty and lack of jobs, grocery stores, banks, and movie theaters led to anger which ultimately exploded in rebellion in 1965. Subsequently, the closure of the Firestone tire and the General Motors automobile factories in nearby South Gate led to a further decline in jobs for Watts residents. When rioting again occurred in South Central in the spring of 1992, the economic frustrations were similar to those of 1965.

However, some major changes had taken place. In Watts the King/Drew Medical Center, the light-rail Blue Line, and a new shopping center had been built in the intervening years. All over South Central, Koreans had replaced the aging white storekeepers, and Latino immigrants made up almost half the population. After the 1992 devastation most of the Korean merchants left and few new jobs appeared, but some supermarkets, stores, and new housing have been built.

Westward shift of the black elite. In the first decades of the century a large area called West Adams, which lies north and west of the University of Southern California campus, was a favored residential location for white professionals and business people, partly because of its numerous architecturally distinguished homes.

About a half-mile to the south, in the West Jefferson area, a mostly black neighborhood of teachers, ministers, lawyers, contractors, and community leaders had emerged by the late 1920s (Fig. 3.1). At first this residential center for the black elite was located south of Jefferson Boulevard and on the east side of Western Avenue.[79] However, in the early 1930s increased crowding of black families in that area led some to move north almost to Adams Boulevard and west as far as Arlington. Later, as white flight opened up the West Adams area, it came to hold an important concentration of leading black families.

The more affluent and educated black families also spearheaded the thrust into all-white areas farther north and west. For example, between 1940 and 1943 black movie stars (Hattie McDaniel, Ethel Waters, Lillian Randolph, and others) and black business and professional people managed to buy some of the spacious, well-landscaped, three-story homes in Sugar Hill, an especially attractive area just north of Adams Boulevard on either side of Western Avenue.[80] Their presence was protested by the West Adams Improvement Association, though ultimately those whites lost.

After World War II white flight opened up Sugar Hill and adjacent neighborhoods to ordinary blacks, but racial tensions over black entry into all-white residential areas remained strong. For example, a few months after the 1948 U.S. Supreme Court decision barring enforcement of restrictive covenants, Nat "King" Cole bought a house in all-white Hancock Park—almost three miles north of the black settlement in Sugar Hill.[81] Cole's purchase led to intimidating letters and telephone calls, offers by whites to buy the house, and threats to revoke the license of the realtor representing the seller.

Black settlement in Sugar Hill has left an important legacy. The area remains the home of the state's largest black-owned insurance company (Golden State Life) and the city's most prestigious church within the black community, First AME (African Methodist Episcopal). However, most of the black elite themselves have moved farther westward from Sugar Hill or left the large, contiguous black settlement area entirely. Many three-story houses have been carved up into small rental apartments.

The westward residential advance of black middle-class families has continued for more than five decades (Fig. 3.12). By 1990, the Windsor Hills and View Park areas west of Crenshaw Boulevard were the areas that had most recently changed from white to black. The adjacent community to the west, Ladera Heights, appeared to be in slow transition between white and black. Reflecting both the forward edge of the black westward expansion and the higher prices of fine homes, these three areas represent the best known concentration of high-income blacks in Southern California.

A corresponding shift of major black institutions also occurred during the 1980s. Political and cultural affairs within Los Angeles' black community have been refocused in Leimert Park and along nearby Crenshaw Boulevard. This is far west of the Central Avenue axis of black leadership and life forty years earlier. The *Los Angeles Sentinel,* the city's leading black newspaper, relocated from Central Avenue to this area in the early 1990s. The Los Angeles Urban League and other predominantly black organizations have their headquarters in or near Leimert Park. In addition, the Baldwin Hills Crenshaw Plaza and the adjacent twelve-screen Magic Theaters (developed by Magic Johnson) have become the leading shopping and entertainment center for middle- and upper-class blacks, thus accentuating the Crenshaw-area focus of the black community in the 1990s.

At the same time, other people were intruding on West Adams—what had once been a neighborhood of the black elite. Latino immigrants rented and bought in what had been almost completely black neighborhoods, and during the 1980s West Adams was partially gentrified as young whites bought up some of the distinguished old houses. Some local black residents appreciated the presence of young, politically connected whites in the area as suggesting possibilities for better city services and the like. However, many others resented what they saw as whites' attempts to direct and control the West Adams neighborhood and its preservation—a pattern uncomfortably familiar to many older people.[82]

Pasadena. Although Los Angeles has easily been the leading center of black settlement, blacks also settled early in outlying areas. In 1900 the U.S. census, which published counts only for the largest cities, found 218 blacks in Pasadena, 195 in Riverside, 84 in San Bernardino, 60 in Santa Monica, and 58 in Redlands. By 1920 development and population growth had been widespread, creating more openings for work in several places outside Los Angeles (Table 3.1), but the largest black population outside that city was still in Pasadena.

The very rapid expansion of Pasadena, like that of so many other places, dates from the coming of the railroad in the mid-1880s. Blacks followed white settlers into this boomtown. Although it may be that some of the seventy-five blacks who arrived before 1890 had planned to become farmers or independent townspeople, most were soon working as servants in the homes of wealthy people.[83] Over the next half-century the black community grew substantially, partly because of advertisements in black newspapers in the East and South that proclaimed Pasadena an ideal destination for black migrants to California. In addition, the surrounding cities (Glendale, Eagle Rock, South Pasadena, San Marino, and Arcadia) effectively prevented home purchase or rental by blacks, so that most of the blacks who worked in those areas were forced to live in Pasadena. Before World War II blacks in Pasadena were typically laborers, truck drivers, and janitors, but others worked for Pasadena's white families as gardeners, butlers, chauffeurs, cooks, and maids.

Table 3.1 Largest Black Populations in Places, 1920

City	Black Population
Los Angeles	15,579
Pasadena	1,094
Watts	652
Riverside	505
Santa Monica	282
San Bernardino	269
Long Beach	142
Monrovia	133
Venice	102
Redlands	77
Oxnard	74
Pomona	46

Source: U. S. Bureau of the Census (1922).

In the 1930s Pasadena had several neighborhoods of blacks, Mexicans, and Asians. Only a few minority families lived outside these areas, all but one of which was west of Fair Oaks Avenue. The one such neighborhood south of Colorado Boulevard once had a mixture of black, Mexican, and Asian families but has since been eliminated by the freeway on-ramps that extend south of Interstate 210. A larger and almost completely black neighborhood lay to the north, tightly bounded by Orange Grove Boulevard on the south, Fair Oaks on the east, and Washington Boulevard on the north. Although geographically separate, this black residential area was not a long walk from the homes of wealthy families, where so many blacks were employed.

In the 1950s blacks dispersed eastward and north into Altadena, where by 1990 black percentages were higher than in Pasadena and where more than three-quarters of blacks were homeowners. Hardly any blacks moved to the west, however. The parks of Arroyo Seco and the Rose Bowl are a racial and social-class boundary, so that the much more expensive section west of the parks is only 2 percent black.

During the past three decades the neighborhood shifts of blacks and the arrival of Latinos in Pasadena have mirrored changes in South Central. In the area north of Interstate 210, blacks moved eastward from Fair Oaks Avenue as Latino immigrants settled into the low-cost housing that blacks were vacating. Although by 1970 not many blacks had moved east of Lake Avenue, the trend continued, so that by 1990 the area another two miles east was becoming more than 10 percent black. Black settlement expansion eastward during this entire period has prompted white flight. South of Interstate 210, such ethnic changes have been minimal, because the affluent white community has retained control of its institutions and residences, many of which are of architectural renown.

Monrovia. This city in the San Gabriel Valley has one of the oldest black communities in Southern California, one with a unique origin. In the mid-1880s the wealthy owner of the Santa Anita Ranch, E. J. "Lucky" Baldwin, was traveling around the United States in connection with his horse-racing operations. He met and hired a black man, John Fisher, to be a blacksmith and to shoe his racehorses. Fisher helped Baldwin recruit additional men to work on the ranch, many as trainers and jockeys.[84] In early 1886, sixty blacks, including some families, arrived by train from North Carolina and South Carolina. Over the next few years more blacks followed this migration chain. Most who were not working with the horses settled in the nearest town, Monrovia, just a few minutes by train from Santa Anita. Men commonly became farm laborers and usually worked in the citrus orchards, but some were employed at Baldwin's winery. Women were typically laundresses and housekeepers for white families in Monrovia.

By 1889 blacks in Monrovia had established a church, which was their early social and religious focus. Although many more blacks arrived and settled in Monrovia during the twentieth century, the church remains active and the community retains a pride in its distinctive, century-old heritage.

As was true elsewhere, in 1960 the black population of Monrovia was strongly segregated residentially, with one census tract that was more than 50 percent black. More recent dispersal has meant that Monrovia's blacks are much less evident in 1990 (Figs. 3.2, 3.12).

Post–World War II concentrations: Pacoima. The development of a major black concentration in the eastern San Fernando Valley did not occur until after World War II.

In the early 1940s only a few black families lived in Pacoima, but in 1946 that began to change when military housing was moved from Griffith Park to Pacoima and set up as temporary public housing for low-income people. Called the Basilone Homes, they were located just downstream from Hansen Dam, which had been designed to capture floods on Tujunga Wash.[85] Because a quarter of its 800 households were black, Basilone Homes became the nucleus of a new black community and served to make Los Angeles blacks aware for the first time of the San Fernando Valley.

Then, in the early 1950s, a large tract of modest homes (the Joe Louis Homes) was privately developed especially for purchase by blacks, some of whom worked at the nearby Lockheed aircraft factory. In those years prior to fair-housing laws this was a prized opportunity for blacks. Two years after that the city housing authority built the permanent San Fernando Gardens project, and in the late 1960s two massive, federally-subsidized apartment complexes (Van Nuys–Pierce Park Apartments) were constructed. These provided much-needed housing in Los Angeles, but they also tended to concentrate poor people in Pacoima. On the other hand, both blacks and whites have bought into the attractive single-family houses in Pacoima's Hansen Hills and, in the late 1980s, the gated Griffin Glenoaks condominium complex. The tensions between the middle class in such developments and the poorer people elsewhere in Pacoima have continued, but in general middle-class black families have been following the earlier exodus of white families from Pacoima, where the numbers of poorer blacks and Latinos have increased.

Post–World War II concentrations: Pomona. In 1900 this town had twenty-seven blacks, working as laborers or laundresses and living close to the railroad tracks.[86] The town grew relatively slowly, and for a half century not many blacks settled there. However, in the late 1940s the city's growth took off. New industrial jobs were snapped up by white residents from Los Angeles, who then bought homes in the many subdivisions newly created from former orange groves. With widespread layoffs at the end of the Korean War in 1953, however, many residents missed payments on their homes, which were then repossessed and left vacant. In the early 1960s the Federal Housing Administration and the Veterans Administration, which had guaranteed the mortgage payments, fixed up the deteriorating homes and listed them with local realtors who agreed for the first time to sell to blacks. Advertisements enticed many black families to move from South Central and buy these inexpensive homes, and the 1965 Watts riot encouraged others to come to Pomona because of less violence and better schools. By 1970 a combination of black suburbanization and white flight had led to a substantial shift in the racial composition of the three separate sections of Pomona in which most of these homes were located.

Since that time, as blacks have moved eastward to places like Fontana and Rialto in San Bernardino County, their places have been taken by Latinos. By 1990 only 14 percent of Pomona's population was black, whereas more than half the city was Hispanic.

People of Jamaican, Belizean, and Nigerian Ancestries

Immigrants came to Southern California from parts of Africa, Central America, and the West Indies. Many identified themselves as black on the census questionnaire, and some migrated from Spanish-speaking areas. The proportion of blacks and Hispanics among people whose ancestry lies in those areas varies from country to country (Table 3.2).

There are relatively few blacks among South Africans, Cubans, and Puerto Ricans in Southern California (Table 3.2). Just the opposite is the case among Trinidadians: Trinidad's population includes approximately equal numbers of Asian Indians and blacks, but blacks easily outnumber Indians among immigrants to Southern California. Although more than a third of Panamanians identified their race as black, their relatively small numbers do not justify special treatment as black immigrants apart from coverage as Hispanic Central Americans.

Our interpretation focuses on the three largest predominantly black immigrant groups. Because their countries were formerly British colonies, most of these immigrants speak English. Distinctive accents in speech and a familiarity with tropical foods and spices distinguish Jamaicans, Belizeans, and Nigerians from U.S.-born blacks. These immigrants' cultural backgrounds have emphasized class distinctions more than racial differences.[87] Most of those from the Caribbean Islands—Jamaicans and Belizeans—refer to themselves as West Indian or Creole rather than black, and they often speak Creole, a language based partly on English and partly on African languages.[88] However, in the United States they are identified as black by most whites.

Belizeans in Los Angeles are ethnically varied. Although the majority are Creole Belizeans, there are two other groups which are somewhat socially and geographically intermixed with the Creoles, more so in Los Angeles than in the country of Belize.[89] One group is Spanish Belizeans, whose families originated in Belize's northern and western parts which border on Mexico and Guatemala (Table 3.2). Many are part Mayan Indian. The other group of Belizean origin living in Los Angeles is a mixed black-Carib Indian population which retains a distinctive identity as Garifuna.

Residential locations. Belizeans, Jamaicans, and Nigerians show two patterns in their distributions (Figs. 3.13, 3.14, and 3.15). First, those who have low incomes or feel more comfortable living among other blacks typically live in South Central. They are mixed residentially with American blacks in areas of low and moderate income and do not settle in enclaves according to their country of origin. A second group of immigrants, discussed at the end of this section, is widely dispersed in predominantly white areas.

Although Belizeans are dispersed over much of South Central, most Belizean markets, restaurants, and other businesses are centrally located on Western Avenue between Jefferson Boulevard and Vernon Avenue (Fig. 3.13).[90] Belizeans tend to meet and socialize at these stores rather than at churches or special ethnic functions. Garifuna Belizeans tend to live east of Vermont Avenue—to the east of most Creole Belizeans.[91] The Spanish heritage of some Belizeans may partly explain their settlement to the east of Jamaicans and Nigerians—closer to the large Hispanic population. Nearly all Belizeans in the strongly Latino cities of South Gate and Lynwood reported themselves as Hispanic. However, within most of South Central, variations among Belizeans in percentage Hispanic are normally not pronounced.[92]

There is a noticeable cluster of Nigerians residing in single-family houses in the middle-income Morningside Park section of Inglewood and in adjacent Hyde Park, within Los Angeles. A few live in the large, gated community on the south side of Manchester Boulevard east of the Forum.

Tracts with relatively high percentages of Jamaicans can also be detected in Inglewood. The larger concentrations are in Morningside Park and to the west, in the tract containing the large Daniel Freeman Memorial Hospital. Jamaican and Belizean niches in hospital employment, especially among women, are pronounced (Table 8.6). The location of Daniel

Table 3.2 Racial and Hispanic Identification among Selected African and Middle American Ancestries, 1990

Ancestry	Percent White	Percent Black	Percent Hispanic
Central American			
Belizean	3.6	87.7	31.9
Honduran	39.2	5.0	98.6
Panamanian	32.6	36.1	85.0
West Indian			
Cuban	64.5	2.1	94.8
Puerto Rican	49.1	3.4	95.1
Jamaican	5.0	92.5	4.3
Trinidadian[a]	5.5	91.8	0.0
African			
Nigerian	4.0	91.2	5.6
South African	94.1	5.3	2.7

Source: U.S. Bureau of the Census (1992).

Notes: Some groups listed are not given special table or map coverage in this book because they have fewer than 5,000 members in Southern California. Those that are listed here are known for being racially mixed or containing two or more different groups. Black and white percentages do not add up to 100 because some people reported their race as "Other," American Indian, or Asian. Because Hispanic persons are identified separately by race in census data, the figures for any one ancestry group often total more than 100.

Where Hispanics and blacks reside in the same neighborhoods (e.g., South Central), percentages of each may be too high. This is because a Census Bureau computer program imputed missing racial and Hispanic identities based on characteristics of nearby households. Because of this, some black persons who did not answer the Hispanic question could be erroneously reported as Hispanic if a Hispanic household was chosen by the computer as the basis for the imputation. In the same way, some Hispanics who did not fill in an answer to the race question may be reported as black when they are not. The problem is illustrated by the Hispanic percentages for Jamaicans and Nigerians, virtually none of whom have some Hispanic heritage.

[a]This ancestry group also includes the smaller numbers of Tobagonians because the two islands are officially one country.

Freeman, Centinela Hospital Medical Center, and Hillcrest Medical Center close to attractive residential areas suggests part of the reason for settlement of these black-ancestry groups in and near Inglewood. Other Jamaicans are scattered in the Crenshaw area and north of Interstate 10, near Washington and Venice Boulevards. The Crenshaw area is to some extent a focus of West Indian society, with its shops, restaurants, and "jerk" chicken places.

The higher incomes and greater acculturation of many West Indian blacks, particularly Jamaicans, enable them to live in outlying suburban areas (see also Fig. 9.9). Jamaicans are widely scattered in such areas, although some slight clustering is evident in tracts within Whittier, West Covina, Pomona, and Montclair. Farther east (beyond the map) more than 150 Jamaicans live near other blacks and many whites in Moreno Valley in Riverside County, a suburban city that grew rapidly during the 1980s. Irvine, Santa Clarita, and Woodland Hills are also home to Jamaicans. Jamaicans residing in tracts composed entirely of university property at the University of California at Irvine, and California State Polytechnic University, Pomona, are students in dormitories. The small concentration of Nigerians in Pasadena is near both Pasadena City College and the California Institute of Technology, where some may be enrolled as students.

Black Median Household Income

Figure 3.16 accentuates important areas of black settlement because only tracts with 100 or more black households are included. Numerous additional black households of varying incomes are actually dispersed in tracts that are not shown on the map. Nevertheless, the large area with tracts of fewer than 100 black households reflects the lower incomes of blacks compared to whites and past exclusion of blacks by whites. In Orange County and eastern Ventura County, the historic absence of black farmworkers in California agriculture helps explain the small black population of those areas.[93]

The lowest-income area is the oldest part of South Central, with its Central Avenue corridor extending south from Downtown and the adjacent Skid Row (Fig. 3.1). At the opposite extreme, upper-income blacks are found in several areas, three of them on the western and southern fringe of the large black-settlement concentration in Los Angeles: the Windsor Hills–View Park–Ladera Heights area, just uphill from Leimert Park and the Crenshaw area; Morningside Park in Inglewood and adjacent areas, which include several gated neighborhoods; and Carson, where black suburbanites are more apt to be living in multiracial neighborhoods. Middle-class and more affluent blacks also live in Altadena, the San Fernando Valley, and in western San Bernardino County.

The map is complex in the area around Pomona and adjacent San Bernardino County, reflecting both long-established black settlement in poorer areas and the black presence in newer suburban areas. Farther east (and not shown) is the city of Moreno Valley, which symbolizes the dispersal of both blacks and whites to distant, affordable developments.

At the top of the map is the old, rural, black settlement of Val Verde, founded in 1924 by black leaders as a resort and retreat from city life and discrimination.[94] Since then many black families have vacationed here or bought property here, some building year-round homes. During the 1940s and 1950s, when an unofficial policy led to black exclusion from Los Angeles city swimming pools except for the day before scheduled cleaning, Val Verde Park, with its open pool, clubhouse, and numerous outdoor activities, was an important summer oasis for black families in Los Angeles. Although by 1990 most of Val Verde's year-round residents were whites, whose incomes were much above those of the older community of blacks, Val Verde remains a well-known symbol of the era of segregation for black families whose roots are in Los Angeles.

Notes

1. The general tendency for immigrants who live in ethnic concentrations to be more recently arrived and less acculturated is part of a general model of immigrant spatial assimilation explained by Massey (1985) and Portes and Rumbaut (1990), chapter 2. For a test of a modified version of this model for 1990 in Southern California, see Allen and Turner (1996b).

2. The theory has been most developed by Schelling (1971) and tested in Los Angeles by Clark (1991, 1992).

3. Massey and Denton (1993), 195.

4. Allen and Turner (1996a), 19.

5. The extent of contemporary housing discrimination is difficult to measure because many people do not realize they have been subjected to it. One technique for identifying discrimination is called testing or auditing. This involves matching minority and white prospective renters or buyers by similar characteristics and recording the nature of the reception given each by realtors, landlords, or apartment managers. Research based on this technique has demonstrated that housing discrimination of one sort or another is still significant and widespread (Turner, Struyk, and Yinger 1991). Janet Sohm, program compliance director of the Los Angeles Fair Housing Congress, estimated that racial and ethnic discrimination in housing, especially rental housing, remains widespread (interviewed January 1993). However, it is more difficult to detect because it is less overt now than it was in the past. Differential treatment by lending agencies is also an issue. Any discrimination involves the application phase of the tenant-selection or mortgage-lending process rather than refusal at initial entry. See Grigsby (1994) for research on the residential-mobility situation facing blacks in different parts of Los Angeles County. Interviews with regional fair-housing directors make it clear that during the 1980s a common type of discrimination involved an apartment manager of a particular immigrant group pressuring tenants who were not members of that group to leave, in order to open up spaces for members of the group.

6. The concentrations in 1940 are based on detailed maps in Hanson and Beckett (1944), which also includes previously unpublished race and ethnic counts by census tract.

7. As of 1960 Asian immigration had just begun to increase, but Asians (primarily Japanese at that time) and the few American Indians were grouped together in these census data as "Other Races." Because no dot is shown in a tract if the ethnic group in that tract numbers fewer than 150, the map slightly underestimates the scattering of ethnic populations within areas dominated by other groups.

8. The origin of these foothill towns is described in McWilliams (1973), 150–154, 205–226.

9. Lothrop (1994), 55.

10. Fogelson (1967), 144–45.

11. McWilliams (1973), 147, 159.

12. McWilliams (1973), 144; Starr (1985), 98–107; Davis (1990), 55–57.

13. McWilliams (1973), 150.

14. McWilliams (1973), 141.

15. Kosmin and Scheckner (1991).

16. Phillips (1986), 138.

17. Russians who are Christian tend to live in the same general areas as some Jews, although the two groups are completely separate socially and impossible to distinguish on the map. In the 1920s several hundred Russian anti-Bolshevik aristocrats from the Czarist period settled in Hollywood (Day 1934), where three Russian Orthodox churches remained active as of 1995. Another Orthodox church is in Tarzana in the San Fernando Valley, where Russian-ancestry adherents are far outnumbered by Russian-ancestry Jews. Contemporary Protestant Christian refugees from the Soviet Union are also too few in number to distinguish in the census data, and members of a non-Orthodox fundamentalist Russian sect known as Molokans who settled on the flats below Boyle Heights in the early twentieth century have long since dispersed (Young 1932).

Also, we treat Jews as an ethnic group rather than as a religious one. Jews vary a great deal in religious perspective, from the majority who do not practice their religion to others who are intensely religious and are affiliated with the Reform, Conservative, or Orthodox branches of Judaism.

18. Sources for early history are Newmark (1970); Vorspan and Gartner (1970); and Stern (1981).

19. Lothrop (1986).

20. Vorspan and Gartner (1970), 109, 118.

21. Vorspan and Gartner (1970), 245.

22. Davis (1990), 119–20.

23. Gabler (1988), 276.

24. Dr. Max Vorspan, University of Judaism, interviewed September 1996.

25. Gottlieb and Wolt (1977), 311–13.

26. Vorspan and Gartner (1970), 127–28, 233.

27. Jews founded the garment industry in Southern California after their earlier experience in New York, and before 1950 many workers in Los Angeles, especially men, at the various cutting and sewing machines were Jewish (Vorspan and Gartner 1970), 116, 124–26.

28. Rabbi William Kramer, University of Judaism, interviewed September 1996.

29. Vorspan and Gartner (1970), 204.

30. Senn (1948).

31. Vorspan and Gartner (1970), 148, 203, 204.

32. Phillips (1986), 132.

33. Phillips (1986), 132.

34. The historical shift of Jews out of their old Westside neighborhoods is described in Vorspan and Gartner (1970), 203–4.

35. Many Sephardic Jews from Turkey and the Greek island of Rhodes settled initially to the southwest of the University of Southern California, near Vermont Avenue and between Vernon and Slauson Avenues. See Chammou (1976), esp. 108, 119.

36. Vorspan and Gartner (1970), 243–44.

37. Arnett Hartsfield, long-time resident of South Central Los Angeles, interviewed February 1992.

38. Phillips (1986), 163.

39. Kaplan, S. H. (1989); Parsons (1993).

40. Sandberg (1986), 44.

41. Gold (1992). This book contains a rich ethnographic study of Soviet Jews in the West Hollywood area.

42. Rabbi Berel Saltzman, a refugee who arrived in the neighborhood in 1980, runs the storefront Chabad-Lubavitch center on Santa Monica Boulevard, interviewed in May, 1990.

43. The pattern of Russian-ancestry concentration on the Westside is very similar to that found in a 1979 survey of Jews in Los Angeles County (Phillips 1986, 140). Bruce Phillips, research director at the Jewish Federation Council of Greater Los Angeles, shared unpublished findings regarding the estimated distribution of Jews according to zip codes. The area within Los Angeles County with the highest percentage of Jews was southeastern Beverly Hills and the adjacent parts of Los Angeles to the south and the east as far as Fairfax Avenue. That area, comprising zip codes 90035, 90048, and 90211, was estimated to be between 61 and 68 percent Jewish. The same survey revealed that Beverly Hills as a whole was 50 percent Jewish. Jewish proportions in these areas probably increased during the 1980s, with the arrival of many Jews from Iran.

44. Davis (1990), 71, 123–25.

45. Phillips (1986), 161.

46. The 1979 survey of Jews in the Los Angeles area indicated variations in Jewish proportions within the Valley (see note 43 above.) The most intensely Jewish area was zip code 91423 in Sherman Oaks, which was estimated to be 44 percent Jewish. The next leading areas were North Hollywood, Encino, and Sherman Oaks, where Jews constituted about one-third of the total population. Jewish percentages have probably increased because many Russian and Iranian Jews settled in the same areas during the 1980s.

47. Gold (1994b) and Gold (1995) are the major sources for the Israeli interpretation.

48. Gold (1995), 269.

49. Gold (1995), 271.

50. Hammam Shafie, West Hills resident and member of the Arab American community, interviewed, June 1996.

51. Two Christian groups from Middle Eastern countries are identifiable by distinctive ancestries in census data and are not included with the Arab aggregation. The first is people of Assyrian or Chaldean ancestry, who represent a large Christian group in Iraq and Iran. Also, Armenians originating in these countries are Christian, but the strength of their Armenian identity makes it highly likely that they would report their ancestry as Armenian rather than the Arabic-speaking country from which they migrated. Despite private efforts by Islamic leaders, no good estimates on the size of the Muslim population in Southern California exist (Kelley 1994, 136).

52. Dart (1995).

53. Dlin (1961).

54. Kelley (1994), 136–37.

55. Kelley (1994), 156, 166.

56. Haiek (1992).

57. Dart (1995).

58. A general introduction to Southern California Armenians which stresses their differing national origins is Der-Martirosian, Sabagh, and Bozorgmehr (1993). Sources for the very early years in Los Angeles are Yeretzian (1923) and Minasian (1982). The material on Montebello is based partly on a telephone interview in 1990 with Dr. Richard Hovannisian of the Department of History, University of California, Los Angeles. In addition, in 1992 and 1993 research by California State University, Northridge, geography students Marsha Otchis, Joanne Quinn, and David Deis uncovered aspects of Armenian communities in Montebello and Pasadena.

59. The East Hollywood settlement is well covered in Stumbo (1980), Arax and Schrader (1988), and Kimble (1989). That in Glendale is described in Holley (1981), in Gordon (1985), and in articles in the *Glendale News-Press* and *The Armenian Observer*.

60. Mehdi Bozorgmehr, sociologist at the University of California, Los Angeles (interviewed June 1990), and Zorah Ramsey of Tarzana (interviewed April 1990) provided comments on both Iran and Iranians in Southern California. Also helpful as

background was *Irangeles: Iranians in Los Angeles,* in which aspects of Iranian life in Southern California are explored in depth, in both text and photos (Kelley and Friedlander 1993).

61. Kelley (1993).

62. Light et al. (1993), 288–91.

63. Dallalfar (1989), 301–11.

64. Bozorgmehr, Sabagh, and Der-Martirosian (1993), 77.

65. Mitchell (1990).

66. Sherwood (1982).

67. The forms of discrimination used against blacks in Los Angeles are detailed in Bass (1960), 69-94.

68. Senn (1948).

69. See Mason and Anderson (1969) for details.

70. Distributional details are from a map based on race counts by enumeration district, as reported in the manuscript schedules of the 1910 U.S. census. The map was produced by Christopher Bruce, Department of Geography, California State University, Northridge.

71. Bond (1936), 70.

72. De Graaf (1970). Bunch (1990) and Moss (1996) also provide fine historical discussions of the evolving black community in Los Angeles. The black concentration in South Central Los Angeles before 1940 is best covered by Bond (1936) and de Graaf (1970); Spaulding (1946) treats the World War II years.

73. *The Crisis* Magazine, August 1913, 194, quoted in Bunch (1990), 101.

74. *Shelley v. Kraemer,* 334 U.S. 1 (1948).

75. Interviews with realtors and black home buyers, as well as details of changes in specific neighborhoods during this period, are reported in Bond (1936). Bass (1960), 95-113, discusses in detail the mechanisms of housing discrimination in Los Angeles and the struggles to counter them.

76. Bond (1936), 144.

77. Early Watts is described in Ray (1985) and Lopez (1994). The importance of this "Red Car" junction point and its little station on 103d Street was appropriately recognized in the recent renovation of the station as a symbol of the early Watts.

78. See Oliver (1992) and Bennett (1993) for Carver Manor and Parkside Manor.

79. Many details of the families in this area are found in Bond (1936), chapter 3.

80. Bass (1960), 105; Moss (1996), 234.

81. Senn (1948).

82. The conflicts over gentrification in West Adams are described in McGee (1991).

83. The situation of blacks in early Pasadena is based substantially on interviews with elderly long-term residents, both black and white, recorded about 1940, in Crimi (1941). The locations of minority families in 1935 are based on a Pasadena Planning Commission map in Crimi's thesis.

84. The recruitment of blacks by "Lucky" Baldwin is covered in Snider (1987), 28. Stephen R. Baker, historian of the city of Monrovia, has examined late-1880s issues of the Monrovia *Messenger* and the 1900 census manuscript schedules. He shared his findings on the origins of Monrovia's black community in telephone conversations, March 1996.

85. Early black settlement in Pacoima is traced in Huling (1978) and to some extent in Mohan (1994). Additional information was provided by Bill Huling, interviewed January 1992; and Ed Kussman, former head of the Valley chapter of the National Association for the Advancement of Colored People, interviewed February 1996.

86. The material on blacks in Pomona is based on Lothrop (1988).

87. Boyer (1985).

88. Arnold (1987). The processes of Trinidadian and Belizean migration to Los Angeles, particularly the role of women, have been explored in depth in Ho (1993) and Miller (1992).

89. Most of the description of Belizean settlement is based on Straughan (1992).

90. Straughan (1995).

91. The distribution as mapped may have omitted many people of Garifuna heritage. This is because people who identified their ancestry simply as Garifuna were coded by the Census Bureau as West Indian rather than Belizean. There are also Garifuna people from Honduras in Los Angeles.

92. These findings are based on our analysis of PUMS data.

93. The historic evolution of the black community in Orange County is clearly presented in Tolbert and de Graaf (1989/1990).

94. Stewart (1994).

4. Distributions: American Indians and Hispanics

In this chapter we explain the changing distributions of Southern Californians whose identity is American in a broader sense than is used by most residents of the United States—people from all of the Americas. We look at American Indians and at the Spanish-speaking nationalities of Mexico, Central America, the West Indies, and South America.

American Indians

With more than 87,000 American Indians counted in 1990, the five-county Southern California area had a larger Indian population than did any other metropolitan area of the United States. It far surpassed the next largest metropolitan centers—Tulsa, Oklahoma City, and New York City, each of which had fewer than 50,000 Indians.

Indians in Southern California have origins in well over a hundred different ethnic groups (or tribes or nations), and many are substantially mixed in their heritage.[1] Only a relative few of these Indians are indigenous to Southern California. This is because nearly all the Indians near the Spanish missions and other white settlements, such as the Gabrielino and the Chumash, were killed, died of disease, or escaped and joined other groups. The Luiseño, Serrano, Cahuilla, and other Indians to the east in San Bernardino and Riverside Counties are few in number, despite their several reservations. The highest percentage-Indian tract in Southern California is part of the Morongo Reservation, near Banning in Riverside County, but it is only 12 percent American Indian (Fig. 4.1). Only three other tracts (none of which is shown in Fig. 4.1) were more than four percent American Indian in 1990. All of them represent indigenous tribes, on or near reservations in San Bernardino and Riverside Counties. Thus, almost all Southern California Indians are migrants or descendants of migrants from other parts of the United States (Table 4.1).

Identities. Because of historic mixing between Indians and Spanish and Mexican in the southwestern United States, 32 percent of the Southern Californians who identified themselves on the census race question as American Indian also reported that they were of Hispanic origin. Similar racial mixing across the country has long occurred between American Indians and both whites and blacks, so that the number of people who wrote in "American Indian" as their first-listed or only ancestry was almost twice the number of those who reported their race as Indian. This appears to reflect more a pride in Indian heritage than a primary social and cultural identity as Indian. At least 68,000 non-Hispanic whites and 7,700 blacks in Southern California listed American Indian as their ancestry.

Specific tribal or ethnic identity is probably less important to Indians in urban Southern California than in the rural and reservation areas of origin, and Indians increasingly have chosen to marry other Indians outside their tribal group.[2] In addition, 60 percent of married Indians in Southern California have white spouses (Fig. 9.17). Thus, multitribal and multiracial backgrounds are common.

Although Indians sometimes prefer not to discuss their tribal affiliation with whites, among Indians the tribal identity or identities remains important.[3] Most social gatherings, however, are not exclusive to certain tribes. This is exemplified in the pan-Indian character of Saturday powwows, the traditional dances and festivities held weekly in one place or another around Southern California. Powwows, begun in Los Angeles in the 1950s, confirm and display the Indian heritage of participants and provide opportunities to develop intertribal friendships.[4] Furthermore, membership in specific Christian denominations and attendance at worship services are also open to all, although in practice they are largely related to past mission activities in various regions. For example, Oklahoma Indians are typically Baptists, Methodists, or other Protestants, whereas many Navajo and Hopi are Mormons. Whatever the Indian social setting, most participants will readily make known their tribal heritage with pride.

Table 4.1 American Indian Populations, 1990

Tribe	Population
Apache	5,316
Blackfoot	1,868
Cherokee	17,500
Chickasaw	1,046
Chippewa	1,602
Choctaw	3,220
Comanche	526
Creek	1,510
Iroquois	1,638
Navajo	5,086
Osage	752
Paiute	761
Pima	703
Potawatomi	748
Pueblo	1,908
Seminole	504
Sioux	2,991
Tohono O'odham	1,076
All other tribes	21,617
Tribe not specified	16,735

Source: U.S. Bureau of the Census (1992), write-in responses to the race question.

Notes: Indians often identify with more specific subgroups of these tribes. Tohono O'odham were formerly called Papago.

Migrants from reservations. Virtually all the families represented in Figure 4.1 migrated from distant, rural Indian homelands, usually officially designated reservations in widely scattered parts of the country. The first arrivals came in the 1930s from Oklahoma, and during World War II and the late 1940s others migrated from varied parts of the country.[5]

Prompted by a Bureau of Indian Affairs program under which Indians were encouraged to leave their reservations and migrate to cities in order to find jobs, Indian migration to Los Angeles increased greatly during the mid-1950s and 1960s.[6] This relocation program was designed to provide vocational training and job placement in urban areas, to reduce unemployment on reservations, and to aid in the general cultural and structural assimilation of Indians into white society. The program was the impetus for other Indians to migrate even without federal subsidies, so that by 1977 only half of a sample of Indians in Los Angeles had received federal assistance in making the move.

Since then many who came to Southern California have been trained, often at community colleges, as welders, diesel mechanics, licensed vocational nurses, or aircraft-assembly-line workers. Many have landed blue-collar jobs in the aircraft, petroleum, and construction industries, and some have built on those experiences to advance themselves educationally and occupationally, but many others have had great difficulty finding stable employment. Most Indians were not prepared for the pace, complexity, and cultural adaptation required in urban life; and adjustment was more difficult than white government officials had imagined. These problems and loneliness in cities and suburbs have prompted frequent visits and return migrations to the reservations. Elderly Indians have been particularly likely to return to the reservations after they retire.[7] Although federal subsides for migration to cities were mostly eliminated in the 1980s, a shortage of work on reservations continues to drive many young Indians to Southern California.

Increasing residential dispersal. Many of the Indian migrants from Oklahoma who came to Los Angeles in the 1930s and 1940s settled where poor whites lived. The major concentration of both Indians and "Okies" was in small cities like Bell, Bell Gardens, Cudahy, Huntington Park, and Lynwood. There, thousands of families settled into urban life in bungalows while the men toiled in nearby glass, meat-packing, aluminum, steel, tire, and automobile factories. These industrial suburbs, as they have been called, thus became the focus of settlement among the Oklahoma-based Cherokee, Creek, Choctaw, and Seminole migrants to Los Angeles during those decades.[8]

Since that early period, the concentration of Indians in the older industrial suburbs has steadily diminished.[9] This is partly because housing and jobs found through the government's relocation program tended to be dispersed across many lower-income areas of Los Angeles. In addition, the varied origins of Indian migrants to Los Angeles have minimized the migration chains that might lead toward tribal or Indian concentrations. Most important, however, cultural assimilation and employment success have made it possible for many Indians to leave low-income areas and move to the suburbs. In 1990 almost 500 Indians still lived in Bell Gardens, which was once known for its Indian concentration and Indian Revival Center (Assembly of God). With the large influx of people of Mexican origin, mostly immigrants, into Bell Gardens, however, that city is hardly distinguishable in Figure 4.1.

By 1990 Indians were widely scattered within a large number of older urban and suburban areas where housing costs were low or moderate. There is no urban Indian enclave in Southern California, but numerous communities have slightly higher than average Indian proportions. As of 1990 the dispersed Indian community received its news and notices of powwows and other events primarily through the Southern California Indian Center, with four branch offices and a headquarters in Garden Grove.

Suburbanization and modest upward occupational mobility are not, however, the whole story. Indian percentages in three tracts are indirect evidence of the adjustment problems that many of them face. In Downtown the tract that stands out as having 3 percent American Indians is Skid Row, where the homeless and jobless try to survive in run-down apartment buildings, in shelters, and on sidewalks. Indians are also somewhat overrepresented in the Los Angeles County Central Jail,

located in the adjacent tract, and in the federal prison on Terminal Island in Los Angeles Harbor.

Mexican and Central American Indians are also included by the U.S. census race data as American Indian. It is likely that the Indians shown in the two very small tracts west of Downtown and Interstate 110 are Mexican or Guatemalan Indians (Fig. 4.1). This is because that Westlake area is home to a large Spanish-speaking immigrant population and because Kanjobal Indians from Guatemala are known to live in other tracts in the same general area, as we discuss later in this chapter. In addition, many Mixtec and Zapotec Indians from Oaxaca, Mexico, migrated during the 1980s into Ventura County, where they have jobs as farmworkers in Oxnard and Camarillo and as landscapers and day laborers in Moorpark and Thousand Oaks.[10]

Like several other ethnic groups in Southern California, Indians retain a strong sense of identity and community, one which is not dependent on residential proximity or the existence of a geographical enclave. Among other ethnic groups, residential dispersal and an absence of enclaves are associated with higher incomes and with life in the newer and better suburbs. Indians remain unusual in that these residential patterns have developed without relatively high levels of education, occupational status, or income.

People of Mexican Origin

Spanish sailors explored the coast of California as early as 1542, and Southern California was part of the settled northern frontier of New Spain from the late 1700s until 1821. At that time Mexicans asserted their independence and this area became Mexican territory. An influx of American adventurers and merchants plus new trade links with the United States led to a growing American recognition of the potential value of California and other parts of Mexico. By the 1840s Mexico's weak military hold on the area made California even more tempting. The United States began the American–Mexican War to take by force the land it coveted.

Only after a contingent of American troops had advanced to the outskirts of Mexico City did Mexico capitulate. In the

1848 treaty, Mexico had to sell the entire northern half of its claimed national territory for $15 million. This included California, from which word of the gold discovery at Sutter's Mill had not yet spread outside the region.

Despite this wrenching of California and other northern territories from Mexican control, the old ties between Mexico and Southern California were never completely severed. Moreover, in the minds of many Mexicans, Southern California has remained an extension of Mexican territory and society. Southern California is geographically close to Mexico, and for most of the twentieth century the United States has not effectively controlled that border. Thus, migration to Southern California has not seemed to Mexicans as drastic and disruptive a step as many Americans believe it should be.

For these reasons, as well as for the more general reasons explained in chapter 2, migration flows from Mexico into Southern California have been and still are far larger than from any other country. The three and three-quarter million people of Mexican origin counted in Southern California in 1990 represented 26 percent of all the region's residents.

Of no less importance than the numbers, however, has been the cleavage between the Mexican and the white communities during most of the twentieth century. In the words of someone raised during the 1950s in the rural Mexican community of Moorpark in eastern Ventura County, Southern California society was "fundamentally structured along 'white' and 'Mexican' lines, determining where one lived and worked as well as one's social status."[11]

Basic geographical patterns. The development of Mexican ethnic concentrations can be explained primarily by the cumulative and inertial effects of population growth and location near employment and in low-cost housing areas. With respect to employment, irrigation agriculture was particularly important during the first half of the twentieth century. In Riverside, San Bernardino, and Ventura Counties the historic association of Mexican immigrants with irrigation farmwork explains most of the ethnic concentrations as of 1990—in cities like Corona, Riverside, Ontario, Cucamunga, and Oxnard and in numerous smaller places. Employment in traditional sectors

of manufacturing has also been very common among people of Mexican origin, which helps explain the concentration of Latinos near industrial areas.[12] In addition, the low average income of people of Mexican origin has meant that those who are employed in service industries and construction also tend, like those in agriculture and manufacturing, to live in areas of less-expensive housing.

Two additional factors have reshaped the distribution of people of Mexican origin in certain areas.[13] First, suburbanization since World War II has redistributed Mexican Americans more widely—a geographical shift which illustrates a widely observed pattern among ethnic populations.[14] The suburban shift has been most prominent in a sector that extends eastward from East Los Angeles into the San Gabriel Valley and beyond. Second, as immigration from Mexico increased in the 1970s and swelled during the 1980s, poor immigrants frequently moved into the lowest-cost housing available, which was in nearby communities that had mostly black populations. The Mexican influx to the east side of South Central was nothing new because Mexican barrios had existed in Watts and Willowbrook since the 1920s. However, by 1990 the leading population had changed from black to Latino, and Latinos had enlarged their areas of settlement. In the process Latinos displaced some of the blacks from their settlement concentrations in South Central, Pasadena, Pacoima, Monrovia, Pomona, Long Beach, and Santa Ana. Such ethnic neighborhood changes have been a common occurrence in American cities, but displacement of low-income blacks by new immigrants is unusual.[15]

The interpretation that follows focuses on the origins of many of the ethnic communities as well as various changes that together explain most features of the distribution (Fig. 4.2).

Early concentration near the plaza. After its founding in 1781 the pueblo of Los Angeles grew slowly during the Spanish and Mexican periods. Its center was the plaza, located adjacent to the modern El Pueblo Historic Park and Olvera Street and just north of Downtown. After California was formally taken over by the United States in 1848, more English-speaking Americans began to arrive. By 1880 they had wrested economic and social dominance away from the Mexican landowning families. With this change of power, nearly all Southern Californians of Mexican origin lost status. Most were relegated by the Anglos to an underclass of laborers together with some artisans—an underclass augmented, especially in the twentieth century, by immigration from Mexico.

Before 1910 newly arrived Mexican immigrants were most likely to settle within a mile of the plaza.[16] This central area also housed most immigrants from Europe and Asia, and the park at the plaza was a center for the hiring of day laborers. Just to the north (in present-day Chinatown) was Sonoratown, the largest Mexican concentration, named for miners from Sonora who came looking for California's gold but settled in Los Angeles instead. To the east of Alameda Street many people of Mexican origin lived on the lower ground of the floodplain of the Los Angeles River.

Beginning about 1910 an increasing number of Mexicans arrived. Most were fleeing economic pressures and the Mexican Revolution or seeking employment in industries that were growing as a result of World War I. Tremendous over-crowding occurred in the plaza area. Many families lived in 300-square-foot houses, sharing toilet facilities and water sup-plies with up to thirty other renter families.[17] In contrast, those members of the old Mexican land-owning families (called Californios) who had substantially assimilated into the Anglo population moved out of the Mexican district and into the Westside.[18]

In recent decades the plaza and Olvera Street remain important sites for both tourists and locals. Next to the plaza is the oldest Catholic church in the city, Our Lady the Queen of the Angels, affectionately known as La Placita. The plaza church holds a special place in the hearts of many Mexican American families, as shown by its popularity for use in wed-dings, baptisms, and other celebrations.[19]

Railroads and industry in outlying colonias. Small Mexican villages, usually called *colonias*, grew up close to indus-trial, railway, or construction work in all parts of Southern California. Little colonias appeared, for example, in Maywood, Bell, and Torrance near steel mills and in Harbor City and Lomita next to the oil refineries.[20] In many such settlements

Mexicans were living close to or somewhat intermixed with immigrants from Europe or with blacks, Japanese, or Chinese. Pockets of such multiethnic neighborhoods were quite com-mon in poorer areas and were usually distinct from neighbor-hoods in which U.S.-born whites lived.

Because the railroad and interurban lines were construct-ed and maintained primarily by Mexican workers, colonias also appeared at junction points, terminals, and freight yards. Railroad companies and the Pacific Electric Company made small amounts of land and shacks, boxcars, or small houses available for Mexican workers, but what little was provided and the workers' low pay meant that housing for these workers was always shabby.[21] The Mexican settlements in Pasadena, Santa Monica, Long Beach, San Bernardino, and Watts all began in this way; and smaller colonias appeared along Pacific Electric line in Alhambra, San Gabriel, El Monte, La Verne, and Colton.

In the decades after 1910, Los Angeles became the most important California center for labor recruitment, as the mas-sive number of arriving immigrants gave it a surplus of unskilled laborers.[22] Wages were often higher for temporary work in railroad construction and in agriculture elsewhere around the state. The net effect was continued net immigra-tion from Mexico but frequent moves in and out of Los Angeles.

The Mexican Eastside. After about 1910 many Mexicans left the plaza area and moved east of the Los Angeles River. This change, together with population growth and geographi-cal consolidation, led ultimately to the creation of the largest and best-known Mexican barrio, the Eastside. The core of the Mexican Eastside is the Boyle Heights part of Los Angeles and East Los Angeles, a portion of county territory (Fig. 3.1).

This shift eastward was due partly to urban renewal and commercial and industrial development in the extremely crowded, more central section near the plaza, but the growing number of Mexicans had to be accommodated somewhere. A sixfold increase in the Mexican population of Los Angeles in the decade after 1910 was followed by a tripling of the city's Mexican residents during the 1920s.[23] Despite repatriation of thousands of Mexicans during the Great Depression, others who had been migrant farmworkers in the Central Valley began to settle permanently in Los Angeles during the 1930s when they were displaced by poor rural whites fleeing the ravages of the Dust Bowl.[24] In addition, the Mexican American population grew from natural increase.

Between 1910 and 1930 the development of new areas for arriving immigrants across the river was aided by the expansion of street railways and interurban lines, opening potential areas of housing for poor people. Italian immigrants were moving northeast into Lincoln Heights, and Boyle Heights was becoming the major center for Eastern European Jews, as well as for Christian Russians (Molokans) and many Armenians, blacks, Japanese, and Mexicans.

At the same time, to the east of Boyle Heights, vacant lots and farmland were being built up into what would later become the large Mexican concentration of East Los Angeles. Low prices on lots and small, single-family houses made this Belvedere area exceptionally desirable for many Mexicans, and it was especially convenient for those who worked at nearby Japanese-run vegetable farms. Without controls on construction and sanitation, Belvedere became a crowded village of small homes and shacks, but at least by 1930, 45 percent of Belvedere's families of Mexican origin were homeowners.[25]

In the 1930s residents of Boyle Heights who were not ethnically Mexican began to depart. Jews had outnumbered other groups there during most of the 1920s, but many successful Jewish professionals and business people were creating new neighborhoods on the Westside and beckoning their friends and relatives east of the river to join them. Those who left found their homes eagerly bought or rented by either Mexican immigrants or their children. By the 1950s people of Mexican origin had expanded their settlement from original villages of Belvedere and El Hoyo Maravilla into all parts of East Los Angeles and into Boyle Heights and nearby City Terrace. By the 1970s, all that remained of the Jewish settlement were one or two kosher shops on Brooklyn Avenue, a home for elderly Jews, and the almost abandoned Breed Street synagogue. The Boyle Heights–East Los Angeles area had coalesced into a single ethnic community. Since then, the Eastside has become more homogeneously Mexican. The exodus of whites, blacks, and some Japanese has continued, and their homes have been eagerly taken by young families and new immigrants from Mexico.

The growing Mexican concentration on the Eastside has reflected the social and economic gulf between whites and "others." After about 1915, when more Mexicans and blacks were arriving in Los Angeles, whites became more concerned with preserving their neighborhoods against encroachment by these groups. Most of the new homes built for whites after 1920 were west of Downtown or, like Glendale and Pasadena, clearly beyond the Eastside. Some cities, like El Segundo and Lynwood, even advertised themselves as excluding Mexicans and other nonwhites. For the vast number of Angelenos the residential areas of whites and Mexicans were coalescing into two very large communities, socially and geographically separate and unequal (Fig. 3.2).

South Central. Between the white Westside concentration and the Mexican Eastside is South Central, an area which has sometimes been thought to be almost all black. In fact, a large Mexican minority has long existed in South Central. Housing there has been low-cost compared with other areas in Los Angeles County, and for Mexicans it offered more individual freedom and less supervision than did the more restrictive Mexican Eastside. In the 1920s and 1930s many intermarried couples and single women of Mexican origin were living in South Central.[26] By 1950 the section north of Slauson Avenue was mostly black, but to the south thousands of Latinos were intermingled with whites and blacks.[27] Far to the south, Watts itself contained more than 7,000 Latinos compared with 26,000 blacks (Figs. 3.1, 3.2).

Altogether, blacks and people of Mexican origin have lived in the same neighborhoods for a considerable time—a situation insufficiently stressed in efforts to identify areas in terms of their leading group.

Industrial employment. Living either west of Alameda Street in South Central or in the Eastside provided good access to jobs in industry for Mexican workers (and for blacks). The largest industrial concentration in Southern California was created in the 1920s just between these two minority residential areas—along Alameda Street in Los Angeles and in the neighboring cities of Vernon and Commerce south to South Gate and Lynwood. In this area were large automobile-tire factories, as well as work in auto assembly, steel and aluminum production, meat packing, brickyards, furniture making, food processing, bakeries, printing, the garment industry, street paving, railroad maintenance, and warehousing.

The strong linkages that developed between Mexican residents and nearby industrial employment have been significant for both workers and employers (Fig. 2.3). Together they have shaped the foremost industrial area in Southern California. At the same time, those workers who were becoming skilled cement finishers or stone and tile workers, plumbers, framers, or roofers were employed more widely in Los Angeles, though many of them still lived in the Eastside or in South Central. However, most families have suffered since the mid-1970s from the replacement of most high-wage, unionized manufacturing jobs by low-wage work in the garment industry, the service sector, and the informal economy.[28]

Farmworker colonias in the San Fernando and Santa Clara Valleys. A geographical continuity between early Mexican settlements and details of the 1990 ethnic distribution is often evident where community origins were more exclusively tied to work in irrigation agriculture. This can be found in parts of the valleys northwest of Los Angeles and in Orange County. Despite a radical shift in occupation away from agriculture and an encroachment of suburban housing, warehouses, and shopping centers, many of the same farmworker colonias remain as barrios—a demonstration of ethnic residential stability amid the swirling currents of urbanization.

Mexican settlement in the San Fernando Valley is as old as Mission San Fernando, founded in 1797. The mission was located a mile west of present-day San Fernando, but neither the town nor the surrounding ranch lands developed a large Mexican-origin population until the latter part of the nineteenth century.

The current ethnic concentration originated with Mexicans working on local fruit and vegetable farms and in the associated packing houses.[29] This agricultural development was based on San Fernando's position on the main rail line from Los Angeles to San Francisco and on its source of water independent from that of Los Angeles. Since mission days San Fernando had been tapping well water and had diverted additional supplies from behind the low hills to its north. Thus in 1913 the residents did not feel compelled to join Los Angeles in order to share in the bounty of that city's new aqueduct water.

After 1913 irrigated farming rapidly expanded in the lands surrounding San Fernando. Mexican laborers worked in the fields of lettuce, carrots, cabbages, onions, and beans as well as in groves of lemons and oranges. Wives and daughters were commonly employed in the four new citrus-packing houses and in the cannery. Most Mexicans lived in a clearly defined Mexican district in San Fernando southwest of the railroad tracks and not far from the fields and packing sheds.

Over the decades workers and their families spilled over into nearby areas like Pacoima, the next stop to the south on the railroad. Since about 1960 many more successful families have moved northward into what had been the strictly Anglo section of San Fernando and into the Mission Hills and Sylmar areas, with their better homes. Agricultural jobs were typically replaced by urban work—construction, manufacturing, trucking, and warehousing. The fact that these sorts of industries were typically located in the eastern San Fernando Valley, often near the railroad tracks, tended to accentuate even more the locational advantages of the east valley for renting and home buying. Moreover, little urban renewal or construction of expensive housing occurred, so the Mexican concentration was not obliterated or diminished.

In the west San Fernando Valley the Canoga Park barrio also had farmworker origins.[30] Soon after aqueduct water from the Sierra Nevada appeared, some growers planted sugar beets but found few Chinese and Japanese laborers to help them. After the United States entered World War I in 1917, demand for farm products increased. The ensuing labor shortage led to widespread recruitment of Mexican farmworkers, who usually camped under tents near the fields. In Canoga Park (then called Owensmouth), in 1918 the American Beet Sugar Company constructed eight adobe houses on Hart Street.

The houses, between Deering and Eaton Avenues, were built to discourage workers from deserting for better wages and conditions elsewhere. The move was effective in that their workers stayed. These homes became the nucleus of a barrio which has persisted and grown for more than seventy years, despite the fact that Latino residents did virtually no farmwork in 1990.

This same locational continuity between irrigation agriculture and a strongly Mexican-origin population in 1990 is even more evident in areas that have retained a rural character, such as the Santa Clara Valley west of Santa Clarita. North of the San Fernando Valley and separated from it by rugged mountains, this valley extends from the ocean at Ventura inland twenty miles to the section shown in Figure 4.2, which includes tiny Piru and the larger town of Fillmore. After the railroad connection between Los Angeles and Santa Barbara was built through this valley in 1887 and control of the flatland passed into the hands of whites, the new landowners experimented with a range of crops and irrigation techniques. By the 1920s citrus had come to dominate the Santa Clara Valley, with picking and packing done mostly by Mexican families who had replaced the earlier Japanese workers. Fillmore was an important packing center for oranges, and to its west was the largest lemon ranch in the world (Limoneira), which for decades was essentially a company town.[31] Agriculture was less intensive in the upper end of the valley, but the Fillmore area had miles of orange groves as well as a variety of field crops, like beans and carrots, worked mostly by Mexican labor.

By 1970 other opportunities had developed, so that few people of Mexican origin continued to be farmworkers. Low and moderate incomes still characterize people in the upper Santa Clara Valley, including the whites, many of whose families had originally migrated from Oklahoma during the 1930s.[32] The Santa Clara Valley's rural setting and its little towns have remained attractive to both Latinos and whites, most of whom commute to Santa Clarita, the San Fernando Valley, Oxnard, or the Ventura area for jobs. In Santa Paula the old labor camps were replaced in the 1980s with attractive new homes, and the incomes of whites and Latinos overlap a great deal, so that any Mexican–white distinction is not primarily economic.

Nevertheless, in 1991 the white and Mexican communities in Santa Paula remained socially and residentially separate. Even membership in the various Protestant and Catholic churches was generally defined by ethnicity.

Farmworker colonias in Orange County. This county's name reflects its heritage in the production of Valencia oranges. These were particularly significant for the development of Mexican farmworker settlements because the season of harvesting and packing lasted between six months and a year and because the growers wanted a large and year-round workforce. Most citrus development occurred in the northern half of the county, and by 1930 more than a dozen Mexican farmworker settlements had appeared close to the packing sheds on the many branch railroad lines built to serve the growers.[33] In addition, Orange County has been important in the production of sugar beets, lima beans, walnuts, and grapes, with Mexican farmworkers primarily responsible for working these crops.

The city of Santa Ana, which appears on the 1990 map as a single, large Mexican-origin concentration, represents the historic expansion and the coalescing of what began as three separate colonias: Delhi (in the southeast, south of Delhi Park), Artesia (in the northwest, centered around Salvador Park), and Logan (in the northeast, west of Logan Park). These colonias, like some others, had not been formally set up for workers but simply represented poor neighborhoods near tracks and packing sheds. In 1960 the Mexican-origin population was substantially segregated. However, the barrios do not appear as ethnic concentrations on Figure 3.2 because of the random placement of dots within census tracts. Although Artesia is now called the 5th Street Barrio, the other two barrios are still known by their original names.

North and west of Santa Ana was Orange County's main citrus-production area. In both Stanton and the city of Orange, tracts with higher Mexican-origin percentage in 1990 identify the local barrios, which are in the same location as the old Stanton and Orange colonias. The most strongly Mexican tracts in north-central Anaheim represent an enlargement of another farmworker colonia, Independencia. Farther north in

La Habra, near the Los Angeles County boundary, the three tracts with highest Mexican-origin proportions are in the same area as Campo Colorado, a virtual company town, and its neighbor, Campo Corona. Although the original housing of both colonias was torn down, the modern barrio remains focused on the Guadalupe Church and park.

Colonias frequently originated as temporary tent camps near citrus-packing houses. They became permanent when landowners later sold house lots to Mexican families, who then built their own homes. In what is now Fountain Valley, Colonia Juarez was created in 1923 in this way—as a residential subdivision restricted to Spanish-speaking people. The modern barrio is in the same location (directly south of the Mile Square Golf Course and west of Ward Street). Suburban development in the large census tract hides the presence of that barrio (Fig. 4.2). Placentia's La Jolla barrio (in the southwestern corner of the city east of the 57 Freeway) also takes its name from the former colonia located in the same place.

Thus, the locations of places which are relatively high in percentage-Mexican origin in 1990 still reflect very much the distribution of Mexican farmworker settlements of the pre–World War II period, despite ubiquitous urbanization. This continuity would not have occurred if entire colonias had been demolished to make room for more expensive housing, as might well have happened if they had been located in areas of much higher urban land values. Equally significant was that the people in most colonias owned their homes and, over the decades, upgraded and embellished them. That there were fewer people of Mexican origin south of Santa Ana in 1990 is due partly to the absence of colonias in that area and partly to the high prices of new housing in Irvine and nearly all the southern half of Orange County.

Low-cost housing. Apart from the large Eastside barrio, which has long been accessible to industrial jobs, and the smaller barrios that originated as farmworker colonias, high percentages of people of Mexican origin are found in areas of low-cost housing. Over the twentieth century landowners and developers have frequently sold land parcels or built modest houses specifically for low-income would-be homeowners. Mexicans

immediately occupied some of these, and their large families and the arrival of their friends and relatives added to the numerous Mexican enclaves.

For example, in Compton inexpensive and undeveloped lots in the Walton Villa subdivision went on sale in 1917.[34] Buyers, mostly Mexican, built low-cost, single-family houses in this tract just west of the Pacific Electric line (the modern-day Blue Line) to Long Beach. For three decades this was Compton's only barrio. By 1950 it was consolidating with an adjacent barrio in Willowbrook, and in 1990 the area is still recognizable for its higher Mexican-origin percentage, compared with surrounding neighborhoods.

More clearly evident in Figure 4.2 is the southern half of the city of Hawaiian Gardens. There, low home prices have resulted in a radical ethnic change, from white to Latino. That area—next to Coyote Creek, which approximates the boundary between Los Angeles and Orange Counties—was long prone to flooding.[35] The land remained cheap, with only scattered farms, when no oil was found in this area during the drilling sprees of the 1920s.

After World War II homes were built on very small lots in the section south of Carson Street, but residential streets remained unpaved until Hawaiian Gardens was incorporated in 1964. Although nearly all of the first residents were whites, the low prices steadily attracted more people of Mexican origin. In 1960 the area was only 20 percent Hispanic, but by 1990 Hispanics represented 76 percent of the same tracts' populations. In Norwalk and adjacent Artesia a large barrio is similarly located in an area of older, modest, single-family houses.

In general, throughout Los Angeles County Latinos in various census tracts tend live in individual blocks with cheaper housing, whether it is single-family houses or apartments.[36] For example, in the central San Fernando Valley the higher Mexican-origin percentage about a mile to the northeast of the Canoga Park barrio is best explained by the presence in that tract of a huge, federally subsidized apartment complex for low-income people.

Other industrial zones. Because low-cost housing is often located close to industry and rail yards, cost of housing

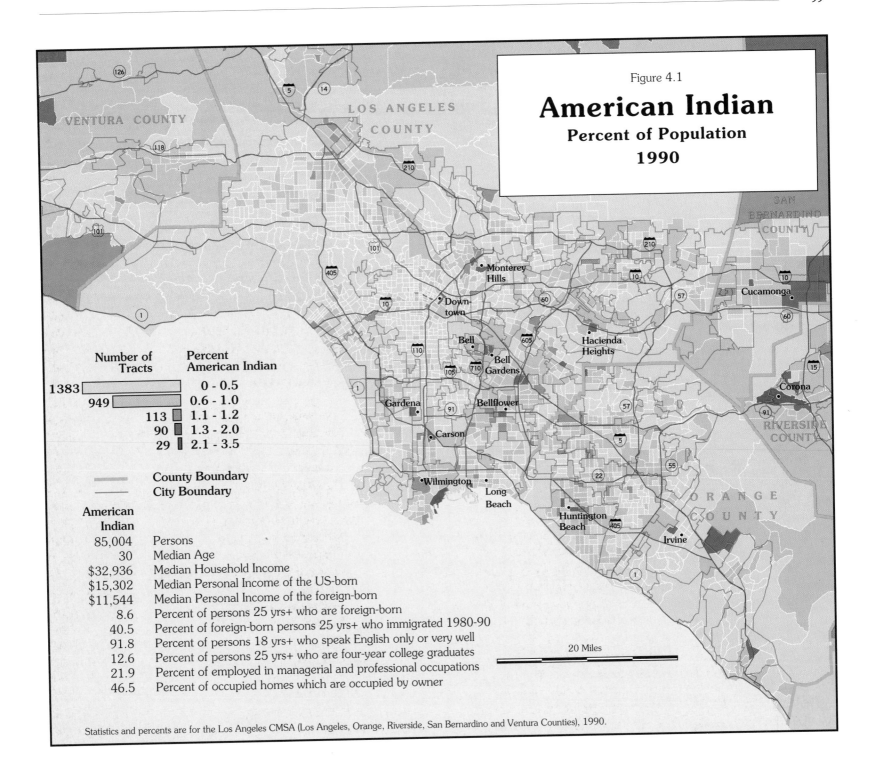

Figure 4.1

American Indian
Percent of Population
1990

Number of Tracts		Percent American Indian
1383		0 - 0.5
949		0.6 - 1.0
113		1.1 - 1.2
90		1.3 - 2.0
29		2.1 - 3.5

County Boundary
City Boundary

American Indian

85,004	Persons
30	Median Age
$32,936	Median Household Income
$15,302	Median Personal Income of the US-born
$11,544	Median Personal Income of the foreign-born
8.6	Percent of persons 25 yrs+ who are foreign-born
40.5	Percent of foreign-born persons 25 yrs+ who immigrated 1980-90
91.8	Percent of persons 18 yrs+ who speak English only or very well
12.6	Percent of persons 25 yrs+ who are four-year college graduates
21.9	Percent of employed in managerial and professional occupations
46.5	Percent of occupied homes which are occupied by owner

20 Miles

Statistics and percents are for the Los Angeles CMSA (Los Angeles, Orange, Riverside, San Bernardino and Ventura Counties), 1990.

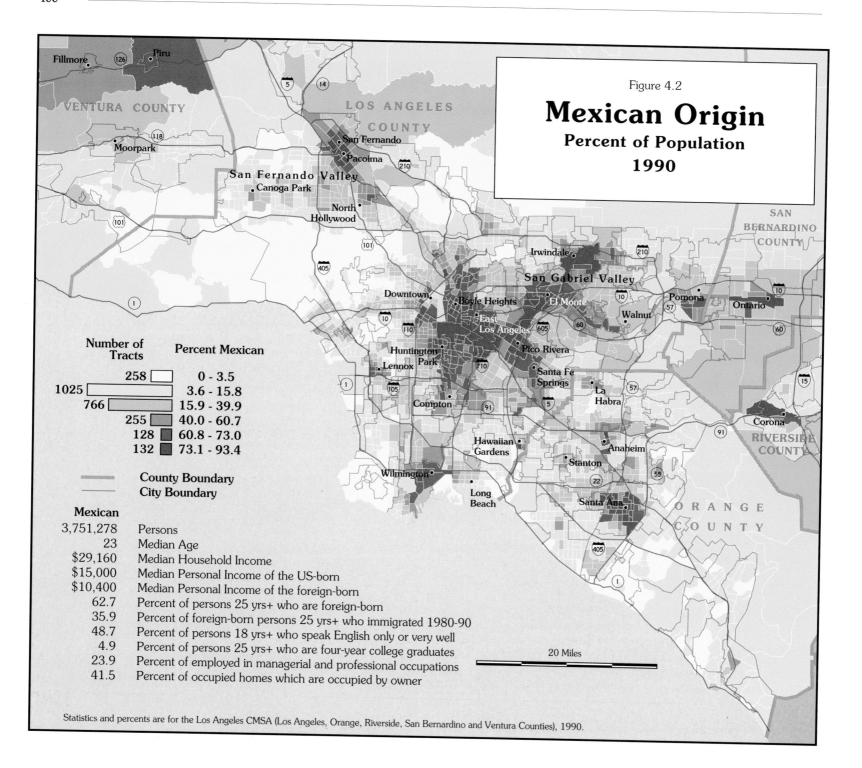

Figure 4.2

Mexican Origin
Percent of Population
1990

Number of Tracts | **Percent Mexican**

258	0 - 3.5
1025	3.6 - 15.8
766	15.9 - 39.9
255	40.0 - 60.7
128	60.8 - 73.0
132	73.1 - 93.4

County Boundary
City Boundary

Mexican

3,751,278	Persons
23	Median Age
$29,160	Median Household Income
$15,000	Median Personal Income of the US-born
$10,400	Median Personal Income of the foreign-born
62.7	Percent of persons 25 yrs+ who are foreign-born
35.9	Percent of foreign-born persons 25 yrs+ who immigrated 1980-90
48.7	Percent of persons 18 yrs+ who speak English only or very well
4.9	Percent of persons 25 yrs+ who are four-year college graduates
23.9	Percent of employed in managerial and professional occupations
41.5	Percent of occupied homes which are occupied by owner

20 Miles

Statistics and percents are for the Los Angeles CMSA (Los Angeles, Orange, Riverside, San Bernardino and Ventura Counties), 1990.

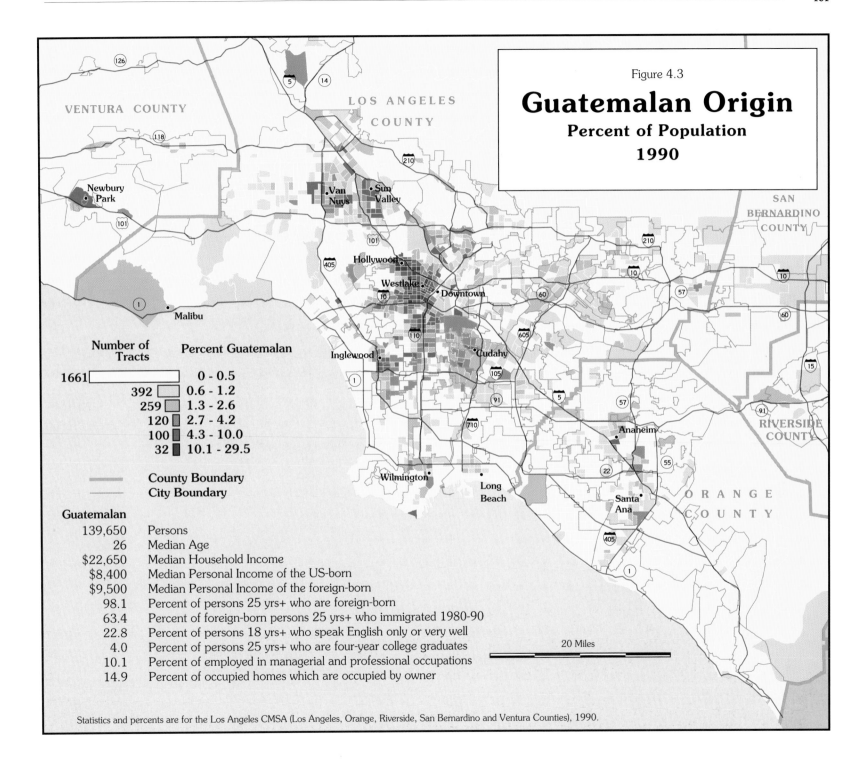

Figure 4.3

Guatemalan Origin
Percent of Population
1990

VENTURA COUNTY

LOS ANGELES COUNTY

SAN BERNARDINO COUNTY

Newbury Park

Malibu

Van Nuys

Sun Valley

Hollywood

Westlake

Downtown

Inglewood

Cudahy

Wilmington

Long Beach

Anaheim

Santa Ana

ORANGE COUNTY

RIVERSIDE COUNTY

Number of Tracts	Percent Guatemalan
1661	0 - 0.5
392	0.6 - 1.2
259	1.3 - 2.6
120	2.7 - 4.2
100	4.3 - 10.0
32	10.1 - 29.5

County Boundary
City Boundary

Guatemalan

139,650	Persons
26	Median Age
$22,650	Median Household Income
$8,400	Median Personal Income of the US-born
$9,500	Median Personal Income of the foreign-born
98.1	Percent of persons 25 yrs+ who are foreign-born
63.4	Percent of foreign-born persons 25 yrs+ who immigrated 1980-90
22.8	Percent of persons 18 yrs+ who speak English only or very well
4.0	Percent of persons 25 yrs+ who are four-year college graduates
10.1	Percent of employed in managerial and professional occupations
14.9	Percent of occupied homes which are occupied by owner

20 Miles

Statistics and percents are for the Los Angeles CMSA (Los Angeles, Orange, Riverside, San Bernardino and Ventura Counties), 1990.

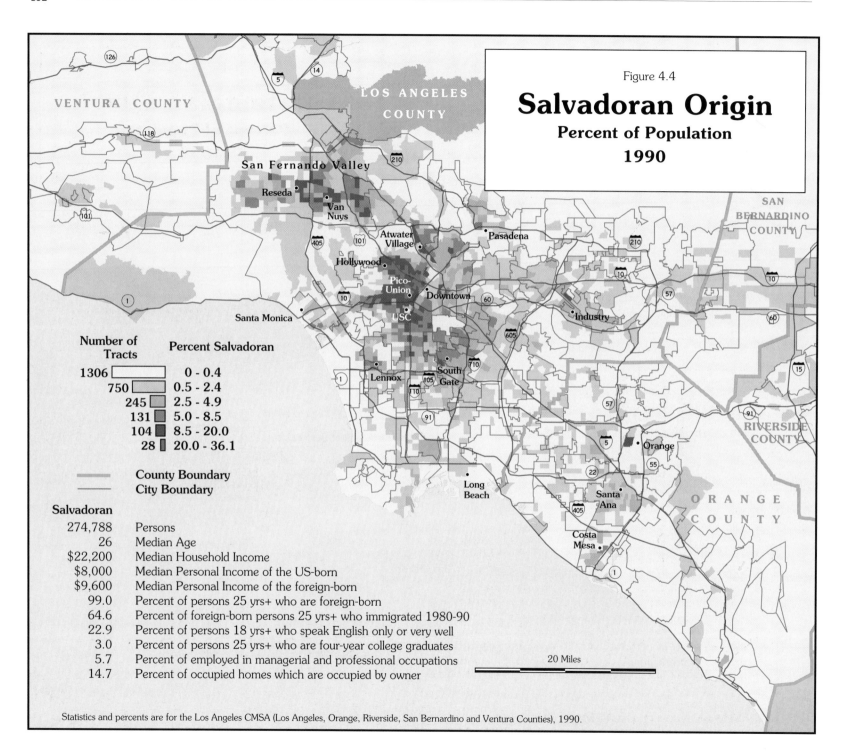

Figure 4.4

Salvadoran Origin
Percent of Population
1990

Number of Tracts	Percent Salvadoran
1306	0 - 0.4
750	0.5 - 2.4
245	2.5 - 4.9
131	5.0 - 8.5
104	8.5 - 20.0
28	20.0 - 36.1

—— County Boundary
— City Boundary

Salvadoran

274,788	Persons
26	Median Age
$22,200	Median Household Income
$8,000	Median Personal Income of the US-born
$9,600	Median Personal Income of the foreign-born
99.0	Percent of persons 25 yrs+ who are foreign-born
64.6	Percent of foreign-born persons 25 yrs+ who immigrated 1980-90
22.9	Percent of persons 18 yrs+ who speak English only or very well
3.0	Percent of persons 25 yrs+ who are four-year college graduates
5.7	Percent of employed in managerial and professional occupations
14.7	Percent of occupied homes which are occupied by owner

20 Miles

Statistics and percents are for the Los Angeles CMSA (Los Angeles, Orange, Riverside, San Bernardino and Ventura Counties), 1990.

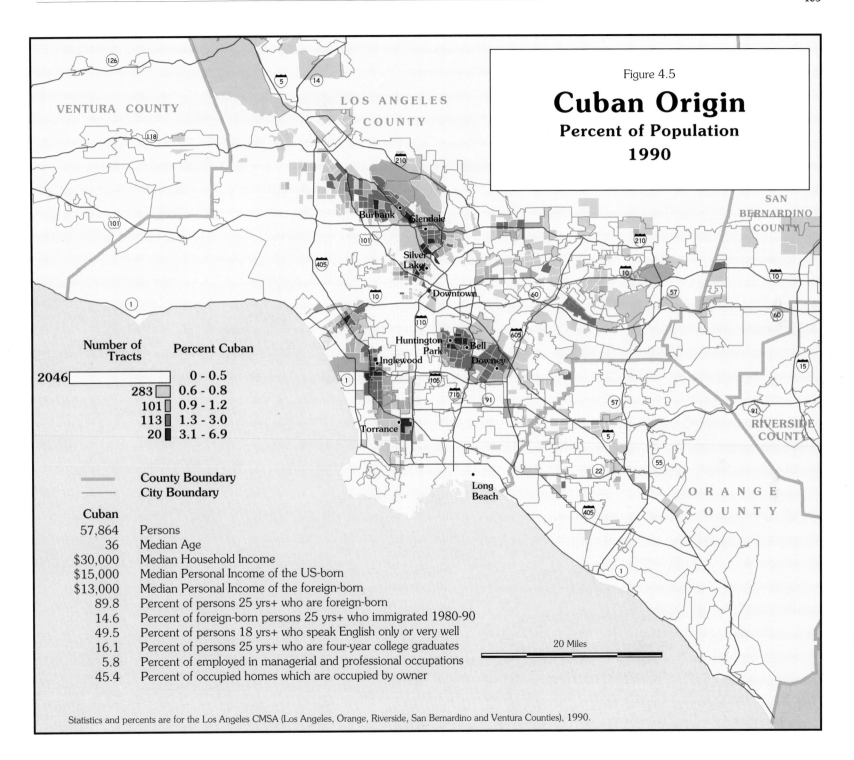

Figure 4.5

Cuban Origin
Percent of Population
1990

Number of Tracts   **Percent Cuban**

2046   0 - 0.5
283   0.6 - 0.8
101   0.9 - 1.2
113   1.3 - 3.0
20   3.1 - 6.9

— County Boundary
— City Boundary

Cuban

57,864	Persons
36	Median Age
$30,000	Median Household Income
$15,000	Median Personal Income of the US-born
$13,000	Median Personal Income of the foreign-born
89.8	Percent of persons 25 yrs+ who are foreign-born
14.6	Percent of foreign-born persons 25 yrs+ who immigrated 1980-90
49.5	Percent of persons 18 yrs+ who speak English only or very well
16.1	Percent of persons 25 yrs+ who are four-year college graduates
5.8	Percent of employed in managerial and professional occupations
45.4	Percent of occupied homes which are occupied by owner

20 Miles

Statistics and percents are for the Los Angeles CMSA (Los Angeles, Orange, Riverside, San Bernardino and Ventura Counties), 1990.

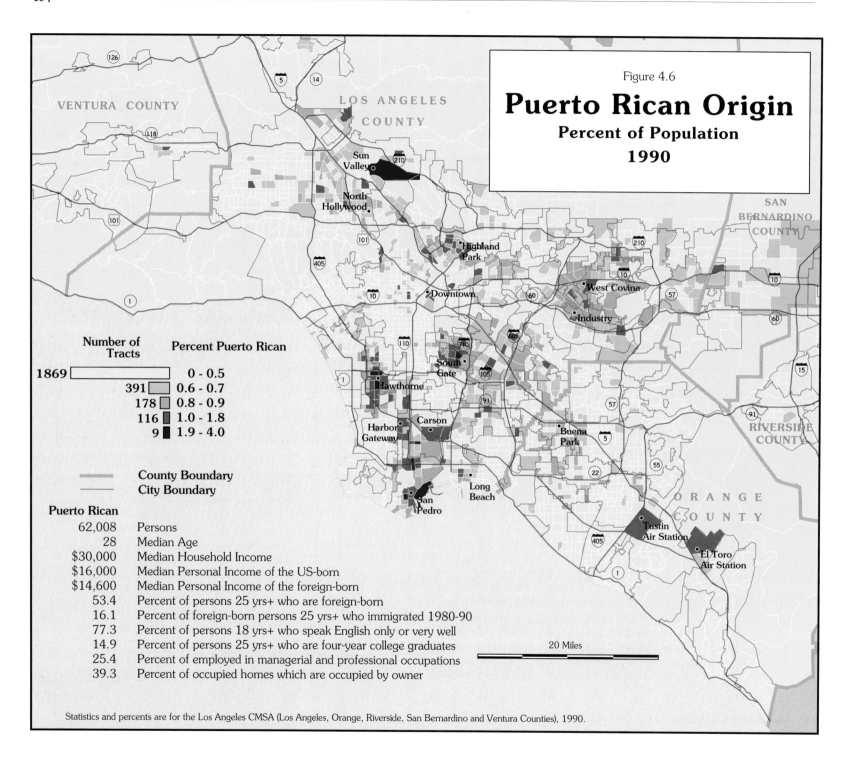

Figure 4.6

Puerto Rican Origin
Percent of Population
1990

VENTURA COUNTY

LOS ANGELES COUNTY

SAN BERNARDINO COUNTY

Sun Valley

North Hollywood

Highland Park

West Covina

Downtown

Industry

South Gate

Hawthorne

Carson

Harbor Gateway

Buena Park

San Pedro

Long Beach

ORANGE COUNTY

Tustin Air Station

El Toro Air Station

RIVERSIDE COUNTY

Number of Tracts	Percent Puerto Rican
1869	0 - 0.5
391	0.6 - 0.7
178	0.8 - 0.9
116	1.0 - 1.8
9	1.9 - 4.0

——— County Boundary
——— City Boundary

Puerto Rican

62,008	Persons
28	Median Age
$30,000	Median Household Income
$16,000	Median Personal Income of the US-born
$14,600	Median Personal Income of the foreign-born
53.4	Percent of persons 25 yrs+ who are foreign-born
16.1	Percent of foreign-born persons 25 yrs+ who immigrated 1980-90
77.3	Percent of persons 18 yrs+ who speak English only or very well
14.9	Percent of persons 25 yrs+ who are four-year college graduates
25.4	Percent of employed in managerial and professional occupations
39.3	Percent of occupied homes which are occupied by owner

20 Miles

Statistics and percents are for the Los Angeles CMSA (Los Angeles, Orange, Riverside, San Bernardino and Ventura Counties), 1990.

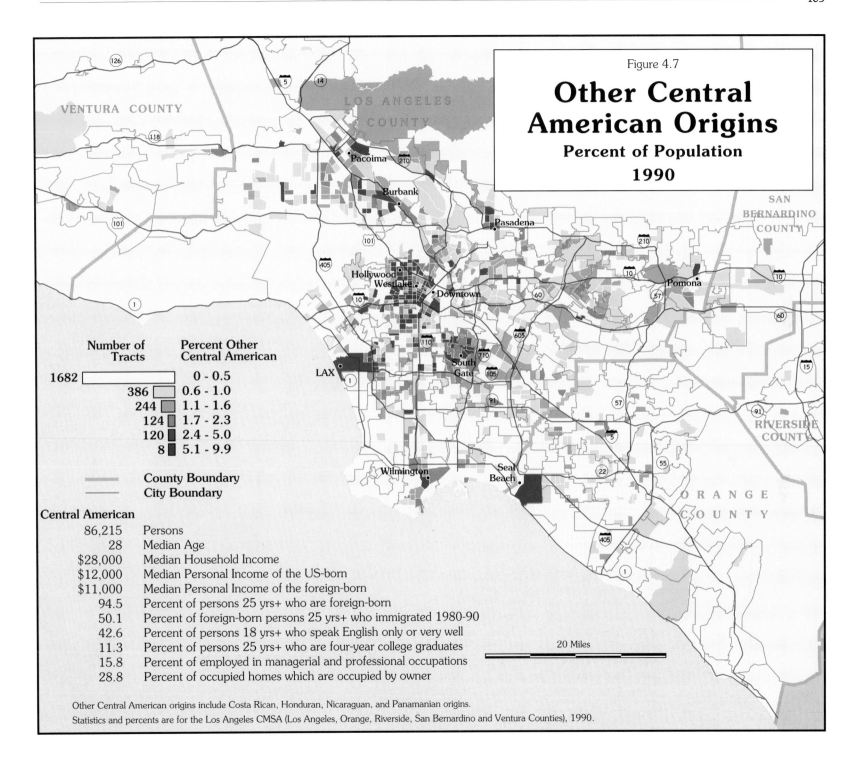

Figure 4.7

Other Central American Origins

Percent of Population

1990

VENTURA COUNTY

LOS ANGELES COUNTY

SAN BERNARDINO COUNTY

Pacoima

Burbank

Pasadena

Pomona

Hollywood
Westlake
Downtown

LAX

South Gate

Wilmington

Seal Beach

RIVERSIDE COUNTY

ORANGE COUNTY

Number of Tracts	Percent Other Central American
1682	0 - 0.5
386	0.6 - 1.0
244	1.1 - 1.6
124	1.7 - 2.3
120	2.4 - 5.0
8	5.1 - 9.9

───── County Boundary
───── City Boundary

Central American

86,215	Persons
28	Median Age
$28,000	Median Household Income
$12,000	Median Personal Income of the US-born
$11,000	Median Personal Income of the foreign-born
94.5	Percent of persons 25 yrs+ who are foreign-born
50.1	Percent of foreign-born persons 25 yrs+ who immigrated 1980-90
42.6	Percent of persons 18 yrs+ who speak English only or very well
11.3	Percent of persons 25 yrs+ who are four-year college graduates
15.8	Percent of employed in managerial and professional occupations
28.8	Percent of occupied homes which are occupied by owner

20 Miles

Other Central American origins include Costa Rican, Honduran, Nicaraguan, and Panamanian origins.

Statistics and percents are for the Los Angeles CMSA (Los Angeles, Orange, Riverside, San Bernardino and Ventura Counties), 1990.

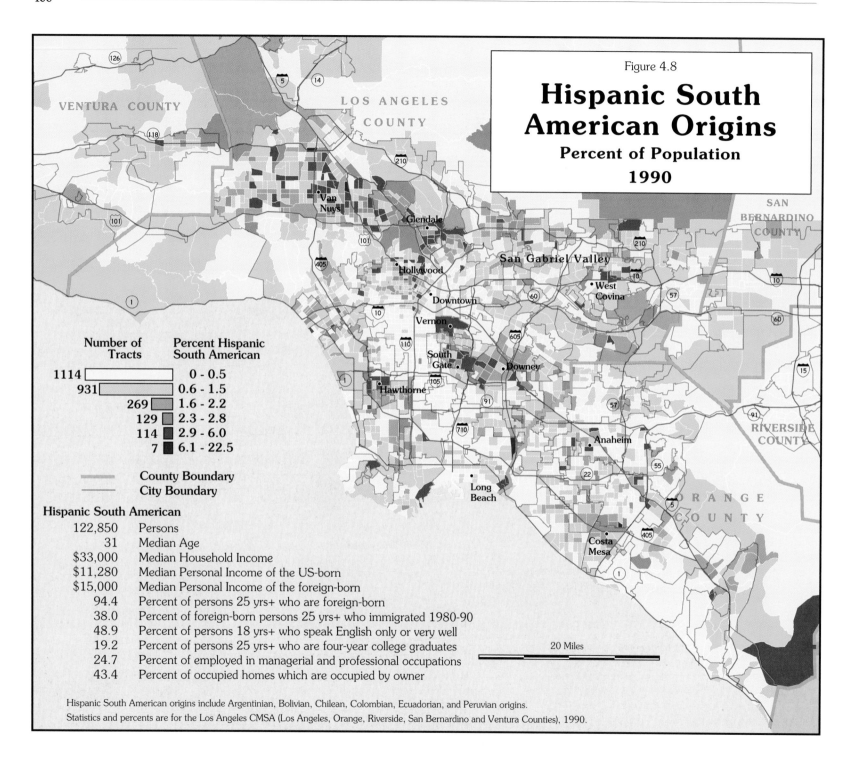

Figure 4.8

Hispanic South American Origins

Percent of Population
1990

Number of Tracts — **Percent Hispanic South American**

Number of Tracts		Percent Hispanic South American
1114		0 - 0.5
931		0.6 - 1.5
269		1.6 - 2.2
129		2.3 - 2.8
114		2.9 - 6.0
7		6.1 - 22.5

—— County Boundary
—— City Boundary

Hispanic South American

122,850	Persons
31	Median Age
$33,000	Median Household Income
$11,280	Median Personal Income of the US-born
$15,000	Median Personal Income of the foreign-born
94.4	Percent of persons 25 yrs+ who are foreign-born
38.0	Percent of foreign-born persons 25 yrs+ who immigrated 1980-90
48.9	Percent of persons 18 yrs+ who speak English only or very well
19.2	Percent of persons 25 yrs+ who are four-year college graduates
24.7	Percent of employed in managerial and professional occupations
43.4	Percent of occupied homes which are occupied by owner

20 Miles

Hispanic South American origins include Argentinian, Bolivian, Chilean, Colombian, Ecuadorian, and Peruvian origins.

Statistics and percents are for the Los Angeles CMSA (Los Angeles, Orange, Riverside, San Bernardino and Ventura Counties), 1990.

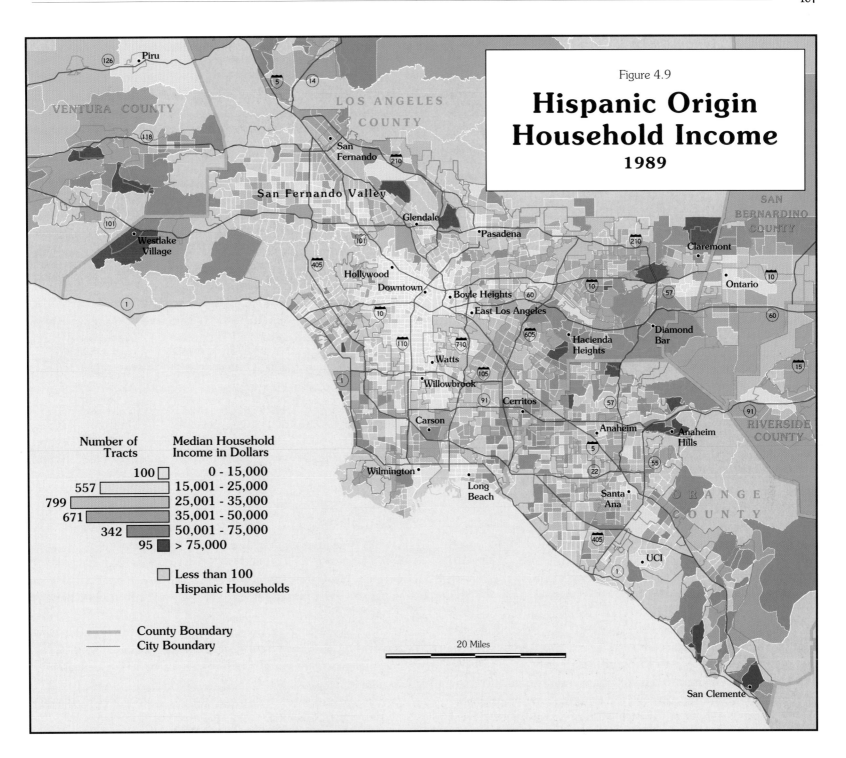

Figure 4.9

Hispanic Origin
Household Income
1989

Number of Tracts — **Median Household Income in Dollars**

Number of Tracts	Median Household Income in Dollars
100	0 - 15,000
557	15,001 - 25,000
799	25,001 - 35,000
671	35,001 - 50,000
342	50,001 - 75,000
95	> 75,000

Less than 100 Hispanic Households

County Boundary
City Boundary

20 Miles

and employment location are often interrelated. Both help explain the distribution of people of Mexican origin. This can be seen most dramatically in the high Mexican-origin percentages frequently found in or near the manufacturing and warehousing corridors that follow the rail lines (Figs. 2.3 and 4.2).

The Alameda Corridor links the central rail yards in Los Angeles and industrial cities like Vernon and South Gate with the massive oil refineries near Wilmington and the joint Los Angeles–Long Beach port facilities. Mexican proportions are highest near the two largest industrial concentrations at either end. Between 1930 and 1950 a sharp racial boundary existed along the broad swath of Alameda Street and the adjacent tracks. To the west were blacks and pockets of Mexicans near Alameda. To the east were whites. In the broad belt of industrial suburbs that stretches south from Huntington Park, Maywood, and Bell Gardens to Lynwood, the few small colonias were hardly evident amid the homes of white industrial workers, many of whom had come from Texas and Oklahoma.

A massive exodus of whites occurred after the mid-1960s, when the large companies began to close operations. Latinos, often immigrants directly from Mexico, eagerly bought or rented the vacated houses. In the 1980s housing became so crowded that the burgeoning Latino population spread west across the tracks, linking up geographically with old barrios in Willowbrook, Watts, and Florence.

The net effect is that the entire area between Downtown and Lynwood and Willowbrook is home to more than 400,000 people of Mexican origin, a high proportion of whom are recent immigrants. As of 1990 the residents of this area outnumbered those of the traditional Eastside, and Huntington Park's popular Latino shopping district along Pacific Boulevard is far larger than any such area on the Eastside or the Latino shopping strip along Broadway in Downtown.

Other industrial zones extend through the flatter lands east and southeast of Los Angeles (Fig. 2.3). One follows the Union Pacific route through the cities of Commerce and Industry. It then swings to the southeast, as both the railroad and a corridor of manufacturing and warehousing follow the valley of San Jose Creek up toward Pomona. A second industrial zone extends southeast through Montebello and Pico Rivera

to the oil-refining and ceramic-manufacturing center of Santa Fe Springs. The association between industry, railroad, and Mexican-origin population can also be seen near the Southern Pacific Railroad tracks which trend northwest from Downtown. An industrial corridor follows the railroad's straight course into the city of San Fernando and beyond, having replaced the earlier agriculture in that area.

Suburbanization in the San Gabriel Valley. During the last fifty years new subdivisions were created again and again out of once-thriving orange and walnut groves, vegetable farms, and ranch land. With the passage of time, acculturation, and improved economic status, many people could afford modest tract homes in many parts of Southern California, but the relatively nearby San Gabriel Valley suburbs were favored. Many thousands of better-educated and often white-collar Mexican American families have moved eastward to new homes in places like Baldwin Park, Covina, Azusa, and Walnut in the San Gabriel Valley. Others have sought lower house prices farther east in the new subdivisions of Riverside and San Bernardino Counties—the Inland Empire.

Even before 1940 some more middle-class Mexican American communities were established in Duarte, El Monte, Irwindale, and La Puente—contrasting with the somewhat poorer and less-educated population in Boyle Heights and Belvedere.[37] After World War II Mexican American servicemen typically returned to Los Angeles with improved English-language skills and a stronger pride in being U.S. citizens. Because of the postwar economic boom and government efforts to overcome discrimination in employment, they often could find more skilled and better-paying jobs than could their parents. However, these jobs were still usually blue collar in nature, as exemplified by work at the Ford automobile factory in Pico Rivera or the Kaiser steel mill in Fontana. Moreover, with the assistance of the G.I. bill, many families could now afford homes in the many subdivisions being created in the San Gabriel Valley and farther east in San Bernardino and Riverside Counties.

Housing discrimination against Mexican Americans slowly diminished after the war, but it was still present after the enforcement of restrictive covenants was outlawed by the U.S. Supreme Court in 1948.[38] After a realtor sold an El Monte home to Mexican Americans in 1948, the San Gabriel Valley Board of Realtors sent an angry resolution to the supervisors of Los Angeles County, stating that "We feel that our citizens are better off when allowed to congregate in districts or settlements, such as Irwindale for Mexicans."[39] Some Mexican American servicemen who attempted to purchase homes in the huge new suburb of Lakewood were refused, and others were told that they would be considered if they would state that their origin was Spanish rather than Mexican.[40]

Suburbanization in the San Gabriel Valley resulted in a merging with older resident Mexican populations—a few descendants of the old California rancho owners and the much larger numbers of people whose families had formerly done farmwork or railroad work.[41] Mexican immigrants had originally come to the northern San Gabriel Valley towns of Asuza, Duarte, Covina, Glendora, and San Dimas to work in the citrus industry or on the Santa Fe Railroad. In 1950 descendants of many of them were still living in small Mexican barrios across the railroad tracks from whites. Pomona's few Californios had been submerged by the tide of Anglos in the 1880s, and they ultimately became part of a low-status Mexican community which grew steadily with the immigration of new railroad and citrus workers.[42] To the south of the Citrus Belt, other families worked the vegetable fields in the lowlands, and especially river bottoms, of the San Gabriel Valley. Some people who owned their homes in the Eastside supplemented their incomes by commuting to harvest work. Others lived in ramshackle colonias near the fields, usually on unincorporated or little-valued land. One such place—on the east side of the San Gabriel River floodplain near Whittier and occasionally flooded out—was Jimtown, commemorated officially as Jimtown Park.

Thus, the San Gabriel Valley represents a mixing of major strains in the Mexican heritage of Southern California: a few descendants of Californio landowners; upwardly mobile, blue-collar families from the Eastside; and those whose roots lay directly in farming and railroad work. In this sense, the San Gabriel Valley best symbolizes the historical and socioeconomic diversity of the Mexican-origin population.

Within the fan-shaped sector of Mexican American settlement which extends eastward from its Eastside base, however, there are surprisingly low proportions of Latinos on the north and east sides of East Los Angeles, not far from Downtown (Fig. 4.2). This is Monterey Park, a mostly hilly and nonindustrial area. Because the city once prided itself on being restricted to whites, Mexican Americans settled in this city later and represented smaller proportions than in cities farther east. In addition, the Latino population in Monterey Park declined in the 1980s as a result of displacement by thousands of Chinese immigrants, who eagerly sought space in the city's apartments or bought homes from Latinos and others.

People of Guatemalan and Salvadoran Origins

Next to people of Mexican origin, those with roots in Guatemala and El Salvador easily constitute the second- and third-largest Hispanic populations in Southern California. More than 400,000 people from these two countries together were counted by the U.S. census. In fact, a substantial undercount is likely because so many arrived here illegally and as of 1990 still had an extremely insecure status. Because even census figures show that these two nationalities constituted 80 percent of all Central Americans in the region, our maps and analyses distinguish these two groups from others.

Guatemalans and Salvadorans differ primarily in that some Guatemalans in Los Angeles are Indians, which is not the case with Salvadorans. Nevertheless, their similarity in settlement and employment patterns and in socioeconomic status justifies treating them together (Figs. 4.3 and 4.4; Tables 8.4 and 8.6). Both nationalities include many people who entered the United States illegally, as well as many political refugees. These groups, as well as Nicaraguans, include people of opposing political allegiances in their countries of origin, but shifts in short-term U.S. government refugee policies have made the position of Salvadorans here particularly uncertain.

There are two keys to understanding the general features of the distribution of these two groups: their low average educational and income levels and the recency of their arrival. No ethnic groups in Southern California have higher proportions of immigrants among their adults. Almost two-thirds of Guatemalan and Salvadoran immigrants arrived in this country during the ten years previous to the census. Both low status and recency of arrival relate to low average ability in English, and all three factors explain their concentrated settlement in declining neighborhoods with housing that costs less than it does in other parts of Los Angeles.

Pico-Union and Westlake. By far the most important area for Guatemalans and Salvadorans is an area just west of Downtown. Since the 1920s, when local whites began to leave for more distant suburbs, it has been an area of initial settlement for Latino immigrants.[43] Many recent arrivals from Mexico have also settled there because it has more apartments and large houses carved into apartments than does the larger traditional barrio of the Eastside (Boyle Heights and East Los Angeles). Compared to the Mexican Eastside, it is also more accessible by bus to jobs serving affluent Westside residents.

The southern part of this area is known as "Pico-Union," for the intersection of Pico Boulevard and Union Street. However, MacArthur Park, with its small lake, is more centrally located within the larger Central American settlement, and the historic name "Westlake" for MacArthur Park has been resurrected as a label for the larger area including Pico-Union. To the northwest of Westlake one wedge of Central American settlement extends into the eastern part of Hollywood; another extends westward from Pico-Union and the University of Southern California into an area known as West Adams. These two westward thrusts of Central American neighborhoods are separated and, to a large extent, blocked by Koreatown.

The main focus of Westlake is along Alvarado Street near the park—a bustling walkway where independent discount shopkeepers, travel agents, courier-service operators, restaurant and bar owners, street vendors, drug dealers and addicts, sellers of phony identity cards, and panhandlers compete for the meager earnings of recent immigrants. Although whites and Koreans own some of the apartment buildings and businesses, most of the entrepreneurs are Latino. To the north, on Hollywood Boulevard, the dance clubs that used to swing for whites have become centers of Central American music and entertainment. From cramped, overcrowded apartments in Westlake, men and women make their way westward by bus to their jobs as maids, nannies, and handymen for affluent whites in places like Beverly Hills and Brentwood, or eastward to sewing work in the garment factories and janitorial jobs in Downtown office buildings. As with other immigrant groups, remittances sent home to Guatemala and El Salvador provide important support for relatives.

First developed more than a century ago as an attractive residential area close to Downtown, Westlake has deteriorated for the same general reasons most inner cities decline—the physical aging of houses and the replacement of middle-class families by poorer people. The absence of whites and the crowding of Central Americans in Westlake has been such that in Los Angeles County as of 1990 these two groups were as segregated residentially from whites as were blacks.[44]

A few thousand Mayan Indians from Guatemala also live in Westlake.[45] The chain migration of the largest group, the Kanjobal, and their association with the garment industry in Los Angeles probably began in 1976, when one Indian was persuaded to come and work in a factory here. At first all of the migrants were men, but then women and children began to follow. By the mid-1980s thousands of Mayan Indians had arrived in the Westlake section of Los Angeles, almost all of them illegally. The main concentration of the Kanjobal developed between 3d and 6th Streets not far west of the Harbor Freeway, and most Indians live near each other in a few apartment buildings, partly because of their inability to speak much Spanish. In this case, Indian linguistic acculturation has been primarily toward Spanish, a process begun in Guatemala.

Other locations. Many Salvadorans and Guatemalans have scattered far beyond Westlake, but this is a function less of assimilation than of the need to be close to the dispersed locations of potential employment—construction and various day-labor jobs, painting, auto repair, and working in car washes and restaurant kitchens (Tables 8.4 and 8.6). Because almost two-thirds of these immigrants arrived in the 1980s and because few came from middle- and upper-class families, not many are living in the better homes and tracts in Southern

California. The few Salvadorans who are found in high-income areas like Malibu and tracts in the Santa Monica Mountains between Santa Monica and the San Fernando Valley are typically live-in maids, nannies, or handymen.

Guatemalans and Salvadorans are proportionately strong in the San Fernando Valley, where they are found mostly in the same general areas as people of Mexican origin. These are areas of lower-cost housing, both apartments and older tract homes, much of which is near old industrial areas. In contrast, few are found in the western, northwestern, or southwestern parts of the San Fernando Valley, where homes are newer and larger. The same general association of these groups with lower-income areas near industry is found in many parts of Southern California. This is illustrated by the modest houses of Lennox just east of LAX and by the Atwater Village strip north of Downtown and next to the Southern Pacific railroad yards.

The fact that Guatemalans and Salvadorans differ in which specific tracts contain higher proportions of them is probably due to differences in chain migration—the social networks of relatives and villagers that direct newcomers to specific apartment buildings and neighborhoods where they know people. For example, in the city of Orange the different tracts that are emphasized on the two maps do not reflect differences in housing costs or other features of the tracts. It is simply that the cumulative effect of separate migration chains has resulted in slightly different locations for the two groups.

People of Cuban Origin

In 1960 the U.S. census reported 4,144 Cubans living in Los Angeles and Orange Counties, but at that time there were no significant concentrations of Cubans and no established Cuban community in Los Angeles.[46] The rapid growth of the Cuban population occurred after 1960, when refugees from Fidel Castro's regime began to settle in Los Angeles. However, as of 1990 approximately 3,800 pre-Castro Cuban emigrants—those who had immigrated to the United States before 1960—were living in the five-county area.[47] These constituted 9 percent of the Cuban immigrants in Southern California.

During the 1960s Cuban refugees flooded into Miami, Florida, and the U.S. government began a program to encourage refugees to disperse outside Miami.[48] The first of several waves arrived in Los Angeles in 1962, and various Catholic and other voluntary service agencies assisted many Cubans who wished to resettle here.[49] Cubans choosing to leave Miami for Los Angeles or elsewhere were often looking for better employment, moving to be close to family, or desirous of a less Cuban-centered environment.[50] Most Cubans in Southern California are not recent immigrants: 58 percent of foreign-born Cubans arrived in the United States between 1960 and 1975, and the last refugee wave occurred in the early 1980s.

Enclaves. As a result of refugee resettlement, the Cuban population in Southern California grew rapidly, to a 1970 total of 40,376 Cubans, and enclaves developed in parts of Los Angeles County. Cuban enclaves appeared to result both from the refugee-settlement efforts of the U.S. government and the voluntary agencies and from chain migration. Initially, the location of jobs and housing arranged by the early sponsors of refugees was probably of greatest importance in shaping the Cuban distribution. During and after the 1970s, a family member or friend often sponsored a Cuban being relocated to Los Angeles, which also tended to accentuate the earlier established pattern of settlement.[51]

In 1970 three enclaves held the largest numbers of Cubans. The first extended from Echo Park to East Hollywood and was focused between Sunset and Beverly Boulevards. The second and third concentrations were in the Bell–Huntington Park area and in the Inglewood-Hawthorne-Lennox area. Each of these three Cuban concentrations had more than 2,700 Cubans in 1970.[52] At that time there were also more than 1,700 Cubans in Glendale, plus more than 500 each in Pasadena, Burbank, Culver City, and Long Beach, as well as in the Palms–Mar Vista and Beverly Boulevard–Vermont Avenue sections of Los Angeles City. Other areas with concentrations of Cubans in 1970 included the southeastern San Fernando Valley, the Atwater Village area east of Interstate 5, and the Harbor Gateway area just south of Interstate 405. Some of these concentrations first appeared when Cubans arriving in the 1960s searched for and moved into areas of less expensive housing but still wished to live near other Cubans.[53] However, the Cuban cluster in the Lennox and Inglewood area also reflected the early employment of many Cuban refugees at LAX, often in the food-service industries. In more expensive areas like Pasadena, Cuban residents are frequently the successful architects, engineers, and business people who were some of the first refugees after Castro's takeover and who today are owners of important Southern California companies.

Nearly all the Cuban concentrations that appear in Figure 4.5 were significant in the distribution of 1970, despite a large new wave of Cubans in the early 1980s. The newcomers—less political refugees than economic migrants—were part of the approximately 125,000 Cubans who fled to Florida from the port of Mariel between late April and September 1980 and have been dubbed the "Marielitos."[54] In Southern California these refugees did not form separate settlements because their sponsors were mostly fellow Cubans who had arrived earlier.

Although Marielitos were living in many parts of Southern California in 1990, they have tended to locate in Cuban enclaves with lower-cost housing. The 5,400 Marielitos represented 9 percent of the 1990 Cuban population total in Southern California. However, within the large Bell–Huntington Park enclave this cohort constituted 15 percent of the enclave's Cubans. In that enclave are popular Cuban restaurants, and the Casa Cuba provided shelter and assistance for Marielitos and other refugees. Similarly, Marielitos made up 20 percent of all Cubans in the southeastern San Fernando Valley and in the Echo Park–East Hollywood area. In contrast, only 4 percent of Glendale's Cubans in 1990 were Marielitos, and Marielitos have been much less likely than other Cubans to live in the newer sections of Orange, Ventura, Riverside, and San Bernardino Counties. Among Cubans the more concentrated settlement pattern of the Marielitos is expected as a result of their later arrival and presumed lower level of acculturation.[55]

None of the Cuban concentrations has been located in a predominantly black area. This is consistent with the fact that only 2 percent of Cubans living in Southern California in 1990 identified their race as black (Table 3.2).

Over the past two decades the Cuban population has grown slowly and the distribution has shifted little. Cubans, like so many Koreans and Central Americans, have tended to leave the older and poorer area between East Hollywood and Silver Lake, and other immigrants have crowded into these neighborhoods. Cubans also extended their settlement into Downey, where the newer homes may have been especially attractive to Cubans who had been living in the Huntington Park area.

Cubans have dispersed widely. This deconcentration reflects their increasing cultural, social, and economic assimilation into the larger society. Although this change is hardly evident in Figure 4.5 (because the map is based on percentages), some Cubans have moved to the newer suburbs of Los Angeles County, and even more have relocated in Orange and the other surrounding counties. Whereas in 1970 Los Angeles County contained 92 percent of Southern California's Cubans, by 1990 only 79 percent lived in the county.

Many Cubans who settled in Los Angeles in the late 1960s have since returned to Miami, where the very large Cuban community permits them to live their lives completely enveloped by a transplanted Cuban culture.

People of Puerto Rican Origin

Puerto Ricans have their origins outside the U.S. mainland, but they are different from immigrant groups in that they are not immigrants in the legal sense. The United States took possession of the island of Puerto Rico in 1898, after the defeat of Spain in the Spanish-American War, and it has remained a U.S. territory. Since 1917 Puerto Ricans have been U.S. citizens, and, as such, they need no visa or other permission to travel to or live in any of the fifty states.

Because Puerto Rico is politically affiliated with the United States, people born in Puerto Rico are not considered foreign-born in the U.S. census. The 3.5 percent of adult Puerto Ricans in Southern California who are considered foreign-born were born in some other country. In many cases these foreign-born are the children of Puerto Rican servicemen in the U.S. military on duty in Germany, Japan, or Korea.

Puerto Ricans arrived in Los Angeles a few years after the United States took over their island. Recruited for work on Hawaii's sugar plantations as early as 1900, they were shipped across the United States by rail and then sent by boat to Hawaii.[56] En route to the West Coast, some laborers decided they had made a mistake. Presumably, these men who jumped the train in Los Angeles or San Francisco either returned home or settled in California. Also, some Puerto Rican plantation laborers came to Los Angeles to live after completing their labor contracts in Hawaii.

By 1910 eight Puerto Ricans (including two women) were living in Los Angeles.[57] At least a few of these may have remained in Los Angeles and acted as magnets for the Puerto Rican migrants who arrived over the following decades. Indeed, both Los Angeles and San Francisco have old, established Puerto Rican populations.[58] Compared with Puerto Ricans in the northeastern and Midwestern United States, those in California were unusual, in that as early as 1970 fewer than half of them had been born in Puerto Rico. In addition to having greater proportions born in one of the fifty states, Puerto Ricans in Los Angeles have had higher socioeconomic status than have Puerto Ricans living elsewhere on the mainland. A clear reflection of their greater mainland experience and higher status is the fact that in 1990 the percentage of Puerto Ricans over the age of 18 who spoke English only or very well was unusually high (77 percent), compared with other Hispanic groups in Southern California.[59]

The high level of cultural and economic assimilation compared with Mexican and Central American Latinos is reflected in the dispersal of most Puerto Ricans across Southern California (Fig. 4.6). In all except nine tracts they represent less than 2 percent of the total population. For example, in the large tract that stands out most in Figure 4.6 (Sun Valley in the eastern San Fernando Valley) there were only 66 Puerto Ricans out of a total tract population of 3,540.

Although Puerto Ricans in general show a great range of racial characteristics, those in Southern California tend to be lighter skinned. With only 3 percent of Puerto Ricans in this area identifying their race as black (Table 3.2), few Puerto Ricans have chosen to live in predominantly black areas.

Weak multitract clustering of Puerto Ricans may be related to the locations of Spanish-speaking areas and employment. Puerto Ricans who live in Highland Park and some of the same localities as Cubans (the Lennox-Hawthorne and South Gate–Huntington Park areas) have chosen less expensive housing in ethnically diverse areas where Spanish is widely spoken. Because so many Puerto Ricans have worked in hospitals and in aerospace manufacturing, they show a very slight tendency to locate near sources of employment. This is the case among Puerto Ricans in the San Bernardino area, where unusually high percentages of them work at the Loma Linda University Medical Center and in other hospitals.[60]

However, the Puerto Ricans in neighborhoods that appear in Figure 4.6 as clusters are outnumbered by those who are more widely dispersed in Southern California. For example, Puerto Ricans living in the area between El Segundo and the Palos Verdes Peninsula are particularly likely to be employed in aerospace manufacturing, but most of them do not live in a Puerto Rican cluster.[61] This geographical scattering is consistent with the complete lack of distinctive Puerto Rican landmarks, neighborhoods, community organizations, and restaurants in Southern California.[62] Although individual and family identity as Puerto Ricans remains important for many, they appear to have little desire or need to create a more formal ethnic community. This lack of community development is presumably related to their high level of assimilation and their secure status as U.S. citizens.

People of Other Central American Origins

In addition to the Hispanic nationalities already discussed, Southern California has attracted people from other countries in Central America and from South America. For purposes of displaying distributions, these populations have been combined into two groups: those with origins in Spanish-speaking Central American countries other than El Salvador and Guatemala; and those from Spanish-speaking countries in South America.

Figure 4.7 includes people who reported the following origins, listed here with their total 1990 populations in Southern

California: Costa Ricans (13,619), Hondurans (25,109), Nicaraguans (39, 110), and Panamanians (7,014).

Three decades ago the total number of all Central Americans in Southern California was only about 6,000.[63] In contrast to the predominance of Guatemalans and Salvadorans among recent immigrants, about half of the Central Americans at that time were Nicaraguans. In one 1960s study most of the fifty-one Nicaraguans interviewed—probably typical of Central American immigrants to Los Angeles at that time—came from larger cities and were literate in Spanish.[64] Although the majority had not attended school and had come to Los Angeles partly to go to school, three women had completed university studies. Some Nicaraguans were clerical workers or professionals, but most had poor skills in English and worked in factories.

After 1960, other Central Americans in Southern California came to include both the wealthy and the poor, as well as political refugees. As people fled abrupt shifts of power during the 1970s and 1980s, Hispanic nationalities in Southern California became somewhat divided politically.

Distribution. The locations of these Central Americans resembles in some ways that of specific groups already covered (Fig. 4.7). The concentration in Huntington Park–South Gate is shared by Cubans and Puerto Ricans, as well as Mexican immigrants, and the varied Hispanic nationalities is reflected in the range of restaurants in the area. Those who live in Lennox and Westchester and in the southeast San Fernando Valley also share those general areas with Cubans and Puerto Ricans. It is likely that some of the residents of these clusters are employed at LAX or Burbank Airport. This is because both Cuban and Puerto Rican men are slightly overrepresented in the air-transportation industry. Costa Rican men are employed in that industry at seven times the rate expected for their population size.

However, other Central Americans who live west of Downtown are not likely to be in the heart of the Westlake and Pico-Union barrio, where Guatemalans and Salvadorans are so concentrated. Rather, Hondurans, Nicaraguans, and others are more typically found farther west—in Koreatown, in Hollywood north of Beverly Boulevard, and in the Country Club Park and Mid-City areas. Some Central Americans living in and near Country Club Park are live-in housekeepers and nannies, but most Central Americans in the area west of Westlake and Hoover Street are immigrants who can afford the somewhat higher rents and better neighborhoods compared with Westlake but who enjoy having Central American markets, restaurants, and shops not far away.

Central Americans are often located in areas that are in transition between black and Latino. The largest such area is south of Interstate 10. Over the previous two decades blacks tended to move westward, as large numbers of Latino immigrants arrived. As of 1990 this zone of greatest black-Latino residential mixing was located on either side of Western Avenue north of Slauson Avenue, but by the late 1990s it may have shifted westward with the continued greater influx of Latinos. The same situation has been occurring in Pasadena and Pacoima; in 1990 the percentage of other Central Americans is particularly high in tracts where Latinos have been replacing black residents.

It is possible that many of the Latinos who led these ethnic residential shifts are Central Americans with darker skins, particularly the one-third of Panamanians who identified their race as black (Table 3.2). In fact, those Panamanians who lived in Inglewood, Pasadena, San Bernardino, and the Crenshaw area were especially likely to have identified their race as black in the census. However, Panamanians living in the southwestern San Fernando Valley, where few blacks live, were also likely to report themselves as black, suggesting that such Central Americans may also be pioneers of black settlement in areas that are mostly white and Latino.

Other tracts with relatively high percentages of Central Americans are evident as isolated neighborhoods in such places as Pomona, Alhambra, Reseda, and Culver City. This pattern may result primarily from varied chain migrations of immigrants, some perhaps focused on only a few apartment buildings in certain tracts. Another tract that stands out is in Orange County (Fig. 4.7). The tract lies within the U.S. Naval Weapons Station, a weapons and ammunition storage facility, and many of its residents are in the Navy.

People of Hispanic South American Origins

The nationalities in this aggregation are: Argentinean (23,298), Bolivian (5,650), Chilean (11, 590), Colombian (31,790), Ecuadorian (22,961), and Peruvian (27,458).[65]

Because South American immigrants have to travel great distances by air, they generally have higher occupational status and incomes than do people from Central America. Thus, they can avoid poor areas like Westlake and South Central.

Many South Americans are well educated and fluent in English. Highly acculturated immigrants have little reason to concentrate geographically, and the map correctly shows South Americans as widely dispersed in Southern California (Fig. 4.8). Nevertheless, areas where South Americans do settle together tend to command moderate or higher home and apartment prices. A few clusters appear in more expensive areas, like the hills of Glendora and Rolling Hills Estates and Toluca Lake, Tarzana, and Northridge in the San Fernando Valley.

South Americans overlap in distribution to some extent with Central Americans, Cubans, and Puerto Ricans. A concentration of South Americans shows up in South Gate, where the other groups are also found, and in nearby Downey, where so many Cubans settled.

To some extent the map legend, showing percentages ranging up to 22.5 percent, is misleading because of the small populations in some tracts. The two tracts with the highest percentages of South Americans had total populations of only 119 and 216. However, the eastern San Fernando Valley does contain two tracts that are important because each tract numbers over 140 South Americans.

South Americans are also overrepresented in the federal prison at the western end of Terminal Island in Los Angeles Harbor. Anyone can speculate as to the crimes for which they were convicted.

Hispanic Median Household Income

Figure 4.9 shows areal variations in the median of total income earned by members of those households in which the householder (or head of household) is of Hispanic origin. As we have observed elsewhere, lower incomes tend to characterize areas of older housing, which are found most commonly in the more central parts of long-established places like Los Angeles, Long Beach, Wilmington, Santa Ana, and Ontario. Incomes of residents tend to increase in areas where homes and apartments are newer and more expensive, with highest incomes typically found in the more distant suburbs.

Areal differences in age and cost of housing explain Hispanic income variations better than does an association between traditional barrios and very low income. With the large influx and widespread settlement of Latino immigrants during the 1980s, historic barrios established in the early twentieth century have diminished in significance and are less distinctive in their poverty. Hispanic household incomes average less than $25,000 in traditional barrios in Wilmington, Long Beach, Ontario, and in the older part of the Mexican Eastside, which comprises Boyle Heights and East Los Angeles. However, to the west and south of Downtown—as far south as Compton—Latinos average similarly very low incomes. These are areas in which the Latino population has been built up since 1970, particularly by the arrival of poor immigrants who found the cheapest housing available without regard to location in a traditional barrio.

The very low income of Latino immigrant areas is illustrated by a large square tract in Willowbrook, an area east of Interstate 110 and just south of Watts. What is unusual about this tract is the large income differential between its ethnic groups. Black households, which constitute about two-thirds of the tract's residents, have a median income of more than $25,000. Other characteristics of the populations help explain the income differences and are a reminder that a single tract or neighborhood may contain ethnic populations which differ substantially in socioeconomic status. Most of the Latinos in the tract are immigrants, typically employed as machine operators in manufacturing, and only 25 percent have graduated from high school. In contrast, the typical black resident of the tract works in a clerical or administrative-support occupation, and 71 percent of black residents are high-school graduates.

Older, traditional barrios are often not the poorest Hispanic areas. Both the Mexican Eastside and the eastern San

Fernando Valley illustrate this point. The city of San Fernando and adjacent Pacoima, to the south, constitute the oldest barrio in the San Fernando Valley. Yet the map shows that Hispanic incomes were higher in all tracts of this area than in some more distant low-rent and industrial areas.

In general, Latino professionals and business people—whether third-generation residents of Southern California or new immigrants from South America—find newer homes in suburban areas, where many of them assimilate partly into the larger white society and are sometimes not recognized as Latino. The most affluent Latinos are found in parts of Manhattan Beach, Westlake Village, Laguna Niguel, Yorba Linda, Anaheim Hills, and La Habra Heights, where the median Latino income is more than $75,000.

Downtown. The lowest incomes of all are found in the industrial and warehousing area just east of Downtown. This zone is sometimes called "The Flats" because its low, flat surface represents the floodplain of the Los Angeles River before its channel was encased in concrete. The low-income area extends right into the older section of Downtown, where buildings date from the early twentieth century. The southern and eastern sides of the Downtown area include Skid Row, the sweatshops on the upper floors of old, run-down office buildings, and dilapidated old apartment buildings. The poor people in this area are ethnically diverse, but Latinos are most numerous.

Downtown property owners and other members of the social and political elite (usually Anglo) have tried to set up various indirect barriers to retard the westward spread of this low-income population, to prevent its intrusion into the zone of much-newer banks, modern hotels, and office buildings.[66] This geographical competition for control of different Downtown zones is not just a matter of rich and poor, because white-Latino differences accentuate the class contrast.

Hill Street and Grand Avenue represent the zone of especially intense conflict—over space, land use, and the types of people who dominate the sidewalks and public spaces during the day. A one-block walk up Bunker Hill from Hill Street or Pershing Square brings the pedestrian to Grand Avenue and entry into the "the Hill"—the middle-class zone of secretaries,

attorneys, bankers, and other business people. Farther east, the Ronald Reagan Office Building represents an attempt to reclaim for middle-class workers the daytime space at least to Spring Street. The ethnic and income contrasts continue after the workday ends, as 80 percent of the residents of the new apartment buildings on Bunker Hill are non-Hispanic whites and their median household income is over $40,000.

Notes

1. The diversity of tribes, subgroups, and intermarriage among Indian groups in Southern California is much greater than is indicated in Table 4.1. Details of identities and change in Los Angeles are discussed in Weibel-Orlando (1991), chapter 3.

2. Weibel-Orlando (1991), 34–42.

3. Weibel-Orlando (1991), 38.

4. Mott (1990); Pulskamp (1990).

5. Price (1968), 169.

6. Price (1968); Weibel-Orlando (1991), 14–18.

7. Citron (1988); Weibel-Orlando (1991), 20–22.

8. Price (1968).

9. Weibel-Orlando (1991), 23–31.

10. Alvarez (1995).

11. Almaguer (1994), 212.

12. The historic association between the Mexican population and industry is less likely to apply to industry based on post-1960 technology. For example, in the northwestern corner of the San Fernando Valley is the large, modern Chatsworth industrial park. Because its high-tech manufacturing is unobtrusive and kept within areas zoned for industry, the surrounding residential areas are still expensive residential areas in which few people of Mexican origin can afford to live.

13. If the ethnic distribution is examined historically and in greater detail than is shown on these maps, displacements connected with freeway construction and urban renewal are evident. Several freeways have been cut through the Mexican Eastside. The city's clearance of poor people also created displacements. The mostly Mexican inhabitants of Chavez Ravine were cleared in the 1950s to make room for Dodger Stadium, and the ethnically mixed population of Bunker Hill was forced out in the early 1960s. See Gottlieb and Wolt (1977) and Acuña (1984) for details. In the 1980s the people evicted from the poor Temple-Beaudry neighborhood

west of L.A.'s Downtown in anticipation of the new Central City West development were mostly Latinos.

14. For the general tendency, see Allen and Turner (1996b).

15. For a vivid demonstration of these changes, see the map of black population change, 1980–1990, in Turner and Allen (1991).

16. Settlement concentrations are based on distribution maps of both U.S.-born and Mexican-born Hispanics as of 1910. These maps were produced by Christopher Bruce of the Department of Geography, California State University, Northridge, from the residents enumerated in the manuscript schedules of the U.S. census. In addition, McEuen (1914) and Sánchez (1993) are useful in understanding early Mexican settlements.

17. Romo (1983), 72.

18. Sánchez (1993), 70.

19. Acuña (1996), 29–30.

20. Examples of colonias connected with industry and the Pacific Electric Railway are from Garcia (1994), 69–70.

21. McWilliams (1973), 217; Sánchez (1993), 80.

22. Romo (1983), 126.

23. Romo (1983), 61.

24. McWilliams (1973), 316.

25. Sánchez (1993), 80, 198. Chapter 3 in Sánchez's *Becoming Mexican American* provides an excellent description of life in the incipient Mexican Eastside before 1930.

26. Sánchez (1993), 141.

27. Ethnic proportions are based on 1950 census data reported in Frank (1955), Table 9. More detailed distributions in 1940, based on unpublished tract-level data for both blacks and Mexican immigrants, can be found in Hanson and Beckett (1944).

28. Economic and social trends in the Mexican Eastside, including the gang situation, are clearly presented in Moore and Vigil (1993).

29. Our discussion of the origins of the San Fernando Mexican community is based on Zierer (1934).

30. Mulholland (1987), 49, 116–20.

31. McBane (1995).

32. Comments on Piru and Fillmore by Martha Menchaca at the University of Texas at Austin were helpful. Details on the limited interaction of the Mexican and white communities in Santa Paula are from her anthropological study (Menchaca 1995).

33. Details of the origins of many barrios in Orange County as farmworker colonias are based on Gilbert Gonzalez's studies (1989–1990, 1994) and discussion with Professor Gonzalez.

34. Camarillo (1971).

35. The historical development of Hawaiian Gardens is covered in Jacobs (1977).

36. Allen and Turner (1995).

37. Shevky and Williams (1949), 70.

38. *Shelley v. Kraemer,* 334 U.S. 72.

39. Senn (1948).

40. Connelly (1951).

41. Rios-Bustamante and Castillo (1986), 144.

42. Peñalosa (1963).

43. The best description of Westlake is provided in Chinchilla, Hamilton, and Loucky (1993).

44. Allen and Turner (1996a), 20, 21.

45. Peñalosa (1986). See also Hernandez (1984). Anthropologist James Loucky identified the location of Kanjobal Indians within the Westlake area. It is likely that the undercount of Mayan Indians in Los Angeles in the 1990 census was unusually large.

46. Gil (1976), 54; Agustin Prado, one of California's commissioners for refugees and a Cuban who settled in Los Angeles in 1960, interviewed April 1996.

47. These figures, as well as others concerning the 1980–1981 refugee cohort (Marielitos), are based on analysis of PUMS data on Cubans in Southern California.

48. Details of resettlement under the Cuban Refugee Program can be found in Boswell and Curtis (1984).

49. Clark (1963); Gil (1976), 52.

50. Gil (1976), 55.

51. Gil (1976), 72, 75, 76.

52. U.S. Bureau of the Census (1972), Table P–2.

53. Agustin Prado, interviewed April 1996.

54. Masud-Piloto (1996), 92–93.

55. Allen and Turner (1996b).

56. Souza (1984), Maldonado (1979). One man who jumped the train in Los Angeles when he heard that pay and working conditions in Hawaii would be less than promised watched his belongings go on to Hawaii without him. He lived a hand-to-mouth existence for months in Los Angeles, hoping somehow to make enough money to return to his home in Puerto Rico (Contract Slave's Pathetic Craving, 1903).

57. In 1910 three of the Puerto Ricans were unemployed; the others worked as a laborer, a cigar maker, a seamstress, a teamster, and a cook. Puerto Ricans in Los Angeles as listed in manuscript census schedules were analyzed by Christopher Bruce, a graduate

student in geography at California State University, Northridge.

58. Fitzpatrick (1980).

59. This figure is based on PUMS data that are discussed in chapter 9.

60. This employment specialization is evident from analysis of PUMS data.

61. The employment specialization in that area is based on analysis of PUMS data.

62. Hernandez (1994).

63. U.S. Bureau of the Census (1962b).

64. Stirling (1968).

65. The smaller nationalities in Southern California, based on PUMS estimates, are not included: 486 Paraguayans; 1,901 Uruguayans; 2,794 Venezuelans; and the 812 who listed "South American." Also, we do not treat the 54,877 who identified their origin as "Spaniard" because they are of direct European origin. Brazilians speak Portuguese and do not consider themselves Hispanic.

66. These conflicts over space in Downtown have been effectively analyzed by Mike Davis (1990), 228–36, (1992).

5. Distributions: Asians and Pacific Islanders

A great range of ethnic groups, most with high proportions of recent immigrants, is included in the category of Asians and Pacific Islanders. The first four groups covered—Chinese, Japanese, Filipinos, and Koreans—were the earliest Asians to settle in Southern California, but by the 1950s representatives of nearly all Asian and Pacific Islander groups had arrived.

Chinese

The Chinese were the first in the sequence of Asian groups that entered Southern California. Most of the earliest Chinese arrivals were men who hoped to find gold and to work hard as laborers for a few years in order to return home rich. U.S. immigration restrictions in the 1880s stopped the immigration of Chinese laborers and of the wives of laborers already here, leading to a decline of Southern California's Chinese population in the early 1900s—just as the numbers of Japanese immigrants were growing.[1] By 1990, however, renewed immigration meant that the Chinese had again become the largest Asian group in the region.

Increasing diversity among the Chinese. Immigrants who have arrived in the United States since World War II represent a varied group in terms of culture, language, and country of birth. In the nineteenth century the Chinese who came to the United States had roots in southeastern China—in villages near the provincial capital of Guangzhou. Because that city was known to Americans as Canton, the early immigrants have been described as "Cantonese" in cultural heritage. In fact, until 1943, when the United States again began to allow some Chinese to enter the country, nearly all Chinese immigrants and their descendants had been of Cantonese origin.

As the numbers of Chinese students, refugees, and immigrants grew slowly in the 1950s and rapidly after 1965, other regions and languages became well represented in Southern California. Most from North China speak what Westerners call Mandarin, the common language of that region but one with many dialect variations. Immigrants from Taiwan speak Taiwanese or Mandarin, but both of those languages are very different from Cantonese, which is still the language of Hong Kong. These differences in regional origin and language have meant that the Chinese in Southern California are divided into multiple social networks.

In addition, thousands of Chinese immigrants to Southern California are members of families that had been living for at least two generations in other countries, usually in Southeast Asia. That experience clearly modified the original Chinese culture. Although the Chinese in Vietnam, for example, constituted a separate, business-oriented ethnic group that did not participate in Vietnamese public institutions, many Chinese who lived in Vietnam identify strongly with that country and speak its language.[2] At the same time, most Chinese in Southeast Asia also speak the language of their family's ultimate origin in China, such as the chao-zhou dialect of eastern Guangzhou, which is spoken by most Chinese in Vietnam.

In order words, what may appear on the surface to be a single Chinese ethnic group is in many ways a set of subgroups. The range of subgroups is indicated in Table 5.1 by the countries of birth of Southern Californians who reported their race as Chinese.

Table 5.1 Leading Countries of Birth of Chinese Immigrants to Southern California, 1990

Birth Place	Number
People's Republic of China	77,628
Taiwan	66,242
Vietnam	33,589
Hong Kong[a]	22,938
Cambodia	4,299
Philippines	3,761
Indonesia	3,150
Burma	2,793
Malaysia	2,466
Thailand	1,637
Singapore	1,565
Korea	1,125
Laos	994

Source: U.S. Bureau of the Census (1992).

[a]Many people born in Hong Kong have parents who were refugees from the People's Republic of China.

Although changes in the origins of Chinese immigrants have been dramatic over the more than 125 years of Chinese residence here, no less important have been changes in their distribution within Southern California.

Historic Chinatowns. In the 1860s Chinese began to settle east of the old city plaza in Los Angeles, in a place which would soon become the first of a sequence of Chinatowns in the city. That tiny enclave was focused on Calle de los Negros (Negro Alley), a narrow street just one block long which became the site of the 1871 massacre of nineteen Chinese. This was almost the only place in the city where Chinese were permitted to live unless they were servants in the homes of white families. The population grew as many Chinese men who had been scattered around Southern California in gangs of farm and construction laborers left that work and headed for a less

itinerant life in Los Angeles. By 1890 a bustling Chinese quarter had grown up southeast of the plaza and just east of Alameda Street.[3]

Many of these early Chinese became farmers, supplying fresh vegetables to city residents. They farmed on land a mile or two to the south, irrigating their crops with water from the nearby Los Angeles River. This early entrepreneurial focus on the production and sale of fresh vegetables led to additional clusters of Chinese close to their farm areas.

In 1910 Chinatown was the clear focus of the Chinese population in Los Angeles, but some Chinese produce sellers still lived near their old vegetable fields, and a few Chinese servants were found in other parts of the city. Although Chinatown remained a residential and business center through the 1920s, Chinese families and many of the elderly bachelors began moving to other sections of the city. In 1933 the demolition of this Old Chinatown began. The space was ultimately used for the new railroad terminal, Union Station, which prompted the relocation of Chinatown in 1938.

Chinatown was resituated about half a mile to the north, between Hill and Broadway. Although this New Chinatown was designed particularly to attract tourists, the poverty of most Chinese and the restrictions on where they could live meant that Chinatown remained the heart of the "old" Los Angeles Chinese community as of 1940.[4] At that time the only other Chinese residential concentration was near produce markets and industry—in the same area where Chinese had farmed forty years earlier, roughly between San Pedro Street and Central Avenue and from 7th Street south to East Adams. Residents of both areas were Cantonese in speech and customs (Fig. 3.1).

Suburbanization after World War II led many residents to move out of Chinatown and other central locations and into the older suburbs, which whites were vacating. These areas, variously pioneered by Japanese and blacks in earlier decades, became Los Angeles' most important areas of multiracial housing during the 1960s. Thus, by 1970 many long-term resident Chinese families had moved into the predominantly black West Adams district and into predominantly Japanese Crenshaw.[5] Others pushed to the east, beyond Lincoln Heights and the Mexican Eastside, into Monterey Park and Alhambra, establishing a foundation for the large-scale Chinese immigration and settlement that would begin during the 1970s.

Contemporary Chinatown. Beginning in the 1960s Chinatown became much more diverse in terms of the backgrounds of its Chinese residents and business people. Immigrants whose numbers grew steadily between the 1950s and 1990 came from many different parts of China, as well as from Hong Kong, Taiwan, and Southeast Asia. Their varied languages, identities, and cultural traditions meant that Chinatown was no longer anything like a cohesive community, and tensions between anti-Communist Taiwanese nationalists and immigrants from the Communist People's Republic of China have been strong, though usually hidden.

Chinatown changed particularly during the 1980s, as more and more Chinese from Southeast Asia opened up businesses. Their bustling malls and shops echo some of the mood of Saigon and contrast with the older, slower-paced, and less prosperous northern part of Chinatown. Chinese-Vietnamese own many of the new food stores, clothing shops, restaurants, and malls in Chinatown. By 1996 about 60 percent of Chinatown's businesses were owned by Chinese from Vietnam, and their successes have stood in sharp contrast to the section north of College Street, where the old businesses started by the Cantonese a half-century ago were not doing well.[6]

Despite the economic rejuvenation of the southern part of Chinatown, those Chinese developers and merchants who are from Vietnam and Cambodia have had great difficulty in being accepted into the traditional business elite of Chinatown. The older Taiwanese and Cantonese leaders consider the Southeast Asian Chinese very different culturally, too clannish, too aggressive, and too willing to take risks in business. In addition, they appeared to have settled in Chinatown initially to take advantage of the social services there.

Residents of modern Chinatown are poorer, less educated, less acculturated, and more recently arrived than the Chinese who live elsewhere in Southern California (Table 5.2). This illustrates the tendency for less-acculturated immigrants to live among familiar people and institutions in ethnic enclaves.

With such a large immigration of Chinese during the 1980s, apartments in Chinatown have been in short supply. Some immigrants have spilled over into surrounding areas, such as the slopes of Alpine Hill or farther on into Echo Park, and others have located east of the Los Angeles River, in Lincoln Heights. Some of Chinatown's elderly residents rent apartments in the government-subsidized Cathay Manor, but when this sixteen-story building first opened in the mid-1980s it could house only about a tenth of the people who applied for residence.[7] On the first floor of Cathay Manor is the Chinatown Service Center, an agency which treats health, language, housing, employment, and psychological problems faced by immigrants.

The census tract within which Chinatown is located is 72 percent Chinese—the most intensely Chinese tract in Southern California (Fig. 5.1). However, if ethnic Chinese from Vietnam and Cambodia who reported their race as Vietnamese and Cambodian were included, the percentage of Chinese in Chinatown would rise to 80 percent.

Chinatown continues to be an important shopping focus for Chinese in the greater Los Angeles area as well as for some tourists. For most non-Chinese it remains the best-known and

Table 5.2 Characteristics of Chinatown Residents and All Chinese Immigrants, 1990

Characteristics	Chinatown	Southern California
Percent Arriving in the United States, 1987-1990	20.1	15.4
Percent Speaking English Only or Very Well	14.7	33.8
Percent High School Graduates	37.1	77.0
Percent Naturalized Citizens	29.4	47.1

Source: U.S. Bureau of the Census (1992).

Notes: Only the foreign-born ages 25-64 are included. Chinatown percentages are those for the PUMA in which Chinatown is located.

symbolic focus of Chinese life in the region. Its lively and bustling markets, offices, restaurants, and walkways make it a unique place in Southern California—and an interesting one to visit. However, Chinatown's poverty and lower level of acculturation make it unrepresentative of the Chinese in Southern California. Moreover, the approximately 9,000 Chinese (including those from Vietnam and Cambodia) who live in the three census tracts of greater Chinatown constitute less than 3 percent of the Chinese population of Southern California.

The San Gabriel Valley. This large valley to the east of Chinatown became the most popular home for immigrants who could afford better housing than Chinatown. So many immigrants have settled in the valley that it reflects contemporary Chinese life in Southern California much better than does Chinatown, now an outdated symbol.

The origin of the Chinese push into the San Gabriel Valley can be traced to a single Chinese immigrant, Frederick Hsieh, who arrived as a student in 1963. Hsieh decided in the 1970s to develop America's first suburban Chinatown, and for this he chose Monterey Park, a suburban city a few miles east of Los Angeles.[8] Advertising Monterey Park as the "Chinese Beverly Hills" in Hong Kong and Taiwan newspapers, he attracted buyers of land, homes, and businesses. Many of these families feared political changes in Hong Kong and Taiwan and wanted a more secure investment.

For this reason Chinese immigration in the 1970s and 1980s included a higher proportion of wealthy people than is usually found among immigrants. A great many Chinese bought homes in and around Monterey Park, and many soon opened businesses in the area, frequently catering to the needs of the growing Chinese population. Other businesses that were located outside Chinese or Asian concentrations tended to serve the general population.

The white population, which had previously dominated Monterey Park culturally and politically, found it difficult to accept the immigrants. Tensions between older residents and Chinese newcomers were partly cultural and partly a function of class differences. Established residents were dismayed and frustrated by the rapid building of entire shopping centers and office complexes by rich Taiwanese. Many of the Chinese were wealthier than the whites and seemed to show little interest in acculturating to white America. Resentment was expressed in the anti-immigrant effort to make English an official language in California and in a slow-growth movement.

The San Gabriel Valley has become the largest, most intensively Chinese settlement within Southern California (Fig. 5.1). By 1990 Monterey Park had experienced such a large in-movement of Chinese and departure of whites and others that it was 36 percent Chinese and was often referred to as Little Taipei. Neighboring Alhambra was 26 percent Chinese.[9] Significant also is the higher proportion of Taiwanese in this area compared with other sections; to some extent a Taiwanese society has been transplanted here. Mandarin has become the common Chinese language in the valley, and immigrants are easily able to live and work comfortably in this area without speaking or understanding English.

Some of the wealthiest Chinese bought homes in San Marino, a small city that had long been a prestigious symbol of gracious living for the white elite. White residents were shocked to find that immigrants were able to afford the lovely homes and estates of this city, but by 1990 more than a quarter of San Marino's population was Chinese.

Other affluent Chinese moved into newer suburban developments in the eastern San Gabriel Valley, in places like Rowland Heights and the cities of Walnut and Diamond Bar. In response to the shopping and service needs of Chinese in these areas, a great many Chinese businesses have located together along a mile-long stretch of Colima Road in Rowland Heights and Industry (parallel to the 60 Freeway). In nearby Hacienda Heights the Taiwanese presence has been accentuated by the palatial Hsi Lai Buddhist Temple and monastery, which has attracted a higher proportion of Chinese to that portion of the valley. However, the Hsi Lai Temple was built not only to serve Chinese people in the area but to enhance understanding between an Eastern culture and that of the West.[10] Some whites have become members of the temple.

All these residents make the eastern San Gabriel Valley the largest center of affluent Chinese in Southern California. Yet they are not isolated from a Chinese-oriented life, for they can find whatever goods and services they need right in the valley. They feel no need to visit Chinatown.

Other areas. Apart from the San Gabriel Valley settlements, the city of Cerritos to the south has been very attractive to many Chinese and other Asians, who value this new city especially because of the excellent reputation of its schools. Some Chinese have moved to the wealthy community of Rancho Palos Verdes in the hills near the coast, and others in Irvine are employed in companies or are students or teachers at the University of California at Irvine campus

In general, Chinese who could afford to do so have moved into expensive suburban homes, not in specifically Asian

Table 5.3   Chinese-Vietnamese in Selected Areas,1990

Area	Percent of Vietnamese Race with Chinese Ancestry	Percent of Chinese Race Born in Vietnam
Orange County	3.2	11.0
Long Beach	11.8	21.9
Cerritos	.8	3.0
Gardena–Hawthorne–Lawndale area	6.7	14.7
West San Fernando Valley	11.8	7.5
Chinatown area	19.5	13.7
Monterey Park–Alhambra–Rosemead area	19.6	22.9
Southern California average	8.1	11.8

Source: U.S. Bureau of the Census (1992).

Note: The data are two separate but only partial indicators of the Chinese-Vietnamese population in Southern California.The total of this group can be estimated from the total of Chinese born in Vietnam (33,589, shown in Table 5.1) plus Vietnamese reporting Chinese ancestry (11,597). However, this total of 45,186 does not include the U.S.born children of the former group. It appears that at least three-quarters of Chinese-Vietnamese reported their race as Chinese on the census questionnaire. This is consistent with findings at the national level (Rumbaut 1995, 245).

neighborhoods but in areas where whites have been the leading group. This is evident in West Hills and in the Granada Hills area of the San Fernando Valley. The many Christians among Chinese immigrants have frequently organized and built churches, thus providing a Chinese institutional center within these mostly white suburbs. Few Chinese have located in the areas beyond those shown in Figure 5.1 because few enjoy living so far from their work and their ethnic communities.

Chinese-Vietnamese. People of Chinese family heritage who had been living in Vietnam are a somewhat distinct group. They are usually called "Chinese-Vietnamese" to distinguish them from the larger group of "ethnic Vietnamese." Although they speak Vietnamese, they have separate social networks from most of the ethnic Vietnamese and partially share an identity with Chinese from other countries. To some extent these various linkages are reflected in differences in residential locations (Table 5.3). The lower percentage of Chinese-Vietnamese in Orange County contrasts with the higher percentages in Chinatown and the Monterey Park area, and Cerritos is exceptional in having both Chinese and ethnic Vietnamese but very few Chinese-Vietnamese.

Japanese

Japanese are exceptional among the Asian groups in that immigrants are less important proportionately than is the long-established community of Japanese Americans. During the past three decades students and businessmen have visited, but the numbers of new immigrants coming to Southern California have been small because income and working conditions in the United States have not been sufficiently better than those in Japan to make migration attractive. For this reason Japanese families who have been Americans for three or more generations also have a larger role than do recent immigrants in defining the distribution of Japanese in Southern California.

Early laborers and families. When Chinese laborers were excluded in the 1880s, the Japanese became the major labor source for Hawaii and the western states. In contrast to the Chinese, however, potential emigrants were screened by the Japanese government, and only men who were healthy, literate, and ambitious were allowed to leave.[11]

From 1890 to about 1900 most Japanese men who came to Southern California worked on farms, citrus ranches, and railroads—doing the physical labor that the Chinese had done in previous decades. The rapidly expanding city of Los Angeles needed construction workers, and many Japanese responded. For instance, the Pacific Electric Railway hired Japanese workers to break a strike of Mexican workers in 1903. Also, more than 2,000 Japanese moved to Los Angeles after the 1906 San Francisco earthquake and fire and because of the increasingly vicious anti-Japanese mood there during those years.[12] Furthermore, business opportunities abounded in Los Angeles, and some Japanese immigrants opened retail shops or restaurants. During the first three decades of the twentieth century, many thousands immigrated directly from Japan or moved from Hawaii or San Francisco.

Through an informal arrangement in 1907 between the United States and Japanese governments, known as the Gentlemen's Agreement, Japan agreed to prohibit the emigration of laborers, while the United States agreed to allow the immigration of merchants, farmers, and the wives and children of Japanese men already here. This led to a large flow of "picture brides"—women chosen on the basis of their photographs to be wives of Japanese men already in this country. At the same time, many of the older single men returned to Japan.

As a result, families were established at an early period, and by 1920 a second generation was appearing. Although the U.S. Congress stopped all immigration from Japan in 1924, the foundation for a Japanese American community had been laid. By 1930 the 35,000 Japanese in Los Angeles County constituted 36 percent of the Japanese in the entire state.

Internment. In early 1942, soon after the Japanese invaded Pearl Harbor, Japanese residents of Southern California and most other parts of the West were forced by the U.S. government to leave their homes. Because they were considered a potential threat in the war against Japan, nearly all the Japanese were required to live in various desert camps for about three years, an experience usually called internment. Two-thirds of those arbitrarily sent to the camps were the U.S.-citizen sons and daughters of immigrants, rather than Japanese nationals.

After 1945 most Japanese returned to Southern California to face huge economic losses. They had not been able to earn income during internment, and many families' property had been either sold in a panic before evacuation or damaged or stolen during internment. Because the internment experience was so demoralizing and such an important watershed in the history of Japanese in Southern California, our interpretation of specific settlements covers first the period before 1942 and then the post-1945 years.

Little Tokyo. Within the city of Los Angeles, the most important early Japanese enclave was centered around 1st Street between Alameda and Los Angeles Streets—an area which, by 1905, Americans were already calling "Little Tokyo." Employment agencies, several boarding houses for Japanese laborers, and train stations were nearby, as were the companies that signed up crews of Japanese to clean people's homes.

Although the first Japanese businesses were not located in Little Tokyo, by 1910 they were clustering more on 1st Street because of its lower rents and its central location for serving the growing concentration of Japanese workers and families. And as more Japanese settled in Little Tokyo, earlier residents tended to move out, and Japanese frequently bought up already established retail shops. By 1915 Japanese owned twelve restaurants, six general stores, nine barber shops, fourteen hotels, and more than fifty other businesses on 1st Street between Central Avenue and Los Angeles Street.[13] These served both neighborhood Japanese and others who would come into Little Tokyo to shop.

The Japanese in Little Tokyo constituted only about a third of the neighborhood residents, but the area continued to be an important residential and business center for Japanese in Los Angeles until 1942 (Fig. 3.1).[14]

Other Los Angeles enclaves. Because of housing discrimination on the part of whites, Japanese residential enclaves appeared only in certain less attractive residential neighborhoods. These were typically near commercial or industrial areas or on low land that was poorly drained. Often they were near black settlements.

Japanese with higher incomes were not allowed to buy or rent in better areas. Thus, Japanese tended to cluster in those neighborhoods where a few earlier arrivals had become somewhat accepted. In part, the choice of enclave was also a function of social networks based on prefecture of origin in Japan.[15] Japanese usually bought or rented from whites who were departing for newer suburbs.

Between 1906 and 1910 Japanese began to move into three neighborhoods. These came to be called the Virgil Avenue (also called Madison Avenue) neighborhood; 10th Street (later, Olympic Boulevard), which was called "Uptown" by the Japanese; and the West Jefferson Street area (Fig. 3.1), identified as "Southwest" by some Japanese.[16] Over the next two decades these developed into Japanese and multiracial enclaves. Most had a Japanese grocery store and a Japanese church and school. Some Japanese residents were clerks, doctors, or restaurant owners; at least half the men were day laborers, nurserymen, or landscape gardeners who worked on the estates of white families in Hollywood or the Wilshire area.

Tensions with the surrounding white population occasionally flared. In 1919 white residents in the 10th Street area attempted with some success to replace all Japanese tenants with whites by raising rents excessively. Although some Japanese moved out of the 10th Street area and some of those who remained hired guards for protection, the enclave persisted. Still farther south was the West Jefferson area. Few whites remained there in the 1920s, when most Japanese were moving in, but its moderately priced and attractive homes made it the premier black settlement in Los Angeles, and black homeowners were willing to rent to Japanese.

Beginning in the late 1920s some Japanese families with higher incomes began to extend the West Jefferson enclave by moving a few blocks to the west. Houses became available when whites anticipated black and Japanese encroachment and chose to leave the area.[17] This spatial expansion of Japanese settlement in the direction of newer residential construction was led by those Japanese with more money. As both Japanese and blacks moved into white areas, home prices generally dropped. By 1940 the Japanese enclave extended as far west as Van Ness Avenue.

Another larger Japanese enclave was in West Los Angeles near Sawtelle Boulevard, between the Veterans Hospital and Pico Boulevard.[18] Almost all of the men were gardeners who tended the grounds of wealthy families in nearby Westwood, Bel Air, Brentwood, and Beverly Hills. Women found other work, for landscape gardening was a man's job. The Sawtelle neighborhood had both boarding houses for single men and bungalows and apartments for families, as well as the usual church and grocery stores.

To the east of Little Tokyo and the Los Angeles River, a Japanese enclave also developed in Boyle Heights.[19] Beginning with the building of a Japanese Buddhist temple in 1904, its early focus was around 2d and Savannah Streets. The temple and the continued availability of land for farms and nurseries just east of the city enticed more Japanese. With numerous new bungalows, Japanese churches, large and well-kept homes, Boyle Heights attracted many former residents of Little Tokyo. It was probably the most attractive and largest of the areas in Los Angeles where Japanese lived during the 1920s, and in 1940 it was home to more than 3,000 Japanese (Fig. 3.1).

Terminal Island. An important concentration of Japanese fishermen existed during these pre-1942 years. Although Italian and Croatian immigrants were also important in establishing the local fishing industry, these Japanese lived and worked by themselves. After the harbor for the city of Los Angeles was improved in the early twentieth century, a Japanese fishing village was developed at Fish Harbor on the west end of Terminal Island, across the main harbor channel from San Pedro. From the early 1920s until 1942 it was home to more than 2,000 people.[20] Most of the mackerel, tuna, and other fish were canned right in the village. Those Japanese who were not fishing or operating restaurants or stores worked in the canneries, and all lived in houses or boarding houses owned by the canneries. The U.S. government took over that part of the island in February 1942 and soon demolished the housing.

When former Japanese residents returned in 1945 to find the village destroyed, they scattered to San Pedro, Long Beach, and elsewhere.[21] Perhaps because nearly all the families had originated from the same prefecture in Japan and because growing up on Terminal Island had been such an indelible experience, the aging former residents and their children still gather at annual picnics and occasionally revisit the island.

Irrigation farming. In the 1890s Japanese immigrants were typically viewed as replacements for earlier Chinese workers on citrus ranches and vegetable farms. However, soon after 1910 Mexicans were taking their places, and many Japanese in Southern California were operating their own farms. Japanese farmers took advantage of the agricultural demand during World War I and raised sugar beets, lettuce, cabbage, celery, various vegetables, and strawberries. Later, many Japanese came to specialize in flowers and nursery stock.

Independent farming of specialty crops not raised by white farmers was a good occupation for Japanese for several reasons. Many had come from farm families in Japan, no direct competition with whites was involved, and English-language skills were not necessary. However, the Alien Land Laws, which began in 1913 and remained in effect until 1948, made it illegal for immigrant Japanese to own or rent land in California. The existence of those laws persuaded some Japanese to leave farming and open nurseries on rented urban land. Although agricultural ownership was possible through U.S.-born children, 90 percent of 1,500 Japanese farmers in Los Angeles County in 1940 were tenants, paying cash rent to use small plots for their horticulture.[22]

Japanese farms were distributed throughout Southern California, but most were in Los Angeles County to the south and southeast of Los Angeles City—from El Segundo and the Palos Verdes Peninsula east to Downey and El Monte. In addition, Japanese constituted three-quarters of the farmers in the Venice and Mar Vista areas, where they specialized in celery, flowers, and nursery products.

Early Gardena. The first independent farming by Japanese in the broad zone south of Los Angeles City was in

Moneta, now a part of the city of Gardena. What became the highly successful and large Japanese farm community of Gardena had its beginnings in 1902, when a Japanese husband and wife arrived from Hawaii and bought some land already planted in strawberries.[23] The crop's success persuaded the husband to lease and buy more acres. By 1906 other Japanese couples had settled and bought land, usually with money saved from work in Hawaii or northern California. Farming was done by family units, and a Japanese cooperative growers' association was formed the next year. Strawberries were profitable because they could be easily shipped to the large city market in Los Angeles via the rail line from Redondo Beach, and after 1909 refrigerated boxcars made possible sales in San Francisco, Chicago, and elsewhere.

After about 1913 Japanese farmers began to grow more vegetables because of a strawberry-plant disease and higher prices for vegetables during World War I. In addition, worry over potential loss of leased or owned land under the new Alien Land Laws made it preferable for farmers to grow crops, such as vegetables, which required a commitment to only a single year of farming on any one plot. With an intensive farming focus already developed in Moneta, new arrivals often found better opportunities elsewhere, and Japanese farming became dispersed over much of southern Los Angeles County.

The foundations of Japanese settlement in the Gardena and South Bay areas were thus laid with early landownership by farm families and the development of organizations for mutual support and marketing. Social networks based on Japanese region of origin were also important. In about 1930, more than 30 percent of Gardena residents had roots in the Hiroshima area.[24] By that time the Japanese community in the Gardena area had its own stores, professionals, publications, cultural organizations, and recreational activities, making it virtually independent of the local white communities.

Orange County farms. Some early Japanese followed railroad or farmwork or letters from friends and headed to counties around Los Angeles, where many families later opened grocery stores or other businesses in small hamlets. Most of them, however, became farmers. In 1930 Orange

County contained 1,600 Japanese, while Riverside, San Bernardino, and Ventura Counties each had nearly 600 Japanese residents.

Several Japanese settlements, all connected with farming, grew up in Orange County.[25] The Seal Beach–Bixby Japanese farm community was spread across the county line but sold its produce in Long Beach. Anaheim was the most important settlement, with a school, church, and several stores to serve the dispersed Japanese community. Irvine Ranch had several villages for its Japanese farmworkers, and other small communities were located in the modern cities of Garden Grove, Orange, Fountain Valley, and Huntington Beach.

Return to Southern California in 1945. After three years of internment, many—but not all—Japanese chose to return to Southern California. They were joined by others who had formerly lived in the Central Valley or elsewhere but had heard about Los Angeles and specific Japanese enclaves during discussions in the camps.

In 1945 and 1946, however, the continued wartime housing shortage and discrimination made reestablishment more difficult. Japanese even had trouble gaining access to houses and shops which they owned, and for a time many lived in trailer camps, abandoned army barracks, or hostels while housing and other claims of losses were sorted out.[26] By the end of 1947, almost 90 percent of Japanese in Los Angeles County had some permanent housing.

In rural areas, the loss of leased Japanese farmland during the war and the rapid subdivision of former farm areas for new homes resulted in a major geographical shift of Japanese from rural Southern California to urban areas. After a few years those newcomers and many old-time residents who could afford to do so moved into or toward newer suburbs. Regional economic expansion and a decline in discrimination made it possible for them to shift out of narrow occupational niches and later to improve their status substantially.

Early enclaves re-created. The old Japanese enclaves of 1940 and 1950 have continued to exist (Fig. 3.2). This remains true despite the decline of Japanese numbers due to reduced immigration and to suburbanization. The various neighborhoods have also seen in-movement by blacks, Mexicans, Central Americans, and Koreans. In 1990 the old enclaves of Boyle Heights, Virgil Avenue, 10th Street, and Sawtelle are still visible (Fig. 5.2), and some have expanded in area.

Although the southern edge of the Virgil Avenue neighborhood was destroyed in the 1950s to make room for the 101 Freeway, more than 250 Japanese remained in that enclave as of 1990. Additional Japanese now live in the enclave's extension to the northeast into Echo Park and Silver Lake. Many residents are the elderly sons and daughters of the early immigrants, but the area is also home to younger families and newcomers from Japan. Two miles to the south, Japanese have been equally persistent in the Olympic Boulevard enclave, despite the settlement of many hundreds of Koreans and Latinos during the intervening decades. Japanese settlement has also expanded somewhat to the west, into the more expensive homes of Country Club Park.

In the case of West Jefferson, a shift to newer housing in contiguous areas to the west, past Crenshaw Boulevard, occurred in the late 1940s and 1950s. The new area was by 1950 the largest and most important in-town Japanese enclave, usually called Crenshaw (Fig. 3.2). Japanese residents shopped at the Japanese-dominated Crenshaw Square, at the intersection of Crenshaw and Jefferson Boulevards. Although in the 1970s and 1980s many Japanese moved out of Crenshaw, in 1990 more than 2,200 were still living there.

The Japanese also returned to Venice, Culver City, and Mar Vista, where farms and nurseries were still common in the mid-1950s.[27] Although farmland was being replaced by housing tracts, many families probably remained in the area as some men became involved in retail sales of nursery goods to new suburban residents.

A bit to the north, in Sawtelle, three-quarters of employed Japanese men in 1946 were landscape or maintenance gardeners on the estates of the wealthy whites. Two-thirds of them had lived in Sawtelle before the war.[28] Work in contract gardening continued to attract young men as apprentices. In the early 1950s the supply of apprentice gardeners was augmented by a special immigration of Japanese refugees from natural disasters.[29] These men, mostly from two towns in Kagoshima, settled into prewar enclaves, particularly Sawtelle. Some men brought families. Single men stayed at the boarding houses, which functioned into the 1960s as employment centers and banks for the new immigrant gardeners.

More recently, the Sawtelle enclave has been invigorated with new stores and offices. It and the Mar Vista enclave have coalesced into a major Japanese population center (Fig. 5.2).

New suburban developments. During the decade after World War II much new housing became available on the fringes of already built-up areas, and many people who could afford the move did so. Also, the anti-Japanese hostility of the prewar period, at least in urban areas, came to be replaced by greater acceptance, and white developers and homeowners were much more willing to sell or rent to Japanese and other minority families than they had been before the war. For the Japanese, recently constructed subdivisions were especially good locations for the nursery business.

Suburbanization opened up lower-cost housing in older areas that had not permitted Japanese residents before the war. For example, in the 1950s many Japanese left Boyle Heights for new homes in Monterey Park, the adjacent part of East Los Angeles, and Montebello—just north and east of the Mexican Eastside. The deconcentration has continued, with Japanese settling in newer homes in Monterey Hills and South Pasadena or much farther east—in Industry and Hacienda Heights.

The modest new homes in the eastern San Fernando Valley also attracted many Japanese, particularly new families being formed by the U.S.-born who had been teenagers or young adults in the internment camps.[30] Some initial settlement was on segregated blocks, but such segregation declined sharply in the 1950s. The low percentage of Japanese in Sun Valley, North Hollywood, and Pacoima as of 1990 is deceptive: Japanese community centers came to be located in these places, and a language school, a Buddhist temple, and annual festivals continue to attract people (Fig. 5.2).

Gardena and Torrance. The most important Japanese suburbanization has occurred in the greater Gardena area. As rural land disappeared, many families who had farmed before the war became suburban dwellers. They were joined by families who moved south from Crenshaw, Olympic Boulevard, and the other enclaves in Los Angeles to the tract homes that were being built. During the 1950s Gardena's Japanese population grew to five times its 1950 total. Nearby cities—primarily Torrance, Redondo Beach, and the Harbor Gateway section of Los Angeles—have absorbed additional growth (Fig. 5.2).

The size of the Japanese American community in and near Gardena makes possible an almost completely Japanese-oriented life for those who wish it. This means attending a Japanese school or judo club; being active in a Japanese church, scout troop, and the Japanese Cultural Institute; celebrating traditional holidays; joining all-Japanese clubs and volleyball and baseball teams; socializing completely with Japanese Americans; and finding a Japanese American spouse.[31] Some Japanese American teenagers from outside Gardena perceive the "Gardena girls" as somewhat distinctive in hair, dress, makeup, and ability to speak Japanese. People raised in the "Japanese ghetto" of Gardena may feel uncomfortable with whites. In contrast, young people who grew up in mostly white neighborhoods elsewhere in Southern California are not apt to think of themselves as Japanese or as different from their white friends.

An important but separate component of the large Japanese population in the Gardena-Torrance area has been Japanese nationals (citizens of Japan) who are living temporarily in the United States.[32] There are musicians, artists, journalists, and entrepreneurs. The most prominent of the Japanese nationals are executive managers of companies like Toyota and Honda. Typically the men are assigned to Southern California for a few years but do not plan to settle permanently.

Most such families live in the more expensive homes of Torrance, Palos Verdes Estates, Rancho Palos Verdes, and various Orange County cities. They enjoy the low, ranch-style houses and ocean views, and the area is easily accessible to the offices of Japanese corporations in Orange County and southern Los Angeles County. The more affluent play golf and tennis, and several dozen of them are members of the Rolling Hills Country Club. They support local Japanese choral societies and shop in the Yaohan supermarket in Torrance.

These Japanese visitors have only superficial contact with local Japanese American families, most of whom are third- or fourth-generation Americans. Because the cultures of each are so different, it is not surprising that they constitute two separate societies. As the children of the visiting managers become partially Americanized, however, their parents often seek to reinforce their Japanese identity by means of private Japanese schooling on weekends. Japanese Americans sometimes consider the newcomers rude, spoiled, or ostentatious, but the wealthy sojourners from Japan have helped fund Japanese American businesses in Gardena, as well as the Pacific Square shopping center.

Modern Little Tokyo. After Japanese residents were ordered to depart in 1942, their apartments and shops in Little Tokyo were taken over by blacks, who had also been suffering a shortage of housing. Japanese returned from the camps and reestablished their ownership of property, but for more than twenty years Little Tokyo remained poor, like other old sections near downtowns in American cities. However, beginning about 1970, urban renewal revitalized and reshaped Little Tokyo into a modern commercial complex, designed both to accommodate visiting Japanese businessmen and tourists and to symbolize the culture and prosperity of Japan and Japanese Americans. The area thrived especially during the 1980s, prior to the economic recession that began in 1990.

Little Tokyo's redevelopment has been supported by individual Japanese Americans, the U.S. government, Los Angeles city government, and Japanese corporations.[33] Over the past twenty-five years the various new hotels and cultural centers, restaurants and banks, walkways and shopping malls, gardens, sculptures, and Buddhist temples have eliminated the look of poverty that characterized old Little Tokyo.[34] At the east end of the row of historic buildings on 1st Street is the Japanese American National Museum, expressly dedicated to preserving and sharing the Japanese American experience.

With the widespread availability of suburban housing after World War II, Little Tokyo was never again a leading residential center for Los Angeles' Japanese. In 1990 it was home to fewer than 700 Japanese, nearly all of whom lived in one of three attractive apartment complexes. Most were foreign born, and many were elderly and had low incomes. For these residents, the Japanese food stores, the accentuation of Japanese culture in renovated Little Tokyo, and the companionship of other immigrants combine to make decent homes for many whose children and grandchildren live in the suburbs.

The geographical stability of Japanese urban enclaves. Most enclaves of pre-1942 settlement remain evident in the 1990 distribution, and most old Japanese neighborhoods have persisted in the same place or have shifted only slightly, despite incomes that permitted mobility. In 1933 a similar observation was made: "They [the Japanese] do not like to move from place to place, but once they move they become settled for a long time."[35] This, as well as the continued gatherings of former residents of the Terminal Island fishing village, suggests that greater emotional links to home places might be a trait found among older Japanese immigrants.[36]

Two additional factors help explain the residential stability of early Japanese enclaves. Compared with the early Chinese in Los Angeles, the higher proportions of married-couple families among the Japanese resulted in greater rootedness in neighborhoods. Also, with diminished immigration from Japan, the proportion of U.S.-born was much higher in 1990 among the Japanese than among the Chinese or other Asians. This indicates the greater role of the earlier settlements in the 1990 residential distribution of Japanese. Related to all this are mobility differences among generations: older immigrants and their children, who themselves were typically elderly in 1990, have been more likely to remain in the enclaves than have the third generation, who typically live in middle-class white areas.[37]

Filipinos

Most Filipinos in Southern California arrived after the major 1965 change in U.S. immigration law. Nevertheless, like the Chinese and Japanese, Filipino settlements existed before that time, and some of them have continued to be important.

As with other Asian ethnic groups, differences over time in the numbers and characteristics of immigrants are primarily a function of changes in U.S. immigration laws. Because the Philippines was U.S. territory, Filipinos were not restricted by the 1924 immigration law which prohibited any immigration from Asian countries.[38] From 1924 until 1934, when another U.S. law limited entry to only fifty Filipinos per year, the Philippines was the only Asian source for agricultural workers in California and Hawaii.

Most Filipino men who came to California during those years were laborers. They planned on staying only for a few years, and few women accompanied them.[39] The men were either single or had left their wives at home. The result was that among Filipinos in California in 1930 men outnumbered women sixteen to one. In contrast, those who were recruited for plantation work in Hawaii often brought their wives and established families there.

Most of the men never returned home, however, partly because they could not afford the passage and partly because meager earnings here would make their sojourn a failure in the eyes of people back home. Some Filipino men married white women out of state since interracial marriage was illegal within California before 1948. Today, many U.S.-born Filipinos are descendants of the early migrants; a few of the old men were still living as of 1990.

There is substantial diversity among Filipinos. Chinese families settled in the Philippines, as they did elsewhere in Southeast Asia, but intermarriage between Chinese and Filipinos has been prevalent enough that the Chinese ethnic distinction is less important in the Philippines than in other Southeast Asian countries (Table 5.1). Nevertheless, regional differences in language within the Philippines remain significant among immigrants in Southern California, as do social connections based on locality of origin. Thus, Filipinos frequently describe themselves as internally divided with respect to language, region of origin in the Philippines, and politics.[40]

Many people who are not Filipinos are unaware of the large numbers of Filipinos in Southern California because their cultural impact has not been large. Few Filipinos have attained higher public offices, and Filipino ethnic organizations tend to focus on internal group matters. Basic landscape characteristics also play a role in a group's visibility. Filipino settlements lack distinctive religious buildings because most Filipinos simply become part of local Catholic or sometimes Protestant churches, and their ethnic institutions are not readily noticed by the general public. Filipino restaurants are small and have never achieved a market beyond the ethnic group itself, and the low percentage of self-employed among Filipinos means that signs promoting Filipino-owned business are not common.

Early settlement. The first large group of Filipino migrants arrived in Los Angeles in the 1920s. Some in this first wave had been superior students who migrated with the intention of continuing their studies in this country—the land that supposedly exemplified democracy, justice, and opportunity. Instead, they found racial animosity. Most Filipino immigrants, however, were not educated. Some who settled in cities became busboys or dishwashers in restaurants, managers of pool halls or barber shops, or servants of rich white families. Other Filipinos ended up as farmworkers. For most, dreams of a better life in California never came true.

A small Filipino section in Downtown was evident by the mid-1920s in its collection of barber shops, pool halls, restaurants, dance halls, rooming houses, and employment agencies. Filipino houseboys and chauffeurs strolled the area when off duty from their work for the elite of Hollywood.[41] In those days many of the Filipino bachelors who gathered on Main Street (near the present-day Children's Museum) left Los Angeles during the summers. They worked in the vegetable fields of the Central Valley or in the fish canneries of Alaska. For that transient population, Los Angeles was essentially a popular wintertime base.

The location of this "Manilatown" in the late 1920s amid the poor and homeless of Los Angeles reflected the poverty of Filipinos. Of no less importance, however, was the fact that this area (including the nearby red-light district) was the only area in the city where whites allowed them to rent. Over the next few years the area within which Filipinos could rent rooms expanded slightly. By 1933 many men had left the old district between Main and Los Angeles Streets and moved north, closer to Sunset Boulevard and Figueroa Street. Others had found apartments and bungalows in immigrant neighborhoods. There

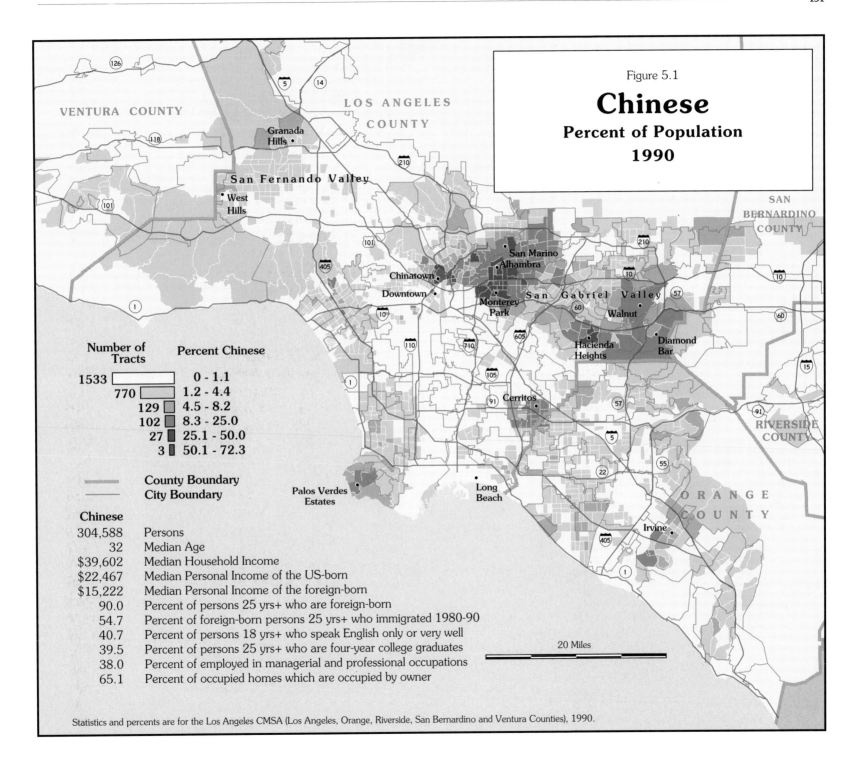

Figure 5.1

Chinese
Percent of Population
1990

VENTURA COUNTY

LOS ANGELES
COUNTY

SAN
BERNARDINO
COUNTY

Granada
Hills •

San Fernando Valley

• West
Hills

San Marino
Alhambra

Chinatown

Downtown

San Gabriel Valley

Monterey
Park

Walnut

Hacienda
Heights

Diamond
Bar

Number of Tracts	Percent Chinese
1533	0 - 1.1
770	1.2 - 4.4
129	4.5 - 8.2
102	8.3 - 25.0
27	25.1 - 50.0
3	50.1 - 72.3

——— County Boundary
——— City Boundary

Cerritos

RIVERSIDE
COUNTY

Palos Verdes
Estates

Long
Beach

ORANGE
COUNTY

Irvine

Chinese

304,588	Persons
32	Median Age
$39,602	Median Household Income
$22,467	Median Personal Income of the US-born
$15,222	Median Personal Income of the foreign-born
90.0	Percent of persons 25 yrs+ who are foreign-born
54.7	Percent of foreign-born persons 25 yrs+ who immigrated 1980-90
40.7	Percent of persons 18 yrs+ who speak English only or very well
39.5	Percent of persons 25 yrs+ who are four-year college graduates
38.0	Percent of employed in managerial and professional occupations
65.1	Percent of occupied homes which are occupied by owner

20 Miles

Statistics and percents are for the Los Angeles CMSA (Los Angeles, Orange, Riverside, San Bernardino and Ventura Counties), 1990.

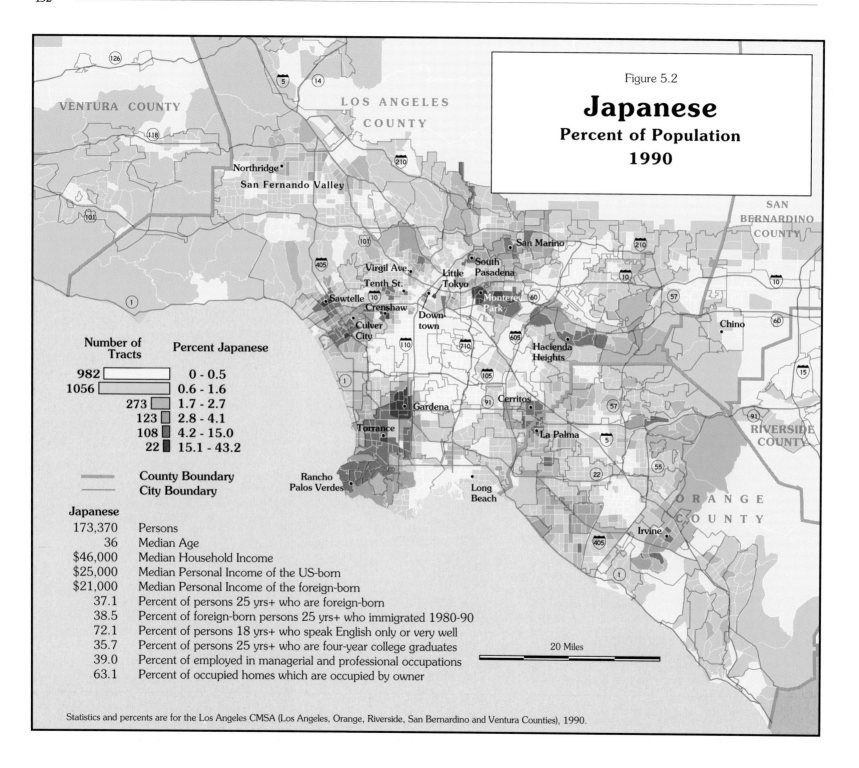

Figure 5.2

Japanese
Percent of Population
1990

VENTURA COUNTY

LOS ANGELES COUNTY

SAN BERNARDINO COUNTY

RIVERSIDE COUNTY

ORANGE COUNTY

Northridge•
San Fernando Valley

San Marino

Virgil Ave.•
Tenth St.•
Sawtelle•
Crenshaw•
Culver City•

Little Tokyo
South Pasadena
Monterey Park
Down-town

Hacienda Heights

Chino

Gardena
Cerritos
La Palma

Torrance

Rancho Palos Verdes

Long Beach

Irvine

Number of Tracts — Percent Japanese

Number of Tracts	Percent Japanese
982	0 - 0.5
1056	0.6 - 1.6
273	1.7 - 2.7
123	2.8 - 4.1
108	4.2 - 15.0
22	15.1 - 43.2

━━━ County Boundary
──── City Boundary

Japanese

173,370	Persons
36	Median Age
$46,000	Median Household Income
$25,000	Median Personal Income of the US-born
$21,000	Median Personal Income of the foreign-born
37.1	Percent of persons 25 yrs+ who are foreign-born
38.5	Percent of foreign-born persons 25 yrs+ who immigrated 1980-90
72.1	Percent of persons 18 yrs+ who speak English only or very well
35.7	Percent of persons 25 yrs+ who are four-year college graduates
39.0	Percent of employed in managerial and professional occupations
63.1	Percent of occupied homes which are occupied by owner

20 Miles

Statistics and percents are for the Los Angeles CMSA (Los Angeles, Orange, Riverside, San Bernardino and Ventura Counties), 1990.

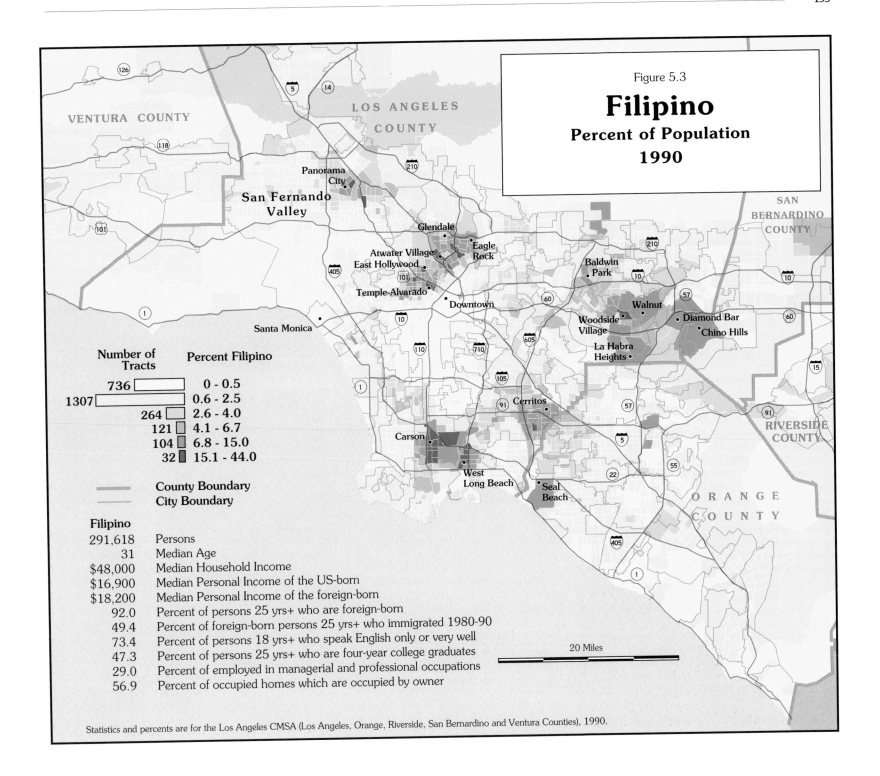

VENTURA COUNTY

LOS ANGELES COUNTY

SAN BERNARDINO COUNTY

Panorama City

San Fernando Valley

Glendale

Atwater Village
East Hollywood

Eagle Rock

Baldwin Park

Temple-Alvarado

Downtown

Walnut

Woodside Village

Diamond Bar

Chino Hills

La Habra Heights

Santa Monica

RIVERSIDE COUNTY

Cerritos

Carson

West Long Beach

Seal Beach

ORANGE COUNTY

Figure 5.3

Filipino
Percent of Population
1990

Number of Tracts   **Percent Filipino**

736	0 - 0.5
1307	0.6 - 2.5
264	2.6 - 4.0
121	4.1 - 6.7
104	6.8 - 15.0
32	15.1 - 44.0

County Boundary
City Boundary

Filipino

291,618	Persons
31	Median Age
$48,000	Median Household Income
$16,900	Median Personal Income of the US-born
$18,200	Median Personal Income of the foreign-born
92.0	Percent of persons 25 yrs+ who are foreign-born
49.4	Percent of foreign-born persons 25 yrs+ who immigrated 1980-90
73.4	Percent of persons 18 yrs+ who speak English only or very well
47.3	Percent of persons 25 yrs+ who are four-year college graduates
29.0	Percent of employed in managerial and professional occupations
56.9	Percent of occupied homes which are occupied by owner

20 Miles

Statistics and percents are for the Los Angeles CMSA (Los Angeles, Orange, Riverside, San Bernardino and Ventura Counties), 1990.

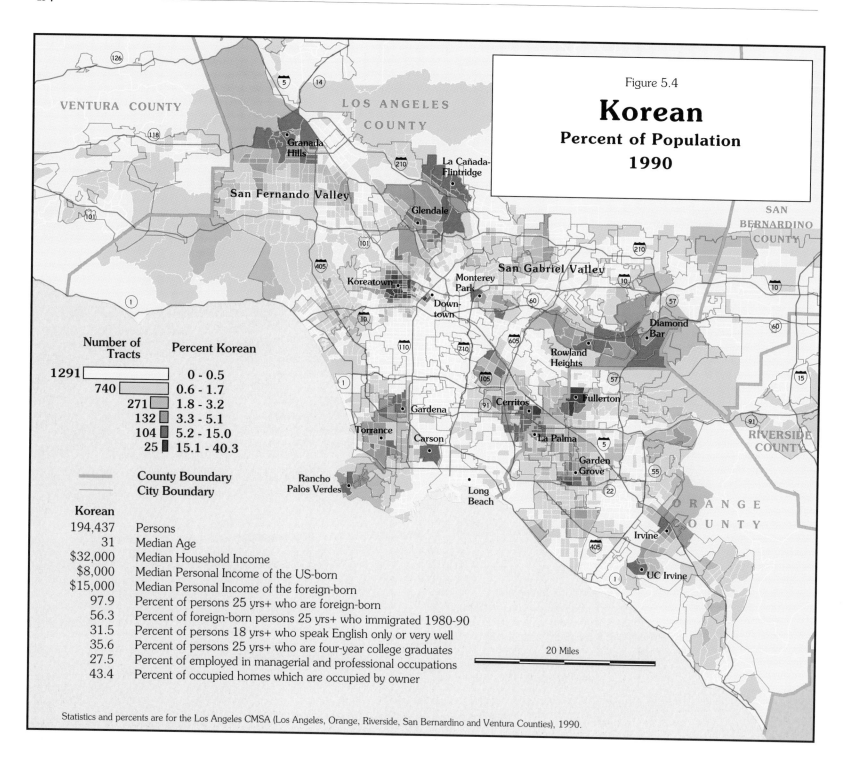

Figure 5.4

Korean
Percent of Population
1990

VENTURA COUNTY

LOS ANGELES COUNTY

Granada Hills

La Cañada-Flintridge

San Fernando Valley

Glendale

SAN BERNARDINO COUNTY

San Gabriel Valley

Koreatown

Monterey Park

Down-town

Diamond Bar

Rowland Heights

Number of Tracts — **Percent Korean**

1291	0 - 0.5
740	0.6 - 1.7
271	1.8 - 3.2
132	3.3 - 5.1
104	5.2 - 15.0
25	15.1 - 40.3

Cerritos

Fullerton

Gardena

Torrance

Carson

La Palma

Garden Grove

——— County Boundary
——— City Boundary

Rancho Palos Verdes

Long Beach

ORANGE COUNTY

RIVERSIDE COUNTY

Irvine

UC Irvine

Korean

194,437	Persons
31	Median Age
$32,000	Median Household Income
$8,000	Median Personal Income of the US-born
$15,000	Median Personal Income of the foreign-born
97.9	Percent of persons 25 yrs+ who are foreign-born
56.3	Percent of foreign-born persons 25 yrs+ who immigrated 1980-90
31.5	Percent of persons 18 yrs+ who speak English only or very well
35.6	Percent of persons 25 yrs+ who are four-year college graduates
27.5	Percent of employed in managerial and professional occupations
43.4	Percent of occupied homes which are occupied by owner

20 Miles

Statistics and percents are for the Los Angeles CMSA (Los Angeles, Orange, Riverside, San Bernardino and Ventura Counties), 1990.

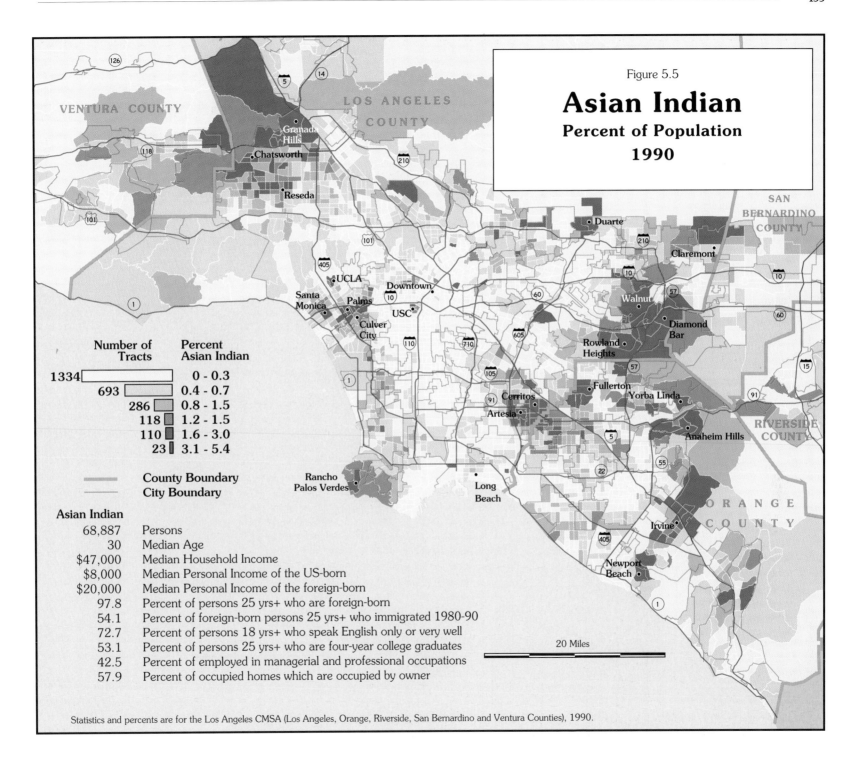

Figure 5.5

Asian Indian

Percent of Population
1990

VENTURA COUNTY

LOS ANGELES COUNTY

SAN BERNARDINO COUNTY

RIVERSIDE COUNTY

ORANGE COUNTY

Granada Hills

Chatsworth

Reseda

Duarte

Claremont

UCLA

Santa Monica

Palms

Downtown

USC

Culver City

Walnut

Diamond Bar

Rowland Heights

Fullerton

Yorba Linda

Cerritos

Artesia

Anaheim Hills

Rancho Palos Verdes

Long Beach

Irvine

Newport Beach

Number of Tracts		Percent Asian Indian
1334		0 - 0.3
693		0.4 - 0.7
286		0.8 - 1.5
118		1.2 - 1.5
110		1.6 - 3.0
23		3.1 - 5.4

—— County Boundary
—— City Boundary

Asian Indian

68,887	Persons
30	Median Age
$47,000	Median Household Income
$8,000	Median Personal Income of the US-born
$20,000	Median Personal Income of the foreign-born
97.8	Percent of persons 25 yrs+ who are foreign-born
54.1	Percent of foreign-born persons 25 yrs+ who immigrated 1980-90
72.7	Percent of persons 18 yrs+ who speak English only or very well
53.1	Percent of persons 25 yrs+ who are four-year college graduates
42.5	Percent of employed in managerial and professional occupations
57.9	Percent of occupied homes which are occupied by owner

20 Miles

Statistics and percents are for the Los Angeles CMSA (Los Angeles, Orange, Riverside, San Bernardino and Ventura Counties), 1990.

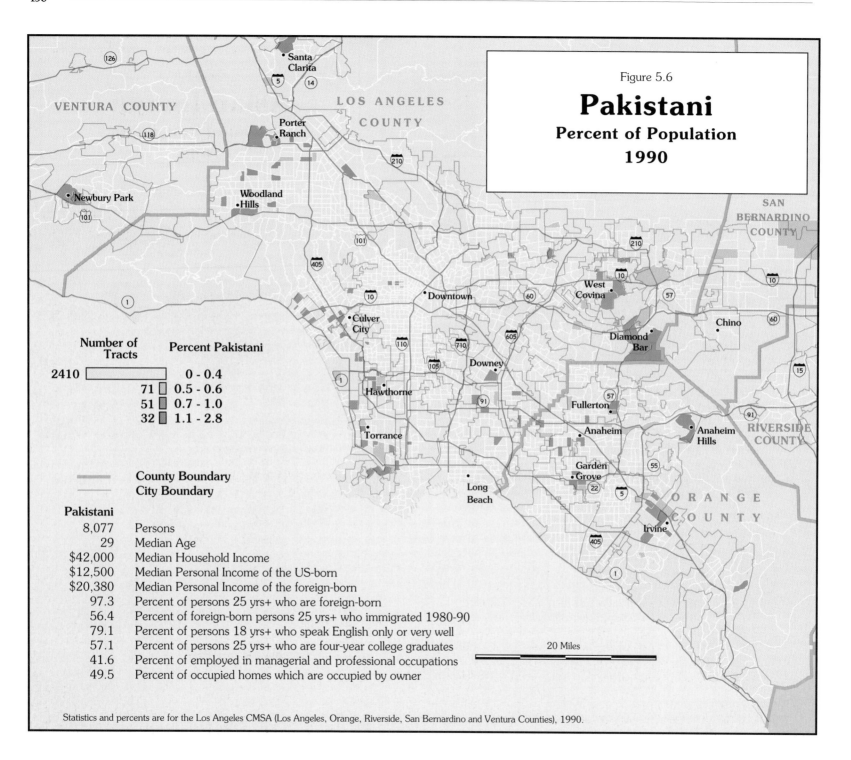

Figure 5.6

Pakistani
Percent of Population
1990

VENTURA COUNTY

LOS ANGELES COUNTY

SAN BERNARDINO COUNTY

RIVERSIDE COUNTY

ORANGE COUNTY

Santa Clarita
Porter Ranch
Newbury Park
Woodland Hills
Downtown
Culver City
Hawthorne
Torrance
Downey
Long Beach
Garden Grove
Anaheim
Fullerton
West Covina
Diamond Bar
Chino
Anaheim Hills
Irvine

Number of Tracts	Percent Pakistani
2410	0 - 0.4
71	0.5 - 0.6
51	0.7 - 1.0
32	1.1 - 2.8

County Boundary
City Boundary

Pakistani

8,077	Persons
29	Median Age
$42,000	Median Household Income
$12,500	Median Personal Income of the US-born
$20,380	Median Personal Income of the foreign-born
97.3	Percent of persons 25 yrs+ who are foreign-born
56.4	Percent of foreign-born persons 25 yrs+ who immigrated 1980-90
79.1	Percent of persons 18 yrs+ who speak English only or very well
57.1	Percent of persons 25 yrs+ who are four-year college graduates
41.6	Percent of employed in managerial and professional occupations
49.5	Percent of occupied homes which are occupied by owner

20 Miles

Statistics and percents are for the Los Angeles CMSA (Los Angeles, Orange, Riverside, San Bernardino and Ventura Counties), 1990.

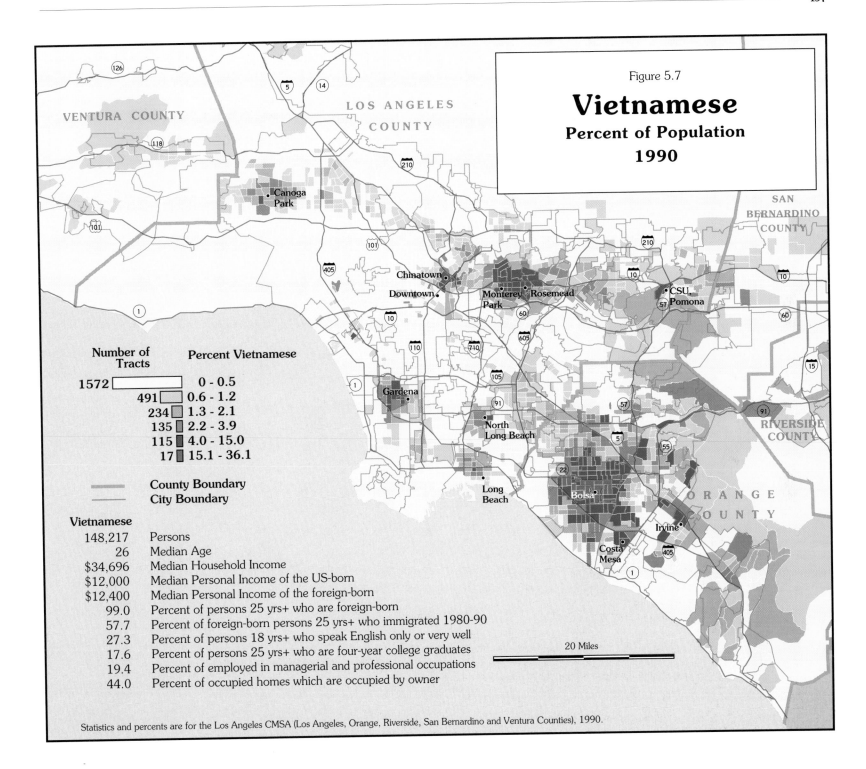

Figure 5.7

Vietnamese
Percent of Population
1990

Number of Tracts

Percent Vietnamese

1572	0 - 0.5
491	0.6 - 1.2
234	1.3 - 2.1
135	2.2 - 3.9
115	4.0 - 15.0
17	15.1 - 36.1

—— County Boundary
—— City Boundary

Vietnamese

148,217	Persons
26	Median Age
$34,696	Median Household Income
$12,000	Median Personal Income of the US-born
$12,400	Median Personal Income of the foreign-born
99.0	Percent of persons 25 yrs+ who are foreign-born
57.7	Percent of foreign-born persons 25 yrs+ who immigrated 1980-90
27.3	Percent of persons 18 yrs+ who speak English only or very well
17.6	Percent of persons 25 yrs+ who are four-year college graduates
19.4	Percent of employed in managerial and professional occupations
44.0	Percent of occupied homes which are occupied by owner

20 Miles

Statistics and percents are for the Los Angeles CMSA (Los Angeles, Orange, Riverside, San Bernardino and Ventura Counties), 1990.

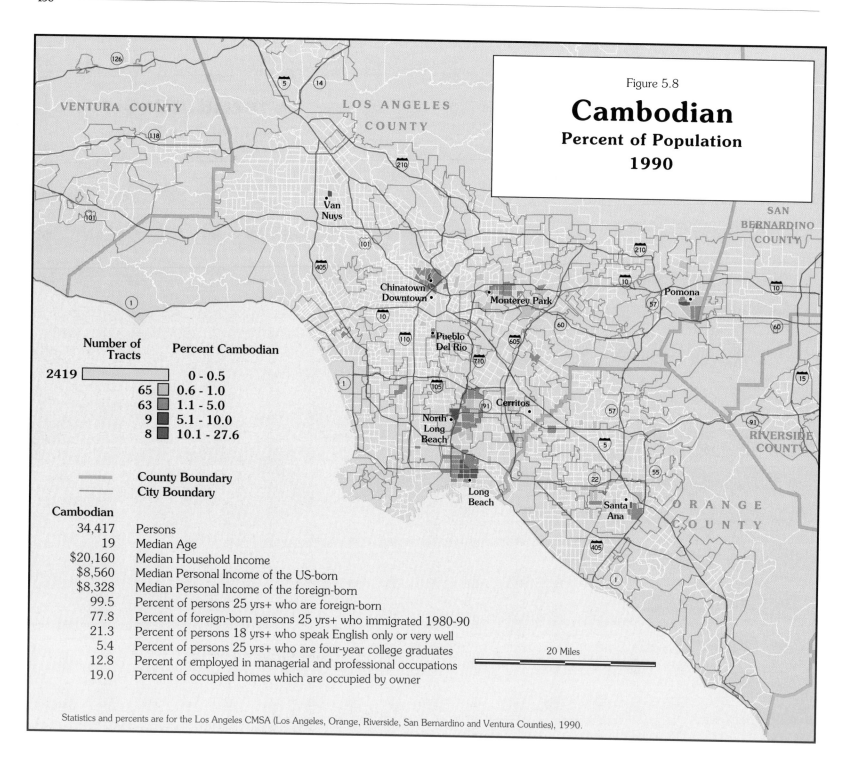

Figure 5.8

Cambodian
Percent of Population
1990

VENTURA COUNTY

LOS ANGELES COUNTY

SAN BERNARDINO COUNTY

Van Nuys

Chinatown
Downtown

Monterey Park

Pomona

Pueblo
Del Rio

Cerritos

North
Long
Beach

Long
Beach

Santa
Ana

ORANGE COUNTY

RIVERSIDE COUNTY

Number of Tracts — **Percent Cambodian**

Number of Tracts	Percent Cambodian
2419	0 - 0.5
65	0.6 - 1.0
63	1.1 - 5.0
9	5.1 - 10.0
8	10.1 - 27.6

County Boundary
City Boundary

Cambodian

34,417	Persons
19	Median Age
$20,160	Median Household Income
$8,560	Median Personal Income of the US-born
$8,328	Median Personal Income of the foreign-born
99.5	Percent of persons 25 yrs+ who are foreign-born
77.8	Percent of foreign-born persons 25 yrs+ who immigrated 1980-90
21.3	Percent of persons 18 yrs+ who speak English only or very well
5.4	Percent of persons 25 yrs+ who are four-year college graduates
12.8	Percent of employed in managerial and professional occupations
19.0	Percent of occupied homes which are occupied by owner

20 Miles

Statistics and percents are for the Los Angeles CMSA (Los Angeles, Orange, Riverside, San Bernardino and Ventura Counties), 1990.

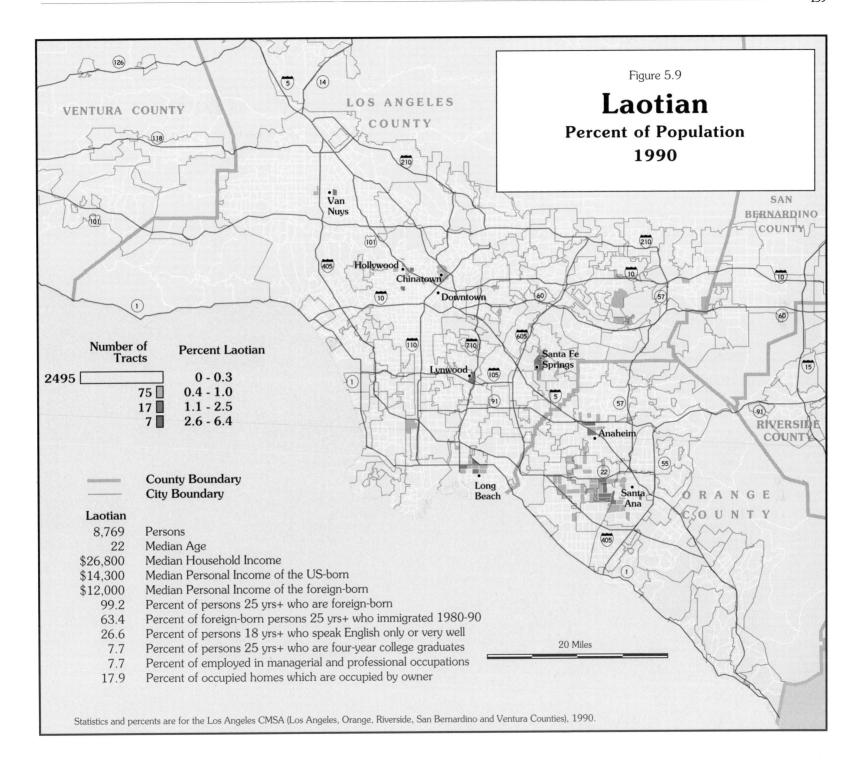

Figure 5.9

Laotian
Percent of Population
1990

VENTURA COUNTY

LOS ANGELES COUNTY

SAN BERNARDINO COUNTY

Van Nuys

Hollywood

Chinatown

Downtown

Lynwood

Santa Fe Springs

Long Beach

Anaheim

Santa Ana

ORANGE COUNTY

RIVERSIDE COUNTY

Number of Tracts   **Percent Laotian**

2495	0 - 0.3
75	0.4 - 1.0
17	1.1 - 2.5
7	2.6 - 6.4

———— County Boundary
———— City Boundary

Laotian

8,769	Persons
22	Median Age
$26,800	Median Household Income
$14,300	Median Personal Income of the US-born
$12,000	Median Personal Income of the foreign-born
99.2	Percent of persons 25 yrs+ who are foreign-born
63.4	Percent of foreign-born persons 25 yrs+ who immigrated 1980-90
26.6	Percent of persons 18 yrs+ who speak English only or very well
7.7	Percent of persons 25 yrs+ who are four-year college graduates
7.7	Percent of employed in managerial and professional occupations
17.9	Percent of occupied homes which are occupied by owner

20 Miles

Statistics and percents are for the Los Angeles CMSA (Los Angeles, Orange, Riverside, San Bernardino and Ventura Counties), 1990.

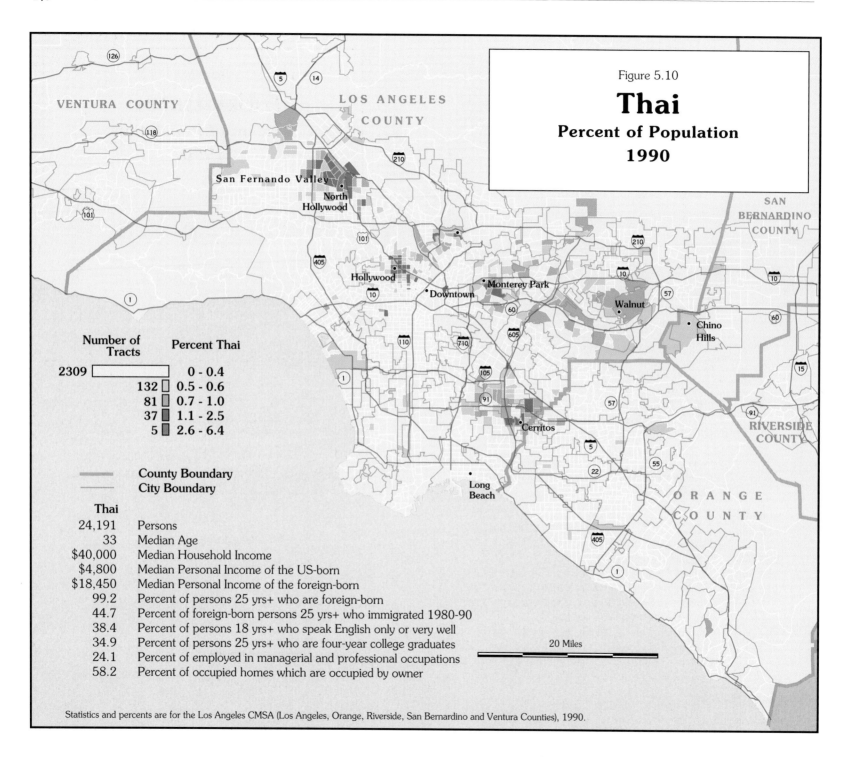

Figure 5.10

Thai
Percent of Population
1990

VENTURA COUNTY

LOS ANGELES COUNTY

SAN BERNARDINO COUNTY

San Fernando Valley

North Hollywood

Hollywood

Monterey Park

Downtown

Walnut

Chino Hills

Long Beach

Cerritos

ORANGE COUNTY

RIVERSIDE COUNTY

Number of Tracts	Percent Thai
2309	0 - 0.4
132	0.5 - 0.6
81	0.7 - 1.0
37	1.1 - 2.5
5	2.6 - 6.4

—— County Boundary
—— City Boundary

Thai

24,191	Persons
33	Median Age
$40,000	Median Household Income
$4,800	Median Personal Income of the US-born
$18,450	Median Personal Income of the foreign-born
99.2	Percent of persons 25 yrs+ who are foreign-born
44.7	Percent of foreign-born persons 25 yrs+ who immigrated 1980-90
38.4	Percent of persons 18 yrs+ who speak English only or very well
34.9	Percent of persons 25 yrs+ who are four-year college graduates
24.1	Percent of employed in managerial and professional occupations
58.2	Percent of occupied homes which are occupied by owner

20 Miles

Statistics and percents are for the Los Angeles CMSA (Los Angeles, Orange, Riverside, San Bernardino and Ventura Counties), 1990.

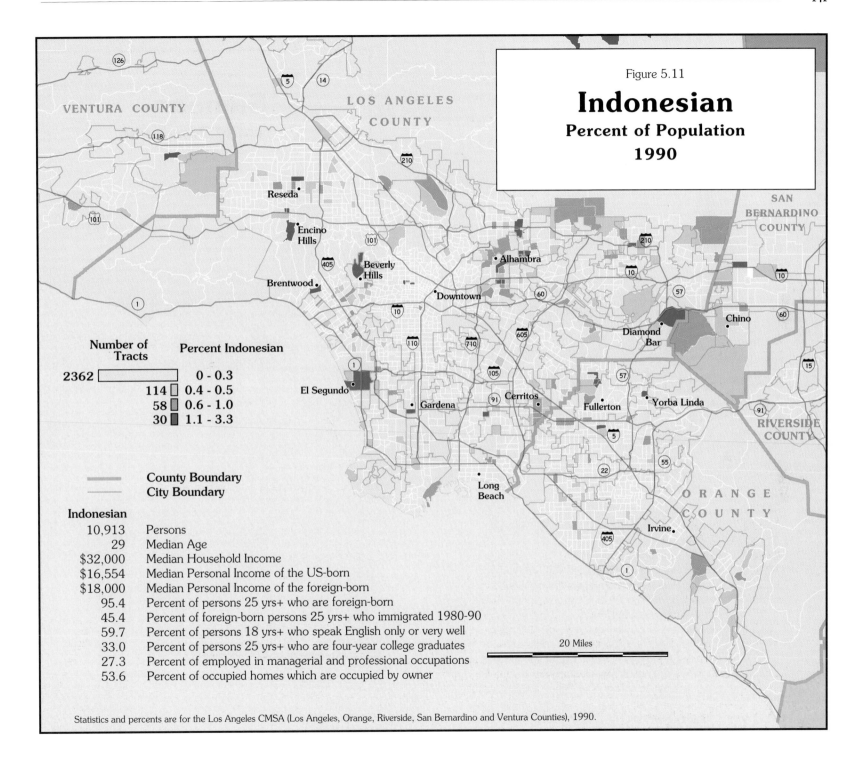

Figure 5.11

Indonesian
Percent of Population
1990

Number of Tracts — **Percent Indonesian**

Number of Tracts	Percent Indonesian
2362	0 - 0.3
114	0.4 - 0.5
58	0.6 - 1.0
30	1.1 - 3.3

County Boundary
City Boundary

Indonesian

10,913	Persons
29	Median Age
$32,000	Median Household Income
$16,554	Median Personal Income of the US-born
$18,000	Median Personal Income of the foreign-born
95.4	Percent of persons 25 yrs+ who are foreign-born
45.4	Percent of foreign-born persons 25 yrs+ who immigrated 1980-90
59.7	Percent of persons 18 yrs+ who speak English only or very well
33.0	Percent of persons 25 yrs+ who are four-year college graduates
27.3	Percent of employed in managerial and professional occupations
53.6	Percent of occupied homes which are occupied by owner

20 Miles

Statistics and percents are for the Los Angeles CMSA (Los Angeles, Orange, Riverside, San Bernardino and Ventura Counties), 1990.

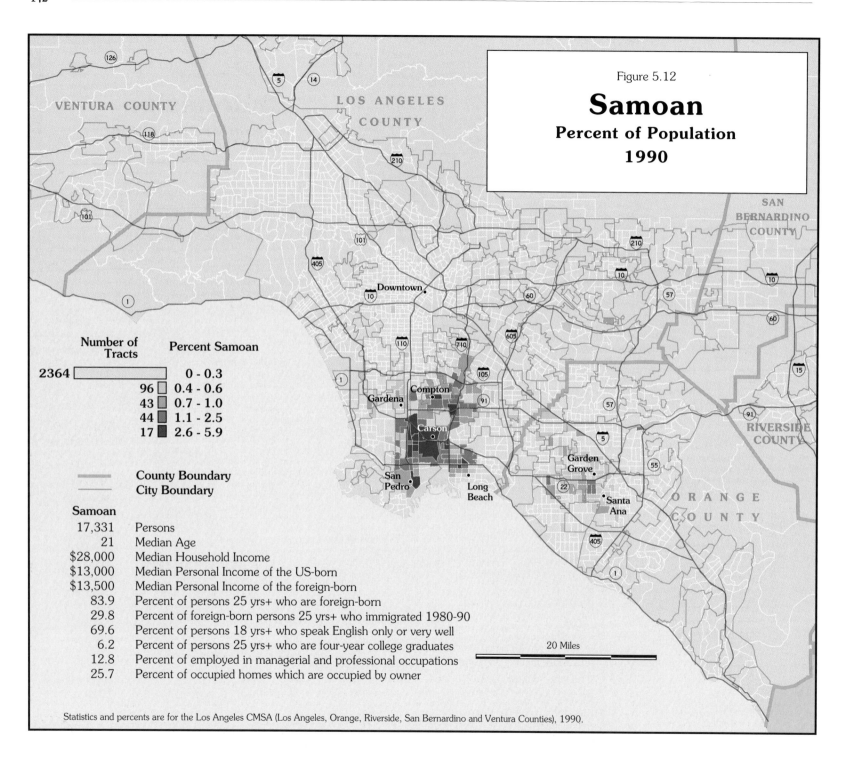

Figure 5.12

Samoan
Percent of Population
1990

Number of Tracts   **Percent Samoan**

2364   0 - 0.3
96   0.4 - 0.6
43   0.7 - 1.0
44   1.1 - 2.5
17   2.6 - 5.9

County Boundary
City Boundary

Samoan

17,331	Persons
21	Median Age
$28,000	Median Household Income
$13,000	Median Personal Income of the US-born
$13,500	Median Personal Income of the foreign-born
83.9	Percent of persons 25 yrs+ who are foreign-born
29.8	Percent of foreign-born persons 25 yrs+ who immigrated 1980-90
69.6	Percent of persons 18 yrs+ who speak English only or very well
6.2	Percent of persons 25 yrs+ who are four-year college graduates
12.8	Percent of employed in managerial and professional occupations
25.7	Percent of occupied homes which are occupied by owner

20 Miles

Statistics and percents are for the Los Angeles CMSA (Los Angeles, Orange, Riverside, San Bernardino and Ventura Counties), 1990.

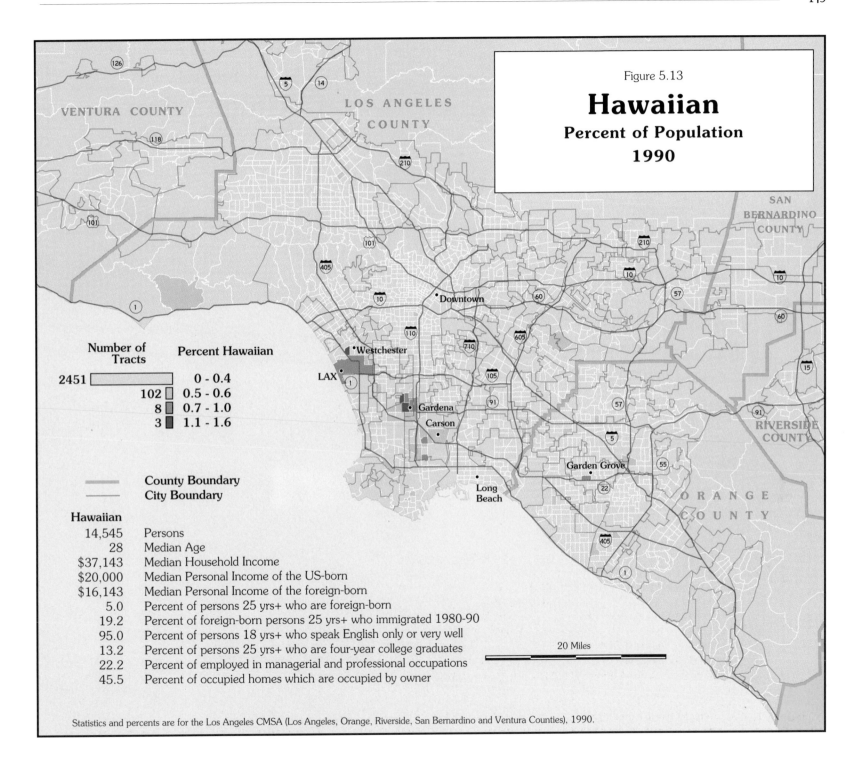

Figure 5.13

Hawaiian
Percent of Population
1990

VENTURA COUNTY

LOS ANGELES COUNTY

SAN BERNARDINO COUNTY

RIVERSIDE COUNTY

ORANGE COUNTY

Downtown

Westchester

LAX

Gardena

Carson

Long Beach

Garden Grove

Number of Tracts | **Percent Hawaiian**

Number of Tracts	Percent Hawaiian
2451	0 - 0.4
102	0.5 - 0.6
8	0.7 - 1.0
3	1.1 - 1.6

County Boundary
City Boundary

Hawaiian

14,545	Persons
28	Median Age
$37,143	Median Household Income
$20,000	Median Personal Income of the US-born
$16,143	Median Personal Income of the foreign-born
5.0	Percent of persons 25 yrs+ who are foreign-born
19.2	Percent of foreign-born persons 25 yrs+ who immigrated 1980-90
95.0	Percent of persons 18 yrs+ who speak English only or very well
13.2	Percent of persons 25 yrs+ who are four-year college graduates
22.2	Percent of employed in managerial and professional occupations
45.5	Percent of occupied homes which are occupied by owner

20 Miles

Statistics and percents are for the Los Angeles CMSA (Los Angeles, Orange, Riverside, San Bernardino and Ventura Counties), 1990.

144

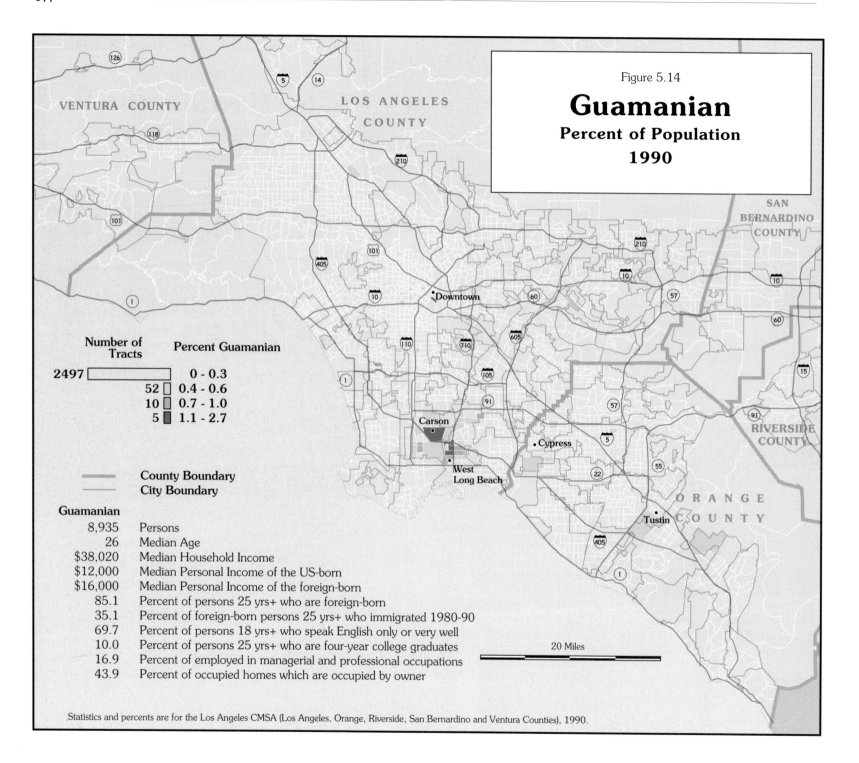

Figure 5.14

Guamanian
Percent of Population
1990

VENTURA COUNTY

LOS ANGELES COUNTY

SAN BERNARDINO COUNTY

RIVERSIDE COUNTY

ORANGE COUNTY

Downtown

Carson

West Long Beach

Cypress

Tustin

Number of Tracts — **Percent Guamanian**

Number of Tracts	Percent Guamanian
2497	0 - 0.3
52	0.4 - 0.6
10	0.7 - 1.0
5	1.1 - 2.7

—— County Boundary
—— City Boundary

Guamanian

8,935	Persons
26	Median Age
$38,020	Median Household Income
$12,000	Median Personal Income of the US-born
$16,000	Median Personal Income of the foreign-born
85.1	Percent of persons 25 yrs+ who are foreign-born
35.1	Percent of foreign-born persons 25 yrs+ who immigrated 1980-90
69.7	Percent of persons 18 yrs+ who speak English only or very well
10.0	Percent of persons 25 yrs+ who are four-year college graduates
16.9	Percent of employed in managerial and professional occupations
43.9	Percent of occupied homes which are occupied by owner

20 Miles

Statistics and percents are for the Los Angeles CMSA (Los Angeles, Orange, Riverside, San Bernardino and Ventura Counties), 1990.

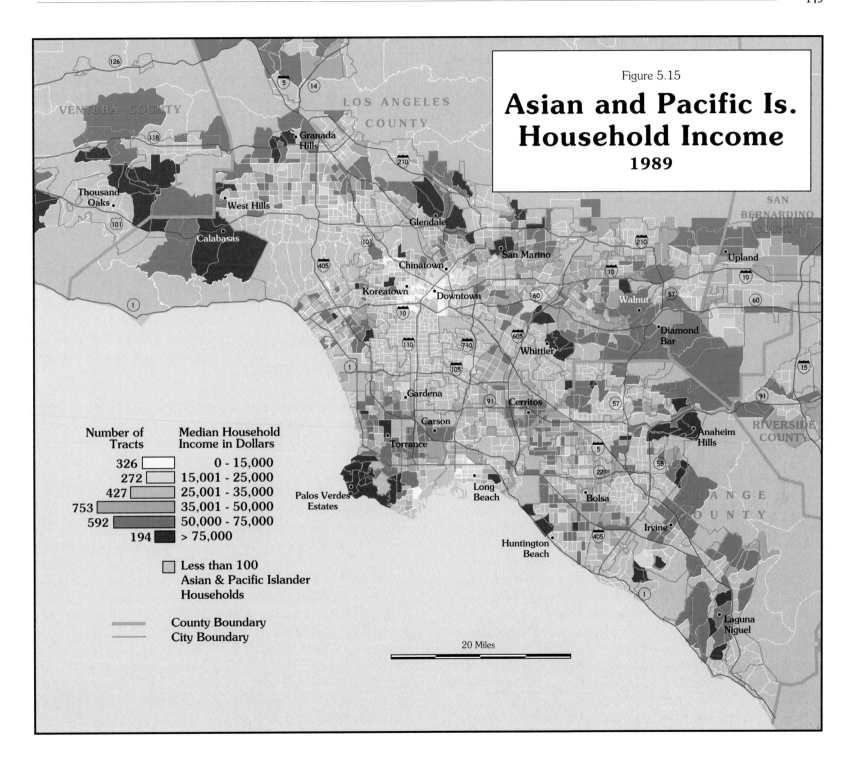

Figure 5.15

Asian and Pacific Is. Household Income
1989

Number of Tracts		Median Household Income in Dollars
326		0 - 15,000
272		15,001 - 25,000
427		25,001 - 35,000
753		35,001 - 50,000
592		50,000 - 75,000
194		> 75,000

Less than 100 Asian & Pacific Islander Households

County Boundary
City Boundary

20 Miles

were several Filipino rooming houses south of Downtown (near Grand Avenue and 25th Street), and other Filipinos lived just to the west, near Temple Street. Filipinos were simply not wanted in white neighborhoods, except as houseboys, valets, or chauffeurs.

By the late 1940s the situation was improving somewhat. New U.S. laws enabled more Filipinos to immigrate. Earlier state laws making marriage with whites illegal were overturned, and much new housing was being built in Los Angeles. Equally important, the U.S. Supreme Court had declared unenforceable the restrictive covenants on property deeds that had legally prohibited homeowners from selling or renting to people who were not white. In 1952 Filipinos who wished to buy a house could still find owners who would not sell to them. Nevertheless, the social and legal changes of the postwar period, combined with the economic growth, made homeownership possible for many Filipinos.[42]

The Temple-Alvarado area. Forty years ago a cluster of homeowners and Filipino businesses and clubhouses was developing near Alvarado Street to the northwest of Downtown. Construction of the 101 Freeway in the early 1950s destroyed part of this Filipino section, shifting it slightly southward to the area near Temple Street and Beverly Boulevard.[43] In the early 1960s this concentration was augmented by the arrival of Filipinos who had been residents of Bunker Hill. (Housing in that once-attractive neighborhood had been deteriorating for decades, and its low-income residents of varied ethnic identities were evicted to clear space for an up-the-hill shift of Los Angeles' more expensive offices, banks, and hotels.)

During the 1970s some newly arrived Filipino professionals settled first in the Temple-Alvarado area but later moved to more desirable areas. By the 1980s this had become the Filipino enclave to which less-acculturated, poorer, and more recent immigrants often gravitated.[44] The oldest ethnic organization, the Filipino American Community of Los Angeles, has always been based in the Temple-Alvarado neighborhood and still functions as a social-service center there.[45]

In 1990 the old Filipino neighborhood around Temple Street, Beverly Boulevard, Alvarado and Rampart Streets remained strong (Fig. 5.3). In that multiethnic and mostly Latino area Filipinos constitute only about a fifth of the population. However, the area has churches (a few identified as Filipino), restaurants, medical clinics, a new Luzon Plaza shopping center, and immigrant social-service agencies that serve poor and elderly Filipinos. Many of the elderly used to be farmworkers, waiters, or hotel bellhops, but others are parents of adult immigrants who were persuaded to join their children in the United States. A wall mural on Temple Street across from Rosemont Elementary School—a collaborative effort by about twenty young Filipino Americans—dramatizes the choices between a good life and a bad one that today's youth must make.

Because this Filipino settlement is the oldest and best-known concentration in Los Angeles, some Filipinos have attempted to have the area officially identified as "Philippine Town" or "Filipino Town."[46] However, many of the better-educated and more affluent immigrants who live in outlying areas have not wanted Filipinos to be associated in the public's perception with a neighborhood as poor as Temple-Alvarado.

The Navy connection. From 1902 through 1992 the U.S. Navy recruited Filipinos into its ranks, primarily as stewards and mess boys.[47] The young men who were selected viewed the Navy as an excellent way to improve their position, and most of them reenlisted for training in technical areas such as jet-engine maintenance. They also saw enlistment as a fast track to U.S. citizenship, which could lead to the entry of their close relatives as permanent residents in this country.

The oldest Filipino settlement based primarily on enlistment in the U.S. Navy is in West Long Beach, and in 1990 this constituted one of the leading Filipino ethnic concentrations. The same harbor area may well have been home to Filipino workers in fish canneries during the 1930s and 1940s. The census of 1940 records several hundred Filipinos in the census tracts very close to the harbor of Los Angeles, but it is not clear to what extent these were cannery workers or Navy personnel.[48] It seems likely that most of them were civilian workers in fish canneries, because the 1950 census counted only ninety-seven nonwhite men in the military workforce and residing in the three tracts closest to the Navy installations.[49]

The number of Filipino enlisted men stationed in Long Beach grew during the 1950s and 1960s, and some returned briefly to the Philippines to choose wives. Some families lived in Navy-owned housing, but most lived nearby in regular homes and apartments. In addition, Filipinos who were not in the Navy were able to immigrate to the United States if they were close relatives of Navy men, their wives, or others who had become permanent residents or citizens of the United States. During the 1970s and 1980s the increase in the non-Navy Filipino population of West Long Beach was much greater than was that of Navy personnel.

The census tract with the highest Filipino percentage in Southern California is in West Long Beach. This strongly Filipino neighborhood includes St. Lucy's Catholic Church, the clear religious focus of the Filipino community. Although the U.S. Navy closed most of its operations in Long Beach after 1990, the West Long Beach Filipino community will persist because it has become substantially independent of direct employment links with the Navy.

Another large concentration of Filipinos is found in Oxnard, which is too far to the west in Ventura County to be shown in Figure 5.3. Filipinos in the military there are stationed at either the Point Mugu Naval Air Station or the Construction Battalion Center in adjacent Port Hueneme. In Oxnard, as in West Long Beach, the direct Navy connection has been dwarfed in recent years by the large immigration of relatives often only distantly related to the original Navy recruits. Filipinos also live and work at the U.S. Naval Weapons Station at Seal Beach and in nearby parts of Orange County.

Nearby suburbs. During the past two decades many Filipinos have moved out of these older concentrations and into more attractive neighborhoods, where they have often been joined by newly arrived immigrants. Many residents of the Temple-Alvarado area or elsewhere became able to rent or buy homes in Silver Lake, Glassell Park, Highland Park, Glendale, and Eagle Rock—areas that were considered suburbs of Los Angeles more than fifty years ago. In Eagle Rock the local schools and Catholic churches experienced a major influx of Filipinos during the 1980s, and new Filipino restaurants and markets suddenly appeared on Colorado Boulevard.[50] Thus, an expanded Filipino enclave has emerged in the area between Temple-Alvarado and Eagle Rock (Fig. 5.3).

Within this area many Filipinos live in East Hollywood. This concentration is strongest near the large hospitals (Kaiser Hospital, Hollywood Presbyterian, and Children's Hospital), where many nurses are employed.

In the San Fernando Valley Filipinos have found the North Hills and Arleta area attractive, because friends, relatives, and an active Catholic parish are nearby. Buying a single-family house is less costly in such older neighborhoods, and a sense of shared Hispanic and Catholic identity with the predominant Latino population makes some Filipinos feel more comfortable in areas like the increasingly Latino East Valley. Many Filipinas in the eastern San Fernando Valley work as nurses in the large Kaiser Hospital in nearby Panorama City.

In southern Los Angeles County, as in the city of Los Angeles, are Filipino enclaves in which an older concentration is matched with a nearby suburban area. In Carson, single-family houses were typically built in the 1960s and are more expensive than are those in Eagle Rock. However, the proximity of Carson to West Long Beach has meant that Filipinos in West Long Beach who wish to reside within an active Filipino community have not had to move far to improve their situation. One out of every six residents of Carson is a Filipino, and five tracts in southern Carson are more than one-quarter Filipino. The high proportion of Filipinos in Carson's population may partly explain why Filipinos there have been more politically involved than they have been elsewhere.

More distant suburbs. As the influx of Filipinos grew after 1970, large numbers of professionals and others with higher incomes began to move into newly built homes in the Cerritos area and the eastern San Gabriel Valley. Moreover, the excellent reputations of the schools there have been an important attraction to Filipinos and other Asians.

During the 1970s Filipinos were particularly directed to the new single-family houses, apartments, and condominiums in the Woodside Village section of West Covina. By 1990 the number of Filipinos in Woodside Village had grown to 2,900, which represented 21 percent of the tract's population.

In the 1980s the eastward thrust of settlement in the San Gabriel Valley continued. Filipinos with relatively high incomes bought homes in nearby Walnut, Rowland Heights, Industry, La Habra Heights, and Diamond Bar. Others moved to new developments in the Chino Hills and elsewhere in Riverside and San Bernardino Counties.

The great range of incomes within the contemporary Filipino population are a striking contrast with the 1930s poverty of Filipinos in Los Angeles. This is reflected in the greater diversity of Filipino settlements today.

Distinctions among Filipino communities. Some Filipino enclaves were once socially distinct because they were settled through separate chain migrations. This is suggested by the fact that Filipino communities in Hawaii and New York developed from two essentially different chain migrations and histories.[51] The former represents family linkages that reach back through plantation-worker connections, whereas the latter derives from the post-1965 immigration of professionals. If a similar distinction is applied to Southern California, the early Filipino community in West Long Beach, with its original Navy connection, may represent different sets of social networks from those in the Temple-Alvarado area.

By the 1980s, however, Filipino communities had become interconnected. Through residential mobility and occasional personal ties in the Philippines, more affluent Filipinos from older settlements (Long Beach–Carson and Temple-Alvarado–Eagle Rock) have joined recently arrived professionals in Cerritos and the eastern San Gabriel Valley.

Koreans

The first Koreans in Los Angeles—laborers and students—came at the beginning of the twentieth century. In 1906 only 60 Koreans lived in Los Angeles County. They established a Presbyterian mission, which symbolized the early Korean presence and served as the focus of their changing distribution.[52]

For more than twenty years the mission was in the Bunker Hill area of Downtown, but in the late 1920s it was relocated to the area west of the University of Southern California. That refocus made sense because many Koreans were students at USC and because the area west of the campus was racially mixed and had low rents. By 1939 the total number of Koreans in the county had risen to 300. Although Korean businesses were dispersed over a wide area, most Koreans lived between Vermont and Western Avenues, from Adams Boulevard on the north to Slauson Avenue on the south.

From the first, the Koreans' path to economic survival and success seemed to be entrepreneurship. Fruit and vegetable stands and grocery stores were the most common forms of self-employment. Some Koreans were wholesalers and retailers of herbs, hats, and novelties. Still others were owners of laundry, trucking, and "Chinese" restaurant businesses. Although many had been trained for professional careers, restrictions on better jobs and discrimination meant that Los Angeles in 1939 had only two Korean doctors and no lawyers, engineers, dentists, or educators.

Origins and expansion of Koreatown. With closer Korean–American ties after the Korean War and increased immigration after the 1965 changes in U.S. immigration law, the number of Koreans in Southern California grew. So did the clustering of their homes in what was coming to be called Koreatown. In 1972 a third of all Korean households listed in Korean directories for Southern California were located in Koreatown, a level of geographical concentration that was understandable for the rapidly growing Korean community.[53]

Over the years the Korean community crept northward. In the 1950s and 1960s this was partly due to the northward expansion of black settlement that followed the elimination of most legal supports of discrimination in housing. By 1972 Koreatown was north of Pico Boulevard. During the 1980s, as the number of Koreans in Koreatown increased from 12,000 to 35,000, Koreatown expanded geographically, reaching north past Wilshire Boulevard and west past Crenshaw Boulevard.[54] This shift was partly a response to the increasing numbers of poorer Central Americans in Pico-Union and Westlake.

Although the movement of Koreatown westward and northward has represented a retreat from the expanding zone of poor Latinos and blacks, it has also permitted more affluent Koreans to remain in the greater Koreatown area but live in more attractive housing in mostly white areas—Hancock Park and Country Club Park. These geographical changes are consistent with both the socioeconomic separation between Koreans and the other groups and the increasing economic success of many Koreans.

Modern Koreatown as a residential area. Despite the name, the majority of Koreatown's residents are not Korean. The proportion of Koreans rose during the 1980s—but only from 11 percent to 16 percent. In most census tracts Latinos are the largest ethnic group, and in only one tract do Koreans outnumber them. Thus, Koreatown's people are less Korean than some might imagine.

For Koreans, however, Koreatown is the most important enclave. It frequently attracts new arrivals, who live there for a few years until they have adjusted somewhat to Southern California.[55] Although most new immigrants settle first near friends or relatives, those without personal ties in Los Angeles and others who wish to minimize the discomfort of contact with the non-Korean world can live in Koreatown.[56] The large numbers of Koreans there make possible the services and institutions that make strangers feel somewhat more at home, and in many ways Koreatown encourages an attachment to Korean culture and society.[57] Elderly Koreans, in particular, enjoy the pervasiveness of Korean culture in Koreatown. This, together with the lower cost of renting apartments there compared to outlying areas, means that Koreatown's residents tend to be older and poorer than most Koreans in Southern California.

In the Downtown area not far from Koreatown is a tract which was 39 percent Korean in 1990. In an old, declining neighborhood (Olive Street between 7th and 8th Streets) a single apartment building with a renovated interior housed 276 Koreans. Even though the area lacks Korean stores and institutions, the apartments are a sought-after residence for low-income, elderly Koreans because rents in this "Section 8" building are federally subsidized.

Koreatown businesses. Koreatown is the center of a wide range of Korean-oriented services. Many banks and accounting, real-estate, insurance, and law firms are located in large Korean-owned office buildings on Wilshire Boulevard, Western Avenue, Olympic Boulevard, and other commercial streets. Other businesses are located in older buildings or in bright shopping centers and minimalls built in the 1970s and 1980s. The largest retailing center is Koreatown Plaza on Western Avenue—a sumptuous, Korean-designed four-story indoor mall.

Koreatown contains more than 400 Korean medical offices, plus numerous providers of herbs and acupuncture. There are also boutiques, beauty salons, travel agencies, gasoline stations, car dealers, clothing and wig stores, laundries, videotape rental shops, book and magazine stores, bakeries, grocery stores, night clubs, and more than 200 restaurants. Organizations have meetings at Korean restaurants, Koreans from the suburbs host wedding receptions and parties there, and every October the Koreatown Festival attracts Koreans from all over Southern California. Almost a dozen hotels serve businessmen, tour groups, and other visitors from Korea.

Korean businesses are often owned by immigrants who were highly educated, often as professionals, but were unable to achieve the success they expected while working for an American-run business or organization.[58] Difficulties with English, lack of sufficient acculturation, and discrimination are likely explanations. In any case, many men obtained enough capital from friends and relatives or Korean rotating-credit associations and banks to finance a business. Most businessmen and women prefer to join Korean trade associations and make business arrangements with other Koreans. This is an understandable reaction to perceived discrimination by white wholesalers and to increases in store rents charged by white landlords after Koreans had made their businesses successful.[59]

In 1986 Koreatown was the location of 26 percent of the Korean businesses in Los Angeles and Orange Counties, which indicates that business operations are slightly more likely to be located in Koreatown than are the Korean people themselves.[60] More significant, however, is the lower rate of self-employment among Koreatown residents and the fact that 59 percent of Korean owners of Koreatown businesses live in the suburbs. Thus, people in business frequently commute from suburban residences to their stores or factories in Koreatown.

Korean storekeepers in South Central. In May of 1992 the acquittal of four white Los Angeles policemen accused of beating a black man precipitated a major riot in South Central. The riot had a major impact on the Korean community.

Within South Central, Korean retailers typically owned gasoline service stations or "mom and pop" stores that sold liquor and some groceries to black and Latino customers. Most owners of these stores would have preferred to be located in an area of higher incomes and less crime but at the time could not afford the higher prices of stores elsewhere. Korean merchants who were successful in South Central typically sold to more recently arrived immigrants. This has meant that Korean store owners in South Central were some of the least acculturated of Koreans, a fact which exacerbated the cultural tensions between blacks and Koreans.

In 1990 Korean men and women were overrepresented in retail liquor operations at seventeen times the average rate (Table 8.6). Nevertheless, fewer than three percent of employed Koreans were working in that industry.

After the rioting in 1992 Koreans found themselves ignored or blamed and have been understandably resentful.[61] The riot also prompted many of them to change their attitude toward living in this country. With their future dependent on increasing sales to others, many Korean merchants have made a stronger commitment to the United States and have resolved to treat non-Koreans in a friendlier manner.

Dispersal to the suburbs. Koreatown is less important for Koreans than in the past. Despite enlargement of the area defined as Koreatown, the proportion of Los Angeles County's Koreans living in Koreatown has dropped from a third in 1972, to 30 percent in 1980, to 24 percent in 1990.[62] Koreans living in Koreatown constitute only 18 percent of the total number of Koreans in Southern California.

As reasons for moving out of Koreatown, Koreans cite a desire to be closer to work or their church or the opportunity

to own a home.[63] Nevertheless, this dispersal has really been made possible by the improved finances of many Koreans and by the growth of Korean enclaves in the suburbs. Most Koreans who still live in Koreatown do so because they cannot afford to live in better areas. Apart from its bright, new stores and offices, Koreatown's older and deteriorating housing correctly reflects its status as a low-income area with much crime.

A shift of Korean businesses out of Koreatown has also occurred. This is partly because merchants want to reach the growing market of suburban Koreans. In Koreatown the merchants traditionally served Korean customers rather than the area's total population, and some of those entrepreneurs simply decided to follow their customers to the suburbs. An even larger factor in the suburbanization of businesses has been a broadening of the customer base. Because by 1989 at least three-quarters of Korean businesses in Los Angeles County were targeting the general population as their primary clientele, moving the business to a high-income suburban area made it easier to reach this general market.[64] Merchants who remain in Koreatown are also trying to reach the non-Korean market.

Suburbanization of Korean entrepreneurs has been even more frequent since 1992.[65] The riot and fear of crime have impelled many to leave Koreatown and South Central.

Suburban enclaves. Korean information networks regarding new housing opportunities tend to lead to the development of suburban enclaves rather than to widespread dispersal in the suburbs. Friends and relatives, real-estate agents (most of whom are Korean), and the *Korean Times* constitute the leading sources regarding housing.[66] New residential clusters are soon noticed by Korean entrepreneurs, who locate to serve that market and thus add to the growth of the enclave.

The development of suburban enclaves is important because these provide Korean-oriented environments almost as complete as Koreatown. Speaking English is still difficult for most adult immigrants, but the growth of Korean stores in those places and the easy availability of Korean television throughout the Los Angeles area mean that immigrants in the suburbs may be living in predominantly white areas but are not at all isolated from Koreans and their institutions.

Although Christianity is a minority religion in Korea, most Korean immigrants to the United States are Christians. Two-thirds of Koreans in Los Angeles attend a Christian church twice a month or more, and Korean church congregations have been likened to an extended family.[67] Thus, the location of Korean churches in the suburbs is an important factor in decisions about moving. Churches are widely found in the areas where Koreans have settled, partly because many congregations have been able to rent facilities during the week from other Protestant churches while planning to build their own.

In 1972 Gardena was the only suburb with a relatively large Korean population, but by 1990 several areas of Southern California had sufficiently large Korean populations to constitute enclaves (Fig. 5.4). In some cases Koreans have selected some of the same areas preferred by other Asians, such as Garden Grove, Cerritos, Rancho Palos Verdes, and Diamond Bar. Such places have seen more Korean settlers since 1992, and some Koreans refer to a section of Garden Grove Boulevard in Garden Grove as "Koreatown South."

In the case of Carson the Korean cluster has been mostly people with low incomes. In 1980 more than 600 Koreans were living at the Scottsdale Townhouses, a relatively low-priced housing complex, but by 1990 those numbers had been cut by more than half.[68]

Many affluent Koreans have settled north of Koreatown, in areas of high-cost homes which are fairly accessible to Koreatown: the Los Feliz district of Hollywood, Glendale and the cities immediately north of it (La Crescenta and La Cañada–Flintridge), and the northern San Fernando Valley.

The San Fernando Valley. During the 1980s Koreans with a wide range of incomes settled in the valley, and their presence encouraged the growth of Korean businesses to serve their needs. The Korean enclave that developed in the north-central part of the valley was home to 4,000 Koreans in 1990.

Korean settlement and an ethnic economy have been more pronounced during the 1990s, especially since the 1992 riots encouraged departure from Koreatown. The more affluent Koreans bought large single-family houses in post-1970 developments in Porter Ranch and Granada Hills, north of the 118 Freeway; many others found attractive homes on the valley floor in North Hills. Fear of crime prompts many to choose houses in gated communities, and Koreans often cluster in a single development, as they have since 1990 in Burnet Villas and Lafayette Villas, just north of Nordhoff Street.[69]

Korean businesses which serve the Granada Hills enclave are most often found just to the south. In the older Van Nuys area rents for Korean businesses are relatively low; and Korean one-story shopping centers, banks, markets, videotape rental stores, and restaurants line Van Nuys Boulevard between Saticoy and Vanowen Streets.[70] Another shopping center, near the intersection of Nordhoff Street and Sepulveda Boulevard, is mostly Korean, and a former Alpha Beta supermarket has become the Korean-owned California Super Market.

Thus, Korean settlement in the San Fernando Valley illustrates the process of business and population dispersal out of Koreatown. The high proportion of immigrants among adult Koreans, unfamiliarity with American society, and widespread discomfort with the English language mean that Korean settlement in outlying areas is often clustered as enclaves rather than being dispersed within those suburbs.

Asian Indians

People whose origins lie in the modern country of India are clearly included in this category, but it also probably includes most other South Asians—those from adjacent Pakistan, Bangladesh, Nepal, and Sri Lanka. The few Asian Indians from Guyana, Trinidad, Fiji, and East Africa presumably also checked this identity. Ancestry data, which identifies specific nationalities, shows that 80 percent of Southern Californians reporting their race as Asian Indian also listed their ancestry as Indian. Another 13 percent indicated Pakistani ancestry, while 5 percent reported they were Sri Lankan and 2 percent, Bangladeshi. This range of South Asian origins in Southern California means that Asian Indians include Hindus, Muslims, Sikhs, Buddhists, and Christians, although Hindus are probably most numerous.

Asian Indian men (Punjabis, mostly Sikhs, from the Punjab region) came to California in the early twentieth century.

Between 1907 and 1911 most found work as agricultural laborers.[71] Later, many were able to lease or buy farmland themselves, especially in the Sacramento Valley. In 1917 Congress barred most Asians, including those from India, from immigrating. Indians who had already arrived were not at first subject to the restrictions of the Alien Land Laws because their racial identity was in question. However, a U.S. Supreme Court decision in 1923 declared that Asian Indians were not whites and thus were not eligible for citizenship or landownership.

After 1946 immigration from India resumed, but the low quota meant that only about 300 entered the United States in an average year. Diverse in their regions of origin, high level of education, and urban orientation, most of these newcomers were a distinct contrast with the rural Punjabis. Many of them settled in San Francisco or Los Angeles, where they were joined by some descendants of the earlier immigrants. In 1960 the U.S. census counted people in terms of foreign stock—those born in another country plus their U.S.-born children. At that time the Indian and Pakistani foreign stock numbered 1,925 and 151, respectively, in Los Angeles County—harbingers of the much larger population that was to arrive after Congress opened the gates to Asian immigrants in 1965.[72] Although most immigrants since 1965 came directly from India or Pakistan, many others lived first in Britain, Germany, Canada, or East Africa.

Dispersed settlements. By 1990 Asian Indians were widely scattered throughout Southern California (Fig. 5.5). Most individual census tracts which appear as having higher proportions of Asian Indians do not represent significant clusters because the number of Indians represented in each is so small. Fluency in English and high levels of educational attainment and income mean that they do not need to live in enclaves.[73] The dispersed nature of Asian Indian communities is also evident statistically. Of twelve major immigrant groups in Los Angeles County in 1990, Asian Indians were least segregated from non-Hispanic whites.[74] Moreover, the diversity of regional origins, languages, and religions included in the relatively small Asian Indian population means that residential enclaves are less likely to develop.[75] Asian Indians' continued emphasis on educational attainment is illustrated by the fact

that the campuses of the University of Southern California and of the University of California at both Los Angeles and Irvine appear as part of the distribution (Fig. 5.5).

Depending on their financial resources and preferences, Asian Indians live in neighborhoods which range from modest to very expensive. None of the Asian Indian concentrations that appear on the map is in a poor area. Slight Asian Indian concentrations are most evident in wealthy areas, many of which lie above the floors of the main basins and valleys where less affluent people live: Rancho Palos Verdes and Cerritos; Anaheim Hills and Irvine in Orange County; and Claremont and Walnut in the San Gabriel Valley. Many residents of these areas came from wealthy families in India; others have simply earned high incomes as professionals or managers in California.

The San Fernando Valley. Most Asian Indians live in the western San Fernando Valley and on its northern fringes. The latter area, including Porter Ranch and Granada Hills, lies just north of the 118 Freeway. (The large tract that is so visually prominent at the top of Figure 5.5 represents a similar development of new homes just west of Valencia. However, this tract should not be emphasized because in 1990 it was home to only forty-seven Asian Indians.) A small Hindu temple in Chatsworth, a Muslim mosque in Northridge, and a Sikh temple in North Hollywood serve worshippers; but these are small, unobtrusive, and located in commercial and industrial areas in order not to arouse antagonism among local residents. There has been much difficulty in gaining approval for additional places of worship that are at all architecturally distinctive and located in residential areas.[76]

The relatively high proportion of Indians in the western San Fernando Valley is partly related to the engineering background and aerospace employment of many South Asian immigrants. In addition, Hindus may be attracted to that part of the valley, as well as to Malibu and eastern Ventura County, partly because of their proximity to the Hindu Temple that was built in the mid-1980s in rustic and narrow Malibu Canyon. The temple is not well located in terms of access from Indian residential areas, but its isolation eliminates many objections to the dramatic South Indian temple style.

The Culver City area. The Palms, Mar Vista, and Culver City settlements of Asian Indians are distinctive in being much more urban than suburban and in being centrally located. The area has an abundance of Asian Indian shops, restaurants, and other businesses. It contains many Pakistanis and Muslims, as well as Hindus from India. Entrepreneurs seem to cultivate a multicultural South Asian spirit which to some extent overcomes the traditional barriers of nation, religion, and region.[77] We expect that the same observations could be made about most Asian Indian shops and businesses because, if for no other reason, their survival in Southern California depends on achieving a broad-based clientele. Family businesses owned by Asian Indians are sometimes managed during the day by the wife while the husband is employed in a larger company, perhaps as an engineer. Such responsibility is not normally given to women in South Asia and represents an improvement in women's status after emigration.

Little India. A shopping area, known as Little India, in southeastern Los Angeles County has become the preeminent Asian Indian commercial center in Southern California.[78] In the 1970s the number of Asian Indian families in the adjacent upper-middle-class suburb, Cerritos, was increasing, because Cerritos had a reputation for excellent schools and was in easy reach of engineering and related employment at McDonnell-Douglas, IBM, and Bechtel. Nearby La Palma and Buena Park in Orange County also attracted many Asian Indians, partly because homes were less expensive.

As more Indians settled in Southern California, particularly in the Cerritos–Artesia area, the potential market for a major Asian Indian shopping center became clearer. Stores and offices along Pioneer Boulevard had been developed in the 1940s, often by merchants of Dutch or Portuguese ancestry who had been originally attracted to the area when it was a center for dairying. However, by the early 1970s these businesses were declining because they could not compete successfully with the large, new malls. Asian Indians steadily bought up older businesses from owners who were usually eager to sell.

By the late 1980s Pioneer Boulevard between 183d and 187th Streets was vibrantly Asian Indian, with many jewelry stores, groceries, restaurants, candy and spice shops, clothing stores, insurance and travel agencies, and videotape rental stores specializing in Indian movies. Little India has become the largest focus of Asian Indian businesses in the western United States, drawing customers from outside California. Not surprisingly, the differences represented by the commercial and population shifts in Artesia—from the earlier conservative and white Americans to the more affluent shoppers and residents from South Asia—have resulted in tensions and barriers between old-timers and newcomers. These have been heightened by the highly visible nature of the ethnic shopping center that is Little India. In Little India the signs, window displays, and types of stores, as well as the dress and appearance of crowds, accentuate the cultural contrasts between Indians and the white merchants and residents.

Social separation. Asian Indian families who are widely scattered in suburbs are unobtrusive and welcomed by most whites, and, as we have pointed out, the level of residential segregation between Asian Indians and whites is low.

Although Asian Indians' English-language skills and high average economic status would suggest much interaction with whites, partially hidden cultural differences are real and result in mostly separate social worlds of Indian and white families. This situation is illustrated in Artesia and by the frequency of white-homeowner objections to Hindu, Sikh, and Muslim places of worship designed in traditional styles.

Pakistanis

Because nearly all people of Pakistani ancestry presumably reported their race as Asian Indian, the distribution of this group is similar in pattern to that of Asian Indians. The history of immigration is similar to that of the Asian Indian group as a whole, especially because no separate country of Pakistan existed before independence from British colonial control in 1947. In that year Pakistan was partitioned as a mostly Muslim country from predominantly Hindu India. For this reason, Pakistani immigrants are highly likely to be Muslim in religion, in contrast to the greater religious diversity within modern India.

Nevertheless, both Muslims from India and Pakistani immigrants are likely to speak a common language, Urdu, such that the two nationalities, which share religion and language, are often considered as a single group, Indo-Pakistanis.[79] Although Muslims believe that their common religion overcomes national differences, Muslims are substantially fragmented by differences of religious tradition within Islam, country and region of origin, and politics. Indo-Pakistanis are estimated to be the second largest religiously active Muslim group in Southern California—smaller in numbers than Arab Muslims but larger than African American members of the Nation of Islam.

Like Indians, immigrants from Pakistan are apt to have middle- or upper-class origins. Of all the immigrant groups we analyze in this book, adults of Pakistani ancestry were more likely to speak English only or very well (79 percent) and to be college graduates (57 percent). Not surprisingly, many Pakistanis were pursuing careers in business, engineering, and various professions.

Although their distribution also shows a dispersal across much of the more attractive residential areas in Southern California, employment with computer, electronics, and aerospace manufacturing may well explain the location of small Pakistani clusters (Fig. 5.6). In contrast to the total Asian Indian population, however, few Pakistanis live in Cerritos and Artesia or in most of the cities of the eastern San Gabriel Valley.

The Palms–Mar Vista section of Los Angeles has probably been the traditional focus for ethnic businesses serving Pakistanis, but it is likely that Pakistanis do most of their specialty shopping at grocery stores and spice shops which serve the larger South Asian and pan-Asian populations across much of middle- and upper-income Southern California.

Vietnamese

Refugees from the War in Indochina entered the United States in large numbers between 1975 and the early 1980s and were joined in the later 1980s by relatives who qualified as immigrants. Vietnamese were the largest group of refugees—outnumbering Cambodians, Laotians, and smaller groups from mountain areas, such as the Hmong.[80]

The fact that most Vietnamese, Cambodians, Lao, and Hmong arrived in the United States as refugees rather than as immigrants has made their adjustment here different from that of other Asian groups. Because refugees did not freely choose to come to this country, they have probably faced greater homesickness, depression, and adjustment difficulties than have most immigrants. Among the refugees, differences in backgrounds have played a major role in adaptation to the United States.

The first wave of refugees. In late April 1975, when U.S. forces were withdrawing from Saigon and South Vietnam, the U.S. government evacuated many Vietnamese who had worked for U.S. organizations or had ties with their personnel. These people together with family members who were able to join the air lifts totaled about 150,000 individuals. They constituted the first wave of Vietnamese refugees.

People in this first wave generally had higher socioeconomic status than did later refugees, were more familiar with U.S. culture, and were more likely to be strongly anti-Communist than were later refugees. Many of them had been educated professionals or managers in Vietnam, and most of the men spoke English, having been part of the South Vietnamese and U.S. war effort. Once in the United States most could not obtain jobs at all commensurate with their backgrounds. Nevertheless by the mid-1980s they were achieving 40 percent higher incomes than were refugees who arrived between 1976 and 1979.[81]

Later arrivals. After 1975 many people continued to leave Vietnam in whatever manner they could. The flow of new refugee arrivals to the United States, which peaked in the 1979–1981 period, is usually referred to as the second wave. The composition of this wave was diverse—ranging from urban businessmen and their families to farmers from the hills—but far fewer were fluent in English or acquainted with U.S. culture than were arrivals in the first wave. The second wave included many Vietnamese who had escaped to Thailand after the 1975 air lift, as well as hundreds of thousands who had fled Vietnam and Cambodia in small boats for the shores of Thailand or Malaysia.

Perhaps the largest part of this second wave was Chinese-Vietnamese—people whose family heritage is Chinese (Table 5.1). (For more on this group, see the final section of this chapter's treatment of the Chinese.) Beginning in 1978, Vietnam's Communist government forced most Chinese-Vietnamese to leave the country, presumably so that their businesses and wealth could be confiscated.

By the 1980s the United Nations and Vietnam had arranged for people who were accepted by the United States as refugees or immigrants to leave Vietnam through an Orderly Departure Program. After 1981 nearly all Vietnamese who entered the United States came under this program. Like the second wave, however, this group included few educated and professional people and few who spoke English. The program ultimately allowed the departure of 61,000 political prisoners and their families, 81,000 Amerasians (children of Vietnamese women and American servicemen) and their accompanying relatives, and 161,000 who qualified as immigrants because they were close relatives of refugees already in the United States.[82]

Formation of the Orange County enclave. In 1975 the large Camp Pendleton Marine training base in northern San Diego County was one of several military installations designated to receive the first wave of Vietnamese refugees.[83] Refugees assigned to Camp Pendleton flew from temporary camps in Guam and the Philippines to El Toro Marine Air Station and were then bussed to Camp Pendleton.

In May a huge city of tents was constructed for processing the refugees. The Red Cross helped reunite families separated during the evacuation. Refugees were examined medically and interviewed, and some rudimentary classes gave refugees a preview of their new life in the United States. However, the primary function of refugee processing at places like Camp Pendleton was to connect each refugee family with a sponsor, who was responsible for arranging housing and jobs for the refugees. Refugees were not permitted to leave Camp Pendleton until approved sponsors were found for them. By the end of October 1975, all the refugees had been assigned sponsors and new homes.

Although sponsors from many parts of the United States were found for the refugees who passed through Camp Pendleton, about one-third of those refugees settled in Orange County.[84] The people and churches of Los Angeles and Orange County were generous in their acceptance of refugees, and some Catholic and Episcopalian churches in Orange County sponsored more than ten large families.[85] Orange County's people and churches were particularly aware of the refugee situation because Camp Pendleton lies just to its south, but the early Orange County focus of Vietnamese resettlement was due to the location of sponsors in Orange County rather than to Camp Pendleton's proximity. Large numbers of refugees may have been accepted more easily in Orange County than in Los Angeles County because the shock of rapid population growth was muted by Orange County's lower density of housing and greater room for expansion.

U.S. government refugee resettlement policy encouraged dispersal across the country in small numbers, but later many refugee families left the isolation of scattered towns to join family members. These Vietnamese migrants typically headed to California, and Orange County was their most favored destination (Fig. 5.7). Migrants moved to Orange County because of its climate, the availability of assembly work in electronics, and the large number of Vietnamese and family members already there.[86] In addition, generous welfare regulations have made California a preferred destination. During the 1980s unemployed parents qualified for Aid to Families with Dependent Children more easily in California than in other states, and a family of four received more cash assistance over a longer period in California than elsewhere.[87]

Orange County was an area of relatively low-cost housing with work possibilities in nearby electronics and garment factories and restaurants. Thus, the refugees usually chose destinations near their relatives in the county. New arrivals also wanted neighborhoods that had bus service and were near friends, schools, and Asian markets.[88] The close proximity of Vietnamese residential and shopping areas resulted from the preference for living within walking distance of a Vietnamese market and the need to buy medicine, cloth, and other goods for shipment to relatives in Vietnam.

By 1990 Orange County contained 12 percent of all the Vietnamese in the United States, with Santa Ana, Westminster, and Garden Grove home to the largest numbers. At the same time that Orange County was attracting migrants from distant parts of the United States, many Vietnamese were dispersing from Orange County to other places within Southern California. The net effect was a strengthening of the general Vietnamese concentration in Southern California. In 1990, 25 percent of the Vietnamese in the United States lived in the five-county Southern California region.

Those who did not live in the leading area of ethnic concentration tended to have slightly higher incomes and be more acculturated.[89] This is illustrated by the Vietnamese who live south of the 55 Freeway in more expensive sections of Tustin and Irvine. First-wave immigrants and their families are also probably overrepresented among these and other Vietnamese residing outside the large enclave.

Little Saigon. Before October 1978 the area that would become the Vietnamese commercial center of Little Saigon was strawberry fields, used-car lots, and machine shops.[90] At first whites resisted the development of Vietnamese stores in the area, but by 1982 six Vietnamese shopping malls, plus other stores and offices, had been built along Bolsa Avenue in Westminster between Brookhurst and Magnolia Streets (Fig. 5.7).[91] The name "Little Saigon" commemorates appropriately the city that had been home to many merchants before the Communists took it over and renamed it Ho Chi Minh City.

Little Saigon is a large cluster of several indoor malls and strip shopping centers oriented primarily to the Vietnamese market. Chinese-Vietnamese, using Chinese capital from different Asian countries, financed and built most of the buildings.[92] A great variety of stores, restaurants, medical offices, and other businesses have appeared, as could be expected in any large shopping district serving an immigrant Asian population. Some small manufacturing plants have also appeared. However, the Vietnamese shopping areas are distinctive from other Asian centers because of the presence of many noodle

houses, restaurants, bakeries, and coffee shops, many of which show a strong French influence stemming from the days of French colonialism.

Surrounding Little Saigon and extending about eight miles across northern Orange County are the single-family houses and scattered apartments of the largest Vietnamese community outside Vietnam.[93] In 1990 over 40,000 Vietnamese were counted in this enclave. Vietnamese proportions are highest between Bolsa and Westminster Avenues close to Little Saigon, but in 1990 the Vietnamese represented no more than forty percent of any tract's population. This is because many of the earlier white residents remained and Latino settlement has expanded into the area from Santa Ana on the east. To the north, however, the 22 Freeway keeps the smaller Korean enclave in Garden Grove separate from the Vietnamese area. Since 1990 the growth of the Vietnamese population by as much as fifty percent has resulted in greater Vietnamese proportions in the enclave and a white exodus.

The entire Vietnamese enclave in Orange County—Little Saigon and its surrounding residential area—is especially important as a cultural home. It is a comforting outpost of the familiar in the very different world of English-speaking Southern California.[94] For Vietnamese who speak little English, it has been the most likely place to look for employment or to start a business.

Enclaves in the San Fernando Valley. The location of most Vietnamese enclaves outside Orange County are probably best explained by specific connections to sponsoring individuals or organizations, although the location of employment has also been important (Fig. 5.7). For example, refugees who moved directly to Long Beach from a camp in Southeast Asia reported that sponsor location was an extremely important factor behind their settlement in Long Beach.[95] Later, despite much movement in and out of Long Beach by Vietnamese families, there was a tendency for friends and relatives to settle near those who remained.

The western and central portions of the San Fernando Valley also illustrate the cumulative effect of the general location of sponsors followed by chain migration. In 1975 some

Catholic parishes in Northridge and Canoga Park helped arrange sponsorship for some Catholic Vietnamese families. These families encouraged others to follow them.[96] The net effect is a strongly Catholic Vietnamese population in the western part of the valley. Another group of refugees moved to the Van Nuys area in 1975 to be near sponsors, and their relatives and other refugees followed. Some of these Vietnamese were Buddhist, for whom a Buddhist Meditation Center was later created in nearby North Hills. In addition, entrepreneurs from Orange County came to the San Fernando Valley because that county was so crowded with Vietnamese businesses that new opportunities there were limited.

Some refugees who settled first in Van Nuys later bought homes in the Canoga Park area.[97] That area was more attractive than Van Nuys, but its home prices were still relatively low compared with some other areas in the Valley. After the initial sponsorship of refugees by individuals who happened to live in the valley, later refugees settling in the western part of the valley were usually sponsored by relatives who already lived there. Work opportunities may have been an additional factor in resettlement there: Vietnamese living in this area have been employed in electronics manufacturing at three times their rate in Southern California as a whole.[98]

As the number of Vietnamese in the western San Fernando Valley grew during the 1980s, immigrants felt more comfortable. Asian food stores serving the diverse Asian communities became more common, and Vietnamese entrepreneurs opened restaurants and other small businesses. Later, Vietnamese Catholics in two parishes were assigned their own priests and are now able to hold a Sunday Mass in Vietnamese. This has increased the attraction of the area for those Vietnamese who are Catholic.

On the northern side of the western San Fernando Valley enclave are some Vietnamese residents of a large apartment complex in which rents for low-income families are subsidized by the federal government. Farther north, outside the enclave, are scattered Vietnamese families who live in single-family houses, as well as some Vietnamese students who live in private apartments while they attend California State University, Northridge.

High-tech employment. Vietnamese may have moved to the Hawthorne, Gardena, and Lawndale area partly because of work in electronics and aircraft factories (Fig. 5.7). The area is a center for that type of manufacturing, and Vietnamese who live in Hawthorne have particularly high rates of employment in aircraft and electronics manufacturing.[99] Northrop Aircraft's large factory in Hawthorne is adjacent to a large, square census tract, where the 222 Vietnamese residents represented 11 percent of the total population. This was the highest percentage of Vietnamese within any tract in Los Angeles County as of 1990. However, reduced defense budgets weakened employment connections after 1990, and some of Hawthorne's Vietnamese have moved to Carson or Gardena, where home prices are lower.[100]

Vietnamese who live in newer housing areas outside enclaves rely more on employment in high-tech industries than do Vietnamese who live in the enclaves. In Ventura County, 28 percent of employed Vietnamese living in Thousand Oaks work in aircraft manufacturing, and 20 percent of those in Simi Valley make computers and related equipment. In southern Orange County, a similar but less-pronounced pattern is found.

Cambodians

In 1975 a group of ruthless, fundamentalist Communists led by Pol Pot took power in Cambodia. The group, the Khmer Rouge, began a three-year reign of terror and destruction. Phnom Penh, the capital city, was emptied as the Khmer Rouge forced its residents, including many skilled workers and managers, into rural areas to work in rice fields. The torture, slaughter, and labor camps they instituted forced Cambodians to try to flee across the Mekong River to Thailand.[101] Minorities in the country—primarily Chinese and Vietnamese—were subject to especially virulent attacks and killings in an effort to wipe out their cultures. In 1978 an invasion by Vietnam and the subsequent guerrilla war led to continued deaths and flight. On average, Cambodian immigrants to the United States spent two years in Thai refugee camps before arriving here.

Many Cambodians were resettled here between 1979 and 1981 as part of the second wave of Indochinese refugees, and others followed during the next few years. By 1985 they had suffered more than other Indochinese groups from split and broken families and an inability to even contact family members who remained in Cambodia. Such problems and the nightmares of atrocities still plague most Cambodian families and have made their adjustment to the United States especially difficult. However, political conditions were stable enough in 1990 for Cambodians to begin to return home to look for relatives and, in a few cases, to stay.

Long Beach. Cambodian settlement in Long Beach began in the early 1960s, when Cambodian students first participated in an exchange program with California State University, Long Beach (Fig. 5.8).[102] The students were well received and exchanges multiplied. Word of Pol Pot's atrocities filtered back to Long Beach, and Cambodians and their friends in Long Beach prepared to sponsor refugees. The U.S. government and the voluntary refugee-resettlement agencies found sponsors in many places in the United States. Because Long Beach may have been the only place with a much earlier Cambodian connection, it is not surprising that it has become the largest local Cambodian community in the United States.[103]

In the early 1980s there were few shops to serve Cambodians, and most were on a small section of 10th Street. By the late 1980s, the focus of the shopping area had shifted north, to East Anaheim Street. The neighborhood had been home to whites in the years before World War II, but over the next decades many whites moved to newer suburbs and were replaced by blacks and Latinos.

Cambodian entrepreneurs have transformed that old commercial strip into an attractive business corridor. The district contains new malls, restaurants, and offices, including the large building that houses the United Cambodian Community, a social-service agency. On side streets all around the business section is the ethnically mixed, older residential area, in which most Cambodian families rent apartments. This enclave in Long Beach is sometimes called Little Phnom Penh for the capital city of Cambodia. In addition, some Cambodians in the city live in northern Long Beach, where a large apartment complex on Long Beach Boulevard was the focus of the largest cluster in 1990 (Fig. 5.8).

Other enclaves. In Orange County a small cluster of Cambodians is located in Santa Ana, in the very poor South Minnie Street area.[104] Many families are headed by women whose husbands were killed during the holocaust perpetrated by the Khmer Rouge in the late 1970s. A Buddhist temple is in the neighborhood, but there are few Cambodian shops or offices. Because most American stores do not stock the rice, fresh fish, and fresh herbs and vegetables Cambodians desire, the women try to arrange rides to either Little Saigon or Long Beach for shopping.

Cambodians clustered in one part of South Central are located in the large Pueblo del Rio public-housing project (Fig. 5.8). Cambodian families took advantage of the high vacancy rate during the 1980s at Pueblo del Rio, and nearly all of them received welfare.[105] Accessibility to Long Beach was direct via the Blue Line commuter railroad, but by the early 1990s many families had moved away, presumably to a less-isolated location. In Pomona, Cambodians live in several of the less expensive tracts, not far from the Buddhist temple and community center on West 10th Street near Hamilton Boulevard.

Although Cambodians have tended to settle in low-rent areas, the specific locations are not as significant as the simple fact of clustering close to relatives and friends. The chain migration that has led to such small pockets of Cambodian settlement may have begun when someone found a particularly friendly and welcoming apartment manager or when a Cambodian wished to move closer to work.[106]

In the central San Fernando Valley, chain migration originating with refugee sponsorship in 1981 led about fifty Cambodian families to a single, large apartment complex (Sunset Point Apartments) on Valerio Street.[107] Most families have remained on welfare. The closest Cambodian Buddhist temple is in a private home in Echo Park, and residents drive to Long Beach twice a month for shopping. This isolated Cambodian settlement persists despite the lack of institutions normally associated with a successful community enclave.

Laotians

People who identified themselves as Laotian in the census were probably ethnic Lao who came from the capital of the country, Vientiane, or farming villages along the Mekong River. Members of other refugee groups, such as the Hmong and the Mien, may have also identified as Laotian because it is the name of their country. However, we assume that the lowland or ethnic Lao predominate in this nationality group.[108]

In Southern California, Laotians tend to be widely dispersed, and few are evident in Figure 5.9. As with Cambodians, the scattered pockets of Laotians in areas of low-cost housing can be explained by the desire of families to live together and by chain migration, often occurring when already settled refugees take on the official sponsorship of later, more recently arrived relatives.[109]

Most evident is the association with Cambodian settlements in Long Beach, Van Nuys, and Pomona. Buddhists in Pomona have built a temple, and the similarity of Buddhist religious traditions in the two ethnic groups may help explain the geographical association. Because many Lao have converted to Christianity in the United States, some clusters may be related to church locations.

In the early 1980s some Laotians were sponsored by people in Riverside County, where they worked in a mobile-home and prefabricated housing factory.[110] These numbers increased sharply in 1987, just after the Whittier Narrows earthquake. Many Lao who had been living in Los Angeles County were frightened by the quake and decided to relocate to Riverside County, where they knew a person who was hiring workers in that area. (This was the same earthquake that led to the overnight flight of several thousand Hmong from Southern California to Fresno and Merced in the Central Valley.) This relocation probably explains most of the several hundred Laotians that were counted in the 1990 census in the city of Riverside and the similar numbers of both Laotians and Hmong in Banning.

Ethnic Chinese are found in both the Cambodian and Lao populations (Table 5.1). Because birth rates are high among these groups and their U.S.-born children are not counted in the above figures, it is clear that well over 10 percent of Cambodians and Lao in Southern California have Chinese family origins. Chinese-Cambodians represent only a small proportion of the large Cambodian community in Long Beach but are much more strongly represented in the Chinatown area.

Thais

Very few people born in Thailand lived in the United States in 1960. As a result, Thais who might have wanted to immigrate after 1965 were unlikely to have relatives here to meet the family-reunification provisions of the 1965 immigration law. However, the establishment of American military bases in Thailand in the 1960s led to increasing contact with Americans and to awareness among Thais of educational and economic opportunities in the United States. Some Thais came initially as temporary visitors to the United States or as students but were later able to change their status to legal immigrants. Others simply remained in this country illegally. Later, once the chains of migration had developed, many Thais chose to live in Southern California because their relatives and friends were already here, they liked the mild climate, and employment opportunities seemed good.

In Southern California 24,191 people identified themselves as Thai on the census questionnaire, and 1,637 Chinese listed Thailand as their birthplace (Table 5.1). It is likely that many in the former group were of Chinese family background, as explained in the section on Chinese. Moreover, there is no reason to believe that the proportion of Chinese-Thais among all Thais has changed since the late 1970s, when a survey of Thais in Los Angeles found that half had at least one Chinese parent.[111] Most immigrants—both ethnic Thai and Chinese-Thai—had been born in greater Bangkok and were thus familiar with life in a large city before they settled in Los Angeles.

East Hollywood. Within Southern California several shifts have occurred in Thai residential and business concentrations. From the 1950s to the 1970s a small Thai enclave existed in Lynwood and a smaller settlement in Culver City, but by 1990 nearly all Thai residents had left those areas (Fig. 5.10).

Some moved to multiethnic East Hollywood, where many newly arrived immigrants were settling.

At first some Thais located near Olympic Boulevard, east of Western Avenue, but by the late 1970s the growing dominance of Korean businesses in that area prompted some Thais to shift their residences and businesses out of Koreatown. Some moved two miles north to East Hollywood, where Thai restaurants, markets, gas stations, travel agencies, a bank, beauty parlors, and newspapers had already been established. The close connection between the neighborhood Thai population and these businesses has been significant, in that Thais are both employees in the businesses and the most important customers for their products and services. Thai settlement in East Hollywood has been enhanced by the presence of large hospitals that employ Thai nurses and of nearby schools that provide technical training in engineering, computer science, and applied sciences.

Although East Hollywood remains an important enclave for the Thai community, in the 1980s many Thais dispersed to the suburbs. Some bought homes or condominiums in Monterey Park and beyond, in the eastern San Gabriel Valley. Others settled in Cerritos or Bellflower. In these moves they have followed other Asians, particularly the Chinese.

North Hollywood. A new enclave in the San Fernando Valley has replaced East Hollywood as the leading geographical focus of Thai life. Because most ethnic Thais are Buddhists, the 1972 completion of a magnificent Buddhist temple and community center in North Hollywood made that location particularly attractive.[112] As the temple, called Wat Thai, steadily gained in popularity as a place of worship and community center during the 1970s and 1980s, more Thais moved to nearby neighborhoods. To quell other residents' objections to the frequent traffic congestion, the temple bought the five houses closest to it.

By 1990 the eastern San Fernando Valley, with more than 1,000 Thais, had eclipsed East Hollywood as the largest Thai enclave in Southern California (Fig. 5.10). The presence of so many Thais in the neighborhood means that the Buddhist monks at Wat Thai can follow the tradition of walking to local Thai homes to receive a Saturday morning food offering, with the person who donates the food gaining religious merit.

No other ethnic group in Southern California has a distribution so strongly oriented to a single religious center. Places of worship and community centers for most other groups are generally located after the faithful have moved into a new area. Among the Thais, however, the temple itself was the key factor behind the geographical concentration.

Indonesians

Indonesia's relative lack of trade with the United States and the low level of historic Indonesian immigration have translated into small numbers of recent immigrants. Even during the 1980s, when immigration from most countries increased substantially, fewer than 12,000 Indonesians were legal immigrants to the United States.[113] The fact that 11,620 Southern Californians identified themselves as Indonesian in 1990 is accounted for by the immigration of some subgroups prior to the 1980s and by the relative importance of Southern California as a destination.

Subgroups of Indonesians. The first Indonesians to settle in Southern California were a distinct group of racially mixed people who called themselves "Indos" but whom others frequently call Dutch Indonesians. They came to United States as refugees by way of the Netherlands.[114] Indos had been marginalized and ostracized in Indonesia, especially during and after World War II. Some—particularly those with Dutch fathers—continued to identify with the Dutch after Indonesian independence in 1949. In the 1950s most migrated to the Netherlands, where they were not well received. Thousands of them later settled in Southern California.

Their numbers in 1990 can be estimated as the population reporting both Indonesian birth and Dutch ancestry. In Southern California 30 percent of the 15,455 people who were born in Indonesia had a Dutch ancestry. Of these, 70 percent were white; the remainder reported themselves as Indonesian on the race question. Thus, people of Dutch ancestry (Indos) remain a distinctive Indonesian group.

Ethnic Chinese are another important subgroup among Indonesians in Southern California. In the late 1960s, after persecution by the Indonesian government, many who were able to leave the country did so. In this way many Chinese-Indonesian professionals and business people came to Southern California, where some families opened restaurants or small delicatessens. In 1990 a total of 1,902 Indonesians identified their ancestry as Chinese, and another 3,150 Chinese reported Indonesia as their birthplace (Table 5.1). This suggests that about a third of Indonesians have Chinese family backgrounds.

The third group, which might be called ethnic Indonesians, generally arrived more recently and may be more affluent than the other subgroups.[115] Many own businesses or are government officials, although the group also includes servants and students.

Thus, three subgroups—Indos or Dutch Indonesians, Chinese-Indonesians, and ethnic Indonesians—comprise the population of Indonesian heritage in Southern California. Here, the three are distinct and have little social contact with each other.

Dispersal. Indonesians have scattered widely (Fig. 5.11). The Indos never clustered together geographically, although in their early years they did so socially.[116] It is not surprising, however, that some lived near Europeans of Dutch ancestry, the largest concentration of which was in Artesia.[117] The PUMS data show a slight tendency for Chinese-Indonesians to locate near other Chinese. Some ethnic Indonesians have their businesses in the Hollywood area and have discussed developing a stretch of Sunset Boulevard near the Indonesian-owned Metropolitan Hotel into a Little Indonesia.[118]

The affluence of some Indonesians is evident from the location of their residences—in places like Irvine and Laguna Hills, in Brentwood and Diamond Bar. Others live in less costly areas such as Upland, Placentia, and the central San Fernando Valley. The fact that hospitals are the leading industry of employment for Indonesian men and women suggests that the Indonesian concentration in Loma Linda in San Bernardino County (not shown in Figure 5.11) may be partly related to employment at Loma Linda University Medical Center.

Samoans

Because American Samoa has been U.S. territory since 1904, Samoans from those islands are U.S. nationals and can travel to the mainland without restriction, as do Puerto Ricans. However, the nearby islands of Western Samoa are an independent country and not U.S. territory. This means that Western Samoans who are considering travel to California cannot migrate or visit as they wish but fall instead under U.S. immigration laws.

World War II abruptly transformed the traditional subsistence life of Samoa.[119] When Samoa became an important staging ground for American forces, the buildup of Navy facilities and the presence of thousands of American servicemen led to the massive infusion of cash into the economy. After the war the old economy was shattered, and almost all available jobs were directly or indirectly tied to the U.S. Navy. The closure of the Navy base in 1951 precipitated the first large out-migration to the United States.

Long Beach, Wilmington, and Carson. When the Navy offered some of its Samoan enlistees the chance to transfer to Hawaii, most took advantage of the opportunity. Those who were later reassigned to Navy bases in California brought their families with them, and others arranged to be "dropped off" at a California base when they completed their service. During the 1950s and 1960s these pioneers were followed by other Samoans, resulting in rapidly growing Samoan communities in and near Long Beach, San Diego, and San Francisco. Thus, settlement in Southern California close to the harbor dates from the Navy connections of the early 1950s (Fig. 5.12).

Over the next two decades tract after tract of new suburban homes was built north of Long Beach. Samoans were among the eager buyers in what would become, in 1968, the city of Carson. In 1990 the distribution of Samoans remains remarkably concentrated in the Carson–Wilmington–Long Beach area. On the northern edge of the concentration, several hundred Samoans live in a single apartment complex in the city of Compton.[120] A separate Samoan enclave is located in Garden Grove and Santa Ana.

Since the 1950s, enlistment in the U.S. Navy has declined.[121] Samoan men frequently work as truckers, security guards, or stevedores, which has allowed them to remain in the area. Samoan settlement can be seen as one part of the larger working-class residential area of southern Los Angeles County. Samoan businesses tend to be family-run retail and food stores, serving Pacific Islanders regardless of nationality.

Adaptation to Southern California may have been particularly difficult for Samoans because of the great differences between their traditional way of life and the world of Southern California. Various Christian churches—most commonly Mormon, Congregational, or Catholic—help ease the transition.[122] Churches are particularly important for Samoans, and much of Samoan social life revolves around them, with frequent weddings and festivals. The importance of social bonds within the Samoan community is also reflected in the strong geographical concentration of its settlement.

Hawaiians

In Hawaii, and presumably among migrants to California, being part Hawaiian in family lineage usually enhances one's status. Because in Hawaii relatively few people trace their ancestry solely to native Hawaiians of Polynesian background, many Hawaiians counted in Southern California probably had mixed ancestries—Hawaiian together with various combinations of Japanese, Chinese, Filipino, Portuguese, Puerto Rican, black, and white, for example. Moreover, the prestige conferred by Hawaiian ancestry may prompt a few to claim this regardless of their actual family heritage.

The total number of Hawaiians in Southern California is so small that only two tracts in 1990 contained more than fifty of them (Fig. 5.13). Nevertheless, their distribution gives hints of likely social and employment connections. First, the tendency of Hawaiians to locate in the southern part of Los Angeles County can be associated with employment in and near the harbors of Los Angeles and Long Beach. Hawaiians may express some preference for living near the ocean, but certainly the harbor area has long had the blue-collar job opportunities that most Hawaiians seek. Second, other Pacific Islanders have located in the same general area of settlement, reflecting perhaps some commonality in background or viewpoint that is expressed in the Pacific Islander festivals. The small restaurants and take-out food stores owned by Hawaiian families are widespread and are patronized by other ethnic groups from Hawaii. Third, the presence of more than 300 Hawaiians in Gardena may well be a function of cultural and personal ties with Japanese from Hawaii. Last, the cluster of Hawaiians near LAX would suggest employment in some aspect of the air-transportation industry.[123]

Guamanians

Guamanians, or Chamorros, began to migrate to California only after 1950, when the U.S. Congress gave them unrestricted right to travel to the United States. Like natives of American Samoa, those who settle in California are not immigrants in the legal sense. Because Spain controlled Guam and other Mariana Islands until the late nineteenth century, most Guamanians, like Filipinos, are Catholics.[124] The early Spanish importation of Filipino labor to replace the dwindling Chamorro population of Guam adds to the similarity in traditional culture between Guamanians and Filipinos.

Because Guamanians, Samoans, and Filipinos share past employment ties with the U.S. Navy, it is not surprising that the earliest Guamanians in Southern California lived in Long Beach. Most of the men had either enlisted in or were working as civilians for the Navy, usually at the large naval shipyard there. Chain migrations of family and friends have directed later migrants to the same sections of Long Beach near Navy housing and the harbor—especially in West Long Beach, where a Filipino community has existed since World War II (Fig. 5.14). Like Filipinos and Samoans, many Guamanians have moved into the newer suburban housing in Carson.

Asian and Pacific Islander Median Household Income

Extremes of wealth and poverty among Asians and Pacific Islanders in different parts of Southern California are striking

(Fig. 5.15). The areas with the poorest Asian population are the best-known Asian ethnic enclaves: Koreatown and the areas close to Chinatown in Los Angeles, and the Cambodian settlement in Long Beach. A closer examination reveals the low incomes in the smaller Filipino enclaves of Temple-Alvarado and West Long Beach. Somewhat better off are Asians in most tracts in northern Orange County, where the Vietnamese are particularly concentrated in Westminster and Garden Grove.

Asians living in Monterey Park, Alhambra, and Gardena tend to have moderate incomes, as do most of the Asians who do not live where their group is concentrated. On the other hand, wealthy Chinese have bought homes in Arcadia and San Marino, to the north and east of Monterey Park. Affluent Asian households in the foothills north of the San Fernando Valley and in Glendale and La Cañada–Flintridge are mostly Korean, but Chinese and other Asians can also be found in these places. Cerritos is a slightly older, upper-middle-class suburban city which has attracted a wide range of Asians, especially Chinese, Koreans, Filipinos, and Asian Indians.

The greatest Asian affluence is generally found in newer housing in the hills surrounding the larger cities. Some of the most expensive Asian homes are on the Palos Verdes Peninsula, in eastern Ventura County (Thousand Oaks), and in Calabasas and other fringe areas of the western San Fernando Valley. Many Japanese executives of Japanese corporations live in Torrance and on the peninsula. The latter has been favored by other Japanese and Chinese families who can afford the homes there.

The largest areas with moderately high Asian incomes are southern Orange County and the eastern San Gabriel Valley, both of which experienced much new homebuilding in the 1970s and 1980s. Walnut and Cerritos have become attractive destinations for many Asians. West Covina, Diamond Bar, Hacienda Heights, and Laguna Niguel are also important Asian middle-income areas.

Asians who desire a new home tend not to move farther east into Riverside or San Bernardino Counties, as would many whites, blacks, and Latinos. This is because most Asians value easy access to larger cities, Asian markets, and institutions of their group over the greater isolation of a distant suburb.

Notes

1. Occupations of the early Chinese are discussed in the case study near the end of chapter 8.

2. Espiritu (1989), 61.

3. Excellent sources on early Chinatown are Mason (1967) and McDannold (1973), but see also Cheng and Cheng (1984) and Rasmussen (1993). Archeological finds from nineteenth-century Chinatown are described in Chang (1990) and Greenwood (1994). Modern Chinatown is covered in Hebert (1972); McMillan (1982, 1990); and Day (1985).

4. Hanson and Beckett (1944).

5. The Chinese distribution in 1970 is based on a map published by I-Shou Wang, Department of Geography, California State University, Northridge.

6. Torres (1996a).

7. Day (1985).

8. For the Chinese in Monterey Park, see Arax (1987b); Horton (1992); and Fong (1994). The characteristics of Chinese in the larger San Gabriel Valley are examined in Waldinger and Tseng (1992) and Tseng (1994, 1995).

9. These statistics understate the Chinese proportion because they do not include Chinese from Vietnam who identified themselves on the census questionnaire as Vietnamese.

10. The temple and its significance are thoroughly examined in Lin (1996).

11. Hing (1993), 28.

12. Coverage of the Japanese in Los Angeles before 1915 is based primarily on Mason and McKinstry (1969).

13. Mason and McKinstry (1969), Appendix. Another very early Japanese focus in Los Angeles was on 6th Street near Pershing Square, but by 1910 this area was being eclipsed by Little Tokyo. The 6th Street Japanese settlement was finally erased as Downtown expanded into that area.

14. Modell (1977), 71.

15. Mason and McKinstry (1969), 20; Strong (1933), 53.

16. The origins of these settlements and descriptions of them, as well as detailed maps, are found in Uono (1927). See also Tuthill (1924). Characterization of these areas is based on the Virgil Avenue enclave, sometimes called the Madison Avenue district, located between Melrose Avenue and Beverly Boulevard. This area lies within tract 1927 of the 1990 census. The area of the 10th Street enclave in 1927 is the area covered in 1990 by census tracts

2132.02 and 2133. West Jefferson, or the 36th Street enclave, was between Jefferson and Exposition Boulevards, from St. Andrews Place on the west to Budlong Avenue on the east, within modern census tracts 2220 and 2225 (Fig. 3.1). These enclaves are shown on the map of Japanese in Los Angeles as of 1940 (Hanson and Beckett 1944).

17. Uono (1927), 124–25; Nishi and Kim (1964), 30; Hanson and Beckett (1944).

18. Nishi (1958), 45.

19. Tuthill (1924); Uono (1927); Strong (1933); Hanson and Beckett (1944); Mason and McKinstry (1969), 29.

20. Broom and Reimer (1949), 154–59; Mason and McKinstry (1969), 26–27; McWilliams (1973), 322.

21. Moffat (1994b).

22. Pre-1942 Japanese farming is covered in detail in Broom and Reimer (1949), 70–75.

23. Hirabayashi and Tanaka (1988).

24. Strong (1933), 19, 53.

25. Liu (1989-1990).

26. Spaulding (1946), 224.

27. Nishi (1958), 41.

28. Broom and Reimer (1949), 120–21.

29. Tsukashima (1995-1996), 60–62.

30. Ronald Tsukashima, interviewed August 1996.

31. Kitano (1988); Fugita and O'Brien (1991), 68–69.

32. Michaelson and Meyer (1982), 7; Hansen (1983); Goodman (1989); Fugita and O'Brien (1991); Moffat (1994a).

33. Nishi (1985).

34. On the north side of 1st Street are brick buildings dating from the early years of this century, with small stores and hotels. This is now the historic district of Little Tokyo. Most of the 700 residents of Little Tokyo live in a high-rise apartment building (Little Tokyo Towers) and two other residential complexes. Poverty is visible only to the south, by the edge of Los Angeles' Skid Row and its the homeless population.

35. Strong (1933), 59.

36. Confirmation of the greater residential stability of Japanese in more recent times is possible with U.S. census data. Different ethnic groups can be compared by means of the percentages living in the same house five years earlier out of all individuals living somewhere in the United States five years earlier. Among Californians in 1970, both Japanese and Chinese had higher percentages living in the same house (59 percent and 55 percent, respectively) five years earlier than did whites (47 percent), blacks (45 percent), Filipinos (49 percent), or people of Spanish surname (47 percent). See U.S. Bureau of the Census (1972), Table 50 and U.S. Bureau of the Census (1973), Tables 5, 20, 35.

37. Ronald Tsukashima, interviewed August 1996.

38. Hing (1993), 34–35.

39. Takaki (1989).

40. For the characteristics and attitudes of Filipinos in Southern California, see Morales (1974) and Kang (1996).

41. The early settlements are described by Bartlett and Bartlett (1932) and Catapusan (1934).

42. Aquino (1952).

43. George Marr, former regional planner, Los Angeles County, interviewed October 1992.

44. Agbayani-Siewert (1993).

45. Espiritu (1992), 33. Because there is no commonly used name for this enclave, we use the term "Temple-Alvarado" because it identifies a key intersection in the area.

46. Espiritu (1992).

47. For discussion of Filipinos in the U.S. Navy, see Quinsaat (1976) and Allen (1977).

48. Hanson and Beckett (1944).

49. U.S. Bureau of the Census (1952).

50. Hamilton (1986).

51. Liu, Ong, and Rosenstein (1991).

52. Some features of early settlement were provided by Eui-Young Yu, Professor of Sociology at California State University, Los Angeles. Additional details are found in Givens (1939), 24. Koreans in Los Angeles in the 1970s are described in Yu, Phillips, and Yang (1982), and fascinating life histories of many Los Angeles area Koreans are reported in Kim and Yu (1996).

53. Park (1984), 62.

54. The 1980 calculations were made by Min (1993), 189, with Koreatown appropriately defined as smaller than in 1990. Koreatown as of 1990 can be easily identified in Figure 5.4. We included as Koreatown the nearly square area that was most strongly Korean, plus the three adjacent census tracts that were more than 5 percent Korean. For a detailed map of Koreatown showing percentage Korean by block, see Allen and Turner (1995).

55. Analysis of 1990 PUMS data showed that 27 percent of Korean immigrants in Koreatown had arrived in the United States after 1986. This was more than twice the average percentage for Korean residents in Southern California.

56. Kim (1986), 75.

57. The description of Koreatown and its businesses is based on a 1986 survey by Min (1993). Another good source on Koreatown is Abelmann and Lie (1995).

58. Characteristics of Korean business operations are covered in Lee (1992).

59. Min (1991), 235.

60. There are also many Korean-owned indoor swap meets and garment factories, but these are usually not located in either Koreatown or a Korean enclave. The other types of Korean business not associated with Korean enclaves have been gasoline service stations, grocery stores, and liquor stores serving black and Latino neighborhoods. The 1992 riots destroyed many Korean businesses.

61. Abelmann and Lie (1995).

62. Kim (1986), 76.

63. Kim (1986), 80, 82.

64. Yu (1990), 12. This source reports the results of a survey of 292 Korean households in 1988–1989 and presents valuable data on topics not covered by the U.S. census.

65. Chua (1994).

66. Kim (1986), 84.

67. Min (1991), 228.

68. Kim (1986), 64.

69. Burke (1994).

70. Kaplan, T. (1989).

71. La Brack (1988).

72. U.S. Bureau of the Census (1962), Table 99.

73. The general principle is that more assimilated immigrants tend to be less clustered residentially (Allen and Turner 1996b).

74. Allen and Turner (1996a), 21.

75. The diversity of regional origins is indicated by the first language spoken by South Asian immigrants to Southern California. It was estimated in 1980 that some 21 percent spoke Punjabi and another 20 percent, Gujarati. Next most important were Urdu (spoken primarily by Muslims), at 18 percent; Hindi, 16 percent; South Indian languages, 12 percent; and Bengali, 11 percent (Mossain 1982).

76. Dart (1993). Norwalk homeowners also objected to the traditional architectural design of a planned Hindu temple in their city. That temple, which serves many Cerritos residents, was redesigned in a Spanish style (Faris 1992).

77. Leonard and Tibrewal (1993), 149, 151.

78. The section on Artesia is based primarily on Harris (1992) and on interviews by California State University, Northridge, student Steve Kennedy.

79. Kelley (1994).

80. Most people identify with the name of their specific ethnic group or country. However, if a wider regional label is used, Southeast Asian is sometimes preferred over Indochinese because of the latter's association with French colonialism.

81. Rumbaut (1995), 249.

82. Rumbaut (1995), 238.

83. Processing operations at Camp Pendleton and links with Orange County sponsors are discussed in Cooper (1992).

84. Desbarats and Holland (1983), 27.

85. Alicia Cooper, former director of the International Rescue Committee office in Santa Ana, interviewed April 1996.

86. Mott (1989); Duong (1983).

87. Caplan, Whitmore, and Choy (1989), 35.

88. Desbarats and Holland (1983), 32. The Vietnamese evaluation of housing in terms of local accessibility is very different from most Americans' emphasis on the size, quality, and cost of the housing.

89. Allen and Turner (1996b).

90. Ngin (1989-1990).

91. Franklin (1983).

92. Gold (1994a), 202.

93. DeWilde (1996).

94. Ngin (1989-1990).

95. Peters (1987); Peters and Chen (1987).

96. The origins of Catholic Vietnamese settlement in the western San Fernando Valley were explained by Loc Nguyen, who was directly involved in arranging sponsorship of these refugees in 1975. Nguyen, director of Immigration and Refugee Department, Catholic Charities of Los Angeles, was interviewed April 1996.

97. The original refugee sponsorships and later chain migration that led to the western San Fernando Valley enclave were described by several Vietnamese ladies at the parish of St. Joseph's the Worker, Canoga Park, with Phuong Pham assisting as interpreter, March 1996.

98. PUMS data shows that 14 percent of working Vietnamese in the western San Fernando Valley were in this industry in 1990.

99. Scott (1993). PUMS data show that Vietnamese living in Hawthorne were employed in these industries at more than twice their average rate in these industries for all of Southern California.

100. This information was provided by neighborhood residents and a postal carrier.

101. Discussion of the chaos beginning in 1975 and the characteristics of refugees in California is based primarily on Rumbaut (1989, 1995) and Kiernan (1990).

102. The early Cambodian connection with California State University, Long Beach, was explained by Elizabeth Koo, youth project director at the United Cambodian Community, in an interview with California State University, Northridge, student Howard Shain, November 1993.

103. A useful source on the Cambodians in Long Beach is a six-part series in the Long Beach *Press Telegram*, December 10–15, 1989.

104. Ngin (1989-1990).

105. Rose Kinsey (program coordinator at the Holmes Avenue School) and Dwieva Hahn (manager of Pueblo del Rio) explained the situation of local Cambodians, February 1992 and January 1993.

106. Cuong Kim, Cambodian-refugee case manager of the International Rescue Committee, Santa Ana, interviewed April 1996. The fact that such neighborhood clusters of Cambodians or Laotians represent social networks and were established by a single person or family is confirmed by Ruben Rumbaut of Michigan State University. In the early 1980s Rumbaut traced the origin of several such clusters in the San Diego area and was always able to identify the specific pioneer who first chose the settlement.

107. Carmen Buenrostro (manager) and Mom Sok (a resident) explained the situation of local Cambodians, interviewed April 1996. See also Nielsen (1984) and Foster (1990).

108. The assumption that the Laotian population represents primarily ethnic Lao is based on the fact that the largest and most distinctive ethnic group from Laos, the Hmong, seem to have identified themselves specifically as Hmong: their census numbers and distribution nationally conform to expectations. Although some Hmong settled in Orange County soon after they arrived in the United States, during the 1980s most moved to Fresno or elsewhere. Because only 1,557 Hmong were counted in all of Southern California in 1990, they are not treated in this book.

109. Sheng Moua, Laotian worker at the International Rescue Committee office in Santa Ana, interviewed April 1996.

110. Alicia Cooper, former director of the International Rescue Committee office in Santa Ana, interviewed April 1996.

111. Details of Thais in Los Angeles in the 1970s and of the older Thai settlements, particularly East Hollywood, are based on Desbarats (1979).

112. Kaplan (1990).

113. U.S. Immigration and Naturalization Service (1991).

114. Kwik (1978).

115. Personal observations on this group and other Indonesians were provided by Stephen Koletty of the Department of Geography at the University of Southern California, interviewed July 1996.

116. Kwik (1978), 291.

117. The Dutch enclave around Artesia developed because of Dutch employment in dairy farming. Prior to its subdivision in the late 1960s, neighboring Cerritos was the single largest dairy center in Los Angeles County and was called Dairy Valley. As land values rose in the 1960s and 1970s, dairying shifted into the Chino area of San Bernardino County, where it remains focused in the 1990s.

118. Brown (1994).

119. For historical connections between migration, the Navy, and the post–World War II economy, see Lewthwaite, Mainzer, and Holland (1973) and Janes (1990), 22–27.

120. According to Margie McKenzie, manager of the Park Village Apartments in Compton, Samoans constituted 85 percent of the total residents (interviewed February 1992). They numbered many more than the 434 reported in the 1990 U.S. census because so many were Western Samoans who were residing in the United States illegally, having overstayed their temporary visitor visas. Park Village was popular with Samoans partly because it qualified for federal rent subsidies for low-income tenants.

121. PUMS data for Southern California show only thirty-seven Samoan men serving in the U.S. Navy in 1990.

122. Kotchek (1978). For general descriptions of Samoans in Southern California, see Bernier (1977); Shu and Satele (1977); and Millican (1991).

123. The PUMS data estimated that 140 Hawaiians in Southern California worked in the air-transportation industry in 1990.

124. Because of the historical influence of Spanish culture, many Guamanians and Filipinos also reported their origin as Hispanic on U.S. census questionnaires.

6. Narrowing the Gap?

How well are blacks, Latinos, and Asian groups in Southern California doing compared with whites? Or, more precisely, how much has the differential or gap in socioeconomic status between whites and minority groups been narrowed over the past three decades?

In this chapter we chart the relative progress of different race and ethnic groups in the four main components of socioeconomic status—educational attainment, occupation, income, and homeownership. Because higher levels of education presumably lead to better occupations, which then make it possible to earn more money, income is probably the most important component of social class. Closely related are the wealth and security represented by owning one's home.

Most research on these matters has been at the national level. In such studies, regional variations in ethnic composition and metropolitan economic differences may be significant influences but are often not controlled. In contrast, our focus on only Southern California means that the results of this chapter are more directly interpretable.

The Remembered Past

The year 1960 is a good baseline from which to measure change in Southern California. It represents the way things used to be in the post–World War II years. It makes a good comparison with 1990 because important demographic, social, and economic changes occurred during the intervening years.

The 1940s and 1950s. Southern California in 1960 had been enjoying the fruits of an economic expansion that began with the growth of defense industries in World War II and the influx of hundreds of thousands seeking such work. After the war men and women who had fought overseas wanted a return to steadier times, and many veterans chose to settle here after having glimpsed California during the war. The war's end unleashed a pent-up desire for goods and services that had not been available since the Great Depression. The seemingly insatiable demand for appliances, automobiles, and homes spurred consumer spending into the 1960s. Despite two recessions, the period from 1941 to the late 1960s was a time of widespread prosperity in Southern California, stimulated in no small way by the continued flow of federal dollars into local defense industries.

Not surprisingly, those were optimistic years. Most Southern Californians saw the region as promising a better life for both themselves and society. For many people life seemed very good indeed. Ozzie and Harriet seemed to personify the American family, Hollywood Boulevard meant movies and glamour, and life in the suburbs of Southern California was a dream being fulfilled.

If this golden era in Southern California is viewed from a different perspective, the domination of the region by English-speaking whites was almost complete in 1960. White proportions in Southern California had been greater in earlier decades, but in 1960 non-Hispanic whites still represented 82 percent of the population. All major decisions affecting life in the region were being made by white men. Most whites knew or cared little about the lives and troubles of blacks, Mexican Americans, and Asian Americans in their midst. The police often seemed to be protecting whites and their more powerful institutions, rather than the whole community. Discrimination in employment and housing was normal practice. Black–white segregation in Los Angeles was the second highest of all large American metropolitan areas.[1] Immigration from other countries was also small during those years, and more than 80 percent of the people of Mexican origin in Southern California had been born in the United States.

Social changes since 1960. In subsequent decades the United States witnessed such profound changes that 1960 represents a watershed. Change was ushered in by the election of President John Kennedy, whose wider vision of American society and this country's potential gave new hope to the poor and minorities. During the 1960s, however, the dreams of Southern California's whites were becoming tarnished. The assassination of President Kennedy in 1963 was followed in successive years by the Berkeley Free Speech Movement, the Watts rebellion, the rising clamor over the Vietnam War, and racial tensions over busing.

At the same time, whites came to acknowledge the fact of racism, and some of them worked to broaden the scope of who would be included in the mainstream of society. The Civil Rights Movement gathered support among whites, especially Jews, and became politically effective. Most whites became aware for the first time of the Mexican American population as a result of television coverage of the marches and struggles of César Chávez and the United Farm Workers. Over the following decades antidiscrimination laws were enacted, courts upheld the rights of minorities, and programs like affirmative action were created to overcome injustices rooted in the past. By the early 1970s it appeared that the social and geographical separation of black and white America was beginning to diminish. The Watts riot of 1965 was becoming, in the minds of most whites, a vestige of the racism of another era.

The late 1960s saw the beginnings of two additional developments that came to change much of the face of Southern California. The first was the ethnic transformation of the region's population, already explained in chapter 2. The second was a polarization of the job market that reduced the opportunities for high-school graduates but opened up new positions requiring either advanced education or very little in the way of education or skills.

Economic changes since 1960. In the late 1960s almost imperceptible changes in the work situations began to occur.[2] Opportunities for highly trained workers increased, while less-educated people experienced a decline in the income their labor could bring. Layoffs and later closings of all the large steel, aluminum, automobile, and tire factories in Southern California forced thousands of industrial workers into early retirement, unemployment, or lower-paying and typically nonunion jobs. At the same time, high-paying jobs opened up in sectors like aerospace, entertainment, and upper-level management, while low-wage jobs expanded in services and in those industries that competed on the basis of cheap labor. Clearly, employment opportunities were becoming more polarized in Southern California. However, the impact of this trend on the various racial and ethnic groups was unknown.

Both the demographic and economic shifts that characterized Southern California were ultimately the result of increasing economic interconnections between countries and the greater population growth in poorer parts of the world. The immigration of many educated and technically trained people; the production of automobiles, shirts, and camcorders by poorly paid workers in other parts of the world; and illegal immigration are all symptomatic of a global restructuring.

Between 1960 and 1990 the economy and population of Southern California continued to expand, but the pace was slower than it had been in earlier decades, especially in the older, more central areas. The overall growth—accompanied by the election of minority political candidates, an apparent nationwide reduction in racial prejudice, and the appearance of improved minority access to education and employment—has made it easy to believe that the differentials in education, occupation, and economic resources between whites and minorities have narrowed significantly since 1960. We now examine to what extent this has been the case.

Data and Methods

In this chapter and much of the next we look at only Los Angeles and Orange Counties. We had to restrict our analysis to these two counties because of limitations of the 1960 census tabulations. In this way we held the geographical area constant for appropriate 1960 and 1990 comparisons.[3] All tables and graphs in this chapter are based on the populations of Los Angeles and Orange Counties only.

People born in Mexico are distinguished from those of Mexican origin born in the United States. There are two reasons for this. First, immigrants from Mexico have had low socioeconomic status, but their adult children and grandchildren have raised their status—a demonstration of the process of assimilation over generations.[4] Secondly, the proportion of immigrants (that is, Mexican-born) among the people of Mexican origin has increased a great deal since 1960, from one-fifth to almost two-thirds. The status of the entire Mexican-origin population (immigrants plus the U.S.-born) could be expected to decline because of this fact alone. Keeping the U.S.-born separate from the immigrants in comparisons over time eliminates this confounding factor. No comparable 1960 socioeconomic figures are available for Asian immigrants as opposed to U.S.-born Asians.

The use of ratios in tables. We used various percentages and medians to measure socioeconomic status. However, because our interest was in comparisons between minority groups and whites rather than in the absolute measures of status, we designed our tables to enhance the comparisons.

Most values shown in each table are ratios between the values of the status indicator for the minority group and for whites. Near the top of the tables are the actual percentages or medians for non-Hispanic whites. In this main portion of the table, the comparative value for whites is always 100, and all listed ratios for other groups represent a percentage of the white value. For any group, the actual income median or a percentage can be calculated simply by multiplying the figure for whites at the top of the table by the group's ratio shown in the main body (expressed as a decimal percentage).

Ratios measure the difference in status between whites and minorities. Thus, in the text the words "gap" and "differential" often appear. These refer to the difference between 100 and any particular ratio. Ratios close to 100 indicate small gaps with whites; lower ratios represent larger gaps.

The Educational-Attainment Gap

This analysis makes use of two appropriate and widely used educational-attainment indicators: the percentage of high-school graduates and the percentage of college graduates. In 1960, when people were much less educated, the former was probably the more important qualification for obtaining a good job. At that time more than half of non-Hispanic white men and women in Southern California were high-school graduates, yet fewer than 15 percent of white men and 8 percent of white women had graduated from a four-year college (Table 6.1). By 1990, however, so many more people were completing higher education that the percentage of graduates from four-year institutions had become a more significant measure of status.

In 1960 blacks and Hispanics were very unlikely to have graduated from college. Black men had graduated from high school at two-thirds the rate of white men, but their rate of college graduation showed a particularly wide gap with white men. The relatively high educational attainment of black women is evident in that fact that white women were half as likely as white men to be college graduates. However, black women had graduated from college at almost twice the rate of black men.

Of the other groups in 1960, Asians were either more highly educated than whites (ratios over 100) or had by far the smallest educational-attainment gaps. These groups, even more than whites, viewed education as the means by which to improve their status. Chinese men and women and Filipino women had unusually high proportions of college graduates.

The high average status of the Chinese shows the effect of the several thousand advanced students from China who were already in the United States at the time of the Communist takeover in 1949, as well as the high educational level of refugees.[5] These new arrivals gave Chinese women something of a head start over Japanese women. Although after World War II many younger Japanese American women attended college, most Japanese women who immigrated during the 1950s were not highly educated and had come to California simply as wives of American servicemen.

Table 6.1 Educational-Attainment Ratios, 1960 and 1990

| | High-School Graduates | | | | College Graduates (4-year) | | | |
| | Men | | Women | | Men | | Women | |
Group	1960	1990	1960	1990	1960	1990	1960	1990
Percentage completion rate								
Non-Hispanic whites (14+)	53.9	–	54.4	–	12.1	–	6.6	–
Non-Hispanic whites (25+)	56.8	88.0	56.9	85.7	14.3	36.7	7.6	25.0
Ratio (percentage of non-Hispanic white completion rate)								
Non-Hispanic whites	100.0	100.0	100.0	100.0	100.0	100.0	100.0	100.0
Blacks	67.6	83.9	73.4	87.0	33.1	42.8	60.6	57.2
Hispanics	47.7	46.4	44.3	46.3	28.0	19.1	25.0	23.2
Mexican Americans	53.3	75.5	50.0	66.5	25.3	28.3	24.5	31.2
Mexican immigrants	22.4	27.3	18.1	32.4	10.5	8.2	9.2	9.6
Japanese	121.3	103.9	120.6	105.1	101.7	119.1	93.9	119.6
Chinese	99.1	88.6	97.8	82.4	158.7	127.0	180.3	130.8
Filipinos	73.8	101.8	101.1	101.4	48.8	124.0	186.4	206.4

Sources: U.S. Bureau of the Census (1962a, 1963a, 1963b, 1992).

Notes: Comparative rates for 1990 and the 1960 Hispanic rate are based on the population aged 25 and older; other 1960 rates are based on the population aged 14 and older. Data are for Los Angeles and Orange Counties.

Among Filipinos, the high attainment of women is mostly due to the immigration of nurses during the 1950s. Under the auspices of the State Department's Exchange Visitor Program of 1948, U.S. hospitals and the American Nurses' Association recruited many graduates of nursing schools in the Philippines.[6] In contrast, the low educational level of Filipino men is due to the large proportion who were migrant farm laborers in their younger days. Typically middle-aged in 1960, many of the men were still single; others had formed families with white women. This meant that Filipino women in Southern California included both U.S.-born daughters of these men and post-1946 immigrants.

The widest of all educational attainment gaps was between whites and Hispanics. The fact that Mexican Americans were between two and three times better educated than immigrants from Mexico represented a dramatic improvement in status as a result of acculturation.

Changes from 1960 to 1990. During these decades all groups in Southern California improved absolutely in their educational attainment. But because the proportion of college graduates more than doubled for white men and tripled for white women, rates of college education among minorities had to increase at least as much in order to close the gap at all. Under these conditions black men and women have made remarkable progress educationally.

Asians continued to show the high educational level that had been so clearly evident in 1960. By 1990 all three Asian groups easily exceeded whites in percentage of college graduates. This development was due to the continued emphasis on education among both Asian families who had been in the United States for generations and immigrants who had arrived since the mid-1960s. The status of Filipino men had almost reversed itself with the dramatic change in immigrant characteristics since the farm laborers had arrived in the early twentieth century. Filipino women, many of whom had graduated from college in the Philippines, continued to have unusually high proportions of college graduates—more than twice the rate of white women.

However, among Hispanics the relative status of immigrants closed hardly at all. In 1990 they were still less than half as likely as whites to have graduated from high school and only a quarter as likely to be college graduates. The relative attainment of Mexican immigrants was the lowest of all; they were less than a tenth as likely as whites to have graduated from college. The higher proportion of Mexican, Guatemalan, and Salvadoran immigrants in Southern California in 1990 compared with 1960 was probably the most important factor in the lack of educational progress for Hispanics relative to whites.

More meaningful in assessing the acculturation and progress of Hispanics is the status of those born in the United States—the Mexican Americans. Their high-school graduation gaps narrowed substantially, but college graduation rates remained large.[7] In 1990 Mexican Americans were still graduating from college at less than a third the rate of whites. In contrast, black men made greater progress in closing the college-graduation gap with whites. This meant that the educational gap between blacks and Latinos had also grown, with blacks in Southern California constituting a measurably better-educated population than Mexican Americans.

The Occupational Gap

Professionals and managers, with administrators and executives included as managers, are the occupations most easily classified in terms of status. These represent the top rungs of the occupational hierarchy, often referred to as "high-status" or "upper-level, white collar" occupations.

Ethnic gaps in percentage working as professionals correlate closely with differentials in educational attainment. This is not surprising because professional qualifications are based so strongly on formal education.[8] In contrast, the qualifications of managers and administrators are often not based on educational attainment. Thus, inclusion of managers and administrators, in addition to professionals, means that our measure of occupational status is less directly dependent on educational attainment and represents a somewhat distinct dimension of status.

Asians in 1960 were somewhat underrepresented as professionals and managers compared with their high educational attainment (Table 6.2). Most of this was due to the legacy of discrimination by whites. During the 1920s and 1930s many white employers refused to hire U.S.-born Chinese, even university graduates, for the jobs and careers for which they had trained.[9] Prior to World War II some whites seemed to believe that success in the professions was too difficult for Asians. In any case, exclusion limited Asian occupational advancement.

In 1960 gender differences in occupational status mirrored in direction and size the gender differentials already observed for education. White men and Japanese men were more likely than white women and Japanese women to hold high-status employment, but for blacks, Chinese, and Filipinos the advantages were reversed. Some gender differences were striking. Black and Filipino women were represented as managers and professionals at more than twice the rate of the men in their ethnic groups. Japanese and Chinese most closely approached whites in upper-level, white-collar employment, with Chinese women even exceeding white women in occupational status.

Progress since 1960. By 1990 the occupational gap had narrowed substantially for black and Asian men. All of these increased their proportions in high-status occupations faster than did whites in the 1960–1990 period.[10] Japanese and Chinese men were even better represented as managers and professionals than were whites. Among black, Japanese, and Filipino women, the gap with white women also narrowed. Mexican American women narrowed the occupational gap substantially, and the men also showed some improvement since 1960 relative to whites.

Thus, since 1960 Southern California has seen an improvement in occupational status among white men and a

Table 6.2 Occupational-Status Ratios, 1960 and 1990

	Men		Women	
Group	1960	1990	1960	1990
Percentage in high-status occupations				
Non-Hispanic whites	30.0	37.5	19.3	35.4
Ratio (percentage of non-Hispanic white rate)				
Non-Hispanic whites	100.0	100.0	100.0	100.0
Blacks	24.5	46.9	49.5	69.0
Hispanics	32.7	23.7	34.0	34.2
Mexican Americans	30.1	38.6	31.7	53.4
Mexican immigrants	19.4	12.6	19.7	17.6
Japanese	84.6	108.7	72.2	93.2
Chinese	78.3	104.4	110.9	86.4
Filipinos	31.4	65.9	73.3	83.2

Sources: U.S. Bureau of the Census (1962a, 1963a, 1963b, 1992).

Notes: Data are for employed persons aged 16 and older. High-status occupations for 1960 were professional, technical, and kindred occupations; and managers, officials, and proprietors. For 1990 the two categories were executive, administrative, and managerial occupations; and professional specialty occupations. In both years engineers, teachers, and physicians were considered professionals. Proprietors and health technicians were included as high-status occupations in 1960 but not in 1990. Data are for Los Angeles and Orange Counties.

very large shift of white women into managerial and professional work. For most minorities the change has been even greater, resulting in a narrowing of the occupational gaps. The greatest improvement has been among blacks and Filipino men. All this constitutes clear evidence of progress toward greater socioeconomic equality. Those groups that showed the opposite trend (Mexican immigrants and Chinese women) had large numbers of recent immigrants with low educational levels and poor English-language skills.

The Income Gap

The indicator appropriate for our research is the annual personal income of men and women. Because its measurement is more fraught with potential hazards than is either education or occupational status, we must explain certain aspects of the data and our method for achieving good comparative ratios.

Quality of the data on income. Income data are for 1959 and 1989 because the census asked people to report their personal income during the previous calendar year.[11] Weaknesses in the data indicate that the ratios we present for Hispanic and black minorities, particularly for the latter, may be a little too high to reflect the reality of group economic differences. Part of this is due to the greater undercount of black and Latino men and of those with incomes below the median. Another important aspect is the fact that the income data for 1989 do not cover as large a proportion of black men as they did in 1959. This contrasts with an increase in the percentage of white men who reported income.[12] This racial divergence suggests that our 1989 black income ratio may be too high to reflect accurately the true economic disparity between black men's and white men's incomes.

The increased percentage of women employed in 1989 compared with those employed in 1959 did not affect the comparisons because the data are based on only people with income. Ethnic differences in the proportion of women working full time could affect the medians, but these were small and had little effect on comparisons between groups or trends.

Income distributions. Most income and other socioeconomic differentials described in this book are based on the average status positions of groups as measured by percentages and medians. However, such indicators cannot show the great range of status within ethnic groups. For this reason we look first at the frequency distributions of men's incomes (Fig. 6.1). (Income figures for women in 1959 are not available.) These graphs make clear the great extent to which the incomes of different groups overlap in the middle portion of the graphs. Except for the 1959 clustering of white men's incomes in the

$7–10,000 range and the 1989 concentration of Mexican immigrants in very low-income categories, all groups include some men who earn low incomes and others with high incomes.

Figure 6.1 also demonstrates that the 1989 income distributions of black and Chinese men are bi-modal: those lines on the graphs show peaks at two different points separated by a trough. Others have also pointed out the growing socioeconomic contrast between poorer people and the more affluent within some Asian immigrant groups and among blacks.[13]

Measuring income ratios. Comparisons of income among groups are usually expressed in terms of median income. Fortunately, published volumes report the 1959 median personal income of men and women in most of the groups.[14] Most 1989 medians were calculated from the PUMS file by a statistical program. Where medians were not available, we calculated them from nine or more income categories using the same method as the Bureau of the Census.

The actual distribution of white men's incomes within the various income categories in 1959 was sufficiently skewed to make the median not entirely satisfactory (Fig. 6.1).[15] Japanese and Chinese men were somewhat similar to whites in their distribution, so their median-based ratios should be better measures. However, because the income distributions of Hispanic, black, and Filipino men were quite different from that of whites, the median-based ratios to white men's income were misleadingly high.

For this reason the ratios most severely affected were supplemented with estimates based on calculations of the Index of Net Difference (ND), a better statistic for comparing differences in frequency distributions.[16] Calculations of ND in 1959 for Mexican American, Mexican immigrant, black, and Filipino men resulted in lower income ratios (Table 6.3).[17] For those groups only we used ND-based ratios in the following text and graphs. However, we also provide the original ratios based entirely on medians.

The income-gap trend. The most important general result was that income gaps between whites and most groups either have remained stable or have increased since 1959. (If the

Table 6.3 Median-Income Ratios, 1959 and 1989

Group	Men 1959	Men 1989	Women 1959	Women 1989
Median income				
Non-Hispanic whites	$5,600	$31,255	$1,969	$16,574
Ratio (percentage of non-Hispanic white median income)				
Non-Hispanic whites	100.0	100.0	100.0	100.0
Blacks	66.8 (54)[a]	56.8	87.7	78.4
Hispanics	77.9	44.0	93.1	57.3
Mexican Americans	81.2 (73)[a]	61.4	97.2	72.8
Mexican immigrants	66.5 (54)[a]	39.2	80.9	52.5
Japanese	85.0	103.2	130.8	108.5
Chinese	72.0	64.2	123.3	74.0
Filipinos	65.2 (53)[a]	63.7	108.8	107.0

Sources: U.S. Bureau of the Census (1962a, 1963a, 1963b, 1992).

Notes: Where possible we used medians for 1959 as reported in census publications. For non-Hispanic white women, however, the median was adjusted from the published white median of $1,957. By weighting according to population sizes, the effect of Hispanic women could be removed from the total of white women. All data are based on individuals age 14 and older who had income during the calendar year. Data are for Los Angeles and Orange Counties.

[a]Revised ratios based on the Index of Net Difference (ND), estimated by interpolation from values of ND.

ND had not been used to improve the income ratios, even the white–black income gap would have been shown as clearly wider in 1989 than in 1959.) The single exception to the trend is Japanese men, whose 1989 median income exceeded that of white men. This is due in part to the higher incomes of many Japanese-born men who are executives of Japanese companies and are based only temporarily in Southern California.[18]

For all other groups, the greater income disparity in 1989 is a striking finding. It indicates that over the past thirty years,

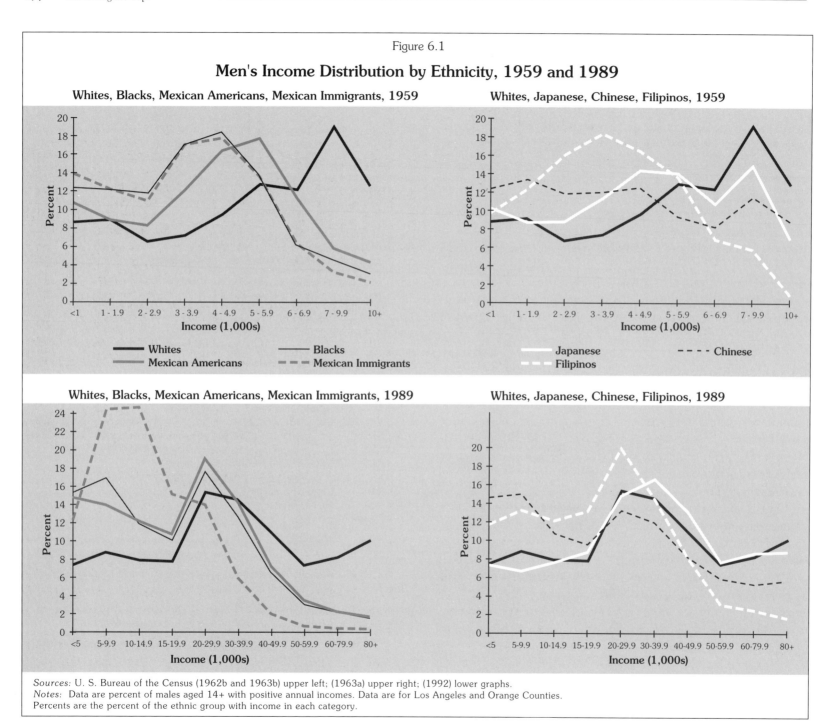

Figure 6.1

Men's Income Distribution by Ethnicity, 1959 and 1989

Whites, Blacks, Mexican Americans, Mexican Immigrants, 1959

Whites, Japanese, Chinese, Filipinos, 1959

Whites, Blacks, Mexican Americans, Mexican Immigrants, 1989

Whites, Japanese, Chinese, Filipinos, 1989

Sources: U. S. Bureau of the Census (1962b and 1963b) upper left; (1963a) upper right; (1992) lower graphs.
Notes: Data are percent of males aged 14+ with positive annual incomes. Data are for Los Angeles and Orange Counties.
Percents are the percent of the ethnic group with income in each category.

despite some convergence between minority groups and whites in education and occupational status, incomes were just as far apart in 1989 as in 1959. Admittedly, the changing characteristics of Asian immigrants have played a role in this trend, and in an absolute sense most of the groups have gained. However, in a relative sense clearly whites have benefited disproportionately from economic and demographic trends.

Changes in the income ratios of blacks, Mexican Americans, and Mexican immigrants are highlighted in Figure 6.2. Bars extending farther toward the left indicate lower ratios or greater gaps with whites. The fact that most income gaps have grown wider since 1959 is indicated by the greater length of the dark bars representing 1989 compared to the lighter narrower 1959 bars. Women of Mexican origin—both the U.S.-born and immigrants—show the greatest drop in income relative to that of comparable whites, but there is also no doubt about the decline among Mexican-origin men. Only black men show a slight narrowing of the income gap.

Apart from Figure 6.2, however, the drop in the percentage of black men reporting any income—from 88 to 82—between 1959 and 1989 means that black and white incomes have really not converged. Moreover, if the 1959 median income ratios had not been corrected for the skewed income distribution of white men by means of the Index of Net Difference, the growing disparity between the incomes of minority and white men over the 1959–1989 years would have appeared even greater than is indicated in Figure 6.2.

The fact that the income differential between whites and Mexican Americans in Southern California has grown substantially since 1959 may come as a surprise. A portion of the income gap in both years can be explained by the fact that working Hispanics are younger on average than are whites. As a result they have fewer of the years of working experience that normally translate into higher pay. In chapter 7, however, we demonstrate that this age difference is not a major factor behind the gap.

This growing income disparity between whites and those other Americans who are not immigrants appears egregiously inconsistent with a basic tenet of the American dream. Many of us assume that the processes of acculturation and economic

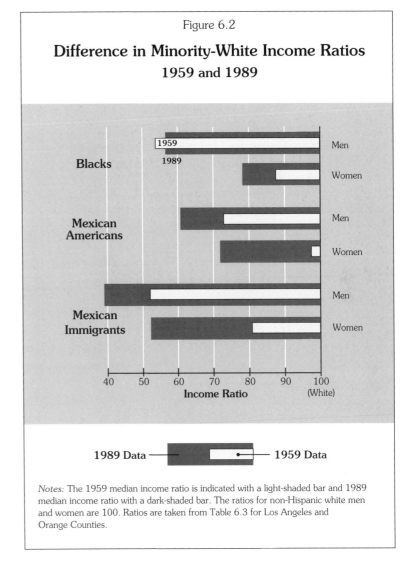

Figure 6.2

Difference in Minority-White Income Ratios
1959 and 1989

Notes: The 1959 median income ratio is indicated with a light-shaded bar and 1989 median income ratio with a dark-shaded bar. The ratios for non-Hispanic white men and women are 100. Ratios are taken from Table 6.3 for Los Angeles and Orange Counties.

growth will result in enough of an income gain among the children and grandchildren of immigrants for the gap to narrow. However, that has not occurred here.

Thus, both immigrants from Mexico and Mexican Americans are doing less well relative to whites than they were in 1959. Moreover, the skewing of the 1989 incomes of Mexican-born men far below the median indicates that the ratio underestimates the real gap (Fig. 6.1 and Table 6.3). The trend is basically the result of a growing disparity in education and skills between whites and Mexican immigrants, but other factors discussed in chapter 7 are also significant. In addition, many Mexican immigrants are residing illegally in Southern California, and studies have found that illegal residents earn about 6 percent less than do Mexican immigrants.[19]

Income Gaps in Relation to Education and Occupational Status

Because educational attainment, occupational status, and income should be interdependent in many ways, we have presented certain ratios in graphic form to clarify these relationships (Fig. 6.3). In these graphs college graduation is used as the measure of educational attainment because an advanced education has become so important for high-income employment. Bars extending above the 100 ratio (which represents whites) indicate status superior to whites.

1960. Ethnic groups differed sharply in the degree to which they were receiving the income commensurate with their educational and occupational attainment. To get an approximate indication of this, compare the length of bars for the three different measures of status for any one group (Fig. 6.3). If the education–occupation–income relationship for whites also characterizes the other groups, the three status bars in the graph will be similar in length and position above or below the 100 ratio.

Incomes for blacks and Mexican Americans in 1959 were higher than expected because in 1959 the economy was providing a larger share of jobs requiring little education. In the 1950s many people had been able to find and hold good jobs—often as blue-collar workers in unionized plants—without having even a high-school education. Many blacks were drawn to Los Angeles by the hope of work in defense industries, while the widespread shift from agriculture to industrial jobs during the 1940s and 1950s positioned Mexican Americans to take advantage of a growing manufacturing sector in Los Angeles.

The percentage of upper-level, white-collar workers was low among most minorities. Chinese women were exceptional

in being better represented in managerial and professional positions than were white women. Nevertheless, Chinese men and women and Filipino women showed much lower proportions in high-status occupations than would be expected from their educational attainment. In large part this is the result of discrimination by whites, which effectively barred many Asians from professional and other higher-status employment.

1990. Both blacks and Mexican Americans still had much lower percentages of college graduates than did whites. However, both groups had higher incomes than would be expected from their percentages of college graduates. Among blacks and Mexican Americans the occupational gap has narrowed somewhat since 1959. The wide gap in education suggests that there is a great need for further increases in rates of college graduation to raise these groups' average incomes.

The frustration that some blacks and Mexican Americans feel at the continuing large income gap may be somewhat mollified by the knowledge that, relative to whites and Asians, their groups had incomes that are higher than could be expected from their educational and occupational status. Indeed, Chinese and Filipino men have average incomes that are very similar to those of black and Mexican American men despite the much higher educational attainment of the Asian men (Fig. 6.3). Chinese women also had incomes commensurate with those of black and Mexican American women although the Chinese had much higher rates of college graduation.

Especially high rates of college graduation among Chinese and Filipinos have generally not resulted in higher incomes in the way they have for whites. Part of this is due to the recency of their immigration, with corresponding low levels of acculturation as well as the lack of recognition by U.S. employers of many degrees obtained overseas. Among Filipinos, the pattern is also related to the many individuals who work in technical occupations classified by the U.S. census as nonprofessional (see occupational niches in Table 8.4).

Japanese are closest to whites in socioeconomic status; there were only small inconsistencies in the size of the three gaps. The fact that most Japanese are not immigrants but are the children or grandchildren of immigrants suggests that

Figure 6.3

Difference in Minority-White Status Ratios
1960 and 1990

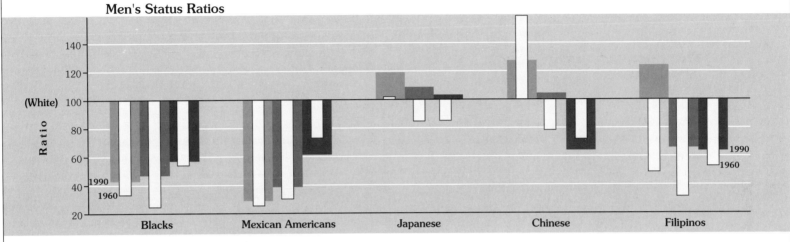

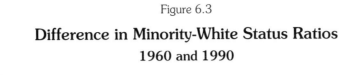

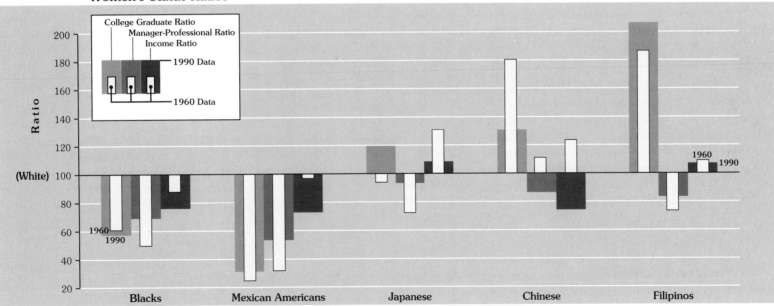

Notes: The 1960 ratios are indicated with light-shaded bars and 1990 ratios with dark-shaded bars.
Ratios are taken from Tables 6.1, 6.2, and 6.3, Los Angeles and Orange Counties.
Income ratios for blacks, Filipinos, and Mexican Americans in 1960 are based on index of net difference rather than median. See text for explanation.

greater acculturation from their longer period of residence has played an important role. The change over the past half-century in the status of Japanese Americans is extraordinary. It would appear that employment and income discrimination against the Japanese in Southern California is no longer significant, although we show one likely exception in chapter 7.

The Homeownership Gap

Owning one's home in America has long been a symbol of success, and group differences in rates of homeownership reflect an important component of gaps in economic status. Because some immigrants to Southern California brought a great deal of money with them and were able to buy housing despite low postmigration incomes, wealth can be somewhat independent of median income. It differs from the previous indicators because it characterizes households, not individuals.

Despite dramatic increases in housing prices in Southern California between the mid-1970s and 1990, most gaps in homeownership rates have not increased since 1960 (Table 6.4).

The fact that the white–minority gap in homeownership rates has not become wider, whereas that of median income has increased, can be explained by the fact that minorities have become homeowners in less-expensive areas than those in which whites have bought houses. During the period of rapid housing inflation, prices increased much more in mostly "white" areas than in other areas. This is shown by the fact that in 1960 the median value of homes owned by blacks and Hispanics in Los Angeles and Orange Counties was about 80 percent that of homes owned by non-Hispanic whites.[20] By 1990, however, the median value of homes owned by blacks was only 56 percent of the median for non-Hispanic whites, and homes owned by Latinos averaged only 67 percent of the value of the homes owned by non-Hispanic whites.

Thus, to some extent the higher incomes of whites were being spent on more expensive housing. The net geographical effect was, of course, to maintain or perhaps increase residential separation between whites and other groups. Gaps in median income tended to reinforce areal differences between homeowners of different ethnic groups.

In terms of specific groups, the tenure gap between blacks and whites has been stable since 1960. The three Asian groups have increased their relative rate of homeownership over the past thirty years, and in 1990 both Japanese and Chinese owned their housing at slightly higher rates than did whites. For Japanese, this change was consistent with the fact that the median income of Japanese men grew faster than did that of whites. Among Chinese, however, the substantial increase in homeownership rate coupled with a decline in median income relative to whites suggests the role of wealth imported by immigrants.

Table 6.4   Homeownership Ratios, 1960 and 1990

Group	1960	1990
Percentage of homeowners		
Non-Hispanic whites	58.2	58.9
Ratio (percentage of non-Hispanic white rate)		
Non-Hispanic whites	100.0	100.0
Blacks	65.0	64.2
Hispanics	82.6	60.4
Mexican Americans	–	85.0
Mexican immigrants	–	53.6
Japanese	91.8	103.4
Chinese	72.1	108.0
Filipinos	83.7	89.2

Sources: U. S. Bureau of the Census (1962d, 1992, 1993a).

Notes: For 1960, published figures indicate a homeownership ratio of 70.0 for both Hispanic and nonwhite households. Values for blacks and specific Asian groups in 1960 were estimated from owner and renter numbers for the State of California from the 1 percent Public-Use Samples adjusted to the published nonwhite numbers. The 1960 figures for blacks and Japanese are good estimates because 52 percent of the state's population of both these groups lived in the Los Angeles and Orange Counties. The figures for Chinese and Filipinos are less reliable because only 20 percent of their state populations lived in these two counties. Data are for Los Angeles and Orange Counties.

The only group whose homeownership rate declined sharply since 1960 was Hispanics. This change is the result of the wider gap in median income, the increasing percentage of poor immigrants among Hispanics, and the higher proportion of young households.

Summary and Interpretation

Several findings have emerged from these analyses. White gains in educational attainment, occupational status, and income mean that minorities must advance even more rapidly than whites in order to realize any closing of the gaps. In most cases there has been much absolute progress, although our intended focus on gaps often obscures it.

By 1990 there were proportionately more college graduates among all three Asian groups than among whites. Filipino women had twice the proportion of college graduates as did white women. The contrast in educational attainment between Asians and both blacks and Hispanics was extreme.

In 1960, when only about 57 percent of white adults in Southern California had graduated from high school, the educational gap between whites and both blacks and Latinos was wide. Blacks and Mexican Americans narrowed their educational gap substantially in terms of percentage of high-school graduates, but rates of college graduation have changed more slowly. Among black women the gap even became wider.

With respect to high-status occupations, the gap narrowed a great deal between 1960 and 1990 for all except Mexican immigrants and Chinese women. In 1990 Japanese and Chinese men were more likely than white men to be managers or professionals. Improved educational attainment, government policies of affirmative action, and partial white acceptance of blacks and Latinos as managers and professionals has presumably made this possible.

Despite this educational and occupational progress, the income gap in Southern California did not decrease for blacks and grew much greater for Mexican Americans. In other words, the average income of blacks compared with whites has not improved since 1959, and the income situation of Mexican Americans has deteriorated substantially.

Although Chinese and Filipinos had higher rates of educational attainment than did whites in 1990, their incomes were much lower than whites' incomes. Clearly Chinese and Filipinos, a high proportion of whom are immigrants, cannot assume that an educational achievement leads directly to higher incomes in the same way it has for whites or for the longer-resident Japanese.

Homeownership rates for blacks and whites have been stable in Southern California. Asians have increased their rate of homeownership, whereas the average Latino household has become much less likely to be a homeowner.

These results confirm in very specific ways what many people may have sensed but have not been able to demonstrate. Most startling are that the black–white income differential has not narrowed and that the gap between whites and Mexican Americans has grown much wider. The reasons for these trends, despite some narrowing of the educational and occupational gaps for those groups, are the subject of the next chapter.

The large income gap may be an underlying but unexpressed source of resentment among some minorities. Whites have probably assumed that substantial economic progress on the part of minorities has accompanied well-publicized educational and occupational progress. Tensions between whites and minorities might be ameliorated, at least in a small way, if whites would acknowledge that the income gaps for minorities did not narrow in the way that most people had anticipated.

Notes

1. Two sources concerning social tensions at that time are Klein and Schiesl (1990) and Horne (1995). Residential segregation in 1960 is based on Allen and Turner (1996a), 19.

2. Soja, Morales, and Wolff (1989); UCLA Research Group (1989).

3. In the 1960 census, our analyses make use of the 25 percent sample data in the published volumes, from which most indicators of socioeconomic status could be calculated. For 1990 the 5 percent PUMS file was used. The 1990 census provides excellent data on the non-Hispanic white population, but an adaptation was necessary to obtain comparable data for 1960. In 1960 it would have

been possible to use data for the white race group except that almost all Latinos were arbitrarily considered to be in that group. Their lower average status compared with non-Hispanic whites meant that figures for all whites would be misleadingly low as indicators for non-Hispanic whites. This problem was solved by returning to the original counts of individuals in various educational, occupational, and income categories and subtracting the numbers of Spanish-surname whites from the total whites in each category.

Although people of Mexican origin and other Hispanics were identified differently in 1960 and 1990, this represented an improvement in coverage (Bean and Tienda 1987), with no likely effect on measures of status. In 1960 Latinos were considered to be those with any of several thousand distinctive Spanish surnames. In addition, an origin in Mexico or another country was based one's stated country of birth or, if born in the United States, on the birthplace of one or both parents. In 1990 there were two separate census questions regarding race and Hispanic origin, resulting in 28 percent of whites in Los Angeles County claiming a Hispanic origin and 42 percent of Hispanics identifying their race as white.

4. LaLonde and Topel (1992).

5. Chan (1991b); Daniels (1988), 300–8.

6. Ong and Azores (1994).

7. The relatively small improvement for U.S.-born men can be partly understood by the fact that both the second generation (children of immigrants) and later generations were included in the U.S.-born aggregation. Other research has shown more recently that only in the third generation (grandchildren of immigrants) do Latinos in Southern California move into white-collar professional and managerial occupations—a move closely linked to their shift from Spanish to English in everyday speech (McCarthy and Valdez 1986).

8. Lieberson and Waters (1988).

9. Takaki (1989), 265–68; Chan (1991a), 113–15.

10. In this chapter and chapter 7 the percentages of persons employed in managerial and professional occupations were calculated from a base that includes the experienced unemployed and those in the armed forces. This produced values that varied slightly from percentages that appear in published 1990 census tables because the tables did not include those groups.

11. Focusing on differentials between groups rather than the actual dollar values made it unnecessary to standardize income in constant dollars to compensate for inflation.

Ethnic differences in income sources may slightly increase income differences between groups. Earnings from rental properties, stocks, and savings accounts, which play a larger role in the income of whites than of blacks, should be reported as income on the census questionnaire (Levy 1995). However, interest and dividends are underreported in the census. In contrast, employer-paid medical coverage or retirement contributions, capital gains, government-paid low-income subsidies for medical care and housing, and noncash welfare benefits (food stamps and school lunches) are not to be reported on the census questionnaire. Unreported income by participants in the underground economy occurs, but its distribution is thought to be similar to that of reported income (Levy 1987). On balance, the results in Table 6.3 probably understate differences between whites and lower-status groups.

In another recent study of gaps in Southern California, income was restricted to wage, salary, and self-employment earnings (Waldinger and Bozorgmehr 1996). The effect of using earnings rather than total income was generally minor although it substantially diminished a few earnings gaps. We believe that total income results in a truer measure of the economic gap between whites and others.

12. To illustrate, of males age 14 and older in Los Angeles and Orange Counties in 1960, 92 percent of whites and 88 percent of blacks reported 1959 income. They were thus included. Unemployment was the major reason for exclusion from these data: at the time of the census, the unemployment rate among whites was 5.6 percent; among nonwhites, 9.4 percent. By 1989, among those age 15 and older, 95 percent of non-Hispanic white men but only 82 percent of black men reported income.

13. Wilson (1978); Liu and Cheng (1994); Grant, Oliver, and James (1996).

14. A median identifies only the middle point of a frequency distribution and does not take into account the nature of distribution above or below that point. Though widely used as a measure of the income gap, compared with the mean it usually minimizes differences between groups (Farley and Allen 1987; Lieberson and Waters 1988). The income of many whites has often been far above the median, as is illustrated in Figure 6.1.

15. Although the median income for white men was $5,600 in 1959, that group had unusually high proportions in the $7,000–$9,999 range. Moreover, there were as many whites with incomes of more than $10,000 as there were with incomes in the $6,000–$6,999 range. Data on women's income distributions in

1959 were not available for similar graphing. The 1989 income distribution for some groups showed a similar tendency, but it was minor (Fig. 6.1).

16. The index and its method of calculation are explained in Lieberson (1975). Assuming that cases from the groups are randomly paired, it measures the percentage of cases in each ordered category in which each group exceeds the other. The values are summed as the index, which ranges from 0 to 1, with 0 indicating that each group exceeds the other in the same number of cases. Thus, the larger the index, the greater the difference between the two groups.

17. Assuming the less-skewed distribution of 1989 as a standard, we estimated better ratios for certain 1959 income differences (Table 6.3) based on the relative ND of groups in relation to the 1989 NDs and ratios. The ND for white-black income of .348 in 1959 and .331 in 1989 indicates a very slight convergence in white-black incomes over the three decades. The ND for whites compared with U.S.-born men of Mexican origin was .206 in 1959 and .300 in 1989, demonstrating a substantial divergence in incomes. The ND for white and Filipino men was .399 in 1959, confirming this as the largest income gap in 1959.

18. The higher income of foreign-born Japanese men was determined from a separate analysis of PUMS data. For a brief discussion of these executive sojourners in Southern California, see the Gardena and Torrance section of the discussion of Japanese in chapter 5.

19. Borjas and Tienda (1993).

20. U.S. Bureau of the Census (1962d, 1993a).

7. Probing the Income Gap

Chapter 6 showed that most differences between whites and both blacks and Hispanics have narrowed with respect to educational attainment and employment in high-status jobs. In contrast, the income differential (or gap) between white men and black men changed little, and the gap between whites and Hispanics widened. This growing income gap characterized not just immigrants but also Mexican Americans (the U.S.-born).

Why have these income gaps become wider? For many Californians and others who placed their faith in the struggle for improved education and fairer access to the better jobs, this finding is unexpected and discouraging. There is no simple answer to the question. However, in this chapter we search for the reasons behind this change by analyzing the income differentials in several ways.

Our first approach is to compare Southern California's 1959–1989 trend with that in the nation as a whole.[1] This comparison demonstrates that the trend has been somewhat different in Southern California. We then examine special factors that might have produced the distinctive trend of this region.

Subsequent analyses deal with Southern California by itself. We look at the possible role of self-employment and government employment as opposed to work in the private sector as an influence on income gaps. After that comes the largest analysis in the chapter. This is a comparison of the median incomes of workers in different ethnic groups after stratifying workers according to characteristics known to affect income. By matching individuals from different groups according to age cohort, educational attainment, U.S. birth, full-time employment, and general category of occupation, we were able to eliminate the influence of these factors. The size of the gap that remains is a better measure of the unexplained ethnic

income differential. Next we study differentials among workers employed in the same specific occupations. Lastly, we show how varying proportions of Mexican immigrants in selected low-skill occupations affect the income distributions of workers from other groups in those occupations.

Most of the analyses focus on income ratios between whites and blacks and between whites and Mexican Americans, but some sections also include Asians. The multiple approaches of this chapter result in a series of findings which together help explain the reasons behind the increased income gap in Southern California.

The National Income-Gap Trend

The question of income differentials between whites and minorities has been of concern to scholars and other Americans for some time. Several studies have traced and analyzed the national trends of ratios and gaps, usually for the income gaps of blacks and Hispanics.[2]

The generally observed nationwide trends are as follows. General economic expansion and productivity growth from the 1940s into the 1970s lifted most people's incomes a great deal. This made possible a narrowing of income differences between whites and minorities. Incomes of Hispanics converged with white incomes until about 1970, and the black–white income gap was closing until about 1980. Thus, the period from 1959 was indeed one of progress in reducing income differentials between groups.

However, since about 1980 income gaps for the United States have widened. The net effect over the entire period since 1959 was still a narrowing of most gaps nationally (see the bottom of Fig. 7.1). This is shown by the shorter length of most dark-toned bars representing 1989 compared to the 1959 light-toned bars in the U.S. portion of the graph.

The timing of the shift toward increased income differentials suggests that a major factor was the income polarization that came to characterize the United States after the mid-1970s.[3] Polarization means that the middle portion of the income distribution declined, resulting in increased proportions of both poor and rich. When ethnic groups are compared, whites are better represented in the upper part of most income distributions whereas blacks and Hispanics more commonly occupy the lower income levels. Thus, increasing white-minority income gaps after about 1980 are not surprising.

Economists attribute this polarization of the 1980s in large part to shifts in national economic policy designed to control inflation, to lower marginal tax rates, and to reduced government regulation of large corporations.[4] Some argue that important additional causes are foreign competition in manufacturing and the increase in imported manufactured goods. The shift of manufacturing operations from the United States to countries with lower labor costs resulted in a surplus of American workers, many of whom lacked even a high-school education. Until the mid-1970s, they had found good work.

Other economists explain wage reductions for less-skilled workers primarily in terms of technological change. Automation and other new technologies, more complex and often computer related, meant that people with advanced education in certain disciplines became more valuable. The opposite was true for the less educated. Although the educational attainment of Americans was rising rapidly, the demand for highly educated workers outpaced the expanding supply, and the demand for less-educated workers was much smaller than their declining numbers.[5] During the 1980s those men with five or more years of college increased their income by 12 percent, whereas those with only a high-school education averaged an income decline of 7 percent. Thus, educational attainment was a major factor in determining the direction of income change. On an average, the gainers tended to be whites and some Asian groups. Blacks and Hispanics were less apt to have jobs in high-growth occupations and industries.[6]

However, the increasing income gaps of the 1980s are probably not simply racial and ethnic fallout from income polarization. Rather, President Reagan's deemphasis on the federal government as protector of minority rights and his desire to let the free market deal with social problems made it possible for the market to become more discriminatory.[7] The growing income gap of the 1980s seemed to indicate that the federal government was needed to enforce laws against discrimination in employment and income. Altogether, the 1980s marked somewhat of a setback nationally in the slow progress toward income equality that had characterized earlier decades.

Differences in Gaps between Southern California and the United States

In 1959 the gender gap in median income (between non-Hispanic white men and non-Hispanic white women) was the same in Southern California as it was in the United States. However, Southern California was distinctive in that the income gap between whites and both blacks and Hispanics was less in 1959 than it was in the country as a whole (Fig. 7.1).[8] In this region black and Mexican-origin women were earning incomes that approximated 90 percent of the income of non-Hispanic white women. In 1959 the gaps were wider among minority men than among women, but Southern California had smaller gaps than the U.S. average.[9]

The higher status of whites, blacks, and people of Mexican origin in Southern California in 1960 was due partly to the very low incomes of blacks in the South and of Mexican Americans in Texas. However, it is likely that the post–World War II period of job growth in Southern California was the primary factor behind the narrower gaps in this region. This is because the differences with the U.S. averages were pronounced and because the era was one of such rapid growth in Southern California.

Los Angeles was the only one of the ten largest central cities in the country in which total employment and manufacturing employment expanded during the 1947–1963 period.[10] The broad-based economic development of those years resulted in improved jobs for people with a wide range of skills. This presumably led to narrower income gaps between whites and other groups. Minorities and whites eagerly migrated to Los Angeles during those years to take advantage of opportunities. Between 1940 and 1960 the Hispanic population tripled, and the black population grew to six times its 1940 size. Despite the exclusion of black workers from most Los Angeles–area unions

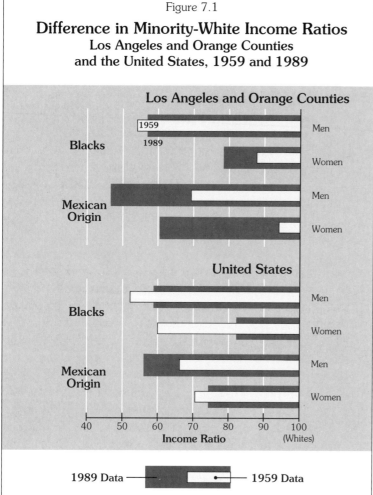

Figure 7.1

Difference in Minority-White Income Ratios
Los Angeles and Orange Counties
and the United States, 1959 and 1989

Notes: The 1959 income ratio is indicated with a light-shaded bar and the 1989 income ratio with a dark-shaded bar. Data are for U.S.-born persons employed full-time in Los Angeles and Orange Counties. The ratios for white men and women are 100. The ratio of women's to men's median income for whites in Los Angeles and Orange Counties was 35.2 in 1959 and 53.1 in 1989. The ratio of women's to men's income in the United States was 34.8 in 1959 and 48.7 in 1989.

and other forms of discrimination, minorities were swept along in the wave of economic expansion.

By 1989, however, the relatively favorable income situation for blacks and Hispanics in Southern California had changed. The income convergence that characterized the national trend until the mid-1970s suggests that the gap may also have been narrowing in Southern California until that time. Thus, comparison of income gaps in Southern California in 1959 and 1989 should not imply a steady rate of change.

Regardless of the ups and downs of an income-gap trend line over the last thirty years, in 1989 Southern California had income gaps that were, if anything, wider than the U.S. average (Fig. 7.1). This is shown by the greater length of the bars (dark-toned) representing Southern California in Figure 7.1 compared to those representing the United States. The disparity between gaps for the United States and Southern California was greater between whites and people of Mexican origin than between whites and blacks.

Any explanation of the increasing white–Hispanic income gap in Southern California must assume that the factors responsible for the nationwide income polarization also played major roles in this region. However, the fact that the smaller gap experienced in Southern California in 1959 was replaced by a wider gap than that found nationwide tells us that regional characteristics must also be important.

Regional Influences on the Wider Income Gaps

Three characteristics of Southern California appear to have played key roles in the unexpected widening of the income gap between Hispanics and whites and the immobility of the gap between whites and blacks. These regional influences are the following: changes in the employment structure, the immigration of large numbers of workers with few skills, and the increase in minority proportions.

Changes in the employment structure. Beginning in the late 1960s Southern California experienced major shifts in the types of employment available. Although this restructuring occurred in many places across America, its sum total may well have been greater in this region. Depending on the ethnic makeup of the workforce in affected industries, the losses and gains in jobs may have widened white–minority income gaps.

Three major changes in employment structure have occurred since 1960. One was the growth of employment in the high-end service sector, particularly in finance, insurance, real estate, and business services. Another was the increase in employment in the low-wage service sector and in low-wage manufacturing. The last component of the restructuring was the decline of high-paying jobs for blue-collar workers in manufacturing.[11] Our examination of trends in these sectors indicates that only the first two were likely to have increased the income gaps in Southern California.

Southern California's employment growth in the high-level service sector benefited whites somewhat more than other groups. By 1990 white men and white women in Southern California were working as managers and professionals in higher proportions than were whites elsewhere across the country. The percentages of blacks, Japanese, Chinese, and Filipinos in upper-level, white-collar positions in Southern California were not very different from the U.S. average for each group. The net effect, however, was a wider white–minority occupational gap within Southern California than elsewhere.

It is also likely that the growth of low-wage jobs in the service sector and in manufacturing has played a role in the increasing white–Hispanic income gap. During the 1980s there was a large increase in Southern California's low-wage workforce, most of whom were recent immigrants who had few special skills but were eager to work. Large numbers of people, particularly Hispanic immigrants, were absorbed into the service sector as day laborers, housekeepers and nannies, kitchen helpers, car washers, lawn-maintenance workers, street vendors, and so forth. Apparel manufacturing, which has been on the decline nationally, grew in Southern California such that employment in the industry increased by 62 percent during the 1980s.[12] In that industry Hispanics, most of whom were in the United States illegally, made up an increasing proportion of workers (at least 69 percent in 1990). There is little doubt that garment factories expanded in Los Angeles because of the growing supply of low-skilled immigrants who were willing to work for wages that were low by California standards.

Although some scholars have thought that blacks and Hispanics bore a disproportionate share of layoffs in high-wage industries since 1960, the effect of that aspect of employment restructuring on white-minority income gaps was small. In representative industries (primary nonferrous metals, fabricated-metal production, electrical machinery, and motor vehicles) the percentage of black employees was virtually the same in 1990 as in 1960.[13] Also, of all men in the durable-goods workforce, Hispanics increased their representation between 1960 and 1990 from 11 percent to 36 percent, whereas blacks dropped only from 6 percent to 5 percent. It was primarily non-Hispanic whites whose departure from the durable-goods industries made room for Hispanic workers. In addition, in the aerospace industry the proportion of minorities among male workers increased between 1960, when only 4 percent were black, and 1990, when 9 percent were black and another 14 percent were Hispanics. Thus, loss of employment in high-wage manufacturing jobs was not a significant factor in white–minority income-gap changes.

The immigration of workers with few skills. If we ignore for the moment the foregoing three facets of employment restructuring, the evidence suggests that the immigration of large numbers of persons without advanced education or special skill has acted to lower the incomes of Hispanics compared with whites.

The arrival in an area of potential workers with few skills generally produces increases in the proportion of low-wage employment.[14] This labor surplus translates into lower wages. To illustrate, in the 1960s unskilled workers earned higher wages in Los Angeles County than in other metropolitan areas, but by the 1980s the average wage was 10 to 15 percent lower.[15] If whites were not competing for the same jobs as low-skilled immigrants, the arrival of large numbers of immigrants could be expected to widen the income gap between the two groups.

Patterns of migration within the United States provide indirect evidence of job competition between low-skilled immigrants and comparable U.S.-born workers, whether white, black, or Latino. This is because migrants move primarily for employment and other economic reasons. Their migration decisions are based partly on the relative opportunities they perceive in different places. The arrival in an area of migrants willing to work at low wages seems to stimulate the outmigration of less-educated, often blue-collar, workers.[16] In contrast, those with a college education tend to move toward areas receiving immigrants.

This is exactly what occurred in Southern California during the last half of the 1980s.[17] If only people moving within the United States are included, between 1985 and 1990 there was a net outmigration from Southern California of U.S.-born Hispanics, blacks, and whites who were not college graduates. However, all three of these ethnic groups showed a net inmigration among those who had graduated from college.

Increases in minority proportions. The increased income gaps are also consistent with the results of previous research that shows wider income gaps between whites and minorities when minority proportions are higher. Three major studies of income inequality in different metropolitan areas found this to be the case.[18] Although the particular mechanisms that are operating are not understood, higher proportions of Mexican-origin or black people in a metropolitan area are associated with larger income gaps between whites and those minorities. This means that minority groups have a tendency to do relatively better economically outside metropolitan areas in which they are concentrated.

Because the proportion of non-Hispanic whites in Southern California dropped from more than 82 percent to 46 percent during the past three decades, a larger income gap could be expected from this trend alone. The greatest change in minority proportions involved Hispanics, who constituted 9.3 percent of the Los Angeles–Orange County total population in 1960 but 34.7 percent in 1990. Because the United States did not experience anywhere near the proportionate increase in minorities that characterized Southern California, the income gap nationwide should not have increased as much as the gap did in Southern California. That was precisely what happened (Fig. 6.2).

The fact that the gap also increased substantially for U.S.-born Hispanics is masked when data for Mexican Americans and Mexican immigrants are combined. However, when the U.S.-born are analyzed later in this chapter, the gap between them and whites also widened.

Summary of regional factors. We have identified the increases in service-sector employment at both the high end and the low end as likely factors behind growing white–minority gaps in Southern California. Of no less importance are the ample supply of low-skilled immigrants and increasing Hispanic proportions in the population. The specific ways in which these factors are intertwined causally are not known, and it may be a mistake to assign precedence to one or another. However, we do believe that developments in Mexico and Central America were sufficiently strong to explain most of the large immigration that the Los Angeles area experienced during the 1980s almost regardless of what was happening in Southern California. In other words, it seems likely that employment restructuring did not precede immigration and that the presence and prospects of low-wage immigrant labor encouraged job growth to take advantage of that labor supply.

At the same time, the net outmigration of less-educated whites and the net inmigration of white college graduates may have raised the median income of whites, thereby increasing the income gaps. As we have already seen, the net outflow of working-class whites was stimulated in part by the arrival of the large number of immigrants.

For all these reasons, it appears to us that the primary regional factors in explaining Southern California's income-gap trends are the ample supply of low-skilled immigrant labor and the increasing proportion of minorities.

Effect of low-skilled immigrants on Mexican Americans and blacks. Incomes of Mexican Americans have been hurt more than have those of other groups as a result of the labor surplus provided by the large numbers of immigrants. We do not know exactly why this is the case. Certainly, the low educational attainment of Mexican Americans did not qualify most of them for the higher-level technical and professional positions that were being created in the 1980s in Southern California. It is also possible that the large number of Hispanic immigrants made it easier for employers to discriminate against Mexican Americans. Employers may have assumed that the U.S.-born had no greater skills than immigrants.

The effect of the immigrants on the incomes of blacks is more complex. In most jobs there may have been little direct competition between blacks and immigrants. The differing occupational niches of blacks compared with people of Mexican origin (Tables 8.4) supports this notion. Moreover, black employment in the public sector has probably increased in response to the growing demand for government services generated by the arrival of so many needy immigrants.[19]

However, where blacks and immigrant Hispanics have overlapped in occupations, it is likely that competition has resulted in wage decline, subsequent avoidance of such jobs by blacks, and migration out of the area. The effect of wage competition is supported by a statistical analysis of wages in various Los Angeles industries as of 1980. The study shows that less-educated workers received lower pay in industries that had a higher proportion of Mexican-immigrant workers.[20] The fact that the same industries were not low-paying in other metropolitan areas is further evidence that job competition from Mexican immigrants is of special regional importance.

The findings of a recent economic study of regional trends in wage inequality in the United States between 1973 and 1991 echo ours.[21] The region that had the greatest increase in wage inequality between low-skilled and high-skilled U.S.-born workers was the West. In this region the wages of low-skilled, U.S.-born workers were reduced by about 10 percent. This was explained as resulting from a labor surplus due to the immigration of low-skilled workers.

Income Differentials by Class of Employment

Workers can be in one of three classes of employment. Some are self-employed, others work for the government, but most are employed by private businesses or corporations. Because ethnic differences in proportions employed in the three classes are substantial (Table 8.3), analyzing how incomes vary by class of employment may help explain income differentials between ethnic groups. We compared income levels among U.S.-born white, black, and Mexican American men aged 25 to 64 who were employed full time. We made separate calculations for three different combinations of educational and occupational status.

The first comparison involves men who did not graduate from college and are in occupations other than managerial or professional (Fig. 7.2). Regardless of type of employer, white men earn substantially higher income than do blacks or Mexican Americans, and blacks make the least. For men who are not college graduates, however, there is little difference in incomes among the three types of employment. The consistency of the ranking of white, black, and Hispanic incomes across all three types indicates that class of employment is not a major factor behind the income gaps already observed.

When the educational and occupational levels are raised, the ethnic differentials already observed still apply to the private sector (Fig. 7.2). However, for these college-graduate managers, two other patterns become evident. Among government workers the groups differ little in income. This may well indicate the success of government in reducing discrimination in its own workplaces. Also, self-employment is associated with much higher incomes for whites and blacks than is either private-sector employment or government work.

Lastly, we look at the median incomes of men who have completed a post-graduate degree program and are practicing professionals (Fig. 7.2). This group includes teachers, social workers, chemists, engineers, and judges, as well as almost all university professors, lawyers, physicians, dentists, and veterinarians. In this high-status group the income benefits of self-employment are dramatic. Although whites still have the highest income, self-employed black and Mexican American professionals average $90,000, approximately twice the income of those who are employed by government.

Government workers show the smallest income differences among the three ethnic groups. The income advantages of self-employment increase greatly as status increases, suggesting substantial earning potential for blacks and Hispanics who complete the necessary education.

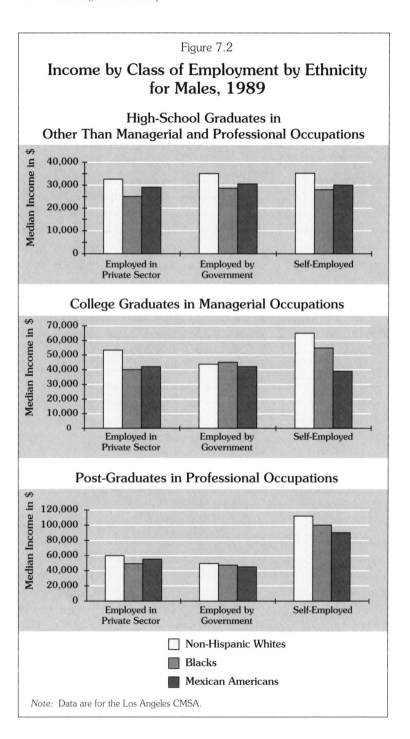

Figure 7.2

Income by Class of Employment by Ethnicity for Males, 1989

High-School Graduates in
Other Than Managerial and Professional Occupations

College Graduates in Managerial Occupations

Post-Graduates in Professional Occupations

☐ Non-Hispanic Whites
▨ Blacks
■ Mexican Americans

Note: Data are for the Los Angeles CMSA.

Income Gaps after Individuals Stratified by Human Capital

To what extent do income gaps result from differences in the characteristics of the various ethnic groups?

Human capital. Such factors as age, employment experience, educational attainment, and cultural skills are often referred to as human capital. This is because they are the resources built up by individuals who must compete in a labor market. The characteristics that people bring to their work are the supply in a supply-demand system that links workers with jobs in any economy. If such factors account for most of the gaps, then improving the human capital of minority workers would presumably eliminate most income differentials.

The problem with this approach is that it is impossible to measure precisely much of the human capital that is important in work success. The census provides the best data because its samples are large enough for such complex testing, but it provides no clues regarding some important characteristics of individuals. For instance, the census cannot measure the quality of education that individuals have received, as opposed to the level of attainment. Nor can it measure motivation, intelligence, or speech and personality characteristics that may be important in many occupations. All of these are human capital factors that may affect hiring and promotion decisions and thus income.

Method of analysis. Despite the imperfect nature of census data, in this section we compare median incomes of ethnic groups while controlling for some important individual characteristics. To control for key human capital characteristics, we stratified ethnic populations into similar subgroups.

We created a series of samples of Southern California workers using the 1990 PUMS. Only U.S.-born workers aged 25 through 64 who were employed year-round and full-time were included. We controlled for work experience by assigning individuals to one of four ten-year age categories, such as ages 25–34. Samples were also matched according to four educational-attainment categories and three occupational categories.[22]

Then the median income was calculated for each matched group. As in chapter 6, the median income for each group was compared with that for the equivalent white group by means of a ratio (Tables 7.1 and 7.2).

To eliminate the possibility that insufficient English language skills were playing a role in the income gap of Mexican Americans, we calculated an additional median-income ratio for those Mexican Americans who spoke English only or spoke it very well. Also, because it is difficult to judge how widely income ratios may vary within an ethnically diverse white population, we included comparable ratios for two important white-ancestry groups.

To distinguish the earlier income ratios in this chapter and chapter 6 from ratios calculated after individuals have been stratified for their human capital, we refer to the latter as "adjusted ratios."

We present adjusted ratios separately for each of three occupational types. This is because ratios may vary according to the status of the occupations and the extent to which professional training is required. The category of managers, which also includes executives and administrators, is distinguished from the other high-status category—professionals. All other occupations constitute the last type.

Results: managers and professionals. The gap in white-minority incomes that remains after controlling for human capital factors is generally less among professionals than in other occupational types. This is presumably because a professional's qualifications to practice are based more directly on completed formal education and licensing or certification than is the case in most other occupations. Among those with postgraduate degrees, such as physicians and lawyers, there are no longer any income gaps for minority women compared with white women. Also, the gaps virtually disappear among college-graduate Asians and among black women.

Nevertheless, Mexican American professionals earn only about 90 percent of the income of comparable whites, an indication that even among professionals factors other than age, educational attainment, and country of birth affect incomes. The widest adjusted income gap among professionals is that for black men, who make only about 80 percent of the income of comparable whites. The size of this income gap after controlling for some human capital characteristics is surprisingly large.

Minority managers and executives experience wider income gaps than do professionals. For men, the gaps seem very wide, and gaps for Asians are comparable with those for blacks and Mexican Americans. Managers who are black earn only about 75 percent of the income of comparable white men, and for Mexican American men the adjusted ratio is about 80 percent. However, for female managers of all minority groups who are college graduates there is no longer an income differential with white women. Among Mexican Americans in high-status positions, differentiating those who speak English very well has virtually no effect on median income.

The fact that the adjusted median income of Russian-ancestry managers and professional men is 19 percent higher than that for comparable whites means that the minority-income gaps may well be explained by whatever differences lie behind the gap between Jews and other whites. The existence of such large gaps between white ethnic groups demonstrates that gaps of this size can result from factors other than racial discrimination. We suspect, but we cannot show, that the higher incomes of high-status Jews compared with most whites can be explained by such cultural factors as exceptional motivation, an especially high quality of human capital in terms of education, and effective mutual assistance.

Japanese men who are managers show an adjusted ratio of only about 81, indicating a much wider gap with whites than in the professions and other occupations. The dramatic inconsistency in the median-income gap for managerial occupations is probably evidence for the existence of a "glass ceiling," a form of discrimination.[23] This refers to the complaint of many Asians that they are often passed over in favor of whites in promotions to better managerial and executive positions. There seems to be an invisible barrier above which they are not permitted to rise. Recall that all these Japanese managers were born in the United States and that many of them are the grandchildren of immigrants. For those reasons they should be perfectly fluent in English and thoroughly at ease with American culture.[24]

Table 7.1   Adjusted Median-Income Ratios of U.S.-Born Men, 1989

Group	Managerial High Sch. Graduate	Managerial College Graduate	Managerial Post- Graduate	Professional College Graduate	Professional Post- Graduate	Other Not H.S. Graduate	Other High Sch. Graduate	Other College Graduate	Other Post- Graduate
Median income									
Non-Hispanic whites	$45,883	$59,562	$68,776	$48,653	$61,238	$29,488	$35,263	$47,410	$52,375
Ratio (percentage of non-Hispanic white median income)									
Non-Hispanic whites	100.0	100.0	100.0	100.0	100.0	100.0	100.0	100.0	100.0
English ancestry	99.8	97.5	107.1	102.7	97.2	106.5	103.5	102.6	109.8
Russian ancestry	122.1	118.8	110.3	116.3	127.5	–	110.0	127.9	132.8
Blacks	73.5	76.6	65.1	80.9	80.4	70.6	77.3	83.8	72.7
Mexican Americans	81.6	79.5	78.7	92.0	85.5	78.0	87.8	81.3	77.3
With very good English	83.3	79.3	77.6	91.4	83.4	79.4	88.1	80.6	78.0
Japanese	81.8	80.7	80.9	105.6	98.3	100.6	101.8	84.0	92.2
Chinese	–	85.6	–	103.5	96.6	–	97.7	88.6	80.0
Filipinos	95.5	60.4	–	–	–	–	89.6	–	–

Table 7.2   Adjusted Median-Income Ratios of U.S.-Born Women, 1989

Group	Managerial High Sch. Graduate	Managerial College Graduate	Managerial Post- Graduate	Professional College Graduate	Professional Post- Graduate	Other Not H.S. Graduate	Other High Sch. Graduate	Other College Graduate	Other Post- Graduate
Median income									
Non-Hispanic whites	$29,231	$36,140	$47,302	$35,050	$40,240	$19,200	$23,326	$29,000	$34,685
Ratio (percentage of non-Hispanic white median income)									
Non-Hispanic whites	100.0	100.0	100.0	100.0	100.0	100.0	100.0	100.0	100.0
English ancestry	100.1	98.9	90.9	101.8	98.8	97.3	91.9	96.6	100.7
Russian ancestry	105.0	103.1	98.1	110.7	111.4	–	108.4	99.3	100.4
Blacks	89.8	98.0	89.8	96.2	100.0	89.1	92.2	103.6	98.0
Mexican Americans	88.4	99.9	94.8	84.7	98.5	81.2	89.7	91.2	92.1
With very good English	87.5	100.7	–	84.7	98.2	83.3	89.7	91.2	92.1
Japanese	106.1	95.5	101.4	100.9	113.9	108.1	108.4	95.0	–
Chinese	–	98.0	–	108.6	118.2	–	110.9	112.0	–
Filipinos	101.8	–	–	–	–	–	99.7	–	–

Source: U.S. Bureau of the Census (1992).

Notes: Insufficient sample sizes are indicated by dashes. Adjusted ratios are for full-time employed persons stratified by occupational type and educational attainment. Data are for Los Angeles and Orange Counties.

Results: other occupations. Adjusted ratios for blacks and Mexican Americans in all occupations other than managerial and professional (Tables 7.1 and 7.2) are also graphed (Fig. 7.3) to emphasize them because the numbers in these ethnic groups and occupations are so large.

In occupations that are not managerial or professional, black men earn even less than three-quarters of the income of comparable white men. When this adjusted ratio is compared with the direct income ratio of 57 for all black men (Table 6.3), it is clear that stratifying by human capital factors eliminates less than half the income gap for black men. Mexican American men had an adjusted income ratio of about 82 or 83, in comparison with the unadjusted ratio of 61 (Table 6.3). This shows that educational level and other measured characteristics explain only a little more than half the income gap. Clearly, a major part of the explanation for men's income gaps must involve influences that we have been unable to measure.[25]

Blacks and Mexican Americans with less education experience wider gaps with whites than do the better-educated members of their groups (Fig. 7.3). This is an expected result of the greater competition from immigrants with little education. It is also consistent with the finding reported earlier in this chapter that less educated U.S.-born workers—especially whites—have left Los Angeles County and Southern California in the face of competition from poorly educated immigrants.

Interpretation of the remaining income gaps. One factor which we were not able to calculate was the greater improvement in educational quality among blacks than among whites since 1940. A major national study has shown that as of 1980 "there is little racial difference in the economic benefits of schooling for younger workers."[26] Although our research describes a single gap experienced in 1989 by Southern Californians who range in age from 25 to 64, it may be true that the adjusted gap is reduced among younger people because of the improved quality of minority education.

In one of the few national studies to distinguish the U.S.-born within the larger Mexican-origin population, Mexican American men had an income ratio of 94 in 1979 after education, age, and full-time employment were controlled through

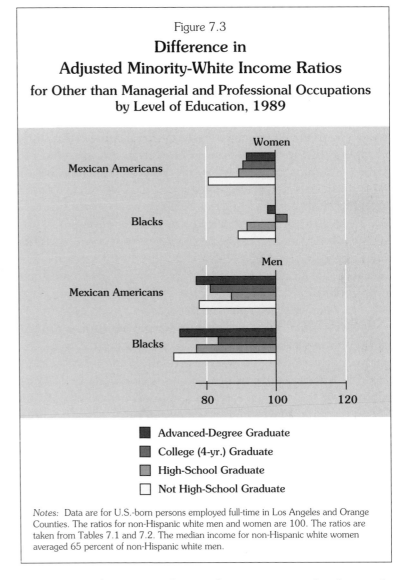

Figure 7.3

Difference in Adjusted Minority-White Income Ratios

for Other than Managerial and Professional Occupations by Level of Education, 1989

Legend:
- Advanced-Degree Graduate
- College (4-yr.) Graduate
- High-School Graduate
- Not High-School Graduate

Notes: Data are for U.S.-born persons employed full-time in Los Angeles and Orange Counties. The ratios for non-Hispanic white men and women are 100. The ratios are taken from Tables 7.1 and 7.2. The median income for non-Hispanic white women averaged 65 percent of non-Hispanic white men.

regression techniques.[27] That result, consistent with other studies from the late 1970s and early 1980s, showed that the Mexican American income gap was mostly explainable at that time by that group's lower level of human capital compared to whites. In comparing that ratio with our results for 1989, some allowance must be made for the increasing national gap during the 1980s as a result of income polarization. However, the adjusted 1979 national gap of 6 compared with the adjusted 1989 Southern California gap of approximately 17 suggests a much greater income gap in Southern California. This is consistent with our previous findings of a wider unadjusted income gap in this region (Fig. 7.1).

Among women in Southern California, the widest remaining income gap is among less-educated black and Mexican American women (Table 7.2). For black female college graduates and for all Asian women virtually no income gap with white women's incomes remains after full-time status, education, U.S. birth, and occupation have been taken into account.

These findings regarding women are important. They demonstrate that, on the average, any discrimination regarding hiring or promotion experienced by U.S.-born Asian women and college-educated black women is due to their sex, not their ethnic identity.

Gaps among men versus gaps among women. Although our focus is on comparisons of ethnic groups, the income differentials between men and women are striking. Even after eliminating part-time and seasonal workers, white women on the average earn only about 65 percent of white men's incomes. The same ratio for full-time workers has been found at the national level, where the gap is smaller for those aged 25 to 34 and for those with college education.[28]

In contrast, most minority men experience larger income gaps than do the women. For Japanese, managers have the largest income gaps. For blacks and Mexican Americans, the gaps are pervasive. They are a clear demonstration that age, educational attainment, and occupational status simply do not account for a large portion the income gaps experienced by blacks and Mexican Americans.[29]

Ethnic Income Differences within Occupations

Specific occupations within the three broad categories of occupations can vary a great deal in pay. For example, lawyers, physicians, and electronics-assembly workers earn more money, respectively, than do nurses, teachers, and operators of sewing machines in the garment industry. If whites, blacks, and people of Mexican origin tend to work at differing occupations which themselves vary systematically in rates of pay, this tendency could account for much or most of the remaining income gaps.

To investigate the role of this factor we measured the median incomes of workers from different ethnic groups in the same occupations. Our first analysis involves a simple comparison of income ratios for selected occupations of moderate or high status. The second examines six occupations requiring less skill to see whether the proportion of Mexican immigrant workers in an occupation is related to the presence of ethnic differences in income in the occupation.

Income ratios in specific occupations. Workers already in an occupation have presumably met any entry qualifications. We must assume that they are performing their work satisfactorily. For these reasons ethnic groups were not stratified in terms of educational attainment, and it was not necessary to analyze only those born in the United States.

However, there is such a range of occupations that the number employed in each is not large. Only a few of the more common occupations could be included, and we compared only three groups: non-Hispanic whites, blacks, and people of Mexican origin (Tables 7.3 and 7.4). To increase our sample size in this and the next analysis, workers were sampled from the entire five-county area of Southern California. We attempted to reduce the effect of higher incomes associated with more experienced (older) men and women by dividing the sample into two age groups: ages 25–44 and ages 45–64. Median incomes and ratios for the two age groups were then averaged.

The income gap is pervasive and substantial across the majority of occupations for both minority groups. Whites have higher incomes in nearly all the listed occupations, and most income ratios are not very different from the adjusted ratios found earlier. This means that the substantial gaps found in adjusted income ratios cannot be explained by ethnic differences in specific occupations chosen.

An important factor in the gaps is the older age of white workers. This means that on the average whites have from four

Table 7.3   Median-Income Ratios of Men in Selected Occupations, 1989

Occupation	Non-Hispanic White Income	Ratio for Blacks	Ratio for Mexican origin
Financial manager	$59,453	75.2	76.1
Marketing manager	$63,138	51.9	72.6
Administrator, education	$54,349	80.7	117.7
Accountant, auditor	$47,142	77.4	76.2
Engineer, aerospace	$52,600	86.3	90.3
Engineer, electrical	$53,400	92.5	89.9
Computer systems analyst	$45,000	91.1	87.4
Physician	$121,302	78.9	69.3
Lawyer	$94,000	67.9	76.9
Computer programmer	$45,501	84.4	83.9
Sales rep., insurance	$57,659	68.1	59.4
Computer operator	$34,113	95.7	85.0
Bookkeeper	$26,343	94.2	71.3
Aircraft mechanic	$35,500	85.6	82.5
Carpenter	$32,500	87.1	87.4
Average ratio		79.4	82.3

Source: U.S. Bureau of the Census (1992).
Notes: Each ethnic group comprises more than 700 men in each occupation. Data are for the Los Angeles CMSA.

Table 7.4   Median-Income Ratios of Women in Selected Occupations, 1989

Occupation	Non-Hispanic White Income	Ratio for Blacks	Ratio for Mexican origin
Financial manager	$59,453	75.2	76.1
Financial manager	$38,800	68.6	64.5
Manager, service organization	$31,954	81.7	88.7
Accountant, auditor	$29,400	89.3	101.4
Registered nurse	$38,363	88.6	83.3
Social worker	$30,950	86.0	73.8
Lawyer	$63,525	60.3	86.5[a]
Sales rep., insurance	$31,700	68.5	70.3
Computer operator	$23,976	104.3	91.5
Bookkeeper	$23,000	88.4	93.1
Clerk, inventory	$22,910	99.4	82.1
Average ratio		83.6	83.2

Source: U.S. Bureau of the Census (1992).

Notes: Each ethnic group comprises more than 700 women in each occupation. Data are for the Los Angeles CMSA.

[a]Only women aged 25–44 are included because of insufficient sample size.

to ten more years of work experience and for this reason should expect somewhat higher incomes. Among the minorities, the average black worker is a few years older than the average worker of Mexican origin.

The white–minority income gaps are less in the more technical occupations. For men the income gaps are generally smaller among computer-systems analysts and aerospace and electrical engineers; minority women who are accountants or computer operators earn closest to the incomes of white women.

At the opposite extreme for men are marketing managers, accountants, insurance salesmen, lawyers, and physicians. In those occupations the gap between whites and others is wide.

Minority women who are financial managers or insurance saleswomen also tend to earn much less than white women. The varied nature of these occupations makes generalization difficult, reinforcing the notion the income gaps are found in the highest-skilled occupations.

The effect of Mexican immigrants on income. Do income gaps vary in low-status occupations according to the supply of workers who are willing to work at relatively low wages? This is particularly relevant where the presence of a large number of Mexican immigrant workers has resulted in job competition among ethnic groups in certain low-status occupations.

To help answer this question we selected for comparison six occupations which require a relatively low level of education and little or no English-language ability. For this reason the human capital differences among individuals and ethnic groups in age, language ability, and education should not be factors in the income differences.

We examined the income distributions for different ethnic groups in the same six occupations by means of a statistical test (analysis of variance) that determined the probability that the several income distributions represented only random variations within a single population. The statistical significance of this probability was estimated by the F-test (Table 7.5). In addition, income distributions were graphed in order to show the large income range within each occupation and the substantial overlapping of incomes for different groups (Figs. 7.4 and 7.5).

In all six occupations immigrants from Mexico earned the least, but statistical results showed that occupations varied in the extent to which workers of different ethnic identities averaged different incomes. When the occupations were compared as to the percentages of workers born in Mexico, those occupations that were less completely dominated by Mexican immigrants were the ones with significant income differences between groups (Table 7.5).

These results indicate that in occupations in which Mexican immigrants make up almost half or more of the workforce the wages of all the ethnic groups are essentially similar. Presumably this is because the incomes of all workers in that occupation are lower due to the high proportion of immigrant workers willing to work at low wages. This is consistent with our earlier findings and with another study, which reported lower wages in those industries in which Mexican immigrants dominated the workforce.[30]

The situations of female electrical-equipment assemblers and male janitors and assemblers are different. Workers in some ethnic groups are earning significantly more than are Mexican immigrants in those occupations, a situation that is sometimes called a dual labor market.[31] The statistic does not make clear precisely which ethnic groups, in addition to whites,

Table 7.5   Ethnic Percentages in Selected Occupations, 1990

	Whites	Blacks	Asians[a]	Mexican Americans	Mexican Immigrants	Probability of No Real Income Difference between Groups
Women						
Electronic equipment assembler	19.3	4.6	23.2	12.5	29.4	.000[b]
Textile, apparel machine operator	6.0	2.8	13.3	4.3	52.8	.083
Men						
Assembler	22.3	6.0	8.2	10.5	42.2	.045[c]
Groundskeeper	19.8	5.8	6.6	9.5	50.8	.170
Janitor or cleaner	27.4	14.9	5.4	10.3	28.9	.000[b]
Machine operator	22.0	5.2	7.1	9.9	46.6	.161

Source: U.S. Bureau of the Census (1992).

Notes: The census codes for the six occupations, in order of their listing, are 683, 738-749, 785, 486, 453, and 753-779. Percentage employed is of only these listed groups. Data are for the Los Angeles CMSA.

[a] Asians include Pacific Islanders.
[b] Differences between the groups are highly significant ($p < .01$).
[c] Differences between the groups are also statistically significant ($p < .05$).

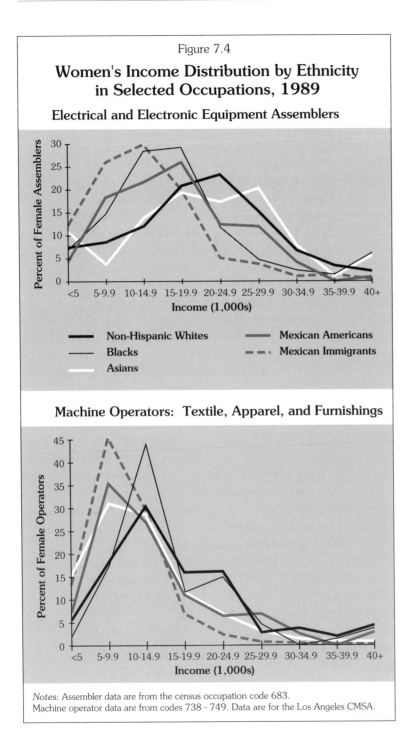

Figure 7.4

Women's Income Distribution by Ethnicity in Selected Occupations, 1989

Electrical and Electronic Equipment Assemblers

Legend:
— Non-Hispanic Whites
— Blacks
— Asians
— Mexican Americans
– – Mexican Immigrants

Machine Operators: Textile, Apparel, and Furnishings

Notes: Assembler data are from the census occupation code 683.
Machine operator data are from codes 738 - 749. Data are for the Los Angeles CMSA.

have incomes significantly higher than those of Mexican immigrants—only that ethnic income differences are significant.

Ethnic differences in the incomes of janitorial and electrical assembly workers may also be due to the fact that certain jobs are protected from competition by lower-cost immigrant workers. For black and white janitors, working for the government probably provides this insulation against competition. Many white and other non-immigrant electrical-equipment assembly workers may earn higher wages because they are unionized or employed in the aerospace industry.

This result does not indicate that Mexican immigrants are being discriminated against, though that may be the case. It is very possible that the ethnic differences are only an indirect reflection of the real factors producing the income differences between groups. Geographical concentrations of labor in certain neighborhoods tend to keep wages down in those areas, so that the location of enclaves in relation to work may be affecting results.[32] Other factors include differences among employees in relative seniority and self-employment, differences in the size of companies, degree of unionization, and type of industry represented. Other occupations in Southern California, of course, may also show ethnic differences in income distributions which are statistically significant.[33]

Summary and Interpretation

This chapter comprises several separate analyses, which lend themselves to a series of findings.

1. In 1959 the income gap between whites and both blacks and people of Mexican origin was less in Southern California than in the nation as a whole. In other words, those minorities in Southern California were earning higher incomes relative to whites than minorities were earning in the rest of the country. This was probably an effect of industrial expansion during the war years and of subsequent economic growth. Despite lack of political power on the part of blacks and Hispanics and blatant discrimination, the economic growth of that period was sufficient to raise wages for both whites and minorities.

2. The increased income differences between whites and minorities in Southern California since 1959 are partly the

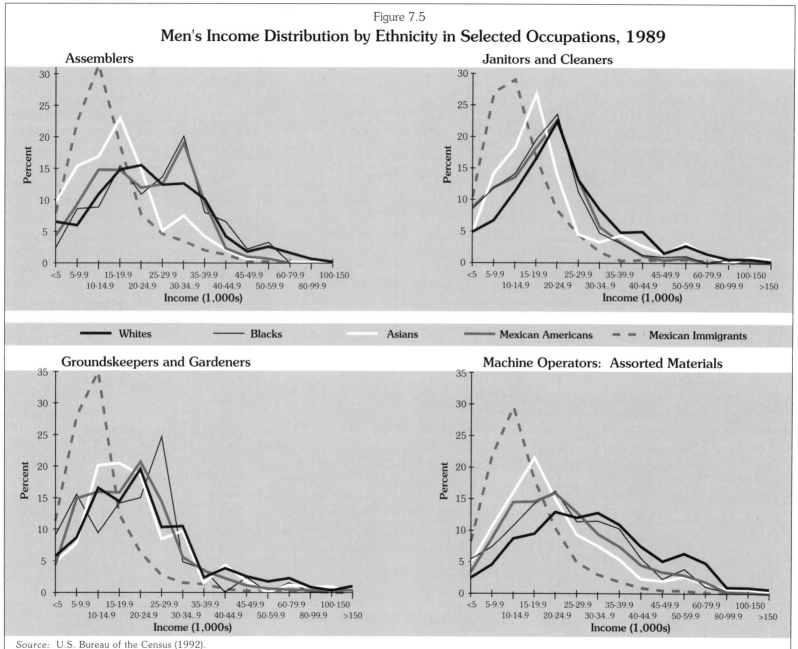

Figure 7.5

Men's Income Distribution by Ethnicity in Selected Occupations, 1989

Assemblers

Janitors and Cleaners

—— Whites   —— Blacks   —— Asians   —— Mexican Americans   — — Mexican Immigrants

Groundskeepers and Gardeners

Machine Operators: Assorted Materials

Source: U.S. Bureau of the Census (1992).

Notes: Assembler data are for census occupation code 785. Groundskeeper and gardener data are for code 486 (farmers not included). Janitor and cleaner data are for code 453 and machine operator data are for codes 753–779. Data are percent of males aged 14+ with positive annual incomes. Percents are the percent of the ethnic group with income in each category. Data are for the Los Angeles CMSA.

result of nationwide trends since the mid-1970s. Nationally, the growing use of technology and the shift of manufacturing to other countries have produced a surplus of less-educated workers and a growing demand for those with higher education. In combination with changes in economic and social policies during the 1980s, this has led to income polarization among Americans. The net effect of all these developments has probably been to increase the relative incomes of whites and Asians (who are generally more educated) compared with those of blacks and Hispanics (who are generally less educated). Despite this trend of the 1980s, over the past thirty years the country as a whole experienced some narrowing of the income gap between blacks and whites. For workers of Mexican origin there has been little change in the gap nationally.

3. Widening income gaps in Southern California are also due partly to regional trends. By 1989 Southern California's blacks and people of Mexican origin had lost the favorable position compared with the rest of the country that they had known in 1959. In 1989 the gaps between these groups and whites were wider in this region than was case nationally.

4. The regional factor that seems to explain most of the growing income gaps in Southern California is the development of a surplus of low-skilled workers, mostly immigrants from Mexico, Central America, and Asia. The arrival of these immigrants spurred the expansion of low-wage manufacturing, epitomized by the apparel and furniture industries, and the low-wage service sector, in which restaurant-kitchen and car-wash employees, lawn-maintenance crews, janitors, and nannies find work. U.S.-born people working in those sectors bore the brunt of competition with the immigrants. The effect of this labor surplus has been to depress wages, not only for immigrants themselves but also for those born in the United States. This has been especially the case among less educated Mexican Americans—those who are not high-school graduates.

In other words, immigrants have played the major role in widening the region's income gap. Whites have tended to benefit economically from the large supply of low-wage labor and the increased gap while the incomes of Mexican Americans compared to other groups have declined. The extent to which immigrants have hurt employment opportunities and incomes

among blacks is not clear, and among Asians the effect probably varied according to the status of the specific group.

5. Differences in median income between the ethnic groups are little influenced by group tendencies toward self-employment and government work. However, if our analyses had identified specific occupations and industries within the three classes of employment, we might have been able to see greater effects on income.

6. Stratifying populations in terms of age, educational attainment, U.S. birth, full-time employment, and occupational type makes it possible to compare median incomes of subgroups matched according to human capital characteristics. This eliminates all of the gaps for U.S.-born Asian women and for black women who are college graduates. Because white women who work full time earn 65 percent as much as do men, the income gap that remains for women is one of gender rather than ethnicity.

7. With the same factors controlled, almost half the income gap for black men is eliminated, and for Mexican American men the gap is reduced by more than half. This shows that human capital (education, age, and U.S. birth) are important factors in the income gap.

8. Income gaps among men do not vary substantially and consistently by level of education. The presence of large gaps across most stratified subgroups suggests the effect of widespread cultural or social processes, the most important of which may be discrimination.

9 . Income gaps among men are somewhat smaller among professionals than among managers and people in other occupations. It seems likely that academic degree requirements and possibly professional licensing provide some protection for minority men against a wider income gap.

10. Japanese American men in managerial occupations have incomes that average only 81 percent of the income of comparable white men. This appears to result from a "glass ceiling" or discriminatory limitations with respect to executive and administrative advancement, about which Asians have frequently complained.

11. Adjusted income gaps between people of Russian ancestry with bachelors and advanced degrees were almost as large as

those between whites and the black and Mexican-origin minorities. This demonstrates that gaps are not automatically explainable by racial discrimination.

12. Japanese and Chinese men who are college graduates and employed professionally earn slightly more than do white men. Similarly, the earnings of Japanese and Chinese women, both those in the professions and others who are not high-school or college graduates often exceed those of white women. This probably relates to certain cultural and social factors which we have not attempted to identify.

13. If specific occupations are examined, the income gap is pervasive, though less so in the more technical occupations. This demonstrates that minority–white income gaps cannot be primarily explained by ethnic group differences in the occupations followed. The large minority presence in some of these occupations may be the result of affirmative action policies. However, the level of wages or salary earned is much less influenced by affirmative action. All this suggests that efforts to increase minority proportions in better and generally higher-paying occupations may reduce the income gap but are not likely to eliminate it.

14. Among selected low-skill occupations, those in which Mexican immigrants constituted fewer than a third of the employees showed at least two ethnically defined income tiers, with Mexican immigrants on the bottom. This is evidence for what is sometimes called a dual labor market in that specific occupation. In contrast, occupations in which more than about 40 percent of the workers were Mexican immigrants did not have two or more income levels. Government employment or work in certain unions or industries has probably protected some workers against wage competition. In other cases, the influence of the immigrant labor surplus has been sufficient to depress wages throughout that occupation. This is additional evidence of the deleterious effect of large numbers of low-skilled Mexican immigrants on the incomes of other residents of Southern California.

To sum up, we have attempted to explain the income gap in several different ways, but with each analysis some portion of the gap has remained, especially among men and especially among people who are not professionals. Additional factors behind the persisting gaps are probably ethnic-group differences in home environments, cultural heritage, attitudes toward work and achievement, family connections which can lead people toward better jobs, and employment discrimination. Separating out the influence of each of these and other possible factors in the explanation of income gaps is extremely difficult, if not impossible, though it has been the subject of much research and much argument.[34]

It is important for all Southern Californians, particularly for whites, to realize the size of the continued income gap among minority men, even among college-educated blacks and U.S.-born Hispanics. Awareness of this is salutary. It may prompt whites to examine their own treatment of minority individuals more carefully and understand with greater patience an underlying reason for the resentment that some minority people feel toward whites.

The existence of income gaps across most educational and occupational groups suggests that some form of discrimination may well be the greatest remaining factor behind the gaps.

Notes

1. Those tables and analyses which are linked to the 1959–1989 trend studied in chapter six and include results for Japanese, Chinese, and Filipinos are based on data for Los Angeles and Orange Counties only. In all other analyses the entire five-county area was used. Differences in area of coverage appear insignificant, however, because factors causing ethnic differentials in medians are presumably the same from one county to another. Also, the lowest and highest median incomes in the five counties are found in Los Angeles and Orange Counties.

2. A thorough national study of changes in income gaps among black and Latino men and women from 1939 to 1989 is Carnoy (1994). Various chapters in Chan (1990) cover Asian groups in California; and Carnoy, Daley, and Ojeda (1993) is excellent on Latino trends. Analyses of income gaps during the 1970s and 1980s are integrated into more comprehensive analyses of economic status at the national level by Levy (1987, 1995) and by Harrison and Bennett (1995).

3. See particularly Harrison and Bluestone (1988) and Levy and Murnane (1992).

4. Taylor (1995).

5. Wetzel (1994).

6. Glass, Tienda, and Smith (1988).

7. Carnoy (1994).

8. Median incomes for groups for the entire United States are available in U.S. Bureau of the Census (1962a, 1963a, 1963b, 1993b, and 1993c). Data for people of Mexican origin in 1959 are available only for the five southwestern states; we used figures reported in Bean and Tienda (1987), Table 10.6.

9. In chapter 6 we adjusted certain ratios based on an improved method of calculation of net group differences (ND) where the median was a less satisfactory measure. Calculation of the black-white index of net difference for the United States showed that the relatively superior situation for Southern California black men in 1959 was greater than appears in Figure 7.1. The ND was .399 for the United States and .348 for Southern California in 1959, demonstrating that the black-white gap was 15 percent wider in the United States than in Southern California. The ND for whites and Hispanics was not calculated because nationwide data were not available.

10. Levy (1987).

11. Soja, Morales, and Wolff (1989); Scott and Paul (1991).

12. For an examination of this regional industry and its work force, see Bonacich (1994).

13. U.S. Bureau of the Census (1962b, 1962c, 1963b, and 1992). The percentage of blacks among all employed men in Los Angeles and Orange counties increased from 5.7 percent to 7.6 percent during the period, and the comparable percentage of Hispanics quadrupled, from 7.5 percent to 32.4 percent.

14. Salinas (1986); UCLA Research Group (1989).

15. Morales and Ong (1993).

16. Filer (1992); Walker, Ellis, and Barff (1992); Frey (1995b).

17. Frey (1995a).

18. Frisbie and Neidert (1977); Reimers (1985); Tienda and Lii (1987).

19. Ong and Valenzuela (1996), 175.

20. Hensley (1989). Using a more specific methodology than that used by most economists, Hensley demonstrated that a real reduction in wages in Los Angeles has occurred in those industries with high percentages of Mexican immigrant workers. He examined specific industries and by comparing relative industry wages in other areas with little Mexican immigration. The largest wage reduction he found was 12.6 percent, in the furniture industry.

21. Topel (1994).

22. With respect to education, the sample was stratified into four groups: people who had not graduated from high school, those who were high-school but not college graduates, college graduates who had not received an advanced (postgraduate) or professional degree, and those who had received an advanced or professional degree. To control for age, we analyzed medians for each of the four ten-year age cohorts (ages 25–34, 35–44, and so forth), then averaged the four medians. Variations among individuals in acculturation were controlled by limiting our sample to U.S.-born people. Where the analysis indicated fewer than 100 persons within any of the categories of matched characteristics for any ethnic group (meaning the sample was actually based on only five individuals), the median income is not reported.

23. Der (1993); Cheng and Yang (1966), 328.

24. The income ratio for all Japanese men, 103.2 (Table 6.3), may seem inconsistent with the lower ratios reported for the U.S.-born (Table 7.1). The difference is due to foreign-born Japanese executives, administrators, and professionals, who averaged 112 percent of the income of comparably educated whites in Southern California and constituted 47 percent of all employed persons born in Japan. Most of these are not immigrants but managers of Japanese corporate offices in Southern California who remain in the area for only a few years.

25. In addition, we investigated whether or not the race of Mexican-origin men played a role in their median incomes. This was done by calculating from our educationally and occupationally stratified populations the median incomes of U.S.-born Mexican-origin men who were white, compared with those of all other races. Nearly all who did not identify their race as white reported it as "Other Race." There were no consistent differences in median income, echoing previous national findings from the 1980s (Reimers 1985). This showed that ethnic identity, rather than race identity based perhaps on skin color, was the important income-related influence for Mexican Americans.

26. Smith and Welch (1989), 560.

27. Carnoy, Daley, and Ojeda (1993).

28. The smaller gender income gaps for younger and college-educated women are demonstrated in Bianchi (1994). For a comprehensive look at characteristics of major ethnic groups, including incomes of full-time workers, see Harrison and Bennett (1994).

29. Carnoy (1994, 118) made a similar conclusion after a comparable analysis at the national level.

30. Hensley (1989).

31. Our analysis relates to the concepts of dual and segmented labor markets in the fields of economics and sociology. Those occupations in which income showed statistically significant differences between ethnic groups are presumably those in which two or more ethnically separate labor markets are functioning. Further explanation of dual labor-market theory and evidence can be found in Dickens and Lang (1988).

32. Scott (1988), 127–29.

33. One study of automobile wheel and battery manufacturers in Los Angeles has confirmed wage differentials based partly on the basis of ethnicity (Morales 1983). In these industries there are substantial wage-scale differences among employers. Some firms develop roughly three pay tiers, with highest pay for workers who are U.S. citizens, midlevel pay for legal immigrants, and lowest wages for immigrant workers who lack any legal status. Also, highly capitalized and more mechanized manufacturers use more U.S.-born and legal-resident workers and pay them more than immigrant workers lacking legal status. The latter typically dominate the workforce in labor-intensive firms where the work is often hazardous. However, in the garment industry a worker's status as a legal resident or an illegal one does not appear to affect his wages (Gill and Long 1989).

34. Most such research makes use of regression analysis to measure statistically the relationship between certain "human capital" characteristics of people and their incomes. Because there are no census data on certain characteristics, the best analyses combine census data with other sources. For example, one study using regression analysis found that the income gap at the national level between black and white men in their twenties was mostly eliminated when work experience, type of industry, and scores on the Armed Forces Qualification Test could be included (in addition to age and educational attainment) as potential influences on the income of individuals (O'Neill 1990). For college graduates the gap was completely eliminated. This means that that the income gap was essentially the result of real differences in the characteristics of individuals and types of work rather than discrimination.

There is contrary evidence of discrimination, however. Differential treatment of whites and blacks that affects the income gap can occur in either initial hiring or in the later work situation. Discrimination in hiring has been demonstrated and measured in Chicago and Washington, DC, by recording the treatment and outcomes of matched and fully qualified white and black men applying for the same jobs. In most cases both received similar treatment. However, in 15 percent of the tests whites were offered jobs when equally qualified blacks were not, and in 5 percent of the tests blacks were offered jobs when equally qualified whites were not (Turner, Fix, and Struyk 1991). Among blacks already employed, evidence of racial discrimination as a factor in the income gap is found in the experiences reported by black men, especially those in the middle class (Feagin and Sikes 1994). The ostensibly innocuous rebuffs, delays, and other subtle barriers experienced by black contractors are described compellingly in Feagin and Imani (1994).

8. Ethnic Niches at Work

When an ethnic group is represented much more strongly than the average of all ethnic groups in a specific occupation or industry, the work is often referred to as an occupational or industrial niche for that group. If members of a group are self-employed or employed by the government to an unusual degree, such tendencies can also be described as niches. If an ethnic group is overrepresented in certain niches, it must be correspondingly underrepresented in other types of work.

Niches demonstrate the influence of ethnic-group networks of mutual support in the inherently competitive world of work. Ethnic work niches often arise when immigrants discover and pursue a specialization as a means of adapting to life in this country, but others result from the differential status and power of racial and ethnic groups, with poorer and weaker groups relegated to the least desirable jobs.[1] Niches change, however, and a group which is leaving a niche for better opportunities is often replaced by another group. For example, as technologically advanced and high-paying industries appeared over the past century and as whites moved into those new niches, their departure from older, stagnating, and lower-paying types of works made it possible for blacks to enter those types of work in substantial numbers.[2] However, many niches are stable over decades and provide specific avenues of somewhat protected employment for the group for generations.

Many of the ethnic groups in Southern California have found distinct niches. These are important because they represent an underlying but half-hidden aspect of the region's employment structure. Because they are difficult to pin down and often the subject of speculation and stereotyping, we measure the main features of ethnic work specialization and attempt to explain the reasons for their development.

Like chapter 7, this chapter comprises several analyses. First we look at changes in some specific niches over the past several decades, with particular attention paid to 1960 and 1990. As in chapter 6, our attempt to keep the geographical area comparable required us to restrict this historical analysis to Los Angeles and Orange Counties. This is followed by the chapter's primary focus—comparative ethnic niches in 1990. For this we measure ethnic-group differences in self-employment and government employment and in specific occupations and industries in the five-county Southern California region. Lastly, a case study of the evolving Chinese niches over the past century and a quarter illustrates how certain conditions lead to a radical transformation of ethnic niches.

Selected Changes in Occupational Niches, 1960–1990

The growth of Los Angeles and Orange Counties since 1960 has meant that the actual numbers of people in nearly all nonfarm occupations has increased. The greatest growth occurred in professional, managerial, and sales occupations, and most dramatic of all has been a tripling of the proportion of female managers and administrators. The area also had more private-household workers and machine operatives in 1990 than in 1960. Under conditions of general job growth, specific ethnic niches often expand but not always is this the case. A niche may diminish because some other ethnic group is getting most of the jobs or because new technology is eliminating certain jobs.

In order to highlight unusually strong or weak niches, many of the tables in this chapter are set up in the form of ratios for easy comparison with the white population, as was done in chapters 6 and 7. A value of 1.0 for an occupation (Table 8.1, for example) means that the percentage of an ethnic group employed in that occupation is the same as the percentage of non-Hispanic whites employed in that occupation. Those occupations with values much higher than one show distinctive minority overrepresentation (or niches), often because whites have tended to avoid them.

Agriculture. The greatest contrast with the white occupational structure in 1960 is that of the Japanese, where men were forty times more likely and women almost twenty times more likely than whites to be farmers or gardeners. For Japanese, farming was a family enterprise, so the high ratio of Japanese women as farm laborers was due to their work on family farms, where the husband was owner or manager.

Many Japanese immigrants in the early twentieth century had origins in Japan as independent farmers.[3] They found vegetable gardening a practical means of advancing in this country. A horticultural specialty was still evident before World

War II, when Japanese farmers grew almost all the celery, peppers, and strawberries in Los Angeles County and raised more than half the cauliflower, cucumbers, tomatoes, spinach, and garlic.

The California Alien Land Laws of 1913, 1920, and 1923, which restricted the right of Japanese to own land, began the shift of Japanese from farming into other lines of work, particularly maintaining gardens and landscapes around the homes of the wealthy. This sort of work provided a good income all year long but did not require a large initial investment. After World War II the rapid suburbanization of Southern California resulted in a continued exodus of Japanese from farming. However, taking care of the gardens of well-to-do Southern Californians remained an important specialty, and new immigrants in the early 1950s often served as apprentices to older gardeners and so continued the trade.[4]

By 1990 the Japanese in Los Angeles and Orange Counties were much less likely to be involved in some type of agriculture. Japanese men were still more prevalent in farming than were white men, but this was primarily due to the estimated

Table 8.1 Selected Occupational Niches, 1960 and 1990

| | Men | | | | | | Women | | | | | |
| | | | | | Mexican Origin | | | | | | Mexican Origin | |
Occupation	Black	Japanese	Chinese	Filipino	U.S.-born	Mex.-born	Black	Japanese	Chinese	Filipino	U.S.-born	Mex.-born
Total employed, 1960	99,777	23,833	13,269	4,310	93,280	37,236	68,130	13,802	3,600	1,164	41,024	13,764
Total employed, 1990	283,453	57,624	86,530	76,416	281,322	605,602	292,725	51,724	80,071	87,179	257,903	338,722
Private household worker, 1960	7.3	6.0	10.4	20.6	.7	1.4	6.3	1.9	.4	.7	.6	2.0
Private household worker, 1990	2.4	2.2	4.6	3.4	1.9	2.9	2.7	1.1	1.9	2.2	1.6	9.8
Other service worker, 1960	3.2	.6	7.0	7.4	1.1	1.7	1.7	.6	.6	1.0	.6	.2
Other service worker, 1990	2.5	1.3	2.6	2.1	1.9	3.6	1.6	.9	.9	1.1	1.3	2.1
Farm manager, 1960	.8	40.9	.1	4.9	1.1	3.2	.2	19.5	.00	11.1	.1	.4
Farm manager, 1990	1.0	5.5	.5	1.1	.8	1.8	.4	1.7	.7	.3	.2	1.1
Farm laborer, 1960	.5	9.8	.2	9.3	3.1	24.8	.2	36.4	.00	8.3	6.2	13.4
Farm laborer, 1990	2.2	9.0	.5	1.0	2.9	9.6	.9	1.1	.6	1.1	1.2	3.6

Sources: U.S. Bureau of the Census (1962b, 1963a, 1963b, 1992).

Note: Data are for Los Angeles and Orange Counties.

3,244 Japanese men who were maintenance gardeners and groundskeepers. The ratio of Japanese women in farming in 1990 was only slightly above that of non-Hispanic white women because maintenance gardening is viewed as man's work, not as a family operation. Japanese who worked in retail nursery operations are not included because that is considered a sales occupation rather than an agricultural one.

Whereas Japanese traditionally had family farms, Mexicans have been the major source of labor in larger farm operations. When the Gentlemen's Agreement of 1908 sharply reduced the emigration of male laborers from Japan and the disruptions during and after the Mexican Revolution of 1910 prompted many thousands of Mexicans to move northward, immigrants from Mexico began to replace the traditional Asian sources of farm labor. Although thousands were forced back to Mexico during the Great Depression, those who returned to Southern California, plus new arrivals, meant that Mexican immigrants continued to provide farm labor in Southern California from the 1940s to the present.

Mexican immigrants far outnumbered those born in the United States—the Mexican Americans—in the farm-labor niche (Table 8.1). The contrast regarding country of birth remained for 1990, but by this time the decline of agriculture in Los Angeles and Orange Counties meant that the farm-laborer category included more than twice as many groundskeepers as farmworkers.

Although eighty years earlier Chinese immigrants in Los Angeles had been the leading suppliers of fresh vegetables, by 1960 almost all of them had left farming. Filipinos, the last of the Asian nationalities hired for farmwork in California, supplemented the Mexican workforce in some areas after about 1925. In 1960 Filipino men were still nine times more likely than whites to be farmworkers in Los Angeles and Orange Counties, but by 1990 they were as unlikely as whites to be doing that work.

Private-household workers. In 1960 Chinese and Filipino men were, respectively, ten and twenty times more likely than white men to be employed as private-household workers. They were houseboys, cooks, general servants, and maintenance workers, usually in the homes of well-to-do whites. Among women, however, blacks stood out for their greater representation in this occupation (Table 8.1). In fact, 23 percent of black women in Los Angeles and Orange Counties in 1960 were maids or servants in private homes—cooking meals, washing dishes and clothes, and scrubbing floors. However, this proportion was much lower than it had been in 1930, when 87 percent of working black women in Los Angeles City were so employed.[5]

Over the past three decades a major shift in the ethnic composition of private-household workers has taken place. By 1990 more than half of all female private-household workers were of Mexican origin, and 89 percent of these women had been born in Mexico. This is an example of an ethnic occupational shift which has been very common in Southern California—the replacement of most whites, blacks, and Asians in low-status positions by workers from Mexico. It is difficult to believe that many others were not essentially displaced from their jobs by the arrival of so many immigrants who were willing to do housework in other people's homes for lower wages.

Other service occupations. This category includes such jobs as waiters, kitchen workers, dental assistants, janitors, barbers, hairdressers, ushers, and welfare-service aides. The high proportion of Chinese men in such services in 1960 was probably related to the presence of Chinese laundrymen, one of the few businesses that the Chinese were permitted to open in the early part of the twentieth century.[6] Filipinos in service occupations in 1960 were more apt to be working as dishwashers, kitchen helpers, busboys, or porters in hotels and restaurants because thirty years earlier these constituted most of the few jobs open to them. By 1990 neither Chinese nor Filipinos were so strongly overrepresented, but men in all the groups worked in these occupations more than white men.

Because ethnic specializations are often tied to very specific occupations, we include similar ratios for a number of such occupations for 1960 and 1990 (Table 8.2). As before, the number represents the proportionate representation of the ethnic group in the occupation compared with the proportion of whites in the occupation.

Self-employment. Self-employed workers include those who work with or for a family member (Table 8.2). Percentages indicate the importance of entrepreneurship in the ethnic group. Over the past thirty years the rate of self-employment in Los Angeles and Orange Counties has more than tripled. This trend is linked to entrepreneurship among immigrants.

Table 8.2 Ethnic Representation in Detailed Occupations, 1960 and 1990

Occupation	Black Men		Black Women		Asian Men		Asian Women	
	1960	1990	1960	1990	1960	1990	1960	1990
Self-employed	.29	.42	.38	.42	1.08	.91	1.37	1.00
Accountant	.15	.47	.20	.61	.97	1.55	.85	1.78
Engineer, aeronautical	.14	.27	–	1.01	1.10	.86	–	1.22
Nurse, professional	–	1.68	1.02	1.03	–	1.99	1.00	1.63
Physician or surgeon	.33	.28	.30	.59	1.05	1.32	.89	2.11
Teacher, elementary or secondary	.56	.70	.59	.81	.58	.51	.74	.47
Mail carrier	3.36	2.95	–	3.75	.30	1.97	–	.74
Insurance or real-estate agent	.30	.50	.35	.49	.42	.72	.31	.72
Retail trade clerk	.31	.89	.21	.98	1.33	1.45	.60	1.25
Carpenter	.58	.75	–	1.04	.32	.36	–	.32
Painter, glazier, paperhanger	.96	1.08	–	.47	.25	.96	–	1.39
Automobile mechanic	1.00	1.01	–	1.93	1.53	1.19	–	.31
Truck driver or delivery person	1.51	1.88	–	1.12	.54	.57	–	.44
Assembler	1.56	2.12	.72	2.59	1.00	2.44	.63	4.64
Janitor, porter	9.17	3.04	7.59	3.42	1.05	1.16	1.02	1.25
Laborer, construction	2.33	1.64	1.89	.89	1.17	.47	1.13	.51
Machine operator, durable goods	1.20	1.56	.60	1.41	.55	1.14	.66	1.01
Machine operator, nondurable goods	1.50	1.23	2.36	2.10	.72	2.02	1.85	7.72
Cook (except private household)	2.06	2.56	1.62	2.22	6.14	4.11	.82	2.38
Waiter, counterperson	1.91	.54	.50	.36	2.81	1.33	.49	.85
Fireman	.17	1.10	–	–	.03	.17	–	–
Police, sheriff, marshal	.51	1.33	–	2.59	.13	.35	–	.31

Source: U.S. Bureau of the Census (1962b, 1992).

Notes: In 1960 this detail is available only for blacks and other non-whites. Ratios for 1960 are based on all whites; ratios for 1990 are based on non-Hispanic whites. The Asian category for both years includes a very small percentage of American Indians. Dashes indicate lack of employment by group or by whites. Data are for Los Angeles and Orange Counties.

Janitors, porters, and cleaning ladies. In 1960 the employment of black men as janitors and porters was what set them off occupationally most from whites.[7] Although in absolute numbers most janitors were white, this occupation was represented among black workers at more than nine times the rate found among whites. At that time black men also worked as garbagemen, elevator operators, mechanics, truck drivers, or in the skilled building trades; others were cooks, waiters, busboys, or Pullman car porters on railroad trains.

Occupations open to black women were greatly restricted in the first half of the twentieth century. This is reflected in the fact that in 1960 black women were still three times as likely as white women to be cleaning ladies or janitors.

Mail carriers. In 1960 black men were employed as mail carriers at three times the rate of whites. This work was an early and very popular avenue for blacks who sought economic and social advancement. Postal work was first opened to a few blacks in the 1880s, when the federal government began to use civil-service examinations as a basis for hiring.[8] By the early 1940s black mail carriers had become common in many places. Promotions, based especially on seniority and experience, had moved many blacks into the post office's bureaucracy, and in 1942 the first black man was appointed superintendent of a post-office station in Los Angeles. Between 1960 and 1990, black women showed dramatic gains in employment as mail carriers, the niche into which black men had moved decades earlier.

Fire fighting and police work. The extremely low ratio for firemen in 1960 is largely due to the efforts of white officials in the Los Angeles City Fire Department to bypass the role of civil service examinations in the hiring of blacks and to maintain segregated engine companies, only two of which were black.[9] The situation was not as bad in police work, for black men were represented as policemen at about half the rate of white men. By 1990 a major shift had occurred, however, in that black men were slightly overrepresented in work as both policemen and firemen. The movement of black women into police work has also been very significant.

Nurses and physicians. Black female professionals were particularly likely to be in nursing, which in 1960 provided employment proportionately equal to that for white women—a striking anomaly at the time (Table 8.2). Aspiring black women had long directed their efforts for advancement in those occupations that required education and training yet provided security, but discrimination in hiring had thwarted most of these efforts. In Los Angeles, however, local political pressure from black leaders and their allies, in combination with a high demand for nurses after World War II, opened up nursing to black women.

The struggle against discrimination in the hiring of nurses began in 1911. Black attendants were employed, and nurses and student nurses were later hired at Los Angeles County General Hospital.[10] In 1950 some black leaders in Los Angeles launched a major effort to document and fight discrimination in other local hospitals, most of which were still discriminating against blacks and Mexican Americans in patient care and staff hiring. Their report may have goaded hospital administrators into making major changes. At least as important, however, was the shortage of nurses in Los Angeles during the 1950s and 1960s as a result of rapid population growth and the need to staff new federal facilities for World War II veterans. By the early 1960s virtually all black women in Los Angeles who had been trained as nurses were employed as nurses.[11] Although racial barriers to nursing-management positions in hospitals were still an issue, an important victory in the struggle against discrimination had been achieved for professional nurses in Los Angeles.

Black men were physicians and surgeons at only one-third the rate of whites, and in 1950 they were generally not permitted to practice, even as interns, in local hospitals. A report by the End-Discrimination Committee may have improved opportunities for these men. To a white observer, the many younger, well-trained black physicians who had moved to Los Angeles after World War II and the lack of any predominantly black hospital in the area seemed to auger well for the professional advancement of black physicians in this area.[12]

Cooks. Among Asian men, the highest ratio involved cooks. This specialty among Chinese men had its origins in the demand for cooks during the Gold Rush days, and since the early twentieth century many Chinese across the country found a niche as cooks and part-owners of Chinese restaurants.[13] By 1920, mostly due to restrictions and pressure from whites, 58 percent of Chinese men in the United States were employed in services, most frequently in the restaurant or laundry businesses.

Manufacturing workers. The many thousands of white migrants to Los Angeles during the 1920s meant that even local automobile and tire manufacturers saw no need to hire black workers as of the early 1930s. Even with labor demands in defense industries during and after World War II, black community organizations in Los Angeles had to struggle almost constantly against white-controlled companies and government agencies to open up employment to qualified blacks.[14]

Employment as machine operators in the manufacture of durable goods is a category which symbolizes blue-collar work in traditional manufacturing. In Los Angeles in 1960 most such jobs were stable, unionized, and relatively high-paying.[15] Work was particularly associated with large operations of major corporations, producing steel, automobiles, tires, aircraft, and guided missiles. Since the 1960s nearly all large-scale, durable-goods factories in industries that are not high-tech have closed.

The statistics show that between 1960 and 1990 the proportions of black men and women working as machine operators in durable-goods manufacturing increased relative to whites. However, such figures are somewhat misleading. In fact, the proportion of blacks in this type of manufacturing has probably declined slightly in relation to total employment in this occupation as a result of both a drop in the number of whites and changes in ethnic categories between censuses. We explain in detail. In the 1960 data Hispanics were included with whites in these specific tabulations. Thus, blacks were somewhat better represented in this work than were whites and Hispanics combined at that time (Table 8.2). What erroneously appears as an increase in black proportions between 1960 and 1990 in relation to white workers is due both to the massive departure of white workers and the fact that the Hispanics who replaced them were not counted as whites in 1990.

The decrease in black proportions among nondurable-goods workers between 1960 and 1990 is also probably greater than that shown in Table 8.2 for the same reason. Moreover, chapter 7 makes it clear that the drop is due primarily to competition with Mexican immigrants. Less-educated, U.S.-born blacks (and whites) in Los Angeles who have the lowest manufacturing wages tend to work in those industries and services that have higher proportions of Mexican immigrants.[16] This effect is substantial in several nondurable-goods manufacturing industries (food, apparel, paper, chemicals, rubber, and plastics) in Los Angeles but is not found nationally. Thus, it is not surprising that many local U.S.-born workers in Southern California have left jobs in those industries.

Self-Employment and Government Employment in 1990

Here we begin our detailed examination of employment niches in 1990. Because comparisons with 1960 are not being made, we use the entire five-county Southern California area and are able to measure niches for a much larger number of ethnic groups. The change in areal coverage from the previous section's focus on Los Angeles and Orange Counties has no significant effect on niche measurement because outlying counties contain both older central cities and newer suburbs and are home to relatively few members of most ethnic groups.

In this first section we focus on differences in class of employment.[17] Because most people work for employers in the private sector (companies or businesses), we examine variations in terms of the alternative classes: self-employment and government employment. With all workers fitting into only three possible categories for class of employment, the numbers in each class are sufficiently large that we can look in more detail at ethnic populations, including ethnic subgroups (Table 8.3).

Immigrants generally take one of two main pathways toward economic success. Most aim to improve of their skills through formal education and take jobs in American companies or government. Alternatively, opening a small business is an option for all but the poorest adults, regardless of their education and language skills. Compared with other countries and metropolitan areas, the United States and Southern California are viewed particularly favorably by potential immigrants who consider opening up a business here, partly because nonentrepreneurial ethnic groups appear to constitute a large portion of the inhabitants of Los Angeles.[18]

Although many Southern Californians associate Asians with self-employment, the fact that Asians and Pacific Islanders are no more likely to be self-employed than are whites was already demonstrated (Table 8.2). The inclusive category of "Asian" clearly disguises the reality of large variations in self-employment rates among different Asian groups.

In nearly all ethnic groups, men are more apt to be self-employed than are women (Table 8.3). Exceptions exist, however, and gender disparity varies a great deal among groups. For Vietnamese, for example, the greater rate of entrepreneurship among women continues a cultural tradition of women taking responsibility for a family's business and financial matters.[19] On the other hand, the 10 percent of Asian Indian women who are self-employed (or helping without pay in a family business) represent a new adaptation, because in India women rarely work as managers or clerks in businesses.[20]

Cultural predisposition toward self-employment. Ethnic differences in self-employment are sometimes the result of cultural backgrounds which predispose some groups more than others to entrepreneurship.[21] The importance of cultural differences is indirectly evident in the fact that a father's self-employment has an important influence in the likelihood of his son following that path. Explanation of entrepreneurship based on cultural tradition is exemplified by Jews and Armenians. Both groups have long-standing traditions of commerce and trading in many countries.[22] Many ethnic groups which have high rates of self-employment share special ethnic resources not available to outsiders, such as information and training about specific business operations, start-up funds from their extended family or from a rotating-credit organization, and personal connections for supplying imported goods.[23]

The self-employment rate of Armenians is slightly lower for those who migrated from what is now independent Armenia but at the time of the census was the Armenian Republic in the Soviet Union. This is probably because they were not permitted to take much money with them when they left the Soviet Union and because entrepreneurship was strongly discouraged during the Soviet period.[24] However, rates for Armenians from the Soviet Union are still higher than those for most non-Armenian groups. This suggests that influences of the Soviet period are less important in adapting here than are their Armenian heritage and the new social and financial support networks developed in Southern California.

Among Latinos, the fact that Cuban and South American men have higher rates of self-employment than do Mexicans and Central Americans points to what are probably real differences in social class and traditions between these groups. However, it is not clear whether the Cubans reflect an entrepreneurial heritage from pre-Castro Cuba or were particularly responsive to the special assistance provided to refugees when they opened a business. Whether or not the self-employed Argentineans in Southern California carry on a business tradition brought by German immigrant families to Argentina is also unknown.[25]

Although a continuity of cultural traditions may appear to explain why some ethnic groups are much more predisposed to self-employment than others, the next section shows many exceptions to this notion.

Self-employment as a new adaptation. The decision of many immigrants to open businesses has nothing to do with any ethnic cultural predisposition. Rather, people frequently choose to become entrepreneurs after finding themselves unsuccessful in the general job market. Many Asians, for instance, who are well educated or were in high-status occupations in their home country have been unable to reach a similar position in this country as long as they worked for a typical American company. Such disappointment and downward mobility often occurs when language skills are insufficient or when degrees and certifications earned in their home country are not recognized here. Discrimination may also play a role.

For example, recently arrived Russian Jewish refugees and Vietnamese have often reported that they opened their own business to avoid taking poor jobs in the general job market.[26]

Table 8.3   Class of Employment, 1990

Ethnic Group	Men Private[a]	Men Government[b]	Men Self[c]	Women Private[a]	Women Government[b]	Women Self[c]
Non-Hispanic White	71.7	12.2	16.2	76.3	13.9	9.8
English ancestry	71.5	12.2	16.3	73.3	15.9	10.7
Russian ancestry	61.6	10.1	28.4	69.7	14.3	16.0
Israeli ancestry	62.2	3.6	34.2	77.2	8.6	14.3
Armenian ancestry	61.7	9.6	28.7	74.6	12.7	12.7
Armenian ancestry born in Iran	65.0	8.5	26.5	76.2	10.3	13.4
Armenian ancestry born in the Soviet Union	63.3	12.0	24.7	70.3	20.7	9.0
Armenian ancestry born in Lebanon	59.4	5.8	34.7	77.0	10.6	12.3
Iranian ancestry	62.2	7.4	30.4	79.0	7.1	14.0
Egyptian ancestry	69.2	13.8	17.0	70.8	18.1	11.1
Lebanese ancestry	67.7	7.4	24.9	77.0	9.8	13.2
American Indian	77.8	13.1	9.0	75.9	17.0	7.0
Black	69.2	23.7	7.1	68.5	27.3	4.2
Belizean ancestry	77.5	13.5	9.0	85.0	10.2	4.8
Jamaican ancestry	68.1	23.6	8.3	76.3	17.2	6.4
Asian Indian	76.1	9.9	14.1	77.2	13.1	9.7
Cambodian	73.4	16.2	10.3	72.7	12.1	15.2
Chinese	73.0	9.8	17.2	76.4	12.7	10.9
Chinese-Vietnamese	77.5	13.1	9.4	82.4	9.9	7.7
Taiwanese	60.8	9.5	29.8	72.2	9.1	18.7
Filipino	76.4	17.5	6.0	82.3	13.6	4.1
Hawaiian	80.0	14.5	5.6	78.9	15.6	5.5
Indonesian	74.8	9.7	15.5	77.1	14.2	8.7
Japanese	71.9	11.5	16.6	74.7	16.9	8.4
Korean	60.1	4.6	35.3	67.1	8.0	24.9
Samoan	79.5	14.9	5.6	82.7	13.0	4.3
Thai	80.6	5.4	14.1	80.2	7.9	11.9
Vietnamese	80.0	10.1	9.8	76.6	12.1	11.3
Mexican	86.3	7.2	6.5	82.9	12.2	4.9
Puerto Rican	74.9	18.1	7.0	80.7	15.6	3.7
Cuban	72.5	10.3	17.2	76.5	15.3	8.3
Guatemalan	90.4	2.8	6.7	85.5	4.5	9.9
Salvadoran	90.9	3.0	6.1	88.3	3.8	7.8
Nicaraguan	87.8	5.3	6.8	83.9	9.0	7.0
Argentinian	72.3	5.6	22.0	71.1	17.1	11.8
Colombian	75.9	7.7	16.4	79.7	9.3	10.9

Notes: The table shows the percentages of workers in each ethnic group employed in each of these classes. All groups and subgroups listed are represented by more than 2,000 employed men or women.

[a]Employed by a private company or organization or by an individual.
[b]Employed by a local, state, or federal government.
[c]Self-employed or working without pay in a family business.

In many cases the ethnic group lacks a cultural tradition of business activities. Similarly, entrepreneurship among Koreans developed only since World War II; it is a means of adapting to the United States that reflects no essential component of Korean culture.[27] For middle- and upper-class Iranian women, the appearance of entrepreneurism is even more recent.[28] In the 1970s some women began to sell goods and services from their homes in Teheran and simply expanded such activities after they arrived in Los Angeles. Selling flowers, pastries, clothing, and beauty services to other Iranian women from their homes reduces business costs and is socially satisfying while being economically profitable.

Variations among subgroups. The ethnic categories for which the census tabulated data may have obscured important differences in self-employment among the religious, social, and regional subgroups within any country. For instance, among immigrant Israelis, who average a high rate of self-employment, the Oriental (Middle Eastern) and Sephardic Jews are much more likely to be entrepreneurs than are the Westernized, often college-educated Ashkenazic Jews, whose orientation toward the professions is greater.[29] Another example of the significance of religious-group differences involves Iranian men, who average a relatively high rate of self-employment in Southern California. A sample survey during 1987–1988 found that Iranian Jews had a rate of self-employment that was more than 80 percent higher than the rates for Iranian Muslims and Armenians from Iran.[30]

Asian Indian immigrants who belong to one of the business-oriented castes in India can be expected to continue to be self-employed in the United States. Nevertheless, subgroup specializations are not necessarily perpetuated. The Patels from Gujarat, who are the leading motel owners among Asian Indians, are not from a business caste, and those Sikhs who operate convenience stores represent a shift from tradition because most Sikh immigrants had their origins in farming or craft castes.[31]

Chinese immigrants, particularly those from Vietnam, have been described as highly entrepreneurial, but such a characterization does not appear to apply to the average Chinese or Chinese-Vietnamese in Southern California.[32] Our data show the Chinese to be only slightly more entrepreneurial than are people of English ancestry (Table 8.3). Despite the impressive international business activities of some Chinese from Vietnam, as a group they have a low rate of self-employment. Among the Chinese, it is those from Taiwan who are especially likely to be self-employed.

Government employment. An alternative to self-employment is government, or public-sector, employment. This has long been a desirable type of employment among blacks, and it has become important for many immigrants, especially those with clerical skills.[33] Among blacks, this preference is well justified by their better economic treatment by the government than in the private sector. Blacks entered this class of employment earlier than did most immigrants. In their quest for government positions, many blacks are helped by being native English speakers or by having been veterans of the armed forces, which gives preference in civil-service hiring.

Thus, it is not surprising that government employment is more common among blacks than among any other ethnic group and that a quarter of employed blacks work for the government (Table 8.3). Although the post office, the armed forces, and various federal programs spearheaded employment opportunities and better pay for a wide range of blacks, black employment has also come to characterize government at the municipal, county, and state levels.

The most recent immigrants often have lower proportions employed by government unless they represent a minority aided by affirmative action or other programs. Many immigrants are unable to qualify for government jobs because of insufficient ability in English. Although legal status as an immigrant (a permanent resident) is sufficient for employment at the state and local levels of government, most federal-government jobs require U.S. citizenship. Thus, ethnic differences in rates of government employment are related to differences in citizenship, veteran status, education, and occupation.[34] However, these factors only partly explain group differences, leaving unknown some important influences on government employment. Immigrant professionals have usually preferred to work for the government, and, like blacks, tend to alert members of their own group to new job openings when they appear.[35] Because of such personal-contact networks, ethnic groups are often clustered in particular government agencies.

A Closer Look at Selected Occupations in 1990

In this section we present ethnic occupational specializations for fifteen ethnic groups. The fact that a total of 501 occupational categories were tabulated means that smaller ethnic groups and subgroups had very few persons employed in most occupations. For this reason we selected only larger ethnic groups and occupations (Table 8.4).

Understanding Table 8.4. The values in Table 8.4 represent percentages of people employed in the five-county region. The extent of disproportionate representation of an ethnic group can be calculated by dividing the group's total percentage of workers in all occupations (top line) into the percentage of an ethnic group working in a specific occupation. For example, white women represent 55.3 percent of all employed women but only 13.3 percent of all women working as private-household servants. This means that white women are found in that occupation at less than a quarter of the average rate of all Southern California women.

Table 8.4 emphasizes both niches and underrepresentation. Boldface numbers show a substantial overrepresentation of the group in any occupation; regular type indicates a pronounced underrepresentation. Where the ethnic group is not very different from the average in the percentage of its people employed in a particular occupation, no number appears.

Ethnic groups are ordered by median household income, from the highest, on the left side of the table, to the lowest, on the right. The order of occupations follows that of the U.S. census: higher-status occupations are listed first; those at the bottom require less education and provide much lower incomes. This design makes it possible to see general patterns of disproportionate representation. The frequent overrepresentation of high-income groups in more prestigious occupations is evident on the upper left-hand side of the table; the

niches of some low-income groups can be compared on the lower right-hand side.

Blacks and Hispanics. The large size and relatively low status of the black and Mexican origin groups suggest comparisons. Both men and women of Mexican origin are underrepresented in almost all listed professional and managerial occupations, but among blacks only men are underrepresented in most of those positions. This indicates that the generally higher occupational status of black women compared with men (chapters 6 and 7) is based on their positions in a wide range of specific occupations.

Table 8.4 shows that black and Mexican workers have very different occupational niches. The only overrepresentation of both groups is among women who are janitors and cleaners. Nevertheless, the fact that the table shows neither underrepresentation nor overrepresentation in many occupations indicates that members of the two groups still frequently hold the same occupations, implying continued job competition. These data cannot show the extent of black occupational displacement prior to 1990 as a result of competition with Mexican immigrants. Nor is it possible to estimate how many more blacks would be working in these occupations if there had been no increase in the number of available Hispanic workers. Thus, the table should not be interpreted as indicating that blacks and Mexicans hold such different occupations that the groups do not compete directly.[36]

Although Table 8.4 demonstrates some dramatic cases of ethnic occupational specialization, in reality some low-status groups may be even more strongly overrepresented than is shown. Percentages of workers from Mexico, El Salvador, and Guatemala in low-level jobs are understated by the census data. This is because many workers from these countries are living in the United States illegally and chose not to complete the census questionnaires. The effect must have been a substantial undercount of illegal or undocumented immigrants, many of whom work in low-status niches.

Among women who are household servants and cleaners, Salvadorans are overrepresented by ten times the expected proportion. They and women from Guatemala constitute one-

Table 8.4 Disproportionate Representation of Ethnic Groups in Selected Occupations, 1990

Men	Employed Men	Russian	Filipino	Asian Indian	Japanese	English[a]	White[b]	Iranian	Chinese	Vietnam	American Indian	Korean	Armenian	Mexican[b]	Black[b]	Guatemalan	Salvadoran
Percent of all employed men, aged 16+		1.6	1.9	0.5	1.3	7.1	53.3	0.6	1.9	0.9	0.6	1.2	0.7	24.3	7.2	1.0	1.8
Executive, Administrative, Managerial																	
Financial manager	22,426	–	–	–	–	–	–	–	–	0.1	–	–	–	4.8	3	0.1	0.6
Marketing, advertising	31,322	–	–	–	–	–	**83.5**	–	–	0.3	0.2	–	–	4.5	3	0	0.2
Food service, lodging manager	38,646	–	–	**2.2**	–	–	–	–	**5.8**	–	–	–	–	–	–	–	–
Manager, administrator, n.e.c.	283,871	–	–	–	–	–	–	–	–	0.3	–	–	–	7.8	3.2	–	0.4
Accountant	52,742	–	**7**	**1.5**	–	–	–	–	–	–	0.2	–	–	5.3	–	0.1	0.5
Professional Specialty																	
Engineer, aerospace	38,524	–	–	**1.7**	–	–	–	–	–	–	0.1	–	–	3.7	3.4	0	0
Engineer, civil	19,860	–	–	**3.9**	–	–	–	**3.4**	–	–	–	–	**2.5**	5.4	3	0.3	0.1
Engineer, electrical, electronic	37,365	–	–	**1.9**	**3.8**	–	–	–	**7.1**	–	–	–	–	3.6	3.2	0	0.1
Physician	30,831	**7.7**	–	**2.7**	–	–	–	**2**	**6.2**	–	–	–	–	2.5	3.2	0	0.1
Lawyer	39,486	**10.0**	0.6	–	–	–	**88.5**	–	–	0.1	0.2	–	–	3.1	3.1	0	0.1
Actor, director	18,523	**8.6**	0	0	0.3	–	**86.1**	0.1	0.3	0.2	0.2	0.1	–	3	–	0.1	0.1
Technical, Sales, Administrative Support																	
Clinical laboratory technician	6,039	–	**16.2**	–	**3.6**	–	–	–	**5.9**	**3.3**	0	–	–	10	–	0	–
Electronic technician	23,900	–	–	–	–	–	–	–	–	**6.3**	–	–	–	11.7	–	–	–
Cashier	58,528	–	–	**2.6**	–	–	–	–	–	–	–	**5**	–	–	–	–	–
Computer operator	18,139	–	**6.8**	–	–	–	–	–	–	–	–	–	–	–	–	–	–
Bookkeeper, accounting clerk	18,834	–	**6.4**	–	–	–	–	–	–	–	–	–	–	–	–	–	–
Postal clerk	12,750	–	**7.4**	–	–	–	–	0	–	–	0.1	–	0.1	–	**28.4**	0.2	0
Mail carrier	14,860	–	**6.1**	0.1	–	–	–	0	–	0.3	–	–	–	–	**16.4**	0.2	0.1
General office clerk	23,996	–	**6.7**	–	–	–	–	–	–	–	–	–	–	–	**14.3**	–	–
Firefighter	13,339	0.1	0.1	–	–	–	–	0	0.2	0.2	–	0	–	–	–	0	0
Police (public service)	23,440	–	–	0	–	–	–	0	0.6	0.2	–	0.2	0.1	–	–	0.1	0.1
Guard, police (private)	57,596	–	–	–	0.4	–	–	0.1	0.4	–	–	0.4	–	–	**21.5**	–	–
Cook	88,040	0.5	–	0.1	–	2.5	20.3	–	**5.9**	–	–	–	0.1	**52.0**	–	–	–
Busboy, kitchen assistant	50,538	0.2	–	–	0.3	2.8	21	0.2	–	–	–	–	0.2	**57.0**	–	**2.7**	–
Nursing aid, orderly	15,610	–	**8.4**	–	0.4	–	–	–	–	0.3	–	0.4	–	–	**19.3**	–	–
Farming																	
Groundskeeper	75,097	0.2	0.5	–	**4.3**	2.3	19.8	0	0.4	–	–	–	–	**60.3**	–	–	–
Precision Production, Repair																	
Painter	50,112	0.4	0.4	–	0.3	–	–	0	0.5	0.1	–	**4.5**	–	–	–	**4.6**	**5.8**
Electronic equipment assembler	11,336	0	–	–	–	3	20.6	0	–	**8.1**	–	–	–	**43.9**	–	–	0
Operator, Laborer																	
Textile sewing machine operator	23,288	0.1	0.2	0	0.1	0.1	3.2	0.1	–	–	0	–	–	**68.4**	0.5	**8.3**	**9.2**
Assembler	70,203	0.2	–	–	–	3.3	22.3	0.1	–	3.2	–	–	–	**52.2**	–	–	–
Bus driver	12,016	–	–	–	–	–	–	0	–	–	0	–	–	–	**33.5**	–	–
Construction laborer	102,045	0.3	0.4	0.1	0.2	–	–	–	0.3	0.4	0	0.3	–	**49.8**	–	–	–

Notes: The figure for an ethnic group in an occupation indicates the percentage of all workers in that occupation who are in the ethnic group. For smaller groups, percentages are shown only where the group's representation is greater than 3 times or less than 0.33 the percentage of all workers in that occupation.
Bold type indicates disproportionately higher representation in the occupation; regular type indicates underrepresentation.

Table 8.4   Disproportionate Representation of Ethnic Groups in Selected Occupations, 1990 (continued)

Women	Employed Women	Russian	Filipino	Asian Indian	Japanese	English[a]	White[b]	Iranian	Chinese	Vietnam	American Indian	Korean	Armenian	Mexican[b]	Black[b]	Guatemalan	Salvadoran
Percent of all employed women, aged 16+		1.7	2.5	0.4	1.4	7.8	55.3	0.4	2.1	0.8	0.6	1.3	0.6	19.7	8.7	1.0	1.9
Executive, Administrative, Managerial																	
Financial manager	24,100	–	–	–	–	–	–	–	–	0.2	0.3	–	–	6.9	–	0	0.2
Marketing, advertising, p.r. manager	15,913	–	–	–	–	–	–	0.1	–	0.1	–	–	–	5.9	3.6	0.1	0
Manager, administrator, n.e.c.	104,649	–	–	–	–	–	–	–	–	–	–	–	–	8.5	–	0.2	0.2
Accountant	65,476	–	–	–	–	–	–	–	6.8	–	–	–	–	6.8	–	0.1	0.2
Professional Specialty																	
Engineer, aerospace	3,605	–	0.7	1.2	–	–	–	0	8.4	0.1	–	0.4	0	5	–	–	0
Engineer, electrical	3,969	–	–	0	–	–	–	–	11.7	4.2	–	0	0	5.5	–	0	0
Computer systems analyst	9,916	0.3	–	–	–	–	–	0	8.2	–	0	–	0.2	8.6	–	0	0
Physician	8,909	5.4	7.7	5	–	–	–	1.3	–	–	0.3	–	0.2	4.3	–	0	0.2
Registered nurse	98,239	–	11.8	–	–	–	–	–	–	–	–	–	–	5.3	–	0.1	0.4
Pharmacist	3,345	–	–	–	4.5	–	–	–	18.2	5.6	0	8.3	–	4.1	–	0	0
Social worker	22,731	–	–	–	–	–	–	–	–	–	–	–	–	–	20.9	–	0.4
Lawyer	15,000	8.2	0.6	–	–	–	–	0	–	0.1	0.2	–	–	5	–	0	0.3
Designer	30,291	–	–	–	–	–	–	–	–	–	0.2	–	–	–	2.2	–	–
Actor, director	12,925	10.1	–	–	–	–	85.1	–	0.5	0.2	–	–	–	2.2	–	–	0
Technical, Sales, Administrative Support																	
Clinical laboratory technician	11,296	–	16	–	–	–	–	–	–	–	0	–	0	6.7	–	0.2	–
Licensed vocational nurse	17,007	–	10.1	–	–	–	–	0	0.5	0.2	–	–	0	–	22.5	–	–
Electronic technician	4,595	–	–	0	–	–	–	0	–	11.2	–	–	0	–	–	–	0
Computer programmer	12,599	–	–	1.3	–	–	–	1.6	14.6	–	0	–	–	6.2	–	–	0.2
Computer operator	24,411	–	–	–	–	–	–	–	–	–	–	–	–	–	13.2	–	–
Bookkeeper, accounting clerk	118,788	–	–	–	–	–	–	–	–	–	–	–	–	–	–	0.2	0.4–
Postal clerk	11,040	0.3	–	–	0.2	3.4	24.7	0.1	6.4	–	0.3	4.3	0.1	–	40.3	0.3	0.1
Child care worker, household	16,031	–	–	–	0.2	–	–	–	–	–	–	0.4	–	9.5	3.6	9.5	11.3
Private household servant	51,644	0	–	–	–	1.7	13.3	0	–	0	–	–	–	35.2	–	12.1	20.8
Guard, police (private)	11,685	–	–	–	–	–	–	0	0.7	–	–	0.2	0	–	23.7	0	–
Nursing aid, orderly	81,361	–	–	–	–	–	–	–	–	0.4	–	–	–	–	22.3	–	–
Janitor, cleaner	49,390	0.1	–	0.1	0.4	2.4	22.4	0	–	–	0.3	–	0.2	38	13.2	5	9.7
Hairdresser, cosmetologist	48,018	–	–	0.1	–	–	–	1.5	–	6.2	–	–	–	–	–	–	–
Farming																	
Farm worker	10,649	0.5	0.1	0	0	1.3	11.6	0	0.1	0	–	0	0	78.4	2.7	0.3	–
Precision Production, Repair																	
Electronic equipment assembler	24,731	0.2	–	–	–	1.8	19.3	0.1	–	5.9	–	–	–	41.9	–	–	–
Operator, Laborer																	
Textile sewing machine operator	69,102	0.1	–	–	–	0.6	4.5	0.1	7.1	–	0.3	–	–	56.7	2.3	3.8	11.4
Assembler	59,373	0.2	–	–	–	1.7	18.6	0	–	3.2	0.3	–	–	51.6	–	–	–
Bus driver	8,280	0.4	0.3	0	0	0	–	0	0	0	–	0.4	0.2	–	35.6	0	0

[a]English ancestry is shown only where greater than two times or less than 0.5 the percentage of all workers in that occupation.

[b]Non-Hispanic white, Mexican origin, and black percentages are shown only where greater than 1.5 times or less than 0.5 the percentage of all workers in that occupation.

third of all household servants in Southern California, with Mexican women making up another third. The similar niches of Salvadorans and Guatemalans suggest communication and networks which interlink these groups, and their shared cultural background, recent migration history, and residential location focused in the Westlake section of Los Angeles make this highly likely. The proximity of this main Salvadoran and Guatemalan concentration to the well-to-do white families on the Westside of Los Angeles is evident on various maps.

Jews. Two other extreme cases of ethnic overrepresentation involve people of Russian-ancestry as lawyers and as actors and directors. Although white men in general are also overrepresented as lawyers, Jewish men are represented at six times the expected rate and Jewish women at nearly five times the expected rate. Among women, overrepresentation as actors and directors is almost as great as the men's niche as lawyers. Acting reflects the cultural heritage of the Yiddish theater in Eastern Europe and America in the late nineteenth century: a Jewish tradition expressive of both a people's ambition and their marginal social position.[37] Although Jewish scholars have long been concerned with both secular and Jewish law, the overrepresentation of Jews among lawyers has probably more to do with the general long-standing Jewish value placed on the intellect and education, combined with changes in twentieth-century America that opened more opportunities in the law for Jews. These changes were the decline of anti-Jewish discrimination in the professions and the growth of both Jewish-owned businesses and an affluent Jewry.[38]

Filipinos. This group's strongest niche occurs among clinical laboratory technicians, where Filipino men and women constitute one-sixth of all such workers in Southern California (Table 8.4). However, among the women, Filipino registered nurses are more widely recognized because they have much greater contact with the public and because the number of nurses is much greater. The niche in nursing is not surprising, considering the 1948 inauguration of a nursing exchange program with the Philippines, the proliferation of nursing schools in the Philippines during the next two decades, the chronic shortage of nurses in the United States, and the willingness of Filipina nurses to work long hours in some of the more difficult positions in American hospitals.[39]

Half of the immigrant nurses who entered the United States between 1965 and 1988 were Filipinos, and 90 percent of the foreign-trained nurses admitted as temporary (nonimmigrant) workers were from the Philippines. Because some nurses have not yet passed their examinations to become registered nurses, they have taken jobs as licensed vocational nurses or nursing aides, which have less demanding requirements. Filipino nurses have higher incomes than do nurses from other ethnic groups because they frequently take evening and night shifts in hospitals or hold positions in two hospitals. The economic independence and advancement represented by these nurses reflect aspects of culture in the Philippine Islands: a greater equality of status between men and women and an encouragement of women who work outside the home.[40]

Filipino men are overrepresented among accountants and in certain clerical occupations. Their good command of English, with special strengths often in reading and writing, makes them well qualified for such work. These language skills also permit those who are citizens to compete well in examinations for federal employment as postal clerks and mail carriers, and veterans of military service (such as from earlier enlistment in the U.S. Navy) are awarded extra points in the competition for such jobs. The tendency of many Filipino men in Los Angeles to work for the U.S. Post Office or in clerical and semiprofessional occupations was noted as early as 1940, although at that time many were aging farmworkers.[41] Thus, the occupational niches found in 1990 are not necessarily new.

In both 1940 and 1990, few Filipinos occupied upper-level management positions. It is said that they lack the advanced degrees, personal contacts, smooth interpersonal skills, and other characteristics needed for such positions.[42] However, America's heritage of employment discrimination against Asians strains the credibility of this sort of comment.

Other Asians. Occupations held by Asian groups in Southern California vary a great deal as the result of different levels of education and differing social networks among the ethnic groups.

At the upper end of the status ranking are some niche occupations which reflect the high level of education and emphasis on science among many Asians. For instance, in Southern California, Asian Indian men are physicians at five times the expected percentage, and Asian Indian women are ten times more likely to be physicians than is the average woman (Table 8.4). Chinese women are pharmacists at eight times the rate expected, and women from Vietnam and Korea are pharmacists at more than six times the expected frequency. That occupation has the status of being a licensed profession and the advantage, for those who are weak in English-language skills, of requiring little direct speaking with the public.

Asian groups with lower average levels of education or difficulty in learning English frequently have lower-status occupational niches. In 1980, 44 percent of employed Vietnamese in the United States worked as machine operators or in precision production work.[43] In Orange County, in particular, a niche in this sort of production is evident in the overrepresentation of Vietnamese as electronic technicians and electrical-equipment assemblers. Vietnamese find that assembling circuit boards or heart valves is similar to weaving and embroidering, with which many are familiar, and assembly pays better than do service jobs. High-tech employers find Vietnamese workers to be reliable and skilled workers and to have good memories. A large amount of aircraft, missile, and electronic-assembly work takes place in Orange County and the southern part of Los Angeles County, not far from the largest Vietnamese concentration in the United States. Vietnamese have many of these jobs.[44]

Mexican origin: U.S.-born compared with foreign-born. The largest number of occupations with disproportionate representation is found among people of Mexican origin. Both men and women are underrepresented in nearly all the listed occupations that are professional and managerial, as well as some technical, sales, and administrative-support occupations (Table 8.4). On the other hand, men of Mexican origin are overrepresented as assembly-line workers, groundskeepers, farmworkers, cooks, busboys and kitchen assistants, and construction laborers.

Among people of Mexican origin, the overrepresented occupations show much higher proportions of immigrants compared with U.S.-born workers (Table 8.5). Half of Southern California's groundskeepers and kitchen assistants are Mexican immigrants, as are more than half of the people operating sewing machines in the garment industry. Considering the substantial undercount among such workers, such niches must be even stronger in reality than these data indicate.

On the other hand, the reverse situation is not true: higher-status occupations are not dominated as completely by those born in the United States. A separate analysis (not shown) found that immigrants constitute 36 percent of the Mexican-origin men in the managerial, professional, and technical occupations listed in Table 8.4.

Table 8.5   Mexican Immigrants and Mexican Americans in Overrepresented Occupations, 1990

Mexican-origin Men's Niches	Foreign-born Men	U.S.-born Men
Cook	44.8	7.1
Busboy, kitchen assistant	50.1	6.9
Groundskeeper	50.8	9.5
Textile sewing machine operator	65.8	2.6
Assembler	42.2	10.5
Construction laborer	39.1	10.7

Mexican-origin Women's Niches	Foreign-born Women	U.S.-born Women
Private household servant, cleaner	30.8	4.3
Janitor, cleaner	30.4	7.6
Farm worker	70.7	7.7
Electrical equipment assembler	29.4	12.5
Textile sewing machine operator	53.1	3.6
Assembler	39.6	12.0

Notes: This table shows the percentages of U.S.-born and immigrant Mexican workers out of the total employment in each occupation. Occupational percentages in Table 8.5 sum to comparable figures in Table 8.4.

Ethnic Niches in Industries

Understanding Table 8.6. Whereas Table 8.4 focused on only a few occupations, Table 8.6 is particularly useful because it includes all industry categories. For each ethnic group, it lists the five numerically largest employing industries out of the 235 industry categories for which data are available. Also included, in italics below the five leading industries, are any other industries in which the group is concentrated at three or more times the rate for all employed men or women.[45]

The importance of these industries for employment of persons in the ethnic group is also shown (in the middle column). For example, 4.1 percent of men of Iranian ancestry are employed in real estate. (Very similar industry concentrations among Guatemalans and Salvadorans and among the largest Spanish-speaking Central and South American nationalities justified combining these into two groups in the table.)

The "Ratio to Total Employed" (the third column) shows the proportion of the ethnic group employed in that industry compared with the proportion in that industry among all employed men or women. It shows the degree of disproportionate representation by an ethnic group in industry niches much as Table 8.4 did. For example, the ratio of 1 for white men in construction means that they are represented at exactly the same rate as all Southern California men; the ratio for Armenian men in automobile repair (2.7) means that they are overrepresented in that industry at 2.7 times the rate for all employed men.

Among extremely large ethnic groups—whites and people of Mexican origin—the ratios to total employed can reflect an ethnic numerical dominance in an entire industry. For example, in the manufacture of guided missiles and space vehicles, the overrepresentation of Chinese, English-ancestry, Puerto Rican, and white men is not proportionately large and suggests something of the ethnic diversity in that industry. But because 53 percent of all men employed in Southern California are white, the 1.4 ratio for whites means that this group constitutes about 75 percent of the total employment in that industry. Similarly, because Mexican men make up 24.3 percent of all employed men, the 2.5 ratio for their overrepresentation in

landscape and horticultural services means that about 60 percent of all men working in that industry are Mexican (either immigrants or U.S.-born).

Ethnic variations in niche importance. A good indication of the degree of ethnic-group specialization in industry can be obtained by summing the percentages represented by the five most important industries. Although that value is not shown in the table, a standard for a low level of ethnic niches could be the 23 percent of white men who work in the five leading industries for whites. In contrast, industry niches are most strongly developed among Israeli men (at 43 percent in the five leading industries) and Chinese-Vietnamese men (with 37 percent in the five industries). Among women, Thais and Guatemalans–Salvadorans are most strongly specialized in their leading industries.

The large number of industry niches is evident from the fact that nearly all groups have at least one or two industries in which they are represented at twice the rate for the total population, and in many cases groups are working in several industries at more than three times the average.[46]

Relationship to occupational niches. Niches can be indicated by both industry and occupation. However, work requiring advanced training or licensing can be performed in different industries and is usually better characterized by occupation. For the self-employed, niches are better described in terms of industry because business people have often built up their experience over a range of occupations within the same industry. In many instances, both occupation and industry have value as means of identifying niches.

Some niches were previously presented in terms of occupation, but the greater detail in Table 8.6 can illuminate the work specialties even more. For example, Vietnamese women (overrepresented as assemblers of electrical and electronic equipment in Table 8.4) are particularly likely to be making electrical machinery, medical and dental instruments, computers, and various types of communications equipment, such as television sets. Likewise, the occupational overrepresentation of Korean men as cashiers (Table 8.4) presumably refers to the

Table 8.6   Leading Industries of Employment, 1990

Men Industry	Number of Employed Men	Percent of Ethnic Group	Ratio to Total Employed	Women Industry	Number of Employed Women	Percent of Ethnic Group	Ratio to Total Employed
White (Non-Hispanic)							
Construction	278,755	11.1	1.0	Elementary, secondary schools	186,076	8.6	1.2
Manufacture, missiles, space vehicles	82,241	3.3	1.4	Hospitals	120,523	5.5	.9
Retail, eating, drinking places	75,810	3.0	.6	Retail, eating, drinking places	107,903	5.0	.9
Real estate	70,974	2.8	1.3	Real estate	82,062	3.8	1.4
Theater, motion picture	64,730	2.6	1.5	Insurance	63,651	2.9	1.2
English Ancestry							
Construction	33,385	10.0	.9	Elementary, secondary schools	31,684	10.4	1.4
Manufacture, missiles, space vehicles	12,918	3.9	1.7	Hospitals	16,882	5.5	.9
Real estate	7,824	3.1	1.5	Retail, eating, drinking places	12,362	4.0	.8
Elementary, secondary schools	7,179	3.0	1.3	Real estate	12,354	4.0	1.5
Manufacture, aircraft, parts	9,021	2.7	1.3	Insurance	8,478	2.8	1.1
Russian Ancestry							
Theater, motion picture	4,646	6.2	3.5	Elementary, secondary schools	5,961	9.1	1.2
Legal services	3,738	5.0	5.3	Theater, motion picture	3,570	5.4	4.2
Construction	3,511	4.7	.4	Hospitals	3,344	5.1	.8
Real estate	3,487	4.7	2.2	Legal services	2,956	4.5	2.8
Colleges, universities	1,950	2.6	1.9	Real estate	2,908	4.4	1.6
				Radio, television	*596*	*.9*	*3.0*
Israeli Ancestry							
Construction	1,123	22.2	2.0	Elementary, secondary schools	483	14.3	1.9
Real estate	388	7.7	3.6	Real estate	192	5.7	2.1
Automobile repair	231	4.6	2.8	Retail, eating, drinking places	145	4.3	.8
Miscellaneous entertainment services	225	4.4	3.7	Hospitals	158	4.7	.8
Manufacture, electrical machinery	198	3.9	2.5	Retail, apparel, accessories	116	3.4	.5
Armenian Ancestry							
Construction	3,267	10.1	.9	Banking	1764	8.0	2.9
Automobile repair	1,418	4.4	2.7	Elementary, secondary schools	1544	7.0	.9
Retail, eating, drinking places	1,016	3.1	.7	Insurance	1001	4.5	1.8
Real estate	1,014	3.1	1.5	Hospitals	986	4.5	.7
Manufacture, durable goods, unspecified	1,005	3.1	7.4	Retail, eating, drinking places	817	3.7	.7
Retail, gasoline service stations	*859*	*2.7*	*5.2*				
Retail, jewelry stores	*856*	*2.7*	*16.6*				

Source: U.S. Bureau of the Census (1992).

Notes: This table shows the five industries or lines of business in which the largest numbers of each ethnic group are employed. Additional industries are shown in italics where the ethnic group employed numbers more than 300 and are represented in an industry at more than three times the rate for the total population. Industry labels are from the 242 categories developed for the 1990 census, originally based on the 1987 Standard Industrial Classification (SIC). In our tables, "Manufacture, electrical machinery" is an aggregation of industry codes 342 and 350.

Table 8.6   Leading Industries of Employment, 1990 (continued)

Men Industry	Number of Employed Men	Percent of Ethnic Group	Ratio to Total Employed	Women Industry	Number of Employed Women	Percent of Ethnic Group	Ratio to Total Employed
Iranian Ancestry							
Construction	2,084	7.8	.7	Banking	987	7.1	2.6
Retail, eating, drinking places	1,651	6.2	1.3	Retail, eating, drinking places	774	5.6	1.1
Real estate	1,097	4.1	1.9	Retail, department stores	773	5.6	2.4
Engineering, architectural services	978	3.7	4.1	Retail, apparel, accessories	759	5.5	3.8
Retail, gasoline service stations	806	3.0	5.9	Elementary, secondary schools	549	4.0	.5
Retail, furniture, home furnishings	*447*	*1.7*	*3.0*				
Black							
Construction	25,523	7.6	.7	Hospitals	35,067	10.4	1.7
Elementary, secondary schools	12,955	3.8	1.7	Elementary, secondary schools	30,910	9.1	1.2
Hospitals	12,532	3.7	2.1	Retail, eating, drinking places	12,299	3.6	.7
Retail, eating, drinking places	10,943	3.2	.7	Insurance	10,415	3.1	1.2
Trucking	10,157	3.0	1.6	Banking	10,220	3.0	1.1
U.S. Postal Service	*8,616*	*2.6*	*3.3*	*U.S. Postal Service*	*7,528*	*2.2*	*4.3*
Bus service, urban transit	*3,852*	*1.1*	*3.2*	*Bus service, urban transit*	*3,065*	*.9*	*4.1*
				Utilities services, electric, gas	*1,313*	*.4*	*3.2*
Belizean Ancestry							
Construction	427	15.5	1.4	Hospitals	440	16.6	2.7
Hospitals	179	6.5	3.7	Private household services	200	7.6	3.7
Elementary, secondary schools	128	4.6	2.1	Banking	181	6.8	2.4
Real estate	115	4.2	2.0	Elementary, secondary schools	145	5.5	.7
Retail, eating, drinking places	96	3.5	.7	Insurance	143	5.4	2.1
				Nursing, personal care facilities	*140*	*5.3*	*7.4*
Jamaican Ancestry							
Construction	212	6.4	.6	Hospitals	535	14.6	2.4
Hospitals	197	5.9	3.3	Elementary, secondary schools	328	8.9	1.2
Automobile repair	148	4.5	2.8	Private household services	204	5.6	2.7
Retail, grocery stores	131	4.0	1.9	Health services, unspecified	186	5.1	3.5
Elementary, secondary schools	129	3.9	1.7	Banking	167	4.5	1.6
American Indian							
Construction	4,654	15.6	1.4	Hospitals	1,539	6.1	1.0
Retail, eating, drinking places	1,391	4.7	1.0	Elementary, secondary schools	1,425	5.7	.8
Trucking	997	3.3	1.7	Retail, eating, drinking places	1,295	5.2	1.0
Retail, grocery stores	594	2.0	1.0	Retail, department stores	802	3.2	1.4
Elementary, secondary schools	587	2.0	.9	Real estate	738	2.9	1.0

Notes: See notes at bottom of first panel of Table 8.6.

Table 8.6   Leading Industries of Employment, 1990 (continued)

Men Industry	Number of Employed Men	Percent of Ethnic Group	Ratio to Total Employed	Women Industry	Number of Employed Women	Percent of Ethnic Group	Ratio to Total Employed
Asian Indian							
Manufacture, electrical machinery	1,306	5.0	3.2	Hospitals	1,759	11.0	1.8
Retail, grocery stores	1,156	4.5	2.2	Retail, eating, drinking places	777	4.8	.9
Construction	1,117	4.3	.4	Banking	682	4.3	1.5
Hospitals	1,017	3.9	2.2	Elementary, secondary schools	674	4.2	.6
Retail, eating, drinking places	982	3.8	.8	Retail, department stores	553	3.4	1.5
Hotels, motels	*773*	*3.0*	*3.2*				
Engineering, architectural services	*748*	*2.9*	*3.3*				
Retail, gasoline service stations	*599*	*2.3*	*4.5*				
Manufacture, computers	*514*	*2.0*	*3.3*				
Cambodian							
Retail, eating, drinking places	424	8.5	1.8	Retail, bakeries	349	8.7	31.6
Retail, bakeries	405	8.1	37.5	Manufacture, apparel, accessories	243	6.1	2.7
Manufacture, apparel, accessories	286	5.7	6.0	Hospitals	208	5.2	2.7
U. S. Postal Service	236	4.7	6.1	Retail, grocery stores	181	4.5	.7
Elementary, secondary schools	234	4.7	2.1	Retail, eating, drinking places	163	4.1	.8
				Manufacture, electrical machinery	*146*	*3.7*	*4.0*
Chinese							
Retail, eating, drinking places	10,065	11.8	2.5	Manufacture, apparel, accessories	6,015	7.6	3.3
Construction	3,119	3.7	.3	Retail, eating, drinking places	5,515	7.0	1.3
Manufacture, missiles, space vehicles	2,894	3.4	1.5	Banking	4,930	6.2	2.2
Colleges, universities	2,872	3.4	2.4	Hospitals	4,085	5.2	.9
Retail, grocery stores	2,519	3.0	1.4	Elementary, secondary schools	2,909	3.7	.5
Manufacture, computers	*1,697*	*2.0*	*3.3*				
Wholesale, prof. communication equip.	*927*	*1.1*	*5.1*				
Wholesale, apparel, fabrics	*598*	*.7*	*3.3*				
Chinese-Vietnamese[a]							
Retail, eating, drinking places	650	15.8	3.3	Banking	331	10.2	3.6
Manufacture, electrical machinery	291	7.1	4.6	Retail, eating, drinking places	222	6.8	1.3
Manufacture, durable goods, unspecified	265	6.5	5.0	Manufacture, apparel, accessories	220	6.8	3.0
U. S. Postal Service	196	4.8	6.2	Manufacture, electrical machinery	205	6.3	6.9
Banking	120	2.9	3.1	Manufacture, durable goods, unspecified	169	5.2	5.0
Taiwanese[b]							
Real estate	493	7.5	3.5	Retail, eating, drinking places	388	7.2	1.4
Wholesale, nondurable goods, unspecified	375	5.7	9.0	Real estate	350	6.5	2.3
Colleges, universities	297	4.5	3.3	Banking	276	5.1	1.8
Retail, eating, drinking places	273	4.1	.9	Hospitals	258	4.8	.8
Construction	265	4.0	.4	Colleges, universities	199	3.7	2.0

Notes: See notes at bottom of first panel of Table 8.6.

[a]Identity based on combined reported race and ancestry.
[b]Includes only those who reported a Taiwanese as opposed to a Chinese racial identity.

Table 8.6   Leading Industries of Employment, 1990 (continued)

Men Industry	Number of Employed Men	Percent of Ethnic Group	Ratio to Total Employed	Women Industry	Number of Employed Women	Percent of Ethnic Group	Ratio to Total Employed
Filipino							
Hospitals	5,975	6.8	3.8	Hospitals	20,381	20.3	3.4
Construction	4,330	4.9	.4	Banking	4,829	4.8	1.7
Retail, eating, drinking places	3,257	3.7	.8	Insurance	3,807	3.8	1.5
Banking	2,426	2.7	2.9	Elementary, secondary schools	3,287	3.3	.4
Insurance	2,269	2.6	2.0	Retail, eating, drinking places	3,183	3.2	.6
U. S. Postal Service	2,187	2.5	3.2	Nursing, personal care facilities	2,339	2.3	3.3
Armed Forces, navy	1,750	2.0	4.9	Public administration, finance, taxation	696	.7	3.7
Health services, n.e.c.	1,388	1.6	3.3				
Nursing, personal care facilities	584	.7	4.9				
Public administration, finance, taxation	399	.5	3.8				
Hawaiian							
Construction	597	12.1	1.1	Elementary, secondary schools	232	6.3	.9
Retail, eating, drinking places	288	5.8	1.2	Real estate	158	4.3	1.6
Retail, grocery stores	205	4.2	2.0	Hospitals	157	4.3	.7
Business services, unspecified	170	3.4	2.5	Retail, grocery stores	152	4.1	2.2
Landscape, horticultural services	164	3.3	2.1	Retail, eating, drinking places	142	3.9	.7
Indonesian							
Hospitals	268	6.8	3.9	Hospitals	289	9.6	1.6
Construction	232	5.9	.5	Colleges, universities	163	5.4	2.9
Retail, eating, drinking places	202	5.2	1.1	Retail, eating, drinking places	140	4.7	.9
Printing, publishing	140	3.6	2.8	Insurance	138	4.6	1.8
Engineering, architectural services	131	3.3	3.8	Elementary, secondary schools	118	3.9	.5
Japanese							
Landscape, horticultural services	3,700	6.0	3.9	Elementary, secondary schools	5,185	8.6	1.2
Manufacture, missiles, space vehicles	2,643	4.3	1.8	Hospitals	2,567	4.2	.7
Retail, eating, drinking places	2,641	4.3	.9	Retail, eating, drinking places	2,469	3.6	.7
Retail, grocery stores	2,150	3.5	1.7	Banking	1,895	3.1	1.1
Construction	1,947	3.2	.3	Colleges, universities	1,793	2.9	1.5
Wholesale, nondurable goods, unspecif.	427	.7	3.9				

Notes: See notes at bottom of first panel of Table 8.6.

Table 8.6   Leading Industries of Employment, 1990 (continued)

Men Industry	Number of Employed Men	Percent of Ethnic Group	Ratio to Total Employed	**Women** Industry	Number of Employed Women	Percent of Ethnic Group	Ratio to Total Employed

Korean

Men Industry	Number of Employed Men	Percent of Ethnic Group	Ratio to Total Employed	**Women** Industry	Number of Employed Women	Percent of Ethnic Group	Ratio to Total Employed
Construction	4,939	8.5	.8	Retail, eating, drinking places	5,683	10.8	2.0
Retail, grocery stores	3,326	5.7	2.8	Manufacture, apparel, accessories	3,631	6.9	3.0
Retail, eating, drinking places	3,161	5.5	1.1	Retail, apparel, accessories	2,609	5.0	3.4
Retail, liquor stores	2,111	3.6	16.9	Hospitals	2,591	4.9	.8
Laundry, cleaning services	1,627	2.8	6.9	Retail, grocery stores	2,555	4.9	2.5
Retail, apparel and accessories	1,098	1.9	4.7	Laundry, cleaning services	1,825	3.5	7.1
Retail, miscellaneous stores	1,086	1.9	3.8	Retail, liquor stores	945	1.8	16.5
Retail, gasoline service stations	931	1.6	3.1	Wholesale, apparel, fabrics	460	.9	3.3
Religious organizations	853	1.5	3.1	Retail, jewelry stores	393	.7	3.3
Wholesale, apparel, fabrics	484	.8	4.0				

Samoan

Trucking	233	7.5	3.9	Hospitals	354	12.9	2.1
Detective, protective services	200	7.7	10.6	Retail, eating, drinking places	196	7.1	1.3
Construction	184	7.1	3.7	Banking	101	3.7	1.3
Retail, eating, drinking places	177	5.2	1.1	Manufacture, furniture, fixtures	97	3.5	9.4
Religious organizations	97	3.7	7.8	Elementary, secondary schools	96	3.5	.5

Thai

Retail, eating, drinking places	933	13.2	2.7	Retail, eating, drinking places	1,365	18.0	3.4
Retail, grocery stores	231	3.3	1.6	Hospitals	780	10.3	1.7
Business services, unspecified	224	3.2	2.3	Manufacture, apparel, accessories	502	6.6	2.9
Construction	216	3.1	1.6	Retail, grocery stores	308	4.1	2.1
Trucking	198	2.8	1.5	Insurance	250	3.3	1.3
Retail, gasoline service stations	188	2.7	5.2				

Vietnamese

Manufacture, electrical machinery	3,160	7.6	4.9	Beauty shops	2195	7.4	6.4
Retail, eating, drinking places	2,234	5.4	1.1	Retail, eating, drinking places	1422	4.8	.9
Manufacture, computers	1,931	4.6	7.8	Manufacture, electrical machinery	2360	8.0	5.6
Manufacture, aircraft, parts	1,654	4.0	.8	Banking	1041	3.5	1.3
Social services, unspecified	518	1.2	3.4	Manufacture, apparel, accessories	1059	3.6	1.6
Manufacture, medical, dental equip.	415	1.0	3.1	Manufacture, medical, dental instr.	883	3.0	7.4
Beauty shop	345	.8	4.5	Manufacture, computers	794	2.7	6.3
Manufacture, scientific instruments	332	.8	3.5	Personal services, unspecified	720	2.4	4.2
				Manufacture, radio, TV, equipment	339	1.1	3.1

Notes: See notes at bottom of first panel of Table 8.6.

Table 8.6 Leading Industries of Employment, 1990 (continued)

Men Industry	Number of Employed Men	Percent of Ethnic Group	Ratio to Total Employed	Women Industry	Number of Employed Women	Percent of Ethnic Group	Ratio to Total Employed
Mexican							
Construction	156,953	13.7	1.2	Retail, eating, drinking places	51,770	6.7	1.3
Retail, eating, drinking places	94,199	8.2	1.7	Elementary, secondary schools	47,300	6.1	.8
Landscape, horticultural services	44,266	3.9	2.5	Manufacture, apparel, accessories	44,925	5.8	2.5
Manufacture, durable goods, unspec.	27,431	2.4	1.9	Hospitals	33,918	4.4	.7
Manufacture, furniture	24,532	2.1	2.3	Private household services	26,701	3.5	1.7
				Agricultural production, crops	*11,213*	*1.5*	*3.3*
				Manufacture, canned, frozen veg.	*3,015*	*.4*	*3.0*
				Manufacture, leather products	*1,309*	*.2*	*3.4*
Puerto Rican							
Construction	1,871	8.9	.8	Hospitals	1,445	8.3	1.4
Hospitals	623	3.0	1.7	Elementary, secondary schools	1,202	6.9	.9
Retail, eating, drinking places	589	2.8	.6	Retail, eating, drinking places	868	5.0	.9
Manufacture, missiles, space vehicles	553	2.6	1.1	Retail, department stores	657	3.8	1.6
Manufacture, aircraft, parts	546	2.6	1.2	Banking	592	3.4	1.2
Cuban							
Construction	1,260	6.0	.5	Elementary, secondary schools	1,593	8.8	1.2
Retail, eating, drinking places	727	3.5	.7	Hospitals	748	4.1	.7
Manufacture, durable goods, unspecified	485	2.3	1.8	Manufacture, apparel, accessories	730	4.0	1.8
Hospitals	481	2.3	1.3	Banking	693	3.8	1.4
Retail, grocery stores	464	2.2	1.1	Retail, eating, drinking places	615	3.4	.6
Guatemalan-Salvadoran							
Construction	19,892	14.5	1.3	Private household services	22,568	20.0	9.8
Retail, eating, drinking places	11,932	8.7	1.8	Manufacture, apparel, accessories	11,667	10.3	4.5
Manufacture, apparel, accessories	6,219	4.5	4.8	Retail, eating, drinking places	7,558	6.7	1.3
Automobile repair	5,558	4.1	2.5	Business, repair services to dwellings	6,909	6.1	6.7
Manufacture durable goods, unspecified	4,482	3.3	2.6	Family child care, at homes	2,907	2.6	3.6
Repair services to dwellings	*3,531*	*2.6*	*3.2*				
Automobile parking, car washes	*2,605*	*1.9*	*5.3*				
Private household services	*727*	*.5*	*3.5*				
Other Central American and South American[c]							
Construction	4,996	9.1	.8	Private household services	3,438	6.6	3.2
Retail, eating, drinking places	2,679	4.9	1.0	Retail, eating, drinking places	3,437	6.6	1.2
Automobile repair	1,408	2.6	1.6	Manufacture, apparel, accessories	3,183	6.1	2.7
Business services, unspec.	1,177	2.1	1.6	Elementary, secondary schools	3,079	5.9	.8
Manufacture, aircraft, parts	1,077	2.0	.9	Hospitals	2,717	5.2	.9

Notes: See notes at bottom of first panel of Table 8.6.

[c]Includes Honduran, Nicaraguan, Argentinian, Colombian, Ecuadorian, and Peruvian identities.

many self-employed Koreans who operate grocery, liquor, and other retail stores (Table 8.6). Most of the Asian Indian managers of food-service and lodging facilities are in the hotel and motel business, and the Asian Indian men who are overrepresented in the manufacture of computers and electrical machinery are more typically engineers than assemblers.

Relationship to status. Specific industry niches are mostly a function of similar networks of personal contact and guidance, but they may also reflect the group's level of education and acculturation and its cultural predispositions. For instance, the Samoan concentration in private protective services, typically as security guards, is partly related to the group's low level of educational attainment. In contrast, the concentration of Iranian women in banking and in department stores and accessory shops clearly relates to their affluence and their consciousness of fashion, both of which represent a transfer of the lifestyle they knew in Iran before the 1979 revolution.[47]

Movies, rugs, and jewelry. Well known to older generations is the importance of Eastern European Jews in creating the movie business.[48] Whereas movies seemed vaguely immoral to Protestant sensibilities, a few Jewish immigrants saw their potential. By 1925 immigrant men like Carl Laemmle, William Fox, Louis B. Mayer, Adolph Zukor, Marcus Loew, Cecil B. De Mille, and Jack and Sam Warner had created a new industry, with Hollywood as its unrivaled center. They founded Universal Studios, Columbia Pictures, Paramount Pictures, Metro-Goldwyn-Mayer, and Warner Brothers. Although carpenters, electricians, and other trade workers in the film industry have usually not been Jewish, movies and later television led to employment for countless Jewish writers, actors, directors, production supervisors, actors' agents and press agents, set designers, studio managers, film distributors, theater managers, and lawyers. In the radio and television industry, a Jewish men's niche is only slightly weaker. However, their representation at only 2.7 times the average means that this industry does not qualify as a niche for Russian-ancestry men in Table 8.6.

Some ethnic niches of the past have receded in importance, often replaced by new niches. The historic association of

Armenians with the rug business in Los Angeles and elsewhere was not sufficiently strong in 1990 to qualify for this table. The concentration of Armenian men in the jewelry business contrasts sharply with the situation in 1920, when there were only five jewelers among the 2,000 Armenian men in Los Angeles whose occupations were surveyed.[49] During the 1980s opportunities in jewelry design, manufacturing, wholesaling, and retailing attracted hundreds of immigrants from both Soviet Armenia and the Middle East, so that by 1989 approximately half the manufacturers in the Jewelry District (6th and Hill Streets) in Downtown were Armenian immigrants.[50] Some men had been jewelers before they immigrated, but many were taught the trade by fellow Armenians after they arrived in Los Angeles. Proud of their role in design, many Armenians also see Los Angeles as well located for the anticipated growth of jewelry sales in Asia.

Doughnut shops, beauty shops, and motels. The most striking case of an ethnic niche in an industry is that of Cambodians who operate retail bakeries. If the census data identified doughnut shops specifically within the broader category of bakeries, this Cambodian specialty would appear far stronger, because Cambodians clearly dominated the business in Southern California in 1990.

Work in a Winchell's doughnut shop was first arranged for Vietnamese through refugee-resettlement offices in 1975, but other Vietnamese did not follow this lead.[51] Cambodians, however, saw an opportunity, and this business niche began in 1977, when a single Chinese-Cambodian immigrant opened a doughnut shop in La Habra.[52] The business was successful, relatives trained with the owner and opened their own shops, and word of these opportunities spread widely within the community.[53] In Orange County, the majority of Chinese-Cambodians own doughnut shops, and many own more than one. Nearly all Cambodians use the spelling *donut* because of its simplicity and the lower cost of store signs.

Doughnuts are completely alien to the Cambodian culture, and many shop owners do not like doughnuts at all: the business is simply a practical means of economic survival. Both husbands and wives put in long hours at the shops, but not much English-language ability is needed. Rotating-credit societies within the Cambodian community made many of the loans that supplemented family savings and enabled immigrants to establish doughnut businesses. Before the early 1990s, when the doughnut market became saturated, the financial success of at least some Cambodians was highly visible in the new Mercedes and sporty automobiles that the owners and their families often drove. Because the shops are widely scattered, most proprietors own homes in nearby white areas rather than in the Long Beach enclave.

Vietnamese women are six times more likely to be working in beauty shops than is the average Southern California woman (Table 8.6). Vietnamese women are attracted to this industry because the work does not require a high-school diploma, the hours are usually flexible, and the women can keep their children with them during the day.[54] Over time they have achieved a reputation as highly skilled manicurists.

Work in a beauty shop provides experience for those who later open their own nail salons, and over time such shops have become widely distributed. In some areas, such as Westwood Boulevard south of Wilshire Boulevard, their proliferation has saturated the market.

The Asian Indian niche in the motel industry is not particularly strong in Southern California compared with many other smaller places, but, as with Cambodians in the doughnut business, the niche appeared when others emulated and received guidance from successful pioneers. It is quite possible that the niche had its origins in 1946 in San Francisco.[55] During World War II an Asian Indian farmworker who was drafted by the U.S. Army leased a hotel for a friend to operate. While he was away in the Army, the hotel showed a profit. News of this success spread in the homeland, especially among those from the same Patel caste in the Gujarat region, so that over the years many others followed and pursued the same dream.

As with doughnut shops, an entire family can help in the motel's day-to-day operations, which require neither an advanced education nor much English-language ability. Gujaratis living in East Africa were also part of these international social networks, so many Gujaratis who had been in business in East Africa become motel owners or followed other business pursuits in California. Running a motel may be similar in many ways to operating a retail grocery business, so the many Asian Indians who manage convenience stores may represent an extension of the motel-industry niche.

Eating and drinking places, apparel, and construction. A group's representation in eating and drinking places and in apparel manufacturing is significant because the former pays the lowest averages wages of any industry and the latter the lowest wages of any type of manufacturing.[56]

The apparel industry provides a niche for women who cannot speak English but can learn to operate a sewing machine with skill. However, the low wages deter many Asians and effectively create more opportunities for Latino immigrants.[57] Although rates of self-employment in specific industries cannot be determined from this table, the self-employed in this industry are presumably making much higher incomes. For example, garment manufacturing is clearly a niche among Korean and Vietnamese women (Table 8.6). In 1989 there were more than 900 Korean and Vietnamese business owners in that industry in Los Angeles and Orange Counties.[58]

Southern California's construction industry is so massive that it provides employment opportunities for many groups. For example, one-fifth of Israeli men work in construction, and Israelis are more specialized in construction than any other ethnic group listed. Construction work is also much more important to Belizeans and American Indians than it is to Asian Indians or Chinese.

The Chinese: A Case Study of Changing Niches

Changes in the characteristics of the immigrants themselves within any one ethnic group and in employment opportunities in Southern California have expanded the potential for new work niches and less extreme specializations. Examination of one ethnic group's employment niches over the past 125 years in Southern California demonstrates how work specializations can change dramatically despite an overall continuity of cultural heritage. The almost complete reversal in Chinese work niches over that time was the result of startling changes in the educational and economic characteristics of those who settled in this region and in the potential for opportunities in Southern California.

Historic Chinese niches. In the 1850s and 1860s boatloads of Chinese men left the southeast coast of China and sailed to California. Most found work only as laborers, and those who ventured into Southern California came after having completed railroad and other construction contracts in northern California or elsewhere.

By the 1870s these Chinese men were building or maintaining early railroad lines, irrigation ditches, orange groves, and vineyards.[59] They lived out of temporary homes in numerous small Chinatowns and rural camps near their farmwork. Until the end of the nineteenth century Chinese in labor gangs, moving around from job to job, supplied most of the cheap labor for construction and farmwork in Southern California. Whites increasingly resented the competition from the efficient and low-cost Chinese and in the 1890s drove many Chinese out of their temporary camps and little Chinatowns, frequently setting the shacks on fire. By 1910 most Chinese had left the small towns and rural camps of Southern California, and newly arrived Japanese and, later, Mexicans replaced the Chinese as laborers.

Many of the Chinese who moved from these rural areas into Los Angeles began to grow vegetables and sell them door to door. By 1880 the 200 Chinese produce farmers constituted 89 percent of all such farmers in Los Angeles County. At the same time Chinese men had commonly worked as washers and ironers in Los Angeles' laundries, and some were later able to pool their savings and enter the laundry business. The larger society of Los Angeles became so highly dependent on Chinese vegetable vendors and laundry workers that anti-Chinese boycotts in the 1880s failed to garner wide support, particularly from local women who recognized that the Chinese freed them from many tasks that their husbands would otherwise expect them to do.

Other Chinese opened small stores, curio shops, and restaurants—another niche in which the Chinese were permitted by white society to operate. Chinese restaurants also

became popular with whites. At first some whites had believed that Chinese food was poisonous, but slowly that notion was overcome. Chinese men were also servants and cooks on ranches and for in-town white families.

In the late 1880s and 1890s the Chinese lost much of the vegetable produce niche to European immigrants. Also, a few years later new railroads linked large San Joaquin Valley farms to eastern cities, thus eroding external markets for local vegetable production.

With restrictions on Chinese immigration since 1882, the Chinese population of Los Angeles slowly declined after 1900. Young Chinese families were replacing the aging, single men whose labor had built so much of California. Because Chinese merchants (but not laborers) were permitted to enter and bring wives into this country, the nucleus of a small, established Chinese community in Los Angeles was built around a few business-oriented families, many of whom had middle-class merchant origins. By 1910 a second generation was growing: 24 percent of the Chinese had been born in the United States. Another twenty-five years later most of the elderly, bachelor laborers had moved elsewhere, returned to China, or died. The younger Chinese who stayed were highly acculturated. However, they still worked mostly in laundries, small food stores, and restaurants—largely because white society continued to restrict access to better opportunities.

Shifts in immigrant characteristics since 1945. Changes in U.S. immigration policy in the 1940s made possible the entry of many more Chinese women, so that 40 percent of the Chinese in Los Angeles in 1950 were females. The Communist takeover of the mainland in 1949 precipitated the flight of Nationalists to Taiwan and the beginnings of an exodus from China of tens of thousands of refugees, as well as equally large numbers of students.[60] Many of those who fled were well-educated government officials, former businessmen or businesswomen, or advanced students in the sciences or engineering. A great many of these ended up in Southern California, often having come via Hong Kong.

During the 1950s these Chinese presented a sharp contrast with the descendants of the earlier immigrants. Many had been part of China's elite. Their educational level and skills, including some English-language ability, made them more employable in higher-level jobs than were the earlier immigrants.

As of 1990 family connections and the legal immigration process remain the major means by which Chinese immigrants settle in Southern California. However, some people with temporary visas to visit the United States as tourists or students have overstayed those visas and have become illegal residents. Also, during the 1990s there has been clear evidence of carefully planned smuggling operations which bring people from China's southeast coast, usually by way of Mexico, into the Los Angeles area.[61]

Real estate, banking, and other businesses. The mid-1970s plan of a Chinese immigrant to change Monterey Park into the first suburban Chinatown was successfully sold to thousands of potential Chinese immigrants. Monterey Park became the hub of a massive settlement of Chinese in Southern California. Many new arrivals were business people, and many, especially those from Taiwan, brought a considerable amount of family wealth with them.

As a result of the importation of this money, Southern California bypassed both San Francisco and New York to become the largest center of Chinese business activity in North America. For example, immigrants to Southern California developed toy-, clothing-, and computer-importing businesses (for example, ABC toys, Bugle Boy clothing, and Acer computers) and innumerable restaurants and grocery stores, including chains like Panda Express and 99 Ranch Markets. By 1992 Chinese owned more than 20 banks and about 900 hotels and motels in Southern California.

Immigrant Chinese entrepreneurs are well educated and have managerial and business experience. Chinese investment in office-building, shopping-center, and high-tech industrial developments in the San Gabriel Valley represents about half of the valley's commercial land transactions in the very late 1980s, and investment continued through the recession of the 1990s. Many U.S. businesses feel unable to compete with Chinese businesses, especially in appeal to Chinese consumers, and some have left the San Gabriel Valley, opening up further opportunities for Chinese immigrants. Computer assembly companies, often closely linked to Taiwan as a supplier of components, have proliferated in the San Gabriel Valley.[62] Many have successfully undercut their retail competitors.

All this investment activity contrasts sharply with the Chinese who immigrated to New York City, who have tended to be blue-collar and service workers from Hong Kong and the People's Republic of China and to live in the older Chinatown section of Manhattan.

Chinese from Southeast Asia. The most recent groups of Chinese to arrive in Southern California have come from Southeast Asia, particularly Vietnam. Many of these "overseas" Chinese come from families which have been successful in business and banking in Southeast Asia.

Ethnic Chinese from Vietnam own about a third of the businesses in Little Saigon, the commercial center in the midst of the large ethnic Vietnamese settlement in Orange County.[63] The business and social ties of the Chinese-Vietnamese link them frequently to Chinese from other countries, who have also provided them with much capital for investment. For example, Chinese-Vietnamese ownership of large Asian supermarkets is widespread, and in the San Gabriel Valley a garment industry is run mostly by Chinese-Vietnamese.[64] Stores and homes have been converted into sweatshops, some hidden from view but others visible, in which refugees and illegal immigrants toil long hours but receive welfare payments—in violation of welfare regulations.

Despite the widespread business experience of Chinese-Vietnamese, census data indicate that the percentage of Chinese-Vietnamese engaged in family-operated businesses in Southern California is lower than that for Chinese. The self-employment percentage (9 percent) would be higher if more family members worked without pay and if Latinos were not so readily hired for low-level tasks.

The general profile of Chinese-Vietnamese compared with other Chinese immigrants is more reflective of their lower educational level and language skills, their arrival here without the capital brought by so many Taiwanese, the turmoil resulting from their involuntary migration, and the difficulties of adjustment usually experienced by refugees. Chinese from Vietnam are more apt to work in manufacturing, particularly the assembly of electrical machinery, or with the post office.

Diversity of work specializations. The variety of work pursued by the Chinese suggests a range of backgrounds, educational levels, and business directions far more diverse than the restricted jobs held by the "old" Chinese—laborers, servants, cooks, laundrymen, vegetable growers, or peddlers.

Some of the work specializations are similar to those of the past. Operating or working in restaurants and grocery stores is still common among men, as in the past, and it is perhaps the most typical work for newly arrived immigrants. Chinese and other Asian grocery stores supply the basic ingredients that Asian immigrants need but cannot obtain in American supermarkets, such as twenty-five-pound bags of rice, low-priced fresh fish, and special herbs and vegetables. And for decades Chinese women have operated the apparel manufacturers' sewing machines—at home and in the sweatshops of Chinatown and Los Angeles' Garment District.

Yet most immigrants with skills and motivation do not want to stock goods in grocery stores, wash dishes, or stitch endless piles of garments. Some Chinese, like some Koreans and Vietnamese, have become contractors and manufacturers in the garment industry.[65] Immigrants with more education have been more apt to work in the aerospace industry (often as engineers) or in colleges and universities (usually as professors), and others have opened up a wide range of businesses, the most prominent of which are suggested in Table 8.6.

Altogether, the recent Chinese immigrants to Southern California represent a highly diverse group whose labor, talent, and wealth have breathed life into local economies. Moreover, their contacts with the international world of Chinese business activities may become the most important of Southern California's growing economic and social ties across the Pacific.

Summary and Interpretation

In this chapter we have measured in much detail ethnic niches in the workplace, as well as ethnic underrepresentation in certain occupations. For some groups, dramatic changes have been observed over the past three decades. In earlier times the extreme occupational concentrations of blacks, Chinese, and Japanese represented the more physically demanding, low-wage, or servant-type jobs—work that was relegated to minorities. By 1990, however, the weakening of discrimination, the loosening of occupational barriers, and the arrival of immigrants from highly varied cultures have made more complex the patterns of ethnic employment specialization in Southern California.

Self-employment is an adaptation widely practiced by immigrants in Southern California, but its importance varies a great deal among ethnic groups. Although in some cases entrepreneurship can be traced and partly explained through the group's cultural tradition, in more cases it is innovative. Self-employment for most immigrants is a useful alternative to other types of work in which there were barriers to success, such as language, cultural differences, and discrimination. Rates of government employment also differ from one group to another, and among blacks government work has been especially popular because hiring and promotion has seemed to be more on the basis of merit there than in the private sector.

We have demonstrated that Southern California's ethnic groups have varied and complex patterns of occupational and industrial niches. Some of the niches show high levels of work specialization, with groups occasionally being represented at seven or more times the rate expected if all people were of similar ethnic heritage. Nevertheless, certain occupation and industry niches may not be as dominated by certain groups as might be expected based on informal observations and estimates.[66] This is because unsystematic observations of ethnic niches, especially when the focus is a particular ethnic group, can too easily lead to exaggerated claims of the proportionate strength of that group within certain occupations. In contrast, our analysis provides a solid basis for comparative statements concerning the degree of work specialization and underrepresentation.

Our stress on ethnic niches must be balanced by the realization that most workers in most ethnic groups are not employed in the leading niches. The apparent importance of ethnic niches depends partly on how they are defined. Although we have chosen to present only the strongest cases of ethnic overrepresentation, more niches are evident when the definition is less exacting.[67]

We cannot fully explain the reasons for ethnic niches. In some cases, they can be understood in terms of a cultural background which predisposes some groups toward certain types of work. However, more common have been ethnic niches which began as new and experimental adaptations and ended up providing some success. Part of the reason for this is the fact that so much work in the world of 1990 involves technology that is new within the last century, in which case a niche cannot represent cultural continuity.

Other factors behind the development of ethnic niches at work have been the great areal extent of the region and the large size of its ethnic populations. Major differences in the settlement patterns of ethnic groups mean that groups differ in their access to employment opportunities. A important aspect of this is the tendency for newer and better jobs to be created in outlying suburban areas, whereas poorer people, especially minorities, are more likely to live in older, more central areas. Moreover, the multitude of communication networks—defined mostly by ethnicity, income level, and location—by which people learn of employment opportunities makes implausible the assumption that all ethnic groups compete equally for employment and wages in a single metropolitan labor market.[68]

Some niches weaken over time, and a few disappear over the course of generations. However, employers' preferences for hiring workers of their own ethnic group and not hiring from certain other groups still play a significant role in the job–worker matching process, as they clearly did during earlier decades. Such patterned discrimination is probably a necessary result of the continued importance of ethnic social networks and the essential competitive nature of matching people with jobs. As long as ethnic identities and ethnically-based networks exist, there will be ethnic work niches.

Notes

1. Presumably, ethnic niches result from a combination of factors: the characteristics (human capital) of an ethnic group, the nature of employment opportunities or other unfulfilled demands in a local area, and the process by which potential workers are matched to specific jobs through ethnic social networks. The most thorough coverage is in Waldinger (1996), but in Los Angeles niches are also treated in Waldinger and Bozorgmehr (1996).

2. Hiestand (1964), 112–18.

3. Sources for Japanese occupations in earlier parts of this century are Bonacich and Modell (1980); Tsuchida (1984); and Nishi (1985).

4. The best sources on the Japanese niche in maintenance gardening are Tsukashima (1991, 1995/1996).

5. Bond (1936), 171.

6. Takaki (1989), 240–45, 317.

7. Major sources for the occupations of blacks during the first half of the twentieth century are Bond (1936); Bass (1960); and de Graaf (1962).

8. Krislov (1967).

9. Hartsfield-Mills (1973).

10. This section on black nurses is based on Bass (1960), Martin (1979), and the recollections of two black nurses, Doris Williams and Ruby Lassiter, who began to work in Los Angeles–area hospitals in 1961, interviewed January 1996.

11. No black nurses were out of work at that time, according to Ruby Lassiter, associate chief of nursing service, Department of Veterans Affairs, West Los Angeles Medical Center.

12. Reitzes (1958).

13. Takaki (1989), 240; Chan (1991a). See also the section on changing Chinese niches near the end of this chapter.

14. These struggles against employment discrimination in Los Angeles are described in great detail in Smith (1978).

15. The best source on changes in manufacturing in Southern California since 1960 is Soja, Morales, and Wolff (1989).

16. Hensley (1989).

17. For our measurement of the three classes see chapter 1.

18. Razin (1993).

19. Finnan and Cooperstein (1983).

20. Leonard and Tibrewal (1993).

21. Sources on general aspects of immigrant entrepreneurship are Waldinger, Aldrich, and Ward (1990); Butler and Herring (1991); Gold (1992); and Nee, Sanders, and Sernau (1994).

22. Kotkin (1992).

23. Light and Bonacich (1988); Waldinger, Aldrich, and Ward (1990).

24. Der-Martirosian, Sabagh, and Bozorgmehr (1993).

25. Sowell (1994), 25, 26, 34–36.

26. Gold (1992).

27. Light and Bonacich (1988).

28. Dallalfar (1994).

29. Gold (1994b).

30. Light, Sabagh, Bozorgmehr, and Der-Martirosian (1993), 587.

31. Leonard and Tibrewal (1993); Light, Bhachu, and Karageorgis (1993).

32. For the Chinese in business, see Waldinger, Aldrich, and Ward (1990). The Taiwanese in business are treated by Tseng (1994). Chinese-Vietnamese entrepreneurs, who have faced special difficulties (Desbarats 1986), are emphasized in Gold (1992) and Gold (1994a).

33. Krislov (1967); Carnoy (1994); and Nee, Sanders, and Sernau (1994).

34. Reimers and Chernick (1991).

35. Waldinger (1994, 1996).

36. An analysis of black and Hispanic competition in manufacturing sectors in Southern California in 1980 reached inconclusive results (Scott and Paul 1990), as did we, but both those authors and we caution against assuming that different niches at one time indicate no history of significant competition in the development of those niches.

37. Kotkin (1992).

38. Ben-Sasson (1976).

49. Ong and Azores (1994).

40. Agbayani-Siewert and Revilla (1995).

41. Aquino (1952).

42. Nee, Sanders, and Sernau (1994), 857.

43. Applegate (1984).

44. For a discussion of these industries see Scott (1993).

45. For an industry to be listed for an ethnic group, there must be a ratio to total employed of at least three, with at least 300 persons from the group employed in the industry. Because our coverage of groups is so broad, we made the ratio requirement unusually stringent. As a result, the table does not include the many industries that are overrepresented for some groups at between two and three times the average.

46. Logan, Alba, and McNulty (1994) found that ethnic entrepreneurial niches were more varied and significant in Los Angeles than in the several other large metropolitan areas they examined.

47. Kelley (1993).

48. Vorspan and Gartner (1970), 132–33; Gabler (1988), 5.

49. Yeretzian (1923).

50. Clark (1989).

51. Loc Nguyen, Director of the Immigration and Refugee Department, Catholic Charities of Los Angeles, interviewed April 1996.

52. Akst (1993).

53. Cambodian doughnut businesses are described in the videotape entitled *Cambodian Donut Dreams*, written and directed by Charles Davis in 1989 (School of Cinematography, University of Southern California). The videotape was loaned to us by Pamela Bunte, Department of Anthropology, California State University, Long Beach. Additional information was provided by Sandy Arun San-Blankenship, president of the Cambodian Business Association in Long Beach, interviewed December 1995. A good source on Orange County's Chinese-Cambodians in the doughnut business is Lee (1996).

54. O'Conner (1989); Johnson (1996); Huynh (1996).

55. Jain (1989).

56. Logan, Alba, and McNulty (1994).

57. Kim, Nakamura, and Fong (1992). The best description of the work and home situations of Latina garment workers in Los Angeles is in Soldatenko (1992).

58. Bonacich (1993).

59. Sources for this description of historic Chinese work specializations are Mason (1967); McWilliams (1973); Cheng and Cheng (1984); Chan (1986); and Lin (1989/1990).

60. Sources for the characterization of the new immigrants and their work niches in the San Gabriel Valley are Arax (1987a, 1987c); Waldinger and Tseng (1992); Schoenberger (1993); Fong (1994); and Tseng (1994).

61. Rotella and Romney (1993).

62. Torres (1996b).

63. Gold (1994a).

64. Arax (1987a, 1987c).
65. Bonacich (1993).
66. Much detail regarding immigrant occupational specialization in New York City can be found in Lorch (1992), but the anecdotal nature of the evidence and the reliance on sources within specific groups and occupations suggests that the strength of ethnic niches may be easily overestimated.

67. Other studies have used a less stringent definition of niche, requiring a minimum representation at only 1.5 times the average rate (Logan, Alba, and McNulty 1994; Waldinger 1996; Waldinger and Bozorgmehr 1996).
68. Galster and Hornburg (1995).

9. A Multiethnic Society?

Is Southern California a multiethnic society—a single society whose people simply vary in their ethnic heritage? If this is the case, then the similarities and social integration of the different ethnic groups outweigh their differences and separatist leanings. Or, is Southern California essentially a collection of separate ethnic societies? This conception means that different ethnic groups are weakly interconnected economically in their work, shopping, and other public activities. However, they are not really integrated residentially, culturally, and socially.

In this chapter we attempt to determine the essential unity or pluralism of Southern California by approaching the question from several different directions. First, we summarize in three different ways the distributions of the larger groups that we covered in detail in chapter 3 through chapter 5. To assess this residential geography we use maps of the leading (largest) ethnic group in each tract, statistics on the level of residential segregation between specific groups, and a table and a map showing variations in ethnic diversity across Southern California. Then we compare ethnic groups with respect to aspects of social class or socioeconomic status. The relative acculturation and recency of the ethnic groups' immigration are examined next.

Last, we look at Southern California as a crucible for creating a multiethnic society. Apart from public and work-related situations, are members of ethnic groups really intermixing? To examine this question, we make use of a very stringent measure of social mixing: intermarriage between ethnic groups. We also look at areal variations in selected intermarriage rates, because the locations of higher intermarriage rates constitute the frontier of what may be an emerging multiethnic society.

The Leading Ethnic Populations

A map of the numerically largest ethnic group in each census tract portrays an important aspect of place-to-place differences in Southern California (Fig. 9.1). It is a simplified version of the ethnic spatial structure. Because the numbers of whites and people of Mexican origin are so large, most tracts show one of these as the leading group. In many such tracts other ethnic groups are also numerous and important, and a map of the second leading ethnic population in each tract helps to show these patterns (Fig. 9.2). Together, these summarize some of the most significant spatial patterns of race and ethnicity in Southern California.

In some areas neither whites nor people of Mexican origin are the largest group. The two maps show the larger enclaves of other groups, such as Chinese in Chinatown and Monterey Park, Japanese in Gardena, Vietnamese in Westminster and Garden Grove, Salvadorans in Westlake, and Filipinos in Carson. Blacks are most numerous in a large area that stretches from north of Crenshaw through Compton. Within Koreatown, people of Mexican origin outnumber Koreans in most tracts, but the second map shows the importance of Koreans in Koreatown as well as in several suburban areas.

Residential Segregation

Different ethnic groups living near each other can be described as unsegregated or having a low level of residential segregation. Conversely, groups with very different residential distributions are highly segregated. It is possible to summarize the differences with a useful statistic, the index of dissimilarity.

Meaning and measurement. Comparison of ethnic distributions is of more than just direct geographical interest. Differences in distribution are thought to result from other differences among the groups—usually cultural, social, economic, or some combination thereof. Ethnic groups of similar income levels presumably live closer to each other than do groups that differ in economic status. Likewise, two groups that share a religious or other cultural heritage are expected to be less segregated from each other than are other groups that have no cultural affinity.

The index of dissimilarity, or D, measures the differences between any two distinct groups. It ranges between 0, meaning no segregation, and 1, which indicates complete segregation.[1] The higher the index of dissimilarity, the greater the presumed social separation or socioeconomic status differences between the two groups. Index values of less than .30 are considered low; those between .30 and .60, moderate; and those over .60, high. The index cannot tell us the reason behind the differences in the two distributions, but the varying income levels, language skills, and cultural affinity of groups provide some clues.

Because the index works best with larger populations and because ethnic populations are larger in Los Angeles and Orange Counties than in the other counties, we measured segregation only in Los Angeles and Orange Counties. Moreover, we studied only those groups that numbered more than 30,000 in those two counties (Table 9.1).

The degree of segregation of a group is often measured in comparison with non-Hispanic whites, because whites usually represent the cultural and economic standard. However, we provide index values for all pairings of groups as indirect geographical indicators of the degree of economic and cultural differences between any two of the groups.[2]

Levels of segregation. Segregation indexes for Los Angeles County are shown in boldface type for each pairing of ethnic groups, in order to distinguish them from Orange County (Table 9.1). Levels of segregation vary over Southern California but are substantially higher in Los Angeles County.[3] That county contains older minority areas and has been the leading destination for immigrants. Differences in segregation are dramatically illustrated by black–white segregation values in Los Angeles (D = .73) compared to Orange County (D = .38). Although Orange County once had a small black ghetto in Santa Ana, black out-movement and Hispanic in-movement during the 1980s, plus the suburbanization of middle-class blacks, have resulted in a low-moderate level of segregation.

At the same time, Orange County has higher rates of Mexican–white segregation than black–white segregation. This situation is unusual in the United States, where blacks have long been the group most highly segregated from whites. It is clearly due to the rapid growth of Orange County's barrios in areas where whites tend not to live.

In Los Angeles County, a major change in relative segregation has also occurred. Blacks are no longer the most highly segregated group. Although part of the explanation involves lower levels of black–white segregation since 1970, an equally important factor was the arrival of poor and unacculturated immigrant groups during the 1980s. By 1990, the great concentrations of Cambodians in parts of Long Beach and of Salvadorans in Westlake made those the groups that were most segregated from whites.

The moderate segregation between various Hispanic groups (such as Mexicans and Cubans) and between various Asian groups (Koreans and Japanese, for example) is a reminder that the social networks of these specific ethnic groups are essentially separate and that their economic status may be quite different. The fact that Asian Indians and Puerto Ricans are least segregated from whites is entirely consistent with their highly dispersed distributions, as shown in Figures 7.6 and 8.5.

Among the white ethnic (ancestry) groups, the degree of segregation from the various Hispanic and Asian groups is high. Because recently arrived white groups have often formed their own enclaves, it is not surprising that their levels of segregation are some of the highest in Table 9.1. Because none of the white ancestry groups has a low median income, segregation between them reflects group differences in social networks and residential preferences much more than group differences in economic status.

232   A Multiethnic Society?

Table 9.1 Residential Segregation Between Ethnic Groups, Los Angeles and Orange Counties, 1990

	Black	American Indian	Chinese	Filipino	Japanese	Asian Indian	Korean	Vietnamese	Cambodian	Mexican	Puerto Rican	Cuban	Salvadoran	Arab	Armenian	English	Iranian	Russian	
Non-Hispanic White	**.73** .38	**.39** .28	**.60** .34	**.52** .32	**.49** .25	**.39** .35	**.54** .43	**.60** .57	**.86** .73	**.64** .54	**.44** .31	**.48** .34	**.74** .69	**.39** .38	**.64** .48	**.12** .09	**.56** .48	**.44** .28	Non-Hispanic White
Black		**.60** .32	**.80** .45	**.70** .30	**.73** .42	**.70** .41	**.78** .45	**.71** .52	**.86** .65	**.60** .39	**.60** .26	**.71** .35	**.64** .57	**.78** .49	**.88** .64	**.74** .42	**.86** .59	**.83** .54	Black
American Indian			**.61** .43	**.45** .32	**.55** .37	**.46** .43	**.59** .48	**.50** .48	**.79** .64	**.35** .38	**.24** .24	**.42** .31	**.55** .60	**.55** .46	**.74** .61	**.42** .31	**.74** .59	**.66** .48	American Indian
Chinese				**.58** .35	**.49** .21	**.55** .29	**.58** .34	**.44** .54	**.81** .72	**.66** .61	**.61** .43	**.62** .42	**.78** .75	**.64** .43	**.80** .50	**.59** .36	**.78** .46	**.74** .40	Chinese
Filipino					**.56** .31	**.47** .31	**.49** .36	**.50** .49	**.80** .67	**.54** .48	**.42** .27	**.45** .32	**.61** .64	**.57** .45	**.71** .56	**.55** .36	**.76** .54	**.72** .48	Filipino
Japanese						**.51** .31	**.51** .35	**.61** .55	**.87** .74	**.66** .60	**.55** .37	**.56** .38	**.75** .73	**.58** .40	**.75** .49	**.49** .28	**.70** .45	**.64** .35	Japanese
Asian Indian							**.46** .34	**.55** .59	**.85** .73	**.61** .58	**.46** .39	**.49** .41	**.70** .73	**.46** .44	**.70** .53	**.42** .38	**.64** .46	**.59** .43	Asian Indian
Korean								**.63** .56	**.89** .75	**.70** .62	**.58** .44	**.56** .46	**.66** .75	**.57** .51	**.68** .59	**.55** .45	**.70** .55	**.69** .51	Korean
Vietnamese									**.73** .62	**.54** .53	**.48** .51	**.55** .51	**.69** .69	**.64** .62	**.79** .70	**.61** .60	**.78** .72	**.77** .67	Vietnamese
Cambodian										**.79** .63	**.80** .66	**.85** .66	**.87** .73	**.90** .77	**.96** .83	**.86** .74	**.95** .86	**.93** .83	Cambodian
Mexican											**.34** .41	**.49** .43	**.48** .41	**.71** .62	**.81** .76	**.65** .56	**.85** .74	**.79** .69	Mexican
Puerto Rican												**.36** .30	**.53** .59	**.54** .45	**.74** .60	**.47** .35	**.75** .57	**.68** .49	Puerto Rican
Cuban													**.58** .62	**.53** .48	**.68** .59	**.50** .37	**.74** .58	**.68** .48	Cuban
Salvadoran														**.76** .75	**.77** .82	**.77** .71	**.86** .82	**.82** .79	Salvadoran
Arab															**.61** .54	**.43** .40	**.59** .54	**.53** .47	Arab
Armenian																**.67** .49	**.71** .56	**.70** .49	Armenian
English																	**.61** .49	**.50** .28	English
Iranian																		**.46** .48	Iranian

Sources: U.S. Bureau of the Census (1991, 1993d).
Notes: Los Angeles County values shown in bold type and Orange County values shown in regular type. Tabled values are calculations from the index of dissimilarity, D, which measures the distributional differences between any two distinct groups. It ranges between 0, meaning no segregation, and 1, which indicates complete segregation. Data are for groups with at least 30,000 persons.

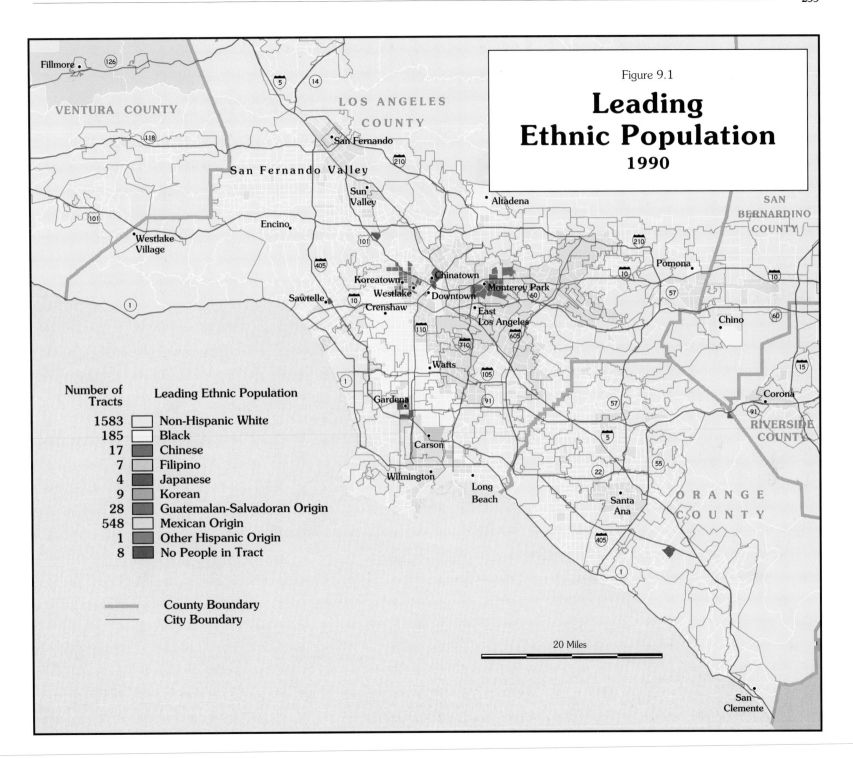

Figure 9.1

Leading Ethnic Population
1990

Number of Tracts		Leading Ethnic Population
1583		Non-Hispanic White
185		Black
17		Chinese
7		Filipino
4		Japanese
9		Korean
28		Guatemalan-Salvadoran Origin
548		Mexican Origin
1		Other Hispanic Origin
8		No People in Tract

County Boundary
City Boundary

20 Miles

234

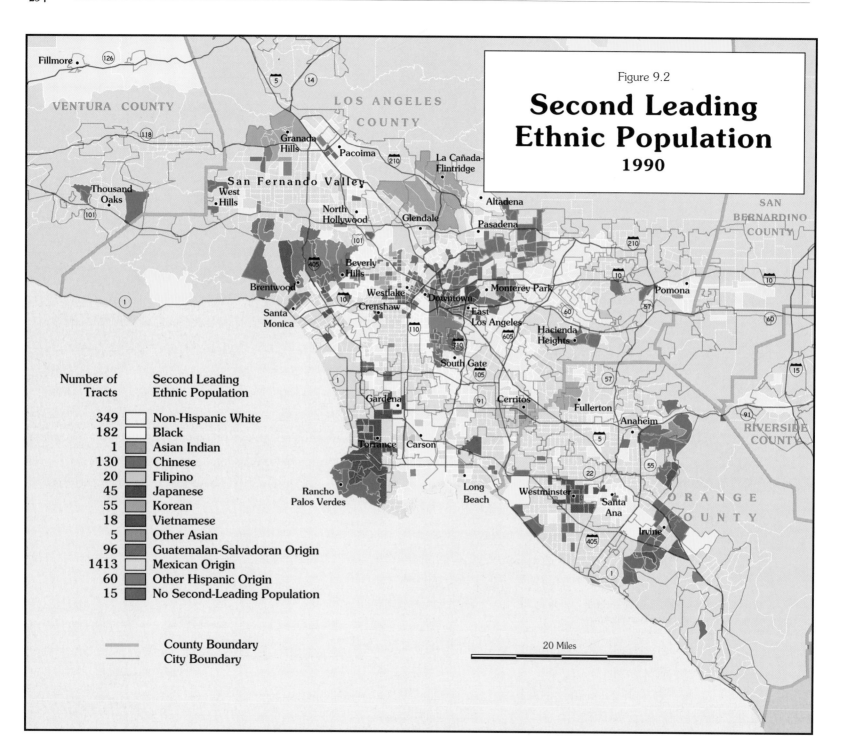

Figure 9.2

Second Leading Ethnic Population

1990

Number of Tracts	Second Leading Ethnic Population
349	Non-Hispanic White
182	Black
1	Asian Indian
130	Chinese
20	Filipino
45	Japanese
55	Korean
18	Vietnamese
5	Other Asian
96	Guatemalan-Salvadoran Origin
1413	Mexican Origin
60	Other Hispanic Origin
15	No Second-Leading Population

County Boundary
City Boundary

20 Miles

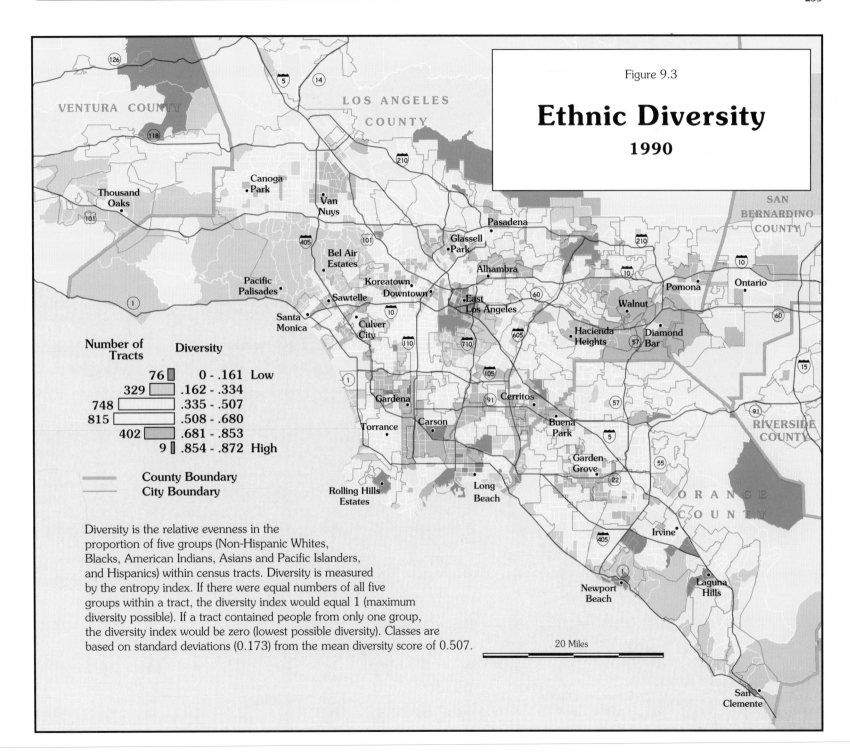

Figure 9.3

Ethnic Diversity
1990

Number of Tracts — **Diversity**

76	0 - .161	Low
329	.162 - .334	
748	.335 - .507	
815	.508 - .680	
402	.681 - .853	
9	.854 - .872	High

County Boundary
City Boundary

Diversity is the relative evenness in the proportion of five groups (Non-Hispanic Whites, Blacks, American Indians, Asians and Pacific Islanders, and Hispanics) within census tracts. Diversity is measured by the entropy index. If there were equal numbers of all five groups within a tract, the diversity index would equal 1 (maximum diversity possible). If a tract contained people from only one group, the diversity index would be zero (lowest possible diversity). Classes are based on standard deviations (0.173) from the mean diversity score of 0.507.

20 Miles

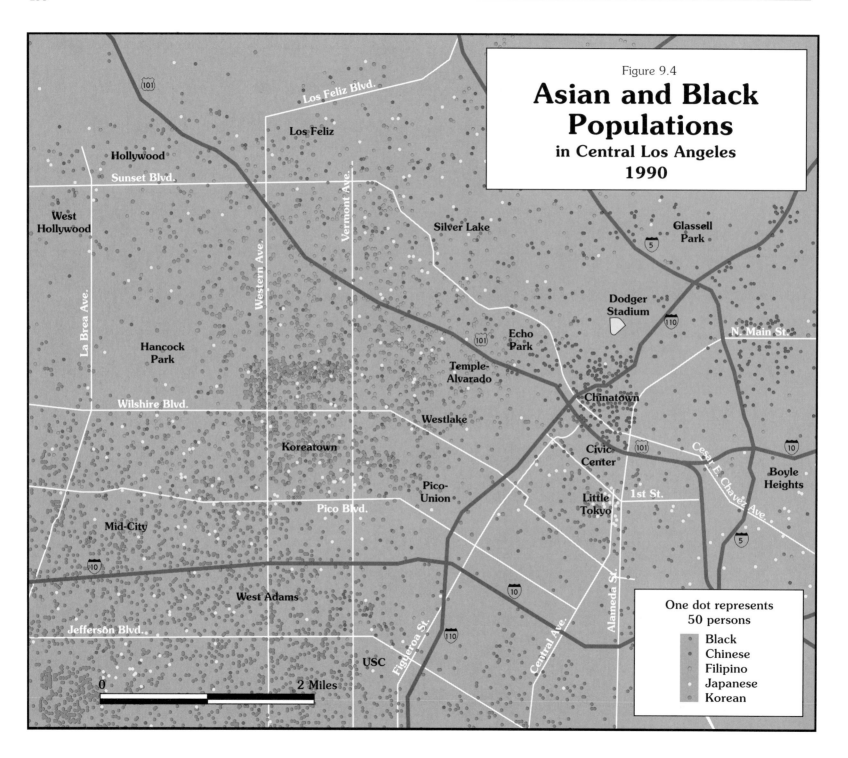

Figure 9.4

Asian and Black Populations

in Central Los Angeles
1990

One dot represents
50 persons

- Black
- Chinese
- Filipino
- Japanese
- Korean

0   2 Miles

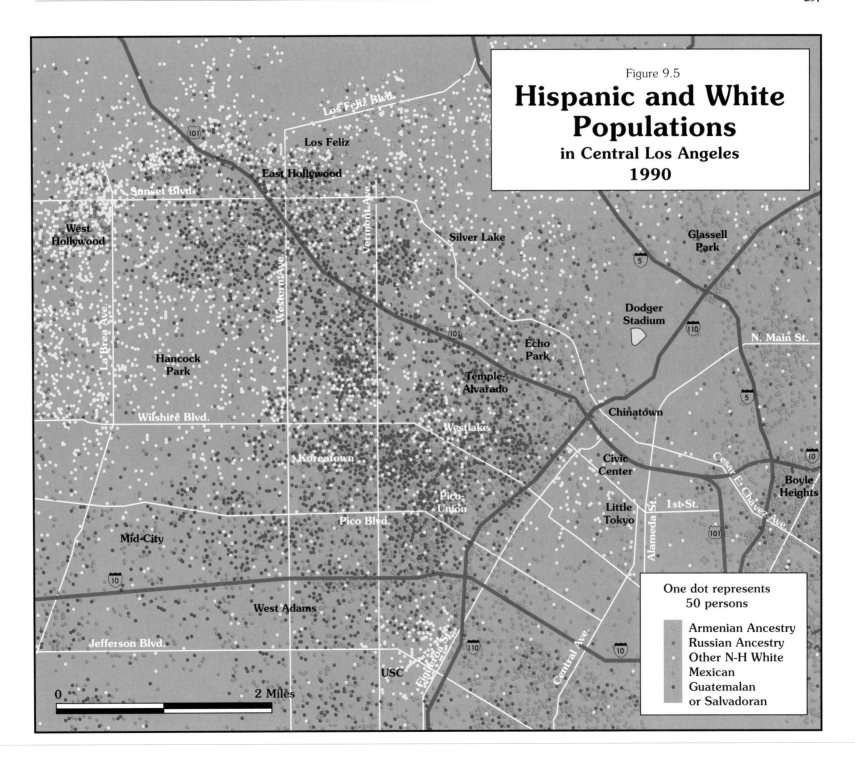

Figure 9.5

Hispanic and White Populations

in Central Los Angeles
1990

One dot represents
50 persons

Armenian Ancestry
Russian Ancestry
Other N-H White
Mexican
Guatemalan
or Salvadoran

238

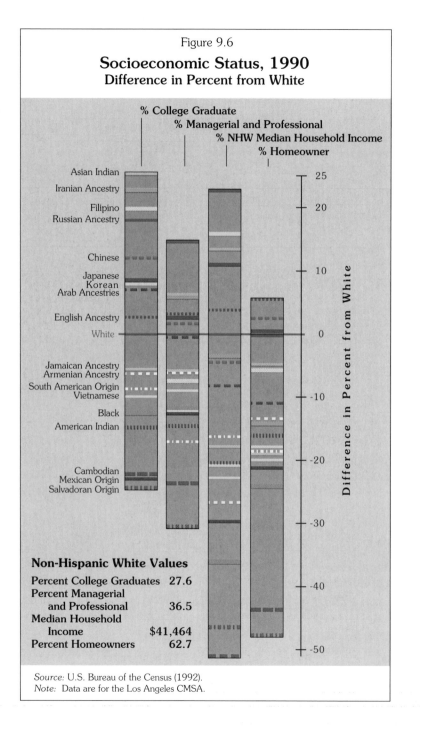

Figure 9.6

Socioeconomic Status, 1990
Difference in Percent from White

% College Graduate

% Managerial and Professional

% NHW Median Household Income

% Homeowner

Asian Indian
Iranian Ancestry
Filipino
Russian Ancestry

Chinese

Japanese
Korean
Arab Ancestries

English Ancestry

White

Jamaican Ancestry
Armenian Ancestry
South American Origin
Vietnamese

Black

American Indian

Cambodian
Mexican Origin
Salvadoran Origin

Difference in Percent from White

25

20

10

0

-10

-20

-30

-40

-50

Non-Hispanic White Values

Percent College Graduates	27.6
Percent Managerial and Professional	36.5
Median Household Income	$41,464
Percent Homeowners	62.7

Source: U.S. Bureau of the Census (1992).
Note: Data are for the Los Angeles CMSA.

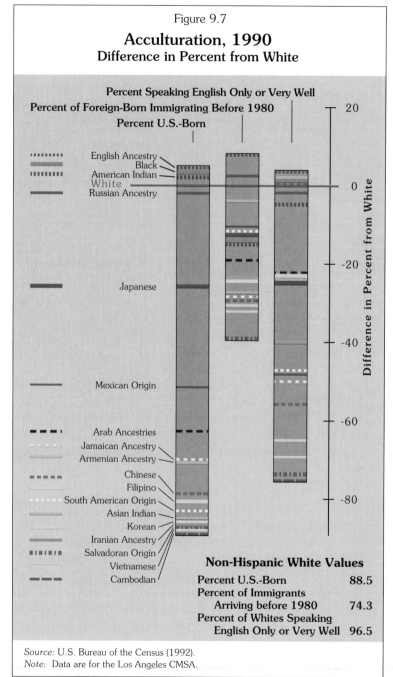

Figure 9.7

Acculturation, 1990
Difference in Percent from White

Percent Speaking English Only or Very Well

Percent of Foreign-Born Immigrating Before 1980

Percent U.S.-Born

English Ancestry
Black
American Indian
White
Russian Ancestry

Japanese

Mexican Origin

Arab Ancestries
Jamaican Ancestry
Armenian Ancestry
Chinese
Filipino
South American Origin
Asian Indian
Korean
Iranian Ancestry
Salvadoran Origin
Vietnamese
Cambodian

Difference in Percent from White

20

0

-20

-40

-60

-80

Non-Hispanic White Values

Percent U.S.-Born	88.5
Percent of Immigrants Arriving before 1980	74.3
Percent of Whites Speaking English Only or Very Well	96.5

Source: U.S. Bureau of the Census (1992).
Note: Data are for the Los Angeles CMSA.

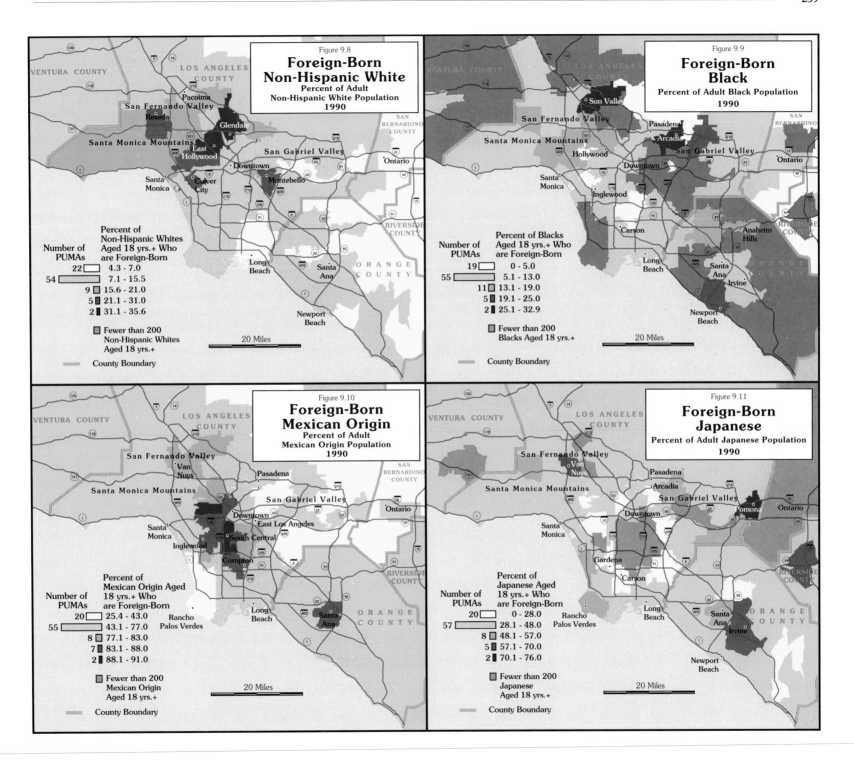

Figure 9.8

**Foreign-Born
Non-Hispanic White**

Percent of Adult
Non-Hispanic White Population
1990

Number of
PUMAs | Percent of
Non-Hispanic Whites
Aged 18 yrs.+ Who
are Foreign-Born

22 — 4.3 - 7.0
54 — 7.1 - 15.5
9 — 15.6 - 21.0
5 — 21.1 - 31.0
2 — 31.1 - 35.6

Fewer than 200
Non-Hispanic Whites
Aged 18 yrs.+

County Boundary

20 Miles

Figure 9.9

**Foreign-Born
Black**

Percent of Adult Black Population
1990

Number of
PUMAs | Percent of Blacks
Aged 18 yrs.+ Who
are Foreign-Born

19 — 0 - 5.0
55 — 5.1 - 13.0
11 — 13.1 - 19.0
5 — 19.1 - 25.0
2 — 25.1 - 32.9

Fewer than 200
Blacks Aged 18 yrs.+

County Boundary

20 Miles

Figure 9.10

**Foreign-Born
Mexican Origin**

Percent of Adult
Mexican Origin Population
1990

Number of
PUMAs | Percent of
Mexican Origin Aged
18 yrs.+ Who
are Foreign-Born

20 — 25.4 - 43.0
55 — 43.1 - 77.0
8 — 77.1 - 83.0
7 — 83.1 - 88.0
2 — 88.1 - 91.0

Fewer than 200
Mexican Origin
Aged 18 yrs.+

County Boundary

20 Miles

Figure 9.11

**Foreign-Born
Japanese**

Percent of Adult Japanese Population
1990

Number of
PUMAs | Percent of
Japanese Aged
18 yrs.+ Who
are Foreign-Born

20 — 0 - 28.0
57 — 28.1 - 48.0
8 — 48.1 - 57.0
5 — 57.1 - 70.0
2 — 70.1 - 76.0

Fewer than 200
Japanese
Aged 18 yrs.+

County Boundary

20 Miles

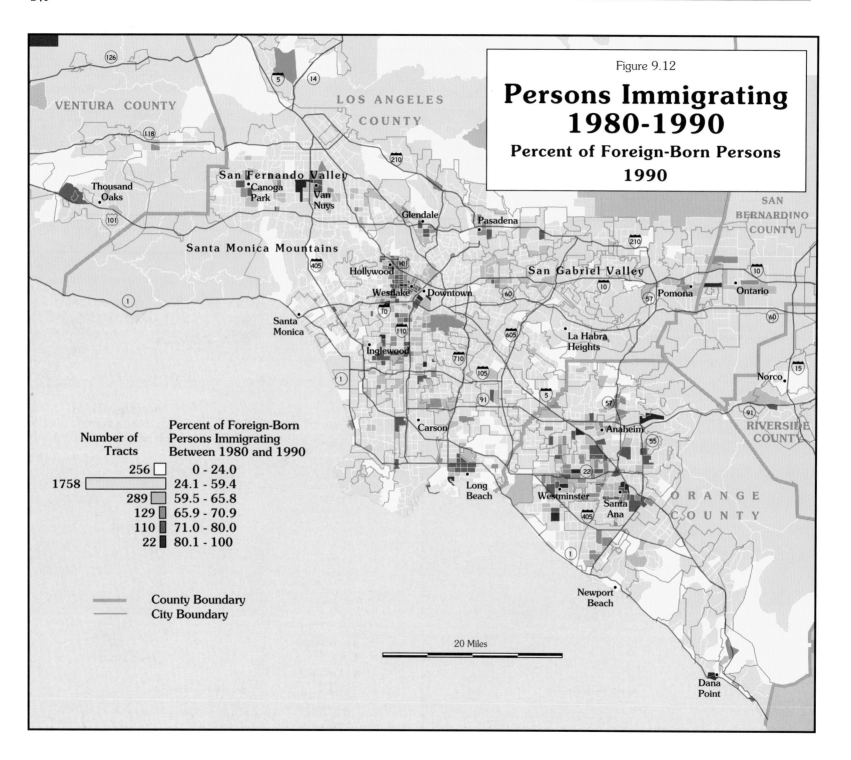

Figure 9.12

Persons Immigrating 1980-1990

Percent of Foreign-Born Persons

1990

Number of Tracts		Percent of Foreign-Born Persons Immigrating Between 1980 and 1990
256		0 - 24.0
1758		24.1 - 59.4
289		59.5 - 65.8
129		65.9 - 70.9
110		71.0 - 80.0
22		80.1 - 100

County Boundary

City Boundary

20 Miles

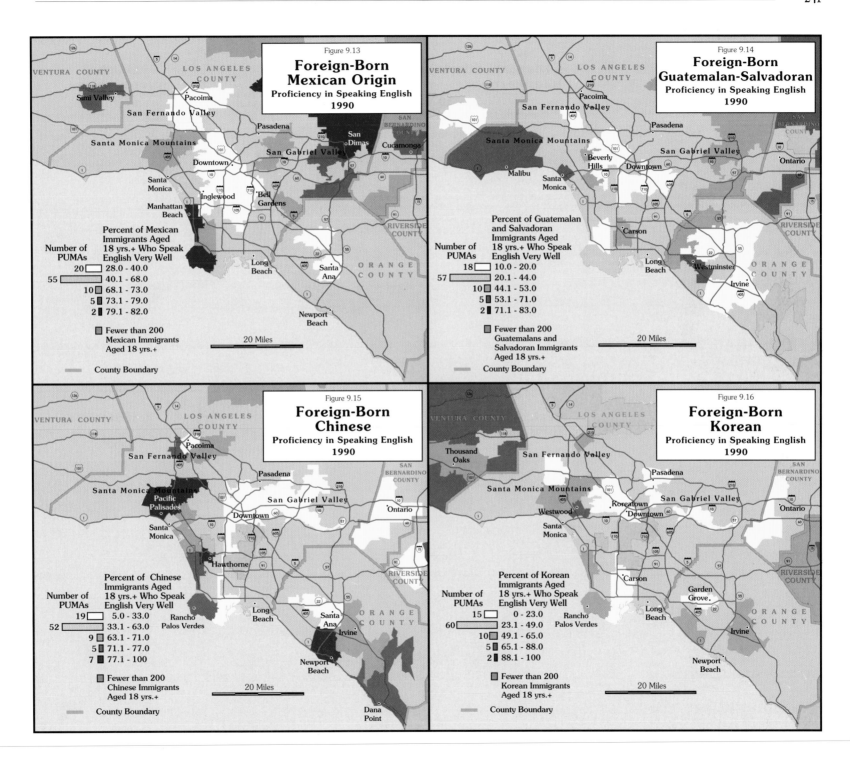

Figure 9.13

Foreign-Born Mexican Origin
Proficiency in Speaking English
1990

Percent of Mexican Immigrants Aged 18 yrs.+ Who Speak English Very Well

Number of PUMAs
20 — 28.0 - 40.0
55 — 40.1 - 68.0
10 — 68.1 - 73.0
5 — 73.1 - 79.0
2 — 79.1 - 82.0

Fewer than 200 Mexican Immigrants Aged 18 yrs.+

County Boundary

20 Miles

Figure 9.14

Foreign-Born Guatemalan-Salvadoran
Proficiency in Speaking English
1990

Percent of Guatemalan and Salvadoran Immigrants Aged 18 yrs.+ Who Speak English Very Well

Number of PUMAs
18 — 10.0 - 20.0
57 — 20.1 - 44.0
10 — 44.1 - 53.0
5 — 53.1 - 71.0
2 — 71.1 - 83.0

Fewer than 200 Guatemalans and Salvadoran Immigrants Aged 18 yrs.+

County Boundary

20 Miles

Figure 9.15

Foreign-Born Chinese
Proficiency in Speaking English
1990

Percent of Chinese Immigrants Aged 18 yrs.+ Who Speak English Very Well

Number of PUMAs
19 — 5.0 - 33.0
52 — 33.1 - 63.0
9 — 63.1 - 71.0
5 — 71.1 - 77.0
7 — 77.1 - 100

Fewer than 200 Chinese Immigrants Aged 18 yrs.+

County Boundary

20 Miles

Figure 9.16

Foreign-Born Korean
Proficiency in Speaking English
1990

Percent of Korean Immigrants Aged 18 yrs.+ Who Speak English Very Well

Number of PUMAs
15 — 0 - 23.0
60 — 23.1 - 49.0
10 — 49.1 - 65.0
5 — 65.1 - 88.0
2 — 88.1 - 100

Fewer than 200 Korean Immigrants Aged 18 yrs.+

County Boundary

20 Miles

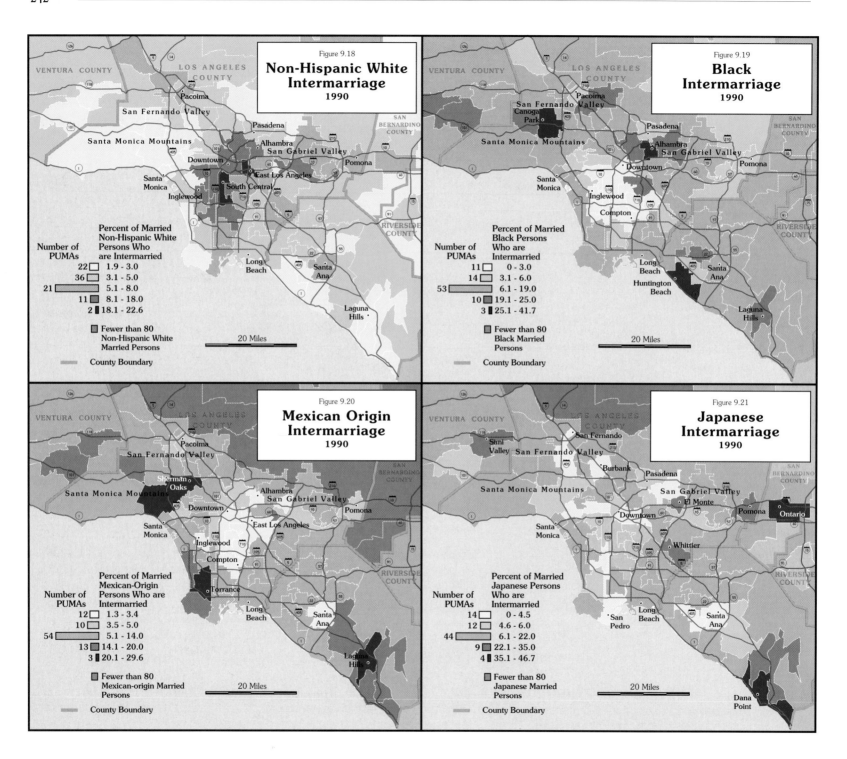

Figure 9.18
Non-Hispanic White Intermarriage 1990

Percent of Married Non-Hispanic White Persons Who are Intermarried

Number of PUMAs
22 □ 1.9 - 3.0
36 □ 3.1 - 5.0
21 ▒ 5.1 - 8.0
11 ▓ 8.1 - 18.0
2 ■ 18.1 - 22.6

▪ Fewer than 80 Non-Hispanic White Married Persons

▬ County Boundary

20 Miles

Figure 9.19
Black Intermarriage 1990

Percent of Married Black Persons Who are Intermarried

Number of PUMAs
11 □ 0 - 3.0
14 □ 3.1 - 6.0
53 ▒ 6.1 - 19.0
10 ▓ 19.1 - 25.0
3 ■ 25.1 - 41.7

▪ Fewer than 80 Black Married Persons

▬ County Boundary

20 Miles

Figure 9.20
Mexican Origin Intermarriage 1990

Percent of Married Mexican-Origin Persons Who are Intermarried

Number of PUMAs
12 □ 1.3 - 3.4
10 □ 3.5 - 5.0
54 ▒ 5.1 - 14.0
13 ▓ 14.1 - 20.0
3 ■ 20.1 - 29.6

▪ Fewer than 80 Mexican-origin Married Persons

▬ County Boundary

20 Miles

Figure 9.21
Japanese Intermarriage 1990

Percent of Married Japanese Persons Who are Intermarried

Number of PUMAs
14 □ 0 - 4.5
12 □ 4.6 - 6.0
44 ▒ 6.1 - 22.0
9 ▓ 22.1 - 35.0
4 ■ 35.1 - 46.7

▪ Fewer than 80 Japanese Married Persons

▬ County Boundary

20 Miles

Ethnic Diversity

Another way to examine ethnic distributions is to look at the extent to which members of several different groups live in the same area. Where ethnic groups are more mixed residentially, there is greater potential for social contact between groups.[4] Such areas are normally described as ethnically diverse.

Measuring diversity. The statistic used most commonly to measure diversity in different places is the entropy index, or H.[5] The value of H increases as the groups approach more even proportions. It reaches its maximum when all measured groups are represented in equal numbers in a place, whereas diversity is zero when the area contains members of only one group. We measure diversity in terms of the relative proportions of five groups: non-Hispanic whites, blacks, American Indians, Asians and Pacific Islanders, and Hispanics. The relative diversity of places is what is important, not the absolute value of the index.

We look first at the diversity of different cities and other urban places (Table 9.2). Then we examine the relative diversity of neighborhoods by calculating the same statistic for census tracts (Fig. 9.3). Entropy index scores were standardized so that if the numbers of each ethnic group in a place are equal, the entropy score for that place would be 1. If only one ethnic group is present, the score would be 0.

Cities and other urban places. In order to set our Southern California findings in a larger context, we calculated entropy indexes for all urban places and for counties in the United States as of 1990.[6] Out of more than 3,100 counties in the United States, all the counties of Southern California are among the 100 most diverse. Los Angeles County was the fourth most diverse in the United States.[7] Among Southern California cities—the focus of this chapter—there are often only small variations in the index of diversity scores. This means that the detailed position of a city in the ranking is usually of little or no significance. However, those few listed at either end of the ranking—as the most diverse or the least diverse—have index values that are clearly higher or lower than those of nearly all others (Table 9.2).

Ethnic diversity is greatest in the cities and older suburbs near industry in the southern part of Los Angeles County and in the newer suburbs of the eastern San Gabriel Valley. The first area's proximity to employment in oil refining and other harbor-area activities has attracted whites and minorities for several decades. The five most diverse cities in Southern California are in this area, and Carson's score shows it to be the most ethnically diverse city in the entire United States. The second area has attracted immigrants, especially from Asia, as well as Americans of all origins who can afford homes in that valley's suburbs, most of which have been built since the early 1970s. Walnut, West Covina, and Rowland Heights are places in the San Gabriel Valley which are particularly diverse.

The least diverse places are either white or Hispanic concentrations. East Los Angeles and the places immediately to its south and southwest are part of the very large, poor Latino barrio that expanded farther to the southwest into Huntington

Table 9.2 Most and Least Ethnically Diverse Urban Places, 1990

Most Diverse		Least Diverse	
Urban Place	Entropy Index	Urban Place	Entropy Index
Carson	.876	East Los Angeles	.182
Gardena	.867	Maywood	.200
Hawthorne	.836	Newport Beach	.209
West Carson	.797	Walnut Park	.212
Alondra Park	.792	Huntington Park	.243
Walnut	.789	Laguna Beach	.247
West Covina	.789	Commerce	.254
Long Beach	.784	Manhattan Beach	.271
Rowland Heights	.784	Seal Beach	.273
Los Angeles	.782	Cudahy	.294

Source: U.S. Bureau of the Census (1992).
Notes: The higher the index, the greater the diversity. Our analysis included all urban places in Southern California with populations of at least 10,000. Calculations are based on five groups: non-Hispanic whites, blacks, American Indians, Asians and Pacific Islanders, and Hispanics. Scores are standardized so that a value of 1 represents the maximum diversity possible: equal proportions of all five groups.

Park and Walnut Park during the 1990s. Just the opposite are the affluent Orange County cities of Newport Beach, Laguna Beach, and Seal Beach—all of which are strongly white. They are places of white retreat from older or deteriorating neighborhoods or from poorer or ethnically different people.

An alternative way of measuring ethnic diversity defines groups in terms of more specific ethnic categories. Instead of aggregating all Asians or all Hispanics together, as in Table 9.2, we now define diversity in different places as the relative proportions of fourteen groups. Because Asian ethnic groups are so sharply separated by language and identity, this measure accentuates that diversity. The fourteen ethnic groups are blacks, American Indians, the largest six groups from Asia, and three white and three Hispanic groups.

We do not present a table of diversity scores for the method using fourteen groups, but when diversity is measured in this more complex way, most of the cities listed in Table 9.2 appear again. However, the city of Cerritos emerges as the most diverse in the entire United States—a position it also held in 1980.[8] In addition, Walnut is ranked second nationally in diversity, and Diamond Bar and La Palma (adjacent to Cerritos) now appear among the ten most diverse urban places in the United States. In all of these places, diversity among the Asian populations is pronounced.

Neighborhoods. Members of different ethnic groups who live in the same neighborhood are more likely to talk and become acquainted than if they did not live nearby. In addition, neighborhoods are often fairly uniform in housing costs, so their residents probably have a similar economic status. All this means that the potential for social contact between ethnic groups is greater when different groups reside in a neighborhood. Census tracts are the areal unit closest to the concept of neighborhood.

Neighborhood differences in ethnic diversity are striking (Fig. 9.3). The lowest diversity is found in areas which are most homogeneously white or Latino. Thus, the very high proportions of whites in the Santa Monica Mountains, the Seal Beach and Newport Beach areas, and parts of southern Orange County make those areas less diverse. A similar low diversity

characterizes Boyle Heights, East Los Angeles, parts of Pacoima, and the Huntington Park area because their Hispanic proportions are so high. Diversity is somewhat greater in much of South Central, where tracts have few if any Asians and whites but where blacks and Latinos have similar proportions.

Many of the urban places previously noted in Table 9.2 as highly diverse are evident on the tract-level map. Within such places more diverse sections can be easily found (Fig. 9.3). For instance, the older, central parts of Long Beach and West Long Beach are much more diverse than is eastern Long Beach, but in Lakewood the two easternmost tracts are highly diverse. This was due to the settlement of black families during the 1980s and the expansion of both Asians and Latinos out of their adjacent enclaves in Cerritos and Hawaiian Gardens.

Central Los Angeles. Neighborhoods in the central part of the city of Los Angeles contain several ethnic enclaves as well as moderate or high ethnic diversity. This makes the area worth investigating in more detail, not by means of an entropy index but by detailed distributions of specific groups (Figs. 9.4 and 9.5). Two maps are necessary for readers to be able to distinguish the colored dots that together represent ten different ethnic groups. The map shows the degree of areal mixing of groups in different sections although the actual residential mixing is probably somewhat less than shown on the map. This is because dots representing tract populations of groups are placed randomly within census tracts by the computer. In reality, there is some ethnic clustering by blocks and probably even smaller areas, like sections of blocks and apartment buildings, which cannot be shown here.[9]

Nevertheless, the maps portray effectively the major areal variations in ethnic composition. Armenian and Russian Jewish settlements, white settlement associated with the University of Southern California, and the long-lived Japanese community in the Crenshaw area are easily distinguishable. Also evident are variations in the degree of ethnic homogeneity between enclaves such as Chinatown, Koreatown, Westlake, Boyle Heights, East Hollywood (Armenians), and Temple-Alvarado (Filipinos). For instance, the low-cost housing in Westlake has as many people of Mexican origin as

Salvadorans and Guatemalans although that area is best known as a Central American barrio.

Over most of the past half century, it was almost predictable that zones lying between strongly white and strongly black neighborhoods were in transition from white to black. However, it is unlikely that these processes of white–black racial transition and resegregation will continue or advance into new areas. This is because of the slowing growth of the black population, its dispersal to nonadjacent suburban areas, and the arrival of so many Latino immigrants.[10]

Comparative Socioeconomic Status

The next two sections of this chapter present basic socioeconomic and acculturation characteristics of the larger ethnic groups. Two graphs summarize these characteristics (Figs. 9.6 and 9.7).

Because social class or status can be measured in several different ways, our graphic description of the relative status of ethnic groups uses four important indicators. Each of these was explained in chapter 1. We generally selected ethnic populations of more than 70,000 for these analyses. However, Cambodians were also included because of their unusually low status and Guatemalans were omitted because their status position was so close to that of Salvadorans. Because the same status indicators are presented on the maps for all 34 ethnic groups, the positions of groups not included on this graph can be approximated by the reader.

The position of groups on different indicators varies substantially (Fig. 9.6). For example, the income of Koreans is relatively low compared to the group's standing on other indicators. Also, the percentage of homeowners among Armenians, Chinese, Vietnamese, people of English ancestry, and people of Mexican origin is higher than is suggested by other indicators. This may be due partly to cultural emphases on the value of homeownership, although the rapid increase in home prices since the mid-1970s makes group differences in the timing of home purchases also a factor.

Contrasts among the groups in socioeconomic status are striking. The general high status of whites, Asian Indians, striking. The general high status of whites, Asian Indians, Filipinos, and Japanese is clear, as it is for people of English and Russian ancestries. The high percentage of college graduates among Asian Indians, Iranians, Filipinos, and people of Russian ancestry make these groups very different from American Indians, blacks, Vietnamese, Cambodians, and people of Mexican origin. Exceptionally low median incomes and home-ownership characterize Cambodians and Salvadorans; and Cambodians, Salvadorans, and people of Mexican origin do stand out in their low percentages in managerial and professional occupations.

Comparative Acculturation

Because acculturation, or cultural assimilation, is increased by time spent in the United States, we first characterize ethnic groups in terms of their recency of immigration and then look at their relative English-language proficiencies.[11] We also look at the relative incomes of immigrants compared to U.S.-born members of the same ethnic groups as an indicator of acculturation. Our expectation is that immigrants have lower incomes than those born in the United States.[12]

Figure 9.7 makes clear some important distinctions among groups in the importance and timing of immigration. Adults in the American Indian, white, black, and English- and Russian-ancestry groups are all less than 15 percent foreign-born. This contrasts sharply with Salvadorans, South Americans, people of Iranian ancestry, and all of the Asian groups except Japanese. In all of these groups, more than 90 percent of the adults in 1990 were foreign-born, and in many groups the figure is more than 97 percent. Moreover, more than half of the foreign-born people in several groups immigrated to the United States during the 1980s. Together, these findings show that ethnic groups differ substantially in the timing of their immigration.

Cambodians are exceptional because such a high percentage arrived in the United States during the 1980s. Recency of immigration is probably the most important reason behind their very low level of English-language skills. This may also account for poorer language skills among Koreans, Vietnamese, Chinese, Armenians, and Salvadorans, so many of whom settled here in the 1980s. At the same time, the high level of

English-language skills among groups with low percentages of immigrants is entirely expected.

Groups do differ in the relationship between immigration timing and English proficiency. For example, a high percentage of Jamaicans speak English very well despite being more than 80 percent foreign-born. This is because English is widely spoken in Jamaica, especially among middle-class Jamaicans, who are more likely to immigrate. Similarly, most Filipino and Asian Indian immigrants gained much experience in English before coming to this country because English is an important language of advanced instruction in their countries.

On the other hand, ability to speak English very well is less common among people of Mexican origin than one would expect, given their immigration history. Immigrants constitute only 63 percent of the adults, and the percentage that arrived in the 1980s is only 35 percent—relatively low compared with many groups. Nevertheless, only 49 percent of Mexican-origin adults speak English very well. It appears that the very large number of Spanish speakers in Southern California reduces acculturation and, perhaps, the incentive to learn English well.

With respect to income differences between immigrants and U.S.-born members of an ethnic group, immigrants generally have somewhat lower incomes. Armenian and Russian immigrants are exceptional, however, in that their very low incomes contrast sharply with the much higher incomes of U.S.-born members of the groups. These are real differences between immigrant generations—differences that may be sources of intragroup tension.

Foreign-born American Indians have substantially lower incomes than do others born in the United States. Almost all of the foreign-born American Indians are from Canada, Mexico, or Guatemala. Their lower incomes are probably due to the especially low educational and occupational status of those who arrived from Mexico and Guatemala, some of whom fled persecution in their home areas. The income differential between immigrant and U.S.-born people of Mexican origin was discussed and documented for specific occupations near the end of chapter 7. On the other hand, among blacks and people of English and Arab ancestries, the incomes of immigrants and the U.S.-born shows little or no differences.

Spatial Patterns of Acculturation

Spatial patterns of acculturation differ among groups depending on their status and on the location of their enclaves. For this reason, we examine selected groups whose patterns of acculturation can be compared with distribution maps in earlier chapters. On the quarter-page maps, acculturation is shown only for PUMAs containing at least 200 members of the ethnic group, to avoid misleading impressions that might result from very small samples.

Percentage foreign-born. Among whites, the percentage of foreign-born is highest in Glendale and Hollywood because of the strong concentrations of Armenians in both places and of Russian Jews in the latter area (Fig. 9.8). The foreign-born make up somewhat smaller percentages of whites in the Westside, the Santa Monica Mountains, and the southern San Fernando Valley. In these areas the largest numbers of immigrants are Jews (Russian, Iranian, and Israeli), Iranians, and Armenians, but the same areas are also attractive to immigrants from many parts of Europe.

Black immigrants tend to live outside the larger black settlements (Fig. 9.9). In more expensive areas like Brentwood, Westwood, and the Santa Monica Mountains they are scattered among a largely white population. The percentage of immigrants among blacks is even higher in areas of more moderate income areas, like northern Orange County, San Gabriel, Temple City, Glendale, and the Sunland–Tujunga section of the eastern San Fernando Valley. In addition, a few clusters of Jamaican and Nigerian immigrants in middle-income black areas like Inglewood show up in Figures 3.14 and 3.15.

The fact that foreign-born blacks, compared with all black adults, tend to live outside areas of black settlement in Los Angeles and Pasadena may well reflect their social distance from the black American community.[13] African immigrants view America as the land of economic opportunities and do not focus on the elimination of white racism as a necessary prerequisite to black advancement. Black immigrants also see American blacks as culturally more like Americans and Europeans than like themselves, whereas American blacks often deride the more Negroid features of recent immigrants from Africa. All these perceptions suggest that many African immigrants see little reason to live within a black settlement area. The low number of immigrants in high-status black areas, such as View Park and Ladera Heights, may also be related to these differences between U.S.-born and immigrant blacks.

Immigrants from Mexico have shown a tendency to settle outside the traditional, large Mexican barrios (Fig. 9.10). This is most clearly seen in the fact that the large barrio of the Mexican Eastside (Boyle Heights and East Los Angeles) has lower proportions of immigrants than do nearby areas to the south: South Central, Huntington Park, South Gate, and Bell Gardens. The reason for Mexican-immigrant settlement beyond the older barrio is very different from the situation among black immigrants. Poor Mexican immigrants, particularly during the 1980s, faced a shortage of housing in the old barrio, but they found that housing was available not far away and that rents were even lower. The same process took place elsewhere. For instance, immigrants moved into inexpensive and often run-down houses and apartments in Westlake and Koreatown. In the eastern San Fernando Valley, new immigrants settled not so much in the large San Fernando–Pacoima barrio but in less-crowded adjacent areas, where blacks and whites had been living: Arleta, North Hills, Van Nuys, and North Hollywood.

Among the Japanese (Fig. 9.11), the percentages of foreign-born are lowest in the long-established Japanese American enclaves: Crenshaw, Culver City, the Sun Valley section of the eastern San Fernando Valley, and Gardena. In contrast, the most distinctive area for foreign-born Japanese is the expensive Palos Verdes Peninsula, where managers of Japanese companies often live while spending a few years on temporary assignment in Southern California.[14]

Recent immigrants. The locations of the foreign-born who arrived in the United States during the 1980s compared with all of the foreign-born show somewhat similar general patterns, although the areal unit permits more detail (Fig. 9.12). Recent immigrants are often quite localized in specific census tracts. This results from personal-contact networks which direct new arrivals to the locations of friends and relatives. As word of housing and work opportunities spreads, newcomers pile into many of the same apartment buildings and census tracts. Unusually high proportions of recent immigrants in certain neighborhoods also suggest that these may be pockets of very low acculturation and English-language proficiency.

The largest portion of 1980s immigrants are from Mexico and Central America. As we noted in the previous section, recent immigrants settled less in Boyle Heights, East Los Angeles, San Fernando, Pacoima, and other older barrios because that housing was already intensely occupied by older immigrants and Mexican Americans. Instead, some of the cheapest available housing was in adjacent or even somewhat distant neighborhoods, often near industrial areas. This is the case in the Harbor City section of Los Angeles City and in the section of Downtown that houses the garment district and produce market. In the San Fernando Valley, a similar area lies between Van Nuys Airport and what was a General Motors automobile plant in Van Nuys.

The pattern is similar among the poorer immigrants from other groups. A large, low-rent area evident in Figure 9.12 is the Westlake-Koreatown area, in which many thousands of immigrant Koreans, Mexicans, and Salvadorans settled in the 1980s.

English-language ability. Immigrants who live in enclaves in which English is rarely spoken feel less need or pressure to improve their skills in English. In contrast, those with the ability to speak English very well tend to live outside ethnic concentrations. This is entirely expected and is consistent with previous research and theory, which has stressed the support provided to new immigrants in an ethnic enclave.[15] Areal patterns reflect both the reduced acculturation in areas of ethnic concentration and the past in- or out-movement of people based partly on their level of acculturation.

The general pattern is well illustrated by Mexican immigrant adults (Fig. 9.13). Low English proficiency characterizes the large area of recent immigration, which extends from Hollywood south into Hawthorne and Lynwood. Other large areas of unusually low English-language skills are the eastern San Fernando Valley, Santa Ana, and Anaheim. Despite the cultural homogeneity of the Mexican Eastside barrio, its residents have somewhat better English because many of them were born in the United States.

Still greater proficiency in English is found among Mexican-born adults who live outside the major enclaves and in places with moderate or expensive housing—Simi Valley, Palos Verdes, Torrance, Redondo Beach, San Dimas, and Glendora. In these areas most of those who speak English very well are second- or third-generation Mexican Americans, although in some areas they are live-in nannies, domestics, and gardeners. Among Guatemalans and Salvadorans, too, the low level of English speech found in the larger concentrations is entirely expected (Fig. 9.14). In contrast, many who live and work as housekeepers, nannies, and aides in Malibu, Santa Monica, and Beverly Hills developed better skills in English because of close contact with wealthy families.

Chinese immigrants in the area from Chinatown through most of the San Gabriel Valley have less ability in English than do Chinese in most other places (Fig. 9.15). This area contains so many Chinese people that it is possible to live an almost completely Chinese-oriented life. Similarly, Koreans in and near Koreatown have less ability to speak English than is found among Koreans in most of the outlying areas, where contact with English-speaking Americans is much greater (Fig. 9.16).

Compartmentalization, Social Integration, and Structural Assimilation

People tend to have most of their highly personal ties with others in the same social class and ethnic group. This social compartmentalization occurs even when people are substantially acculturated in terms of language ability and other aspects of culture. However, when people choose close friends from ethnic and class groups other than their own, compartmentalization weakens and social integration begins.

Social integration proceeds much more slowly than does acculturation. Most of the children of immigrants are perfectly fluent in English, for instance, but their own ethnic identity remains a powerful influence on whom they select as their close friends and spouses.

There is no established threshold that divides groups who are socially integrated from those that are ethnically compartmentalized. Only a continuum stretches between complete compartmentalization (social contact only within an ethnic group) and complete social integration (close friendships primarily with people in other ethnic groups).

Measuring social integration and structural assimilation. The best indicator of an ethnic group's relative compartmentalization and social integration is the rate at which its members marry outside the group. This is known as intermarriage. In intermarriage the spouse can be from any other ethnic group. High rates of intermarriage demonstrate weak compartmentalization and strong social integration.

Because most people are married to someone in their ethnic group, rates of intermarriage are generally low. Whites in the United States have very frequently married outside their European-ancestry groups, but the spouse is usually white. Moreover, analyses show that ethnic identity is still important in the choice of marriage partners—even for people whose families have lived in this country for several generations.[16]

Because whites are culturally and socially dominant in the United States, they are the group toward which others shift during structural assimilation. Thus, we measure the degree of structural assimilation of a non-white ethnic group by its rate of intermarriage with non-Hispanic whites. Groups with higher rates intermarriage with whites are more structurally assimilated.

General factors affecting rates of intermarriage. The likelihood of a person marrying outside one's ethnic group depends on the number of available mates within the group.[17] If the ethnic group is small in numbers or the sex ratio very unbalanced in any area, some people who would prefer to marry within their group will be unable to find a suitable mate from the group, so intermarriage rates will be high. On the other hand, members of large groups have little trouble finding mates within their group, so rates of intermarriage tend to be low. Also, ethnic intermarriage is uncommon among immigrants but increases with subsequent, U.S.-born generations.

More opportunities for social contact outside the ethnic group are found in Southern California than in countries of immigrant origin. Thus, intermarriage should be more common among younger members of immigrant ethnic groups because younger people are more likely to have married in Southern California. Here, too, increasing social receptivity concerning other ethnic groups may play a role in increased intermarriage. For these reasons, we also calculated rates of intermarriage for younger couples by selecting all married householders under the age of 35 and their spouses.[18]

We could not determine the cumulative effect of low levels of past mixing of ethnic populations. Presumably, many people who checked one racial response on the census were themselves of multiracial background. This means that there has been slightly more mixing than the rates suggest (Table 9.3).

Group differences in intermarriage rates. Rates of intermarriage are generally low—reflecting substantial social separation between groups (Table 9.3). Smaller, more acculturated ethnic groups have higher rates of intermarriage.

Younger couples have consistently higher rates of intermarriage, but age differences are usually not large. Among blacks and whites, the higher rates of intermarriage among younger people do indicate more recent weakening of compartmentalization and greater social integration. Younger Japanese, Samoans, and Cubans show much higher intermarriage rates than older members of their groups. This could reflect either marriage in the United States or a change in cultural attitude among younger people toward intermarriage. In either case, the large age difference in intermarriage rates suggests recently increasing social integration but also a likely source of intergenerational family tension.

Rates of intermarriage between groups should be greater among groups which share a cultural affinity, as has been demonstrated at the national level.[19] This is seen most clearly in the high rates of intermarriage among Hispanic groups, all of whom share a Spanish-language heritage (Fig. 9.17). Cubans and Puerto Ricans marry people of Mexican origin almost as often as they marry non-Hispanic whites. Guatemalans and Salvadorans are married to people of Mexican origin at four

times the rate that they are married to whites. This can be explained partly by their shared culture, but also important are the low status of both groups and their residential proximity.

The high degree of ethnic compartmentalization evident for Cambodians and Vietnamese is consistent with their high percentage of immigrants and their exceptionally low level of English-language skills. In addition, it seems reasonable that Cambodians, Vietnamese, and other groups in which refugees constitute a large proportion of the immigrants have low rates of intermarriage because their past experience has shown the importance of preserving a tight community to help guard against an uncertain future.

The fact that whites have a low intermarriage rate is partly due to the presence of so many whites as potential marriage partners for other whites. However, history suggests that some

Table 9.3 Ethnic Intermarriage Rates, 1990

	All Married Persons in Group		Married Persons Under Age 35
	Percentage Married Outside Group	Percentage Married to Non-Hispanic Whites	Percentage Married Outside Group
Cambodians	3.6	1.1	5.5
Vietnamese	6.5	3.6	8.3
Non-Hispanic whites	6.6	93.4	11.1
Koreans	6.7	4.5	10.2
Blacks	8.7	5.0	12.3
Asian Indians	8.9	5.8	14.1
Chinese	10.3	5.9	15.8
Mexicans	14.0	9.9	14.8
Samoans	17.1	10.4	30.2
Filipinos	18.7	12.3	27.4
Guatemalans-Salvadorans	22.2	3.3	23.3
Japanese	25.1	17.8	42.7
Thais	30.7	19.1	31.7
Cubans	34.2	15.5	62.5
Puerto Ricans	58.2	25.3	69.4
American Indians	79.1	60.6	82.1

Source: U.S. Bureau of the Census (1992).

sense of racial exclusiveness may also be operating. Strong white concerns about racial mixing and negative attitudes toward other races are still with us.

On the other hand, more than half of the Puerto Ricans and American Indians and almost a third of the Cubans are married to someone outside their ethnic group. All of these groups are small in numbers and widely scattered throughout Southern California, making intermarriage more likely. Their high degree of social integration is a striking contrast to that of whites and some of the Asian groups.

Among most groups, half or more of all intermarriages are with whites. This is because whites are such a large population and because some people gain status by marrying a white. The groups which have been most strongly assimilated with the white population are American Indians, Puerto Ricans, Thais, Japanese, and Filipinos; but people of Mexican origin and some other groups have rates that are not much lower.

Relationship between acculturation and structural assimilation. A correlation analysis permits us to better understand how certain variables introduced earlier in this chapter relate to intermarriage rates with whites—the indicator of structural assimilation. To what extent do groups' average level of acculturation and status correlate with structural assimilation?

The Spearman rank-correlation technique is useful in examining these relationships (Table 9.4). The correlation coefficient, r, varies between 1 and –1. The former indicates that a group is ranked exactly the same on two variables while the latter indicates an opposite ranking. Correlations closer to zero show weaker associations between the variables.

The analysis demonstrates certain relationships quite clearly. First, structural assimilation is highly correlated with total intermarriage rate because marriage with whites is the most common type of intermarriage. Second, the correlation between level of residential segregation and the rate of intermarriage with whites is not statistically significant, although it is in the expected direction. This is because the close social relationships of people extend far beyond their neighborhoods of residence.

Especially significant is the fact that the relative status of ethnic groups in terms of educational attainment, occupation, and income gives absolutely no indication of the level of structural assimilation of immigrant groups. On the other hand, the associations between aspects of acculturation and structural assimilation are strong and statistically significant. Those ethnic groups with better English proficiency and those who immigrated less recently were much more likely to be intermarried with whites. This analysis suggests indirectly that social linkages between immigrant groups and whites can be expected to increase with greater acculturation of the immigrant groups. Conversely, residential location and status will probably have little effect on structural assimilation.

Trends and Spatial Patterns of Intermarriage

Because intermarriage between whites and other racial groups was prohibited by state law from 1901 until 1948, it makes little sense to measure interracial marriage before 1948 except in the case of Filipinos, who until 1933 were permitted to marry whites.[20]

Table 9.4   Structural Assimilation and Related Characteristics, 1990

Variables	Spearman's r
Rate of total intermarriage	.86[a]
Residential segregation from whites	-.43
Acculturation variables	
Percent of adults foreign-born	-.81[a]
Percent of foreign-born immigrating in 1980s	-.96[a]
Percent of adults speaking English very well	.76[a]
Socioeconomic status variables	
Percent college graduates among adults	-.06
Percent in managerial-professional occupations	.05
Median household income	.06

Source: U.S. Bureau of the Census (1992).

Notes: Structural assimilation is defined as the rate of intermarriage with non-Hispanic whites. N = 13 ethnic groups.

[a]The correlation is statistically significant (p < .01).

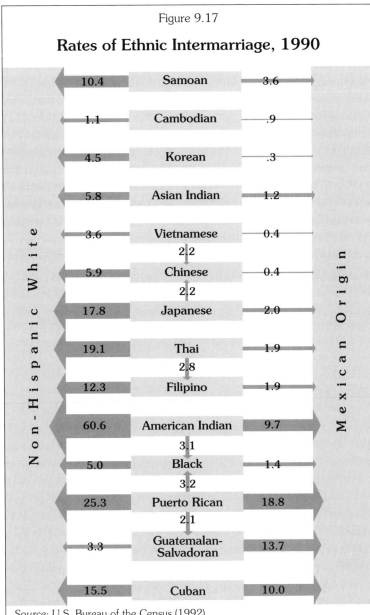

Figure 9.17

Rates of Ethnic Intermarriage, 1990

Non-Hispanic White		Mexican Origin
10.4	Samoan	3.6
1.1	Cambodian	.9
4.5	Korean	.3
5.8	Asian Indian	1.2
3.6	Vietnamese	0.4
	2.2	
5.9	Chinese	0.4
	2.2	
17.8	Japanese	2.0
19.1	Thai	1.9
	2.8	
12.3	Filipino	1.9
60.6	American Indian	9.7
	3.1	
5.0	Black	1.4
	3.2	
25.3	Puerto Rican	18.8
	2.1	
3.3	Guatemalan-Salvadoran	13.7
15.5	Cuban	10.0

Source: U.S. Bureau of the Census (1992).
Notes: Numbers show the percent of married people in groups listed in center column married to whites (left) and to people of Mexican origin (right). For example, 19.1% of married Thais are married to a white and 2.8% of married Thais are married to a Filipino. In addition, 9.9% of married people of Mexican origin are married to a white spouse and 3.3% of married whites are married to a spouse of Mexican origin. Linkages between the center column groups under 2.0% are not shown. Data are for the Los Angeles CMSA.

Trends. Of the blacks who applied for marriage licenses in 1959, 2.2 percent in Los Angeles County and 2.7 percent in Orange County married outside the black community.[21] Thus, the 12 percent intermarriage rate for Southern California blacks who were married as of 1990 represents a major increase in social integration since about 1960. It may result from diminishing criticism of racially mixed couples by blacks and whites since that time, but it could also reflect a greater tolerance for such marriages in Southern California than elsewhere.

A different trend appears, however, for people of Mexican origin in Los Angeles County. In this case, rates calculated for four periods show rising rates of intermarriage during the period from the 1920s through 1963 but a likely decline in intermarriage since 1963. Of Mexican-origin people who applied for marriage licenses in Los Angeles County between 1924 and 1933, 9 percent married outside their ethnic group.[22] Among Mexican immigrants who applied for naturalization before 1940, 17 percent were married to non-Hispanic whites.[23] Marriage-license applications for 1963 show that 25 percent of people of Mexican origin were marrying outside their group.[24] As expected, immigrants had lower rates of intermarriage and the grandchildren of immigrants had much higher rates. The period of the early 1960s seems to represent the high point of a trend toward increasing social integration of the Mexican community with the larger population in Southern California.

By 1990, however, only 14 percent of all married people of Mexican origin were married to someone from another group.[25] This reversal of what had been a trend toward greater intermarriage among people of Mexican origin is most directly explained by the much larger numbers of Mexican immigrants who have arrived in Southern California. Most unacculturated immigrants have settled primarily in Mexican concentrations; as a result, the level of residential segregation has increased, and the general level of acculturation of Southern California's Latino population has decreased. These geographical and cultural trends are consistent with the decreased social integration measured by intermarriage rates.

Between 1924 and 1933, 70 percent of the Filipinos who applied for marriage licenses in Los Angeles County married outside their ethnic group, and most of these married whites.[26]

The unusually high rate of intermarriage during those years is directly explainable by the shortage of Filipino women in California at that time.

Spatial patterns. People who have married outside their group are more likely to live outside the group's geographical concentrations. The presence of different ethnic groups in the same neighborhoods and regions within Southern California should enhance the opportunities for contact which can lead to intermarriage. On the other hand, areas of ethnic homogeneity presumably reduce the likelihood of intermarriage, because contact between different groups is less common. In addition, ethnic groups which are highly segregated from each other can be expected to have low rates of intermarriage.

Patterns of varying rates of intermarriage support these expected relationships. Intermarriage rates are higher outside each group's areas of concentration and where ethnic social structures are weaker and more fluid (Figs. 9.18–9.21). For example, in comparison with all whites, intermarried whites tend to live in the poorer, more central parts of Los Angeles. On the other hand, blacks married to someone other than another black are less likely to live in South Central than in outlying areas. Pasadena, Glendale, Huntington Beach, and parts of the San Fernando Valley show relatively high rates of intermarriage among their blacks. Similarly, ethnic intermarriage among Japanese is more common where the Japanese are fewer in number.

We believe that the maps show the leading areas where close relationships are cultivated between people in different ethnic groups. The residents of these areas have been the most active in reducing the ethnic compartmentalization of contemporary Southern California. These areas are the geographical frontier of social change.

Is Southern California a Multiethnic Society?

The evidence presented in this chapter suggests that the answer to this question is no. Rather than a multiethnic society, Southern California is better described as a collection of ethnic societies. On the surface—in the public and commercial arenas—the ethnic groups work together. In a superficial sense the people who mix in malls and schools and on the job can be described as constituting a single multiethnic society. A deeper look must acknowledge that most ethnic societies are highly compartmentalized, moderately separated residentially, and in some cases not well acculturated to the dominant English-speaking culture.

No more than a quarter of the married adults in most ethnic groups are married to anyone outside the group. It appears that only American Indians and Puerto Ricans live in a truly multiethnic society, because less than half the married people in those groups are married to someone in their same group. Cambodians, Salvadorans, Vietnamese, and Koreans have very low rates of both English proficiency and intermarriage.

Most ethnic groups are moderately segregated, but a few —Cambodians, Salvadorans, and blacks—are very highly segregated. Acculturation and economic progress have operated to reduce residential segregation over time, and even the traditionally high rate of black–white segregation has diminished.

The recent arrival of immigrants is a major impediment to acculturation and social integration of ethnic groups. Immigrants account for over 90 percent of the adults in many groups; and in several, more than half the immigrants arrived after 1980. Because of massive immigration, the residential segregation of people of Mexican origin has increased since 1960. Also, in 1990 the segregation of Cambodians and Salvadorans was higher than that of blacks because immigration into ethnic enclaves has overwhelmed the processes of assimilation.

It is encouraging that acculturation increases over time.[27] In addition, our finding that social integration is somewhat greater among people under the age of 35 suggests that the social barriers between ethnic societies are weakening. The cities and neighborhoods with greater ethnic diversity will provide more opportunities for close social contact among groups, and geographical zones between ethnic concentrations are the areas of both greater diversity and greater intermarriage.

For acculturation and social integration to take place, the pace of the immigrant influx must slow. Then, those immigrants already here and their children can have greater opportunities for acculturation and integration. If new immigrants continue to arrive in the large numbers that settled here in the 1980s, Southern California will remain as compartmentalized as it is today—a set of separate societies rather than a single society of varied ethnic identities.

Notes

1. D is the most commonly used of a group of indexes known as segregation indexes. For its properties compared with others, see White (1986).

2. The index does not distinguish between economic and cultural differences as the primary reason behind residential segregation. However, it is possible to control for economic differences between groups by measuring the segregation of households within a limited income range. In an earlier 1990 study of Los Angeles County we found that black and white households with incomes over $50,000 were almost as segregated from each other (D = .71) as were low-income black and white households (D = .75). This shows that black-white segregation cannot be explained by the groups' different income distributions (Allen and Turner 1996a, 20).

3. Comparative figures for Riverside, San Bernardino, and Ventura Counties can be found in Clark (1996).

4. Blau (1994).

5. The entropy index and its properties are explained in White (1986).

6. Our results for 1990 can be compared with those for 1980 using the same methods (Allen and Turner 1989).

7. Only New York City's Queens County, an Aleutian Island borough in Alaska, and San Francisco County are more ethnically diverse than Los Angeles County.

8. Allen and Turner (1989), 537.

9. For an analysis and a map of percentage Koreans by block within Koreatown, see Allen and Turner (1995).

10. Black dispersal during the 1980s is shown clearly on maps of the changing distribution of blacks (Turner and Allen 1991).

11. The best evidence for the acculturation and economic progress of immigrants in Southern California is Myers (1995), especially chapters 4 and 7. In contrast to most analyses of immigrant adaptation, Myers tracked specific white, Asian, and Latino immigrant cohorts from one decade to the next. In this way the 1990 characteristics of immigrants who arrived in the 1970s are not confounded by the arrival of new immigrants during the 1980s. For measures of the very rapid language shift toward English among children of immigrants in Miami and elsewhere, see Portes and Schauffler (1994).

12. This income comparison is inappropriate, however, where there are very few U.S.-born adults because nearly all the U.S.-born are much younger than is the average immigrant. Income comparisons between the U.S.-born and the foreign-born for other groups are not graphed in Figure 9.7 but are based instead on the statistics included on earlier maps of the groups.

13. Emoungu (1992).

14. Moffat (1994a).

15. See Massey (1985) and Allen and Turner (1996b) for the theory and research results.

16. Lieberson and Waters (1988), 171–75.

17. Alba and Golden (1986); Blau (1994), 54–57. For a general summary of theory, history, and empirical research on intermarriage, see Spickard (1989) and Root (1992).

18. Because men were four times more likely than women to be designated the householder and are more apt to marry younger women, a high proportion of the married people in our under-35 sample are under the age of 35.

19. Alba and Golden (1986).

20. In 1948 the California Supreme Court ruled, in *Perez v. Sharp*, that the state's law prohibiting interracial marriage was unconstitutional.

21. Heer (1966), 269.

22. Panunzio (1942), 693.

23. Sánchez (1993), 139.

24. Grebler et al. (1970), 406–9.

25. The inclusion of the four outlying counties in the 1990 sample had probably no significant effect, because the area contains both large Mexican concentrations and dispersed, suburban Mexican Americans, as does Los Angeles County.

26. Panunzio (1942), 695.

27. Neidert and Farley (1985); Lieberson and Waters (1988), 94–116; Myers (1995).

10. Conclusion

Our goal has been to understand the varying spatial and status positions of ethnic groups in the larger social structure of Southern California. To help us in this quest, we explicitly compared the largest groups in terms of their socioeconomic positions and geographical locations. We also examined the extent of acculturation, overrepresentation and underrepresentation in different types of work, and social integration among the various ethnic groups. In the process, we charted major trends since 1960 and were able to explain most of the changes and patterns we observed.

Our method made it possible to interweave the various ethnic populations and their class positions and distributions together into a three-dimensional description of Southern California's population structure—an ethnic quilt, so to speak.

The maps in this book demonstrate that profound differences exist among many of the localities and neighborhoods of Southern California. Variations from place to place in environment, land use, housing, social class, and age characteristics are significant and are interrelated with the settlement patterns of the various ethnic groups.

Distributions

Although the maps and text regarding distributions lend themselves more to local details than general statements, we can describe some broad patterns and processes of settlement and change.

Persistence of ethnic enclaves. Ethnic distributions and the location of residential enclaves are usually slow to change. Although new housing opportunities may prompt residents to leave their neighborhoods, other members of the ethnic group usually remain, and still others move in. All of this means that most features of the 1990 distributions shown in our book should be valid for twenty or more years.

The oldest distinctive concentrations we uncovered were those of blacks in Los Angeles, Pasadena, and Monrovia, all of which were established before 1890. In the first few years of the twentieth century, Armenians settled in Pasadena, and a Japanese presence was established in Little Tokyo, Boyle Heights, and Gardena. All these areas retain some of their ethnic populations today.

The foundations of the present-day Mexican distribution were laid in the nineteenth century near Los Angeles' plaza. Today Olvera Street and Our Lady the Queen of the Angels church (La Placita) commemorate this heritage. In the early twentieth century urban renewal near the plaza displaced Mexicans eastward across the Los Angeles River to locations like Belvedere and Boyle Heights. These later expanded and coalesced into the large Mexican Eastside barrio. Today this is still the best known Mexican American enclave.

In rural Southern California the expansion of irrigated agriculture at the time of World War I and the increasing use of Mexican immigrants as farmworkers led to the appearance of new Mexican colonias. Although later urbanization destroyed the continuity of some of these, contemporary barrios in Orange County, San Fernando, Canoga Park, and the Santa Clara Valley had their origins in those farmworker villages more than seventy years ago.

In the 1930s modern Chinatown was built. During the next decade the Filipino enclaves of Temple-Alvarado and West Long Beach appeared, and Russian Armenian refugees settled in Montebello. Soon after World War II, blacks found homes for the first time in Pacoima, and Jews moved into their present area of concentration on the Westside. All these enclaves persist today.

From the early 1920s until the late 1940s, blacks, Mexicans, Filipinos, Japanese, and Chinese were usually not permitted to buy or rent apartments or houses in most parts of Southern California. At that time whites were legally able to keep those minorities out of white neighborhoods, and minorities were forced to live in less attractive areas. Some minority settlements from those days have persisted to the present—geographical reminders of the blatant racism of a half-century ago. During the 1960s exclusion based on race became illegal, and rapid suburbanization led to the elaboration of older distributions and the creation of new ones.

Changes since the mid-1960s. The distribution of ethnic populations arriving since the mid-1960s is most clearly related to their socioeconomic status, their relative acculturation, and special locations of employment. Groups that settled here in both the early decades of the twentieth century and after the mid-1960s have mixed distributions, with the new distribution typically grafted onto the older one. This combination of old and new patterns can be seen among Filipinos, Japanese, Chinese, Koreans, people of Russian and Armenian ancestry, and people of Mexican origin.

Competition for low-cost housing has meant that certain older enclaves near city centers have shifted somewhat. This occurred because the numbers of new arrivals who sought housing in the low-rent areas were often so large that the new group displaced earlier inhabitants. Cambodians in Long Beach, Salvadorans in Westlake, Koreans in Koreatown, Armenians in East Hollywood, and Chinese in areas near Chinatown have produced such displacements.

By far the most important such displacement and distributional change has involved the historic black concentrations in South Central and in outlying areas—Pasadena, Pacoima, Pomona, Long Beach, and Santa Ana. Because these areas usually had the lowest-cost housing available, they were particularly attractive to low-income groups. As poor Mexican immigrants arrived in the 1970s and 1980s, different families often pooled their earnings to rent or purchase a house. The result was that many blacks were displaced. By 1990 these areas had become mostly Hispanic, and the large black concentration of South Central had shifted westward from the historic Central Avenue area to a new focus around Leimert Park and the Crenshaw district.

The importance of social networks which interconnect members of ethnic groups is demonstrated indirectly by the substantial differences in group distributions. If ethnic identity and its social networks were not significant, ethnic groups of similar income would have similar distributions. However, this is not the case. Groups with a high median household income (Japanese, Filipinos, Asian Indians, people of Russian ancestry, and people of English ancestry) have very different distributions. Similarly, the ethnic concentrations of the lowest-income groups (Cambodians and Salvadorans) are spatially far apart. These distinctive settlement patterns would not have occurred without a tendency for many of the people who share an ethnic identity to stick together residentially.

The large size of the white, black, and Mexican-origin populations, the separate locations of their settlements, and the much greater affluence of whites compared to the other two groups are powerful features of Southern California's ethnic geography.

Ethnic Work Niches

Ethnic populations vary substantially in their representation in different types of employment. The work specializations of low-skilled immigrants are probably even more concentrated than U.S. census data show because many illegal or undocumented residents were working in those niches but did not fill out the census questionnaires.

Because the purpose of our research on this topic was to establish an empirical basis for comparing groups, the details of work niches are more important than any generalization. For instance, Korean men are six times more likely than Filipino men to be self-employed, and black women are six times more likely than Salvadoran women to work for the government.

Similarly, the fact that 22 percent of Israeli men are employed in construction and that Armenian men are five times more likely than the average employed man to be working in gasoline stations helps characterize the position of these groups in the Southern California economy. The particular niches which groups have created are usually new adaptations to Southern California, but in some cases the group's niche reflects aspects of its traditional culture.

There are substantial variations in work specialization between various ethnic groups of similar educational or income status. When the groups are equal in socioeconomic status, the explanation of work niches must involve ethnically defined social networks that guide members toward certain types of work and not others.

Gaps or Differentials in Socioeconomic Status

Educational attainment. Because white men and white women increased their educational attainment substantially between 1960 and 1990, it has been difficult for minorities to increase their attainment at an even faster rate. Nevertheless, our examination of Los Angeles and Orange Counties in 1960 and 1990 showed a clear narrowing of the educational-attainment differential for black men and for Mexican Americans. For Filipino men the gap has been eliminated. With respect to high-school graduation, black men and black women have cut the 1960 differential with whites in half, and progress has been almost as great among U.S.-born men of Mexican origin. These are major accomplishments.

Nevertheless, rates of college graduation are more important today than rates of high-school graduation. Japanese, Chinese, and Filipino men and women are now more likely than whites to be college graduates. However, a very large differential in college-graduation rates remains between whites and both blacks and Mexican Americans. Blacks are college graduates at about half the rate of whites, and the rate for Mexican Americans is less than a third that of whites. These gaps retard the efforts of many people to improve the occupational and income status of blacks and Mexican Americans in Southern California.

Occupational status. This is where affirmative-action programs have presumably played their greatest role. The gap has narrowed substantially for blacks. The 1960 black–white differential in percentage of managers and professionals had been reduced by 30 percent for black men and 60 percent for black women as of 1990. Among Mexican American women the progress was similar: the 1960 differential was reduced by 33 percent. For Mexican American men, however, the gap was reduced by only 12 percent during the 1960–1990 years, and for immigrant Mexicans the differential with whites widened.

Men in all three Asian groups have shown much progress in narrowing the occupational gap, with Japanese and Chinese by 1990 exceeding whites in percentage in managerial and professional occupations. Among women, convergence has been less, and the lower educational attainment of recently arrived Chinese women compared with those who arrived in the 1950s probably explains much of the wider occupational status gap for them.

Income. This book contains findings that can be used to show the economic success of many blacks, Mexican Americans, and immigrants. The fact that all groups contain men who in 1989 earned incomes over $50,000 demonstrates this achievement. It is useful to realize that some people in most ethnic groups have "made it."

Nevertheless, more penetrating analyses are possible by comparing medians of income distributions. Ethnic differences in economic status are dramatic. Asian Indians, Filipinos, Japanese, whites, and people of Russian ancestry have usually attained very high median incomes. At the other extreme, Cambodians and Salvadorans have the lowest.

Whereas there has been some narrowing of education and occupation differentials between whites and both blacks and Mexican Americans, the income gaps have not narrowed significantly. Considering the lower percentage of black men with income in 1989 compared with 1959, the actual black-white income gap among men has probably widened somewhat since 1959. Moreover, the nature of the median as a statistical measure, the greater undercount of lower-status minorities, and the underreporting of certain types of incomes mean that differences between whites and lower-status groups are probably greater than what is revealed in U.S. census data.

Some may assume that improved access to education and better occupations on the part of minorities would result in income convergence with whites. But that has not been the case in Southern California. These minorities were farther from whites in 1989 than they were in 1959. The situation is better described as the continued layering or stratification of Mexican Americans and blacks compared to whites.

We believe that it is especially important for whites to recognize the widening of income gaps between themselves and both blacks and Mexican Americans in Southern California. Awareness of this trend may help whites to better understand one source of resentment on the part of lower-income minorities, who probably expected that improved civil rights and the passage of time would bring them closer to whites in income levels.

Why Has the Income Gap Become Wider?

In the United States as a whole, the gap in median incomes between whites and both blacks and Hispanics narrowed between 1959 and 1979, and the divergence during the 1980s did not negate the general nationwide trend toward greater income equality over the past thirty years. However, the income convergence that the nation experienced since 1959 was not found in Southern California. The fact that income gaps in this region did not follow the U.S. trend but instead grew wider indicates that regional factors must have been especially significant in Southern California.

Employment restructuring and immigration. The exceptional growth of high-level service-sector employment in Southern California since the 1960s has raised the incomes of whites compared to less educated minorities in this region. The loss of high-wage blue-collar manufacturing jobs had a negligible effect on the gaps. On the other hand, expansion of low-wage manufacturing and service-sector employment has been an important factor behind the increased gaps in 1989 compared to 1959.

It is likely that new, low-wage service and manufacturing jobs were created only after it was clear to entrepreneurs that immigrants were arriving in such numbers that new jobs could be filled at low wages. In other words, the presence in Southern California of a large supply of eager workers was probably a necessary factor behind the increase of low-wage jobs.

Several different sources of evidence reveal that the lack of income convergence in Southern California between whites and both Mexican Americans and blacks is best explained by the unusually large number of low-skilled and low-wage workers who settled here in the 1970s and 1980s. Most of these are immigrants from Mexico, although many are from El Salvador or Guatemala and some are from Asian countries, such as Vietnam and China.

Large numbers of immigrants who are willing to work for low wages have driven down the incomes of Mexican Americans (the U.S.-born) compared with whites. The detailed mechanisms by which this divergence has taken place are not known, but they involve processes of matching a surplus of poorly educated workers with jobs.

Relative sizes of income gaps. After controlling for education, age, full-time employment, and U.S. birth within three broad categories of occupation, we found that substantial differences remain between the median incomes of white men and both black men and Mexican American men. In occupations other than professional specialties, black men average about 75 percent of the income of white men, and Mexican American men earn about 80 percent of the income of white men. The gaps are smaller among professionals.

These income differentials are not due to ethnic differences in specific occupations. Even within the same occupations, black men and Mexican-origin men earn only about four-fifths of the incomes of white men. Because white workers tend to be older than Hispanic workers and, to a lesser extent, black workers, the explanation of the income gaps in specific occupations must acknowledge the greater years of experience of the average white worker. However, apart from this, the sizes of the gaps that remain seem to point toward wage and salary discrimination as the most likely explanation.

The size of the white–Asian income gap among men is much less than the white–black and white–Mexican American gaps. However, Japanese American managers earn only 81 percent of the income of U.S.-born white managers, which suggests a "glass ceiling"—an invisible barrier that excludes many Asian Americans from higher executive positions.

The incomes of Russian-ancestry (Jewish) men are about 20 percent above the median income of all white men in comparable occupational categories. Jews were once discriminated against by other whites, but by 1990 they were earning more than other whites. It is difficult to explain this reversal by anything other than aspects of Jewish ethnic culture and social networks which have resulted in enhanced earnings. Our methodology makes it impossible to zero in more closely on the explanation for the various income gaps, but the Jewish example suggests that cultural differences may be strong influences.

Income gaps between women in the different ethnic groups are much smaller than they are among men. They are quite minor compared with the great discrepancy in median incomes between men and women. Among U.S.-born whites who are employed full-time, women's incomes are only 65 percent as high as men's.

Prospects for narrowing the gaps. Progress in narrowing the occupational status and income gaps has been slow and is likely to be so in the future. Part of this is because employers—regardless of ethnic identity—are generally predisposed to hire and promote either members of their own ethnic group or those members of other groups who are not very different culturally. Because U.S.-born whites retain control of most hiring and promotional decisions in Southern California, members of their group and others who are highly acculturated to the culture of that group will tend to be favored.

The fact that this is a natural tendency does not imply that anti-discrimination laws should not be enforced. Indeed, because laws prohibiting discrimination have been only marginally effective, we favor still stronger enforcement and a search for new approaches toward reducing discrimination.

It is understandable and appropriate that many minority people wish to diminish or eliminate the economic dominance of whites. Many work toward this goal by mobilizing politically, developing new businesses in the ethnic communities, and accumulating capital in order to gain control of a larger portion of the region's wealth. We believe that a broader base of economic power among the region's ethnic groups would narrow the income gaps and reduce interethnic tensions. At the same time, it is not surprising that many whites resist this effort in a competitive economic environment.

Another approach to narrowing the occupational and income gaps involves cultural change on the part of minorities. Blacks, Mexican Americans, and other minorities might consciously attempt to follow the examples of Jews, Japanese Americans, or other high-income ethnic groups. These two groups have become successful after earlier periods of low status and of discrimination. Both groups have placed great emphasis on achieving a superior education and business ownership as means to economic betterment. In the early years, the occupational and income benefits that Jews and Japanese hoped to gain were thwarted by discrimination, but they persisted in their efforts. Ultimately, these have been rewarded.

Ethnic Polarization in Southern California

The last thirty years have seen increased divisions between ethnic groups and social classes. The most important factor behind that trend has been the arrival of large numbers of immigrants willing to work for low wages. The social and economic gaps between poor immigrants and other residents are exacerbated by the many immigrants living here illegally.

The high proportion of immigrants coming from Mexico and the traditionally high birth rate among Mexican immigrants means that people of Mexican origin are by far the largest ethnic population apart from non-Hispanic whites. Contrasts between whites and people of Mexican origin have grown such that Southern California is being polarized by a combination of ethnicity and class. Thus, although one aspect of the ethnic transformation of Southern California is its greater diversity compared to the earlier dominance by whites, an equally important feature is its increasingly dichotomous character.

The shape of Southern California in the future depends in many ways on the size and characteristics of the immigrant flow. This, in turn, is dependent on three key factors: the region's opportunities compared to those in immigrant source countries, the trend of birth rates in source countries, and the nature of U.S. immigration policy and enforcement.

The first half of the 1990s showed a general continuation of the demographic trends of the 1980s. Southern California's economic recession resulted in a slightly lower rate of immigration and a sharply increased rate of net outmigration after about 1992.[1] As in the 1980s, less educated whites, blacks, and Hispanics have been overrepresented among those departing. Those replacing them include many well-trained and affluent people from many countries. However, the new immigrants are commonly less-educated people from Mexico. This means that social class differences between the remaining whites and people of Mexican origin are, if anything, becoming greater.

Thus, these distinctive patterns of net migration into and out of Southern California have continued during periods of both economic expansion and contraction. Moreover, similar patterns are found in other metropolitan areas that are important immigrant destinations, but they are not found elsewhere. This confirms our conclusion that the numbers and characteristics of immigrants are the primary influences on the migration flows and on the increased ethnic and class polarization.

If the number of new arrivals willing to work at low wages is not substantially reduced in future years, the ethnic transformation will continue. Changes in tax laws or other political changes in the current patterns of income distribution could reduce class polarization, but no major change in this direction seems likely at this writing. Acculturation does diminish differences between people. However, education and the intermarriage of immigrants take place too slowly to counteract the growing polarization between more affluent whites and poorer people of Mexican origin. Trends of the recent past suggest that Southern California will see increased differentiation by class, a continued exodus of whites, and much greater proportions of immigrant Hispanics and their children.

There is also a strong geographical dimension to the ethnic and class polarization. Affluent whites tend to live in newer suburbs and in scattered high-status enclaves. These are very different places from older, more central areas which house poor black, Mexican, Salvadoran, and Cambodian populations. This ethnic-class-spatial differentiation is epitomized in the contrast between Westside Los Angeles, southern Orange County, and Thousand Oaks on the one hand and the Mexican Eastside, South Central Los Angeles, Santa Ana, and Pico-Union on the other. Such powerful and disturbing differences between places remind us of the need to look at all three of the dimensions of structure outlined in chapter 1 and developed throughout the book.

Uncovering the Hidden Side of Ethnicity

Evidence for the continued geographical, social, and economic significance of ethnic identity in Southern California is overwhelming. There are natural tensions between ethnic groups which can be expected and which can be reduced but not completely eliminated. These tensions arise from differences in culture and social networks and from economic competition between both individuals and ethnic groups.

Thus, it seems unrealistic to expect that Southern California could be a "melting pot" or that all groups should live together with no tension between them. The cities that come closest to the metaphor of a melting pot are those which are the most ethnically diverse—Carson, Gardena, Hawthorne, Cerritos and Walnut.

A marked reduction in the rate at which immigrants have been arriving in Southern California would provide essential time for the acculturation of those who are already here and would probably reduce the separation between groups.

Rates of intermarriage measure patterns of very personal ties among people. In three-quarters of the sixteen ethnic groups we examined, fewer than 20 percent of the married people had selected a spouse from outside their group. These low rates mean that most ethnic groups are substantially separate from each other in terms of family matters. This is the most powerful evidence that Southern California is not a multiethnic society but rather a collection of ethnic societies. Intermarriage is least common among Koreans, Cambodians, and Vietnamese and most common among American Indians, Puerto Ricans, and Cubans. Groups with higher rates of intermarriage tend to be those with greater English-language skills and lower proportions of recent immigrants. The degree of social separation between most groups is lessening, however. Higher rates of intermarriage among younger couples indicate that barriers are weakening slightly.

People's decisions about where they live are also highly personal. Although some people select a residence without regard to the general ethnic character of the neighborhood, the fact that the distributions of most groups are substantially different demonstrates that ethnic identity and the ethnic character of various places do play a role in these very private, family-based decisions. Moreover, lack of any direct contact means that residents of widely scattered neighborhoods and cities remain substantially separated.

Altogether, Southern California's social structure is a quilt—fascinating in its colors and arrangements but with a patchwork of ethnic blocks stitched together loosely and tentatively. Moreover, the essential character of the fabric of those different components is mostly hidden from those who are not close friends and family. This book has probed beneath the surface of Southern California, exposing and measuring patterns of an underlying social reality that is normally not very visible.

Uncovering the often-unacknowledged similarities and differences among groups in locations of settlement, work niches, acculturation, and socioeconomic status should make all of us more familiar with Southern California's ethnic diversity. It is our hope that this knowledge will help the inhabitants of this much loved but troubled region learn to treat each other with greater mutual respect and understanding.

Notes

1. Frey (1996); California Department of Finance (1996).

References

Abelmann, N., and J. Lie. 1995. *Blue Dreams: Korean Americans and the Los Angeles Riots*. Cambridge, MA: Harvard University Press.

Acuña, R. F. 1984. *A Community under Siege: A Chronicle of Chicanos East of the Los Angeles River, 1945-1975*. Los Angeles: Chicano Studies Research Center, UCLA.

———. 1996. *Anything But Mexican: Chicanos in Contemporary Los Angeles*. New York: Verso.

Agbayani-Siewert, P. 1993. Filipino American Immigrants: Social Role Strain, Self-Esteem, Locus of Control, Social Networks, Coping, Stress, and Mental Health Outcome. Ph.D. dissertation, University of California, Los Angeles.

Agbayani-Siewert, P., and L. Revilla. 1995. Filipino Americans. In *Asian Americans: Contemporary Trends and Issues*, P. G. Min, ed., 134–68. Thousand Oaks, CA: Sage Publications.

Akst, D. 1993. Cruller Fates: Cambodians Find Slim Profit in Doughnuts. *Los Angeles Times*, March 9: D1, 6.

Alba, R. D., and R. M. Golden. 1986. Patterns of Ethnic Marriage in the United States. *Social Forces* 65 (1): 202–23.

Allen, J. P. 1977. Recent Immigration from the Philippines and Filipino Communities in the United States. *Geographical Review* 67 (2): 195–208.

———. 1990. Migration into and out of Los Angeles County in the 1980s. *Perspective* (CSU Northridge) 7 (2): 2–6, 16.

Allen, J. P., and E. Turner. 1989. The Most Ethnically Diverse Urban Places in the United States. *Urban Geography* 10 (6): 523–39.

———. 1995. Ethnic Differentiation by Blocks within Census Tracts. *Urban Geography* 16 (4): 344–64.

———. 1996a. Ethnic Diversity and Segregation in the New Los Angeles. In *EthniCity: Geographic Perspectives on Ethnic Change in Modern Cities*, C. C. Roseman, G. Thieme, and H. D. Laux, eds.: 1–29. Lanham, MD: Rowman and Littlefield.

———. 1996b. Spatial Patterns of Immigrant Assimilation. *The Professional Geographer* 48 (2): 140–55.

Almaguer, T. 1994. *Racial Fault Lines: The Historical Origins of White Supremacy in California*. Berkeley: University of California Press.

Alvarez, F. 1995. A Hard Life for Mixtec Laborers. *Los Angeles Times*[a], July 27: B13.

Applegate, J. 1984. Indochinese Swelling Work Force: Majority of Orange County's Refugees Get High-Tech Jobs. *Los Angeles Times*[a], October 2: IV1, 17.

Aquino, V. R. 1952. The Filipino Community in Los Angeles. M.A. thesis, University of Southern California.

Arax, M.. 1987a. Many Refugees Work While Getting Welfare. *Los Angeles Times*[a], February 9: I1, 16, 17.

———. 1987b. Monterey Park: Nation's 1st Suburban Chinatown. *Los Angeles Times*[a], April 6: 1, 3, 18, 19.

———. 1987c. Refugees Called Victims and Perpetrators of Fraud. *Los Angeles Times*[a], February 10: I1, 3, 26.

Arax, M., and E. Schrader. 1988. Soviet Emigres: Armenians Find Refuge in Hollywood. *Los Angeles Times*[a], April 25: I1, 3, 16.

Archdeacon, T. J. 1983. *Becoming American: An Ethnic History*. New York: The Free Press.

Arnold, F. W. 1987. Ethnic Identification, Ethnicity, and Ethnic Solidarity in Los Angeles County's West Indian-American Community. Ph.D. dissertation, University of California, Los Angeles.

Bartlett, L., and V. S. Bartlett. 1932. *Los Angeles in 7 Days, including Southern California*. New York: Robert M. McBride and Co.

Bass, C. A. 1960. *Forty Years: Memoirs from the Pages of a Newspaper*. Los Angeles: Charlotta A. Bass.

Bean, F. D., and M. Tienda. 1987. *The Hispanic Population of the United States*. New York: Russell Sage Foundation.

Ben-Sasson, H. H., ed. 1976. *A History of the Jewish People*. Cambridge, MA: Harvard University Press.

Bennett, P. 1993. Feeling of Home Rests on Mutual Respect. *Los Angeles Times*[a], May 2: L2, 12.

Bernier, L. 1977. Samoans in the Southland. *Los Angeles Herald Examiner,* August 16: A8, 9.

Bianchi, S. 1994. Changing Economic Roles of Women and Men. In *State of the Union: America in the 1990s,* Vol. 1, *Economic Trends,* R. Farley, ed., 107–54. New York: Russell Sage Foundation.

Blau, P. M. 1994. *Structural Contexts of Opportunities.* Chicago: University of Chicago Press.

Bonacich, E. 1993. Asian and Latino Immigrants in the Los Angeles Garment Industry: An Exploration of the Relationship between Capitalism and Racial Oppression. In *Immigration and Entrepreneurship: Culture, Capital, and Ethnic Networks,* I. Light and P. Bhachu, eds.: 51–73. New Brunswick, NJ: Transaction Publishers.

———. 1994. Asians in the Los Angeles Garment Industry. In *The New Asian Immigration in Los Angeles and Global Restructuring,* P. Ong, E. Bonacich, and L. Cheng, eds.: 136–63.

Bonacich, E., and J. Modell. 1980. *The Economic Basis of Ethnic Solidarity: Small Business in the Japanese American Community.* Berkeley: University of California Press.

Bond, J. M. 1936. The Negro in Los Angeles. Ph.D. dissertation, University of Southern California.

Borjas, G. J. 1990. *Friends or Strangers: The Impact of Immigrants on the U.S. Economy.* New York: Basic Books.

Borjas, G. J., and M. Tienda. 1993. The Employment and Wages of Legalized Immigrants. *International Migration Review* 27 (4): 712–47.

Boswell, T. D., and J. R. Curtis. 1984. *The Cuban-American Experience: Culture, Images, and Perspectives.* Totowa, NJ: Rowman and Allanheld.

Boyer, E. J. 1985. American Dream: Caribbeans—Driven Migrants. *Los Angeles Times[a],* April 25: 1, 20, 22, 23.

Bozorgmehr, M., G. Sabagh, and C. Der-Martirosian. 1993. Beyond Nationality: Religio-Ethnic Diversity. In *Irangeles: Iranians in Los Angeles,* R. Kelley and J. Friedlander, eds.: 59–79. Berkeley: University of California Press.

Broom, L., and R. Reimer. 1949. *Removal and Return: The Socio-Economic Effects of the War on Japanese Americans.* Berkeley: University of California Press.

Brown, S. S. 1994. Little Indonesia Taking Root around Sunset Boulevard Hotel. *Los Angeles Times[a],* October 2: B11, 14.

Bunch, L. G. 1990. A Past Not Necessarily Prologue: The Afro-American in Los Angeles. In *20th Century Los Angeles: Power, Promotion, and Social Conflict,* N. M. Klein and M. J. Schiesl, eds.: 101–30.

Burke, A. 1994. Koreans Forming Valley Enclaves. *Los Angeles Daily News,* May 8: 1, 8.

Butler, J. S., and C. Herring. 1991. Ethnicity and Entrepreneurship in America: Towards an Explanation of Racial and Ethnic Group Variations in Self-Employment. *Sociological Perspectives* 34: 79–94.

California Department of Finance. 1996. *Race/Ethnic Population Estimates: Components of Change by Race, 1990-1994.* Sacramento: California Department of Finance.

California Department of Health Services. 1994. *Vital Statistics of California 1992.* Sacramento: California Department of Health Services.

Camarillo, A. M. 1971. Chicano Urban History: A Study of Compton's Barrio, 1936–1970. *Aztlan* 2 (2): 79–106.

Caplan, N., J. K. Whitmore, and M. H. Choy. 1989. *The Boat People and Achievement in America: A Study of Family Life, Hard Work, and Cultural Values.* Ann Arbor: University of Michigan Press.

Carnoy, M. 1994. *Faded Dreams: The Politics and Economics of Race in America.* Cambridge, UK: Cambridge University Press.

Carnoy, M., H. M. Daley, and R. H. Ojeda. 1993. The Changing Economic Position of Latinos in the U. S. Labor Market since 1939. In *Latinos in a Changing U. S. Economy: Comparative Perspectives on Growing Inequality,* R. Morales and F. Bonilla, eds.: 28–54. Newbury Park, CA: Sage Publications.

Catapusan, B. T. 1934. Filipino Occupational and Recreational Activities in Los Angeles. M.A. thesis, University of Southern California.

Chammou, E. 1976. Migration and Adjustment: The Case of Sephardic Jews in Los Angeles. Ph.D. dissertation, University of California, Los Angeles.

Chan, S. 1986. *This Bittersweet Soil: The Chinese in California Agriculture, 1860-1910.* Berkeley: University of California Press.

———. 1991a. *Asian Americans: An Interpretive History.* Boston: Twayne Publishers.

———. 1991b. *Asian Californians.* San Francisco: MTL/Boyd and Fraser.

———. 1990, ed. *Income and Status Differences between White and Minority Americans.* Lewiston, NY: Edwin Mellen Press.

Chang, I. 1990. Metro Rail Excavation Casts New Light on "Old Chinatown." *Los Angeles Times[a],* November 14: B1, 10.

Cheng, L., and S. Cheng. 1984. Chinese Women of Los Angeles, A Social Historical Survey. In *Linking Our Lives: Chinese American Women of Los Angeles,* L. Cheng, S. Cheng, J. Chu, et al.: 1–26. Los Angeles: Chinese Historical Society of Southern California and UCLA Asian American Studies Center.

Chinchilla, N., N. Hamilton, and J. Loucky. 1993. In *In the Barrios: Latinos and the Underclass Debate*, J. Moore and R. Pinderhughes, eds.: 51–78. New York: Russell Sage Foundation.

Chiswick, B. 1978. The Effect of Americanization on the Earnings of Foreign-Born Men. *Journal of Political Economy* 86: 897–921.

Chua, L. 1994. Opening up for Business: Koreatown Looks to Other Ethnicities for Post-Riot Patrons. *Los Angeles Times*[a], April 25: D1, 2.

Citron, A. 1988. Aging Indians Finding They Can Go Home Again. *Los Angeles Times*[a], March 6: I1, 34, 36.

Clark, C. 1989. How the Armenians Came to Hill Street. *Modern Jeweler* March: 42–48.

Clark, L. E. 1963. The Social Adjustment of Cuban Refugee Families. M.A. thesis, University of Southern California.

Clark, W. A. V. 1991. Residential Preferences and Neighborhood Racial Segregation: A Test of the Schelling Segregation Model. *Demography* 18 (1): 1–19.

———. 1992. Residential Preferences and Residential Choices in a Multi-Ethnic Context. *Demography* 29 (3): 451–66.

———. 1996. Avoidance, Assimilation and Succession: Residential Patterns in a Multi-Ethnic Metropolis. In *Ethnic Los Angeles*, R. Waldinger and M. Bozorgmehr, eds.: 109–138. New York: Russell Sage Foundation.

Clark, W. A. V., and M. Mueller. 1988. Hispanic Relocation and Spatial Assimilation: A Case Study. *Social Science Quarterly* 69 (2): 468–75.

Contract Slave's Pathetic Craving. 1903. *Los Angeles Times*, February 27: 18.

Connelly, P. M. 1951. Behind the Bias at Wyverwood. *Daily People's World*, February 6. (In the Archives of the Jewish Federation Council of Greater Los Angeles's Community Relations Committee, Urban Archives/Special Collections, California State University, Northridge.)

Cooper, A. 1992. Interview with Alicia Cooper, Director, International Rescue Committee. In *The Vietnamese Community in Orange County: An Oral History*, Vol. 3, 113–30. San Ana, CA: Intercultural Development Center, California State University, Fullerton, and Newhope Branch of the Santa Ana Public Library.

Crimi, J. E. 1941. The Social Status of the Negro in Pasadena, California. M.A. thesis, University of Southern California.

Dallalfar, A. 1989. Iranian Immigrant Women in Los Angeles: The Reconstruction of Work, Ethnicity, and Community. Ph.D. dissertation, University of California, Los Angeles.

———. 1994. Iranian Women as Immigrant Entrepreneurs. *Gender and Society* 8 (4): 541–61.

Daniels, R. 1988. *Asian America: Chinese and Japanese in the United States since 1850*. Seattle: University of Washington Press.

Danielson, M. N. 1976. *The Politics of Exclusion*. New York: Columbia University Press.

Dart, J. 1993. Long Way from Home: Sikhs Persist in Quest to Locate Temple in Residential North Hills. *Los Angeles Times*[a], August 1: B1, 4.

———. 1995. From Cairo to California. *Los Angeles Times*[a], December 23: B1, 9.

Davis, M. 1990. *City of Quartz: Excavating the Future in Los Angeles*. New York: Verso.

———. 1992. Chinatown, Revisited? The "Internationalization" of Downtown Los Angeles. In *Sex, Death, and God in L.A.*, D. Reid, ed.: 19–53. New York: Pantheon Books.

Day, A. 1992. Troubling Times for U.S. Jews. *Los Angeles Times*[a], January 23: A1, 26–27.

Day, G. M. 1934. *The Russians in Hollywood: A Study in Culture Conflict*. Los Angeles: University of Southern California Press.

Day, R. L. 1985. Redevelopment in Chinatown: The Role of Immigration in Class and Ethnic Conflicts. M.A. thesis, University of California, Los Angeles

De Graaf, L. B. 1962. Negro Migration to Los Angeles, 1930–1950. Ph.D. dissertation, University of California, Los Angeles.

———. 1970. The City of Black Angels: Emergence of the Los Angeles Ghetto, 1890–1930. *Pacific Historical Review* 39 (3): 323–52.

Der, H. 1993. Asian Pacific Islanders and the "Glass Ceiling"—New Era of Civil Rights Activism? In *The State of Asian Pacific America: A Public Policy Report*, S. Hune and P. Ong, eds.: 215–30. Los Angeles: Leadership Education for Asian Pacifics and UCLA Asian American Studies Center.

Der-Martirosian, C., G. Sabagh, and M. Bozorgmehr 1993. Subethnicity: Armenians in Los Angeles. In *Immigration and Entrepreneurship: Culture, Capital, and Ethnic Networks*, I. Light and P. Bhachu, eds.: 243–58. New Brunswick, NJ: Transaction Publishers.

Desbarats, J. 1979. Thai Migration to Los Angeles. *Geographical Review* 69 (3): 302–18.

———. 1986. Ethnic Differences in Adaptation: Sino-Vietnamese Refugees in the United States. *International Migration Review* 20 (2): 405–27.

Desbarats, J., and L. Holland. 1983. Indochinese Settlement Patterns in Orange County. *Amerasia* 10 (1): 23–46.

DeWilde, S. R. 1996. Vietnamese Settlement Patterns in Orange County's Little Saigon. M.A. thesis, California State University, Long Beach.

Dickens, W. T., and K. Lang. 1988. The Reemergence of Segmented Labor Market Theory. *American Economic Review* 78 (2): 129–34.

Dlin, N. 1961. Some Cultural and Geographic Aspects of the Christian Lebanese in Metropolitan Los Angeles. M.A. thesis, University of California, Los Angeles.

Duong, P. C. 1983. Facing New Life: The Vietnamese Family. In *Second Lives: The Contemporary Immigrant/Refugee Experience in Orange County: The Shaping of a Multi-Ethnic Community*, V. Smith and M. B. Dixon, eds.: 27–30. Costa Mesa, CA: South Coast Repertory.

Emoungu, P.–A. 1992. Africans and Black Americans in the United States: Social Distance and Differential Acculturation. *Ethnic Forum* 12 (2): 69–79.

Espiritu, A. F. 1992. The Rise and Fall of the Filipino Town Campaign in Los Angeles: A Study in Filipino American Leadership. M.A. thesis, University of California, Los Angeles.

Espiritu, Y. L. 1989. Beyond the "Boat People": Ethnicization of American Life. *Amerasia Journal* 15 (2): 49–67.

Faris, G. 1992. Hindus' Plan for Temple in Norwalk Encounters Unfriendly Neighbors. *Los Angeles Times*[a], July 21: B7.

Farley, R., and W. Allen. 1987. *The Color Line and the Quality of Life in America*. New York: Russell Sage Foundation.

Feagin, J. R., and C. B. Feagin. 1994. Theoretical Perspectives in Race and Ethnic Relations. In *Race and Ethnic Conflict: Contending Views on Prejudice, Discrimination, and Ethnoviolence*, F. L. Pincus and H. J. Ehrlich, eds.: 29–47. Boulder, CO: Westview Press.

Feagin, J. R., and N. Imani. 1994. Racial Barriers to African-American Entrepreneurship: An Exploratory Study. *Social Problems* 41 (4): 562–84.

Feagin, J. R., and M. P. Sikes. 1994. *Living with Racism: The Black Middle-Class Experience*. Boston: Beacon Press.

Fein, D. J. 1990. Racial and Ethnic Differences in U.S. Census Omission Rates. *Demography* 27 (2): 285–302.

Filer, R. K. 1992. The Effect of Immigrant Arrivals on Migratory Patterns of Native Workers. In *Immigration and the Work Force: Economic Consequences for the United Sates and Source Areas*, G. J. Borjas and R. B. Freeman, eds.: 245–69. Chicago: University of Chicago Press.

Finnan, C. R., and R. Cooperstein. 1983. *Southeast Asian Refugee Resettlement at the Local Level*. Menlo Park, CA: SRI International.

Fitzpatrick, J. P. 1980. Puerto Ricans. In *Harvard Encyclopedia of American Ethnic Groups*, S. Thernstrom, A. Orlov, and O. Handlin, eds.: 858–67. Cambridge, MA: Harvard University Press.

Fogelson, R. M. 1965. *The Fragmented Metropolis: Los Angeles, 1850–1930*. Berkeley: University of California Press.

———. 1967. *The Fragmented Metropolis: Los Angeles, 1850–1930*. Berkeley: University of California Press.

Fong, T. P. 1994. *The First Suburban Chinatown: The Remaking of Monterey Park, California*. Philadelphia: Temple University Press.

Foster, R. D. 1990. A Clash of Cultures, Cambodian-Style. *Los Angeles Times*[a], September 20: E15A, D.

Frank, E. R. 1955. *Background for Planning*. Los Angeles: Welfare Planning Council, Los Angeles Region.

Franklin, R. L. 1983. Ethnicity and an Emerging Indochinese Commercial District in Orange County. *Yearbook of the Association of Pacific Coast Geographers* 45: 85–99.

Frey, W. H. 1995a. Immigration Impacts on Internal Migration of the Poor: 1990 Census Evidence for US States. *International Journal of Population Geography* 1 (1): 51–67.

———. 1995b. Migration of Latinos, Asians and Blacks: Toward Assimilation or Balkanization? Paper presented at the annual meeting of the Association of American Geographers, Chicago.

———. 1996. Immigration, Domestic Migration, and Demographic Balkanization in America: New Evidence for the 1990s. *Population and Development Review* 22 (4): 741–763.

Frisbie, W. P., and L. Neidert. 1977. Inequality and the Relative Size of Minority Populations: A Comparative Analysis. *American Journal of Sociology* 82 (5): 1007–30.

Fugita, S. S., and D. J. O'Brien. 1991. *Japanese American Ethnicity: The Persistence of Community*. Seattle: University of Washington Press.

Gabler, N. 1988. *An Empire of Their Own: How the Jews Invented Hollywood*. New York: Crown Publishers.

Galster, G. C., and S. Hornburg. 1995. Access to Opportunity: Understanding Its Influence on Urban Lives. *Housing Policy Debate* (U.S. Office of Housing Research, Fannie Mae) 6 (1): 1–297.

Garcia, M. T. 1994. *Memories of Chicano History: The Life and Narrative of Bert Corona*. Berkeley: University of California Press.

Garreau, J. 1991. *Edge City: Life on the New Frontier*. New York: Doubleday.

Gil, V. E. 1976. The Personal Adjustment and Acculturation of Cuban Immigrants in Los Angeles. Ph.D. dissertation, University of California, Los Angeles.

Gill, A., and S. Long. 1989. Is There an Immigration Status Wage Differential between Legal and Undocumented Workers?: Evidence from the Los Angeles Garment Industry. *Social Science Quarterly* 70 (1): 164–73.

Givens, H. L. 1939. The Korean Community in Los Angeles County. M.A. thesis, University of Southern California.

Glass, J., M. Tienda, and S. A. Smith. 1988. The Impact of Changing Employment Opportunity on Gender and Ethnic Earnings. *Social Science Research* 17 (3): 252–76.

Gold, S. 1992. *Refugee Communities: A Comparative Field Study.* Newbury Park, CA: Sage Publications:

———. 1994a. Chinese-Vietnamese Entrepreneurs in California. In *The New Asian Immigration in Los Angeles and Global Restructuring*, P. Ong, E. Bonacich, and L. Cheng, eds.: 196–226. Philadelphia: Temple University Press.

———. 1994b. Patterns of Economic Cooperation among Israeli Immigrants in Los Angeles. *International Migration Review* 28 (1): 114–35.

Gold, S. J. 1992. *Refugee Communities: A Comparative Field Study.* Newbury Park, CA: Sage Publications.

———. 1995. Gender and Social Capital among Israeli Immigrants in Los Angeles. *Diaspora* 4 (3): 267–301.

Gonzalez , G. G. 1989/1990. "The Mexican Has Played the Role of . . . Atlas": Mexican Communities in Orange County, 1850–1990. *Journal of Orange County Studies* 3/4 : 19–27.

———. 1994. *Labor and Community: Mexican Citrus Worker Villages in a Southern California County, 1900-1950.* Urbana and Chicago: University of Illinois Press.

Goodman, A. 1989. On Palos Verdes Peninsula: Asian Buyers Fuel Boom in Real Estate. *Los Angeles Times*[a], March 4: III18, 19.

Gordon, L. 1985. New Church Is Source of Pride for Armenians. *Los Angeles Times*[a], April 21: III13.

Gordon, M. M. 1964. *Assimilation in American Life: The Role of Race, Religion, and National Origins.* New York: Oxford University Press.

Gottdiener, M., and G. Kephart. 1991. The Multinucleated Metropolitan Region: A Comparative Analysis. In *Postsuburban California: The Transformation of Orange County since World War II*, R. Kling, S. Olin, and M. Poster, eds.: 31–54. Berkeley: University of California Press.

Gottlieb, R., and I. Wolt. 1977. *Thinking Big: The Story of the Los Angeles Times, Its Publishers and Their Influence on Southern California.* New York: G. P. Putnam's Sons.

Grant, D. M., M. L. Oliver, and A. D. James. 1996. African Americans: Social and Economic Bifurcation. In *Ethnic Los Angeles*, R. Waldinger and M. Bozorgmehr, eds.: 379–411. New York: Russell Sage Foundation.

Grebler, L., J. W. Moore, and R. C. Guzman. 1970. *The Mexican American People: The Nation's Second Largest Minority.* New York: The Free Press.

Greenwood, R. S. 1994. News from the Underground: History and Archeology Meet at the Station. In *Origins and Destinations: 41 Essays on Chinese America*, S. Mu, ed.: 477–82. Los Angeles: Chinese Historical Society of Southern California and UCLA Asian American Studies Center.

Grigsby, J. E. 1994. African American Mobility and Residential Quality in Los Angeles. In *Residential Apartheid: The American Legacy*, R. D. Bullard, J. E. Grigsby, and C. Lee, eds.: 122–149. Los Angeles: Center for Afro-American Studies, University of California, Los Angeles.

Haiek, J. R. 1992. *Arab-American Almanac* 4th ed. Glendale, CA: News Circle Publishing House.

Hamilton, D. 1986. Filipinos Bring a New, Exotic Touch to Eagle Rock. *Los Angeles Times*[a], May 11: S9.

Hamilton, N., and N. S. Chinchilla. 1991. Central American Migration: A Framework for Analysis. *Latin American Research Review* 26 (1): 75–110.

Hansen, A. A. 1983. *Shosha* Spouses Speak Up: The American Sojourn of Wives in the Japanese Business Community of Orange County. In *Second Lives: The Contemporary Immigrant/Refugee Experience in Orange County: The Shaping of a Multi-Ethnic Community*, V. Smith and M. B. Dixon, eds.: 93–96. Costa Mesa, CA: South Coast Repertory.

Hanson, E., and P. Beckett. 1944. *Los Angeles: Its People and Its Homes.* Los Angeles: Haynes Foundation.

Harris, S. 1992. Little India. *Los Angeles Times*[a], September 1: B1, 7.

Harrison, B., and B. Bluestone. 1988. *The Great U-Turn: Corporate Restructuring and the Polarizing of America.* New York: Basic Books.

Harrison, R. J., and C. E. Bennett. 1995. Racial and Ethnic Diversity. In *State of the Union: America in the 1990s.* Vol 2, *Social Trends*, R. Farley, ed.: 141–210. New York: Russell Sage Foundation.

Hartsfield-Mills, A. B. 1973. *The Old Stentorians*. Los Angeles: published by the author, at 8745 S. Harvard Boulevard, Los Angeles, CA.

Hebert, R. 1972. The Hidden City behind Chinatown's Facade. *Los Angeles Times*[a], November 26: B1, 5.

Heer, D. M. 1966. Negro–White Marriage in the U.S. *Journal of Marriage and the Family* 28 (3): 262–73.

Hensley, D. G. 1989. The Effects of Mexican Immigration to Los Angeles on the Wages of Native Workers. Ph.D. dissertation, University of California, Los Angeles.

Hernandez, E., Jr. 1994. Puerto Ricans: One of L.A.'s Best-Kept Secrets. *Los Angeles Times*[a], October 30: B14.

Hernandez, M. 1984. Kanjobal Indians: Guatemala to L.A.—Bid for Survival. *Los Angeles Times*[a], September 24: I1, 3, 12.

Hiestand, D. L. 1964. *Economic Growth and Employment Opportunities for Minorities*. New York: Columbia University Press.

Hing, B. O. 1993. *Making and Remaking Asian America through Immigration Policy, 1850-1990*. Stanford, CA: Stanford University Press.

Hinojosa-Ojeda, R., M. Carnoy, and H. Daley. 1991. An Even Greater "U-Turn": Latinos and the New Inequality. In *Hispanics in the Labor Force: Issues and Policies*, E. Melendez, C. Rodriguez, and J. B. Figueroa, eds.: 25–52. New York: Plenum Press.

Hirabayashi, L. R., and G. Tanaka. 1988. The Issei Community in Moneta and the Gardena Valley, 1900–1920. *Southern California Quarterly* 70 (1): 127–58.

Hise, G. 1993. Home Building and Industrial Decentralization in Los Angeles: The Roots of the Postwar Urban Region. *Journal of Urban History* 19 (2): 95–125.

Ho, C. G. T. 1993. The Internationalization of Kinship and the Feminization of Caribbean Migration: The Case of Afro-Trinidadian Immigrants in Los Angeles. *Human Organization* 52 (1): 32–40.

Holley, D. 1981. Armenian Enclave Finds Prosperity in Glendale. *Los Angeles Times* (Glendale/Burbank edition), August 23: IX: 1, 8.

Horne, G. 1995. *Fire This Time: The Watts Uprising and the 1960s*. Charlottesville: University Press of Virginia.

Horton, J. 1992. The Politics of Diversity in Monterey Park, California. In *Structuring Diversity: Ethnographic Perspectives on the New Immigration*, L. Lamphere, ed.: 215–45. Chicago: University of Chicago Press.

Huling, W. E. 1978. Aging Blacks in Suburbia: Patterns of Culture Reflected in the Social Organization of a California Community. Ph.D. dissertation, University of Southern California.

Huynh, C. 1996. Vietnamese-Owned Manicure Businesses in Los Angeles. In *Reframing the Immigration Debate: A Public Policy Report*, B. O. Hing and R. Lee, eds.: 195–203. Los Angeles: Leadership Education for Asian Pacifics (LEAP) and UCLA Asian American Studies Center.

Jacobs, T. 1977. *Hawaiian Gardens: An Informal History*. Hawaiian Gardens: Gale Brandon and Associates.

Jain, U. R. 1989. *The Gujaratis of San Francisco*. New York: AMS Press.

Janes, C. R. 1990. *Migration, Social Change, and Health: A Samoan Community in Urban California*. Stanford, CA: Stanford University Press.

Jasso, G., and M. R. Rosenzweig. 1986. Family Reunification and the Immigration Multiplier: U.S. Immigration Law, Origin-Country Conditions, and the Reproduction of Immigrants. *Demography* 23 (3): 291–311.

Johnson, T. 1996. Cash in Hand. *Los Angeles Times*[a], June 28: E1, 3, 4.

Kang, K. C. 1996. Filipinos Happy in U.S., but Lack a United Voice. *Los Angeles Times*[a], January 26: A1, 20.

Kaplan, S. H. 1989. Sensitivity Needed to Retain Fairfax Area's Sense of Place. *Los Angeles Times*[a], December 17: K2.

Kaplan, T. 1989. Seoul of the Valley. *Los Angeles Times*[a], October 22: B3, 8.

———. 1990. Bending Like a Bamboo. *Los Angeles Times*[a], February 3: B3, 8.

Kelley, R. 1993. Wealth and Illusions of Wealth in the Los Angeles Iranian Community. In *Irangeles: Iranians in Los Angeles*, R. Kelley and J. Friedlander, eds.: 247–73. Berkeley: University of California Press.

———. 1994. Muslims in Los Angeles. In *Muslim Communities in North America*, Y. Y. Hadded and J. I. Smith, eds.: 135–67. Albany: State University of New York Press.

Kelley, R., and J. Friedlander, eds. 1993. *Irangeles: Iranians in Los Angeles*. Berkeley: University of California Press.

Kiernan, B. 1990. Cambodian Genocide. *Far Eastern Economic Review*, March 1: 18.

Kim, E. H., and E-Y. Yu. 1996. *East to America: Korean American Life Stories*. New York: The New Press.

Kim, H. H. 1986. Residential Patterns and Mobility of Koreans in Los Angeles County. M.A. thesis, California State University, Los Angeles.

Kim, R., K. K. Nakamura, and G. Fong. 1992. Asian Immigrant Women Garment Workers in Los Angeles. *Amerasia Journal* 18 (1): 69–82.

Kimble, B. 1989. *Impact of Soviet Armenian Immigration in Los Angeles County*. Report of the Commission on Human Relations, County of Los Angeles, April 10.

Kitano, H. H. L. 1988. The Japanese American Family. In *Ethnic Families in America: Patterns and Variations*, D. H. Mindel, R. W. Habenstein, and R. Wright, Jr., eds.: 258–75. New York: Elsevier Science Publishing.

Klein, N. M., and M. J. Schiesl, eds. 1990. *20th Century Los Angeles: Power, Promotion, and Social Conflict*. Claremont, CA: Regina Books.

Kling, R., S. Olin, and M. Poster. 1991. The Emergence of Postsuburbia: An Introduction. In *Postsuburban California: The Transformation of Orange County since World War II*, R. Kling, S. Olin, and M. Poster, eds.: 1–30. Berkeley: University of California Press.

Kosmin, B. A., and J. Scheckner. 1991. Jewish Population in the United States, 1990. In *The American Jewish Yearbook, 1991*, D. Singer and R. R. Seldin, eds., 204–24. New York and Philadelphia: American Jewish Committee and Jewish Publication Society.

Kotchek, L. 1978. Migrant Samoan Churches: Adaptation, Preservation, and Division. In *New Neighbors: Islanders in Adaptation*, B. Shore and R. Franco, eds.: 286–93. Santa Cruz: University of California, Center for South Pacific Studies.

Kotkin, J. 1992. *Tribes: How Race, Religion, and Identity Determine Success in the New Global Economy*. New York: Random House.

Krislov, S. 1967. *The Negro in Federal Employment: The Quest for Equal Opportunity*. Minneapolis: University of Minnesota Press.

Kwik, G. 1978. The Indos of Southern California: A Preliminary Study of Ethnicity and Assimilation among Refugee-Immigrants. Ph.D. dissertation, Syracuse University.

La Brack, B. 1988. *The Sikhs of Northern California: 1904-1975*. New York: AMS Press.

LaLonde, R. J., and R. H. Topel. 1992. The Assimilation of Immigrants in the U.S. Labor Market. In *Immigration and the Work Force: Economic Consequences for the United States and Source Areas*, G. J. Borjas and R. B. Freeman, eds.: 67–92. Chicago: University of Chicago Press.

Lee, D. O. 1992. Commodification of Ethnicity: The Sociospatial Reproduction of Immigrant Entrepreneurs. *Urban Affairs Quarterly* 28 (2): 258–75.

Lee, E. S. 1966. A Theory of Migration. *Demography* 3 (1): 47–57.

Lee, G. L. 1996. Cambodian-Owned Donut Shops. In *Reframing the Immigration Debate: A Public Policy Report*, B. O. Hing and R. Lee, eds.: 205–219. Los Angeles: Leadership Education for Asian Pacifics (LEAP) and UCLA Asian American Studies Center.

Leonard, K. B., and C. S. Tibrewal. 1993. Asian Indians in Southern California. In *Immigration and Entrepreneurship: Culture, Capital, and Ethnic Networks*, I. Light and P. Bhachu, eds.: 141–57. New Brunswick, NJ: Transaction Publishers.

Levy, F. 1987. *Dollars and Dreams: The Changing American Income Distribution*. New York: Russell Sage Foundation.

———. 1995. Incomes and Income Inequality. In *State of the Union: America in the 1990s*. Vol. 1, *Economic Trends*, R. Farley, ed.: 10–57. New York: Russell Sage Foundation.

Levy, F., and R. J. Murnane. 1992. U. S. Earnings Levels and Earnings Inequality: A Review of Recent Trends and Proposed Explanations. *Journal of Economic Literature* 30 (3): 1337–81.

Lewthwaite, G. R., C. Mainzer, and P. J. Holland. 1973. From Polynesia to California: Samoan Migration and Its Sequel. *Journal of Pacific History* 8 : 133–57.

Lieberson, S. 1975. Rank-Sum Comparisons between Groups. In *Sociological Methodology 1976*, D. R. Heise, ed.: 276–91. San Francisco: Jossey-Bass.

Lieberson, S., and M. C. Waters. 1988. *From Many Strands: Ethnic and Racial Groups in Contemporary America*. New York: Russell Sage Foundation.

Light, I., and E. Bonacich. 1988. *Immigrant Entrepreneurs: Koreans in Los Angeles, 1965-1982*. Berkeley: University of California Press.

Light, I., P. Bhachu, and S. Karageorgis. 1993. Migration Networks and Immigrant Entrepreneurship. In *Immigration and Entrepreneurship: Culture, Capital, and Ethnic Networks*, I. Light and P. Bhachu, eds.: 25–49. New Brunswick, NJ: Transaction Publishers.

Light, I., G. Sabagh, M. Bozorgmehr, and C. Der-Martirosian. 1993. Internal Ethnicity in the Ethnic Economy. *Ethnic and Racial Studies* 16 (4): 581–97.

Lin, I. 1996. Journey to the Far West: Chinese Buddhism in America. *Amerasia Journal* 22 (1): 107–32.

Lin, P. 1989/1990. Perspectives on the Chinese in Nineteenth-Century Orange County. *Journal of Orange County Studies* 3/4 : 28–36.

Liu, J. M. 1989/1990. A Centennial Retrospective of the Asian American Legacy in Orange County. *Journal of Orange County Studies* 3/4 : 37–45.

Liu, J. M. and L. Cheng. 1994. Pacific Rim Development and the Duality of Post-1965 Asian Immigration to the United States. In *The New Asian Immigration in Los Angeles and Global Restructuring*, P. Ong, E. Bonacich, and L. Cheng, eds.: 74-99. Philadelphia, PA: Temple University Press.

Liu, J. M., P. M. Ong, and C. Rosenstein. 1991. Dual Chain Migration: Post-1965 Filipino Immigration to the United States. *International Migration Review* 25 (3): 487–513.

Logan, J., R. D. Alba, and T. L. McNulty. 1994. Ethnic Economies in Metropolitan Regions: Miami and Beyond. *Social Forces* 72 (3): 691–724.

Lopez, R. J. 1994. From Earliest Days, Change Has Come Slowly for Residents of Watts. *Los Angeles Times^a*, July 20: B13.

Lorch, D. 1992. Ethnic Niches Creating Jobs That Fuel Immigrant Growth. *New York Times,* January 12: 1, 14.

Los Angeles Department of City Planning. 1991. *1990 Census— Preliminary Results.* Report of 8 April. Los Angeles: Department of City Planning.

Lothrop, G. R. 1986. The Bittersweet Tale of Los Angeles and Her Jews. *The Californians* 4 (2): 24–25.

———. 1988. *Pomona: A Centennial History.* Northridge, CA: Windsor Publications.

———. 1994. *Los Angeles Profiles: A Tribute to the Ethnic Diversity of Los Angeles.* Los Angeles: Historical Society of Southern California.

Lou, R. 1990. Chinese-American Agricultural Workers and the Anti-Chinese Movement in Los Angeles, 1870–1890. In *Labor Divided: Race and Ethnicity in United States Labor Struggles, 1835-1960,* R. Asher and C. Stephenson, eds.: 49–62. Albany: State University of New York Press.

Maldonado, E. 1979. Contract Labor and the Origins of Puerto Rican Communities in the United States. *International Migration Review* 13 (1): 103–21.

Marchand, B. 1986. *The Emergence of Los Angeles, 1940-1970: Population and Housing in the City of Dreams.* London: Pion Limited.

Martin, H. E. 1979. *History of the Los Angeles County Hospital (1878-1968) and the Los Angeles County-University of Southern California Medical Center (1968-1978).* Los Angeles: University of Southern California Press.

Mason, W. 1967. The Chinese in Los Angeles. *Museum Alliance Quarterly* (Los Angeles County Museum of Natural History) 6 (2): 15–20.

Mason, W. M., and J. Anderson. 1969. Los Angeles Black Heritage. *Museum Alliance Quarterly* (Los Angeles County Museum of Natural History) 8 (2): 4–9.

Mason, W. M., and J. A. McKinstry. 1969. *The Japanese of Los Angeles.* Los Angeles: Los Angeles County Museum of Natural History.

Massey, D. S. 1985. Ethnic Residential Segregation: A Theoretical Synthesis and Empirical Review. *Sociology and Social Research* 69 (3): 315–50.

Massey, D. S., and N. A. Denton. 1993. *American Apartheid: Segregation and the Making of the Underclass.* Cambridge, MA: Harvard University Press.

Massey, D. S., J. Arango, G. Hugo, A. Kouaouci, A Pellegrino, and J. E. Taylor. 1994. An Evaluation of International Migration Theory: The North American Case. *Population and Development Review* 20 (4): 699–751.

Masud-Piloto, F. R. 1996. *From Welcomed Exiles to Illegal Immigrants: Cuban Migration to the U.S., 1959-1995.* Lanham, MD: Rowman & Littlefield Publishers.

McBane, M. 1995. The Role of Gender in Citrus Employment: A Case Study of Recruitment, Labor, and Housing Patterns at the Limoneira Company, 1893 to 1940. *California History* 74 (1): 68–81.

McCarthy, K. F., and R. B. Valdez. 1986. *Current and Future Effects of Mexican Immigration to California.* Report R–3365–CR. Santa Monica, CA: Rand Corporation.

McDannold, T. A. 1973. Development of the Los Angeles Chinatown: 1850–1970. M.A. thesis, California State University, Northridge.

McEuen, W. W. 1914. A Survey of the Mexicans in Los Angeles. M.A. thesis, University of Southern California.

McGee, H. W., Jr. 1991. Afro-American Resistance to Gentrification and the Demise of Integrationist Ideology in the United States. *The Urban Lawyer* 23 (1): 25–44.

McKenny, N., C. Bennett, R. Harrison, and J. del Pinal. 1993. Evaluating Racial and Ethnic Reporting in the 1990 Census. *Proceedings of the Section on Social Science* (American Statistical Association) 88 (423): 65–74.

McMillan, P. 1982. Vietnamese Influx: It's Chinatown, with Subtitles. *Los Angeles Times^a*, February 14: I11.

———. 1990. Newcomers Changing Face of Chinatown. *Los Angeles Times^a*, January 28: B1, 11.

McWilliams, C. [1946] 1973. *Southern California Country: An Island on the Land.* New York: Duell, Sloan, & Pearce. Reprinted as *Southern California: An Island on the Land.* Salt Lake City: Peregrine Smith Books.

McWilliams, C. [1948] 1968. *North From Mexico: The Spanish-Speaking People of the United States.* New York: Greenwood Press.

Menchaca, M. 1995. *The Mexican Outsiders: A Community History of Marginalization and Discrimination in California.* Austin: University of Texas Press.

Michaelson, J., and R. E. Meyer. 1982. L.A.'s Japanese-Americans: Breaking into the Mainstream. *Los Angeles Times*[a], April 19: III, 5, 7, 8, 12.

Miller, L. R. 1992. Bridges: Garifuna Migration to Los Angeles. Ph.D. dissertation, University of California, Irvine.

Millican, A. 1991. Samoans Speak Out. *Los Angeles Times*[a] (South Bay edition), October 13: B3.

Min, P. G. 1991. Culture and Economic Boundaries of Korean Ethnicity: A Comparative Analysis. *Ethnic and Racial Studies* 14 (2): 225–41.

———. 1993. Korean Immigrants in Los Angeles. In *Immigration and Entrepreneurship: Culture, Capital, and Ethnic Networks*, I. Light and P. Bhachu, eds.: 185–204. New Brunswick, NJ: Transaction Publishers.

Minasian, E. 1982. *The Armenian Community of California: The First One Hundred Years*. Los Angeles: Armenian Assembly Resource Center.

Mitchell, J. L. 1990. Iranian Jews Find a Beverly Hills Refuge. *Los Angeles Times*[a], February 13: B5, 6.

Modell, J. 1977. *The Economics and Politics of Racial Accommodation: The Japanese of Los Angeles, 1900-1942*. Urbana: University of Illinois Press.

Moffat, S. 1994a. No Longer an Island: Economic Woes, Crime Fears Encroach upon Cloister of Southland's Japanese Nationals. *Los Angeles Times*[a], April 4: B8, 9.

———. 1994b. A Paradise Lost, Never Forgotten. *Los Angeles Times*[a], January 5: A1, 12, 13.

Mohan, G. 1994. Pacoima: Joe Louis Homes Gave Hope for Housing. *Los Angeles Times*[a], February 22, B2.

Moore, J., and J. D. Vigil. 1993. Barrios in Transition. In *In the Barrios: Latinos and the Underclass Debate*, J. Moore and R. Pinderhughes, eds.: 27–49. New York: Russell Sage Foundation.

Morales, R. 1983. Transitional Labor: Undocumented Workers in the Los Angeles Automobile Industry. *International Migration Review* 17 (4): 570–95.

Morales, R., and P. M. Ong. 1993. The Illusion of Progress. Latinos in Los Angeles. In *Latinos in a Changing Economy: Comparative Perspectives on Growing Inequality*, R. Morales and F. Bonilla, eds.: 55–84. Newbury Park, CA: Sage Publications.

Morales, R. F. 1974. *Makibaka: The Pilipino American Struggle*. Los Angeles: Mountainview Publishers.

Mossain, M. 1982. South Asians in Southern California: A Sociological Study of Immigrants from India, Pakistan, and Bangladesh. *South Asia Bulletin* 2 (1): 74–83.

Mott, P. 1989. Little Saigon: Immigrants Cling to Culture While Adapting to a New, Fast Way of Life. *Los Angeles Times*[a], February 13: IX1.

———. 1990. Powwow Will Unite Dozens of Tribes. *Los Angeles Times*[a], August 16: E13.

Moss, R. 1996. Not Quite Paradise: The Development of the African American Community in Los Angeles through 1950. *California History* 75 (3): 222–235.

Mulholland, C. 1987. *The Owensmouth Baby: The Making of a San Fernando Valley Town*. Northridge, CA: Santa Susana Press.

Myers, D. 1990. Filtering in Time: Rethinking the Longitudinal Behavior of Neighborhood Housing Markets. In *Housing Demography: Linking Demographic Structure and Housing Markets*, D. Myers, ed.: 274–96. Madison: University of Wisconsin Press.

———. 1995. *The Changing Immigrants of Southern California*. Los Angeles: School of Urban and Regional Planning, University of Southern California.

Nagel, J. 1995. Resource Competition Theories. *American Behavioral Scientist* 38 (3): 442–58.

Nee, V., J. M. Sanders, and S. Sernau. 1994. Job Transitions in an Immigrant Metropolis: Ethnic Boundaries and the Mixed Economy. *American Sociological Review* 59 (6): 849–72.

Neidert, L. J., and R. Farley. 1985. Assimilation in the United States: An Analysis of Ethnic and Generational Differences in Status. *American Sociological Review* 50 (6): 840–49.

Nelson, H. J. 1959. The Spread of an Artificial Landscape over Southern California. *Annals of the Association of American Geographers* 49 (3, special suppl.): 80–100.

———. 1983. *The Los Angeles Metropolis*. Dubuque, IA: Kendall/Hunt Publishing Co.

Newmark, H. [1916] 1970. *Sixty Years in Southern California, 1853-1913*. Los Angeles: Zeitlin & Ver Brugge.

Ngin, C. S. 1989/1990. The Acculturation Pattern of Orange County's Southeast Asian Refugees. *Journal of Orange County Studies* 3/4: 46–53.

Nielsen, J. 1984. Modern Pilgrims Give Thanks for U.S. Sanctuary. *Los Angeles Times*[a], November 23: II8, 10.

Nishi, M. 1958. Japanese Settlement in the Los Angeles Area. *Yearbook of the Association of Pacific Coast Geographers* 20: 35–48.

———. 1985. Japanese Americans. In *Ethnicity in Contemporary America: A Geographical Appraisal*, J. O, McKee, ed.: 169–93. Dubuque, IA: Kendall/Hunt.

Nishi, M., and Y. I. Kim. 1964. Recent Japanese Settlement Changes in the Los Angeles Area. *Yearbook of the Association of Pacific Coast Geographers* 26: 23–36.

O'Conner, C. 1989. Nailing It: In Mini-Malls across the Valley, Vietnamese Refugees Find Their Niche as Manicurists. *Los Angeles Times*[a], June 8: V20, 23.

O'Neill, J. 1990. The Role of Human Capital in Earnings Differences between Black and White Men. *Journal of Economic Perspectives* 4 (4): 25–45.

Oliver, M. T. 1992. Quiet L. A. Neighborhood in Eye of Storm. *Los Angeles Times*[a], August 30: K2, 4, 5.

Olzak, S., and J. Nagel. 1986. *Competitive Ethnic Relations.* New York: Academic Press.

Omi, M. and H. Winant. 1986. *Racial Formation in the United States: From the 1960s to the 1980s.* New York: Routledge and Kegan Paul.

Ong. P. 1990. Uncertain Economic Progress: Racial Inequality among Californian Males, 1940–1980. In *Income and Status Differences between White and Minority Americans: A Persistent Inequality*, S. Chan, ed.: 29–55. Lewiston, PA: Edwin Mellen Press.

Ong, P., ed. 1993. *Beyond Asian American Poverty: Community Economic Development Policies and Strategies.* Los Angeles: Leadership Education for Asian Pacifics.

Ong, P., and T. Azores. 1994. The Migration and Incorporation of Filipino Nurses. In *The New Asian Immigration in Los Angeles and Global Restructuring*, P. Ong, E. Bonacich, and L. Cheng, eds.: 164–95. Philadelphia: Temple University Press.

Ong, P., and J. M. Liu. 1994. U.S. Immigration Policies and Asian Migration. In *The New Asian Immigration in Los Angeles and Global Restructuring*, P. Ong, E. Bonacich, and L. Cheng, eds.: 45–73. Philadelphia, PA: Temple University Press.

Ong, P., and A. Valenzuela, Jr. 1996. The Labor Market: Immigrant Effects and Racial Disparities. In *Ethnic Los Angeles*, R. Waldinger and M. Bozorgmehr, eds.: 165–91. New York: Russell Sage Foundation.

Panunzio, C. 1942. Intermarriage in Los Angeles, 1924–1933. *American Journal of Sociology* 47 (5): 690–701.

Park, S. 1984. Settlement Patterns: Residential Distribution and Mobility. In *Korean Immigrants in America: A Structural Analysis of Ethnic Confinement and Adhesive Adaptation*, W. M. Hurh and K. C. Kim, eds.: 61–68. Cranbury, NJ: Associated University Presses.

Parsons, R. 1993. Cooks' Walks: Fairfax. *Los Angeles Times*[a], May 20: H10, 11.

Passel, J. S., and K. A. Woodrow. 1984. Geographic Distribution of Undocumented Immigrants: Estimates of Undocumented Aliens Counted in the 1980 Census by State. *International Migration Review* 18 (3): 642–71.

Peñalosa , F. 1963. Class Consciousness and Social Mobility in a Mexican-American Community. Ph.D. dissertation, University of Southern California.

———. 1986. Trilingualism in the Barrio: Mayan Indians in Los Angeles. *Language Problems and Language Planning* 10 (3): 229–52.

Peters, G. L. 1987. Migration Decision-making among the Vietnamese in Southern California. *Sociology and Social Research* 71 (4): 280–86.

Peters, G. L., and K. H. Chen. 1987. Vietnamese Refugees in Long Beach, California. *Sociology and Social Research* 71 (3): 231–37.

Peterson, J. 1989. Filipinos—A Search for Community. *Los Angeles Times*[a], May 24: A1, 14.

Phillips, B. A. 1986. Los Angeles Jewry: A Demographic Portrait. In *American Jewish Yearbook, 1986*, M. Himmelfarb and D. Singer, eds.: 126–93. New York: American Jewish Committee, and Philadelphia: Jewish Publication Society of America.

Portes, A., and R. G. Rumbaut. 1990. *Immigrant America: A Portrait.* Berkeley: University of California Press.

Portes, A., and R. Schauffler. 1994. Language and the Second Generation: Bilingualism Yesterday and Today. *International Migration Review* 38 (4): 640–61.

Price, J. A. 1968. The Migration and Adaptation of American Indians to Los Angeles. *Human Organization* 27 (2): 167–75.

Pulskamp, J. R. 1990. Intertribal Powwows in the Greater Los Angeles Area. Research paper, Department of Geography, California State University, Northridge.

Quinsaat, J. G. 1976. How to Join the Navy and Still Not See the World. In *Letters in Exile: An Introductory Reader on the History of Pilipinos in America*, J. Quinsaat, ed.: 96–111. Los Angeles: UCLA Asian American Studies Center.

Rasmussen, C. 1993. L. A. Scene: The City Then and Now. *Los Angeles Times*[a], August 30: B9. Reprinted as "Chinatown's Saga as an Urban Enclave" in Rasmussen, C. 1995. *L. A. Scene: The Southland Then and Now*: 22–23. Los Angeles: Los Angeles Times.

Ray, M. E. B. 1985. *The City of Watts, California: 1907-1926.* Los Angeles: Rising Publishing.

Index

A

accountant, 193, 204, 211–212

acculturation, xi, 6–7, 9, 74, 86, 92, 108, 110, 112, 122, 149, 170–171, 175–176, 178, 199, 222, 230, 245–248, 250–255, 259–260

actor, 211–212

adjusted median-income ratios, 190

aerospace industry, 46, 113, 152, 154, 168, 185, 193, 195, 211–212, 226

affirmative action, 168, 179, 198, 209

Afghans, xiv

African Americans. *See* blacks

Africans, xiv, 4, 8, 81, 84–85, 154, 246–247. *See also* Nigerians, South Africans

age of housing, 14

age of population, 3–4, 10, 14, 32–34, 39, 113, 115, 173, 175, 180, 182, 188–189, 191–192, 194, 197, 199–200, 249, 252–254, 257

agricultural workers. *See* farmworkers

agriculture. *See* farming

aircraft industry, 11–12, 48, 80, 83, 91, 157, 193, 206, 214, 216, 220–221

Alameda Street, 12, 78–79, 94–96, 108, 120

Aleuts, xiv

Algerian ancestry, 71

Alhambra, 94, 114, 121–122, 163

Alien Land Laws, 126, 152, 202

Alondra Park, 243

Altadena, 72, 83, 86

Alvarado Street, 110, 146

American Indians, 10, 34, 41, 87, 90–92, 94, 96, 98–99, 108, 110, 112, 114, 116, 118, 204, 223, 243–246, 249–250, 252, 260

American Samoans, 161–162

Anaheim, 18, 72, 97, 116, 127, 152, 158, 247

Anaheim Hills, 116, 152

Anglos, 4, 8, 69–70, 94, 96, 109, 116

Antelope Valley, 14

Apache, 91

apparel industry, 12, 18, 185, 194, 197, 206, 211–212, 214, 216–218, 220–221, 223, 226

Arab ancestry, 57, 71–72, 88, 154, 232, 246

Arcadia, 82, 163

Argentineans, 115, 207–208, 221

Arleta, 72, 147, 247

Armenian ancestry, 4, 18, 20, 39, 58, 71–76, 88, 207–208, 215–216, 222, 232, 244, 246

Artesia, 97–98, 153–154, 161, 165–166

Asian Indians, 84, 151–153, 163, 209, 223, 231, 245, 249, 255–256

assembler, 194, 204, 211–212, 214

assimilation, xi, 6–7, 9, 38, 76, 86, 91–92, 110, 112–113, 169, 238, 245. *See also* acculturation, structural assimilation

Assyrian ancestry, xiv, 74–75, 88

Atwater Village, 111

Avalon, 15

Azusa, 76, 109

B

Bahais, 74–76

Bahraini ancestry, 71

bakeries, 96, 149, 156, 218, 222

Baldwin Hills, 82

Baldwin, Lucky, 82–83, 89

Baldwin Park, 108

Bangladeshi, xiv, 151, 165

banking industry, 216–222, 225

Banning, 90, 159

Baptists, 91

barrios, 16, 45, 94, 96–98, 110, 114–116, 243, 245, 247–248, 254

Basilone Homes, 83

Bel Air, 69, 125

Belizean ancestry, 63, 84–85, 89, 208, 217, 223

Bell, 79, 92, 94, 108, 247

Bell Gardens, 79, 92, 108, 247

Bellflower, 72, 160

Belmont Shore, 17

Belvedere, 95, 108, 254

Bengalis. *See* Bangladeshi

Beverly Hills, 17, 50, 69–70, 75–76, 88, 110, 122, 125, 248

birth rates. *See* fertility

Bixby Knolls, 17, 46, 48

Blackfoot, 91

Blacks, 1, 4, 8, 16, 34, 40, 43–46, 66–68, 77–86, 89, 93, 95, 112–115, 117, 120, 125, 148, 150, 162, 165, 168–173, 175–176, 179–180, 182–187, 189, 191–193, 195, 197–200, 202–206, 208–210, 212, 217, 227–228, 231–232, 236, 244–247, 251, 253, 255–257, 259

Bolivians, 115

Bolsa Avenue, 77, 156

Boyle Heights, 16, 18, 34, 46, 50, 67–69, 73, 75, 79, 87, 94–95, 108, 110, 115, 125, 127–128, 244, 247, 254

Bradbury, 77

Brazilian ancestry, xiv, 118

Brea, 11, 34, 48, 69

Brentwood, 69, 75, 110, 125, 161, 246, 252

British ancestry, 35, 47, 84, 153. *See also* English ancestry

Buddhists, 122, 125, 128–129, 151, 157–160

Buena Park, 153

Bunker Hill, 14, 34, 41, 116, 146, 148

Burbank, 12, 14, 70, 111, 114

Burma, 120
Burmese, xiv
busboy, 211, 214

C

Cahuilla, 90
Calabasas, 46, 163
California Alien Land Laws, 202
California State Polytechnic University, Pomona, 16, 86
California State University, Long Beach, 16, 158, 166, 228
California State University, Northridge, xiii–xiv, 88–89, 117–118, 157, 163, 165–166
California Supreme Court, 77–79, 253
Californios, 94, 109
Camarillo, 92, 117
Cambodia, 120
Cambodians, 16, 39, 154, 157–159, 166, 222–223, 231, 245, 249, 252, 255–256, 259
Camp Pendleton, 39, 155, 165
Canoga Park, 74, 96, 98, 157, 165, 254
Cantonese, 119–121
Carson, 15, 34, 86, 98, 147, 151, 157, 161–162, 230, 243, 259
Central Americans, 39, 42, 84–85, 92, 105, 109–110, 112–115, 127, 148, 207, 221, 245
Central Avenue, 50, 67, 74, 77–79, 82, 86, 120, 124, 255
Century City, 13, 34, 69
Cerritos, 123, 147–148, 151–154, 160, 163, 165–166, 244, 259
Chaldean. *See* Assyrian ancestry
Chamorros. *See* Guamanians
Chatsworth, 116, 152
Chavez Ravine, 41–42, 116
Cherokee, 91–92
Cheviot Hills, 15, 46, 68–69, 77
Chickasaw, 91
Chileans, 115
China, 10, 35, 37–38, 40, 119–121, 169, 224–225, 257
Chinatown, 94, 120–123, 159, 163, 225–226, 230, 244, 248, 252, 254–255
Chinese, 4, 8, 35, 44–45, 68, 94, 96, 109, 119–124, 126, 129–131, 148, 155–157,

159–164, 169–173, 176, 178–179, 185, 190, 198, 201–203, 205–206, 208–209, 211–212, 214–215, 218, 223–228, 230, 232, 245, 248–249, 252, 255–256
Chinese-Cambodians, 159, 222, 228
Chinese-Indonesians, 161
Chinese-Thais, 159
Chinese-Vietnamese, 39, 121, 123, 155–156, 208–209, 215, 225, 228
Chino, 11, 16, 46, 148, 166
Chippewa, 91
Choctaw, 91–92
Christians, 4, 5, 9, 36, 49–50, 70–72, 74, 87–88, 91, 95, 123, 151, 157, 162, 165, 228.
Chumash, 90
Citrus Belt, 45, 109
citrus groves, 45, 83, 97, 109, 124, 126
city of Orange, 97, 111
City Terrace, 67, 95
civil rights, 168, 257
Claremont, 16, 45, 152; Claremont Colleges, 16
class of employment, 6, 187, 206, 208–209
class, 2–3, 8, 10, 13, 16–18, 74, 76, 78, 80, 84, 116, 122, 167, 187, 200, 206–209, 230, 245, 248, 254, 258–259
clerk, 193, 204, 211–212
CMSA (Consolidated Metropolitan Statistical Area), xii, 193–194
Colima Road, 122
college graduates, 6, 17–18, 27, 154, 169–171, 176, 179, 186–187, 189, 192, 197–200, 245, 250, 256
Colombians, 115, 208, 221
colonias, 94, 96–98, 108–109, 117, 254
Colton, 94
Comanche, 91
Commerce, 96, 108, 207, 243
compartmentalization, 3, 6–7, 248–249, 252
competition, 1, 8, 69, 116, 126, 183, 185, 187, 191, 193, 195, 197–198, 206, 210, 213, 224, 228, 255, 259
Compton, 46, 78, 80, 98, 115, 161, 166, 230
computer industry, 4, 46, 85, 154, 160, 183, 193, 211–212, 225, 244
concentration, geographical. *See* enclave

construction industry, 11–14, 17, 23, 75, 78, 91, 93–96, 110, 116, 120, 124–125, 146–147, 204, 211, 214–221, 223–224, 256
cook, 44, 117, 204, 211, 214
Corona, 93, 98
correlation technique, 250
Costa Mesa, 48
Costa Ricans, 114
Country Club Park, 114, 127, 149
Covina, 86, 108–109, 148, 163, 243
Crenshaw area, 34, 81–82, 86, 114, 120, 127–128, 148, 230, 244, 247, 255
Crenshaw Boulevard, 81–82, 127, 148
Creole Belizeans, 84–85
Cubans, 84, 103, 111–112, 117, 207, 231, 249–250, 260
Cucamunga, 93
Cudahy, 92, 243
cultural assimilation. *See* acculturation
Culver City, 15, 111, 114, 127, 153, 159, 247

D

Dana Point, 76
Dana Strand Village, 18, 34
deconcentration, 13, 40, 46, 76, 112, 128
defense industries, 11, 79–80, 157, 167, 176, 206
demographic, 167–168, 175, 259
developers, 10, 12, 45, 47, 80, 98, 121, 128
Diamond Bar, 47, 122, 148, 151, 161, 163, 244, 252
discrimination, 5, 44, 50, 67, 86–87, 89, 108, 124, 127, 148–149, 167, 171, 176, 178, 183–184, 187, 189, 192, 195, 197–198, 200, 205, 207, 213, 226–227, 257–258
dissimilarity index, 230–232
diversity, 5–7, 10, 17, 41, 43, 109, 116, 119, 130, 148, 152–153, 165, 215, 226, 230, 235, 243–244, 252, 258, 260
doughnut industry, 222
Downey, 11–12, 16, 112, 115, 126
Downtown, Los Angeles, 11–14, 16–18, 34, 45–46, 48–50, 67, 69, 72, 75, 77–79, 86, 92–93, 95, 108–111, 114–118, 130, 146, 148–149, 163, 222, 247
Druze, 71

Duarte, 108–109
durable-goods manufacturing, 75, 206
Dutch Indonesians, 160–161
Dutch, 153, 160–161, 166

E

Eagle Rock, 82, 147
earnings, 180. *See also* income
East Anaheim Street, 158
East Hollywood, 16, 73–74, 88, 111–112, 147, 159–160, 166, 244, 255
East Los Angeles, 34, 47, 93–95, 109–110, 115, 128, 243–244, 247
East Tustin, 48
Eastern European Jews, 46, 49, 67, 95, 222
Eastside, 94–96, 98, 108–110, 115–117, 121, 128, 247–248, 254, 259
Echo Park, 111, 121, 127, 158
Ecuadorans, 115
education, 1–2, 6–7, 17, 47, 70, 74, 76, 92, 152, 167–172, 175–177, 182–183, 185–189, 191–194, 197, 199, 205–206, 209–210, 213–214, 222–223, 226, 256–259
Egyptians, 5, 71
El Hoyo Maravilla, 95
El Monte, 94, 108–109, 126
El Pueblo Historic Park, 93
El Salvador, 39–40, 42, 109–110, 113, 210, 257
El Segundo, 11, 95, 113, 126
elderly, 34, 68–69, 77, 89, 91, 95, 120–121, 127, 129, 146, 149, 224
electronics, 194, 211–212, 214–215
employment, 7, 18, 36, 43–44, 46, 70–71, 77, 85, 91–96, 108–113, 118, 121, 124, 128, 130, 147, 152–154, 156–157, 159, 161–162, 166–168, 171, 176, 178, 182–188, 191, 197–198, 201, 204–209, 213–223, 226–227, 243, 255, 257
Encino, 70, 74–75, 88
enclaves, 12, 37, 43–45, 48, 50, 68–69, 71–72, 76–79, 81–83, 85–86, 88–89, 91–98, 110–112, 114–115, 120–121, 124–125, 127–129, 146–148, 150–152, 156–158, 160–165, 173, 195, 213–214, 222, 230–231, 244, 246–248, 252, 254–255, 259
engineers, 152–154, 160, 193, 204, 211–212, 217–219, 224

English ancestry, 4, 47–49, 54, 190, 208–209, 216, 245, 255
English language, 10, 108, 126, 153, 172, 194, 214, 223, 225, 245–247, 249, 260
English speech, 4, 7, 9, 37, 45, 84, 93, 121, 150, 154, 156, 167, 189, 223, 241, 246–248, 250, 252
entrepreneurs, 75, 110, 128, 150, 153, 157–158, 187–188, 207, 209, 225, 228, 257. *See also* self-employment
entropy index, 243–244, 253
Eskimos, xiv
Ethiopians, xiv
ethnic diversity, 10, 41, 43, 215, 230, 235, 243–244, 252, 260. *See also* diversity
ethnic-identity labels, 8
ethnic niches, work. *See* niches
ethnic transformation, 10, 12, 14, 16, 18, 34, 36, 38, 40–42, 168, 258–259
European ancestries, 4, 37–38, 161, 246, 248
executives, 128, 172, 181, 189, 197, 211–212, 258

F

Fair Housing Act, 44, 78
Fairfax Avenue District, 34, 67–70, 88
farm laborer, 202
farm manager, 202
farming, 11, 45, 86, 93–94, 96–97, 108–109, 126–127, 159, 164, 166, 176, 202–203, 209, 211–212, 254
farmwork, 93, 97, 109, 126, 203, 224
farmworkers, 40, 96–98, 117, 130, 212, 214, 223, 254
Federal Correctional Institution, Terminal Island, 16, 92, 115
fertility, 10, 35, 37, 40–42, 159, 259
Filipino Town, 146
Filipinos, 8, 119, 129–130, 133, 146–148, 162–163, 166, 169–173, 176, 178–179, 181, 202–203, 208, 211–213, 219, 232, 246, 249–252, 254–256
Fillmore, 97, 117
firefighter, 204, 205, 211
Florence, 108
Fontana, 84, 108
Fountain Valley, 98, 127

freeways, 11–12, 44, 46, 70, 73–74, 83, 98, 110, 116, 122, 127, 146, 151–152, 156
Fullerton, 17
furniture industry, 96, 197, 199, 217, 220–221

G

Gabrielino, 90
gaps in socioeconomic status, 11, 17, 167–176, 175–177, 178–189 188–200, 256–258
Garden Grove, 92, 127, 151, 156, 161, 163, 230
Gardena, 45, 80, 126, 128–129, 151, 157, 162–163, 181, 230, 243, 247, 254, 259
Garifuna, 85, 89
garment manufacturing industry, 16, 87, 96, 110, 155, 165, 185, 192,194, 200, 211–212, 214, 223, 225–226, 228, 247. *See also* apparel industry
gender, 171, 183, 197, 199, 207
glass ceiling, 189, 197, 258
Glassell Park, 147
Glendale, 13–15, 50, 72–75, 77, 82, 88, 95, 111–112, 147, 151, 163, 246
Glendora, 45, 72, 76, 109, 115, 248
globalization, 35, 39
government, 6, 11–13, 16, 36, 38–39, 74, 91–92, 108–109, 111, 124–125, 129, 154–155, 157–158, 161, 179, 182–183, 187, 195, 197–198, 201, 205–210, 224, 226, 255
government employment, 182, 187–188, 198, 201, 206–207, 209, 226
Granada Hills, 77, 123, 151–152
grocery stores, 76, 78, 81, 125–126, 148–149, 154, 165, 217–223, 225–226
groundskeeper, 194, 211, 214
group quarters, 16
Guamanians, 162, 166
Guangdong, 35
Guangzhou, 119
Guatemalans, 18 ,92, 101, 109–111, 114, 171, 208, 213, 215, 221, 245, 248–249
Gujaratis, 223
Guyanese, xiv

H

Hacienda Heights, 47, 122, 128, 163, 252
hairdresser, 212
Haitians, xiv

Hancock Park, 17, 77, 81, 149
Harbor City, 94, 247
Harbor Gateway, 111, 128
Hawaiian Gardens, 98, 117, 244
Hawaiians, 162, 166
Hawthorne, 12, 157, 165, 243, 247, 259
Hemet, 14
Hermosa Beach, 48
high-school graduates, 70, 74, 115, 121, 169, 170–171, 179, 199, 256
high school, 70, 74, 115, 121, 169, 171, 179, 199
Highland Park, 113, 147
Hindus, 151–153, 165
Hispanic origin, 4–5, 8, 15–17, 35, 40–42, 84–85, 90, 92, 94, 96, 98, 107–108, 110, 112, 114–118, 169–173, 175, 178–180, 182–187, 195, 197–199, 206, 210, 243–244, 257, 259
Hispanic South Americans, 106, 115, 245
Hmong, xiv, 39, 154, 159, 166
Hollywood, 15–16, 46, 50, 67–74, 87–88, 110–112, 114, 125, 128, 130, 147, 151–152, 159–161, 166–167, 222, 244, 246–247, 252, 255
homeownership, 1, 6, 15, 47, 146, 167, 178–179, 245
Hondurans, 114
Hong Kong, 120
Hopi, 91
hotel business, 13, 36, 69, 77, 116, 124, 129, 146, 149, 164, 203, 218, 225
household income, 6, 44, 61, 66, 76, 86, 107, 115–116, 145, 162, 210, 250, 255
housing, 6, 8, 10–18, 25, 34, 37, 40–46, 50, 68–70, 73, 76–78, 80–81, 83–84, 87, 89, 92–96, 98, 108, 110–113, 115, 120–122, 124–125, 127–129, 146–151, 155, 157, 159, 162–163, 165, 167, 178, 180, 244, 247–248, 254–255
housing construction, median year of, 14
Hsi Lai Buddhist Temple, 122
human capital, 188–189, 191, 194, 197, 200, 227
Huntington Beach, 11, 15, 46, 48, 77, 127
Huntington Park, 16, 79, 92, 108, 112, 243–244, 247
Hyde Park, 85

I
illegal immigration, 5, 8, 39–40, 126, 130, 146, 168, 176, 200, 210, 225, 255
Immigration Act, 37–39
immigration, 5, 7–8, 10, 34–40, 42, 71, 74, 87, 93–94, 109, 119, 121–122, 124, 127, 129–130, 147–148, 152–153, 159–161, 165–166, 168, 170, 176, 184–187, 199, 224–225, 228, 230, 240, 245–247, 252, 257, 259
income, 2–3, 5–9, 12–13, 15–18, 43–44, 46, 61, 66, 76, 85–86, 92–93, 107, 109, 115–116, 123–124, 145, 152, 162, 167–169, 172–173, 175–200, 202, 210, 227, 231, 245–246, 250, 253, 255–259
income distribution, 175, 181, 183, 259
income ratios and gaps, 173, 175–177, 179, 182–189, 191–193, 197–199, 256–258
index of dissimilarity, 230–232
index of net difference, 173, 175, 181, 199
Indian (American), 4–5, 10, 89–92, 211–212, 214, 217,
Indochinese, 39–40, 158, 165
Indonesia, 120
Indonesians, 141, 160–161, 208, 219
industrial niche, 201
industry, 3, 10–14, 17–18, 37, 41, 46, 79–80, 84, 91–96, 98, 108, 111, 112, 157, 165, 167–168, 176, 183, 185, 187, 194, 195, 197–201, 206, 215–221, 223, 225–226, 228, 247
Inglewood, 12, 14, 46, 50, 80, 85–86, 112, 114, 246
insurance industry, 81, 149, 153, 185, 193, 204, 216–217, 219–220
intermarriage, ethnic, xi, 4–7, 9, 47, 95, 116, 130, 230, 242, 248–253, 259–260
internment, 124, 127–128
interurban, 11, 16, 80, 94–95
Iranian ancestry, 5, 49, 59, 74–76, 88–89, 208, 209, 215, 217, 245–246
Iraqi ancestry, 71
Iroquois, 91
Irvine, 13–15, 76, 86, 98, 123, 127, 152, 156, 161
Irwindale, 14, 108–109
Islam, 71, 73–74, 88, 154
Israeli ancestry, 56, 70–71, 88, 208, 215–216, 223, 246, 256

J
Jamaican ancestry, 64, 84–86, 208, 217, 246
janitors, 82, 194–195, 197, 203, 205, 210
Japanese, 8, 34, 37, 45, 78–79, 87, 94–97, 119–120, 123–129, 132, 162–164, 169–173, 176, 178–179, 181, 185, 189–190, 192, 197–199, 202–203, 208, 211–212, 219, 224, 226–227, 230–232, 244–245, 247, 249–250, 254–256, 258
jewelry industry, 74–75, 122, 153, 216, 220, 222
Jews, 4–5, 9, 34, 37, 39, 44, 46, 49–50, 67–71, 74–76, 79, 87–88, 95, 168, 189, 207, 209, 213, 222, 244, 246, 255, 258
Jordanian ancestry, 71

K
Kanjobal Indians, 92, 117. See Mayan Indians
Khmer Rouge, 39, 157–158
kitchen workers, 185, 203, 211, 214
Korea, 120
Korean War, 84, 148
Koreans, 81, 110, 112, 119, 127, 148–151, 163–164, 209, 222, 226, 230–231, 245, 247–249, 252–253, 255, 259
Koreatown, 16, 69, 110, 114, 148–151, 160, 163–165, 230, 244, 247–248, 253, 255
Ku Klux Klan, 50, 80
Kurdish ancestry, 75–76
Kuwaiti ancestry, 71

L
La Brea, 34, 69
La Cañada–Flintridge, 48, 73, 151, 163
La Crescenta, 151
La Habra Heights, 48, 77, 116, 148
La Habra, 48, 77, 98, 116, 148, 222
La Palma, 153, 244
La Placita, 94, 254
La Puente, 108
La Verne, 94
labor market, 188, 194, 198, 227
laborers, 117, 202, 204, 211–212, 214
Ladera Heights, 82, 247
Laguna Beach, 48, 243–244
Laguna Hills, 34, 161

Laguna Niguel, 75, 116, 163
Lakeview Terrace, 48
Lakewood, 15, 48, 72, 109, 244
Lancaster, 14, 47
land use, 3, 10–11, 13, 21, 116, 254
Lanterman Developmental Center, 16
Laos, 120
Laotians, 139, 154, 159, 166
Latin Americans, 4, 10, 36–38
Latinos, 8, 16, 34–35, 40–41, 46–47, 70, 77–78, 81–84, 93, 95, 97–98, 108–110, 113–117, 127, 146–147, 149, 156, 158, 163, 165, 167, 171–172, 178–180, 198, 207, 225, 244. *See also* Hispanic origin
laundry, 148, 206, 220, 224
Lawndale, 123, 157
lawyers, 18, 50, 81, 148, 187, 189, 192–193, 213, 222
Lebanese ancestry, 5, 71–72, 208
Leimert Park, 82, 86, 255
Leisure Village, 34
Leisure World, 34, 48
Lennox, 111–112, 114
Libyan ancestry, 71
Lido Isle, 48
Lincoln Heights, 18, 95, 120–121
Little Armenia, 73
Little India, 153
Little Indonesia, 161
Little Phnom Penh, 158
Little Saigon, 156, 158, 225
Little Taipei, 122
Little Teheran, 75
Little Tokyo, 16, 124–125, 129, 163–164, 254
Loma Linda, including University Medical Center, 113, 161
Lomita, 94
Long Beach V. A. Medical Center, 16
Long Beach, 12, 14, 16–18, 34, 39, 43, 46, 48–49, 77–78, 80, 82, 93–94, 98, 111, 115, 123, 126–127, 146–148, 156, 158–159, 161–163, 166, 223, 228, 231, 243–244, 254–255
Los Angeles city, 15, 41, 67, 86, 111, 126, 129, 203, 205, 247. *Other references to the city are too numerous to identify here*
Los Angeles CMSA (Consolidated Metropolitan Statistical Area), xii, 193–194

Los Angeles County Central Jail, 16, 92
Los Angeles County General Hospital, 205
Los Angeles Harbor, 92, 115
Los Angeles International Airport, 13
Los Feliz, 15, 72–73, 151
low-skilled, 182, 185–187, 197–198, 255, 257
Luiseño, 90
Lynwood, 46, 85, 92, 95–96, 108, 159, 247

M

MacArthur Park, 110
machine operator, 9, 194, 204, 211–212, 214
Madison Avenue, 125, 163
mail carriers, 204, 211. *See* postal workers
Malaysia, 120
Malibu, 46, 77, 111, 152, 248
managerial occupations, 6, 12, 17–18, 28, 36, 50, 97, 128–130, 152, 154, 172, 176, 180, 187, 189–191, 197, 201, 210–212, 214, 225, 245, 256
Manhattan Beach, 48, 116, 243
Manilatown, 130
manufacturing, 11–12, 18, 48, 75, 93, 96, 108, 113, 115–116, 154, 156–157, 176, 183, 185, 197, 206, 222–223, 226–228, 257. *See also specific industries*
Mar Vista, 18, 111, 126–128, 153, 154, 252
Marina Del Rey, 14–15, 77
Mayan Indians, 85, 92, 110, 117. *See also* Kanjobal
Maywood, 94, 108, 243
measurement of ethnic diversity. *See* entropy index
mechanic, 193, 204
median household income, 6, 76, 86, 115–116, 162, 193, 210, 250, 255
median-income ratios, 173, 190, 193
merchants, 1, 49, 72, 81, 92, 121, 124, 150, 153, 156, 224. *See also* entrepreneurs
Metropolitan Detention Center, 16
Metropolitan State Hospital, 16
Mexican Americans, 8, 46, 93–95, 108–109, 117, 167–168, 171, 173, 175–176, 178–179, 182–183, 186–187, 189, 191–192, 197, 199, 254, 256–257
Mexican Eastside, 94–95, 110, 115–117, 121, 128, 247–248, 254, 259

Mexican immigrants, 5, 8, 18, 38, 45, 78, 93–95, 109, 114, 117, 169–173, 175–176, 178–179, 182, 186–187, 193–195, 198, 203, 206, 210, 214, 247, 251, 254–255, 258
Mexican-origin population (U.S.-born plus foreign-born), 8, 40, 92–98, 100, 108–109, 111, 116, 168–169, 175, 180–181, 183–184, 186–187, 191–193, 195, 197–199, 214, 202–203, 210, 212, 214–215, 230, 244–246, 249–252, 255–259
Mexicans, 8, 10, 18, 36–37, 39, 45–46, 78–80, 83, 92–96, 98, 108–109, 126–127, 203, 207, 210, 224, 231, 247, 249, 254–256
Mid-City, 114
Middle Eastern ancestries, 4, 36, 72, 85, 88, 209. *See also* Armenian, Iranian, Israeli, Turkish, *and* Arab ancestries
middle-class, 2, 36, 46, 80–81, 84, 86, 108, 110, 116, 129, 224, 231, 246
migrants, 10, 12, 36–37, 39, 45, 48–49, 70, 79–80, 82, 90–92, 110, 112–113, 130, 155–156, 162, 186, 206
minorities, 6–8, 12, 17, 35, 40–44, 46–47, 74, 76, 157, 168–170, 172, 176, 178–179, 182, 184–186, 193, 195, 198, 226–227, 243, 255–258
Miracle Mile, 50, 69
Mission Hills, 96
Mission San Fernando, 96
Mission Viejo, 34
Mixtec Indians, 92
Molokans, 87, 95
Moneta, 126. *See also* Gardena
Monrovia, 11, 45, 72, 78, 82–83, 89, 93, 254
Montclair, 86
Montebello, 73–74, 88, 108, 128, 255
Monterey Hills, 128
Monterey Park, 47, 109, 121–123, 128, 160, 163, 225, 230
Moorpark, 92–93
Moreno Valley, 14, 47, 86
Mormons, 91, 162
Morningside Park, 85–86
Moroccan ancestry, 71
Morongo Reservation, 90
motion picture (movie) industry, 18, 153, 167, 213, 216, 222

Mount Washington, 46
multiethnic society, 7, 230, 232, 244, 246, 248, 250, 252, 259
Muslims, 5, 70–71, 74–76, 88, 151, 152–154, 165, 209. *See also* Islam

N

nannies, 110–111, 114, 185, 197, 248
Naples, 48
Navajo, 91
Navy. See U.S. Navy
Nepalese, 151
New Spain, 10, 92
New York, 5, 49, 67, 72, 87, 90, 148, 225, 229, 253
Newport Beach, 13, 46, 48, 75, 77, 243–244
Nicaraguans, 109, 114
niches, 6, 8, 70, 75, 85, 118, 127, 176, 187, 201–206, 208, 210, 212–229, 255–256, 260.
Nigerian ancestry, 84–85
Non-Hispanic white, 4, 7–8, 20, 34–35, 40–41, 45, 47, 49, 53, 61, 76, 90, 116, 152, 167, 169–170, 172–173, 178–180, 183, 185–186, 190, 192–193, 202–204, 208, 216, 231–232, 243, 248–251, 258. See also white
Norco, 16
North Hills, 147, 151, 157, 247
North Hollywood, 70, 72, 88, 128, 152, 160, 247
Northridge, 18, 70, 77, 88–89, 115, 117–118, 152, 157, 163, 165–166
Norwalk, 11, 16, 98, 165
nurses, nursing, 91, 147, 160, 170, 192, 205, 211–213, 219, 227

O

occupational gap, 171, 176, 185, 256
occupational status, 17, 92, 115, 171–172, 175–177, 179, 187, 192, 210, 246, 256, 258
occupations, 1, 2, 5–6, 9, 17–18, 29, 38–39, 41, 75, 92, 96, 115, 126–127, 163, 167–168, 171–172, 175–177, 179–180, 185, 187–190, 192, 197–198, 201–203, 205, 210, 213–215, 226, 229, 246, 256, 258
oil industry, 11–12, 74, 94, 98, 108, 243
Okies, 91

Oklahoma Indians, 91
Olvera Street, 93–94, 254
Ontario, 93, 115
operator, machine, 9, 193–194, 204, 211–212, 214
Osage, 91
Other Central American origin, 105
Our Lady the Queen of the Angels, 94, 254. *See* La Placita
out-movement, 43, 68, 231, 247
overcrowded housing, 15–16, 37, 94, 110
overrepresented occupations. *See* niches
Oxnard, 82, 92–93, 97, 147

P

Pacific Electric Railway, 80, 89, 94, 98, 117, 124
Pacific Islanders, 4, 35, 119–120, 122, 124, 126, 128, 130, 146, 148, 150, 152, 154, 156, 158, 160, 162, 164, 166, 194, 207, 243
Pacific Palisades, 46, 48, 69, 77
Pacoima, 16, 18, 46, 78, 83–84, 89, 93, 96, 114, 116, 128, 244, 247, 255
Paiute, 91
Pakistanis, 136, 151–154
Palestinian ancestry, 70–71
Palmdale, 14, 47
Palms, 69, 76, 111, 153, 154
Palos Verdes, 11, 46, 48, 67, 74–77, 113, 123, 126, 128, 151–152, 163, 247–248
Panamanians, 84, 114
Panorama City, 147
Papago, 91
Paraguayans, 118
Pasadena, 11–14, 43, 45, 48, 72–73, 77–78, 82–83, 86, 88–89, 93–95, 111–112, 114, 128, 246, 254–255
Peruvians, 115, 221
pharmacists, 212
Philippines, The, 36, 40, 42, 120, 130, 147–148, 155, 170–171, 213
physicians, 18, 36, 172, 187, 189, 192–193, 204, 205, 211–212, 214
Pico Rivera, 108
Pico-Robertson, 68–70
Pico-Union, 110, 114, 148, 259
Pima, 91

Piru, 14, 97, 117
Placentia, 98, 161
polarization, 17, 168, 183–184, 191, 197, 258–259
police, 18, 78, 167, 204–205, 211–212
Pomona, 11, 16, 43, 78, 82, 84, 86, 89, 93, 108–109, 114, 158–159, 255
Port Hueneme, 147
Porter Ranch, 17, 70, 74, 151–152
postal workers, 166, 205, 211–213, 217–219
Potawatomi, 91
poverty, 15, 17–18, 31, 34, 42, 78, 80–81, 115, 120, 122, 129–130, 148, 162, 164
powwows, 90, 92
private household workers, 202
private sector, 182, 187, 206, 209, 226
professionals, 6, 12, 17–18, 28, 36, 45, 50, 67, 72, 73, 76, 79, 81, 95, 114, 116, 126, 146–149, 152–155, 161, 171–172, 179–180, 185–187, 189–191, 197–199, 204–205, 209, 210–212, 256–257
Public Use Microdata Areas (PUMAs), xii–xiii, 3, 41, 121, 246
Public Use Microdata Sample (PUMS), 3, 7, 41, 89, 117–118, 161, 164–166, 173, 179, 181, 188
pueblo, 11, 18, 77, 91, 93, 158, 166
Puente Hills, 11, 46
Puerto Ricans, 35, 84, 104, 112–115, 117, 161, 231, 249–250, 252, 260
PUMAs. *See* Public Use Microdata Areas
Punjabis, 151–152, 165

Q

quilt, ethnic, 254, 260

R

race, ix, 1, 3–5, 10, 38, 84–85, 87, 89–92, 112–114, 119, 121, 123, 151, 153, 160, 167, 180, 199, 218, 230, 255
race question, 4, 85, 90–91, 160
radio and television industry, 216, 220, 222
railroads, 3, 10, 12–13, 45–46, 49, 73, 78, 80, 82, 84, 94, 96–97, 108–109, 111, 120, 124, 126, 158, 205, 224
Rancho Los Amigos Medical Center, 16
Rancho Palos Verdes, 123, 128, 151–152